EMBATTLED DREAMS

AMERICANS AND THE CALIFORNIA DREAM

Americans and the California Dream, 1850–1915

Inventing the Dream
California Through the Progressive Era

Material Dreams
Southern California Through the 1920s

Endangered Dreams
The Great Depression in California

The Dream Endures
California Enters the 1940s

Embattled Dreams
California in War and Peace, 1940–1950

EMBATTLED DREAMS

California in War and Peace, 1940–1950

KEVIN STARR

OXFORD
UNIVERSITY PRESS

OXFORD

UNIVERSITY PRESS

Oxford   New York
Auckland   Bangkok   Buenos Aires   Cape Town   Chennai
Dar es Salaam   Delhi   Hong Kong   Istanbul   Karachi   Kolkata
Kuala Lumpur   Madrid   Melbourne   Mexico City   Mumbai   Nairobi
São Paulo   Shanghai   Taipei   Tokyo   Toronto

Copyright © 2002 by Kevin Starr

First published by Oxford University Press Inc., 2002
First issued as an Oxford University Press paperback, 2003
198 Madison Avenue, New York, New York 10016

www.oup.com.

Oxford is a registered trademark of Oxford University Press

Library of Congress Cataloging-in-Publication Data
Starr, Kevin.
Embattled dreams : California in war and peace, 1940–1950
/ by Kevin Starr.
p. cm.—(Americans and the California dream)
Includes bibliographical references and index.
ISBN 0-19-512437-5 (cloth) ISBN 0-19-516897-6 (pbk.)
1. California—History—1850–1950.
2. World War, 1939–1945—California.
I. Title.
F866.S786   2002   979.4'052—dc21   2001036047

1 3 5 7 9 8 6 4 2
Printed in the United States of America

For the physicians, medical support teams,
and administrative staffs of
Kaiser Permanente, San Francisco

Preface

Historians have properly emphasized the continuities between one era and the next: from the Depression to the war years, for example, through the post-war years of return and growth; and it is proper and correct for them to do so. No historical epoch, after all, can be completely self-referencing or stand upon an exclusive set of premises. Social changes occur across time; and time — if it is anything at all — is a process and a continuity. Hence it is important to understand the decade 1940 to 1950 in terms of prior and ongoing American and Californian continuities. The war years, in fact, can in many ways be seen as an intensification of prior developments rather than a beginning. The great underground river of history frequently gushes to the surface in times of cataclysm and crisis; but even at such times — and a great world war would certainly qualify as such a time — the vast subterranean river of social and imaginative experience never fully surfaces. It continues to flow, rather, from past to present to future, with much of its power hidden beneath the surface of even the most dramatic of events.

From this perspective, the sheer act of beginning this chronicle of California in 1940 and ending it in 1950 is an arbitrary convenience of calendar date. The war itself, it must be remembered, had its origins two decades earlier with the Treaty of Versailles and in its Asian dimension had already become violent years before either Europe or the United States came into the conflict. And as far as the domestic scene of California was concerned, which is the exclusive focus of this book, in sector after sector of social experience — the role of women, the emergence of minorities, the steady rise in population, a growing sense of California as a significant instance of the American experiment — the war years and the post-war era only intensified developments already under way during two previous decades.

Yet no one, even historians chronicling continuities, could truly say that it would ever be the same. Something more than the passage of time lies between calendar years 1940 and 1950: something that was not only transformative in a social sense but gave to time itself an almost physical quality of differentiation. Soon, such phrases as "before the war" and "during the war" and "after the war" emerged as time-and-place-marks of momentous significance, despite the fact that they embraced something less than a decade in duration. And that was because, for all the continuities that must be chronicled, everyone knew that it would never be the same, either for California or the nation, especially in view of the national role California had played during the war as Arsenal of Democracy, training ground, staging area, and port of embarkation.

No, California would never be the same: not after the federal government had spent more than $35 billion in California between 1940 and 1946 (a sum exceeded only in New York and Michigan), multiplying the manufacturing economy of the state by a factor of 2.5, tripling the average personal income between 1939 and 1945; not after some 1.6 million Americans had moved to California to work in defense-related industries; not after millions of young Americans had been trained in California for the military, with so many of them vowing to return after the war. It could never be the same for the women of California who had worked in the shipyards and aircraft factories or entered public life. It would never be the same for the minorities of California who had their worlds shattered or transformed.

On the negative side, the Japanese-Americans of California suffered the trauma and indignity of an incarceration that represented the most massive violation of the constitutional rights of any single ethnic group in this nation after the ending of slavery. For the Chinese-Americans of California, by contrast, these war years represented an unprecedented de-ghetto-ization and upwardly mobile release of talent as Chinese-Americans served alongside their white counterparts in the military and on the home front. For Mexican-Americans in California, these years represented a comparable experience of de-*barrio*-ization and upward mobility, although the path in this direction was far from smooth, especially on the California home front. During these years as well, California became an important center of African-American culture as hundreds of thousands of African-Americans flocked into the state seeking defense work. Even more, perhaps, than was the case for Mexican-Americans, the pathway of African-Americans to their new identity as Californians was filled with repressions and hurt; yet by 1950 California was something that it had not been before the war: a significantly African-American place, especially in the Bay Area and Los Angeles.

Marginal or marginalized white groups, meanwhile, were experiencing a comparable process of assimilation and upgrade. The despised Okies, for example — which is to say, more than one million white migrants from the Dust Bowl — were absorbed in unprecedented numbers into the defense industry and for all practical purposes disappeared as a denigrated minority as prosperity allowed them to realign themselves alongside other whites. Conversely, California was showing signs during the war of becoming significantly Dust Bowl–ized in its popular culture as, among other symptoms, music with a Texas-Oklahoma flavor became increasingly characteristic of mainstream entertainment. By 1950, in fact, Bakersfield would be second only to Nashville as a center of country-and-western music. In instance after instance, the despised Okie was being absorbed by California and was in turn enriching the social and cultural mix of the Golden State.

No, nothing would ever be the same. A University of California that had played a major role in releasing the power of the atom would never be the same. Corporations that had accelerated themselves into almost unthinkable levels of productivity would never revert to business as usual. Architects and planners who had, almost overnight, housed millions of military personnel and defense workers were now dreaming of new cities and suburbs for a rapidly expanding population centered on the very same urban and suburban places that had sustained the defense industries. A motion picture industry that had helped mobilize an entire nation and sent its emissaries into the forward zones of war had experienced a power even greater than it had known in the Depression and, once the war was over, plunged itself into the effort of imaginatively reconstructing (as well as deconstructing) the American identity.

From the beginning, California had been a direct creation of the national will as expressed in the doctrine and practice of Manifest Destiny. During the War Between the States, the national will, as expressed by the federal government, had linked California to the nation via a publicly subsidized transcontinental railroad. Since the Conquest of 1846, the military had long sustained an abiding interest in California, with its strategic relationship to the Pacific. During the 1940s California became even more federalized in its governance and economy and even more national in its social, cultural, and economic significance. In this period, among other things, millions of Americans determined that becoming a Californian was the best way for them to possess or repossess the American Dream. Acting on that assumption, they transformed California into not only the most populous state in the union (by 1962) but a place, almost a state of mind, offering an increasingly impressive American paradigm. Thus when the United States entered upon the Cold War, California did more than its part—the Hollywood Ten, the Tenney Committee, the Loyalty Oath controversy, the rise of Richard Milhous Nixon—in playing out the larger American reaction to the realities and delusional fears of Communism as a foreign and domestic threat. In the later years of the 1940s, tensions and antagonisms put on hold during the war, some of them anti-Semitic, resurfaced within the intensified and intensifying context of the Cold War. New tensions and antagonisms, meanwhile—especially as to just exactly who would control and profit by the post-war California boom—now surfaced and added their virulence to prior anxieties about Communism.

A decade that opened with a war ended with a war, hot and deadly in Korea, cold and compulsive across a newly descended Iron Curtain. Geared up for war in the first half of the decade, California entered the 1950s even more super-charged by defense spending. Indeed, much of the business of California in the 1950s—the sheer total business of not just the economy but of society itself—would be defense related. As dramatic (and frequently poignant) as were the demobilizations and homecomings of 1946 and 1947, California would experience peacetime conditions and attitudes for only a few short years. War, hot or cold or a combination thereof, had become an American, hence a Californian, way of life.

The perception, finally, that it would never be the same was most powerfully a personal judgment. However historians might connect the mobilizations of the New Deal to the mobilizations of the Second World War, to the mobilizations of the Korean and Cold wars, any Californian living in California between 1940 and 1950, or any American with significant experience of California during this period, knew full well that he or she had passed through a transformative experience. The pre-war ambitions of California had served, or so it would seem by the 1950s, as only a prologue to what California now envisioned itself to be in its economy, its program for higher education, its ambitions for the built environment and for quality of life. Prior to 1940 the ambitions of California had been relatively modest and in many instances provincial. California, it was hoped, would continue to grow at a steady pace, with agriculture remaining the lead element in its economy. Although agriculture would continue to pace the economy of California for the next half century, no one by 1950 was envisioning California as a modest agricultural state. Something vibrant, explosive, inchoate even, had entered the California experiment. The inner landscape of California—which is to say, California as a shared social and imaginative identity—had been fast-forwarded into futurity even beyond the rate of acceleration brought about by the Gold Rush. Californians of all sorts, including the first wave of new immigrants, were now wanting more of everything, and certainly more than the modest expectations of the Depression era: more and better homes and schools, more and better-paying jobs; more highways, more freeways, and more and better automobiles; more educational opportunities; more glamour, more sexuality, more entertainment, more fun.

So much of this expectation was hype, destined to remain unfulfilled—indeed, destined to give California a dubious reputation among the more modest and stabilized portions of the United States. Yet even when confronted with the dubiousness, the hype, the unreality of the California Dream, Californians who had experienced life in the Golden State in the 1940s might very well insist that they had already seen it happen. Had they not witnessed an entire society in transformation and upheaval? Had they not seen a still-remote Pacific Coast state become a strategic center of global importance? Had they not experienced California brought to new levels of social, economic, and planning mobilization? Even more important, had they not learned—especially those who had left California to serve overseas and those who had come to California from less advantaged places—what a promising place the Golden State could be? Having experienced this—having,

that is, either lost and regained California or found it in the first place—they
could be expected as the 1940s became the 1950s to see in California the possibilities for their own fulfillment and the creation of an even more challenging
and paradigmatic American place.

Los Angeles, San Francisco, Sacramento   K.S.
March 2001

Contents

Even in wartime, Hollywood was concerned with positioning itself. Through its films, stars in uniform, and USO entertainments at home and at the front, Hollywood made sure that World War II remained a celebrity event.

Homecoming had its anxieties and adjustments as well as its elations and triumphs. The fact that so many returning veterans were choosing California as the place to come home to only compounded the drama. Simultaneously, California was serving the needs of those who wanted to fit back in as soon as possible and those who were nursing a rebellious resentment.

In the sad life and tragic death of one damaged V-girl, the underside of home-front and post-war Los Angeles stood revealed. Still, for all its shoddiness, the City of Angels possessed a certain sassy, savvy energy. It was, among other things, a Front Page kind of town where life was lived by many on the edge, and that made for good copy and good film noir.

While Earl Warren was steering California through the post-war era, his photogenic family was helping forge a new way of communicating political value. When youngest daughter Honey Bear contracted polio, all California held its breath and waited. Honey Bear, after all, embodied the post-war hopes of an entire state.

Reactivated by the Cold War, the Depression-era clash of Reds and Red-hunters resurfaced with a vengeance. When it came to Red-baiting, no one could outperform a portly ex-bandleader state senator from the Folks. It was not a pleasant time.

As the 40th Division of the California National Guard shipped out for Korea, the regents of the University of California were pursuing a police action of their own. At stake, among other things, was the question of just exactly who was going to control California and its university.

EMBATTLED DREAMS

1

1940 * A Matter of Life or Death

L IKE most philosophers, Sigmund Freud struggled throughout his life with the problem of evil. From Freud's perspective, that of a practicing psychiatrist with ambitions equally clinical and speculative, evil meant aggression, which is to say, all forms of destructive behavior. For various reasons, Freud long resisted the notion that aggression was possessed of its own separate existence, its own ontology, in the human psyche. Aggression rather—or so Freud struggled to believe—came as a by-product of those suppressions of instinct that were necessary for civilization itself. And yet, in surveying the terrible destruction of the First World War, Freud had his doubts. Was there not ample evidence of a persistent death instinct in human behavior as well? True, death was the inevitable *terminus ad quem* of life; but such a perception of death kept it in balance with the life instinct in an ambivalent but inevitable partnership. What was one to say, though, when the death instinct raged beyond its normal boundaries and became an overriding force in human behavior? Freud called the life instinct *eros*. Never in print, only in conversation, he called the death instinct *thanatos*, perhaps reluctant to use so mythic and metaphysical a term in clinical discourse.

Contemplating the Great War, in part through discussions with Albert Einstein, Freud edged, reluctantly, toward an admission, as his biographer Ernest Jones puts it, "of a *primary* aggressive or destructive instinct, one which when fused with sexual impulses becomes the familiar perversion called sadism." By the time he wrote *Civilization and Its Discontents* (1930) in the summer of 1929, Freud was willing to admit his error. "I can no longer understand," Freud admitted, "how we could have overlooked the universality of non-erotic aggression and destruction, and could have omitted to give it its due significance in our interpretation of life."[1] Freud struggled to come to terms with the balances and imbalances of the life instinct and the death instinct—when out of kilter, running rampant, as aggression

3

and destruction — in human affairs. But something else, something more dark and terrible, something loving violence and death, could also erupt into personal and social experience. Fleeing Vienna for London in the wake of the Nazi invasion of Austria on 11 March 1938, dying of throat cancer through 1939 as Europe entered into darkness, Freud had time to contemplate the final question of *Civilization and Its Discontents*. "The fateful question for the human species," Freud had written, "seems to me to be whether and to what extent their cultural development will succeed in mastering the disturbance of their communal life by the human instinct of aggression and self-destruction. It may be that in this respect precisely the present time deserves a special interest. Men have gained control over the forces of nature to such an extent that with their help they would have no difficulty in exterminating one another to the last man. They know this, and hence comes a large part of their current unrest, their unhappiness and their mood of anxiety. And now it is to be expected that the other of the two 'Heavenly Powers,' eternal Eros, will make an effort to assert himself in the struggle with his equally immortal adversary."[2]

Eros and *thanatos*! The forces of life, Freud was suggesting simply but power-fully — love, sexuality, appetite, joy in the pageant and mystery of creation — were now on a worldwide basis coming under massive threat from *thanatos*: the forces of death and darkness, abnegation and annihilation. Now was unfolding across Europe and Asia a reversion to a dawn world of primal conflict and indiscriminate slaughter made even more fearsome by the new technologies of war. Cities would be destroyed from the sky, with hundreds of thousands killed. Great armies would meet in conflict, and young men would die unto the millions or have their bodies reduced to clotted knots of pain. An entire race of people, together with dissidents and other undesirables, would be fed into ovens more horrible than the fiery furnaces of Moloch that consumed the ancient Hebrews. And when it would be ended by the deaths of an entire generation and the ferocious preventative of two atom bombs, some sixty million people would have lost their lives, devoured by the forces of *thanatos* that had in the first half of the 1940s reached an intensity of scale unprecedented in human history.

This, then, was the world in 1940: a world at war, save for the Americas, yet a world still only in the early stages of combat and slaughter. By the end of 1940, only Great Britain and its allies, which is to say, its Commonwealth nations, stood against the German Reich; and it remained a matter of conjecture just exactly how long this situation could last or, more ominously, whether it was now time for Great Britain itself to be invaded or to sue for peace. Nineteen forty had been a year of triumphant aggression by Nazi Germany on the Continent. Only Great Britain and Greece had managed to maintain their independence, and this at a terrible cost of life. True, the Battle of Britain, which had begun in July, had maintained British mastery over British airspace, and this in turn would make the invasion of Britain less probable, especially after Hitler had turned his attention to the invasion of the Soviet Union; but for Londoners on the receiving end of the firebombs, or Americans listening to the descriptions of these attacks by radio commentator Edward R. Murrow, the prospect of Great Britain failing, or suing for a separate peace, remained a possibility as 1940 turned to 1941. Already, now, millions had died in Europe and Asia. Great cities—Warsaw, Rotterdam, London—had been bombed. Britain had lost a battleship, the *Royal Oak*, to a German submarine and had barely managed to evacuate its army from the Continent. Death was everywhere, and a great Nazi darkness had descended on Europe.

All this seemed so remote, so irrelevant to far-off California, even more remote and irrelevant than it seemed to other parts of the United States, given the isolation of California on a still sparsely settled Pacific Coast, separated from Europe by the American continent itself and the Atlantic Ocean and from Asia by a Pacific Ocean whose vastness had always intimidated the American imagination. And besides: as of 3 October 1939, with the passage and signing of the Neutrality Act, the United States was officially on the sidelines, although the very next month, on 4 November, Congress passed an amendment to the Neutrality Act allowing the United States to sell arms to European democracies on a cash-and-carry basis. On 3 September 1940 the United States transferred to Great Britain fifty antiquated destroyers in exchange for ninety-nine-year leases on naval and air bases in Newfoundland and the West Indies.

Nominated for an unprecedented third term, with Henry Wallace as his running mate, President Franklin Delano Roosevelt was taking a risk with the exchange of destroyers for leases because he, like Woodrow Wilson in 1916, was explicitly promising in his campaign to keep the United States out of the European conflict. Still, there was the destroyer deal to reckon with and the passage by Congress a mere thirteen days later, on 16 September, of the Selective Service Act authorizing the first peacetime draft in American history: nine hundred thousand selectees to be taken each year from a pool of all men between the ages of twenty and thirty-six, who were now required to register. Their length of service: one year—but this was quickly extended to eighteen months in August 1941. No matter what Roosevelt was saying about staying out of the war, the Selective Service Act of September 1940 conveyed another message entirely in bold, unambiguous terms.

Nor was the national media absent from this psychological buildup toward war. The year 1940 witnessed a steady rise in articles on both the European war and American preparedness. *Look* magazine was especially active in this regard, publishing articles by General Hugh Johnson, who had administered Roosevelt's National Recovery Act in the 1930s, World War I ace Captain Eddie Rickenbacker, military theorist Major Leonard Nason, and Colonel William Donovan, soon to organize the Office of Strategic Services, on various aspects of American preparedness. Eric Sevareid, meanwhile, was reporting on the Battle of Britain and the bombing of London, and commentator Dorothy Thompson was pounding away against arguments for continuing American neutrality. The California dimension of all this talk of preparedness and the coming war did not so much involve the Pacific Fleet, which had recently left San Diego and Long Beach for Pearl Harbor;

nor did it involve the Army or the Marine Corps, still a scaled-down presence on the West Coast. In the buildup of American aviation at Douglas, Northrop, Lockheed, North American, and Consolidated in Southern California, however, and the first efforts to train pilots for the war that would surely happen, California was accorded more than its share of media coverage. In May 1940 Roosevelt called for the building of fifty thousand war planes within the next calendar year, the first step in what would later emerge as the President's concept of the United States as an Arsenal of Democracy. In early 1940 the Army Air Corps established pilot training programs at the Ryan School of Aeronautics in San Diego and Hemet, the Cal-Aero School in Glendale, and the Allan Hancock College of Aeronautics in Santa Maria. Mechanics were to be trained at the Curtiss-Wright Technical Institute in Glendale. Privately owned, these flight and technical schools were under contract to the Army Air Corps to produce the first generation of pilots and mechanics for the possible entry of the United States into the world conflict. In April 1940 Major General Henry Arnold, chief of the Army Air Corps, conducted an official visit to these facilities. Shortly, Arnold would establish bombardier and bomber crew training programs at various sites in Riverside County.

Resistance to this growing involvement in the war effort—the cash-and-carry amendment to the Neutrality Act, the draft, the fifty destroyers, the fifty thousand aircraft, the impending Arsenal of Democracy concept—surfaced in 1940 in various anti-war groups: Keep Out of the War, Youth Committee Against War, the North Philadelphia Peace Council, and, most effectively, the America First movement. Founded in the spring of 1940 by a group of students at the Yale Law School that included future President Gerald Ford, future Supreme Court Justice Potter Stewart, and future Yale president Kingman Brewster, the chairman of the *Yale Daily News*, the America First movement soon developed into a nationwide organization attracting a variety of anti-interventionists. While the movement included such a liberal figure as *New Republic* columnist John Flynn, the basic membership and certainly the leadership of America First was soon dominated by Midwestern Republicans of wealth. Its acting chairman was General Robert Wood, chairman of the board of Sears, Roebuck in Chicago. Here was no fringe group. Here was, rather, a consolidation of some sixty thousand Republicans organized in eleven local chapters, many of them former Progressives, still traumatized by what they considered to be America's unnecessary entrance into the First World War and the heroic casualties of that misadventure. Supporters of the movement in one degree or another of affiliation or mere friendliness included Ray Lyman Wilbur, president of Stanford University, architect Frank Lloyd Wright, Captain Eddie Rickenbacker, and former President Herbert Hoover. In California, two prominent women, film and stage star Lillian Gish and novelist Kathleen Norris, assumed leadership positions. Throughout 1940, then, the America First Committee functioned, basically, as a generally Republican Progressive-oriented and largely Midwestern opposition to Roosevelt and the pro-interventionists.

On 17 April 1941, however, sometime Californian Colonel Charles Lindbergh, the Lone Eagle, joined the national committee. Lindbergh's notoriety was good news for America First. The bad news, Lindbergh's adamantly anti-British attitudes and his citation of Zionism as one of the forces dragging the United States into the conflict, would soon reveal itself. As far as California was concerned, the high point of Lindbergh's campaign consisted in two rallies in the summer of 1941 in Los Angeles and San Francisco. On the evening of 20 June more than thirty thousand people filled the Hollywood Bowl and surrounding hillsides to hear Lindbergh, Gish, Norris, and Republican Senator D. Worth Clark of Idaho denounce the increasing involvement of the United States in the European conflict. Eleven nights later, the same group appeared at a similar rally attended by a full house of twelve thousand in the Civic Auditorium in San Francisco. Following the San Francisco rally, Lindbergh and his wife, Anne, spent three days at Wyntoon on the McCloud River with publisher William Randolph Hearst, whose newspapers were also advancing an anti-interventionist message.

At each of these rallies, Kathleen Norris spoke with notable effectiveness. Having launched her career with the best-selling novel *Mother* (1911), Norris took precisely that stance—a mother not wanting her sons destroyed—in her support of the America First crusade. However naive from a strategic point of view, Norris was at least talking about the ancient war between life and death, *eros* and *thanatos*, and in her own straightforward way was making her choice as an American, a mother, and a spokesperson for motherhood. Did the mothers of America, Norris asked—Jewish and Christian mothers alike—wish to see their sons killed or maimed in a foreign war, if it could be avoided? Lindbergh was getting most of the attention. But were his strategic and racial theories any more pertinent or compelling than the simple questions being asked by Norris? Remaining simple, focused on life over death, focused on the sheer fact of biological generation and survival, Kathleen Norris chose her side most clearly in that ancient battle between life and death which Sigmund Freud saw in 1940 as holding the world once more in its grip.

So too in the popular entertainment of 1940, so much of it originating in California, did the desire for amusement, fantasy, humor, and escape resist the dawning recognition that the United States would soon be entering the conflict. Popular music, for example, ranged from the sheer nonsense of the "Woodpecker Song" to the escapism of "South of the Border," "Oh, Johnny," "Scatterbrain," "In an Old Dutch Garden," and "Careless." While there was some recognition of partings and leave-takings to come in "I'll Never Smile Again," the predominant mood was optimistic and hopeful, as testified to by the hit song of the year, "When You Wish upon a Star," sung by Jiminy Cricket in Walt Disney's *Pinocchio* (1940). Soon, Johnny Mercer and Hoagy Carmichael would be composing "Skylark," perhaps the most purely poetic song in all of American popular music: a song that spoke most powerfully to the desire to escape into a place of beauty and peace.

This same desire for escape, for transcendence even, so evident in "Skylark," pervaded national radio, then in the apogee of its golden age. True, *The March of Time* provided serious news documentary and dramatization. Edward R. Murrow was broadcasting from ground zero of the London blitz, and Murrow had gathered around him a CBS team — Bob Trout, Eric Sevareid, Charles Collingwood, Howard K. Smith, Winston Burdette — who would dominate broadcast journalism for the next forty years; and Elmer Davis, H. V. Kaltenborn, and Fulton Lewis Jr. were providing hard-hitting commentary on a variety of subjects; and even Walter Winchell was taking off after Hitler and the Nazis. Yet the general tenor of national radio was dominated by comedy. Most of the radio comedy shows now considered classics, in fact, were flourishing in 1940. A few of them — *The Abbott and Costello Show, Duffy's Tavern* — made their debut in that year, as did the humorous quiz show *Truth or Consequences,* the escapist crime program *Suspense,* and Gene Autry's *Melody Ranch.* Other comedy classics — *The Aldrich Family, Amos 'n' Andy, Blondie,* George Burns and Gracie Allen, *The Edgar Bergen/ Charlie McCarthy Show, Fibber McGee and Molly, The Red Skelton Show* — were running at full tide, filling the airwaves with nonsensical humor based on the premise that ordinary American life was rich in comic implications. Add these shows to such mega-classics as *The Bob Hope Show, The Eddie Cantor Show, The Fred Allen Show,* and *The Jack Benny Program,* with the dueling egos of Allen and Benny cross-referencing each other in an Irish-Jewish confrontation of sass and *shtick* that affirmed each sensibility — and you can make the case that 1940 was witnessing a near-obsession with comedy on the part of the American people. In a world grown murderously anti-Semitic on the European continent, there was even a program devoted to Jewish-American humor, with Gertrude Berg as Molly Goldberg holding forth from her kitchen in the Bronx in America's first Jewish comedy and a rare example of Jewish humor for national consumption. Even such ambitious quiz programs as *Information, Please,* moderated by the polished polymath Clifton Fadiman, were good-humored in their presentation. *Double or Nothing* was explicitly comic in intent.

Americans wanted comedy on the airwaves, and they wanted music: remote broadcasts of big bands from glamorous locations throughout the country — Abe Lyman, Artie Shaw, Benny Goodman, David Rose, Duke Ellington, Guy Lombardo, Glenn Miller, Sammy Kaye, Count Basie, the Tommy Dorsey Orchestra, Woody Herman, Jimmie Lunceford, each of them broadcasting from one of the nightclubs, hotel ballrooms, casinos, or skyscraper sites high atop American cities, so that, cumulatively, it seemed as if, on the radio at least, all of America was dancing. Then there was *The Bing Crosby Show, The Dinah Shore Show, The Kate Smith Hour,* and such upper-middle-brow efforts as *The Ford Sunday Evening Hour, The Standard Hour, The Texaco Star Theater,* and the Saturday broadcasts of the Metropolitan Opera hosted by Milton Cross. For lovers of country music the Grand Ole Opry was broadcasting from radio station WSM in Nashville. There was even a comic musical quiz program, the wacky *Kay Kyser's Kollege of Musical Knowledge*.

Even Hollywood was resorting to comedy in dealing with Adolf Hitler in Charlie Chaplin's 1940 film *The Great Dictator*. Sixty years later, living in the full knowledge of who Hitler was and the vast evil he managed to accomplish, Chaplin's satire, for many at least, lands with a thud—it being next to impossible to make a monster seem funny—but from the perspective of 1940, *The Great Dictator* shows the hope, however subliminal, that Hitler might be kept in check if only he were to be properly ridiculed by the greatest film comic of all time. One senses, however, in the popular media of 1940 a certain ambivalence toward *The Great Dictator*, as if the joke were already falling flat. Audiences stayed away in droves, and Chaplin's career never fully recovered. Much more successful were the thoroughly American screwball comedy *My Favorite Wife* (1940) and the quintessentially American *My Little Chickadee* (1939), starring Mae West and W. C. Fields, two total icons of American identity.

Even the most cursory analysis of Hollywood releases in 1940 reveals the dichotomy of war (and by implication interventionism) and heartland America (and by equal implication minding one's own American business). *Gone with the Wind* (1939), first of all, was continuing to pack in audiences through 1940. *Gone with the Wind* can be considered an anti-war film in which men play war games and kill each other while women endure, and Rhett Butler observes it all with detached cynicism. From this perspective, the continuing popularity of *Gone with the Wind* through 1940 can be considered an asset in the isolationist camp. So too does *Citizen Kane* (1940), perhaps the greatest American film, seem for all its cinematic sophistication a profoundly American, and by implication isolationist, statement. Indeed, many of the films released in 1940—*Citizen Kane, Abe Lincoln in Illinois, The Grapes of Wrath, Of Mice and Men, Northwest Passage, Our Town, Kitty Foyle, The Philadelphia Story*—were powerful instances of American settings and values in which Europe and England were totally absent.

The Grapes of Wrath, in fact—both John Steinbeck's novel, which continued on the best-seller list through 1940, and the John Ford film—was provoking a most American-centered debate, given the fact that the so-called Okies and other Dust Bowl migrants could trace their lineage to colonial times and were, if anyone could make that claim, a virtually unadulterated American Protestant folk. Throughout 1940 discussion of the plight of the Okies constituted in California, and to a lesser extent elsewhere in the nation, the last unfinished business of the Great Depression. Franklin Roosevelt talked about the Joads as if they were real figures. First Lady Eleanor Roosevelt and Secretary of Labor Frances Perkins toured California on fact-finding missions regarding the migrants' plight. The First Lady took every opportunity to praise the migrants and to challenge California to do right by them. The House of Representatives established a Select Committee to Investigate Interstate Migration of Destitute Citizens under the chairmanship of John Tolan, a Democrat from Alameda County. Throughout the second half of 1940, the Tolan Committee traveled twenty thousand miles and heard testimony from five hundred witnesses as it investigated not just the plight of Okies in California but the whole question of migrant labor in the United States. Following the success of Ford's film, Hollywood found itself in a condition of Okie-mania, and a number of *Grapes of Wrath* knockoffs were quickly produced, including *You're Not So Tough*, in which the Dead End Kids join the Okies in the California fields, and *Gold Rush Maisie*, in which an Okie heroine retraces the migration of the Joads along Route 66. Okie-mania, or whatever it should be called, was most definitely American, which is to say, domestic in focus, hence by implication isolationist.

On the other hand, *The Fighting 69th*, telling the story of a crack New York City–recruited infantry division in World War I, can be seen as an interventionist argument, as can *That Hamilton Woman* ("England expects each man to do his duty," this before Trafalgar) and *The Sea Hawk*, in which Errol Flynn, representing England, takes on Philip II of Spain, standing in for Hitler's Germany. The Oscar for the Best Picture of 1940 went to *Rebecca*, a film thoroughly Anglophilic in tone and value. On the other hand, James Stewart won the Oscar for Best Actor in *The Philadelphia Story*, and Ginger Rogers won Best Actress for *Kitty Foyle*, two aggressively Philadelphia-set films concerned with America's efforts to deal with the challenges of social class. What is interesting, however, is a certain repudiation of the genteel in the up-and-coming female stars of 1940. True, Deanna Durbin was allowed her first on-screen kiss that year in *First Love*, given by Robert Stack; but Durbin was essentially a mid-1930s figure, a teenaged Shirley Temple with an operatic voice. The stars emerging in 1940, by contrast—Rita Hayworth, Ann Sheridan, Ida Lupino, Lupe Velez, Marie Wilson, Lana Turner, Lizabeth Scott—each possessed a certain hardness, an invisible shield of attitude and defense, that suggested that times were getting serious and that comedy would not be able to handle all the issues. Even English import Vivien Leigh had this defensive quality, as did comedienne Lucille Ball, who could never fully hide her sadder but wiser flintiness behind a smokescreen of gags.

Later, Americans were to learn some of the causes of this damaged quality, this tough-gal attitude (incest, sexual abuse, battery by boyfriends); but what was important from the perspective of 1940 and the developing war scenario was the fact that these women managed to communicate, however subtly, that they had been through the mill and knew the story. Just a few years earlier Hollywood had been presenting the wisecracking platinum blonde, frank, sexy, self-actualizing. Now, with the war, that insouciance had become hard-boiled. With the exception of Lucille Ball, none of the new female stars of 1940 was humorous or even comic by implication. In their hard looks and defensive attitudes, they tended, rather, to resemble such real-life counterparts as party girl Virginia Hill, later the love of Bugsy Siegel's life, who had eloped at fourteen and by 1940 had three ex-husbands and was a figure in the demimondes of New York, Chicago, and Hollywood.

The most European-oriented film of them all that year, Walt Disney's *Fantasia*, was also the most troubled. True, *Fantasia* had its benevolent side, with Mickey Mouse as the Sorcerer's Apprentice and the cute little Chinese mushrooms dancing to Tchaikovsky's *Nutcracker Suite*. Yet there is as well a ferocious battle unto death between a stegosaurus and a tyrannosaurus rex: their eyes aglow with fierce hatred, their flashing razor teeth. At the conclusion of this sequence, dinosaurs march into extinction in a world that is dying. Even the intended comedy of hippopotamuses dancing to the ballet from the opera *La Gioconda* by Amilcare Ponchielli is offset by the ominous crocodile seducers, Nazi-like figures filled with evil intent. The next to last sequence of *Fantasia*, the tone poem *Night on Bald Mountain* by Modest Mussorgsky (a piece of music so frightening that it was never performed in its composer's lifetime), is dominated by the grimacing head of Chernobog, the god of evil in Slavonic mythology. Drawn for Disney by artist Vladimir Tytla, Chernobog communicates a sense of absolute evil incarnate, reinforced by other menacing spirits, grotesque dancing, and bizarre images of cemeteries, crows, and death: a mood that cannot be fully dissipated by the candlelight procession of worshippers in the last sequence, moving at dusk to the strains of Franz Schubert's "Ave Maria."

In general, then, to judge from radio and motion pictures, a pattern was asserting itself: there could be oblique or displaced references to the war but no head-on consideration. The world of books proved no exception to the rule. No best-seller of 1940, whether fiction or non-fiction, was directly connected to the war, with the exception of *American White Paper* by Joseph Alsop Jr. and Robert Kintnor. As in the case of the movies, however, certain displaced references can be discerned. Jan Struther's *Mrs. Miniver* was strongly Anglophilic, hence interventionist; and Kenneth Roberts's *Oliver Wiswell* told the Loyalists' side of the American Revolution. Richard Llewellyn's *How Green Was My Valley* was set in Wales, hence vaguely interventionist by implication; even Van Wyck Brooks's *New England: Indian Summer* underscored the compelling Anglo-American foundations of the national culture. And was not Ernest Hemingway's *For Whom the Bell Tolls* most fundamentally about the war against fascism? Out in California, where F. Scott Fitzgerald and Nathanael West died the same day, 22 December 1940, the single most enduring novel of 1940 to emerge, Budd Schulberg's *What Makes Sammy Run?*, concerned itself with the backstage, behind-the-scenes Hollywood in which Fitzgerald and West had spent their final years.

No specifically anti- or pro-interventionist regional best-seller surfaced in California that year, although Carmel poet Robinson Jeffers was writing vociferously anti-war poems and, in the course of an Eastern tour, arguing against American involvement. San Francisco poet Kenneth Rexroth, soon to surface as a pacifist, seemed ethereally disconnected from international events in the poems gathered as *In What Hour* (1940). And California's best-known writer, William Saroyan, was, as usual, remaining apolitical in *My Name Is Aram* (1940), a collection of autobiographical short stories published in December to enthusiastic reviews, and in his Broadway play *The Time of Your Life*, which won the 1940 Pulitzer Prize for drama. If Saroyan had any political opinions, they could be discerned in the mournful pacifism of his unproduced play *The Well-Known Soldier*, written in September 1939 when Hitler invaded Poland and optioned in mid-1940 by José Ferrer for a summer tryout at the Bucks County Playhouse.

Then there is the question of denial: the desire to distance oneself from the war in the hopes that it might go away or in some fashion or another work itself out. One can find this dynamic everywhere in the 1940s, nationally and in California. *Sunset* magazine, for example, was throughout 1940 running ads featuring cruises on the American President Line to Japan, China, and the Philippines. The Matson Line, meanwhile, another San Francisco–based company, was offering cruises to Hawaii, New Zealand, and Australia via Samoa, New Zealand, and Fiji. Most poignantly, the Java Pacific Line was in February 1940 advertising cruises to Bali and Java, Sumatra, and India on ships flying the neutral Netherlands flag: this just before the invasion of the Netherlands by the Nazis. The NYK Line (Japan Mail), with offices on Market Street in San Francisco and 6th Street in Los Angeles, was advertising tours to Japan for the cherry blossom season and other vacation opportunities. In 1940, the ad suggested, Japan was celebrating the 2,600th anniversary of the accession to the throne of Jimmu Tenno, the country's founding emperor. There would be, the NYK ads promised, many festivals and pageants American tourists would enjoy. In October 1940 the exclusive San Francisco Golf Club arranged a welcoming reception for Captain Shunji Ito, skipper of the NYK Line ship *Tatuta Maru*, who was accompanied by T. Satow, consul general for Japan in San Francisco. The docks of Long Beach, meanwhile, remained piled high through 1940 with American scrap iron headed for Japan.

Even Captain Fritz Wiedemann, the German consul general in San Francisco, remained throughout 1940 a quasi-acceptable local celebrity, frequently covered in Herb Caen's gossip column in the *Chronicle*. A handsome, elegant man, impeccably tailored in the British style, Wiedemann had been Corporal Adolf Hitler's commanding officer in the First World War. Hitler liked and respected his former company commander and recruited him into the diplomatic service in the late 1930s, posting him to San Francisco. According to the House of Representatives Committee for Investigation of Un-American Activities, headed by Martin Dies, a Democratic congressman from Texas, Captain Wiedemann was the number one Nazi representative in the United States, with the San Francisco consulate at 26 O'Farrell serving as a clearinghouse for spying and networking throughout North and South America. In July 1940, in fact, Wiedemann stood on the edge of prosecution for violation of the United States Foreign Agent Law when an unregistered German courier carrying sensitive information on Latin America was arrested in Los Angeles. On 31 December 1940 *Look* magazine called Captain Wiedemann "probably the most dangerous Nazi in the country." And yet Wiedemann was charming, as everyone knew at the Olympic Club in San Francisco, where he was a member, or down the peninsula in Hillsborough, where the captain maintained a suburban villa at 1808 Floribunda Avenue. Wiedemann's son Edward was attending Burlingame High School, where he lettered in swimming and water polo and was popular with his classmates. The captain could be found, at various times, at any number of Hillsborough soirees or in the grand dining room of the Burlingame Country Club.

Wiedemann, in other words, was as popular as one might expect a Nazi representative in the United States to be in 1940—and a little bit more so, given his personal charm and his ability to pop up in the Herb Caen column. Perhaps there was even a surge of sympathy in San Francisco in 1941 when Wiedemann sought a draft deferment from the German army for the son of one of his key staffers. And it did seem rather decent of the captain, in 1939, to advise German-Americans to stay out of the German-American Bund, although after the war Wiedemann was himself accused of trying to recruit German-Americans into the German army. In any event, Wiedemann left for Lisbon via New York in late 1941 and was posted first to Tokyo, then to Tientsin and Nanking in China. After the war, he was taken into custody in China and flown to the United States for interrogation. Whether Wiedemann cut a deal and sang like a canary may never be known; in any event, the man once described as the most dangerous Nazi in the United States was declared a minor Nazi by a German de-Nazification court in 1948 and fined a paltry $600.

The forces for life were manifesting themselves in a number of ways throughout 1940. One of them, perhaps the most obvious, was an epidemic of marriage. An estimated 1.4 million Americans out of a population of 131,669,275 were married in 1940, with the average age for men being twenty-four and for women twenty-one. Among the 1940 newlyweds: screen stars Ronald (Dutch) Reagan and Jane Wyman, and musician Artie Shaw and screen star Lana Turner. That same year, novelist John P. Marquand made the issue of early marriages among young people facing war the central theme of his best-selling novel *So Little Time*. Honeymoons and honeymooners generated a number of national and California-based magazine layouts. At UCLA four undergraduate married couples leased Falkirk House, near the campus, together. Each couple paid $48 a month for their own bedroom, but all shared meals in common and gave parties together in what the national media featured as a unique inter-gender fraternity-sorority house where nice girls did stay over.

In a direct interfacing of *eros* and *thanatos*, life and death, magazines returned again and again to photographs of attractive young women with young men in the military, whether the Navy wives and girlfriends of Coronado or the hundred-plus young women invited to graduation ceremonies at the Ryan School of Aeronautics in Hemet. Among many such pictorial layouts showing young women visiting soldiers and sailors and air cadets, dancing with them, romping with them on the beach, two featuring nineteen-year-old starlet Jane Russell visiting soldiers at Camp Roberts and sailors at the San Diego Naval Training Station underscore most vividly the *eros* versus *thanatos* theme of 1940 moving into 1941. Few Hollywood stars could better emanate *eros* than the beautiful and full-figured Russell as she stood atop a platform in shorts and T-shirt before hundreds of young men, leading them in their early morning calisthenics.

The introduction of nylon stockings in 1940 provided further opportunity for the erotic, which is to say, the life force dimension, to surface and be celebrated. Women's stockings are by their very nature highly eroticized garments. The invention of mass-manufactured nylon stockings as competition for expensive silk stockings fostered, in effect, a democratization of *eros* in that now millions of women could associate themselves with a highly glamorous and sexualized garment. While the silk hosiery industry responded with a national advertising campaign promoting the more traditional fabric, the magazines lost no opportunity to feature ambitious layouts of women modeling the new nylon stocking stories that allowed multiple opportunities for eroticized photographs of attractive women in various stages of putting on or taking off or merely displaying the new nylons.

Two forces — eroticization and regimentation — vied for dominance of women's fashions in 1940. On the one hand, 1940 witnessed the introduction of the strapless and the open-midriff two-piece bathing suit. Leisure and casual wear exploded in colorful floral patterns that seemed to present a woman's body as a harmonious part of nature herself: as if each woman, in leisure, were emerging from a lush floral arrangement, like Dorothy Lamour in a Crosby-Hope *Road* comedy. Then, on the other hand, there was the uniform, or regimental, impulse, destined to gain preeminence by late 1941. Members of the Women's Ambulance and Defense Corps of America, for example, five thousand strong in Southern California, wore a smart, regimentally sexy khaki uniform that looked forward to the couture-designed women's military uniforms of the war years.

A renewed emphasis, indeed a fixation, upon youth accompanied all this attention to *eros*, sex, marriage, nylon stockings, and fashion. Just as the 1930s seemed obsessed with the figure of the impoverished pensioner, the year 1940 witnessed an even more compelling obsession with young people of high school and college age. Even Shirley Temple, child star of the 1930s, made a tentative entrance into this category with her eleventh birthday on 6 May 1940, when she was allowed to wear her first long dress. Much of the concern with youth represented a lingering legacy of the Depression. By 1940 some 1.8 million young people were coming into a still-depressed job market each year. At a time when the vast majority of young people went to work after high school or left high school to go to work full-time, some four million unemployed Americans were teenagers. The publication that year of Gunnar Myrdal's *An American Dilemma* and Richard Wright's *Native Son* focused new attention on the special problem of African-American youth, young males especially, for many of whom chronic unemployment led to crime or to a numbing despair at the beginning of adult life from which they never recovered. In California, there was renewed media interest in the Sherman Institute at Riverside, a two-hundred-acre campus centered on a Mission Revival building where some 650 young Native Americans were being educated and trained for the work world in a state-run prep and vocational school.

High school was becoming a bigger and bigger deal in 1940, if one is to judge from media attention. In retrospect, high school students seem older in 1940 than their counterparts a half century and more later: more adult in their facial demeanor and hairstyles, their dating habits, and their social rituals. A significant percentage of high school students, after all, would soon be looking for work, which is to say, beginning their adult lives, marrying early (in so many cases someone known from high school), and having children. For 1940, in other words, high school was the equivalent of college in a later era: the last moratorium, the last encounter with a formalized youth culture, before the realities of adult life.

No two film stars better expressed the interest of the nation in young people of high school age—indeed, in high school as a charged and pivotal time of life— than did Mickey Rooney and Judy Garland, stars of the 1940 release *Strike Up the Band*, a musical comedy that further strengthened the genre "Gee! Let's fix up this old barn and give a show" introduced the previous year in *Babes in Toyland*. The avuncular presence of Paul Whiteman, whose orchestra was the band being struck up, framed Mickey and Judy in a context of approval by the older generation. Legally emancipated and living in his own home in Hollywood, Mickey Rooney represented a significant instance of the eighteen-year-old as adult. When President Roosevelt celebrated his fifty-eighth birthday with a ball in Washington, D.C., on 30 January 1940, he invited Rooney, who managed to upstage such other Hollywood guests as Edward G. Robinson, James Cagney, Dorothy Lamour, Gene Autry, and Olivia de Havilland.

When *Strike Up the Band* was in the can, Rooney and Garland gave a cast party at Garland's home in Hollywood: swimming, dancing, a barbecue—and jitterbugging, with Mickey on drums and Ray Hirsch, the national jitterbug champion, doing his thing. Nowhere was the inner emotional and psychological landscape of young people in 1940 more evident than in the jitterbug: a dance, a style, a craze fraught with all sorts of implications. Coming from a generation soon to be fed into the maw of war, the jitterbug was wild, frenetic, and anti-authoritarian. It also released enormous reservoirs of emotional energy. The jitterbug was not so much erotic, as the tango or even ballroom dancing can be erotic, as it was an absolute explosion of emotionalized individualism on the part of athletic young people dancing a dance that only they could do: a dance that by its very nature emphasized personal freedom and autonomy. In Nazi Germany, the jitterbug had been immediately banned as subversive. German kids who danced the jitterbug were, from the perspective of 1940, celebrating life by putting their own lives at risk. In the United States, many, including bandleader Artie Shaw, condemned the jitterbug as anarchistic. Tommy Dorsey, by contrast, defended the dance and pointedly attacked the notion that jitterbugging was a form of juvenile delinquency.

The jitterbug—indeed, the entire emphasis upon high school–age youth in

1940 — represented a subliminal apprehension on the part of an entire generation of young people who were realizing that they might soon be in harm's way. In February 1940 an American Youth Conference, some five thousand strong, descended upon Washington to argue in favor of non-intervention. Roosevelt pointedly told the young people that they were all wet, slyly alluding to the raw weather, although Eleanor Roosevelt arranged for the housing of hundreds of conference members in the midst of a bitter Washington winter. *Eros* and *thanatos*, the jitterbug and the war: some eight years' worth of young people in high school between 1936 and 1944 were entering a zone of risk. Even those in high school during the war were in danger. Thousands of young men entering high school in 1940 and graduating in 1944, for example, might very well find themselves by the end of their graduation year or in 1945 as riflemen in the Battle of the Bulge or in the fierce fighting in northern Italy or in such Pacific-theater man-killing maws as Guadalcanal and Iwo Jima. Indeed, most of the young American men who would die in military service in the Second World War would lose their lives in the final year of the conflict.

While the enlisted men and women of this conflict would come from a wide variety of social backgrounds, college graduates and undergraduates provided a favored recruiting ground for the officer corps. In 1940 high school was broadly based and democratic. College was still an elite opportunity, with a mere 165,000 young Americans earning a bachelor's degree in 1940. Throughout the year, the national media began to show an increasing interest in college-oriented stories, although not to the level of interest it had in high schools. In Southern California, the seven-day spring break in Balboa Beach, which attracted more than twelve thousand college students, with up to thirty young men or co-eds taking over a four-room house for a week of frolic, offered a ready-made opportunity to follow the sons and daughters of privilege as they cavorted on the beach by day and danced at night in Rendezvouz Hall. Over at the Ryan School of Aeronautics in Hemet, meanwhile, college boys were being transformed into a first generation of pilots. Media coverage of the young men frequently mentioned individual cadets' college affiliation; indeed, the Ryan School was organized, in part, as an extension of the college campus.

The Balboa Beach spring break also stressed a notable Southern California link between college students and the beach. *Life* magazine that year had no fewer than three Southern California beach stories: beach life in Venice, UCLA social life on the beach, and the annual Santa Monica lifeguards' beach party. Each story provided ample opportunity for photographs of gloriously fit young people in minimum attire, swimming in the surf, lounging in the sun, as if their youth would last forever and life would always be this glorious day on an unspoiled Southern California beach. Each year, the Reverend Frederick Crane, an Episcopal rector from Beaumont near Palm Springs, took the young people of his parish for a weekend at the beach, organized around St. Christopher's Chapel, which Rector Crane established in a trailer pulled up on the sand. The 24 September 1940 *Look* feature article on this annual encampment charmingly juxta-poses images of piety—the young people gathered in prayer before the trailer chapel at sundown—with images of sun-drenched merrymaking by attractive young people in swim trunks and bathing suits.

In a few short years, these same young people, many of them at least, would be remembering such idylls as they performed their duties in various danger spots throughout the globe. Stanford students—such as Francis Carney, flying missions over Germany in 1944—would be remembering the exquisite, magical co-eds at the Stanford sorority house where he was hashing his way through college or the scent of his date's gardenia as they danced on a warm moonlit night near the Quad. Amidst its depictions of campus life in a setting of almost country-club sheen, the Stanford yearbook for 1940, *The Quad*, reveals only minimal awareness of an impending war, unless the extensive coverage *The Quad* gave to ROTC be brought into evidence. On the other hand, the dedication of the yearbook to peace and non-intervention was electric. "May it never be necessary," wrote *Quad* editor Newton Russell, "for the youth of America to contribute blood, sinew, or brains to 'this generation of conflict' in order to demonstrate 'the utter futility of war.'"

Former President Herbert Hoover would be saying almost the same thing on campus that year at the dedication of the Stanford University–based Hoover Library on War, Revolution, and Peace. The Hoover Library, the former President stated at dedication ceremonies held on 20 June, was devoted to the study of war so that peace might be preserved. As the leading member of his generation of California Progressives, an orientation he shared with his classmate Stanford president Ray Lyman Wilbur, Hoover was highly suspicious of the interventionist policies of his successor in the White House. Just two decades earlier, after all, the United States had taken terrible casualties in slightly more than a year of fighting. If such had been the case then with a European war, what would a more completely global conflict do to those golden boys and girls now sauntering across the Stanford campus, en route to Professor Margery Bailey's lectures on Shakespeare or to meetings of the Rally Committee, the Pan-Hellenic Council, the Inter-Fraternity Council, the Glee Club, the Choir, the Stanford Axe Society responsible for the preservation and security of the axe awarded each year to the victor of the Big Game between Stanford and Cal?

Stanford had had a terrible season in 1939, losing all six of its conference games; nevertheless, hope springs eternal, and *The Quad* accorded fifteen lavishly illustrated pages to the football team, which, in a startling reversal of its previous performance, won nine straight games in 1940, including a 13–7 victory over Cal. UCLA had tied with USC in the fall 1939 season, but USC won the vote of the Pacific Conference to go to the Rose Bowl on New Year's Day 1940, where USC coach Howard Jones won his fifth Rose Bowl victory, 14–0, over Tennessee. By 1940 UCLA, now in its twelfth year at its impressive Westside Los Angeles campus, was coming into its own in more than football. Visiting professor Bertrand Russell, age sixty-eight, British mathematician and philosopher, for example, was lecturing to jam-packed classes. Selected students could attend graduate seminars at the third Earl Russell's home near the campus, where sherry was served as part of the proceedings. UCLA students loved the easy flow of Russell's lectures and the fact that such an eminent, if controversial, academic kept scrupulous office hours. Set like a magical city atop a mesa in Westwood, the beautiful Italian Romanesque quadrangle of UCLA was part of a University of California that had now grown statewide beyond its original Berkeley campus. Along with Berkeley and UCLA, there was the Farm, as the Cal agricultural campus at Davis near Sacramento was known; the Medical Center in San Francisco, with schools of medicine, dentistry, pharmacy, and nursing; the Hastings College of Law and the California School of Fine Arts, also in San Francisco; the Lick Observatory atop Mount Hamilton near San Jose; the W. K. Kellogg Institute of Animal Husbandry near Pomona in Los Angeles County, and the Scripps Institution of Oceanography at La Jolla in San Diego. The seventeen-thousand-student University of California, in short, was en route to becoming the multi-campus university it would become in the post-war era.

Yet as of 1940—and within the context of the emergence of UCLA, which would not gain its full independence as a self-governing campus until after the war—the University of California most fundamentally meant Cal, which is to say, the Berkeley campus, which alumna Joan Didion would later describe as California's best idea of itself. Such a self-identification, although years into the future, certainly emanated from the Charter Day ceremonies held on 28 March 1940 in the Men's Gym on campus or the white-tie banquet that followed, with California governor Culbert Olson and Harvard president J. B. Conant, Charter Day speaker, flanking President Robert Sproul. Certainly one might feel a compelling idea of California surveying the grand array of Classical Revival buildings, dominated by a majestic campanile, set on the still-sylvan campus with a straight-line view of the Golden Gate. Presided over by Provost Monroe Deutsch, an alumnus, the Cal faculty included such luminaries as Max Radin and Roger Traynor (later chief justice of California) in law, Joel Hildebrand in chemistry, George R. Stewart in English, Herbert Eugene Bolton in history, Robert Oppenheimer in physics, and Ernest Bloch in music, with Arthur Bliss a visiting professor in the same department. On 29 February 1940 special ceremonies were held in Wheeler Auditorium at which Carl Wallerstedt, consul general of Sweden in San Francisco, presented the 1939 Nobel Prize in physics to Professor Ernest Lawrence, inventor of the cyclotron and director of the radiation laboratory. Because of the war, the ceremonies could not be held in Stockholm.

Tax supported, Cal nevertheless catered to the privileged middle and upper-middle classes, although it was entirely possible, as frequently happened, for scholarship students to hash and otherwise scrounge their way through to a degree. Yearbook photographs, however, reveal a general prosperity. Cal male undergraduates wore slacks or corduroy pants and cardigan sweaters or coats and ties and sometimes smoked long-stemmed pipes as a mode of statement. Cal co-eds wore white or saddle shoes, knee-length skirts, frequently pleated, and cashmere sweat-ers. At their sororities they gathered each week for formal candlelit dinners on a campus at which fraternities and sororities constituted a major component of un-dergraduate culture.

Like *The Quad* at Stanford, the 1940 *Blue and Gold* suggests a collegiate idyll before the storm. True, there were reverberations from the outside world. In the spring of 1940, for example, Charles Bell, editor of the *Daily Californian*, was writing aggressive pro-peace editorials and pushing for the abolition of compulsory ROTC. Bell's sentiments met with the approval of the UC Peace Committee and the Senior Peace Committee, also active that year. Yet Army and Navy ROTC programs continued without a hitch, commissioning at year's end a generation of ensigns and second lieutenants who would by the time of Pearl Harbor be available for the middle ranks of military management.

But all that was for the future; and even a future that was only two or three years away could seem a remote future indeed to someone who was young at Cal in 1940: a young person, for example, getting ready for the annual Assembly Dance in the gym, with Ray Noble and his orchestra doing the honors; or the Spring Informal at the Claremont Hotel in Oakland; or any of the mixers held on campus each Friday during the academic year. What did it signify if a world was at war if one was busy polishing one's skis in preparation for the 1940 Winter Ski Weekend at the Norden Ski Lodge in the Sierra Nevada, or traveling east to Poughkeepsie, New York, as part of the top-ranked Cal crew for the annual Intercollegiate Rowing Association regatta, or taking the Southern Pacific Owl overnight to Los Angeles for the annual UCLA game, playing poker till dawn in the club car with laughter, talk, and the sounds of a jam session filling the night? For Senior Week, the Class of 1940 took "The Land of Oz" as its theme. "Anything can happen in Oz," stated fliers inviting students to a "Land of the Munchkins" picnic in Marin County and a Graduation Ball with an "Emerald Palace of Oz" theme, to be held at the Palace Hotel in San Francisco. True, anything could happen in Oz; but the Oz of 1940, even 1941, an Oz of youth and privilege, would soon be yielding to new realities.

In the meanwhile, the home, as place and ideal, was, like youth itself, assuming greater and greater importance in American life; and nowhere was this more true than in California. Domestic architecture in California in 1940 was displaying a revived historicism in contrast to the Moderne and the International Style, which had held sway just five years earlier. Now, in 1940, as if to reinforce the notion of a retreat into American circumstances, the architects of California were recovering a variety of American traditions—New England Colonial, mid-Atlantic Dutch, Federalist, antebellum Greek Revival—each of these styles bespeaking, at least metaphorically, an earlier era of domestic stability and peace. Even the ranch house designs of Cliff May for 1940 can be seen in this context, adapting, as they did, the Spanish hacienda to contemporary usage. To drive today up Coldwater or Laurel Canyon in Beverly Hills is to encounter in the earlier phases of ascent home after home from 1940 or thereabouts constituting an almost museum-like display of traditional American styles adapted to Southern California. Even office construction — Paul R. Williams's Federalist Revival headquarters for the Music Corporation of America in Beverly Hills, for example — shows this drive toward a recovered Americanism.

As far as the interiors of these houses were concerned, there was in the year 1940 a concomitant drive toward comfort and domesticity: a renewed interest in the fireplace, for example — its design and placement, the new use of raised fire-places adjacent to kitchens to create a warm, den-like atmosphere in the kitchen and family room — all this putting the hearth and everything that the hearth sym-bolized at the core of the house itself. So too was the kitchen emphasized, not only in terms of the efficiencies of food preparation and service but as a room in its own right, the center of the home, a place of nourishment and nurture. In-creased attention, meanwhile, was being paid to the patio, an outdoor living space incorporating aspects of the kitchen, the living room, the family room, and the den and reflecting the growing popularity of the barbecue. Photographs of interiors from 1940 show a softening of the streamline in favor of a certain cozy comfort, a quality almost Dutch Colonial in its emphasis upon domestic warmth. Furniture has returned to traditional styles, and curtains, drapes, and lamps are almost fussy in their neo-traditionalism. At the same time, a new generation of building ma-terials — plywood, fiberboard, plastic, linoleum — was making household construc-tion easy and more efficient; and a new generation of household appliances — stoves, refrigerators, toasters, pressure cookers, deep-freeze lockers, washing ma-chines — was making domestic life easier. At a time when millions of Americans still preserved their food with blocks of ice, companies such as Kelvinator and Philco were introducing refrigerators that in their dramatic design and varied and capacious storage arrangements suggested a world of domestic abundance. Zenith, Philco, and RCA Victrola, meanwhile, were introducing entertainment consoles for the living room incorporating both a radio and a phonograph with an automatic record changer handling up to twelve 78 rpm discs.

Like the 1940 home itself, the foods coming from the kitchens of 1940, as judged from cookbooks, menus, and *Sunset* recipes, seem (at least in retrospect) to be serving almost self-consciously ambitions of nurture, solace, and comfort. Sixty years later, a nutritionist might blanch at these high-fat, cholesterol-laden foods — the casseroles, dripping in butter and cheese sauce (tuna noodle casseroles, mac-aroni and cheese, tamale pie); the creamed tuna on toast, made with Campbell's cream of mushroom soup; the cholesterol-rich luncheon meats, bologna and liv-erwurst, the Velveeta cheese, the canned Treat and Spam made from fat-laden pork and beef by-products; the mayonnaise that was everywhere, in deviled eggs, potato salad, shrimp Louis dressings, and tunafish sandwiches; the waffles, pan-cakes, custard cornbreads; the Crisco-crusted pies, chocolate cakes, donuts, snails, and butterhorns; the Jell-O salads, peanut butter and jelly sandwiches, fried chicken, meat loaf and mashed potatoes and gravy, the vegetables drenched in creamy sauces. Certain less rich foods were making their appearance — oleomargarine, for example, from Nucoa; frosted (frozen) foods from Libby's; Sanka coffee, 97 percent caffeine free — but the basic American diet of 1940 remained an orchestration of abundance that must, in some way, be placed in contrast to the dwindling caloric intake of Asia, Europe, and the British Isles. Were Americans in 1940 conscious of this superfluity of calories? Were they deliberately creating such domestic menus as a counter-statement to the war-induced scarcities abroad? Or was it merely a matter of the Depression being over and hence of a renewed evocation of plentitude taking hold in the American kitchen? Were all these steaks, chops, hamburgers, hot dogs, meat loaves, sausages, and bacon-and-egg breakfasts merely American preferences resistant to interpretation; or were the food habits of the United States also reflecting a dialectic of plenty versus scarcity, nurture against destruction, life against death?

Then there was the question of drink. Advertisements for hard liquor were common in national magazines. Most ads for hard liquor tried in one way or another to link their product with some aspect of the aristocratic tradition: gentlemen sipping bourbon beneath the portrait of an antebellum ancestor, clubmen with their scotches before a roaring fire, golfers enjoying gin drinks on the nineteenth hole. A survey of bar menus, such as that of the Marco Polo restaurant at the Golden Gate International Exposition on Treasure Island, revealed a number of drinks (martinis, manhattans, daiquiris, whiskies and soda of various sorts) which would survive the century, together with another array of drinks (the gin sour, the whiskey sour, the gin rickey, the Tom Collins, the pink lady, the old-fashioned) that now seem period pieces, evocative of another era. Beer — Regal, Rainier, Blatz, Budweiser, Miller's, Pabst Blue Ribbon, and dozens of local California brands such as Acme and Lucky Lager — also reinforced the prevailing mood of Dutch-like abundance.

Americans were not yet drinking much wine, less than half a gallon per person per year, as opposed to fifty-five gallons per person per year in pre-war France; but Californians were drinking three gallons of wine a year, suggesting the consumption patterns of a much later era. Nineteen forty witnessed the death of the Burgundy-born Paul Masson, last of the founders of California wine; yet Masson's colleague Martin Ray, then in his mid-thirties, was producing pinot noirs that, just before the war, were earning the respect of France itself. The Livermore Valley–based Cresta Blanca line of wines advertised itself nationally on the radio. Over at the Christian Brothers winery in the Napa Valley, two refugees from Nazi Germany, Alfred Fromm and Franz Sichel, were making plans for national distribution; thanks to their marketing efforts, while the wining of America would await the post-war era, the Christian Brothers were producing and selling an impressive two hundred thousand gallons of wine nationally by 1941. Other California labels — Gallo, Petri, Cresta Blanca, Paul Masson, Italian Swiss Colony, Guild, Foppiano, Cribari — were also making inroads into the popular national market. As of 1940 wine was still an exotic beverage, associated, paradoxically, with both the upper and the lower ends; but the very fact that Norman Rockwell was featured in a series of national magazines that year, telling one and all that he served wine in his home as beverage of choice, suggested an impending change.

No such ambiguity clung to another aspect of domestic life in 1940, and that was the automobiles of the era: sleek, assured, elegant in their shaped grilles and aerodynamic forms. The automobiles of 1940 — all of them, up and down the price range — flowed as one harmonious form as opposed to being a composition of separate parts. This was the influence of the airplane, of course; but it was something more as well: a recognition by Detroit (or, in the case of Studebaker, South Bend, Indiana) that the automobile had become the primary expression of taste and imaginative possibilities for the American household and had hence become not just a machine for travel but a sculptural form expressive of freedom and release. Even the lower-priced automobiles — the Fords, Chevrolets, and Plymouths in the $600 range — showed an elegance akin to that of the more high-priced models: the Studebaker in the $700 range; the DeSotos, Pontiacs, Mercurys, and Dodges in the $800 range; the Hudsons, Chryslers, Oldsmobiles, and Buicks in the $900 category; and the Packards, Lincolns, and Cadillacs selling for $1,000 and more. Certain automobiles — the Willys, the Crosley, the LaSalle — would not survive the war years. Other models — the Oldsmobile with Hydra-Matic drive, the Hudson with overdrive — were introducing innovations ahead of their time. Then there were those customized automobiles that were especially evocative of the poetry of American life. The Chrysler Highlander convertible, for example, featured Scots plaid upholstery and was in everything but name a sports car, as was the Lincoln Zephyr Continental Cabriolet convertible, whose hood stood seven inches lower than the standard Continental's. The 1940 Buick Super Estate Wagon, a wood-paneled town-and-country station wagon, jauntily evoked the suburban good life still being enjoyed by many Americans in the second year of a great world war.

Here, then, were the automobiles, from Plymouths to LaSalles, that promised and delivered a new mobility, a new prosperity: cars for the family, for city and beach, cars for business, cars for first dates, cars that in California, with its 2,606,590 registered vehicles (second only to New York), had become a way of life. Each month, *Westways*, the magazine of the Automobile Association of Southern California, featured the California car of the month: a Chrysler Royal Windsor Cabriolet convertible for March, for example, a wood-paneled station wagon with ash panels without and natural mahogany within. The association considered such featured cars objects of art in and of themselves but also automobiles especially suited to the Southern California lifestyle. *Westways* was also interested in what kinds of automobiles movie stars drove. Jackie Cooper of Universal Pictures, for example, was featured at the wheel of his Lincoln Zephyr Continental Cabriolet. A little lower down the socio-economic scale, the towed camper-trailer, forerunner of today's recreational vehicle, had been growing in popularity throughout the second half of the 1930s. And there was plenty of gas for everyone, despite the war in Europe: gas dispensed in California from shiny and omnipresent Richfield, Texaco, Ethyl, Mohawk, Shell, and Mobil stations by uniformed attendants who wore chauffeur hats and bow ties. And there were roads and highways, plenty of them: most recently the new Arroyo Seco Parkway joining Los Angeles and Pasadena, which opened in August 1940 and to this day remains not only a public works tribute to the automobile but the harbinger of the post-war freeway culture to come.

Projects such as the Arroyo Seco Parkway were intended, in part, as public works projects creating employment, hence battling the Depression. The Depression was not over by 1940; far from it. The investigations of the Tolan Committee that year revealed a continuing migration of destitute Americans into the farm fields of California; indeed, it was still common in 1940, at any given railroad junction, to see hundreds of transients riding the rails into California in search of work. In 1938 Californians had elected Democrat Culbert Olson governor, the first Democratic governor in forty years. Tall, physically impressive, gray-maned and leonine, Olson was a paradox: a Democratic governor in a predominantly Republican state, a free-thinker born and raised in Utah who had attended Brigham Young University before taking a law degree at Columbian (later George Washington) University, a former Utah state senator who had left his Utah constituency and career behind in 1920, moving to Los Angeles, where he helped spearhead across the next decade and a half the rise of a Democratic majority in Los Angeles County. Culbert Olson came from the liberal, even utopian, wing of his party. Upton Sinclair's End Poverty in California (EPIC) campaign of 1934 propelled him into the state senate.

Another utopian measure, the Ham and Eggs pension plan, had energized and driven over the top Olson's 1938 run for governor. Yet he and Lieutenant Governor Ellis Patterson were the only Democrats in statewide office, and Patterson was no friend of Olson, in whom the New Deal had come, belatedly, to California — before stumbling badly. In his inaugural address on 2 January 1939, Olson promised to bring the New Deal to California. Five days later, in the same assembly chamber, Olson granted Tom Mooney, the radical Socialist convicted on trumped-up evidence for the Preparedness Day bombing in San Francisco that killed ten and injured forty bystanders, a full and unconditional pardon in a session that was nationally broadcast. Later that afternoon, Olson collapsed at the California state fair, and by the end of his first week in office the first Democratic governor of California in the twentieth century was hospitalized for nervous prostration. Sadly enough, Olson also lost his wife in the first year of his governorship.

By 1940, his second year in office, Culbert Olson had launched a number of reform initiatives, including the reform of San Quentin and other California prisons. Olson's liberal agenda, however, was getting nowhere. By 1940, in fact, Olson was enduring his third recall attempt statewide and in Sacramento was being bested by Republicans and conservative Democrats. Lieutenant Governor Patterson bitterly broke with Olson on various party matters. When the Democrats regained control of the assembly, it was the pro-Patterson, anti-Olson Democrats who held power. Olson's first budget, for 1939–40, had resulted in the largest state deficit of the decade. Far from launching an array of New Deal–like programs, Olson was forced to spend the remaining years of his term struggling for ways to dig himself out of the deficit. More and more, the Republican attorney general of California, Earl Warren, was looking like the next governor of the state.

Olson's inability to gain control of California was only in part a matter of his troubled health, the death of his wife, and the controversial pardoning of Tom Mooney. The very election of Olson and Patterson had been made possible, almost freakishly, by the Ham and Eggs pension plan mania of 1938 (the very same movement, incidentally, that turned against Olson and launched one of the three recall efforts). Culbert Olson, quite simply, did not possess a mandate. In terms of state government, at least, California was highly ambivalent about jumping onto the Roosevelt–New Deal bandwagon. From this perspective, the forces resisting Olson were the very same forces resisting Roosevelt's interventionism. The Republicans, in other words, who were opposing Olson in Sacramento were also, by and large, anti-interventionist in their sentiments as of 1940. Like the rest of the nation, California was ambivalent to FDR. The state could accord Roosevelt a third term in the 1940 presidential election while at the same time opposing practically every move of Roosevelt's most vigorous champion in Sacramento, the lonely and embattled Democratic governor. This divided sensibility was part of a larger American pattern: the nation by and large trusted Roosevelt domestically but was less confident about his interventionist policies.

In contrast to the volatile 1930s, the California of 1940 was not about politics. With the exception of the Tom Mooney pardon, which was a 1930s-oriented event, Olson had trouble getting the attention of California. Indeed, most of state government seems invisible in this period as Californians turned their attention more and more to the satisfactions and diversions of local life and the ongoing distractions of radio and motion pictures. Almost defiantly, 1940 was about ignoring the continuing presence of the Depression, as much as possible, and focusing upon the pleasures of life in the Golden State.

Like baseball. Nineteen forty, after all, was at the mid-point of a golden age for the Pacific Coast League, which included the Seattle Rainiers, the Portland Beavers, the Sacramento Solons, the Oakland Oaks, the San Francisco Seals, the Hollywood Stars, the Los Angeles Angels, and the San Diego Padres. Each of these Pacific Coast teams was playing in an intimate and accessible urban stadium to large and steady crowds of devoted fans for whom the prospect of the West Coast becoming major league territory was not even an issue, much less an aspiration. No comparable minor league was producing as many major league players as the Pacific Coast League or providing as many major league players with an extension of their careers after their best days were over. And besides: fans in Pacific Coast League cities enjoyed an intimacy with their teams, asking them not to be major league but to be the best possible Pacific Coast League, which testified to the enduring regionalism — some would say provincialism — of life on the Coast.

In any event, while very few Californians were feeling much, if any, rapport with Culbert Olson, they certainly knew who pitcher Tony Freitas of the Sacramento Solons was, a diminutive left-hander and the most consistent pitcher in the league; or Lou Novikoff of the Los Angeles Angels, otherwise known, variously, as the Mad Russian or the Scourge of the Steppes, who in 1939 had led the league in runs (147), hits (259), home runs (41), and runs batted in (171) and was named Minor League Player of the Year; or Showboat Bill Schuster, also of the Angels, a wild and crazy guy as comedian Steve Martin might describe him, a player not above indulging in *shtick* on the ball field: lifting the hat and kissing the bald head of a man who heckled him (the umpire ejected Schuster for fraternizing with spectators), pretending to faint when another umpire called him out on a close play, waving his handkerchief as a sign of surrender to a pitcher who was obviously trying to dust him off home plate.

Then, of course, there was the greatest Pacific Coast League player of them all, Joe DiMaggio, formerly of the San Francisco Seals, now setting records with the New York Yankees, leading the American League in batting average in 1939 and 1940 and being voted Most Valuable Player. Born in Martinez across the Bay, the eighth of nine children, and raised in North Beach, San Francisco, Joe DiMaggio had joined the Seals as an eighteen-year-old in 1933 and was soon followed on the team by his brothers Vince and Dom. Headquartered in Seals Stadium at 16th and Bryant, one of the most successful baseball stadiums on the Pacific Coast in terms of its sightlines, weather, and access to public transportation, the Seals were managed by the legendary Frank (Lefty) O'Doul, an Irish-American native of the Butchertown district near Hunters Point who after a solid record in the majors had settled in with the Seals and developed the baseball talents of all three DiMaggio brothers. In late 1934 the New York Yankees had signed Joe, effective in the 1936 season, for $25,000 and five Yankee players: a true testimony to the excellence of this regional team.

While he became a legend in New York, Joe DiMaggio remained attached in one way or another to San Francisco for the rest of his life. In 1937 the brothers DiMaggio opened DiMaggio's Grotto on Fisherman's Wharf, run by brother Tom. Brother Mike was working off the Wharf as a fisherman. Joe was making his headquarters at the family restaurant throughout February and early March 1940 when he was supposed to be en route to the Yankee training camp in St. Petersburg, Florida, but was lingering in San Francisco with his starlet wife Dorothy Arnold DiMaggio, whom he had married on 19 November 1939 at a nuptial mass at Sts. Peter and Paul Church in North Beach. DiMaggio was asking for a $32,500 contract, which represented a $5,000 increase over his 1939 salary, and the Yankee front office was balking. On 7 March 1940, however, the Yankees agreed to DiMaggio's terms, and the Yankee Clipper and his wife left San Francisco by automobile for St. Petersburg, with Dorothy at the wheel: a true home-town boy, a North Beach boy, Joe had only learned to drive in 1939 and never really liked doing so. Motoring to Florida, DiMaggio was tracing the same route he had taken in 1936 when he had first joined the Yankees. He was also, in great measure, driving into history, into legend, for reasons social and cultural historians will never tire of trying to understand in the context of his life and times and the broader concerns of American culture. Suffice it to say that for Californians following Joe DiMaggio's contract negotiations in February 1940, the issues were not about a European war or an American intervention therein. The issues were about baseball, an almost impenetrable symbol of American identity, and a young man who meant more to most Californians than any elected official.

In the *eros* versus *thanatos* dichotomy of Sigmund Freud, baseball was definitely on the side of life. Baseball, in fact, represented an almost pure presentation of American life and values. So too was the Golden Gate International Exposition on Treasure Island in San Francisco Bay seeking to make its statement about life and the arts of peace with a series of courts and colonnades keyed to themes of prosperity and peace presided over by the gigantic statue of Pacifica intended to evoke a dawning era of Asia/Pacific cooperation, commerce, and culture. Opening in 1939, the exposition was kept in operation throughout 1940. Despite the seriousness of its architecture, the exposition was also a popular festival. On Treasure Island, Sally Rand's Nude Ranch, with its scantily clad cowgirls, and the water nymphs of Billy Rose's Aquacade, including eighteen-year-old Esther Williams, were attracting much more attention than any of the reform initiatives of Culbert Olson.

Visitors to the exposition could come by car across the newly completed San Francisco–Oakland Bay Bridge or, if coming from out of state, arrive by train or plane in Oakland or San Francisco. Nineteen forty would prove a peak year for tourism into California, and what better way to arrive than in the elegant modernity of a transcontinental train or aircraft? It was the penultimate era of the transcontinental train as a primary means of access to the West Coast. The war would militarize train travel, and the post-war era would see the transcontinental train lose out to airplanes and the automobile. In 1940, however, transcontinental train travel was experiencing a time of near-final incandescence.

Four major lines—Western Pacific, Union Pacific, Santa Fe, and Southern Pacific—served the Coast. The Exposition Flyer of the Western Pacific left San Francisco daily for Chicago and St. Louis via the Colorado Rockies. The Union Pacific Challenger connected California with Chicago across the northern route. Each day from Los Angeles, the Santa Fe Chief or Super Chief left for Chicago with stopovers at the Grand Canyon and connecting service to Kansas City. The Super Chief was one of the two fastest of the dailies—thirty-nine hours and forty-five minutes from Los Angeles to Chicago. Next to the Twentieth Century Limited of the New York Central, the Super Chief was the most glamorous train in America, favored by the Hollywood elite, especially the stars, as filmdom traveled to and from the East Coast via Chicago. The Southern Pacific offered a number of routes. Its Sunset Route moved through the Southwest to New Orleans. The City of San Francisco connected that city with Chicago, matching the time of the Super Chief. The Southern Pacific also ran two other routes, the Overland Limited and the Pacific Limited, connecting the heartland with the West Coast. (A round-trip ticket to New York for the World's Fair in 1940 on the Southern Pacific cost $90.) Starting in 1937, the Southern Pacific Daylight and Owl connected San Francisco and Los Angeles. These transcontinental and coastal trains represented, in effect, luxurious hotels in motion, with comfortable overnight accommodations, full-service dining cars, vista lounges for sightseeing, and cocktail lounges for evening entertainment. A sojourn aboard one of these streamlined behemoths was the equivalent to a day or two in a first-class hotel at a time when the American economy could sustain a full spectrum of service jobs. Each detail of service, in the dining room and club car, in the overnight Pullman section, was supervised by a cadre of largely African-American porters, chefs, waiters, and other attendants who had found in these positions a livelihood, a vehicle for their own upward mobility, and a rising sense of group solidarity through their union movement.

Overhead, meanwhile, four-engine Boeing Stratoliners bearing the Pan American or Trans World logo were forging a dawning era of trans- and intercontinental passenger flight. The year 1940 witnessed the dedication of a new $38 million New York Municipal Airport, more commonly called La Guardia Field, on Long Island six miles by taxi from Times Square. From this new facility, a plane took off every sixteen minutes of the working day, many of them headed for California. On 15 May 1940 United Airlines marked the tenth anniversary of the inauguration of a new profession, the air stewardess, with a series of celebrations in San Francisco. Each United Airlines stewardess, it was pointed out, was a registered nurse, starting with Ellen Church, a nurse at the French Hospital in San Francisco, who in 1930 designed the first stewardess uniform and wrote the first stewardess manual. In an era not attuned to civil rights, stewardesses were required not only to be nurses, but to remain unmarried. That requirement, in turn, precipitated a high turnover. "I guess I have acted as best man at more weddings than any man in the world," United Airlines regional traffic manager for Northern California S. A. (Steve) Simpson told the San Francisco *Chronicle* at the tenth anniversary celebration.[3] The same issue ran a photograph of some twenty stewardesses lined up beneath a United Airlines DC-3 Mainliner, all in identical uniform and shoes, holding open umbrellas and seeming on the verge of breaking into a Busby Berkeley kickline.

Such might have been appropriate, given the festival nature of California life. Tourists and Californians alike had before them in 1940 a year-long pageant of festival events expressive of the outdoor nature of California life: events as remote as possible from the realities of the European war. The cavalcade began on New Year's Day itself, with the annual Tournament of Roses parade in Pasadena. Edgar Bergen and Charlie McCarthy served as grand marshal for this year's parade, entitled "The Twentieth-Century in Flowers." Each of the floral floats expressed one or another aspect of peace, progress, and the love of nature. No float made reference to the war in Europe. That afternoon, USC triumphed over Tennessee in the Rose Bowl. It was USC coach Howard Jones's fifth Rose Bowl victory and final game, for he passed away in mid-1941. USC place kicker Jimmy Jones would lose his life in the war. That same afternoon, up in San Francisco, the annual Shrine East-West Game was played in Kezar Stadium, with proceeds going to the Shrine Hospital for Crippled Children in the city.

In mid-March, the thirtieth annual National Orange Show in San Bernardino attracted two hundred thousand visitors. Rudy Vallee and his orchestra offered musical entertainment. As in the case of the Tournament of Roses, citrus displays at the show were organized according to theme. This year, instead of the usual Old California Spanish motifs, the Orange Show keyed its exhibits to the general theme of America, which suggested an awareness of the world beyond California, including the war in Europe. One display, the Dove of Peace, dominated the competition. In April the eighteenth annual Ramona Pageant was held in an outdoor amphitheater set in the rugged hills near Hemet, San Diego County, with the snowy slopes of Mount San Jacinto splendid in the distance. Actress Jean Inness played Ramona that year, and her husband Victor Jory played her husband Alessandro; the total cast numbered 215. More than fifty thousand Californians attended the annual All-States Picnic in Ontario on 1 June. Thousands of people ate lunch at a continuous table, marked off alphabetically from Alabama to Wyoming, whose cumulative length was a mile and a quarter. Picnickers brought their own lunches to the mammoth table, and coffee and orange juice were provided free, together with entertainment by strolling musicians. The spectacle of a jam-packed mile-and-a-quarter picnic table of Californians celebrating their state of origin suggested something very important about the inner landscape of Southern California, still in 1940 the land of the Folks, and the pageantesque quality of California life.

California, Southern California especially, was horse country, as evidenced by the numerous rodeo and other horse-oriented events unfolding across the spring and the summer. The annual horse show at the Palm Springs Field Club, held over the weekend of 17–18 February 1940, started the season. For the annual Intercollegiate Rodeo at Victorville in San Bernardino, ranch- and riding-oriented undergraduates from UCLA, USC, and as far away at the University of Texas converged on the town for an exhaustive schedule of competition in riding, roping, and other rodeo arts on 13 and 14 April. More than 350 horses were entered into competition that summer at the thirteenth annual Coronado Horse Show, which ran for six days and nights, 23–28 July. Film star Leo Carrillo, riding a spirited black charger, led the opening day parade of the annual Old Spanish Days festival in Santa Barbara, running from August 14 to 17, featuring costumes, pageants, parades, dances, and horse shows. To end the horse season, the annual Pendleton Round-Up, 11–14 September 1940, billed itself as one of the leading rodeos in the nation, attracting the best buckaroos, bulldoggers, and lasso artists in the country. A re-created pioneer village was set up outside town, and a contingent of Native Americans in full costume and headdress was invited to lead the opening parade.

Friday, 13 September 1940, saw the opening of the Los Angeles County Fair in Pomona. The livestock displays, ranch and farming events, draft horse competitons, citrus fruit exhibits, and displays of California wines all testified to the surprising fact that agriculture remained the lead element in the Los Angeles County economy. On Admission Day, 9 September 1940, the city of Escondido in San Diego County held its annual Grape Day, the second largest, second most successful, and second oldest festival of its kind after the Pasadena Tournament of Roses. Some fifteen thousand visitors jammed into Escondido to enjoy exhibits, band concerts, a floral-grape parade, and a competition between high school marching bands. Equally people-oriented was the eighteenth annual Halloween Festival in the central city park of Anaheim in Orange County, an event designed to contain Halloween pranks and bring some order to a frequently unruly evening. The opening parade of floats ridden by costumed children extended two miles in length, making 1940's the most successful parade of its kind ever. In an era not overly disturbed by the separation of church and state, the Los Angeles City Playground Department, come the Christmas season, offered on the night of 20 December at the Coliseum a program of plays, folk dances, and choral singing oriented toward the holidays. Nearby Exposition Park, meanwhile, was illuminated with its annual Christmas Tree Lane of lights. Christmas 1940 also saw on nine nights, 16–24 December, a series of La Posada processions in the Olvera Street district adjacent to the Plaza. Processionists began at the historic Avila Adobe and moved throughout the entire district of restored Spanish and Mexican adobes.

As far as resorts were concerned, 1940 proved a banner year for such establishments as the Hotel Del Monte at Pebble Beach, where manager Carl Stanley, who had worked his way up from bellman, was delighted by a record occupancy rate. United Airlines had recently inaugurated Mainliner service to Monterey, with connections to the Midwest and East via San Francisco or Los Angeles; and a large number of non-Californians could now enjoy the world-class golfing and tennis available on the Pebble Beach peninsula. So successful was the resort culture of Pebble Beach, it warranted its own magazine, *Games and Gossip*, replete with photographs of events and visitors. The Ahwahnee Hotel in Yosemite was reporting a boom business in honeymooners, as well as some forty thousand guests in the 1940 summer season at Camp Curry, as reported by Mrs. D. A. (Mother) Curry, owner and manager. DeWitt Hutchings, a polished hotelier with degrees from Princeton and Oxford, was equally gratified with the traffic at the Mission Inn in Riverside, founded by his father-in-law Frank Miller at the turn of the century. February 1940 saw the opening of the new Arrowhead Springs Hotel below Lake Arrowhead in the San Bernardino Mountains: a sumptuous up-to-date resort for skiing and other winter sports, spring mountaineering, and summer sports on the lake. Rita Hayworth spent a week there in September.

Nineteen forty was a boom year for winter sports, from the mountains of San Diego County to the Inyo-Mono Heights of the Sierra Nevada at such places as Snow Valley and Keller Peak, Badger Pass and Squaw Valley. In Inyo County alone, between Bishop and Lee Vining, there were five lifts varying in length from 1,200 to 2,200 feet. So busy were the lifts, floodlights were installed for nighttime skiing. Over the weekend of 3–4 February, the Yosemite Winter Club held its first invitational ski meet, challenging invitees to take on the established record of a run to the Badger Pass finish line in two minutes and fifteen seconds for a gold ski, four minutes for a silver. Because 1940 was an excessively wet winter, snow remained late into the spring; *Firnschnee* it was called, spring snow, corn snow, the kind of snow skiers loved because it came as an unexpected gift one last time in April, allowing them to schuss down the slopes one last time before, once and for all, the snow melted. Moreover, due to the heavy rainfall over the winter, orange-gold poppies were ablaze throughout the state by April, together with the white-blooming popcorn flower and patches of blue brodea and bush lupin. In the desert, the primrose, desert mallow, and sunflowers were especially luxuriant. Even so ominous a place as Death Valley seemed to be solidly ablaze in sunflower yellow.

Nineteen forty represented the high point of an ice-skating craze in California and the rest of the country as well, much of it inspired by the films of the Norwegian skater Sonja Henie. The Blue Jay Resort at Lake Arrowhead in the San Bernardino Mountains, among many other places in Southern California, featured a large outdoor rink. So did the Yosemite, where ice-skating instructor Jimmy Bourke was giving lessons to Mr. and Mrs. Walt Disney over a winter weekend. In the Bay Area, there were ice-skating rinks at Sutro Baths at Ocean Beach and at Winterland in the Western Addition. The St. Moritz Skating Rink in Oakland was equally busy. The Persian Room at the Sir Francis Drake Hotel in San Francisco was featuring that winter an indoor ice-skating review entitled *Naughty but Ice*, in which professional skater Red Bennet thrilled the dinner crowd with a six-barrel jump. So too did the Ice Follies skating review pack in the crowds in both San Francisco and Los Angeles, where the Westwood Rink had recently opened.

With California being horse country, it was not surprising that horse racing—at Del Mar, Hollywood Park, and Santa Anita in Southern California, and Golden Gate Fields and Bay Meadows in the Bay Area—flourished. On 2 March 1940 Seabiscuit won the Santa Anita Handicap with a new track record of two minutes, one and one-fifth seconds. Seabiscuit won $86,650 in the race, for total wins of $437,730 in six years of racing: not bad for the ugly grandson of Man o'War, thought to be a no-win horse by the time he was three and sold for a mere $2,500 to a Buick distributor.

Californians loved to fish; and it was a beautiful fishing season that opened in May 1940 on the eastern slopes of the Sierra, with most lakes and streams below nine thousand feet free of ice and teeming with hungry fighting trout. Deer season opened in mid-August. Throughout the spring and summer, the surf was up at the San Onofre Beach in Orange County and elsewhere along the Southern California coast. Especially popular were overnight surfing parties of young people, gathered on the beach in ramshackle camps, their boards heavy and long, twice the height of a surfer, planted in rows in the sand to create a surfers' Stonehenge. Given California's climate, offshore yachting continued all year, with the California and Los Angeles Yacht Clubs hosting their fourteenth annual mid-winter regatta the week beginning 22 February. From 5 to 11 August, the Balboa Yacht Club and Newport Harbor sponsored their annual Newport-Balboa Regatta on behalf of the Southern California Yachting Association. The St. Francis Yacht Club, Corinthian Yacht Club, and other yachting organizations, meanwhile, were equally active on San Francisco Bay.

The Tahoe Tavern resort, a spacious gabled hotel first opened in 1901 a half mile south of Tahoe City on a knoll above the lake, opened for the 1940 summer season on 20 June, with full occupancy expected through Labor Day. Gene Englander and his ten-piece orchestra and the Thomas Mack dancers were returning for the third time as evening entertainment, offered after a day golfing on the Tahoe Tavern course, lounging by the swimming pool, hiking in the nearby forests, or sailing on the lake itself. Over in Lake County, Hoberg's Resort offered a similar, if less expensive, program catering to San Francisco Bay Area residents, as did many popular resorts along the Russian River from Rio Nido to Guerneville to Monte Rio to Occidental. At Monte Rio the Bohemian Club of San Francisco was holding its annual encampment at the Bohemian Grove in late July, featuring a wide array of member-produced musical and dramatic events. The Low Jinks comedy revue that year was entitled *Streamlined Harem*, and the thirty-ninth annual Grove Play, *Saul*, enlisted the efforts of hundreds.

The Hollywood Bowl had an especially successful season that summer with appearances by Lily Pons, John Charles Thomas, Grace Moore, Kirsten Flagstad, and others. Nelson Eddy, Marian Anderson, Lotte Lehmann, and Paul Robeson toured the state that year, and the Ballet Russe de Monte Carlo made the circuit in February. The San Francisco Symphony Orchestra, Pierre Monteux, conductor, and the Los Angeles Philharmonic under the direction, until 1939, of Otto Klemperer enjoyed equally successful seasons with guest appearances by Jascha Heifetz, Fritz Kreisler, and Artur Rubinstein. Easter morning services drew thousands to Mount Rubidoux, the Rose Bowl, the Hollywood Bowl, and Palm Springs. At the Rose Bowl Easter services, some three hundred white-robed singers from the Lutheran Choral Union previewed a new hymn, "Behold the Sun," by Los Angeles resident Carrie Jacobs Bond. The Hollywood Bowl Easter services attracted some thirty-five thousand worshippers. Restaurants in the area remained open all night to serve the crowds, some people arriving as early as four-thirty.

Given the fact that California was a long way from New York, it is surprising just how much good theater was available that year. January saw a production of the Rodgers and Hart musical comedy *I Married an Angel* at the Biltmore Theater in Los Angeles, followed by a production of S. N. Behrman's *No Time for Comedy*, with Katharine Cornell, also at the Biltmore, and this was followed, again at the Biltmore, by a production of George S. Kaufman and Moss Hart's *The Man Who Came to Dinner*, with Alexander Woollcott playing the leading role, a character based on himself. The Pasadena Community Playhouse, meanwhile, was mounting productions of the new play *Young April* by Aurania Rouverol, *Father Malachy's Miracle* by Brian Doherty, based on the novel by Bruce Marshall, and Thornton Wilder's *The Merchant of Yonkers*. In May 1940 Raymond Massey appeared in a production of Robert Sherwood's 1939 Pulitzer Prize–winning *Abe Lincoln in Illinois* at the Pasadena Civic Auditorium. The Geary Theater in San Francisco opened its season in January with a production of *Hedda Gabler*, followed by a *Hamlet* starring Maurice Evans. In August the annual Pilgrimage Play depicting the life of Christ in ten scenes with dialogue taken verbatim from the King James Bible opened in the Hollywood Hills at the outdoor Pilgrimage Theater. Promoters made mention of the fact that now that the Passion Play at Oberammergau in Bavaria was not being held, the Pilgrimage Play represented the only survival of this tradition.

The war, announced San Francisco Opera impresario Gaetano Merola on 5 February 1940 at a press conference at the Fairmont Hotel, was making it difficult to recruit singers from Europe. As a result, Merola was making an extra effort to recruit America-based singers—Lily Pons, Lotte Lehmann, Risë Stevens, Ezio Pinza, and Lawrence Tibbett—for the 1940 season. For the ninth straight year, moreover, the NBC Red Network would broadcast performances live to a national audience. Merola did manage to recruit the American talent he named at the press conference, but also on hand for the 1940 season were such European standouts as Jussi Bjoerling (*Ballo in Maschera*) and Alexander Kipnis (*Der Rosenkavalier*). The San Francisco cast, interestingly enough, refused to sing *Der Rosenkavalier* in English as originally announced and performed the opera in German, which may or may not be taken as a sign of anti-interventionism. Of all the young singers debuting that year with the San Francisco Opera, Suzanne Sten, a slim and attractive Wagnerian soprano from Germany, in residence in the United States for the past two years and soon to be taking out her American citizenship, seemed to attract the most press, including a lyrical photograph of her atop the Empire Hotel waving to the San Francisco skyline. "I left because there is not for anyone room left in Europe," Miss Sten told the *Chronicle* in her German-accented and German-word-order English, "but please let us again about music talk."[4]

San Francisco was a dancing—as well as an opera—town. Even DiMaggio's Grotto on Fisherman's Wharf featured dancing every night but Monday. The Rose Bowl Room of the Palace Hotel that year featured, among other performers, Artie Shaw and his dance band, offering a suave, sophisticated sound definitely not intended for jitterbuggers. Down in Los Angeles, opportunities for dancing were equally available at the Cocoanut Grove at the Ambassador Hotel on Wilshire, with music by Horace Heidt and His Musical Knights; the Florentine Room at the Beverly Wilshire Hotel, with the music of Ray Noble and his orchestra; the

Blossom Room of the Hollywood Roosevelt Hotel, where Harry Ownes and His Royal Hawaiians were appearing; and the Cafe Lamaze on Sunset Boulevard, featuring Hal Chanslor and his orchestra, with Judy Starr as featured singer. Further into town, the Zebra Room at the Town House on Wilshire and Commonwealth, a spot favored by the smart young set from Hancock Park, was featuring the Rhythm Rascals, with vocals by Lila Dean, and at the Hollywood Plaza on Vine, Don Roland and the Tunesmiths were providing the music. For those preferring a Latin beat, there was the Bomba Club on North Spring Street in the downtown, the Capri Club on Pico at La Cienega, and the Trocadero on Sunset Boulevard, featuring Eddie Durante and His Rumba Band. Earl Carroll's on Sunset Boulevard advertised sixty of the world's most beautiful chorus girls.

Hungry Los Angelenos could dine at Lawry's Prime Rib on La Cienega, featuring exactly that, served from silver carts; Perino's on Wilshire, offering the most distinguished cuisine in town; or Chasen's on Beverly Boulevard, the "21" of the West Coast, owned, interestingly enough, by Harold Ross, editor of *The New Yorker*. For booze, drinks, laughs, there was Slapsie Maxie's nearby on Wilshire; or the raffish Tail o' the Cock on La Cienega; or the Cock 'n' Bull on Sunset catering to English expatriates; or the Bublichki, also on Sunset, famous for its gypsy music, sour-milk bread, and vodka cocktails.

Enjoying nights at such places, or other establishments around the state, Californians talked of a thousand things, as people are wont to do when enjoying life. The prospect of the war in Europe or Asia involving the United States must have surfaced in these conversations as an ominous motif, a grim possibility—but also as something for the future, to be postponed as long as possible, certainly beyond this year of Our Lord 1940: this time-out year between the Great Depression and a world war. As Sigmund Freud wrote just before his death, *thanatos*, the forces of darkness, had seized Europe. *Thanatos* had been seizing Asia as well throughout the 1930s. Yet in a place called California, so far from the scenes of destruction, all this might easily be missed, ignored, even actively denied amidst the rhythms and joys of ordinary life. In retrospect, the year 1940, if one is to judge by its media and popular expression, seems almost willfully, in California at least, keeping an acknowledgment of the inevitability of war at bay. The life force, after all, is not about war; and California was about the life force, about *eros* and appetite, enjoyment and festival. In doing this, in behaving this way, California was as usual part of a larger American pattern. The attack on Pearl Harbor would end this ambiguity. For the time being, however, California drifted through 1940 as in a haze of distraction, its people focused on the satisfactions of daily life and the sheer miracle of being alive in a world focused on death.

2

1941 ✴ Shelling Santa Barbara

S UCH a mood of willfully oblivious, even defiant, well-being persisted into 1941, although as the year went on there seemed to be more and more military-oriented articles in popular magazines. This mood, this belief that somehow it would all work out without American involvement, ended abruptly on the morning of 7 December 1941 with the Japanese attack on Pearl Harbor and the formal declaration the next day of war against Japan. Was Pearl Harbor the beginning, Californians asked, of an assault on the American mainland itself: an assault that would turn California into a battleground? Abruptly, the denial of 1940 and the increasing unease of 1941 turned into the justified paranoia of December: a mood of fear intensified by the depredations of Japanese submarines off the Pacific Coast in late December 1941.

On 22 December, for example, fifteen days after the attack on Pearl Harbor, submarine I-17 of the Japanese Imperial Navy, under the command of Commander Kozo Nishino, arrived at latitude forty-five degrees north off the coast of Salem, Oregon. The next day, Commander Nishino sank a tanker, then proceeded north to intercept shipping off the coast of Washington State. For three weeks I-17 and the other eight submarines of the Submarine Force Detachment of the First Submarine Group, Rear Admiral Sato Tsutomu commanding, harassed shipping off the Pacific Coast.

A graduate of the Japanese naval academy and naval submarine school, Commander Nishino had been active in the submarine service since 1923. Submarine I-17 was his eighth command. Launched in July 1939, I-17 represented the pride of the Japanese submarine force. (Eyewitnesses who later beheld the I-17 gliding arrogantly through the Santa Barbara Channel en route to the open sea marveled at its size, comparing it to a surface ship of the cruiser class.) Modeled on a German prototype, the 348-foot, 1,950-ton vessel was indeed the pride of the First

Submarine Group. Cruising at sixteen knots and capable of twenty-four, the I-17 could remain at sea for ninety days with its crew of ninety-four officers and men and had a surface cruising range of up to sixteen thousand nautical miles. Armed with six forward torpedo tubes, the I-17 also carried a deck gun and a machine gun on the conning tower; even more impressive, the submarine maintained its own hangar and reconnaissance plane in the forward section of the deck. The I-17, in other words, was a compact paradigm of the entire Japanese Imperial Navy, capable of underwater, surface, and air action.

In the recent raid on Pearl Harbor, Commander Nishino had conducted a screening operation off the island of Oahu. His next assignment: to move with eight other submarines of his squadron and disrupt shipping and communication off the Pacific Coast of the United States. From Washington, Commander Nishino took I-17 south to Cape Mendocino on the Northern California coast, then proceeded south to San Francisco. Operating off San Francisco in mid-January, I-17 sank an American freighter before rejoining the Sixth Fleet of the Japanese Imperial Navy at Kwajelein, a coral atoll in the Marshall Islands, for resupply by the submarine tender *Aratama Maru*.

Sometime after 10 February 1942 Commander Nishino received orders to depart for the coast of Southern California and commence operations. On 20 February I-17 made landfall off San Diego, then proceeded north to Santa Barbara, running submerged by daylight, cruising on the surface past the lights of the California coast in the evening hours. Shortly after seven o'clock on the evening of Monday, 23 February, in the Santa Barbara Channel, Commander Kozo Nishino stood in the conning tower of the surfaced I-17. Raising his binoculars to his eyes, Nishino scrutinized the Santa Ynez Mountains, beneath which nestled the city of Santa Barbara.

At this point, Commander Nishino and his submarine were capable of perpetrating a most dramatic event: the shelling, strafing, and torpedoing of an American city at the very moment when President Franklin Delano Roosevelt was addressing the nation by radio. Occurring less than three months after Pearl Harbor, such an attack on an American city would have instantly earned its place in American history: no foreign power, after all, had directly attacked an American city since the War of 1812. It would have driven Americans into even further fury—and Californians into further paranoia regarding a large-scale Japanese attack on the coast.

Already, the military was claiming that the Japanese had been operating in California airspace. The day after the attack on Pearl Harbor, Brigadier General William Ord Ryan, commanding officer of the 4th Interceptor Command, had confirmed that a large number of unidentified aircraft had approached the Golden Gate in the late hours of 7–8 December but vanished after searchlights from the Presidio of San Francisco flooded the sky. "They came from the sea," Ryan was reported to have said, "[and] were turned back, and the Navy has sent out three vessels to find where they came from. I don't know how many planes there were, but there were a large number. They got up to the Golden Gate and then turned about and headed northwest." General Ryan personally confirmed the sighting to Mayor Angelo Rossi of San Francisco.

Lieutenant General John L. DeWitt, commander of the 4th Army and Western Defense Command, confirmed the sighting—and expanded upon General Ryan's report. According to DeWitt, the planes had penetrated Bay Area airspace as far as the Navy installation at Mare Island in the northeast quadrant of the Bay. Fighters from Interceptor Command had tracked the planes, DeWitt declared, but were unable to follow them back to their carrier. "I don't think there's any doubt they came from a carrier," DeWitt stated, "but the carrier would have moved after they were launched and they would rendezvous in another spot." The Pentagon, by contrast, was more cautious. Just before noon, Pacific Standard time, on the morning of the 8th, the office of General George C. Marshall, chief of staff of the Army, issued a cautionary statement: "From information received up to the present time, we cannot confirm the presence of any hostile planes."

ENEMY PLANES SIGHTED OVER CALIFORNIA COAST headlined the Los Angeles *Times* on the morning of 9 December 1941.[1] Generals Ryan and DeWitt were quoted extensively. Mayor Fletcher Bowron of Los Angeles began to plan even further emergency measures with the municipal Defense Council. Already, on the night of December 7, a blackout had been put into effect on a fifteen-mile front centered on the harbor at San Pedro. Army troops and private guards had taken up positions at aircraft manufacturing plants, and Coast Artillery units pointed their anti-aircraft guns skyward. As early as the afternoon of the 7th, within hours of the attack at Pearl Harbor, scenes prophetic of the next four years had been enacted as hundreds of soldiers, sailors, and Marines, ordered back from leave, reported to their bases in a flurry of goodbyes to families and loved ones.

Despite the reported sightings, however, and the general mood of panic, General Marshall's skepticism was justified. No Japanese planes had approached the Golden Gate. No Japanese carrier was lurking offshore. But the attack on Pearl Harbor, so swift, so lethally effective, had made such a scenario entirely plausible to Californians, and they—even the seasoned generals among them—sustained fears, which soon became convictions, that the Japanese, having launched such a bold attack, were quite logically en route to the Coast.

And besides: Pearl Harbor had struck the deepest possible chord in the collective psyche of California. For forty years, California had been at war with the Japanese, foreign and domestic, although this war had never made the history books. Not until 1944, in fact, would it be first and clearly called by its proper name in print, the California-Japanese War of 1900–41, a term first used by the Southern California journalist and historian Carey McWilliams. While this war remained officially undeclared, it had nevertheless played an important role in precipitating the conflict—the deep and fearsome antipathy between the peoples of Japan and the United States—which, among other causes, had now brought submarine I-17 to its shelling position in the channel off Santa Barbara.

Long before Washington had declared war on Tokyo, California had declared war on Japan: the worst possible kind of war, born of fierce racial hatred, uncompromising and annihilating in intent. Along with other white-only movements — White Australia, White New Zealand, White Canada — the White California crusade had poisoned the well between Japan and the United States. The California-Japanese War had shamed and humiliated Japanese residents on the Pacific Coast and offended and enraged the Japanese people. It had continually disrupted diplomatic efforts by Washington and Tokyo to find a common ground between the two emergent Pacific powers. Within two months of Commander Nishino's arrival off Santa Barbara, the California-Japanese War, now a war within a war, would encourage one of the most egregious violations of civil rights in American history: the rounding up and deporting to concentration camps of some hundred thousand Japanese residents on the Coast, the majority of them American citizens.

All wars have their ironies and lost possibilities, and the California-Japanese War was no exception. In another possible scenario, one unmarred by racial antagonism and clashing imperialisms, California and Japan might have achieved at a much earlier date the synergy, interdependence, and mutual self-identification that would by the 1990s create a California-Japan nexus that was its own distinctive social and economic place. Similar in physical configuration — Japan, an island in a sea; California, a mountain and sea-block island on the western North American coast — the two commonwealths faced each other across the North Pacific, as antithetical yet synergistic intensifiers and intensifications of each other's traditions. Each civilization had been precipitated into modernism by the same cluster of ideology and events. Manifest Destiny, the Mexican War, and the Gold Rush had delivered the United States of its Pacific identity with the ferocious midwifery of war, conquest, and mass migration; and this had made California an American commonwealth and the United States a Pacific power, and this in turn had brought the black ships of Commodore Matthew Perry steaming into Tokyo Bay on 8 July 1853. Among his dispatches Perry carried a letter to the Shogun from President Fillmore making specific reference to the rich mineral wealth of California and the maritime trade between California and Asia as reasons to promote a relationship between the two countries.

As California itself came of age as an American commonwealth, it played no small part in stimulating the rise of Japan into an industrialized power. It was California, specifically the Gold Rush, that allowed Nakahama Manjirou to earn enough money in the mines, $600, to return home. Shipwrecked in 1841 at the age of fourteen off Torishima Island, Manjirou had been rescued by an American whaling vessel and taken to New England, where he was educated in seamanship and navigation. Ten years later, in 1851, California gold provided Manjirou his return passage. Purchasing a small sailing boat in Hawaii, Manjirou, a first-class seaman, headed home: a Japanese-American of sorts, or at the least the first person to bridge the two cultures. Under the Meiji government, Manjirou became a professor of navigation at the Kaisei School, later Tokyo University, and made two trips back to the United States as an official interpreter. From the arrival of the first official Japanese delegation on the American frigate *Powhatan* on 9 March 1860, with Nakahama Manjirou aboard as interpreter, San Francisco served as the port of arrival and departure for travel between the two nations. In January 1867 the Pacific Mail Steamship Company established monthly service linking San Francisco, Yokohama, and Hong Kong with the wooden side-wheeler *Colorado*. The company later added the *Great Republic, China, Japan,* and *America* to this service. At 360 feet in length and weighing 4,352 tons gross, these side-wheelers were the largest wooden merchant steamers ever to operate on the high seas.

Although there were only a handful of Japanese in California—no more than fifteen hundred or so, out of a total mainland population of slightly more than two thousand—Californians of the educated classes, especially the citizens of Berkeley, Palo Alto, and San Francisco, were noticeably Japanophilic in their tastes throughout the 1880s and early 1890s. David Starr Jordan, the founding president and later chancellor of Stanford University, traveled from Palo Alto to Japan in 1900 and 1911 and made a special effort to recruit Japanese students. Thanks to Jordan's efforts, Stanford ranked second only to Harvard as the university of choice for Meiji-era students eager to sharpen their professional and technical skills.

In the *fin de siècle*, the aesthetics of Japan held a special appeal for San Franciscans. Brought to San Francisco in 1894 from the Columbian Exposition at Chicago, the Japanese Pavilion was permanently emplaced in Golden Gate Park as an instantly popular tea house and public garden. Gump's, a San Francisco department store, did a thriving trade in screens, statuary, and *objets d'art* from Japan. *Japonaiserie* was all the rage. Novelist Gertrude Atherton describes San Francisco society matrons entertaining in elegant kimonos and decorating their homes with Buddhas, screens, vases, and other forms of *japonaiserie*. Sailing to Japan on two separate expeditions, San Francisco artist Theodore Wores returned with a pioneering portfolio of Japan-inspired canvases. Bay Area architects such as Bernard Maybeck redeployed the Japanese wood-building tradition to Northern California redwood. At night, Japanese lanterns illumined Bay Area gardens; and David Belasco's New York drama that inspired Puccini's *Madama Butterfly* was said by many to have had its origins as a play first performed at the Bohemian Club in San Francisco.

As a formal expression of such interest in Japanese culture and aesthetics, David Starr Jordan joined San Mateo attorney Henry Pike Bowie to form the Japan Society of Northern California in October 1905. Other early members included the noted architect Willis Polk, designer of many San Mateo County residences, and Eugene DeSabla, co-founder of the Pacific Gas & Electric Company. Over the next four decades, until Pearl Harbor, the Japan Society maintained a busy schedule of lectures, exhibitions, study-travels, and other cultural activities. In and of himself, the socially prominent Henry Pike Bowie epitomized the Japanophilic tastes of upper-class California. Having lived and studied in Japan in 1893 and become skilled in the language, Bowie had kept a close personal connection with the country, which he visited a number of times in the following decade. In 1899 Bowie married Komako Hirano, a highly placed woman attached to the imperial court. An adept painter in the Japanese style, Bowie placed respectably in Tokyo competitions. In 1911 he published *On the Laws of Japanese Painting*, a reference book in use to this day. He was transforming, meanwhile, Severn Lodge, his Burlingame estate, into a virtual museum of Japanese art and culture. While at home, Bowie spoke only Japanese to his wife and Japanese servants and frequently wore traditional Japanese dress. Even more boldly, he erected a memorial gate on his property in honor of the valor of Japanese soldiers and sailors during the Russo-Japanese War.

All this (with the exception of the memorial gate) was more than a little *raffiné*, however, hence somewhat fragile and irrelevant, before the onslaught of military and economic competition and the geopolitics that followed. Throughout these years, the empire of Japan was rising as an industrialized naval power, with a number of its top naval officers trained at Annapolis and a significant percentage of its engineers and industrialists trained at American universities. The United States, meanwhile, was becoming progressively more conscious of itself as a Pacific power, urged in this direction by, among others, historian Brooks Adams and naval theorist Alfred Thayer Mahan, who exercised such a persuasive influence over a young Assistant Secretary of the Navy by the name of Theodore Roosevelt. In contrast to his brother Henry, who believed that the United States had no long-range interests in the Pacific, Brooks Adams urged an American expansion into the Pacific Basin as a means of detaching the United States from the inevitable decline of Europe and Great Britain. For Captain, later Rear Admiral, Mahan, the United States had no choice but to establish itself as a naval power in the Pacific to offset the growing presence of the Japanese. Brooks Adams published *The Law of Civilization and Decay* in 1896, and Captain Mahan published his *Interest of America in Sea Power* in 1897. With the acquisition of the Philippines through the Treaty of Paris of 1898, the United States became, virtually overnight, a Pacific power.

From the viewpoint of Japan, the acquisition of the Philippines brought the United States disconcertingly close to Nippon. Conversely, the American annexation of Hawaii that very same year brought Japan disconcertingly close—a mere 2,090 miles—to the United States. Forty-three years later, Carey McWilliams would describe the annexation of Hawaii as the Pearl Harbor of the undeclared California-Japanese War. In 1886 the then Kingdom of Hawaii had entered into an agreement with Japan to allow for the importation of Japanese laborers. By 1890 there were some 12,360 Japanese in the Hawaiian Islands. In 1899, a year after annexation, some 12,000 more Japanese laborers arrived. By 1900 there were 61,111 Japanese resident in the islands. Thus when the United States formally declared Hawaii a territory in 1900, it incorporated *en bloc* its large resident Japanese population. Added to the 24,326 Japanese living on the mainland by 1900, these

61,111 Japanese in Hawaii suddenly gave the United States a Japanese population approaching the 100,000 mark. Not only had the population of Japanese on the mainland United States increased itself tenfold in a decade, this population had in turn been quadrupled by the annexation of Hawaii.

Not only were the Japanese arriving in great numbers, they were bringing their ships of war with them. In April 1897 two Japanese cruisers arrived in Hawaii on a diplomatic mission, a visit that sent a shudder of fear throughout the American naval establishment, including Assistant Secretary of the Navy Theodore Roosevelt, who wrote a long memo to President McKinley describing the possible deployment of American ships in the Pacific if the two Japanese cruisers signaled the impending arrival of a larger naval force. Indeed, the cruisers' visit facilitated the annexation of Hawaii shortly thereafter. In May 1905 the Japanese fleet that Roosevelt and others feared in 1897 destroyed the Russian fleet at Tsushima Strait. For the first time an industrialized Asian nation had defeated a European antagonist. The triumph of the Japanese in the Russo-Japanese War dovetailed with the growing Japanese population in Hawaii and California to create an impression of aggressive ascendancy that a certain sector of white California found frightening, along with their counterparts in Australia, New Zealand, and British Columbia.

Thus Japan emerged after the Russo-Japanese War as the fact and symbol of Asian expansion into white territory and prerogatives. In California, that dubious distinction had previously been held by the Chinese, who first emerged as scapegoat of choice during the rise of the Workingmen's Party in the 1870s. Thanks in large part to California agitation, the United States passed the Chinese Exclusion Act in 1882. Ironically, this act had first encouraged white California farmers to recruit Japanese laborers to replace the excluded Chinese. Possessing a special intensity when it came to Asians, the fierce and persistent racism of California, especially among the embattled and incipiently dispossessed (the upper classes, it must be remembered, loved their Hispanic stablemen, Japanese gardeners, and Chinese houseboys!), shifted easily from the Chinese to the Japanese as objects of obsession.

San Francisco, scene of the Chinese Must Go! crusade of the 1870s, emerged in the early 1900s as the center of anti-Japanese agitation. As the capital city of organized labor on the Coast, San Francisco teemed with organizations and individuals for whom the specter of Japanese labor migrating *en masse* into California represented their worst nightmare come true. In 1888 the Coast Seamen's Union initiated an opening skirmish in the California-Japanese War when it successfully opposed a proposal by the Shipowners Association of San Francisco to hire Japanese seamen on American ships. Throughout the 1890s the union and its publication, the *Coast Seamen's Journal*, together with *Labor Clarion* and *Organized Labor*, publications of the San Francisco Building Trades Council, spearheaded the anti-Japanese movement with a torrent of paranoid invective.

Not surprisingly, the rank and file occasionally edged into violence. In 1890 members of the Shoemakers Union assaulted Japanese cobblers in San Francisco. The next year, members of the Cooks and Waiters Union trashed a Japanese restaurant. Once again, as in the anti-Chinese agitations of the 1870s, working-class San Franciscans tormented themselves, and were in turn tormented by their leadership, with the specter of Asian workers taking their jobs. When Japan signed a treaty and naval alliance with Great Britain in 1902, paranoia quickened in the heart of Irish Catholic working-class San Francisco; for now their two most dreaded enemies—the English, who had seized their homeland, and the Japanese, who wanted their jobs—had formed an alliance that had every possibility of controlling the sea lanes of the Pacific.

Lest too much responsibility for the California-Japanese War be laid at the feet of workingmen and -women of Irish Catholic descent in San Francisco, it must be said that the more established sectors of Bay Area life, operating out of a variety of motives, did their best to fan the flames of paranoia. The *Argonaut*, for one thing, the magazine of the nativist Right, carried on a consistently anti-Japanese policy. Its editor, Jerome Hart, spoke for all those for whom the Japanese represented just one more intrusion—like the Irish!—of the unassimilable into a California commonwealth that would be best governed by the old mercantile ascendancy.

The Progressives thereupon joined the fray, seeing in the specter of cheap Japanese labor the means by which the nineteenth-century oligarchy, which it detested, could continue its hold. The single most powerful anti-Japanese utterance from this period came not from a labor leader, nor even from a member of the old Bourbon mercantile elite, but from Stanford sociology professor Edward Ross, a leading Progressive reformer. Speaking before an anti-Japanese rally sponsored by the San Francisco Labor Council on 7 May 1900 (in the the first mass anti-Japanese demonstration of its kind), Ross provided the California-Japanese War with its marching orders and ideological *raison d'être*. The Japanese, Ross told the rally, were unassimilable. Working for low wages, they undermined the American workingman. They were able to work so cheaply because of their lower standard of living. And last—and in the long run most damnable—"they lacked a proper political feeling for American democratic institutions."

Coming from a Stanford professor, such opinions corroborated the instinctive hostility of Ross's working-class audience. But the Progressive professor went even further in his rhetoric. "Should the worst come to worst," Ross thundered, "it would be better for us if we were to turn our guns upon every vessel bringing Japanese to our shore rather than permit them to land."[2]

Sharing the platform with Ross was another Progressive, San Francisco mayor James Duval Phelan. Privileged and patrician, Phelan was but one generation, possibly one and a half, removed from his Irish Catholic audience, having been born in San Francisco in 1861 to an Irish Catholic family that had become rich in the Gold Rush. Phelan's money, however, his education at St. Ignatius College and the Hastings College of the Law, his European travels, his presidency of the

Bohemian Club, had not so totally removed him from his audience that he could not quickly identify in their anti-Japanese resentment a continuing source of political support for his own career and, even more darkly, something that also spoke to his own instinctive fear of Asia. Phelan saw in Asia and Asians, most intensely represented by the Japanese, something vast and terrible, something totally at odds with the European Catholic Mediterranean tradition, which he believed was the social metaphor with which emergent California should align itself. Without drastic action, Phelan told his audience of carpenters, bricklayers, hod carriers, draymen, and stevedores, "these Asiatic laborers will undermine our civilization and we will repeat the terrible experience of Rome."

The moment had its ironies and incongruities. Within a few short months these very same workingmen would temporarily destroy Phelan's political career with a general strike, but for the time being the mayor was doing his best to tell them what they wanted to hear. Two months earlier, in fact, Phelan had launched a most terrible preemptive strike in the rapidly developing California-Japanese War. Citing an alleged outbreak of bubonic plague in San Francisco, Phelan had ordered the quarantine of both the Chinese and Japanese districts in the city. This quarantine was followed by the forced, frequently brutal, mandatory inoculation of the Chinese and Japanese population.

Anti-Japanese hatred possessed a circularity. The unions scapegoated the Japanese because workers feared for their jobs and harbored deep suspicions that the upper classes of California would prefer, in the long run, Asian to white labor. Upper-class Californians such as Phelan and *Chronicle* publisher Michael H. de Young, in turn, scapegoated the Japanese to please the masses. Politicians like Phelan, in turn, bearded the Japanese to please de Young and the *Chronicle*. Brought to San Francisco in 1854 as a child, Michael Harry de Young had spent the past decade seeking election to the United States Senate. De Young's primary weapon in this campaign was the *Chronicle*, the San Francisco newspaper he and his brother had founded in 1865 as a drama and arts review. Like Phelan, like so many California oligarchs, in fact, de Young had been jumped up in life from ambiguous origins by sudden wealth. As a newly minted Republican patrician, however, de Young still needed a direct connection to the masses, the unions especially, if he was to attain his goal of a Senate seat. Personally cultivated, de Young, like Phelan, enjoyed playing philanthropist and patron of the arts. Political power, however, was partly but significantly in the hands of a more rough-hewn lot, Irish Catholic unionists; and so de Young made the *Chronicle* a vicious and vociferous castigator of the Japanese in the hopes of winning the backing of labor and propelling himself into the Senate.

Thus the *Chronicle* began to editorialize against the Japanese as early as 1891. In 1893, when revolution broke out in Hawaii, the *Chronicle* argued that the islands should be annexed before they were seized by the Japanese. Otherwise hostile to the unions, the *Chronicle* gave extensive coverage to the anti-Japanese remarks of the trade union leadership. Editor John Philip Young directed this campaign on behalf of his boss, filling the paper with innumerable anti-Japanese articles through the early 1900s.

In early 1905, as candidates positioned themselves for election to the United States Senate by the state legislature, the *Chronicle* outdid itself. Among its headlines that February were BROWN MEN ARE AN EVIL IN THE PUBLIC SCHOOLS, JAPANESE A MENACE TO AMERICAN WOMEN, and BROWN ASIATICS STEAL BRAINS OF WHITES. On 23 February 1905 the editorial pages, abandoning all pretense at an economic argument, reached new intensities of invective. "Japan sent us," opined the *Chronicle* in an editorial most likely written by Young, "not her fittest, but her unfittest; she has sent us the scum that has collected upon the surface of the boiling waters of her new national life, the human waste material for which she herself can find no use."[3]

In May 1905 the California-Japanese War, inflamed by such headlines and editorials in the *Chronicle*, reached a new point of escalation. On 6 May the San Francisco school board passed a measure placing all students of "Mongolian descent" in a separate school. At the time, there were only ninety-three Japanese students in attendance out of a total school population of twenty-five thousand. No written or oral evidence against these Japanese pupils had been offered the school board. On the contrary, teachers tended to praise their Japanese students for their diligence, neatness, and courtesy. The following evening, labor held a mass rally at Lyric Hall in which such speakers as Andrew Furuseth, president of the International Seamen's Union of America, denounced the imminent possibility of a massive influx of Chinese and Japanese labor into California. That month as well, the California Federation of Labor helped form a Japanese Exclusion League dedicated to a complete ban on Japanese immigration to the Coast. A raft of anti-Japanese bills was soon pending in the state legislature. During the earthquake and fire of April 1906, nineteen cases of assault against Japanese residents of San Francisco were reported, despite the fact that the Japanese government had sent funds to aid the stricken city.

At this point, as San Franciscans rebuilt their city, anti-Japanese agitation surfaced for a number of complicated, interactive reasons. The mayoral administration of Eugene Schmitz, for one thing, was in deep trouble. Elected in 1902 as a candidate from the newly organized Union Labor Party, Schmitz took his orders from Abraham Ruef, a dapper attorney who served as political boss of San Francisco. A genial orchestra leader of Irish-German Catholic heritage, Schmitz served as front for an elaborate network of bribery and corruption orchestrated by Ruef. On the verge of being indicted for felony bribery, Schmitz turned to that old standby, anti-Japanese agitation, as a way of salvaging his declining fortunes. Passed in May 1905, the school board resolution segregating the Japanese had remained unenforced. On 11 October 1906 Mayor Schmitz put the resolution into effect.

Now Mayor Schmitz had something in common, hostility to the Japanese, with the man who was doing the most to put him behind bars, former mayor James Duval Phelan. And President Theodore Roosevelt, who had backed Phelan's efforts to get Schmitz and Ruef indicted, was now in the awkward position of finding himself literally on the verge of war with Japan because of the grossly insulting nature of the San Francisco school board ordinance.

Outraged by what he considered a "wicked absurdity," Roosevelt sent Secretary of Commerce and Labor V. H. Metcalf, a Californian, out to San Francisco to investigate. In a report dated 18 December 1906 Secretary Metcalf said that there was no justification whatsoever for the segregation of Japanese children in the schools of San Francisco. Metcalf also documented the nineteen cases of violence against Japanese residents of the city during the earthquake and fire. Just before Christmas 1906 Mayor Schmitz, now under indictment, linked his prosecution by the federal government with the pro-Japanese stance taken by President Roosevelt and Secretary Metcalf. The indicted mayor conjured up an image of a war with Japan, in which he was unafraid to lay down his life. Labor leader P. H. McCarthy, head of the Building Trades Council, who would soon succeed Schmitz as mayor, argued that the states west of the Rocky Mountains should unilaterally go to war with Japan, which they could whip at a moment's notice.

In February 1907 the American public was treated to the *opéra bouffe* spectacle of an indicted mayor, Eugene Schmitz, together with the president of the San Francisco school board and the superintendent of schools, meeting with President Roosevelt in the White House as if San Francisco, in its war on Japan at least, were a sovereign state. Indeed, Schmitz negotiated with Roosevelt as if San Francisco had every right to its own foreign policy when it came to the Japanese; and for the moment, the indicted mayor dealt with Roosevelt, who had helped indict him, as a near-equal.

In exchange for withdrawing the offensive ordinance, which Schmitz did in March 1907, Roosevelt issued an executive order prohibiting further Japanese immigration to the United States by way of Hawaii, Canada, or Mexico. This was followed by a so-called Gentleman's Agreement with Japan, put into effect in 1908, in which the Japanese government promised not to issue any further passports to laborers seeking to immigrate to the United States. In its war against Japan, California had succeeded in forcing President Roosevelt to implement its foreign policy.

Agitation did not cease, however, once the Gentleman's Agreement came into effect. Among other things, the San Francisco Police Commission refused to license any new Japanese restaurants. Eugene Schmitz was tried, convicted, removed from office, and later had his conviction overturned on appeal; Abe Ruef went off to San Quentin; but the reforming politicians who replaced these colorful, if corrupt, characters continued their anti-Japanese crusade. In 1910 reformer Hiram Johnson, who had served as special prosecutor against Schmitz and Ruef in the courtroom, ran for the governorship as a Lincoln-Roosevelt Progressive firmly wedded to an anti-Japanese program. By the early 1910s so many anti-Japanese organizations had proliferated in California (there was even an Anti-Jap Laundry League founded in March 1908 by the Laundry Drivers Union in San

Francisco), it became necessary to establish a coordinating organization called the Associated Anti-Japanese Leagues.

From the first, the anti-Japanese crusade in California wrought havoc with diplomatic relations between the United States and Japan. In his annual message to Congress on 4 December 1906, President Roosevelt denounced the San Francisco school segregation order. Roosevelt took very seriously the ability of this local event to influence relations between two otherwise friendly nations. The following April, Secretary of State Elihu Root denounced the San Francisco school board in a speech delivered in Washington. Both Roosevelt and Root realized that the empire of Japan, fresh from its victory over Russia, was in no mood to be baited by a group of corrupt politicians in San Francisco; and when, sadly, this occurred, Mayor Schmitz, Boss Ruef, and the other Japanese-baiters thus succeeded — not for the last time — in poisoning Japan's perception of the United States.

As outrageous as the San Francisco school board issue was, matters became even worse in 1908 when the Great White Fleet sailed into Yokohama Harbor. Outraged by such a show of friendship by the United States toward Japan, Japanese-baiting politicians in California introduced a series of measures into the state legislature to segregate all Japanese children in all the public schools of California. Other measures called for prohibiting Japanese from owning land (this anticipating the Alien Land Law of 1913) or serving as directors of corporations and for segregating all Japanese into specified residential sections. Once again, Theodore Roosevelt was outraged. Here was his Great White Fleet in Yokohama Harbor on a goodwill mission, and California was subverting this national diplomacy with an outrageous series of proposals. On 16 January 1909 Roosevelt wired Governor James Gillett protesting California's subversion of national policy. Two weeks later, a mob in Berkeley assaulted some Japanese residents. In 1911 Roosevelt's successor, William Howard Taft, was forced to deal directly with California legislators in an effort to head off yet another cluster of anti-Japanese bills. While the California legislature was entertaining the Alien Land Law of 1913, President Wilson sent Secretary of State William Jennings Bryan to Sacramento to plead against its passage. Progressive Governor Hiram Johnson rallied the anti-Japanese lobby, however, and the bill passed, despite statements by both the President and the Secretary of State that this law offered insult to the Japanese people and their government.

The very next year, not content with this local victory, California took the anti-Japanese crusade to Washington itself when California congressman John Raker introduced a bill to replace Roosevelt's Gentleman's Agreement with a formal exclusion of Japanese from the United States. Once again, Secretary of State Bryan interceded, begging Raker to withdraw the bill for the good of the nation. Good soldier that he was in the California-Japanese War, Raker refused; but fortunately, the House rejected his bill as not being in the national interest.

In April 1919 Secretary of State Robert Lansing found himself embarrassed before the Japanese at the peace conference in Paris. At the conference, the Japanese and the United States were allies; yet Lansing found himself chagrined by the anti-Japanese Alien Land Initiative then being debated in California, further discussion of segregating Japanese schoolchildren, coming this time from Sacramento, and the outrageous speeches of James Duval Phelan in the United States Senate. Once again, a Secretary of State was forced to appeal directly to the California state legislature, asking it to drop the three anti-Japanese measures it was debating, lest the United States be placed at a disadvantage before the Japanese in Paris. Fortunately, the legislature agreed to drop two measures, and Governor William Stephens squelched the most insulting third, calling for the segregation of Japanese pupils; but, once again, anti-Japanese behavior in California was poisoning diplomatic relations between the United States and Japan.

In 1924, as Congress contemplated a comprehensive act restricting immigration, California's Senator Samuel Shortridge twisted the dagger in the wound when he succeeded in having an amendment attached to the act excluding from immigration "all aliens ineligible to citizenship." Since the United States Supreme Court had decided in November 1922 that the Japanese were ineligible aliens, Shortridge had thus deftly succeeded in banishing the Japanese forever from the United States, without exception. Japanese ambassador Hani Hara wrote a letter of protest to Secretary of State Charles Evans Hughes. In his letter, Hani Hara referred to the "grave consequences" that would follow the passage of the Shortridge amendment. Hughes concurred and publicly stated that the insulting Shortridge amendment would nullify all good will between Japan and the United States. Senator Henry Cabot Lodge, however, a staunch isolationist and opponent of Japan, used Hani Hara's mention of "grave consequences" to incite both the Senate and the House to fury. Japan, Lodge declaimed, was threatening the United States. The House and the Senate kept the Shortridge amendment in the Immigration Act of 1924, thus permanently banishing the Japanese from immigration; and once again, despite the pleadings of a Secretary of State, California had helped convince many Japanese that the United States was an irreconcilable, racially motivated enemy it could never placate: an enemy that loathed the Japanese people in their very physical being and wished them banished from its midst.

All this enmity had arisen, moreover, despite constant efforts on the part of the Japanese government between 1907 and 1919 to accommodate white California. As early as 1901, when Governor Henry Gage protested the influx of Japanese into California, the Japanese government had held back on issuing passports to contract laborers wishing to go to the United States, and the number of Japanese arriving in California fell off by 50 percent. In 1907 the Japanese had agreed not to issue any more passports to laborers, followed in 1919 by a decision to issue no more passports to the so-called picture brides, which is to say, female immigrants coming to the United States for pre-arranged marriages. In 1924, in an effort to placate the United States, the Japanese Diet had amended the law of nationality of Japan, which held that any child born of Japanese parents was automatically a Japanese subject. Under the new law, Japanese parents living abroad would have to declare within fourteen days of the birth of their child their intention to have the child remain a Japanese national.

These legal concessions were matched by efforts to promote harmony between the two nations. In 1913, for example, disturbed by the rising tide of anti-Japanese sentiment in California leading to the first Alien Land Law, the Japanese government sent a Commission of Conciliation to California in an effort to determine the exact cause of the anti-Japanese sentiment and, if at all possible, to make recommendations promoting harmony. One of the commissioners was J. Soyeda, an official of the Associated Chambers of Commerce of Japan. A graduate of Tokyo University who had studied at Cambridge and Heidelberg, Soyeda was a lifelong admirer of American culture and institutions. Upon his return to Japan, Soyeda wrote a pamphlet entitled *Survey of the Japanese Question in California* (1913). In his report Soyeda took the high ground, urging Japanese in California to make every effort to understand American culture at its best—and begging white Californians to extend the same sympathy to the Japanese immigrants in their midst. On 2 October 1913 an editorial in the San Francisco *Examiner* mocked Soyeda's pamphlet in the most derogatory and racist terms, belittling his proposals and questioning the right of any Japanese person to make any recommendations whatsoever to white California.

A similar prejudice was leveled against K. K. Kawakami, secretary of the Japanese Association of America and a prolific writer on Japanese-American affairs, who was based in San Francisco. Carey McWilliams later speculated that Kawakami was in the pay of the Japanese government, which may very well have been the case—but which has nothing to do with the sound sense of Kawakami's prolific commentary between 1903, two years after he arrived in San Francisco from Japan, and the early 1920s. Whether subsidized or not, each of Kawakami's books—*Political Ideas of Modern Japan* (1903), *American Japanese Relations* (1912), *Asia at the Door* (1914), *Japan in World Politics* (1917), *Japan in World Peace* (1919), *The Real Japanese Question* (1920)—made every effort to harmonize with American interests the rise of Japan as a modern nation-state. In retrospect, it is poignant to witness Kawakami struggle in these books to banish the specter of racism from the debate, replacing it with the infinitely more malleable concept of economic competition, which certain demagogues in California had come forth to exploit. In spite of all the propaganda, Kawakami was arguing as late as January 1921, there was little evidence that average Californians harbored an enduring hatred for the Japanese in their midst.

All in all, very few Californians raised their voices in opposition to anti-Japanese behavior and propaganda. David Starr Jordan was one of these. Having traveled and lectured in Japan and shepherded numerous Japanese exchange students through Stanford, Jordan respected the energy and intelligence of the Japanese and the exquisite intricacies of their culture. The implicit basis of Jordan's defense of Japan and the Japanese and his repugnance at the undeclared California-

Japanese War came from a sense of class identification. Upper-middle-class Californians who formed the pro-Japanese California Committee of Justice and the Japan Society of Northern California identified, either consciously or subconsciously, with the hierarchical structure and energy of Japanese society. Thus the oligarchy of Southern California rarely, if ever, joined the anti-Japanese war. In 1905 the Los Angeles Chamber of Commerce went so far as to go on record against Japan-baiting.

Ironically, given the anti-Japanese attitudes of the Irish working class, the most effective defender of the Japanese on the Pacific Coast was an Irish Catholic eponymously named Colonel John Irish, a seventy-seven-year-old (in 1919) Democratic Party satrap whose close personal friend President Grover Cleveland had some thirty-plus years earlier tucked him away into a cushy federal job attached to the Port of San Francisco. In the years that followed, Colonel Irish had prospered in agriculture in the East Bay and was well known in both Oakland and San Francisco Democratic Party circles. Among prominent Irish Catholic Californians, only Colonel Irish seemed to have the courage to say, among other things, that the persecution of the Japanese by white California resembled the Tsarist persecution of the Jews and the English persecution of the Irish. When the congressional Committee on Immigration came to California to hold hearings in the summer of 1919, Irish was conspicuous in his solitary and outspoken defense of the Japanese as good farmers and good citizens. In the fall of 1920 Irish organized the California Committee of Justice in an effort to defeat the Alien Land Initiative before the voters. In this effort Irish enlisted the help of fifty-one noted Californians, including presidents David Starr Jordan of Stanford and Benjamin Ide Wheeler of the University of California. Despite the fact that Irish personally distributed handbills on Market Street in San Francisco, the initiative passed. Noncitizen Japanese were henceforth prohibited from owning property in California. The good news, Colonel Irish consoled himself, was that twenty-two thousand California voters, although submitted to an unprecedented barrage of anti-Japanese propaganda, had voted against the initiative.

Irish's defense of the Japanese, while laudable, was too little and too late. Throughout the first two decades of the twentieth century a perception was growing among the Japanese in Japan that California, and by implication the United States, held them in contempt. Incrementally, an anti-American poison was entering the Japanese soul. Prior to these agitations in California, the Japanese had considered the United States to be *Dai On Jin*, the land of the great friendly people. In 1921, despite everything, such surviving Meiji figures as Viscount Kaneko, a Harvard-trained diplomat, was still holding to this view in a lengthy profile in the magazine *The Outlook*. A privy councilor, holder of a doctorate in law earned at Harvard in 1878, a personal friend of Theodore Roosevelt (whose picture hung just beneath that of Emperor Meiji in the viscount's reception room), a distinguished diplomat in numerous assignments in the service of his nation: Viscount Kaneko epitomized the pro-American point of view of so many Japanese leaders who had emerged during the Meiji era. Throughout the interview, Viscount Kaneko displayed a deep and sympathetic view of American history and sought constantly to draw parallels between Japan and the United States, especially in the matter of cultural assimilation. "In this respect," noted the viscount of his people, "the Japanese very greatly resembled the Americans. They possess the power of assimilating and harmonizing."[4]

But even as Viscount Kaneko was struggling to remain optimistic, his fellow diplomat Baron Shimpei Goto, formerly Minister for Foreign Affairs and a continuing member of the Diplomatic Advisory Council of the cabinet, was being pulled in another direction. Surveying two decades of anti-Japanese agitation in California, Baron Goto asked the question: had the United States lost its way? Was it turning its back on its founding ideals? "Thirty years ago when the stream of the Japanese immigrants began to pour into the Golden Gate," Baron Goto observed, "America welcomed it with a true Walt Whitman spirit, 'I am large; I contain multitudes.' The process has since been reversed."[5]

Other Japanese had been, and continued to be, more overtly angry. Ominously, the California-Japanese War inspired thoughts of retribution, even armed response, among many Japanese. During the San Francisco school board crisis of 1905–6, the naval and army staffs of each country drew up plans for a possible conflict. During the agitation leading to the Alien Land Law of 1913, a war party, stung by the insult being offered in California, surfaced in the Japanese government, and representatives of this group began to scout the possibilities of a loan to finance a war against the United States. Eighteen years before Pearl Harbor, in other words, and well before the seizure of power by the fascist clique in the Japanese cabinet, the Keep California White! campaign had succeeded in provoking a number of highly placed people in the Japanese government to view war with the United States as the only adequate response to the racial insults that were being offered. It was even suggested at the time that Japan declare war only on California and not the rest of the United States!

The Alien Land Initiative of 1920 provoked a similar response. As outrage grew in Japan over the initiative, Baron K. Shidehara, Japanese ambassador to the United States, protested to Secretary of State Bainbridge Colby. Meeting in Tokyo on 21 September 1920, the Japanese cabinet had instructed Baron Shidehara to demand that the United States government protest the California initiative on the basis that it violated the declaration of racial equality contained in the charter of the League of Nations. Speaking in the House of Peers on 26 September 1920, Baron Sakatani, formerly the Minister of Finance, brought the California initiative up for extensive discussion. The law being considered in California, declared former premier Marquis Okuma during the deliberations, could lead to similar restrictions against Japanese ownership in Australia, Canada, New Zealand, and elsewhere. On 6 October 1920 the American Association of Tokyo and the American Association of Yokohama sent a cable to Secretary of State Colby warning of the "intense feeling aroused throughout Japan by the present action in California." At a rally held at the Tokyo YMCA there was talk of war. When the initiative passed, two previously pro-American peers, Marquis Okuma and Viscount Takahira Kato, protested what Marquis Okuma called "the unlawful attitude of the California Americans."[6] Then came a roundup and deportation of Japanese workers in Turlock, California, on grounds that they had no right to be in the United States, followed by a Supreme Court decision affirming the action, followed by the Shortridge amendment in the Immigration Act of 1924, banishing all Japanese from immigration to the United States forever.

Sweeping in its exclusion and implied contempt, the Immigration Act of 1924, more commonly known as the Oriental Exclusion Act, provoked a deep sense of insult and rage. Two Japanese committed suicide in protest. At a dance at the Imperial Hotel in Tokyo on 7 June 1924, a number of Japanese dressed as samurai disrupted the dancing and berated those present for dressing and dancing like the Americans who had just excluded them. Three weeks later someone successfully penetrated the American embassy, lowered the American flag, and ripped it into pieces. The Oriental Exclusion Act, moreover, could not have come at a worse time for the Japanese, its insult being added to the misery caused by the earthquake of 1 September 1923, which had left more than two hundred thousand Japanese dead and vast parts of Tokyo in ruins.

This, then, was the very same California whose Santa Barbara coast submarine commander Kozo Nishino surveyed through his binoculars on the evening of Monday, 23 February 1942: a California where so many citizens had for forty years been doing their best to poison relations between the two nations. True, California had not caused the war between Japan and the United States; and true, Japan itself was guilty of criminal genocide in China. Yet Pearl Harbor and the presence of submarine I-17 off the Santa Barbara coast had come to be, in part, because of the attitudes toward the United States that the White California movement had helped encourage in Japan. By poisoning the well between two peoples, by helping drive Japan into a fascist paranoia that was by no means inevitable, California had played a not inconsiderable role in bringing about the present conflict.

Why did the Japanese inspire such fear and loathing among so many whites, and how did Californians justify such hatred? A number of inter-related motivations, none of them edifying—racism, most obviously, but also envy and Yellow Peril theory—were at work. Promulgated as a concept by none other than Kaiser Wilhelm of Germany in the mid-1890s, Yellow Peril theory predicted an inevitable clash on the field of battle between white and Asian civilizations. Charles Pearson, an Englishman living in Australia, provided the Yellow Perilists with their founding texts in his 1893 book *National Life and Character*. White people, Pearson argued, do not do well outside temperate climates. Black and yellow peoples, by contrast, could sustain a wider variety of climatological conditions. White people had already expanded as far as possible into the temperate zones. They now must defend these regions against an encroaching Yellow Peril. In 1895 Kaiser Wilhelm personally drew a cartoon depicting the dragon of Asia, with a Buddha on its back, locked in fierce combat with the West.

Yellow Peril obsessions soon centered on the Japanese, especially after Japan emerged as a co-equal with the Great Powers in the First World War. T. Lothrop Stoddard's *Rising Tide of Color Against White World Supremacy* (1920) represents the high-water mark of post–World War I Yellow Peril thought. The recent war, Stoddard argued, was a suicidal civil war among whites, which had allowed Japan to assert itself against China and to enter the circle of European nations as an equal power. Since the Japanese did not react well to the tropics, they would now be tempted to expand into the temperate zones occupied by white civilization.

The anti-Japanese lobby had no doubts that Japan had considered the conquest of California a strategic goal. Like scenarios engendered in a later era by the Cold War, the anti-Japanese lobby consistently predicted a military invasion of California. After the Russo-Japanese War of 1904–05 provided a stunning debut for the Japanese army and navy, the San Francisco–based *Organized Labor* predicted that California would be next. Returning from covering the Japanese invasion of Manchuria, Jack London warned in both reportage and fiction that Japan had its eye on even larger prey. Writing in *Cosmopolitan* for June 1908, Congressman Richard Hobson predicted that the Japanese would someday land a million-man army on the Pacific Coast within six months of war breaking out between the United States and Japan. The 1909 film *The Japanese Invasion* depicted a Japanese valet of an American Army officer stealing military secrets. In another film, *The Engine of Death*, released in 1913, Japanese agents steal the formula for a high explosive.

The Hearst newspapers pursued such predictions repeatedly. William Randolph Hearst was himself convinced that the Japanese would one day launch a military action against California via Mexico. On 26 September 1915 the New York *American* and other Hearst newspapers printed an article that purported to outline plans for such an invasion. The article was illustrated with photographs allegedly showing Japanese troops practicing amphibious landings in preparation for an assault on the California coast. It was later discovered that the document on which this story was based was not an official Japanese military publication, as was alleged, but a fictional story lifted from a popular Japanese magazine and distorted in translation. The pictures turned out to be doctored photographs of Japanese troops in action during the Sino-Japanese War twenty years earlier.

Reports of a Japanese plan to assist Mexico in regaining its lost territories north of the Rio Grande were entered into evidence before the Senate Foreign Relations Committee in 1915, despite the fact that Japan was a wartime ally. This Mexican-Japanese link-up surfaced repeatedly in the Hearst press. Hearst's film company, meanwhile, released a serial entitled *Patria* in which the Japanese perform sabotage against the United States and eventually invade the country from Mexico. President Wilson was forced to ask that the serial be recalled since it was offensive to an ally.

The most complete expressions of this invasion scenario came in 1909 from

Homer Lea, a Southern Californian, and the English naval strategist Hector By-water in 1925. Born in Denver in 1875, and moving with his family to Los Angeles in 1892, Homer Lea was one of those eccentrics touched by genius whom one frequently encounters in turn-of-the-century Southern California. Despite his diminutive stature (five feet) and a curved spine, which earned him the nickname "Little Scrunch-Neck" among his classmates at Los Angeles High School, Lea dreamed of a military career (as did his contemporary George Smith Patton Jr., then attending a private academy in Pasadena). Educated at Occidental and Stanford, Lea became involved with Chinese students committed to the overthrow of the imperial system and the establishment of a republic. In July 1899, just before the outbreak of the Boxer Rebellion, Lea sailed for China in search of further involvement. Concealing his republican sympathies, he seems to have wrangled some sort of military commission in the army of the Emperor. In any event, he appeared at the relief of Peking in the last days of the Boxer Rebellion wearing the uniform of a lieutenant general (the rank authorized in his imperial commission, presumably) and directing a ragtag army of reform volunteers.

When it became apparent that there would be no republic in China, not yet at least, Lea returned to Los Angeles in 1901 wearing his general's uniform. He spent the next few years working on behalf of Chinese republicans in California and writing and lecturing on military matters. Among other activities, Lea drilled Chinese students in military fundamentals, in the hopes of preparing them to serve as officers in a revolutionary republican army. Lea's assistant and chief drill master was Ansel O'Banion, a leather-lunged former sergeant in the United States Cavalry who had later secured a commission in the Philippine constabulary. Lea returned to China in 1904 on behalf of the republican movement, and he was in Nanking in 1911, the only white man in the room, when Dr. Sun Yat-sen, with whom Lea had worked closely in Sun Yat-sen's California exile, was elected President of the newly formed Republic of China. Three years before his death in 1912, Harper & Brothers published Homer Lea's *The Valor of Ignorance* (1909), the result of long study and extensive reconnaissance of the Pacific Coast he and O'Banion had conducted after his return from China.

In the first third of *The Valor of Ignorance* Lea developed the thesis that war between Japan and the United States was inevitable because of economic competition. Lea was no crude Japan-basher. On the contrary, he admired the Japanese for their intelligence, enterprise, and military skill. Lea devoted the middle third of his book to a discussion of Japanese military capabilities on land and at sea. Japan, Lea observed, was capable of fielding an invasion army of 1.25 million men. Its navy was the finest on the planet, and it was capable of transporting in one troop transport ship more soldiers than the British had brought to the United States during the entire War of 1812. A military invasion of the Coast, Lea concluded, was fully in the reach of the Japanese from the point of view of their population and industrial capacity, the skill and training of their general staffs and officer corps, and the technical capacities of their army and navy. As important as any of this, the Japanese possessed *bushido*, the code of the samurai, an instinctive affinity for the sword (in Franz Boas's later term) running parallel to their love of the chrysanthemum.

In the final third of *The Valor of Ignorance*, Lea sketched a scenario of Japanese invasion, which later read as an almost eerie prediction of the course of the Second World War in the Pacific. First, Lea argued, the Japanese would seize and occupy the Philippines. From there, they would move on Samoa, Hawaii, the Aleutians, and Alaska, establishing in each a center of overlapping strategic spheres, which would give them control of the entire Pacific. The attack on the Pacific Coast would come on three axes: Washington State, the San Francisco Bay Area, and Los Angeles and the South Coast. With extensive detail and maps, the result of his and O'Banion's surveys, Lea described how the Japanese could land at Santa Monica Bay, seize Los Angeles, and rapidly seal off most of Southern California. Landing in Monterey Bay, the Japanese would move north and encircle San Francisco, bombarding it from strategic heights around the Bay until it surrendered. Eventually, a Japanese army of more than 1.25 million men would establish a defensive perimeter in the Sierra Nevada. It would take years, perhaps a decade, for an American army to be raised, trained, and successfully employed against the invaders.

As a prophetic document, *The Valor of Ignorance* gained credibility, indeed great power, through its detailed plausibility. Lea envisioned the Japanese invasion of California down to the emplacement of specific artillery batteries. He had personally surveyed landing beaches and deployment routes and had reviewed all relevant military maps to back up his assertions. Lea also grasped the essential isolation of California, sealed off as it was by the Sierra Nevada and the Great Basin beyond: an isolation that meant California could be seized and defended by Japanese invaders.

The general staffs of the United States and Japan each took Lea's scenario seriously enough to incorporate it into their own contingency plans. Dining with a group of Army officers in Manila in October 1941, correspondent Clare Booth Luce was treated to a description by Colonel Charles Willoughby of how the Japanese would soon be moving on the Philippines. Luce asked Willoughby his source of information. The colonel laughed. "Just quoting military gospel," he told her, "according to Homer Lea."[7] Willoughby went on to describe how his generation of officers had first encountered Lea in their readings at West Point. Among staff officers in the Philippines, *The Valor of Ignorance* was considered established doctrine. Luce returned to the United States and wrote an article on Lea for the *Saturday Evening Post*, which Harper & Brothers used in 1942 as an introduction to a reissue of a book whose prophecies—an attack on Hawaii, the siege of the Philippines, a deployment into Southeast Asia—were now in the process of coming true.

In 1909 the plausibility of *The Valor of Ignorance* was especially high among Californians. Homer Lea might be a shadowy and eccentric figure, but no one less than Lieutenant General Adna Chaffee, the retired chief of staff of the United States Army, wrote the preface to the first edition of Lea's book. Chaffee was not only a retired chief of staff, he was a Los Angeleno as well — someone, that is, fully capable for reasons other than his military career of saying that, yes, the Japanese would one day invade the Coast. This was no fantasy, Chaffee argued, merely an inevitability Homer Lea had envisioned and analyzed.

Brilliant in his depictions of the land war in California, Homer Lea was rather sketchy when it came to details of the Japanese naval strategy in the Pacific. This scenario was left for Hector Bywater, an English civilian naval intelligence specialist based in London. In 1925, in his book *Sea Power in the Pacific: A Study of the American-Japanese Naval Problem*, Bywater outlined a complete naval strategy for Japan in the Pacific in the event of a war with the United States. Almost matter-of-factly, Bywater suggested that the war would begin with a surprise attack by Japan on Pearl Harbor. For the United States to contain Japan in the Pacific, Bywater wrote, it would have to establish a naval base and fleet in the Philippines, with secondary bases at Midway and Wake islands. As matters stood, the Philippines presented the United States with its only foothold in the Far East and its only base of operations for a blockade against Japan. Although he doubted Homer Lea's contention that the Japanese could launch a major assault on the Pacific Coast, Bywater's Pearl Harbor scenario greatly impressed a young Harvard-trained Japanese naval captain, Isoroku Yamamoto, then serving as a naval attaché in Washington. Yamamoto submitted a detailed report on Bywater's scenario to naval officials in Tokyo and lectured on Bywater's book when he returned to Japan. Fifteen years later, Admiral Yamamoto put many of Bywater's strategies into practice, beginning with an attack on Pearl Harbor.

In 1927 Los Angeles novelist Charles Downing added a new dimension, air power, to Lea's land-based and Bywater's sea-based strategies. As early as 1907, in his novel *War in the Air*, reprinted in 1922, H. G. Wells had envisioned the rise of Japan as an air power. In *War in the Air*, Japan and China launch an air attack on the Pacific Coast: which is the central scenario of Downing's *The Reckoning*, locally published in Los Angeles in 1927. In that novel, the Japanese launch a surprise air attack on the cities of the Pacific Coast, dropping incendiary and poison gas bombs. "We are confronted with a crisis so grave," states one Pacific Coast official amidst the carnage, "it seems beyond human power to even conceive the gigantic and horror-ridden cataclysm that has sunk its poisonous talons into the very heart of our Christian civilization."[8]

The plausibility of such scenarios, even those of melodramatic fiction, cannot be exaggerated. As a writer, Charles Downing cannot be mentioned in the same breath as H. G. Wells. As a Southern Californian, however, Downing, in his depiction of the devastation of the Pacific Coast by Japanese bombers, provides yet another example of Japanophobia. But then again: even more reputable commentators were saying the same thing. In 1921, for example, strategic affairs commentator Walter Pitkin published a book with the incendiary title *Must We Fight*

Japan? Pitkin's answer was yes. War between Japan and the United States, he argued, was inevitable. In such a war, the anti-Japanese lobby argued, the hundred thousand Japanese living on the Pacific Coast would spring into action as a fifth column. Even American-born Japanese, Senator Phelan argued, regarded the Emperor as a divine leader whose will must be obeyed. Technically speaking, Phelan pointed out, every Japanese, even those living abroad, remained liable to call-up between the ages of seventeen and forty. Every Japanese in California was a possible soldier or, even worse, a possible spy.

Despite the hostility they encountered, the Japanese continued to prefer California to any other state. By 1930 some 70 percent of all Japanese resident in the United States lived in California, most of them in Los Angeles County, where they showed the same trend toward urbanization as their white counterparts. By 1935 there were 41,382 Japanese living in Southern California, 32,714 of them in Los Angeles County alone. Fifty-eight percent of these were *Issei*, or Japanese born; 42 percent were *Nisei*, second-generation American citizens. The city of Los Angeles had thirteen thousand Japanese residents by 1935, most of them centered in the Little Tokyo district in the Downtown near City Hall. Paradoxically, anti-Japanese agitation was less intense in the Southland, there being no powerful union movement in this region to carry on the crusade.

The Japanese came, initially, as agriculturalists, moving as rapidly as possible to self-employment on leased properties. As early as May 1910 the state labor commissioner issued a report praising the Japanese as farmers. (The state senate moved rapidly to repudiate the report.) The career of potato king George Shima epitomizes the energies on a larger-than-life scale of this first generation of farmers. Arriving in California in 1889 as a penniless laborer, Shima by 1913 controlled twenty-eight thousand acres and 85 percent of California's potato crop. (He also wrote and published poetry in his native language.) Dying in 1926, Shima left an estate valued at $15 million. By the close of 1934 Japanese farmers had brought nearly two hundred thousand acres under intense cultivation, nearly half of it in Southern California. Cultivating less than 4 percent of California's farmland, the Japanese maintained a 50 to 90 percent position in such crops as celery, peppers, strawberries, cucumbers, artichokes, cauliflower, spinach, and tomatoes. By 1940 there were some 5,135 Japanese-run farms in California, for a total of 226,094 acres, with an estimated value of $65.8 million. Forty-three percent of all employed Japanese on the West Coast were in agriculture. The city of Los Angeles was almost exclusively dependent upon Japanese farmers for its fresh vegetables and much of its berries and fruits; the Wholesale Terminal Market downtown had $10 million of its $70 million in annual business handled by Japanese. Nearly a thousand Japanese fishermen worked out of San Pedro and San Diego harbors.

Like other Southern Californians, the Japanese formed associations based on place of origin. *Ken* designated the prefecture they came from, *kenjin* meant one's fellow countrymen, and *kenjinkai* designated the self-help associations based on home regions they organized in California, in Southern California especially, in a manner directly paralleling the Iowa Society, the Kansas Society, the Nebraska Society, and other similar organizations in the Southland. Like these groups, the *kenjinkai* promoted fellowship, operated savings and loan societies, and provided illness and burial benefits. The *kenjinkai* also sponsored annual picnics at such favored Los Angeles County picnic grounds as White Point, Brighton Beach, Pico Picnic Ground, Arroyo Seco Park, Lincoln Park, and Luna Park, where Japanese Californians would gather for traditional foods, folk dances, magic acts, one-act plays, and displays of martial arts. In Little Tokyo Japanese theater and vaudeville flourished. Noted entertainers from Japan frequently crossed the Pacific to perform in California. In the mid-1930s, for example, the Japanese tenor Yoshie Fujiwara toured the Southland with much success.

Running parallel to the *kenjinkai* were the *mujin*, less formal mutual aid associations based more on shared economic activities or local neighborhoods than places of origin in Japan. *Mujin* members were especially active in providing funerals for single Japanese men who died alone and far from home, a proper funeral being most important in Japanese culture, even for the impoverished. When the Buddhist minister in El Centro became ill in the early 1930s, the local *mujin* paid his bills at a sanitarium in Monrovia, then paid his passage for a recuperative visit to Japan.

Buddhism played an important role in Japanese California. *Jodo Shin Shu* represented the largest sect of Buddhism in California and the United States. In 1898 a priest of the *Jodo Shin Shu* organized the first Buddhist church in California in San Francisco, modeling it upon the Christian parishes of the city. The very use of the word *church* to designate Buddhist places of worship in California underscores the repatterning Japanese Buddhism experienced there. By 1935 there were thirteen Buddhist temples in Southern California and fifteen Shinto shrines, each of them with a fixed church, an employed minister carrying the title Reverend, ladies' auxiliaries, Boy Scout troops, and the other characteristics of Christian parish life.

Indirectly, through a generation of Japanese gardeners, Buddhism helped shape the settled landscape of Southern California. In Buddhism there is no personified deity. God is envisioned, rather, as the cosmos, the universe. Consequently, the arts of landscaping and floral arranging are charged with deep spiritual significance. Each garden is seen as the world in miniature, a delicate re-creation, through the interaction of lawns, trees, stones, waterfalls, lanterns, pathways, bushes, and flower beds, of creation itself. By the mid-1930s an estimated 2,500 Japanese gardeners were at work in the gardens of the residential districts of Los Angeles and surrounding communities. Subtly, but powerfully, these Japanese gardeners translated something of their Buddhist-inspired vision of serenity and order, balance and harmony, to the gardens they were attending.

Los Angeles alone supported more than one hundred Japanese florists by the mid-1930s. The Los Angeles flower market was significantly Japanese in ownership and operation. If Southern California was the land of sunshine and flowers, which it was, Japanese floral farmers, wholesalers, and florists tutored white Southern California in its growing taste for public and private floral arrangements.

Against these people, *Issei* of the first generation, *Nisei* of the second, a number of charges continued to be leveled as the California-Japanese War continued down through the teens, the twenties, the thirties. Among other things, the Japanese were perceived as an economic threat, foreign and domestic; unassimilable; arrogant and cocky; breeding at a dangerously rapid rate; and, most tellingly, incapable by culture and religion of loyalty to the United States, hence a permanent fifth column ready to spring into action when Japan invaded California.

The economic argument against the Japanese surfaced at a very early date, when there were but a few hundred Japanese in the United States. Why allow Japanese students to study in the United States, the San Francisco *Chronicle* had editorialized as early as February 1890? Why allow them to master American engineering and business techniques so that they could return to Japan and transform their country into a fearsome competitor? Was not the United States committing economic suicide by educating this Japanese elite?

In 1894, when Japan won its war against China, John Young of the *Chronicle* returned to the fray with the dire warning that this first important victory by Japan signaled not just military prowess but the economic prowess of Asia's first industrialized nation. In 1896 the National Association of Manufacturers expressed its concern that in the case of certain products—textiles, most noticeably, but also mattings and silks—the Japanese were outperforming Americans. Association economist Robert Porter pointed out that the Japanese showed an alarming ability to design their own machinery or to replicate American designs. In 1897 Sacramento department store owner David Lubin appeared before the House Ways and Means Committee and argued that an industrialized Japan would soon be outperforming the United States because of its lower wages and higher productivity.

This formula of Japan plus industrialism outperforming the United States frequently occurs in the more rational, less vitriolic anti-Japanese utterances issued in the 1920s. It irked the anti-Japanese lobby that by 1920 the United States was annually buying a half billion dollars in Japanese imports, with no comparable reciprocal market in Japan—and that there were fewer Japanese working for white people in California than there were white people working for Japanese.

This emergence of Japanese as employers of whites should logically suggest a high degree of assimilation of the Japanese into the socio-economics of California life. County histories from the teens and twenties, especially those dealing with Southern California counties, speak for themselves. Frequently, a separate section would be devoted to the Japanese community. Photographs depict self-respecting *Issei* and their *Nisei* offspring, everyone wearing his or her Sunday best, posing for the camera, eager to have this visual documentation of their Americanized existence included in the annals of their community. In some cases, the very photo-

graphs of Japanese immigrants counter the stated argument of certain writers that
they were unassimilable. Writing in the *World's Work* in October 1920, Lothrop
Stoddard, grand vizier of Yellow Perilism, goes on endlessly as to how the Japanese
in California can never assimilate. The photographs accompanying Stoddard's text,
however, tell an entirely different story. Japanese schoolchildren in bib overalls
and gingham dresses stand proudly in front of their public school. Another group
of children, dressed in Fauntleroy suits or pinafores, the girls with oversized bows
in their hair, pose proudly with their Presbyterian Sunday school teacher. A Japanese farmer from Florin, a small town outside Sacramento with a large Japanese
population, stands proudly beside his new Model T Ford. Dressed in high-top
shoes, sturdy dark pants, a starched white shirt, a bow tie, and assertive suspenders,
the *Issei* farmer seems more Norman Rockwell than unassimilated alien. The
entire town of Florin, in fact, had become by 1920 an Our Town in the idiom of
Japanese California. If the Japanese citizens of Florin — with their Model T Fords,
their barbershop and pool hall, their Christian and Buddhist places of worship,
their local baseball team, their Boy Scouts and 4-H organization — were unassimilable to American life, then no one had bothered to tell them, except of course
the perennial skirmishers in the California-Japanese War.

Not so! exclaimed the anti-Japanese lobby. Despite all evidence to the contrary,
the charge first leveled against the Japanese by Professor Ross — that they were
unassimilable — was repeated and repeated for four decades by such organizations
as the Asiatic Exclusion League, the Native Sons of the Golden West, and the
American Legion, to mention a few. Even Woodrow Wilson, the high-minded
former president of Princeton, ran with the anti-Japanese pack when seeking California votes in 1912. "We cannot make a homogeneous population," Wilson told
a California audience, "of a people who do not blend with the Caucasian race."[9]
Thousands of copies of this statement were distributed by the Democratic Party
up and down the state.

Arguments in support of this position ran from crude attacks to sophisticated
presentations based on cultural analysis. The fact that Japanese immigrants to
California universally tended to register with the consuls general of Japan was
frequently cited as proof of unassimilability. From the Japanese perspective, such
registration was accepted practice with Japanese nationals abroad. In the midst of
a new, frequently hostile, society, the Japanese farmers and artisans who came to
California tended naturally to want the protection of their homeland. Coming
from a mono-ethnic, scarcity-based culture, Japanese immigrants found themselves
thrust into a vast, culturally heterogeneous society. Early Japanese immigrants were
actually frightened by the scale of everything in California. The people seemed
so big. There were so many large buildings. And the vast spaces, and the thousands
and thousands of trees: all this in such contrast to their intimate and ordered
homeland. Quite naturally, in the midst of this frightening new environment, the
first generation of immigrants clung to home, to family, to religion, to Japanese
culture and the protection of the Japanese government. By Japanese law, they

were required formally to renounce their Japanese citizenship at the office of the consul general or otherwise remain, in the eyes of the Empire, Japanese subjects. Few *Issei* bothered formally to renounce their Japanese citizenship. The flourishing of Japanese-language schools was especially galling to the anti-Japanese lobby. Here, they argued, was proof positive that the Japanese did not want to become Americans. They were sending their children after school, on their own time, to learn Japanese! Critics such as V. S. McClatchy of the *Sacramento Bee* had no objections, however, to comparable programs in the Italian community subsidized by Mussolini's government and featuring fascist-inspired textbooks.

The racial pride of the Japanese and the role of the Emperor in Japanese religion seemed especially to arouse ire. As humble as were their origins, Japanese farmers shared in the Japanese pride of race. Coming to California, they stuck together. Very soon, they organized protective associations and agricultural workers' unions through which they negotiated collective contracts with American farmers a half century and more before such a practice became even thinkable in California agriculture. When working for whites, the Japanese respected themselves, and, what was particularly infuriating, they refused to tug their forelock to local squires. There was iron in the Japanese soul, something reserved and autonomous. Japanese immigrants knew who they were, and they went about their business possessed of a certain strength that came from that knowledge, and this self-confidence infuriated white Californians, so many of whom had come from elsewhere and were intensely insecure in their identity and social status.

In order to denigrate Japanese self-sufficiency, white Californians called them arrogant, cocky. San Francisco (later New York) writer Wallace Irwin spoke to this perception in a series of short stories first published in *Collier's* in 1907, later reissued as *Letters of a Japanese Schoolboy* (1909). Irwin's central character is Hashimura Togo, a buck-toothed, horn-rimmed exchange student of uncertain age who repeatedly uses such phrases as "Honorable Sir" and "So sorry please." Irwin later wrote the novel *Seed of the Sun* (1921), first serialized in the *Saturday Evening Post*, in which equally arrogant Japanese agriculturalists undermine white agribusiness in California.

Politically, Wallace Irwin was a Progressive, the Stanford classmate and chum of Herbert Hoover. So too was was Chester Rowell, who had studied philosophy at Berkeley and in Germany before settling in as columnist and chief editorial writer for the San Francisco *Chronicle*. As someone who combined philosophy with the career of a working journalist, Rowell sought to upgrade the unassimilability argument, purging it of its racist overtones. The Japanese, Rowell frequently wrote, were a superior, not an inferior, race. It was their very talent that made them unassimilable. "Our people have learned their racial lessons in a dangerous school," wrote Rowell of the anti-Japanese Californians. "We have dealt with two inferior darker races, but never with an equal one, and we have dealt always unjustly. We have dealt unjustly with the Negro and he submits. We have dealt unjustly with the Indian and he is dead. If we have many Japanese, we shall not know how to deal otherwise than unjustly with them, and very properly they will not submit. The only real safety is in separation. Nature erected a barrier which man will overpass only at his peril."[10]

Among their other talents, the Japanese impressed white California as being dangerously prolific. Critics frequently accused Japanese women of being little more than breeding machines. In 1910, they pointed out, Japanese births represented one out of every forty-four children born in California. In 1919 they represented one out of every thirteen. In 1917 there were only 295 whites born in Hawaii, as opposed to 5,000 Japanese. The growth of the Japanese population in Hawaii and California was part of a larger pattern, ran the demographic argument. When Commodore Perry sailed into Japan in 1853, the Land of the Rising Sun had approximately twenty-seven million residents. By 1918 fifty-seven million Japanese were living in a land mass 8,335 square miles smaller than California. Among many side effects of the Meiji era had been improved nutrition and health care. Japanese were living longer and having more children, and these children were surviving into adulthood.

In California the baby boom of the late 1910s and early 1920s resulted from the migration of some five thousand Picture Brides between 1910 and 1920. The picture bride system represented a trans-Pacific extension of naka-dachi, in which elders arranged marriages for young people. The first wave of immigrants to California were single men. By the teens these men had established themselves and wished to marry. Ancient custom came into play across the Pacific. Middlemen in Japan would arrange to show photographs of Japanese men in California to unmarried women in their home region and vice versa. Each party then agreed to a marriage by proxy, and the Japanese government issued a passport to the bride.

Newspapers and magazines of the period frequently ran photographs of these picture brides as they arrived by ship in San Pedro or San Francisco. In their elaborate kimonos, their faces whitened with heavy applications of rice powder, their lustrous dark hair piled into high pompadours held in place with elaborate brooches, the picture brides seemed exotic creatures from another planet. In 1911 the Chronicle openly called them prostitutes. Their defenders, such as University of Southern California professor Kiyo Sue Inui, one of the few Japanese to hold academic rank on the Pacific Coast, argued that the picture brides were honorable women looking for a new life in California. "Proud Virginians and noble Carolinians," Professor Inui argued, ". . . resorted to a similar picture bride system, and many a woman crossed the Atlantic to become the bride of a pioneer immigrant."[11]

Arrived in California, the picture bride joined her husband's household. She worked beside him in the field, and year by year she provided him with sons and daughters. For the Japanese, as for agriculturalists everywhere, children were not a mode of expense but a form of wealth. Seeing his sons and daughters around him, the Issei farmer knew that he had truly sunk his roots into American soil.

The willingness of Japanese women to work in the fields alongside their husbands especially irked anti-Japanese critics. The white farm wife, Senator Phelan pointed out in the *Overland Monthly* in November 1920, devoted her time to the home, to her children, to church, and to the community. The Japanese wife, by contrast, worked from dawn to dusk alongside her husband, Sundays and holidays included. No wonder Japanese farmers were outperforming their white counterparts!

In February 1920, under pressure from Washington, which was under pressure from California, the Japanese government ceased to issue passports to picture brides, although those having passports continued to immigrate through August of that year. Phelan played a major role in closing this immigration loophole. In late 1919 Phelan had brought the House and Senate Committees on Immigration out to California to take testimony on what he and others considered the runaway growth of the Japanese population. One photograph, widely distributed, showed a group of congressmen questioning a cluster of diminutive, kimono-clad Japanese women practically dying of shyness before the distinguished gentlemen towering over them.

The anti-Japanese lobby did not want Japanese immigrants to have Japanese wives, lest they produce too many Japanese children; and of course the lobby bristled at the possibility that Japanese men might turn to white women for wives rather than remain in the enforced celibacy that characterized the Chinese experience in nineteenth-century California. Throughout the nineteenth century, Chinese men had been symbolically castrated by white California by its refusal to allow Chinese women to immigrate, with the exception of prostitutes. Thousands and thousands of Chinese men spent lonely lives in imposed solitude, socially and psychologically kept boys (as in houseboy) in a world of white men and unavailable white women.

Refusing to accept a similar fate, Japanese men shattered the stereotype of complacent asexuality into which their Chinese predecessors had been forced and consorted with white women, including instances of cohabitation and legal marriage. In response to this sexual assertiveness on the part of Asian men, white California branded Japanese sexuality in general as something loathsome and degenerate, with special reference to immoral white women and sexually aggressive Japanese men. Perhaps the most volatile film to be produced in early Hollywood outside D. W. Griffith's *The Birth of a Nation* was Cecil B. DeMille's *The Cheat* (1914), in which a white married woman is forced to agree to become the mistress of a Japanese villain played by Sessue Hayakawa. When the woman reneges, the villain brands her on the shoulder, and this mark—at once the symbol of rejection and sadomasochistic possession—becomes the later proof of her resistance.

Obsession with inter-breeding peaked between 1915 and 1924, although the first skirmish of the campaign occurred in February 1905 when a farmer from Elk Grove outside Sacramento testified before a committee of the California legislature. His Japanese neighbor, the farmer told the committee, had a white wife.

"That woman is carrying around a baby in her arms. What is that baby? It isn't white. It isn't Japanese. I'll tell you what it is. It is the beginning of the biggest problem that ever faced the American people."[12] When the Japanese government demanded a statement of racial equality at Versailles in 1919, Senator Phelan claimed that this demand was primarily intended to secure equality and marital rights in California. One can almost hear Phelan's snort of contempt when in February 1920 he wrote in the *Grizzly Bear*, the magazine of the Native Sons of the Golden West: "Imagine a Japanese seeking the hand of an American woman in marriage!" Such marriages, warned the senator, would result in a "mongrel and degenerate population."[13]

Nisei born in the baby boom of the early to mid-1920s were thus forced to come to maturity in a society in which they held citizenship but which had also said, "No more of your kind!" No other group of American citizens was faced with the necessity of coming to maturity amidst such a rejection. By their very nature the laws and agreements under which they lived—the Gentleman's Agreement of 1908, the Alien Land Law of 1913, the Alien Land Initiative of 1920, and the Immigration Act of 1924—qualified the value of Japanese-American citizenship.

By the late 1930s a poignant division had surfaced between *Issei* parents and *Nisei* offspring. Stung by the denial of citizenship, embittered by the racist hostility of the anti-Japanese lobby, the *Issei* regarded with suspicion the American ambitions of their *Nisei* California offspring and clung instead to a memory of a Japan that no longer existed. The *Nisei*, meanwhile, wanted corduroy pants, saddle shoes, plaid skirts, bobby socks. They wanted to drink Cokes and eat hamburgers and jitterbug and go to USC or UCLA. They wanted out of farming and small shops and into business and the professions. Considering the *kenjinkai* old hat, they joined the YMCA, the YWCA, and the Japanese-American Citizens League. A wall had descended between them and their parents, as was also common in other immigrant groups; only in their case, the *Nisei* could not say with full certainty, "We are different from our parents because we are Americans"; for they too, despite their American birth and their citizenship, felt the barriers and rejections all around them.

By December 1941 life had become increasingly more restrictive, more paranoid, for *Issei* and *Nisei* alike. Educated *Nisei*, many of them college graduates, were increasingly limited in their employment opportunities. How long could this continue? How long could they endure being torn between an ardent desire for Americanization and the confining, claustrophobic racism that surrounded them, driving them into tighter and tighter communities and restricted and more restricted neighborhoods? By December 1941, Carey McWiliams suggests, Little Tokyo had become suffocating for young American men and women of Japanese descent. Pearl Harbor came at a time when the entire psychological situation of the Japanese in California was reaching a breaking point. Was this why they had come to the United States? To be huddled into ghettos? To be despised in their culture and their very physical presence by white California, which had dropped such poison into their souls?

Commander Nishino raised his binoculars. Should he shell these Californians who had offered his nation such insult? If Commander Nishino had come in vengeance for the White California campaign, such a shelling of Santa Barbara, like Pearl Harbor itself, might be considered a justifiable act of revenge for fifty years of insults. It would also have been a most effective act of psychological warfare. Two months later, Lieutenant Colonel Jimmy Doolittle would bring his bombers screaming over Tokyo in fiery destruction. A comparable attack on Santa Barbara would have represented an equally effective attack as far as psychological warfare was concerned, one bringing the war to the mainland of America, a feeble but symbolic gesture of the invasion predicted in 1909 by Homer Lea.

But Commander Nishino had other orders — the harassment of industrial properties — and so he sailed I-17 twelve miles north of Santa Barbara to the storage tanks of the Bankline and Barnsdall oil companies at Ellwood and from there, eight miles offshore, fired twenty-five five-inch shells across the Pacific Coast Highway in the direction of the oil tanks. The salvo finished, I-17, uncontested, sailed brazenly out of the channel into the Pacific. Operating between San Francisco and Cape Mendocino in the following two weeks, Nishino sank two more American cargo ships, then headed across the Pacific to the home port of I-17 at Yokosuka.

SUBMARINE SHELLS SOUTHLAND OIL FIELD, ran the Tuesday morning headline in the Los Angeles *Times*, which gave the attack three times the play it gave the Japanese drive into Burma and the Dutch East Indies. Throughout the day, tension mounted in the Los Angeles area. After all, a minister visiting Montecito Monday evening, the Reverend Arthur Basham of Pomona, had reported that he had seen the Japanese submarine heading in the direction of Los Angeles. More ominously, Reverend Basham stated, the submarine was flashing signal lights to the shore.

Already, Ventura County sheriff's deputies had taken four Japanese and one Italian into custody. The Japanese men had been apprehended, the *Times* reported, riding around in a station wagon filled with guns. At 7:58 P.M., the 4th Interceptor Command ordered a total blackout of the Santa Barbara and northern Ventura County coasts and a precautionary alert from San Luis Obispo to the Mexican border. For two hours after the I-17 raid, the *Times* reported, brilliant yellow flares were seen to burst over the darkened Ventura County shoreline, as if someone were signaling the submarine.

That day, imperial headquarters in Tokyo issued a radio broadcast praising the attack on "military establishments" along the coast of California and claiming the raid to be "a great military success." The same Tuesday, Representative Alfred Elliott from Santa Barbara County rose in the House and, making reference to the Santa Barbara attack, called for the removal of all enemy aliens in California to inland points of concentration. "We must move the Japanese in this country into a concentration camp somewhere, someplace, and do it damn quickly," Elliott told the House. "Don't kid yourselves and don't let someone tell you there are good Japs."

Santa Barbara district attorney Percy Heckendorf traveled north to San Francisco to make a personal appeal to Lieutenant General John L. DeWitt, commanding general of the Western Defense Command, that Santa Barbara County be made a restricted area, forbidden to all Axis nationals. "Enough has been learned as to shore signals in Monday night's Japanese submarine attack," Heckendorf told the press, "to make such a measure more imperative than ever before. We want absolute control of aliens and American-born Japanese alike."[14]

In the late hours of Tuesday, 24 February, and the early hours of Wednesday, 25 February, military units in greater Los Angeles went on alert; and the city was put under blackout between 2:25 A.M. and 7:21 A.M. on the morning of the 25th. Although it has never been firmly established, the trigger for the alert was most likely a report from mid-level sources in the Western Defense Command or the 4th Interceptor Command that unidentified aircraft had been sighted over Los Angeles.

At 3:12 Thursday morning, anti-aircraft units of the Los Angeles–based 37th Coast Artillery Brigade began firing into the darkened sky. Searchlights swept the inky horizon. Over the next hour, until a cease-fire was called at 4:14 A.M., the anti-aircraft units fired 1,430 shells against unidentified aircraft alleged to be over the city. For that hour, as sirens wailed and yellow tracer bullets pierced the blackness, and anti-aircraft barrages exploded overhead in fiery orange bursts of shrapnel, and paths of light crisscrossed overhead in search of enemy aircraft, Los Angeles enjoyed a make-believe version, a Hollywood version, of the London blitz.

For the five citizens of Los Angeles County who died in the blackout—three from traffic accidents, two from heart attacks—the ersatz blitz proved as dangerous as any real attack. A number of homes in Long Beach were damaged by falling shrapnel. Duds fell on Santa Monica and the Rancho Golf Course near Long Beach. Given the amount of shells bursting overhead, it was miraculous that no one was killed by falling shrapnel. The only reported casualty was Clyde Lane, age thirty-two, of 1950 South Locust Avenue in Long Beach, who suffered an eight-inch scalp laceration when a shell hit the sidewalk in front of the Bank of America at the intersection of Market and Long Beach Boulevard where he was standing. At Pearl Harbor, by contrast, falling shrapnel had killed a number of civilians.

The next morning, the *Times* reported that sheriff's deputies had arrested thirty suspicious persons during the night and morning. Twenty of them were Japanese. FBI agents, meanwhile, had taken three Japanese nurserymen, two *Issei* and one *Nisei*, into custody at their greenhouse and floral store in West Los Angeles. Yosuke Yamado, age sixty, an *Issei*, and Sukeichi Yokoyama, forty-three, an *Issei*, were arrested by sheriff's deputies when suspicious lights—a series of three white followed by three red—were reported coming from their vegetable ranch. Deputies also arrested four members of a Japanese family in the Bell Garden area when it was reported that flares were being shot from their home at 6143 Buel Street.

A debate broke out in Washington, meanwhile, between Secretary of War Henry Lewis Stimson and Secretary of the Navy Frank Knox, who had described the entire event as a false alarm. Stimson, by contrast, revealed that the Army had indeed released a report that as many as fifteen Japanese planes might have been flying in the direction of Los Angeles at altitudes from nine thousand to eighteen thousand feet. Indeed, Stimson all but confirmed the report in a memorandum released on the 27th, which claimed that "unidentified airplanes, other than American Army or Navy planes, were probably over Los Angeles and were fired on by elements of the 37th Coast Artillery Brigade (that is, anti-aircraft guns) between 3:12 and 4:14 A.M. . . . As many as fifteen airplanes may have been involved."[15] Within a month, on 18 March 1942, President Roosevelt signed Executive Order 9102 calling for the roundup and incarceration of all Japanese, both citizens and non-citizens, on the Pacific Coast. After fifty years of trying, the White Californianists at long last had California emptied of its Japanese residents, *Issei* and *Nisei* alike.

3

1942 ✶ Garrison State

PRIL 1942 found Major General George Smith Patton Jr. training his men in the Desert Training Center east of Riverside in Southern California. With a land mass approximately the size of Pennsylvania, the Desert Training Center bestrode parts of California, Nevada, and Arizona and closely resembled in climate and terrain the North Africa to which Patton and his soldiers would soon be heading. Throughout the spring of 1942, Patton drove his men through exhaustive maneuvers of tanks and motorized infantry and artillery as he sought to instill in his troops the flair and mobility of the Afrika Korps commanded by Field Marshal Erwin Rommel, whom Patton longed to meet on the field of battle, one gentleman professional against the other. Resplendent in jodhpurs and spurred riding boots, a crop clenched tightly in one hand as a swagger stick, an ivory-handled pistol in his polished holster, Patton epitomized the style and esprit of the Cavalry in which he had been commissioned as well as the past, present, and Cold War future of California as garrison state.

Rommel's victories in Libya and Egypt in early 1942, together with the Europe First strategy already decided upon by the Allies, had rapidly yielded an important conclusion. The United States, if it was to be of use to the British in North Africa, had to get into the tank and armored infantry business as soon as possible and in significant numbers. That meant the creation of a coordinated armored force command in Washington on an overall Army level and the immediate field training of armored units in desert warfare. This, in turn, meant (after a fierce and sometimes bitter debate in the Pentagon, for Patton had his critics) the assignment of Major General George S. Patton Jr., currently stationed in Fort Benning, Georgia, to the training effort; for Patton was the highest-ranking and best-known Army officer with World War I experience in tank training and combat. By early March Patton and his staff officers were flying over the vast stretches of government-owned desert—an area 180 miles long and 90 miles wide, covering some 162,000 square miles—in the region where California, Nevada, and Arizona came together, getting a sense of the landscape of the newly authorized Desert Training Center. The region was vast, rugged, hot, dry, and sparsely settled. It would allow for large-scale tank and mechanized infantry maneuvers, including extensive artillery and air support. Establishing his headquarters at a site twenty miles east of Indio in Riverside County (his staff wanted the general to ensconce himself in a hotel at Indio, but Patton wanted to be in the field with his troops), Patton was soon joined by the first contingent, eight thousand officers and men, of armored troops. The very day they arrived, the thermometer hit 120 degrees; and that defined the challenge for the exacting months of training to come.

The sudden establishment of the Desert Training Center recapitulated and reanimated California's long involvement with the military. It also prophesied the next fifty years. It was by military conquest that the United States seized California from Mexico in 1846; and the military administered California as an occupied territory until statehood was granted in September 1850, with the senior military officer in California serving as civil governor. The Army and the Navy brought American institutions to California in the pre–Gold Rush era. A Navy officer, Walter Colton, founded and edited the first newspaper and in Monterey constructed the first important public building. An Army captain, Henry Halleck, served as the first secretary of state. An Army captain on leave, William Tecumseh Sherman, pioneered banking in San Francisco during the 1850s alongside Halleck, then also on leave, while Army Captain Ulysses Simpson Grant was spending a dreary year at Fort Humboldt on the North Coast. During the War Between the States, Halleck, Sherman, and Grant went on to larger things, as did David Farragut, the first commander at the Mare Island Navy Yard in north San Francisco Bay. The state these officers left behind, however—established as a garrison in the late 1840s, developed in part by military men on leave in the 1850s—would always in one way or another remain closely connected to its military origins.

Established as a Navy Yard in 1854, for example, Mare Island remained for the next ninety years the Navy's most ambitious drydock and ship repair facility on the Pacific Coast. During the First World War, more than fifty vessels were constructed on Mare Island, including the USS *California*, the deepest-draft battleship in the American fleet. The Union Iron Works in San Francisco, meanwhile, had already established its reputation with the construction of the USS *Olympia*, flagship of Admiral Dewey at the Battle of Manila Bay, and the USS *Oregon*, another distinguished ship of the line in the war with Spain. In the twentieth century Long Beach and San Diego boosted growth through seeking and attaining a profitable relationship with the Navy and Marine Corps.

In 1942 the implications of California as garrison state, present since the 1840s, exploded into full maturity. The United States was at war in the Pacific, for one thing, and California was the preeminent American presence in the Pacific. California also possessed the available land mass, a suitable topography and climate, the port, rail, and highway infrastructure, the energy resources (Hoover Dam had become operational in the late 1930s), and the industrial and social infrastructure to make it one of the two principal training and staging zones throughout the duration of the conflict. (Texas was the other.)

Annus mirabilis 1942 witnessed the regarrisoning of the garrison state. North, south, and central: literally hundreds of training centers, air and naval bases, supply depots, and administrative headquarters were established by the War Department. In some cases, existing facilities were expanded or reorganized. In most instances, entirely new facilities were acquired and rapidly brought into operation. The Marine Corps, for example, acquired through federal court order and later purchase the sprawling 122,798-acre Rancho Santa Margarita y Las Flores forty-five miles north of San Diego and almost overnight turned it into Camp Joseph H. Pendleton, named in honor of a beloved Marine general who had died that year. Throughout the spring of 1942, some five thousand construction workers, working in three shifts around the clock, six days a week, created a training facility that would in the course of the next three years train three full Marine divisions — the 3rd, the 4th, and the 5th — together with thousands of replacements for all six Marine divisions and such other Marine units as the all-African-American 52nd Defense Battalion, Carlson's Raiders, and the 4th Raider Battalion, commanded by Marine Lieutenant Colonel James Roosevelt, eldest son of the President. By 1944 nearly eighty-seven thousand Marines, sailors, and civilians were stationed in Camp Pendleton. The filming of such a morale-boosting movie as *Guadalcanal Diary* (1943) at Camp Pendleton also contributed to the war effort.

The Marines, meanwhile, were gearing up their Recruit Depot in San Diego, established in 1914, for basic training prior to advanced training at Pendleton. Marine Air established stations at El Toro near Santa Ana, at Goleta near Santa Barbara, at El Centro in the Imperial Valley, and in the Mojave Desert. The year 1942 also witnessed the establishment of a naval air station at Santa Ana, a naval air base on the Salton Sea in Imperial County, and the Pacific Coast headquarters for the naval construction corps (Seabees) at Port Hueneme in Ventura County. The following year, in the summer of 1943, at the Salton Sea Naval Air Base, Navy and Cal Tech scientists began experiments on rocketry and, later, the technology of jet-assisted take-off.

All this — together with the already established Navy presence at San Diego, Long Beach, and Wilmington–San Pedro — would seem to make Southern California Navy and Marine Corps country, were it not for the equally impressive establishment in April 1942 of the Army Air Forces West Coast Training Center at the Santa Ana Army Air Base, where some twenty thousand cadets would soon be in pre-flight training, followed by pilot, bombardier, or navigator instruction at the nearby Victorville Army Flying School, at Army Air Forces Advanced Flying School at Mather Field in Sacramento, or elsewhere throughout the Southwest.

From this perspective, the rapid establishment of the Desert Training Center prefigured the next three years, during which millions of young men and women would be trained, staged, shipped, or returned in one way or another to, from, in, or through California. Patton's presence as commanding general at the training center was also of regional significance. Patton was a Southern Californian. He came, in fact, from the absolute center of the Southern California establishment: the San Marino–Pasadena nexus of land-rich families who rode to the hounds at the Valley Hunt Club in Pasadena, played polo in Santa Monica and Riverside, angled for game fish out of the Tuna Club on Santa Catalina Island, had large families, sent their children to Eastern schools, and in general conducted themselves as a flourishing land-based oligarchy in pre–income tax America. Patton's maternal grandfather, Benjamin Davis Wilson, had come west from Tennessee on the Santa Fe Trail in 1841 at the age of thirty, married into the land-owning Yorba family, and finished his days as Don Benito, a rich and powerful property owner in the San Gabriel Valley. The cities of Pasadena, Alhambra, San Gabriel, and San Bernardino, and the San Pedro and Westwood districts of the City of Los Angeles, were all once, wholly or in part, Wilson properties.

Patton's paternal grandfather had fallen on the field of battle as a colonel in the 22nd Virginia Infantry during the Civil War. From his father's side, Patton absorbed a self-conscious military tradition, Southern style; and from his mother's side, a sense of Southern California heritage, possessed of equally aristocratic overtones. Growing up on the Lake Vineyard estate of Henry Edwards Huntington in San Marino (which his father, the former district attorney of Los Angeles County, managed), young Patton lived a life that was at once horsey and bookish. Throughout Patton's life, those who got to know him, or even came into his physical presence for any length of time, quickly sensed a quality of vast emotionalism, hysteria even, seething just beneath the surface demeanor of the spit-and-polish cavalryman. Like Julius Caesar, whom he so much resembled, and Napoleon as well, Patton had a strong feminine streak in his makeup, a strain of nervous refinement that only the most *macho* posturing could conceal—and not very well at that. Patton's greatness—which above anything else was a greatness of temperament, of an intuitive preference for action and forward drive as a means of dispelling ambiguity—rested on a paradox: he was both kick-ass cavalryman and temperamental impresario. Although he cussed and swore and swaggered and more than occasionally played the bully, Patton never truly left behind the refinements of his class or escaped the subtle femininity of his temperament.

Marrying into a wealthy Beverly Farms, Massachusetts, family who summered on Catalina, Patton lived well and conspicuously throughout his entire Army career with the help of his wife's income. Even as a second lieutenant, he kept polo ponies and belonged to the Metropolitan Club of Washington. Patton's Army career paralleled the civilian career of another Californian, Herbert Hoover, in its ambience of brilliant achievement and steady rise through a combination of accomplishment and social connection: Hoover in Australia, becoming rich as a mining engineer; Patton in Mexico, aide-de-camp to Brigadier General John Pershing, a widower all but engaged to Patton's sister; Hoover in World War I, heading the Committee for the Relief of Belgium; Lieutenant Colonel Patton in France, performing brilliantly as a staff officer, founding the Army's first tank training center and soon becoming the first American officer to lead tanks into battle.

With the exception of Sir Richard McCreery, an Anglo–Santa Barbaran who would later command the British Eighth Army in Italy, Patton would be the only Southern Californian to rise to an Army-level command in World War II. He was to become, in fact, one of the two or three greatest field army commanders in American history. As the most notable figure in the landscape of California as garrison state in mid-1942, then, Patton invites social and cultural, as well as psychological, construal. His horsey country club snobbery, his ultra-right politics and anti-Semitism, his eccentric spiritualism (he might very well have literally believed himself to have been the reincarnation of soldiers and great captains from the past), his Hollywood swagger, his love of costume and masquerade: trait after trait suggests interpretations that are cross-referenced to Southern California.

The very appointment of Patton to the Desert Training Center had been controversial. A number of top-ranking generals in the Pentagon had had grave doubts as to whether Patton would be able to work smoothly with the British in North Africa, which would be a necessity should Patton be assigned field command in the forthcoming Operation Torch. Patton's letters from the Desert Training Center are filled with anxiety over the ever-present possibility that he would not be assigned a field command in North Africa but would, rather, be kept in a training command for the rest of the war. The longer he remained at the training center, the more ferocious became his talk about killing the enemy. "I wish to God that we would start killing somebody," Patton wrote an influential friend a mere twenty-three days into the Desert Training Center exercise, "somewhere soon, and I trust that if we do, you will use your best influence to see that I can take a hand in the killing."[1] On 30 July 1942 Patton was summoned to Washington to be briefed upon the forthcoming invasion of North Africa, code-named Operation Torch. Five days later, he was flying to London, where he reported to Eisenhower, who was in overall command. Three and a half years later, Patton would be swaggering and swearing before a crowd of a hundred thousand jammed into the Coliseum in Los Angeles, the most celebrated returning soldier in the region.

What Major General George S. Patton Jr. was to Southern California, the representative native son risen to celebrity flag rank, Rear Admiral Daniel Judson Callaghan was to the San Francisco Bay Area and Northern California, especially Roman Catholic Northern California. Like Patton, Callaghan was the one gallant military figure who seemed most vividly to embody the best possibilities of the region. Born in 1892 in San Francisco and raised in Oakland, Callaghan had graduated in 1907 from the Jesuit-staffed St. Ignatius High School in San Francisco, an academically distinguished institution founded by Italian Jesuits in 1855. There, along with Latin and Greek, Callaghan had absorbed a gentlemanly de-

meanor and unpretentious religiosity that would last him for his entire life. Graduating from the United States Naval Academy at Annapolis in 1911, Callaghan
(who had come, in part, from a Navy family, at least through marriage) settled
into a naval career. Whereas Patton was privileged, flamboyant, profane, and self-
regarding, Callaghan was steady, unassuming, pious (avoiding alcohol but smoking
like a chimney), and thoroughly devoted to the welfare of his men, who tended
to call him Uncle Dan behind his back. As Patton was devoted to tanks, Callaghan
was devoted to the art of gunnery. While other naval colleagues bespoke the future
in terms of airplanes and submarines, Dan Callaghan devoted his career to per-
fecting the art and science of gunnery from surface ships.

After one near-disaster (a court-martial for administrative neglect in which he
was totally exonerated), Callaghan had risen steadily through the ranks of the inter-
war surface Navy: a tall, solid figure, prematurely gray, a Spencer Tracy look-alike,
known to the men of the fleet as well as to the brass as a commandingly steady
figure, the representative naval officer of his era. After serving in the prestigious
post of professor of naval science in the Naval ROTC unit at UC Berkeley, Callaghan had been selected in 1938 for an even more prestigious assignment: naval
aide to President Franklin Delano Roosevelt. Across the next three years, the solid
and steady Irish Catholic naval officer and his mercurial and patrician
commander-in-chief became, by Roosevelt's own admission, close personal friends.
In 1941 Callaghan, now promoted to captain, was given command of the 9,950-
ton heavy cruiser *San Francisco*, launched from Mare Island in March 1933 and
based in Pearl Harbor. On the morning of 7 December 1941, the *San Francisco*
came under fire but was not severely damaged. Eleven months later, promoted to
rear admiral, Callaghan was back on the *San Francisco* after a half year on the
staff of Vice Admiral William Halsey, this time as commander of Section One—
five cruisers and six destroyers—of the Espiritu Sancto Group operating off
Guadalcanal.

At forty-one minutes after one on the morning of Friday, 13 November 1942,
Callaghan's section came into contact off Savo Island north of Guadalcanal with
a fast-approaching Japanese naval force under the command of Vice Admiral
Hiroaki Abe. Maneuver was difficult, and the *San Francisco* lacked the latest radar;
but whether this was the cause for what followed or rather whether what followed
was due in some measure to Callaghan's gunnery-oriented spirit of the attack,
the American force literally sailed into the middle of the Japanese force, as if
running a gauntlet. What ensued was perhaps the last ship-to-ship naval engagement
in military history as the American ships and the Japanese ships fought through
direct searchlight-guided gunfire. As Samuel Eliot Morison would later write in
his official history of the engagement, the Japanese and American ships "mingled
like minnows in a bucket," each ship at once on the attack and fighting for its
survival. "We want the big ones!" Callaghan commanded over voice radio, meaning
the Japanese battleships.[2] Shortly thereafter, a salvo from the Japanese battleship
Hiei smashed the bridge of the *San Francisco*, killing Callaghan and his staff and

mortally wounding Captain Cassin Young, a Medal of Honor winner at Pearl Harbor. Altogether, a hundred officers and men were lost that night on the *San Francisco*.

For San Franciscans, the death of Rear Admiral Callaghan was especially resonant with meaning, given the fact that this native of San Francisco had met his brave end on a flagship named in honor of his home city. Since the admiral had been buried at sea, no casket stood in the sanctuary of St. Mary's Cathedral on Van Ness Avenue on the morning of 27 November 1942 as Captain William A. Maguire, senior chaplain of the Pacific Fleet and a recognized hero of Pearl Harbor, celebrated a solemn requiem mass, with John J. Mitty, Archbishop of San Francisco, presiding on the episcopal throne. A choir of five hundred gathered from the seminaries, schools, and religious houses of the archdiocese chanted the ancient Gregorian plainsong of the funeral mass.

On 11 December 1942 a battered USS *San Francisco* steamed beneath the Golden Gate Bridge, her shattered superstructure prefiguring, like Callaghan's funeral mass, terrible things to come. Admiral Ernest J. King, commander-in-chief of the United States Fleet, was on hand to present the Medal of Honor to Lieutenant Commander Bruce McCandless, who had taken command of the *San Francisco* after Callaghan, Young, and the other officers were killed. King cited McCandless for his great courage, superb initiative, and distinguished service above and beyond the call of duty in continuing to fight the severely damaged heavy cruiser under withering enemy fire without benefit of a command and control center. A few days later, another officer from the *San Francisco*, Lieutenant Commander Herbert Schonland, received his Congressional Medal of Honor from President Roosevelt in a White House ceremony. Roosevelt praised Schonland for keeping the *San Francisco* afloat while working waist-deep in dark, flooded compartments, guiding himself with a hand lantern while the battle raged on deck.

On 16 December 1942 the crew of the *San Francisco* paraded up a crowded Market Street from Pier 16 on the Embarcadero to a packed Civic Auditorium, where they were greeted by Governor-elect Earl Warren, Mayor Angelo Rossi, a bevy of ranking Navy and Army officers, and the San Francisco Symphony under the leadership of Pierre Monteux, which welcomed the arriving bluejackets with a performance of "Pomp and Circumstance," as if this were a high school graduation. After speeches and presentations, the crew of the *San Francisco* was taken to the Whitcomb Hotel across Market Street for three hours of drinks, eats, and entertainment from nearly every nightspot in town, followed by a dance in the nearby Veterans Building. In the days that followed, a local San Francisco bond drive raised twice as much money (a total of $5.3 million) as it would cost to repair the damaged cruiser at Mare Island. The Navy allocated the surplus funds to the construction of another ship of the line. Eventually, the shell-ridden bridge of the USS *San Francisco* was emplaced on the Land's End shoreline of the city overlooking the Pacific as a memorial to the men who had lost their lives in this early great naval battle of the war.

As 1942 edged into 1943, the San Francisco Bay Area was emerging as the premier military command center and port of embarkation and supply on the Pacific Coast. The entire Bay Area was peppered with an integrated array of military commands suitable to the headquarters city of what was, after all, an officially designated war zone. At the Presidio Lieutenant General John L. DeWitt presided over the Western Defense Command established four days after Pearl Harbor. The entire West Coast, in effect, had been declared a theater of war, with DeWitt possessing, as commanding general, a certain proconsular authority, which remained latent in his dealings with civilian elected officials but would soon come forward in its true nature during the forcible evacuation of a hundred thousand Japanese-Americans from the theater. Also headquartered at the Presidio: the 4th Army, which DeWitt commanded, with its maze of supply, military police, intelligence, transportation, technical, and other support battalions. Staff officers shunted to and fro across the dramatically situated and beautifully forested military reservation, established by the Spanish in 1776 on the shores of San Francisco Bay. Troops held formation and drilled in the spacious parade grounds surrounded by PWA-constructed buildings in the Spanish Revival style. At night, after duty hours, the bar at the Officers Club (the building included the adobe walls of the first Presidio) was packed solid with men in khaki and brass, pinks and greens, highballs in one hand, Lucky Strikes or Camels in the other, the room electric with the excitement of a city, a state, a nation, a world at war. The Army Air Corps maintained its 4th Fighter Command at Hamilton Field on San Pablo Bay just north of San Francisco in Marin County. Hamilton Field also served as a key point of arrival and departure for Air Corps flights of every sort to and from the Pacific, while Crissy Field adjacent to the Presidio served command, staff, and administrative flights.

Paralleling the 4th Army command structure, and administered in part by it, was a vast network of forts, arsenals, warehouses, wharves, and piers under the jurisdiction of an Army command calling itself the San Francisco Port of Embarkation. This multi-sited, multi-jurisdictional command maintained its main operations at Fort Mason adjacent to the Presidio, on the northern shore of San Francisco facing Alcatraz. Other piers were attached to the Oakland Army base at the eastern terminus of the San Francisco–Oakland Bay Bridge, on Alameda Island just south of Oakland, at Benicia in the North Bay, on Carquinez Strait, at the city of Stockton, an inland port on the San Joaquin River seventy miles east of San Francisco, and on Humboldt Bay, 250 miles to the north. An intricate array of warehouses and staging facilities—Fort Mason itself, the Oakland Army base, the Alameda In-Transit Depot, the Ordnance Corps shops at Emeryville, the Richmond Parr Terminals, the Benicia Arsenal, not to mention the Presidio itself—

served these piers as centers of storage, staging, stevedoring, and shipment. All ammunition intended for the Pacific was funneled through Port Chicago on the Carquinez Strait north of San Francisco, midway between the cities of Benicia and Pittsburg.

Also near Pittsburg: Camp Stoneman, forty miles northeast of San Francisco where the San Joaquin River flows into the Carquinez Strait. For three years, Camp Stoneman remained one of the best-kept secrets of the war. All in all, a million soldiers were processed en route to the Pacific through Camp Stoneman between 25 May 1942 and 11 August 1945. Covering one thousand acres, Camp Stoneman (named in honor of Civil War general George Stoneman, the fifteenth governor of California) billeted an average of thirty thousand troops each day of the war. Soldiers were housed in endless rows of two-story olive drab barracks extending as far as the eye could see on a plain bordered in the distance by rolling hills. Here in this intricately organized military city, ever the same yet ever different in its shifting khaki-clad population, was the nerve center for the deployment of troops to the Pacific. Although the realities of war were on the mind of each and every soldier, Camp Stoneman could also possess a strangely recreational aspect, since its residents were living, however briefly, in a transitional state between individual and unit training and the voyage across the Pacific that would take them into the combat zone. Discipline at Stoneman, while maintained, was neither harsh nor overpowering. Every effort was made to keep "chickenshit" (harassment) to a minimum. There was an active athletic program and nightly movies and frequent USO shows. The goal of Camp Stoneman was to process men as smoothly and soothingly as possible in the full knowledge of what awaited them in the Pacific.

Ringing the San Francisco Presidio was a network of attendant installations: Fort McDowell on Angel Island in the Bay, for example, conveniently located across the water from Fort Mason, where the troop ships were embarking. Fort McDowell also served as the processing center for prisoners of war. By 1943 members of Rommel's Afrika Korps were arriving in groups of three to four hundred, having been shipped by the British to Australia, then up to San Francisco on American transport for processing to POW camps in the interior. One batch included a German full general, a lieutenant general, and a major general, each of them captured by the British in Tunisia, who were en route to a POW camp in New Mexico. More than 2,200 German prisoners remained permanently in detention at nearby Camp Stillman, with another three hundred remaining at Fort McDowell for KP and other voluntary assignments.

When Italy surrendered in 1943 and became, instantly, a co-belligerent, Italian POWs were given the option of joining Italian Service Units, which performed non-combat duty for the United States Army. Italians volunteering for such duty wore Army uniforms, minus Army buttons, with an ITALY patch on the left shoulder. Many such Italians had relatives in the North Beach and Excelsior districts of San Francisco, whom they visited on leave. By 1945 the Italians were moving freely throughout San Francisco, not that different in uniform and demeanor from ordinary GIs. If a member of an Italian Service Unit broke the rules or otherwise misbehaved, he was transferred back to POW status. A number of Italian Service Unit men married local girls and returned to the Bay Area as permanent residents after the war.

Combat units on active duty in the San Francisco Bay Area belonged for the most part to the Coast Artillery. Headquartered at Fort Winfield Scott on the southern edge of Marin County, the Coast Artillery maintained active batteries in a ring of installations—Fort Scott itself, Fort Barry, Fort Baker, Fort Funston, Fort Miley, Fort Cronkhite—ringing the Golden Gate headlands and San Francisco Bay. The Golden Gate, in fact, both bridge and headlands, was believed to be the most fortified site in the continental United States. Covered in camouflage (strips of burlap laid over chicken wire), the great guns roared by night in dress rehearsal against an invasion that would never come but was possessed nevertheless, through 1942 at least, of a certain plausibility. Occasionally, at night, the Coast Artillery would activate its giant searchlights, with their eight-hundred-million candlepower; and these sweeping paths of light, together with the booming of the great guns, reminded San Franciscans—sipping drinks in the Top of the Mark or snug in their beds in the Sea Cliff district near the Golden Gate—that for all the eclectic, electric gaiety of the city, the world was, after all, at war.

In general terms, the Bay Area and Northern California were Army country during World War II while Southern California belonged to the Navy and Marine Corps. Although this distinction has some validity, the Navy was significantly present in the Bay Area as well. The entire Western Sea Frontier, together with the 12th Naval District, in fact, was headquartered on Treasure Island between San Francisco and Oakland, a site reclaimed from the shoals and mud flats for the Golden Gate International Exposition of 1939–40. Brass shunted in and out of the Administration Building of the exposition, designed by the talented Timothy Pflueger and now one of the busiest naval headquarters in the nation. Also headquartered on Treasure Island were the Coast Guard and Marine district headquarters, a number of Navy and Coast Guard patrol and convoy escort units, a naval brig and disciplinary barracks, and an assortment of training commands, including a Merchant Marine Officers Training School and a Navy boot camp. Capable of feeding six thousand enlisted men in forty minutes, the mess hall on Treasure Island was the largest single mess hall in the Navy. Also headquartered in the Administration Building was the West Coast office of Pan American Airways, whose Flying Clippers were now crossing the Pacific under contract to the War Department.

The Navy also maintained key ship repair facilities at Hunters Point on the southern edge of San Francisco and on Mare Island in the North Bay. Established in 1854, the Mare Island facility was a direct legacy of the conquest of California by the Navy during the Mexican War. (From 1854 to 1858, Commander David Farragut, Civil War hero and the first American naval officer to be promoted to the rank of vice admiral, commanded the facility.) By late 1942 Mare Island, the largest naval repair facility in the United States, had been manhattanized into a naval city where thousands of uniformed personnel, civilians, ship repair workers, and hospital staff lived and worked. Ten thousand civilians were employed in its shipfitting facilities, brought to and from the job site by nearly three hundred chartered buses. Row upon row of cruisers, destroyers, corvettes, submarines, and submarine tenders ringed the island, either awaiting repair, under repair, or preparing to rejoin the fleet. The destroyer USS *Shaw*, for example, took a direct hit at Pearl Harbor in its forward section. Hastily furnished with a temporary bow, the *Shaw* sailed from Pearl to Mare Island, where it was refitted for further service.

From 1942 onward, the skies over San Francisco were heavy with military air traffic, and the Bay teemed with military ships. The 4th Fighter Command monitored this traffic in its situation room at Hamilton Field: the traffic in and out of Hamilton Field itself, the flights in and out of Crissy Field on the northern edge of San Francisco, the myriads of patrol craft and naval blimps from Moffett Field down the peninsula, the Pan Am Clippers taxiing out from Treasure Island for their long take-off on San Francisco Bay, including one plane, the *Philippine Clipper*, that bore a golden V on its bow for having come under aerial attack by the Japanese as it escaped from Midway Island on 7 December 1941.

Given the frequency of military traffic, it is not surprising that few San Franciscans noticed — or if they noticed, were able to interpret — the significance of the fact that when the aircraft carrier USS *Hornet* sailed beneath the Golden Gate Bridge shortly before noon, 2 April 1942, it carried sixteen normally land-based B-25 twin-engine bombers on deck. The mission of these sixteen bombers and their crews, for which planning and training had been under way since January, was nothing less than an attack on Japan itself: an attack that was way out ahead of any American ability to bring the war to the Japanese mainland but nevertheless would shock the Japanese into recognizing that their assault on Pearl Harbor would have fateful consequences.

In command of this specially trained unit was another local favorite son, the Alameda-born James Harold Doolittle, a 1922 graduate of the University of California at Berkeley. Lieutenant Colonel Doolittle was not a career officer, nor was he from a conventional background. As a boy, he had been taken to Alaska for the Gold Rush and grew up in that rough-and-ready environment. Later, while in high school in Los Angeles, he won a statewide boxing championship and seriously considered a career in professional boxing. As a junior at UC Berkeley when America entered the First World War, Doolittle enlisted in the Army Signal Corps as a pilot. After the war, he finished his Cal degree and took an M.A. and a Ph.D. in aeronautical engineering from MIT, all while on active duty. He was also an inveterate stunt flier and test pilot: the first flier, in fact, to achieve an outside loop and the first to fly blind, guided only by instruments, in a completely covered cockpit. Doolittle left the Regular Army in 1930 to pursue a dual career as a prize-winning airplane speed racer and an executive for the Shell Oil Company, where he helped develop 100-octane aviation gasoline. He returned to active duty in May

1940 as a test pilot and in January 1942 was given the super-secret assignment of planning and executing the air raid on Tokyo. The success of that raid on 18 April 1942, despite the loss of all sixteen bombers and some crew, won Doolittle the Medal of Honor and a double promotion to brigadier general. It also set standards—and this from a local man—for the many air cadets who were preparing for future combat at places like Moffett Field or the Alameda Naval Air Station.

Hastily constructed on East Bay tidal shoals when the war broke out, Alameda Naval Air Station, one of the largest airfields in the world, was a city unto itself, with its vast array of runways, hangars, machine shops, and training schools into which and out of which daily marched thousands of men in training, their notebooks clasped uniformly in their hands. Alameda accounted for much of the military traffic over the Bay Area as innumerable planes of the Naval Air Transport Service headquartered there shuttled to and from Pearl Harbor.

Naval pre-flight training in Northern California was headquartered in yet another 1942-created installation, the Navy Pre-Flight School on the campus of St. Mary's College in Moraga in Alameda County across the Bay, one of the four pre-flight training centers conducted by the Navy in the United States. The first cadets reported for duty on 9 June 1942, delighted, no doubt, by the Spanish Revival beauty of their new campus in the Moraga hills. The first ambition of the school was instruction in such pre-flight subjects as navigation, communications, engine mechanics, and the theory of flight. Yet at least half the program at St. Mary's Pre-Flight consisted of physical conditioning, conducted by expert instructors in football, basketball, boxing, soccer, track and field, gymnastics and tumbling, swimming, wrestling, and martial arts. In addition to this in-house training and athletic competition, St. Mary's Pre-Flight fielded varsity teams in a variety of sports competing against other Pacific Coast colleges and other military teams. On Sundays, dances were held for the cadets, with co-eds being invited from nearby Mills College and the University of California at Berkeley. This fusion of military and collegiate culture also characterized Navy V-12 and Army Specialized Training (AST) programs at other colleges and universities throughout California. In the V-12 and AST programs, students continued their accelerated college studies as enlisted men in uniform. When they graduated, they were sent on to Officers Candidate School. The V-12 program alone produced some sixty thousand Navy and Marine Corps officers.

Most young men, of course, prepared for combat in much less elite circumstances and were expected to serve dutifully in the ranks. In contrast to the collegiate ambience of V-12, AST, or Navy or Army pre-flight programs, these young men were moved rapidly and in great numbers through a course of training that seemed all too brief, given what they would soon be facing. If they were to face such dangers in the Pacific, their port of embarkation, especially if they were Army, was San Francisco. Throughout the war, beginning in 1942, convoys of troopships and freighters, an increasing number of them Liberty ships built in Richmond and Marin shipyards, embarked on a weekly, daily, hourly basis from Fort Mason or any of the other 272 wharves and piers ringing the Bay. The sight of helmeted GIs carrying their rifles and duffle bags up gangplanks to transport ships at Pier 45 on Fort Mason in the Marina district of the city—a Women's Army Corps band playing, Red Cross women handing out coffee and donuts, wives, girlfriends, brass, and politicians on hand to say goodbye—became almost commonplace. Troops began their journey early in the morning with a ferry-boat ride down the Carquinez Strait from Camp Stoneman, past Mare Island in San Pablo Bay, then headed directly south across San Francisco Bay to Pier 15 or 45 on the Embarcadero. Toward the end of the war, when the invasion of Japan remained a fearsome possibility, the shipment of troops reached staggering proportions. On one day alone, for example, 1 November 1945, a total of 22,676 men were processed through five piers by the Port of Embarkation. Red Cross volunteers were on hand that day with a thousand gallons of coffee and thirty-four thousand donuts.

Even now, more than a half century later, it is difficult to comprehend the million men and women and the mega-tons of equipment and supplies the San Francisco Port of Embarkation command processed and sent across the Pacific. The entire rail and highway system of the Bay Area was mobilized as part of this shipping infrastructure. Shipping experts such as Roger Lapham, president of the American Hawaiian Steamship Company, elected mayor of San Francisco in 1943, lent their expertise to the military. After all, many of their own ships (four Matson liners alone) were now carrying troops and equipment. Just about every man, woman, weapon, bullet, torpedo, vehicle, foodstuff, medical supply, and piece of mail intended for the Pacific passed through the San Francisco Port of Embarkation. Approximately two hundred thousand military vehicles of one sort or another—jeeps, trucks, half-tracks, tanks—were given pre-combat checkouts and prepared for shipment at the Ordnance Automotive Shop in Emeryville in the East Bay near Berkeley, where up to one hundred vehicles per day (the record was 360) were prepared for combat in the Pacific.

Working in cooperation with the air arms of the Army and Navy, the port developed an increasingly sophisticated delivery service for crucial medical supplies. By the Battle of Okinawa whole blood was reaching combat troops forty-eight hours from the time it was donated in California. San Francisco also functioned as an important medical center, especially for the Navy and Marine Corps, whose Mare Island and Oak Knoll naval hospitals soon became filled with wounded from the early battles of the Pacific: Pearl Harbor, Guadalcanal, Java, Coral Sea, Midway. In 1944 President Roosevelt would visit wounded sailors at Mare Island Naval Hospital. That same year, Mrs. Roosevelt also made a visit, chatting quietly with the more presentable of the wounded in their wheelchairs, lined up as if in formation. Behind the wheelchair of each sailor stood a medical orderly in starched naval whites.

Each day, weekends especially, the roads and highways into San Francisco were lined with young men in uniform hitchhiking into the city on pass. San Francisco

was considered one of the best liberty towns in the country. A certain egalitari-
anism in the psychology of San Francisco, the legacy of its hundred-year vitality
as a port city, made it especially hospitable to enlisted men. *Chronicle* columnist
Lucius Beebe reported with glee the spectacle of the maître d' at the Garden
Court of the Palace Hotel waving a group of enlisted sailors to their table while
a four-striper captain stood glumly in line with his lady guest. The USO Hospitality
House at Civic Center had been constructed and dedicated four months before
the bombing of Pearl Harbor, so convinced had San Franciscans been that the
United States would soon be getting into the war and San Francisco would soon
be getting into the hospitality business. Throughout the war, thousands of young
men on leave found in the Hospitality House opportunities for a shave, a shower,
a game of pool or Ping-Pong, conversation with a young lady from one or another
San Francisco organization, and other chaperoned social events. Later in the war
the city of San Francisco would hold an open house in Civic Center Auditorium
for ten thousand men in uniform and an equal number of invited young women.
It would be the largest USO dance of its kind during the conflict. For the more
rebellious, young sailors especially, a score of tattoo parlors lined Market and
Kearney streets and adjacent environs, where a man on leave might secure in the
early morning hours—usually after a number of beers—a rose, a panther, a naval
eagle, a battleship, a woman's name, that for the rest of his life would memorialize
these wartime years.

Indeed, the very youthfulness of these San Francisco pleasures—roller-coaster
rides, corn dogs, cotton candy and Its-It ice cream sandwiches at Playland-at-the-
Beach; bike rides in Golden Gate Park (the sight of sailors on bicycles proved
especially intriguing, as if fundamental metaphors were being mixed); the pinball
and arcade games at the Fun Center on the ground floor of the Bank of America
Building at Powell and Market in the downtown (also there was the opportunity
to have your picture taken in front of a cardboard mock-up of a battleship or with
your arm draped around a cardboard girl in a hula skirt)—poignantly emphasized
the fact that the vast majority of these soldiers, sailors, airmen, and Marines were
themselves only in, or barely out of, their late teens.

Human nature being what it is, less wholesome fun was available in the bars
of the Tenderloin district. An increasingly large number of these bars were placed
off-limits as the war progressed. Other establishments—the Pirate's Cave, for example, or the Silver Dollar, Finocchio's, the Lankershim Hotel Tavern Bar, Mc-
Carthy's, Club Alabam, and Jack's Tavern—spent time on the off-limits list, mostly
for serving under age or after hours, but managed to regain good standing with
the authorities. In certain districts of the city—the Tenderloin, North Beach, the
International Settlement—military police and the Shore Patrol passed to and fro
in open jeeps or made sweeps through suspected establishments. Young (and
sometimes not so young) soldiers, sailors, airmen, and Marines who could not
hold their liquor or who succumbed to fisticuffs or other expressions of social
disturbance soon found themselves in MP or SP vans headed for the military tank

at the Hall of Justice on Kearney Street, where San Francisco police chief Charles Dullea, quite early in 1942, negotiated a smooth working arrangement with his military counterparts.

Getting the feel of San Francisco for an article in *Harper's* magazine, novelist John Dos Passos spent an evening in a bar just off the Embarcadero, south of Market. He noted, however, that most of the people in the noisy crowd, calling for beers and boilermakers, seemed to be longshoremen and other defense workers, all of them making good money, as opposed to youngsters in uniform. An estimated 250,000 war workers flooded into San Francisco and adjacent communities, starting in 1942, many of them housed in hastily constructed projects, such as that on Potrero Hill overlooking the city. It was the well-paid defense workers who could afford such places as Bimbo's 365 Club in North Beach, where a seemingly nude young lady cavorted in what appeared to be a fishbowl. Out in the Mission district the bars were packed with Bethlehem Steel workers. Dago Mary's was a favorite with civilian workers at the naval shipyard at Hunters Point. In order to avoid such well-heeled competition, as well as the MPs and the Shore Patrol, many enlisted men favored neighborhood places, such as the Persian Aub Zam Zam on Haight Street near the entrance to Golden Gate Park or the Kezar Club a few blocks away on Stanyan.

Military personnel tended to go to places where they felt comfortable; and this depended in great measure upon their rank. Naturally, there were other distinctions and divisions as well, proceeding in part from the military class system. The military separation of managers from rank and file, of white collars from blue, of privates and seamen who grew up in inner-city ethnic neighborhoods or the boondocks from college kids wearing an ensign's gold stripe or a slick Air Corps uniform, bars on the shoulders, wings on the left chest, only made explicit what civilian life concealed: America had a class system, and in wartime it tended, by and large (there were many exceptions, especially after battlefield commissions began to be granted), to manifest itself in rank. Beginning in 1942, the more privileged echelons of San Francisco extended themselves enthusiastically to the task of entertaining the military, providing, in most instances, they were officers. Clubs—the Bohemian, the Pacific Union, the Olympic, the Concordia-Argonaut—extended guest privileges, even honorary memberships, to ranking officers in the area. Socially prominent women arranged innumerable dinner parties, even dates, for officers, junior and senior, properly referred to their network. Social scion Templeton Crocker donated his two-masted schooner yacht *Zacca* to the Navy for the duration for use as a training ship. In 1943 a socially prominent San Franciscan told John Dos Passos that his set had welcomed the war because it put on hold the intense class conflicts of the city that had surfaced in the bitter maritime strikes of the 1930s.

The entertaining of officers was centered in the finer hotels of the city, such as the Mark Hopkins, where Ensign Willis Keith's socially prominent mother entertains her twenty-three-year-old son, a junior officer on the USS *Caine*, in the novel *The Caine Mutiny* (1949) by Herman Wouk, or the St. Francis Hotel on Union Square, which by August 1944 was reserving five hundred of its seven hundred available rooms for servicemen and -women, with an unstated but effective preference accorded commissioned officers. Popularly called the Frantic, the St. Francis Hotel was, for officers at least, the number one spot in San Francisco because of its central location, its great bars, and its non-stop dancing in the Mural Room. Soon, in fact, the St. Francis would have to construct another 125 rooms, using plywood in previous storage space, to handle its business. The Fairmont, meanwhile, constructed, again with plywood, sleeping quarters for an additional 350 military transients.

It is to the St. Francis that four naval aviators arrive in February 1943 in Frederic Wakeman's novel of wartime San Francisco, *Shore Leave* (1944). Temporarily furloughed from combat duty in the Pacific, the three lieutenants and one lieutenant commander take a suite of rooms in the St. Francis—and the party begins! For days on end, the pilots' suite is the scene of twenty-four-hour action, with waiters from room service equally resourceful in their around-the-clock provision of glasses, ice, soda water, cigarettes, and whiskey. Bottle upon bottle is emptied, and ashtray upon ashtray is filled, cleaned, refilled, as the aviators hold open house. For rest and recuperation from the St. Francis party, which is itself rest and recuperation from war, the pilots venture forth into San Francisco. One of them, Lieutenant Andy Crewson, a Columbia man from Great Neck, Long Island, a non-stop drinker, womanizer, and all-round party animal (not to mention a skilled combat dive-bomber), fascinates the narrator of the novel, an older air intelligence officer, as much as he does the women of San Francisco, including the Junior Leaguer from Pacific Heights who brings him home to meet her parents. Crewson epitomizes the college boy as combat pilot, an elite within an elite. ("Mastery of an airplane," says the narrator, "seems to set men apart in certain very subtle ways, just as the shared experiences of combat seem to pull men together.") For Crewson and his pals—products of Annapolis, Harvard, Columbia, and Tulane—shore leave in San Francisco, like pilot training at Pensacola, represents just another instance of the all-consuming present they have learned to live in as combat pilots. "On duty, it would be a mission; on shore leave, it would be getting drunk or laid, depending on the opportunities. . . . No matter how complicated or dangerous their mission or how involved or mixed-up their shore leave seemed—essentially it was a very simple way to live life, because they were not concerned with the responsibilities laid on them by the past or the prospects promised by the future."[3]

African-American servicemen were not segregated in San Francisco—not formally, at least, although prejudice could easily be detected in many establishments: the maître d' who never finds time to seat you, the bartender who ignores your call, the taxi driver who refuses to stop. To feel more welcomed, black servicemen might, for a better time, hit any number of bars and bebop joints in the Fillmore district or take their leave in Oakland, where a significant African-American com-

munity was developing out of thousands of black shipyard workers recently moved
to the West Coast. Thus, African-American sailor-stevedores from Port Chicago
favored such black-friendly districts as Black Diamond Street in Pittsburg, 7th
Street in Oakland, and the Fillmore district of San Francisco, where in such places
as Club Seven, Club Alabama, Club Havana, Sweet's, and the Club Jet they could
forget the war and the color line that cast such a pall on their military service.

Gay servicemen and -women might try the Black Cat Café near the International Settlement or Li-Po's in Chinatown, or the Silver Rail or the Silver Dollar
in the Tenderloin, or Techau's Cocktail Lounge near Union Square, or the nearby
Mona's, a favored lesbian hangout where an all-girl orchestra played on weekends
(another favored lesbian place was the Rickshaw in Chinatown, just around the
corner from Li-Po's), or Finocchio's in North Beach, with its famed female im-
personators and drag chorus line. The butch set favored the Old Crow in the
Tenderloin or the Silver Rail, where blue-collar civilians and their military counterparts could talk tough together. Jack's Baths, also in the Tenderloin, catered to
a down-to-basics crowd, while the nearby YMCA Hotel on Golden Gate Avenue
offered more subtle opportunities for erotic adventure. Further up the social ladder, the Top of the Mark on Nob Hill maintained an even more discreet gay scene
that floated in a much larger sea of heterosexuality. With the exception of the Top
of the Mark, which did not have an overtly gay identity, places catering to gay
servicemen and -women were continually vulnerable to crackdowns by civilian or
military police. From the summer of 1942 through 1943, some sixty-three San
Francisco nightspots, including a number of gay clubs, such as Finocchio's, lost
their liquor licenses and were declared off-limits. By 1944, however, the cops,
civilian and military, seem to have lost interest; and for the rest of the war gay
night life, while not exactly out of the closet, flourished in San Francisco.

Gay or straight, San Francisco was a great town for leave and for night life,
especially after 1942 when the evening blackouts lessened and streets returned to
neon brightness. For four years, the party continued: in the sleazy array of bars,
tattoo parlors, and locker clubs in the Tenderloin and downtown, where soldiers
and sailors could illegally rent civilian clothes in order to hit off-limits joints; in
Ray and Bee Goman's Gay Nineties Club in the International Settlement, where
a dancer named Yvette doffed significant portions of her costume with the help
of a live parrot who pecked open the knots fastening her sarong. Upstairs at Izzy
Gomez's on Pacific Avenue, Izzy himself, resplendent in apron and hat, now
welcomed servicemen and -women to his establishment for food, drink, and dancing just as he had welcomed bohemia before the war. At Charlie Low's Forbidden
City in Chinatown, Chinese-American chorus girls danced, and after the show
they would patriotically swarm around soldiers and sailors in uniform for
photographs.

The truly rakish—if they were also civilian and affluent, it must be added—
might visit Sally Stanford's establishment at 1144 Pine Street, convenient to the
hotel district and the major men's clubs of the city. Sally Stanford had been in

the hospitality business since the 1920s, and this was her last and most elegant establishment in San Francisco before she devoted her energies exclusively to her Valhalla restaurant in Sausalito. The outbreak of the war brought a temporary restraint to Sally's business, as both the district attorney and the chief of police began cracking down on all houses in San Francisco, no matter how well behaved, at the insistence of General DeWitt. During the war, Sally served thirty days in the county jail: not for running a disorderly house, however, but for running afoul of the Office of Price Administration for the rents she was charging on some of her properties. Wartime visitors to 1144 Pine Street, so Sally Stanford later remembered, included Errol Flynn, who had stayed for two weeks while dodging bad publicity arising from a fight he had gotten into with a Marine; Humphrey Bogart, whom Sally disliked; and assorted military officers, clubmen, public officials, newspaper columnists, and the like. Stanford also provided room service, dispatching girls by taxicab to the Fairmont, the St. Francis, and the Sir Francis Drake.

Throughout the war, the hotels and restaurants of San Francisco remained packed. In one record day in 1943, the restaurants of the Palace Hotel served 4,200 lunches. Equally popular: Trader Vic's across the Bay, where Victor Bergeron presided over open hearth–barbecued spare ribs and an astonishing array of rum drinks. In San Francisco, there was Solari's on Maiden Lane, Julius' Castle atop Telegraph Hill, Slapsie Maxie's on O'Farrell, the Cliff House overlooking the Pacific, Sam's and Jack's and Tadich's in the financial district, and Omar Khayyam's on the corner of Powell and O'Farrell, where restaurateur George Mardikian presided and a line of hungry customers usually extended around the block.

A line usually extended as well through the lobby of the Mark Hopkins Hotel, this one for revelers, fully half of them in uniform, anxious to enjoy a drink at the Top of the Mark penthouse bar. Opened in 1939, the Top of the Mark had been decorated in an Art Deco chicness of leather and chrome by architect Timothy Pflueger. Located on the nineteenth floor of the hotel, which was itself located atop Nob Hill overlooking the city, the Top of the Mark afforded a 360-degree view of greater San Francisco: city, bay, and, on a clear day, the distant hills and suburbs. The custom grew for servicemen to sign a dollar bill, then leave it with the bartender to be reclaimed upon return from the Pacific. The Top of the Mark was, by informal arrangement, officer country, although enlisted men were not made to feel unwelcome. Other packed hotel bars included the Patent Leather Lounge in the St. Francis, another Timothy Pflueger creation, the Cirque Room in the Fairmont, with its festive circus murals by Antonio Sotomayor, the Persian Room and the Starlite Roof at the Sir Francis Drake, the Prado Room in the Plaza Hotel on Union Square, and the Redwood Room at the Clift. The Pied Piper Bar at the Palace, dominated by its great Maxfield Parrish mural, and the Happy Valley Bar in the same hotel maintained their attractiveness for local oligarchs. Pflueger himself, a noted *bon vivant*, favored the Happy Valley Bar, where during the war years he would join such cronies as City Controller Harry Ross, *Chronicle* publisher George Cameron, and Mayor Angelo Rossi for early evening cocktails.

Hearst lawyer John Francis Neylan, *Chronicle* columnist Chester Rowell, and the
Honorable Phil Gibson, chief justice of the Supreme Court of California, favored
the Palm Court at the Palace for their weekly lunches. All these spots buzzed by
day and by night with wartime excitement: the hotel bars packed with men in
uniform and women in hats and veils and the high hemlines of the war years.
Everywhere there was music and talk and laughter, the tinkle of ice cubes in
glasses, the shaking of martini pitchers, the cries of bellhops paging this or that
guest. In its bars and restaurants, its hotel lobbies and hotel rooms, San Francisco
became a city of poignant interludes between training and battle, romances that
might or might not last, sudden hellos that became, almost immediately, lingering
goodbyes.

Occasions for goodbyes were not lacking. All in all, a total of 1,647,174 passengers — 90 percent of them Army personnel, the rest Navy, civilians, American Red
Cross, and Allied forces — sailed from San Francisco for the Pacific between December 1941 and August 1945. For each individual, combat personnel especially,
every minute, each detail, of that last leave, those final goodbyes in San Francisco,
remained fixed in mind amidst the boredom and dangers of war. Visiting San
Francisco in 1943, John Dos Passos dined one evening at the Cliff House and
caught all around him the drama of wartime interludes and departures. A young
Army Air Corps major and his equally elegant female companion proceeded
through a meal that began with cocktails and oysters and continued through ab-
alone steaks, sourdough French bread, salad, and chilled white wine, as if the
meal itself were a departure ceremony. At another table, a man and woman in
late middle age sat with their son, an Army first lieutenant in khaki, whom Dos
Passos thought barely old enough to be in high school. Sometimes, at this table,
the conversation came completely to a halt as the three stared into their food,
caught for a moment in sheer anxiety over what might lie ahead. Everywhere
throughout San Francisco, from 1942 onward, the restaurants in the city abounded
in similar scenes as parents and children, husbands and wives, the newly in love
or the temporarily amorous, dined and said goodbye.

Leave patterns in Southern California lacked the geographical concentration of
the North. Los Angeles, for one thing, was a different kind of city than San Francisco, which is to say, a much more suburbanized and private place. Yet while
Los Angeles lacked the dense *mise-en-scène* of its sister city to the north, its downtown places, the Biltmore Hotel on Pershing Square especially, witnessed action
comparable to that of the St. Francis on Union Square. Although downtown Los
Angeles was tough to reach on a brief twenty-four-hour pass, the Biltmore was a
popular spot for the more than twenty thousand Army Air Force cadets in pre-
flight training at nearby Santa Ana. Passes were issued from Saturday noon until
the Sunday parade at three o'clock, so cadets had to move quickly if they were to
catch any of the action in downtown Los Angeles or Hollywood. The Men's Bar
of the Biltmore provided a gay rendezvous. "Frequently, I'd eat dinner at the
Biltmore Hotel," later recalled Burt Miller, then a twenty-one-year-old ensign from

Seattle stationed just outside Los Angeles. "One night after dinner, I walked through the bar—about 75 percent of the men were in uniform—and I asked myself, 'Can what I think is going on here *be* going on?' I stopped to find out, and sure enough it was! I was in that bar every night." [4]

Just down from the Biltmore extended a zone of honky-tonk bars, burlesque theaters, cheap movie houses, dance halls, and tattoo parlors, most of it centered on Main Street. Military Police and Shore Patrol patrolled constantly, and on weekends thousands of sailors were on the street, as they were in Long Beach and Wilmington–San Pedro. In San Bernardino, the police cordoned off the downtown on weekends to accommodate the thousands of young soldiers on leave from Camp Irwin and the Desert Training Center. In Riverside, weekend action rocked the bar and restaurant of the Mission Inn as flight trainees from Victorville and a half dozen other Air Force bases flooded into town on a weekend pass. In late 1942 Army Air Corps cadet James M. Brown of San Francisco and a group of his pals made a major discovery while in pre-flight training at Santa Ana: the Big Bear resort district in the San Bernardino Mountains. Brown and his friends enjoyed a couple of weekends at Big Bear, delighted to find the resort undiscovered by their fellow cadets. Returning to base, they kept their secret. A few weeks later, the word got out, and Big Bear was crawling with aviation cadets for the rest of the war.

San Diego, being Navy and Marine Corps country, had thousands of young sailors on pass each weekend, joined by a comparable number of Marines from Camp Pendleton, El Toro Marine Air Base, and the Marine Corps boot camp in San Diego. In 1942 Hollywood helped the war effort along by producing *The Shores of Tripoli*, set in the San Diego Marine Corps Recruit Depot. In the film, Randolph Scott played a senior non-com doing his best to instill a knowledge and love of the Corps in recruits John Payne, Eddie Bracken, and others, while Maureen O'Hara provided love interest as a Navy nurse. After the war, writer Leon Uris, who went through a much more realistic version of Marine boot camp than that depicted in *The Shores of Tripoli*, took up the same theme in the best-selling novel *Battle Cry* (1953). Skillfully, Uris depicted the weekend scene in and around Oceanside and San Diego, especially the poignancy of young Marines out on pass. "They say it is easy to spot a new Marine," writes Uris of the young men wandering up and down the streets of San Diego. "He has that boot camp stare. They knew the stare in San Diego, and had become rich on it. It takes a year of wear for the wool nap of Marine greens to wear down and acquire the knifelike sharpness of a veteran. The boots' uniform wrinkles easily and fits badly. It is easy to see the awe of a boy who has never been away from home. You can spot him in a minute."[5]

War placed a terrible strain on marriages. There were more of them, for one thing. In the first three months of 1942 alone, the sale of wedding rings jumped by 300 percent. Many of these marriages were the results of whirlwind courtships, intensified by a sense that life might not last that long. In the interim, wives left behind lived existentially, from moment to moment, hour to hour, day to day, fearful of the dreaded telegram or military officer at the door. By the end of the war, more than 2.7 million American women were heading their own households. Many such women were also raising "goodbye babies," conceived before their husbands shipped out. The simplest private's wife received a minimum of $50 a month as an allotment, $22 of it deducted from her husband's pay. Should her husband be killed in action, there was a onetime $10,000 payment. Many women lived alone or returned home to their families, if possible; others, such as the defense workers in director Edward Dmytryk's *Tender Comrade* (1943), screenplay by Dalton Trumbo, set up housekeeping together while their husbands were away. Produced by David Selznick and directed by John Cromwell, *Since You Went Away* (1944) was the ultimate home-front movie, focusing as it did on the trials and temptations of women left behind. Being alone in a condition of enforced celibacy was for many a great trial. For others, the worst was the uncertainty—an uncertainty that lasted from moment to moment—as to whether their husbands would make it back. Dr. Jacob Sergi Kasanin, chief psychiatrist at Mt. Zion Hospital in San Francisco, identified a neurotic syndrome in wives left behind—depression, colitis, heart palpitations, diarrhea, frequent headaches—that represented its own home-front form of battle fatigue. Many women developed drinking problems or formed extramarital relationships that were themselves further causes of stress. Yet despite all this, the war could also bring to many young couples the most poignant, exultational moments of their relationship: moments and memories that would last a lifetime, such as those documented in the wartime correspondence of Robert and Jane Easton published in 1991.

Robert Easton, Harvard College and Stanford Law graduate, aspiring writer, met Jane Faust, daughter of Hollywood screenwriter and novelist Frederick Faust (writing under the pseudonym Max Brand), on the platform of the Southern Pacific station in Santa Barbara in late August 1939. Thirteen months later, as bombs rained on London, they were married in Berkeley at St. Mark's Episcopal Church on Bancroft Way just opposite the campus, where Bob's grandfather had been rector in the 1890s. The young couple were romantics. They envisioned themselves as ranchers, with Bob continuing to write on the side. Piling into Bob's Dodge after the wedding reception, a JUST MARRIED sign attached to the trunk, they headed north to Rio Vista on the Sacramento River, where Bob had a job as a cattle manager on a large ranch. Bob began to write, according to plan, and sold some stories to the *Atlantic*. Later, when in uniform, he would have a novel, *The Happy Man: A Novel of California Ranch Life* (1943), published by Viking. Listening to a broadcast of the New York Philharmonic on their Zenith portable radio while lunching at the kitchen table in their cottage on Sunday morning, 7 December 1941, the Eastons heard, along with the rest of the nation, the familiar voice of announcer John Daly breaking into the broadcast to give news of Pearl Harbor. Rather than wait for the draft, Robert Easton enlisted, and Jane moved back to Brentwood to live with her parents.

At this point, their correspondence began. For the next four years, they would write to each other at a constant rate: their letters becoming part of a vast and democratic epistolary literature now flowing into libraries and archives and in certain cases reaching publication. Inducted into the Army at Fort MacArthur in San Pedro, Bob was sent to Camp Roberts near Paso Robles in San Luis Obispo County, three hours north of Santa Barbara, for basic training. Accustomed to the outdoor life as a ranch foreman, he did well in the Army and was promoted to corporal in June 1942 and to sergeant in July, responsible for forty-eight men and earning $78 a month. Shortly thereafter, Easton was sent to Officers Candidate School at Camp Hood, Texas — their baby girl Joan was born while he was there — and was commissioned a second lieutenant of infantry in November 1942, assigned to the 825th Tank Destroyer Battalion at Camp Gruber, Oklahoma. When Robert was commissioned, Jane acquired a copy of *The Army Wife* so she could fulfill her obligations at various posts in Oklahoma and Texas.

On 27 May 1944, back in California, Jane received a postcard from the War Department notifying her that her husband had been shipped overseas and that from now on she must address letters to him through a designated APO number. Desperately, she rushed across the country by train, no easy feat in wartime, hoping to say goodbye to Bob in New York, but she missed him by the same few hours they hoped to spend together. In May 1944 Bob shipped overseas to England, together with thirteen thousand other men, on the *Queen Elizabeth*. From then on, their correspondence was by airmail and V-mail, a system that reduced letters to microfilm.

For the duration of the war, Jane, along with daughters Joan and Katherine, born before Bob's departure, lived at a home the couple had purchased at 34 East Padre Street in Santa Barbara. Jane's letters are filled with the day-to-day details of Joan and Katherine as they grow up: their eating habits, their first crawls, standings, and steps. Bob is with his unit in Europe in August 1944 when Jane writes on the 26th: "Katherine has stopped blowing her cereal, and eats very nicely, flat on her back, and now has vegetables (pureed) for her lunch as well as the eternal bottle. She likes carrots and hates peas because they stick to the roof of her mouth. I hated them as a child, too. Her appetite is excellent, and her laughter my great joy."[6] She describes the details of food rationing: red stamps for meat, green stamps for vegetables, blue stamps for sugar, brown stamps for coffee. She writes of her days in Santa Barbara: caring for her two small daughters, having tea with her mother and mother-in-law, reading *Henry IV* aloud with her parents and *Tartuffe* in French with her sister-in-law. She gardens, listens to music, cooks, cleans, sews, volunteers with the Red Cross at a local Army hospital where she cares carefully for young men who have suffered the wounds she fears for her husband.

Her letters reveal the constant necessity, for women left behind, to structure time by an almost preternatural focus on the day-to-day activities of household management. Each moment, each event, seems caught in a quality of slow motion because it bears the burden, not just of its own time present, but of time past as well, and time future, which may or may not be. At any one moment, after all, that Jane Easton is fixing lunch for her children, reading to them, sitting with them in the garden, her husband may be in danger of his life or perhaps losing it: especially now that Bob has volunteered to transfer from a rear-echelon tank destroyer battalion in a defensive perimeter for front-line duty with Company K, 116th Infantry, part of the 29th Infantry Division, which in turn is part of Patton's 3rd Army driving toward the Rhine. Jane cries for ten minutes when she reads the news, but she writes him on 4 January 1945 that she is deeply proud of his decision, despite the increased danger.

Jane is bluffing, keeping up a good front. Already, her family is a Gold Star family of sorts; for on the night of 11–12 May 1944 her father, Frederick Faust, serving as a war correspondent in Italy, was struck on the chest by a mortar shell fragment and killed while accompanying a platoon of the 88th Infantry Division in an attack on a German strong point in the mountains north of Naples. Throughout 1945 Jane follows Robert's every move on the drive to Berlin. "Tell me all, all, everything," she writes on 9 January. "From how dirty you are to what a foxhole smells like and what you dream about when you *do* sleep and what death is like so close, and how cold your hands grow, and anything and everything that you can possibly take time to write me. . . . I hate to think of how dirty you'll get and how tired and how sore your feet. I simply cannot grow accustomed to your suffering. But I shall have to go on living in this strange, indistinct way, half alive, until I can be in your arms once more."[7]

For 160 Pearl Harbor widows and 125 fatherless children living in Long Beach, such a moment of reunion would never come. On 22 February 1942 a memorial service for Long Beach men killed at Pearl Harbor was held in the Municipal Auditorium, with Governor Culbert Olson on hand to give the principal address and Jeanette MacDonald singing religious and patriotic songs. As the home port of the United States fleet in the Pacific, where the war assumed major dimensions as swiftly as early 1942, Long Beach experienced an early and intense number of casualties. Chief Warrant Officer Gaynor Connolly, Chief Yeoman Frank Head, Chief Storekeeper L. F. Weller, Chief Turret Captain Lawrence Nelson, Chief Machinist Mates McClellan Taylor Roberts and Ralph Derrington, Chief Signalman Wilbur Yost, Chief Boatswain's Mate Joseph Anthony Williams, Chief Electrician's Mate John Calvin Greer: the loss of such career warrant and chief petty officers, the heart and soul of the Navy, men well known in Long Beach, the sort who coached teams and belonged to local bowling clubs, drove swiftly home to the people of Long Beach that it would be a long, long war. In one month alone, January 1942, nineteen Army Ferry Command pilots based in Long Beach lost their lives, fifteen of them when an airliner crashed in Nevada on the night of 16 January.

The aircraft companies in the Long Beach area gave employment priority to military widows. In 1942 the presence of women in either the military or the industrial sector was minimal in comparison to the explosions of female enlistment and industrial employment that began in 1943 and continued through 1944. Women, meanwhile, were being mustered into all military branches of the service. In February 1943 a Women's Army Corps (WAC) base was established in the heart of San Francisco in Funston Park in the Marina District. Twelve hundred WACs lived here through the course of the conflict, assigned to the Presidio, neighboring forts and bases, and the Port of Embarkation; a WAC band attached to Special Services sent off, and later welcomed home, the troops. In addition to the WACs, some six thousand civilian women worked at the Port of Embarkation, white-collar equivalents of their (temporarily) blue-collar counterparts in the shipyards and aircraft factories. Women also drove and conducted the streetcars and cable cars of San Francisco. A number of colorful female conductors earned the affection of enlisted men for the humorous barbs they directed at ranking officers venturing onto the cars. "Hurry up, dearie," this to a naval captain, hesitating at entering a streetcar full of sailors. "Don't you know there's a war on?"

Photographs from the war years, in *Life*, for example, almost invariably depict soldiers and sailors with dates: beautiful young women in bobby socks, short skirts, cashmere sweaters, and Andrews Sisters hairdos. More than a little propaganda characterizes these photos. Not every GI or sailor invariably found a date, much less one with a starlet's good looks; yet this was not for lack of trying. With hundreds of thousands of men passing through California each year, the matching up of young women and young military men for social purposes became a cottage industry. "I belonged to a little church," later remembered Jean Bartlett, a Berkeley high school student when the war broke out. "The minister would go out on Sundays and bring in young sailors, Marines, that were roaming around with nothing to do. The ladies of the church would give them supper. I would go with my girlfriends to this little church every Sunday. We became the best churchgoers. We couldn't wait til Sunday to see what new crops would come in. . . . We'd pick out a few we liked and invite 'em home. . . . Most of them were from small towns. I had one little Marine from Alabama. As soon as he got in the house, he took his shoes off. He said, 'My feet are killing me. I never wore shoes until I got in the service.' A lot of these boys had just grits and greens and never had a cheese sandwich. It was just a lot of fun meeting these different boys."[8]

Nisei teenagers and young adults, by contrast, were forced to carry on their socializing behind barbed wire. By 5 June 1942 nearly a hundred thousand Japanese, two-thirds of them from California, had been deported to relocation centers or, to use a harsher term, concentration camps. The forces and events that converged behind the evacuation of Japanese-Americans in the spring of 1942 represented the inevitable outcome of fifty years of anti-Japanese agitation in California and the persistent fantasy of a Japanese invasion of the state. Pearl Harbor and the shelling of Santa Barbara by submarine I-17 only reinforced that belief. On the other side of the Pacific, after all, Japanese soldiers were advancing in an arc of conquest — the Philippines, Malaya, Burma, Indonesia, numerous islands in the South Pacific—which by mid-1942 had extended the Japanese empire from New Guinea to the Aleutian Islands. The loss of the Philippines, an affiliated American commonwealth, represented a disaster to American arms second only to Pearl Harbor; and the Aleutian Islands—Attu, Kiska, and Agattu—which the Japanese had seized in June 1942 after bombing the American Navy base at Dutch Harbor, represented an incursion into American territory itself. The Aleutians, in fact, belonged to the Western Defense Command headquartered in San Francisco.

If the Philippines could fall, why not California? If the Aleutians could be seized, why not Cape Mendocino? If Manila, Hong Kong, and Singapore (especially Singapore, so powerfully garrisoned and fortified by the British!) had now become Japanese-held cities, could not the same thing happen to San Francisco and Los Angeles? A half century and more later, such fears might seem overwrought; but in the winter and spring of 1942, with both Germany and Japan at the apogee of their conquests, the possibility of a Japanese invasion, which had for so long been part of the fantasy life of California, became possessed of a reality of its own. Not only did xenophobes and Japan-bashers believe in it—the palpable, gut-wrenching possibility of an attack on the Pacific Coast—the Best People of the State, as General DeWitt described them, believed it as well, especially after the shock of Pearl Harbor.

And if an invasion was a real possibility, was not the possibility of a fifth column equally plausible? Even before Pearl Harbor, *Newsweek* magazine ran an article on 14 October 1940 regarding the threat posed by Japanese living around military installations in Hawaii and California. On the day of Pearl Harbor itself, the FBI, assisted by sheriff's deputies, began rounding up suspected Japanese aliens in Los Angeles County. By 9 December 1941 some five hundred were in federal custody on Terminal Island in Los Angeles Harbor after being booked, fingerprinted, and photographed.

Ironically, Kenji Nakauchi, the dapper Japanese consul general in Los Angeles, was allowed to return to his office in the Chamber of Commerce Building under the watchful supervision of Los Angeles police officer Gene Renaker. A graduate of Clark University who had spent considerable time on assignment in Washington and Chicago, Nakauchi opened his spacious home at 7425 Franklin Avenue to the press on the very day of the attack to say that he was "quite sorry" about Pearl Harbor. "I feel so at home in America," said the thirty-nine-year-old diplomat as photographers popped flashbulbs in his face. "All this is very hard to believe." When asked by reporters whether he thought Japanese living in Los Angeles should be interned, the consul general referred to his previous assignment in Vancouver: when Canada went to war with Germany and Italy, he pointed out, Germans and Italians living in Vancouver were not locked up.[9]

Consul General Nakauchi, who had been out for a Sunday morning stroll when the attack on Pearl Harbor came, was underestimating the situation. Although German and Italian aliens were included in the early phases of the post–Pearl Harbor roundups (FBI director J. Edgar Hoover reported a total of 2,295 arrested nationwide by 10 December), these were, as California attorney general Earl Warren later suggested, white people, and the Japanese were not white people, and, as Warren was arguing by indirection, one might more easily determine the loyalty of Caucasians than the loyalty of Japanese. In the first months of the war, a number of suspicious German aliens were apprehended in California; but despite evidence of German sabotage on the East Coast, it never even crossed the minds of Californians—not once, if one is to judge by the public record—to contemplate the wholesale roundup and deportation of the thousands of non-citizen German residents in California, much less the hundreds of thousands of American citizens of German ancestry.

California, moreover, was even more Italian than it was German. The city of San Francisco—Angelo Rossi, mayor—and the Bay Area in general were significantly Italian, citizen and non-citizen alike. The parents of Joe DiMaggio, for example, had never filed for citizenship, a common occurrence among older Italian immigrants whose English was shaky. In the early months of the war, FBI sweeps in Northern California resulted in the arrest of a couple of dozen Italian aliens, and a smaller number of suspicious figures were taken into custody in Southern California. Italian aliens were required to register themselves with the government; and in San Francisco and Los Angeles, it became rather embarrassing to see hundreds of elderly Italians, including a number of respected figures, waiting in line to be registered as enemy aliens.

By April 1942 General DeWitt was reporting back to Washington that he saw no need for any full-scale evacuation, relocation, and internment of German or Italian aliens. And besides: by March, DeWitt and the Best People already had in motion the evacuation of the Japanese they so desired. Its dress rehearsal came on 15 February 1942 when the Western Defense Command sent soldiers into the Japanese fishing colony on Terminal Island in the Port of Los Angeles and, with only a twenty-four-hour notice, removed five hundred families from their homes and impounded their craft. Two days later, on the evening of the 17th, the Japanese-American community of Los Angeles held a rally in the Maryknoll Catholic Mission in Japantown. More than 1,500 Japanese-Americans attended to hear speaker after speaker protest their loyalty and to urge calm on the part of the Japanese-American community: calm—and trust in the ultimate fairness of the system. "Our greatest friend," stated one *Nisei* leader, "is a man who is the greatest living man today—our President, Franklin Delano Roosevelt."[10]

Two days later, on 19 February 1942, Roosevelt signed Executive Order 9066, which allowed the War Department to remove suspicious or possibly dangerous persons from military areas. Even then, hope remained among many Japanese-Americans; for, while Executive Order 9066 authorized the removal by the military of a generically defined individual or type if it became necessary, it did not call specifically for the removal of Japanese-Americans from the Pacific Coast. In the fields of California, Japanese-American farmers continued to plant crops that they hoped to harvest in the spring.

Takeo Yuchi, the most prominent Japanese-American farmer in the Salinas Valley, for example, had already sold his spring crop of onions, an estimated seventy thousand bags, to the Navy. Yuchi had orders in hand for 2,700 carloads of lettuce (one-tenth of the lettuce grown in the Salinas Valley) and three hundred acres of sugar beets for the nearby Spreckels refinery. Well known locally since his days as a sprinter at Salinas High School, Yuchi had a white partner by the name of Tom Bun and was known among farm workers as a fair employer. His brother-in-law Hideo Abe was already in the Army, and his younger brother Masao had been called up by the local draft board for his physical—after Pearl Harbor. Another Salinan, Joe Yamamota, the brother-in-law of Dr. Harry Kita, Salinas's leading *Nisei* dentist, was also serving in the Army. Dr. Kita's wife Fumiko and her brother Joe had been born and raised in nearby Watsonville.

As February 1942 edged into March, the entire Japanese-American community of Salinas—the Yuchis, the Kitas, the Yoshitos (rancher Kenzo Yoshito held a dual degree from the University of California in commerce and agriculture), the Tandas (Henry Tanda was a Stanford man, which is where he met his wife Margaret Ushida), the Endos (druggist Richard Endo had taken his pharmacy degree from the University of California in San Francisco), the Yurabes (John Yurabe held his degree in engineering but had turned to an automobile dealership and real estate subdivision)—and all the other Japanese-Americans in the Salinas Valley and up and down the state waited for the other shoe to fall.

The official history of the evacuation, written by Stetson Conn and issued by the Center of Military History of the United States Army in 1990, portrays an initially skeptical DeWitt being edged closer and closer toward the decision to launch a full-scale evacuation and relocation after consultation with political leaders or, as the general described them, the Best People. Governor Culbert Olson, Attorney General Earl Warren, Mayor Angelo Rossi of San Francisco, Mayor Fletcher Bowron of Los Angeles, Senators Hiram Johnson and Sheridan Downey, the entire California membership of the House of Representatives, the publishers and editors of the state's leading newspapers: each of these Best People underscored the threat allegedly posed by possible fifth columnists among Japanese residents of California; and on the national level their opinions were seconded by such formidable personages as Secretary of War Henry Stimson, the well-known and respected columnists Walter Lippmann and Westbrook Pegler, even the ever-compassionate Mayor Fiorello La Guardia of New York. DeWitt, meanwhile, a commissioned officer since he was eighteen, had witnessed the disgrace after Pearl Harbor of his fellow flag officers Admiral Thomas Kimmel and Lieutenant General Walter Short and was hence in no mood to have the same thing happen to him should he screw up while at the helm of the Western Defense Command.

On 25, 26, and 27 February 1942 the Los Angeles *Times* ran prominent articles calling for the removal of the Japanese. From 21 February to 2 March, the House Committee on Defense Migration, chaired by Congressman John Tolan of Alameda County, held hearings on the question of the removal of the Japanese from the Pacific Coast. Since Tolan was a well-known liberal, whose committee had recently played a major role in documenting the plight of migrant workers in California, both the Japanese-American community and such sympathizers as Carey McWilliams initially welcomed his committee to California, believing that it would take testimony that would counter the pro-evacuation argument. The exact opposite occurred. In both San Francisco and Los Angeles, the preponderance of testimony was in favor of evacuation. Testifying on the opening day of the hearings in San Francisco, Attorney General Earl Warren, the chief law enforcement officer of California, who planned to run for governor the following year, made the strongest argument for the evacuation of all Japanese, including American citizens. Coming as it did from the chief prosecutor of the state, Warren's testimony both expressed and intensified pro-evacuation sentiment.

Ironically, even as Warren testified in Civic Center, in the nearby Presidio of San Francisco, the Army was assembling a top-secret *Kisei* (*Nisei* who had been educated in Japan) intelligence unit to be used as radio interceptors and psychological warfare personnel in the Pacific. A number of other *Nisei* and *Kisei*, moreover, were already serving in the Army. Inexplicably, for whatever reasons, these men escaped segregation and were allowed to fight through the war in all-white units. Paul Sakai, for example, fought as an enlisted man in North Africa, was later commissioned, and made the Army his career. Sergeant Ben Kuroki, a Nebraska farm boy, flew thirty missions as a gunner on a Liberator bomber in North Africa and Europe, including the raid on the Ploesti oil fields in Rumania. Having flown five more missions than was necessary in Europe, Sergeant Kuroki flew another twenty-eight combat missions in B-29 bombers in the Pacific. Early in 1944 Kuroki, now holding the Distinguished Flying Cross with two Oak Leaf Clusters and the Air Medal with five clusters, was invited to address the Commonwealth Club in San Francisco, where he received a standing ovation.

Even as the Tolan Committee was holding its hearings, Japanese submarine I-17 shelled Santa Barbara on the evening of 23 February, and Los Angeles experienced its imagined air raid in the early hours of the 25th. Needless to say, testimony before the Tolan Committee in Los Angeles following these two incidents grew still more anxiety-ridden, even hysterical. The very fact that the Los Angeles Japanese-language newspaper *Rafu Shimpo* was continually expressing the loyalty of the Japanese community in Los Angeles to the United States, testified Mayor Fletcher Bowron, was proof positive that sabotage was in the offing. By this time, evacuation and relocation had become an inevitability. Even before the Tolan hearings were concluded, General DeWitt had made up his mind. Since January, in fact, a member of DeWitt's staff, Major Karl Bendetsen, chief of the Aliens Division of the Office of the Provost Marshal, had been preparing plans for the evacuation of the Japanese from the Pacific Coast.

By early February Bendetsen, promoted to lieutenant colonel, was representing DeWitt in Washington in the discussions that led to the proclamation of Executive Order 9066 on 19 February. On 1 March 1942 DeWitt issued Proclamation Number One designating the western half of California, Oregon, and Washington and the southern third of Arizona as military zones from which all Japanese were to be removed. On 11 March, one day before the Tolan hearings concluded, DeWitt established the Wartime Civil Control Administration, headquartered in the Whitcomb Hotel on Market Street with Lieutenant Colonel Bendetsen as director. DeWitt ordered Bendetsen to carry out the evacuation program being planned since January. On 18 March, on the advice of the Tolan Committee, Roosevelt issued Executive Order 9102 creating a civilian War Relocation Authority, headed by Milton Eisenhower, brother of the general, to establish and administer the relocation camps. With both the military and civilian components of the program in place, Lieutenant Colonel Bendetsen got to work. Four months later some 110,000 Japanese-Americans were behind barbed wire, and Karl Bendetsen was on the verge of becoming one of the youngest full colonels in the American Army.

It would take a half century and hundreds of books, together with thousands of pages of congressional debate and newspaper commentary, to chronicle and probe the meaning of this mass evacuation, which had transpired in four months with hardly a hitch and with barely a murmur of dissent from those being evacuated. Quietly, stoically, the Japanese-Americans accepted their fate. Was it because California had already betrayed them—had already devalued the worth of their citizenship through fifty years of suspicion and hostility? Yes and no. Some whites, after all, did protest the evacuation—the Quakers, a few courageous union leaders, a handful of rabbis, the odd clubwoman angered at the loss of a gardener or maid—but they were a minority: not enough to stifle, much less heal, the hurt.

Nearly sixty years later, a further irony emerges from any examination of documents and photographs of life in the internment camps—or concentration camps, as a more militant later generation of Japanese-American activists insisted on calling them. Everybody and everything seem so American. The baseball games and Saturday night movies seem so American, as do the jazz and dance bands. The Boy Scout troops seem so American, as do the bobby soxer attire of the teenagers and the upturned, smiling faces of the kids in the classrooms. The elected camp councils seem so American. (Only American citizens, in fact, were allowed to run for and hold office.) While Buddhism remained a somewhat exotic religion in the United States, Christian internees attended church on Sunday, just as they would in their home towns. All these people and things seem so American because they were American. If sixty years later the fundamental American-ness of these interned Japanese-Americans leaps from the printed page and from photographs as a massive, tragic irony, it must have been evident as well in the 1942–46 era, despite the racism and hysteria of the period, the stereotypes of wartime anti-Japanese propaganda, and the hostility Americans were feeling toward Japan.

And certainly, above all else, the Japanese-American men and women who served in the Army and the Women's Army Corps seem so very American: American in their uniforms, their farewells and departures, their deaths or maimings in combat. Nine (nine!) children of Mr. and Mrs. Ginzo Nakada, evacuated from their home in Long Beach, served in the military. Five of Mrs. Haruye Masaoka's six sons saw combat with the famed all-Japanese-American 442nd Regimental Combat Team in France and Italy. One died. Another suffered 100 percent disability. Altogether, the two largest Japanese-American units, the 100th Infantry Battalion and the 442nd Regimental Combat Team, suffered 9,486 casualties in the course of seven major campaigns, including 650 killed in action, and were awarded one Congressional Medal of Honor, 560 Silver Stars, 9,486 Purple Hearts, and seven Presidential Distinguished Unit Citations. If they had been one unit, it would be the most decorated unit for its size and length of service in the entire history of the United States.

Commentators and historians of the relocation have amply described the losses in homes, property, farms, and businesses experienced by Japanese-Americans in 1942. Less difficult to ascertain is the deep sense of shame and hurt that afflicted nearly everyone, except perhaps the very young, as men and women left behind their homes and piled onto buses or onto trains, their fellow Americans — in uniform with fixed bayonets — providing an armed escort. Here they were, Americans, uprooted, tagged for shipment, facing the loss of three, nearly four years, the best years, in many cases, of their lives, their hurt and shame kept contained behind the stoic reserve that was so characteristic of them as a people: the same self-control with which they had absorbed the fifty-plus years of rejection that had led to this moment. They had struggled for an American identity for so long against such great odds, only to have it now so brutally swept away, their citizenship reduced, in General DeWitt's terms, to "a scrap of paper" that could not dispel the fact that, as he put it, "a Jap's a Jap. They are a dangerous element, whether loyal or not."[11]

The relocation began in hurt and shame, and it got worse. In her classic account of the incarceration, *Farewell to Manzanar* (1973), Jeanne Wakatsuki Houston recalls the shame that gripped her father, an *Issei*, in the camp: a shame that only stupefying draughts of home-brewed rice wine or apricot brandy could still. In one drunken rage Papa threatened to strike his wife — and then Jeanne's teenaged brother Kiyo sprang across the room and punched Papa in the face. "No one had ever seen such a thing before," Jeanne Wakatsuki later remembered. "Papa's arms went limp. The cane fell clattering to the floor. He reached up and touched his nose. Blood was pouring onto his shirt, dripping down onto Mama's dress. Kiyo stepped back, crouching, staring at the blood. This was like bloodying the nose of God."[12]

4

1943 ✶ *Zoot Suit*

B Y 1943 the United States was at war with itself as well as with the Axis powers. The mobilization of American society for war was bringing into close contact disparate groups of Americans who feared, distrusted, even hated each other. Nowhere was this more true than in California. The war itself, after all, was for much of white California a racially motivated conflict with Japan: a conflict already a half century in duration before it broke into actual hostility. By the end of 1942 California had imprisoned most persons of Japanese ancestry and was serving as the central training and staging zone for the fierce war—a fierce racial war—against Japan in the Pacific. In the final phases of that war alone, more than seventy-five thousand Americans and an estimated one million Japanese would lose their lives in terrible, no-holds-barred, hand-to-hand island battles lasting until the bitter end. The invasion of Okinawa in April 1945, for example, cost the Japanese 103,000 dead out of a 120,000-man garrison. Thirteen thousand Americans died, and another thirty-five thousand were wounded in the three-month struggle. American B-29s, meanwhile, were flying massive formations over Tokyo, destroying 46 percent of the city, with an estimated ninety thousand civilians killed.

As plans for the invasion of Japan solidified, the prospect of genocidal warfare between Japan and the United States became a vivid possibility. It was estimated that it would cost one million American casualties to invade Japan, including hundreds of thousands of dead. Already, an estimated 1,219,000 Japanese, military and civilian, had lost their lives. Toward the conclusion of the war, the United States War Department was listing more than a million casualties in all theaters: 600,000 wounded, 60,000 missing in action, 75,000 prisoners of war, 250,000 killed in either battle or training accidents. While the full extent of casualties on both sides remained unknown in 1943, Americans were recognizing by that year that they were in for a long and very dangerous war in which one major enemy was perceived in racially hostile terms. So much hostility could not help but destabilize the home front. Whipping themselves into a racially focused frenzy against the Japanese, Americans could not help but intensify and destabilize racial antagonisms in their own society. In 1943 such tensions erupted into riot.

It began in Los Angeles. By 1943 there were three million people of Mexican descent living in the United States, most of them in the Southwest or in Southern California, with some two hundred thousand in Los Angeles County. The Mexican-American *colonia* was divided into a number of *barrios*: Dogtown, Alpine, the Flats, Happy Valley in East Los Angeles, and other unincorporated areas of Los Angeles County. Only five thousand Mexican-Americans had found jobs in the war industries of greater Los Angeles by early 1943, the Congress of Industrial Organizations reported. So what else was new? For most of the twentieth century, the Mexicans of greater Los Angeles, Mexican nationals and Mexican-American citizens alike, had been living on the margins of white Los Angeles, the forgotten founders of the city.

While white California, Southern California especially, was willing to sentimentalize Old California, as in the Ramona myth, neither they nor the Mexican population of the Southland (with the exception of a few surviving Old California families) saw any continuity between the Spanish and Mexican founders of California and the present population of the state. Even the Roman Catholic Church, to which most Mexicans adhered, had become an English-speaking entity, hence psychologically part of the Anglo-California that existed on the other side of a great cultural and ethnic divide. Had Southern California been heavily industrialized, which it was not, Mexican immigrants might have been forced to accommodate themselves to—and be accommodated by!—the dominant Anglo culture. But Southern California lacked an integrative industrial system and so remained an assemblage of ethnic enclaves, each of them self-contained, each of them excluding and being excluded up and down the social scale. The Mexicans of Los Angeles, along with blacks and Asians, were restricted to certain districts by custom and real estate covenants; were assigned to a separate second-tier, even third-tier, school system ("Why teach them to read and write and spell?" the principal of a Mexican school in the San Fernando Valley asked social worker Beatrice Griffith. "Why worry about it? . . . They'll only pick beets anyway"); were excluded from public swimming pools on all but one day a week (the day before the pool was to be drained); were turned away at the door of numerous theaters and dance halls and saw the sign SE SIRVE SOLAMENTE A RAZA BLANCA (White Race Only Served) in numerous restaurants. Seeing a primarily Mexican group of passengers gathered on a corner, Los Angeles streetcar drivers would frequently pass by rather than stop.[1]

Los Angeles, in short, was a Jim Crow town in which numerous nobodies—failures, drifters, downwardly mobile Folks, those expelled from their previous communities—had one thing and only one thing going for them, either consciously or subconsciously: they were white. As racial hatred against the Japanese surfaced into respectability—indeed, became a vehement proof of patriotism—such Los Angelenos began to identify their whiteness with America itself and with the war effort.

With the Japanese removed into camps, Mexicans provided the next obvious target for racial hatred. Like the California war against the Japanese, foreign and domestic, the California war against Mexicans, foreign and domestic, was rooted in racial antipathies as old as California itself. A white people was looking down upon a brown people of Indian ancestry. A Protestant people was looking down upon what it considered religious superstition. An industrialized people was looking down upon peasants. Among the many charges leveled by whites against Mexicans was their alleged proclivity for violence. Captain Edward Duran Ayres, chief of the Foreign Relations Bureau in the office of the sheriff of Los Angeles County, spoke for many white Southern Californians in a 1942 report to the county's grand jury. As Indians, Captain Ayres reported, Mexicans were descended from "Oriental" ancestors and hence had the "Mongolian" tendency to violence. The human sacrifices of the ancient Aztecs testified to that. To this day, Ayres argued, Mexicans had a tendency to resort to knives or lethal weapons when in a fight, as opposed to Anglo-Saxon youths, who were content to use their fists. Chillingly, a Los Angeles police official was surfacing publicly with the notion that all Mexicans were of racially debased stock and were possessed of a biological orientation toward criminal behavior. They were, in fact, to be linked in ancestry to the Japanese and were, like the Japanese, to be considered an enemy, both foreign and domestic.

Once again, the racism of California caused international embarrassment. Mexico, after all, was an ally with the United States against the Axis: the very same Mexico Captain Ayres, in a report covered widely in the press, described as the homeland of a biologically tainted people. Once again, as in the case of anti-Japanese agitation during World War I, the State Department shuddered at the insult California was offering an ally. Axis radio and the pro-Axis Unión Nacional Sinarquista party in Mexico cited the Ayres report as proof positive that Mexico was on the wrong side of the conflict. American liberals, meanwhile, drew obvious comparisons to the anti-Semitism of the Nazis.

A significant percentage of the officers of the Los Angeles police and sheriff's departments, by contrast, agreed. For years, in fact, the LAPD and the sheriff's department had been making war on young men of Mexican descent in the continuing belief that such young men were by definition criminal in fact and intent. The sheer presence of young Mexicans on street corners in the *barrio*—the localized result of a time-honored preference for street life tracing itself to the social customs of Mexican villages—was seen by patrolling police or sheriff's deputies as *de facto* proof of a crime in process or about to happen. Again and again, young Mexican men found themselves hauled into jail for seventy-two hours on mere suspicion, then released. Beatings were frequent, as were frame-ups of young Mexican men who talked back or otherwise resisted arrest. An impressive number of young Mexican men were shot dead in the street by trigger-happy officers. No white police or sheriff's deputies in the Deep South of the period kept the local black population under a more intense level of intimidation through violence.

Central to this perception of the young Mexican-American as violent gang member were the figures of the *pachuco* and *pachuca* and the zoot suiter. Not every *pachuco* was a zoot suiter (*pachucas* had their own stylized attire), and not every zoot suiter was a *pachuco*. Evolving in the *barrios* of Los Angeles, *pachuquismo* represented a more fundamental condition than the mere wearing of a zoot suit. The *pachuco* was a young male Mexican-American caught between two worlds and belonging to neither. Like later analogues—the hipster, the beat, the hippie—the *pachuco* was in a condition of generalized revolt born of alienation. Cut off from both the village life of Mexico, which had nurtured his parents or grand-parents, and the glittery life of contemporary Los Angeles, from which he was banned, the *pachuco* retreated into a stance of defiant isolation broken only by loyalties to other *pachucos* in associations invariably seen by the police as criminal gangs. Interestingly enough, given the deracination of the *pachuco* in American society, the *pachuco* was reaching back into Spanish tradition in the creation of his argot: an idiosyncratic blend of Calo (the perennial language of the underground and underworld, having its origins in medieval Spain), gypsy, Ladino (Iberian-Hebrew), Mexican tough-guy talk, jive, Anglicized Spanish, and Hispanicized English, together with numerous linguistic terms of strictly Los Angeles coinage. *Pachuquismo* also brought to Los Angeles its own ballad tradition, the ballads being mainly about the Los Angeles Police Department beating *pachuco* heads. *Pachucos* were given to tattoos—crosses mainly, surmounted by initials—which the Los Angeles press invested with near-cabalistic significance.

Pachuquismo represented a defiant response on the part of many young men who belonged to neither Mexico nor the United States. Having been excluded from the center, the *pachuco* embraced his marginality and made of it a defiant style. In certain cases (not every case!) *pachuquismo* could lead to petty crime; but it was no more intrinsically criminal than the hip, beat, or hippie identities among blacks and whites in years to come. From the perspective of Mexicans in Mexico, the *pachuco* was a highly gringoized figure, his style and speech redolent of the streets of Los Angeles alone, not the villages, towns, and cities of the homeland. From the perspective of white Los Angeles, the *pachuco* was its worst nightmare come true: the avenging Mexican—dark, fierce-eyed, Indian, bent on violence and revenge.

The *pachuca* expressed more style than revolt. She was, in fact, little more than a Mexican-American version of the Anglo-American V-girls who had emerged by 1943 as a social type in the American city. Like the V-girl, the *pachuca* featured a stylized version of popular dress: saddle shoes, bobby socks, skirts at or above the knee, sheer blouses, cardigan sweaters, heavy lipstick drawn square above the lip, black hair shaped into astonishingly high pompadours. The *pachuca*, in short, was little more than the American female teenager, Mexican-American style, experiencing the tensions, excitements, and social dislocations of wartime.

By 1943 the white female teenagers whom the press dubbed V-girls constituted a major sector of middle-class America in revolt. While delinquent behavior was not typical of all Anglo teenagers who adopted the V-girl style, numerous V-girls hung around bus terminals and train stations, picked up servicemen, and engaged in promiscuous sexual activity, contributing to an alarming VD rate. If the truth be told, *pachuca* teenagers were noticeably less delinquent than many of their V-girl counterparts in Anglo culture. The Los Angeles press, however, did its best to degrade the *pachuca* just as it was demonizing the *pachuco*. The report went out that *pachucas* frequently concealed knives in their pompadours. Even defenders of Mexican-American youth repeated this ridiculous assertion. The arrest rate for young Mexican-American women in Los Angeles in the early 1940s was practically non-existent. No police report has ever surfaced describing *pachucas* with knives in their pompadours or connecting them in any way with criminal activity.

More tellingly, the Los Angeles press, especially the two Hearst papers, suggested that *pachuca* girls were little more than the sexual servants of the gangs with which they were affiliated. This too was a canard, and bitterly resented by the young Mexican-American women, who were, if anything, held by Mexican custom and the Catholic religion to high standards of sexual conduct. In one instance, a group of *pachuca* girls, incensed by press reports that they provided sexual aid and comfort to *pachuco* boys, demanded in a letter circulated to all Los Angeles newspapers that they be examined *en masse* by competent medical authorities so as to establish their virginity. No randomly selected group of V-girls from the Anglo world could make such a claim or pass such a test, and, in any event, no Los Angeles newspaper ran the letter. The attack against *pachuca* chastity repeated a long-established slur against Mexican women, whom the Anglo world held unchaste because of their dark complexions. (A similar suggestion was attached to Jewish women in nineteenth-century American fiction.) The white world considered promiscuity in *pachucas* in tandem with violence in *pachucos*: just another biological trait. The white world was also obviously compensating for its own teenaged girls running amuck.

On the other hand, it must be admitted that *pachucas* emanated an explosive sexuality. "A bravado and swagger accentuated the dark beauty of these girls," Beatrice Griffith writes in *American Me* (1948), the classic account of Mexican-American Los Angeles. "They had an impudence attractive to all males, light or dark. Many of these *Pachuquitas* were 'little tornadoes' of sexual stimuli, swishing and flouncing down the streets."[2] Among the admirers of the *pachucas* — with their sheer blouses, trim figures, dangling earrings, and pouty lipsticked mouths — were the fifty thousand or so young servicemen on leave in Los Angeles on any given weekend in 1943; and therein arose a tension that would eventually erupt into riot.

In his 1942 report to the grand jury, Captain Ayres had warned against Mexican gangs. He had recommended, in fact, that young Mexican-American men over the age of sixteen who were not in the armed forces should be swept up from the streets preemptively and sent to labor camps. The fact is, the United States in general experienced a surge of juvenile delinquency in 1943, the direct result of wartime conditions: absent fathers, working mothers, the general frenzy into which society was whipping itself. Statistics of juvenile delinquency for young Mexican-Americans in Los Angeles, however, were below the national average. Yet police departments and the press harped continually about the developing problem of Mexican-American youth-gang violence in Los Angeles, city and county. Defenders of the Mexican-American community countered with the charge that the term *gang* was being applied by the police and the press to any grouping of Mexican-American youth. Fifty years later, social historian and critic Mike Davis would be making the same objection, claiming that reports of gang activity in the Mexican-American community were deliberately exaggerated by police and press out of a persistent proclivity to see all Mexicans as violent and conspiratorial.

Ayres's pseudo-anthropological report to the grand jury was intended, among other things, to justify the most egregious persecution of Mexican-Americans in the history of American criminal courts—the mass arrest, trial, and conviction of the Sleepy Lagoon defendants. On the night of 1 August 1942 a group of young Mexican men drove out to an abandoned gravel pit and swimming hole on the Williams Ranch in East Los Angeles. For some time the site had offered swimming and a nighttime hangout for young Mexicans. Earlier that evening, one of the group, Henry Leyvas, and his girlfriend had been harassed by another group of Mexican-American young men. Leyvas was now returning with his friends from 38th Street to reconfront the troublemakers, if they could be found. Finding the gravel pit deserted, the 38th Street group crashed a party at a nearby house, rented by the Delgadillo family. Some scuffling broke out; the 38th Street group left the party. Sometime later one of the young men from the Delgadillo party, Jose Diaz, left the house with two of his friends. Early on the morning of 2 August, Diaz was found unconscious on a dirt road near the Delgadillo house and was taken to Los Angeles General Hospital, where he died without regaining consciousness.

The police and the press had their story. Its elements—an alleged clash of Mexican gangs, the death of Jose Diaz, the gravel site and swimming hole, which an enterprising reporter dubbed the Sleepy Lagoon after a popular song of the same name, giving the place a suggestion of nighttime sexual activity—spoke perfectly to the Anglo perception of Mexican Los Angeles as sexually volatile and given to gang violence. Astonishingly, twenty-four members of the alleged 38th Street gang were arrested, brought before the grand jury, and indicted for murder. From the point of view of police procedure and probable cause, the Sleepy Lagoon indictments were a scandal. For one thing, it was not even certain how Jose Diaz had died. An autopsy revealed a high level of blood alcohol, together with bruises and contusions on his hands and face. It is possible that Diaz, wandering drunk on an unlit back road, was hit by an automobile. He might have gotten into an altercation after he had left the Delgadillo house—and then been hit by an automobile. In any event, the two young men who had left the Delgadillo house with Diaz were never called before the grand jury to give their version of what had happened that evening.

Rather, the police and the district attorney presented a preposterous case. Because Diaz showed bruises and contusions, he was said to have been beaten to death. Because the 38th Street group had gone to both the Sleepy Lagoon and the Delgadillo party with the intent to fight, they were responsible for Diaz's death, in that Diaz had undoubtedly fallen afoul of gang violence. In terms of evidence, neither the Los Angeles Police Department nor the district attorney had a case, but the grand jury returned indictments on charges of first degree murder against nineteen alleged members of the alleged 38th Street gang. Prior to the grand jury sessions, a number of the young men were beaten by the police, in one instance just before offering testimony. Two had the presence of mind to demand separate trials (this was granted, and the charges were later dropped), but the other seventeen stood trial together in the largest mass trial for murder in American jurisprudence. Lasting several months and filling six thousand pages of transcript, the Sleepy Lagoon trial was a farce. Superior Court Judge Charles W. Fricke, already notorious for his vindictiveness against Mexican defendants (Fricke had recently sentenced two Mexican men to 250 years each on charges of rape in a very shaky case in which he had influenced the jury), refused to allow the young men to groom themselves and dress properly for court. Day in, day out, they sat together in their soiled clothes, their dark faces and unkempt appearance proof positive, as Judge Fricke intended, of their guilt.

Far from being gang members or criminals, the seventeen Sleepy Lagoon defendants were in reality aspiring, hard-working young men, employed as furniture-makers, ranch hands, and, one of them, a defense worker. Two were married and the fathers of children. Two had already joined the Navy and were awaiting induction. One of them, Victor Rodman Thompson, aged twenty-one, was not even Mexican but an Anglo youth who had become Mexicanized while growing up in the *barrio*. After an outrageously biased trial, the Sleepy Lagoon defendants were convicted on 13 January 1943: three for first degree, nine for second degree murder. These twelve were sent to San Quentin. Convicted of simple assault, five were released for time served. Five were acquitted. It took nearly two years before the Second District Court of Appeal reversed the convictions and ordered the defendants freed. In its decision, the Court of Appeal chastised Judge Fricke for his conduct of the trial. Yet the damage to seventeen young men had been done. Anglo Los Angeles, a good portion of it at least, had sent them an unambiguous message: with the Japanese-Americans gone, Mexican-Americans were now the enemy within.

University of Southern California historian Mauricio Mazón, who is also a practicing psychoanalyst, links the Sleepy Lagoon affair to the imagined attack on Los Angeles by Japanese aircraft on 25 February 1942. Los Angeles imagined the attack, Mazón argues, in a collective hysteria that approached a dream state. It now turned to the Mexican-American community with the same hysterical response. Only a community in a form of trance, Mazón argues, could have sustained such mass indictments on such non-existent evidence and the phantasmagoric trial that followed. Wartime Los Angeles, in short, was approaching a condition of delusional paranoia.

Paradoxically, Mazón's thesis applies equally to the Sleepy Lagoon Defense Committee. Its paranoia, however, had another focus: the Los Angeles oligarchy, police, and press in general and in particular William Randolph Hearst, whom the committee accused of working, almost consciously, on behalf of the Axis. Chaired by state housing and immigration commissioner Carey McWilliams, a brilliant voice and prolific pen on the left (and the single finest non-fiction writer on California—ever), the Sleepy Lagoon Defense Committee, headquartered at 129 West 2nd Street in Los Angeles, brought together Communists, the far Left, liberals, and the merely outraged (such as Orson Welles) into a strong anti-fascist front. The Sleepy Lagoon trial, Hollywood screenwriter and novelist Guy Endore wrote in a pamphlet issued during the appeal process, fed so powerfully into Axis propaganda, especially the pro-Axis Unión Nacional Sinarquista, that one was tempted to ask whether pro-fascist subversive elements had helped bring the defendants to trial in the first place in an effort to embarrass the United States and to drive a wedge between it and its ally Mexico.

Since the Hearst newspapers had been the most viciously anti-Mexican and the most sensational during the Sleepy Lagoon trial, Endore stopped short—barely short!—of calling William Randolph Hearst a Nazi sympathizer. Endore traced the anti-Mexican campaign and the subsequent Sleepy Lagoon prosecution to a memo from a top Hearst staffer originating in the Hearst castle at San Simeon and suggesting that Hearst editors launch an onslaught against the Mexican-American community. Endore's conspiracy theories indicate just how psychopathic, how dislocated and paranoid, Los Angeles had become. Certainly, Endore had a point regarding the Sinarquistas, who played up each and every detail of the Sleepy Lagoon trial and other instances of anti-Mexican behavior in Los Angeles. Endore also had another interesting point: the pipeline that Axis radio seemed to have into the Los Angeles community. At the time of the Sleepy Lagoon trial, for example, the Los Angeles police beat up a young Mexican-American, the president of the Boys Athletic Club at Clelland House, merely because he was standing on the street talking to friends in a car. In one sense, this was your average everyday beating by L.A. cops of Mexican-American young men, no big deal; yet Axis radio had the story almost immediately and played it for all that it was worth as just one more element of proof that Mexico was on the wrong side of the war, that people of color had no stake in fighting for the United States. Obviously, Endore believed, somebody was deliberately fomenting these incidents so as to feed into the propaganda mill of the Axis and the Unión Nacional Sinarquista, which had a colony in Baja California and some four hundred members throughout Southern California.

In many instances, the Sinarquistas had incidents aplenty to justify their anti-Yankee propaganda. On 10 August 1942, for example, a dragnet organized by the LAPD, the sheriff's office, and the California Highway Patrol swept through Los Angeles County and arrested more than six hundred young Mexican-American men on a variety of trumped-up charges. Now that the Japanese had been interned, the Sinarquistas claimed, Los Angeles County was preparing a similar fate for its Mexican-American community. The infamous sweep—hundreds of uniformed officers moving through *barrio* after *barrio* in well-rehearsed movements, sirens wailing, patrol cars flashing their lights along unimproved back roads, the cries of Mexican-American mothers whose sons were being torn from them, the spectacle of hundreds and hundreds of young Mexican-American men being marched into jails—easily confirmed the Sinarquista charges.

Thus tension built in Los Angeles on multiple levels into mid-1943 as the oligarchy, the police, the district attorney, the courts, and the Hearst newspapers continued to depict the Mexican-American young male as a subversive and criminal element. The Left, for its part, as represented by the Sleepy Lagoon Defense Committee and other organizations, sensed a *de facto* pro-Axis conspiracy in this persecution of Mexicans. The Hearst newspapers continued their attack, meanwhile, and the cops and sheriff's deputies of Los Angeles continued to make arrests and beat heads.

By now, mid-1943, many Mexican-American young men, *pachucos* and non-*pachucos* alike, were wearing the zoot suit. Even more than *pachuquismo*, which it overlapped, the wearing of the zoot suit held multiple layers of identity, pro and con, for Mexican-Americans and their enemies. Whereas *pachuquismo* had one important level of meaning, the defiant alienation of young men caught in a cultural and psychological borderland, the zoot suit had many possible interpretations; for it was not confined exclusively to the Mexican-American community, and it eventually made its way, with modifications, into mainstream fashion. The zoot suit consisted of a long frock jacket, with wide lapels and pronounced shoulder pads, and pleated trousers, high-waisted and pegged at the cuff. Triple-soled shoes, an overlong watch or key chain, and a wide-brimmed hat completed the outfit. Zoot suiters did or did not wear ties. In any event, shirt collars were oversized. A heavily pomaded ducktail haircut, with waves swept to a meeting point at the back of the head, was also *de rigueur*.

Never has one fashion meant so many things to so many different people, at either the gut or most rarified levels. Most basically, the zoot suit had arisen out of the jitterbug cult. The suit itself had evolved so as to make the athletic movements of jitterbug dancing easier. From this perspective, the zoot suit was an icon of youth perceived as a sub-group or cult, organized around jitterbugging. Only young people, after all, could perform the jitterbug properly, just as only young people could truly Charleston in the 1920s. Worn by a young Mexican-American in Los Angeles, the zoot suit declared style, independence, and a level of personal control that foreshadowed the coolness of the hipster, the detachment of the beat, the drug-assisted transcendence of the hippie. Rejected by an alien environment, the Mexican-American in his zoot suit (his drapes, as he called his attire) reasserted his individualism, paradoxically, through a uniform. Kept on the other side of the good life, the young Mexican-American defied the narrowness of his circumstances by spending up to a hundred dollars on his outfit. For Octavio Paz, a Mexican diplomat and poet assigned to Los Angeles in the early 1940s, both the *pachuco* and the zoot suit phenomena represented a form of disguise on the part of young people who were psychologically in flight from a world that baffled them. From this perspective, the zoot suit served as an existentialist icon: a way of stabilizing an uncertain identity via one of the most extreme male fashions to emerge in the First World in the twentieth century. (Before, of course, the advent of punk and grunge in a later era.) Others, such as Mauricio Mazón, see the semi-fetishistic zoot suit in terms of the delayed maturity theories of Harvard psychologist Erik Erikson as developed in *Childhood and Society* (1950) and *Young Man Luther* (1958): as a way, that is, of prolonging late adolescence through stylized stasis and delaying adult identity. Mazón's perspective dovetails with another interpretation: the Last Fling syndrome, in which the zoot suit is interpreted as a conspicuous garment worn by a young man in generalized defiance before going into the military.

The cops, deputies, prosecutors, and press of Los Angeles County, by contrast, considered the zoot suit yet one more proof of hooliganism and the gang cult. Worn by Mexican-Americans, the zoot suit drove police officers into a frenzy, which was most likely intended, consciously or subconsciously, by the young men featuring the attire. The fact is: some of the criminal element—street corner toughs, small-time numbers runners, the misdemeanor crowd—did wear zoot suits; but it would be ridiculous to believe, as Los Angeles newspapers and law enforcement were claiming, that big-time criminals would attire themselves in such a conspicuous getup.

For the young sailors, soldiers, and Marines stationed in and around Los Angeles in 1943 or coming into the city on weekend leave, the zoot suit had a similarly provocative effect. Here these young men were, in uniform, regimented, their heads shaved, deprived of prior identities; and there were the zoot suiters, glorious in their plumage, out of the military, free to stand on street corners and flirt with Mexican-American girls in sheer blouses and high pompadours. Competition for females, in fact, must be seen as a major cause of tension. Just three weeks prior to the outbreak of the Zoot Suit Riots on 3 June 1943, two sailors made moves on two Mexican-American girls at a dance in the seaside Venice district of Los Angeles and provoked a full-scale brawl between young sailors and young Mexican-American men, some of them in zoot suits.

It was a volatile time in general. Hundreds of thousands of young men were being trained in Southern California by the Army, the Army Air Force, the Navy, and the Marines. They were being brought to a fever pitch of fitness and aggression. Within Los Angeles County, the Navy alone maintained large installations on Terminal Island, at Long Beach in San Pedro, and at Chavez Ravine just north of Chinatown in the city. On any given weekend in 1943, up to fifty thousand servicemen would come into Los Angeles on pass.

Stripped of their individuality, these young servicemen were also scared. The war for which they were being prepared, after all, held forth a high possibility, almost a probability, of death or serious injury. Tensions were growing among the servicemen themselves and between servicemen and civilians. A new figure, the draft dodger, had made his appearance. In May 1943 the FBI arrested 638 alleged draft dodgers in a nationwide sweep. The nation, in other words, was emphasizing the mandatory nature of military service to its young men in mass arrests that could not help but put young men not in uniform at a disadvantage. Were they not draft dodgers as well, the question might be asked — indeed, was frequently being asked in military-civilian encounters that were growing increasingly serious.

It had become, in any event, a tense time in the garrison state. In the two weeks prior to the Zoot Suit Riots, there were eighteen serious incidents involving servicemen in Southern California. Seven of these resulted in fatalities. A soldier killed a sailor. A sailor killed a civilian. A civilian killed a sailor. A civilian knifed a soldier to death. A civilian killed a soldier. A hit-and-run driver killed a Marine. Two sailors killed a taxi driver. At the same time, a number of taunting and jeering sessions, together with a few minor fights, were reported between servicemen and zoot suiters. While the eighteen incidents involving servicemen and other servicemen or servicemen and civilians had resulted in seven deaths, the punch-ups and scuffles between zoot suiters and servicemen had resulted in no fatalities and only a few minor injuries. Already, a pattern of symbolic clash between the two groups, zoot suiters and servicemen, was being established. The Zoot Suit Riots would soon prove themselves as stylized as the zoot suit itself.

Early on Thursday evening, 3 June 1943, a group of eleven sailors and a number of Mexican-American young men got into a fight on the 1700 block of North Main Street in a predominantly Mexican-American section of the city. One sailor was hurt in the scuffle. The rest suffered minor cuts and bruises. Another group of young Mexican-Americans, meanwhile — the Alpine Club, named in honor of their *barrio* district — was holding a meeting at (of all places) a local police station, where they were planning social and athletic activities. As the meeting was in progress, a young Mexican-American sailor stopped by and informed the members of the Alpine Club that some two hundred sailors were coming over to Alpine, the *barrio* district, looking to avenge the defeat of the Navy in the initial scuffle. The police drove the members of the Alpine Club home in squad cars. When the police left, members of a rival club — not Mexican-Americans and not sailors in uniform — got into a scuffle with the Alpines.

Thus far there had been one documented clash between sailors and Mexican-Americans, one false report of two hundred sailors returning to Alpine in vengeance, and one gang or club clash involving only civilians. It took the Los Angeles

Police Department and the Los Angeles press to whip this incident into a full-scale riot. Late on the night of the 3rd, a group of off-duty police officers, under the command of a detective lieutenant, organized a self-described Vengeance Squad to go into Alpine and arrest Mexican-Americans who were allegedly attacking sailors. Such attacks were not happening. When the police swept into Alpine, they found no one on the street, no disturbances. The press, however, luridly reported beatings of sailors by zoot suiters and depicted the vigilante raid of the Vengeance Squad as a desperate attempt by the LAPD to protect sailors from zoot suiters.

All day Friday, 4 June, rumors of a full-scale counter-attack by zoot suiters swept Los Angeles. The sailors at the Chavez Ravine arsenal, adjacent to a major *barrio*, were driven to intense excitement. That evening, a caravan of twenty-nine taxicabs formed outside the arsenal, and two hundred sailors piled in. Just who organized this taxicab brigade, as the press would soon be calling it, is uncertain. For the rest of the evening, the taxicab brigade snaked through the Downtown and the Belvedere district on the east side of the city. Sighting a zoot suiter, the sailors would stop the caravan, pour out into the street, and surround the hapless victim. Four Mexican-American young men were severely beaten.

All day Saturday, 5 June, newspaper stories covered the Taxicab Brigade, now capitalized, as if it were a *bona fide* military maneuver by a legitimate armed forces unit. Headlines proclaimed a planned counter-attack by zoot suiters. That Saturday evening, hundreds of sailors and Marines marched through the Downtown, four abreast, stopping Mexican-American young men in zoot suits and telling them to remove the offensive garment by the next day or be in big trouble. Other groups of sailors ventured into East Los Angeles. Encountering a zoot suiter, they submitted him to pantsing, which is to say, they stripped their victim of his pants and shredded the rest of his garments. Some zoot suiters, those resisting, were beaten. Six carloads of sailors, in all, beat eight zoot suiters on Brooklyn Avenue and trashed a bar on Indiana.

Sunday the 6th remained relatively quiet, save for the screaming headlines and lurid press reports that five hundred zoot suiters were organizing a counter-attack — a fabrication for which there was no evidence whatsoever. On the evening of Monday the 7th, servicemen from throughout the Los Angeles area and civilians, whipped into a state of carnival excitement by four days of lurid rumors and press reports, were milling in the Downtown by the thousands. Streetcars were stopped and searched for zoot suiters, who, if found, were pulled onto the street, pantsed, and beaten. Gangs of servicemen and civilians roamed through the theater district on Broadway, forcing managers to stop the film and turn up the house lights. The servicemen would then fan out through the theater looking for zoot suiters. Any discovered were stripped and beaten. The following week, *Life* magazine published photographs of the crowds on Main Street surrounding a stopped streetcar, the prostrate figure of a beaten Mexican-American youth on a sidewalk, zoot suiters in a line-up, and a pantsed zoot suiter in a police station where he had fled for safety.

The photo of the zoot suiters in the line-up underscored the response of Los Angeles police to events. As far as the LAPD was concerned, it was the Mexican-American zoot suiters, not the servicemen, who were doing the rioting. On the night of the taxicab caravan, the police arrested nine sailors, who were quickly released. From then on, the police seemed content to follow the rioting servicemen at a distance in their squad cars, then arrest any Mexican-Americans in the vicinity, even those pantsed and beaten, after the servicemen had departed. When sailors beat teenagers in East Los Angeles and wrecked the bar on Indiana Street on Sunday, 6 June, the police swept in after the event and arrested forty-four Mexican-Americans. Al Waxman, editor of the *Eastside Journal*, happened upon a scene at 12th and Central that typified police behavior in the first days of the riots. "Police were swinging clubs and servicemen were fighting with civilians," Waxman reported. "Wholesale arrests were being made by the officers. Four boys came out of a pool hall. They were wearing the zoot suits that have become the symbol of a fighting flag. Police ordered them into arrest cars. One refused. He asked: 'Why am I being arrested?' The police officer answered with three swift blows of the night stick across the boy's head and he went down. As he sprawled, he was kicked in the face. Police had difficulty loading his body into the vehicle because he was one-legged and wore a wooden limb."[3]

On the night of the seventh, the police arrested twenty-four servicemen and a hundred zoot suiters. During the first two nights of the rioting, novelist Chester Himes reported in *Crisis*, the national magazine of the NAACP, "no policemen were in evidence until the gangs of sailors, outnumbering the pachucos two-three-four to one, had sapped up on the pachucos with belt buckles and knotted ropes. When the sailors departed in their cars, trucks, and taxicabs, furnished them no doubt by the nazi-minded citizenry, the police appeared as if they had been waiting around the corner and arrested the Mexican youths who had been knocked out, stunned, or too frightened to run."[4]

Carey McWilliams suggested that the Los Angeles Police Department was delighted by the Zoot Suit Riots, which it let develop, because they distracted attention from the trial of LAPD officer Compton Dixon, then in progress, for allegedly kicking to death a detainee in the Central Jail. "Shortly after the riots," McWilliams reported, "a Hollywood police captain told a motion picture director that the police had touched off the riots 'in order to give Dixie [Dixon] a break.' By staging a fake demonstration of the alleged necessity for harsh police methods, it was hoped that the jury would acquit Dixon."[5] If true, the strategy worked; for the jury failed to reach a verdict, and on 2 July 1943 the charges against Dixon were dismissed. Neither Mayor Fletcher Bowron nor Chief of Police C. B. Horrall intervened in any visible way during the first days of the rioting.

Strangely enough, for all the commotion, no one was killed during the rioting and there was only one major injury. An African-American defense worker, not even a zoot suiter, was pulled from a streetcar, and someone gouged one of his eyes out with a knife. However horrible and racist this incident, it could not compare to the race riots erupting in Detroit a week later in which thirty-one people died, mostly African-Americans, fifteen of them gunned down by the police. What, then, was really happening? The most ingenious, and compelling, explanation has been given by Professor Mazón. The Zoot Suit Riots, Mazón argues, represented a mass outburst of symbolic annihilation.

First of all, young servicemen read the comic pages. Between 11 April and 23 May 1943, the nationally syndicated *Li'l Abner* comic strip by Al Capp featured a storyline entitled "Zoot Suit Yokum." Not only was the Capp comic filled with images of death and annihilation, it raised the zoot suit to an intense level of social symbology as a suspicious, conspiratorial garment, used in the cartoon to manipulate and cynically exploit the American people. At the end of the comic-strip storyline, mobs destroy clothing stores selling zoot suits. The young servicemen roaming the streets of Los Angeles, Mazón points out, themselves constituted the same genre of uniformed gang they and the press saw in the zoot suiters. But while their uniform symbolized the surrender of their individuality to the military and the possibility of their annihilation, the zoot suit symbolized freedom from the military and a luxuriant, almost narcissistic assertion of male individuality and self-esteem.

And besides, the zoot suiters had girls, plenty of them: gorgeous *pachucas* in short skirts, sheer blouses, high pompadours, bracelets, earrings, and heavily lipsticked mouths pouty with erotic promise. From this perspective, the young servicemen envied the zoot suiters. They, after all, were free, civilian, cocky, even arrogant, while the servicemen were caught in the web of military discipline. *Pachucos* had ducktail haircuts. The servicemen had their heads shaven. Zoot suiters had *pachucas* with whom to dance the jitterbug and do other things, and plenty of time to stand around on corners and hang out with their buddies, with no sergeants or petty officers on their case. The servicemen did not want to kill the zoot suiters or even seriously harm them, Mazón argues; otherwise, they could have easily done so, given their overwhelming numbers and the clubs, saps, and cables many of them were carrying. What the servicemen wanted was the symbolic annihilation of the zoot suiter through the pantsing ritual. Pulling off a zoot suiter's pants, shredding his frock coat, taking a scissors to his ducktail haircut, the servicemen made the zoot suiter into one of them. One gang was erasing the symbols of another.

Writing in the aftermath of the Sleepy Lagoon case and fully aware of the long history of anti-Mexican repression in Los Angeles, Carey McWilliams reported on the Zoot Suit Riots as if they were a full-scale race riot analogous to the Detroit riot or the riot that broke out in Harlem on 1 August, in which six people were killed and three hundred were injured. Not so, argues Mazón. Photographs of the Zoot Suit Riots, such as those that appeared in *Life*, depict an atmosphere that could almost be described as festive. "There was no looting, burning, raping, or killing," Mazón writes. "What transpired was a carnival-like atmosphere in which servicemen and civilians acted out inhibitions about the war in a complex series of symbolic rituals of death, rebirth, initiation, and role-reversal."[6]

Even military authorities, Mazón argues, seemed initially willing to allow their young servicemen to take a holiday from the realities of military discipline. After all, in the first few days of the riots, hundreds, perhaps thousands, of servicemen, sailors especially, were absent without leave. If the military authorities had wished to push the point, these AWOL servicemen could have been declared to be in a state of insurrection bordering upon mutiny. That such an awareness of possible mutiny charges had actually surfaced is evident in a confidential memorandum dated 11 June 1943, written by Major General Maxwell Murray, commanding general of the Southern California Sector of the Western Defense Command. "It is obvious," noted General Murray, "that many soldiers are not aware of the serious nature of riot charges. Convictions in a recent serious riot have resulted in sentence to death or a long confinement."[7] No such charges were ever brought against any servicemen involved in the Zoot Suit Riots, and not until 9 June did Rear Admiral D. W. Bagley, commanding officer of the 11th Naval District, declare Los Angeles off-limits to naval personnel, which effectively ended the disturbances.

The brass recovered itself when the servicemen's riots spread to San Diego and sailors began to beat up civilians, whom they accused of being draft dodgers. It was one thing to rough up and de-pants Mexican-American zoot suiters in Los Angeles; it was another thing entirely to attack non-Mexican-Americans in San Diego. On 10 June 1943 San Diego city councilman Charles Dail wrote Rear Admiral Bagley a stinging letter of protest regarding the persecution of civilians by young servicemen on the streets of the city. Among other instances, Dail complained, a Marine had beaten up an official of the Consolidated Aircraft Company after calling him a draft dodger. The official was unable to return to his duties because of the seriousness of his injuries. Admiral Bagley immediately got the point. The Zoot Suit Riots in Los Angeles stood in danger of precipitating an outburst of resentful young servicemen against civilians. The Navy clamped down, and there were no more disturbances.

The word was also reaching the military that Washington was displeased as well. Once again, as in the case of the long California-Japan War, racial incidents in California were affecting American diplomacy. Mexico, after all, was an ally. The United States Navy was using naval bases in Baja California. By the fall of 1943 some 233,000 Mexican nationals—called *braceros*, or the strong-armed ones—were working in the fields of California, harvesting crops. Another 3,325 Mexican nationals were working for the Southern Pacific, comprising 72 percent of its track-maintenance force. By the end of 1944, more than eighty thousand Mexican nationals were engaged in railroad work in the United States. Without this agricultural and railroad labor from Mexico, California's wartime economy—indeed, the food supply of the entire nation—would have been seriously impaired. And yet, on 9 June 1943 the consul general of Mexico in Los Angeles, Señor Alfredo Elias, was being forced to issue an official warning to all Mexicans in Los

Angeles, nationals and American citizens alike, to remain in their homes as protection against violence from servicemen. The affront to Mexico was instantane-
ous. The Mexican ambassador to the United States, Dr. Francisco Castillo Najera,
personally protested to Secretary of State Cordell Hull. Nelson A. Rockefeller,
coordinator of inter-American affairs at the State Department, issued a warning to
Los Angeles officials, as did Guy Nunn of the War Manpower Commission.
Eleanor Roosevelt described the Los Angeles riots in her syndicated newspaper
column as a race riot against Mexicans, similar to the riots against blacks in
Detroit.

Stung by the national perception of Los Angeles as a race-rioting city subversive
of the wartime alliance between the United States and Mexico, the Los Angeles
oligarchy got on its high horse. The Los Angeles *Times* chided Mrs. Roosevelt for
daring to suggest that Los Angeles nurtured any emotion other than reverence for
Mexico and the Mexicans. After all, the *Times* opined, Southern California had
once been part of Mexico and considered itself a continuing participant in the
legacy of Mexican civilization. In the aftermath of the riots, Mayor Bowron appointed a Committee for Home Front Unity, the Board of Supervisors of Los
Angeles County established a Committee for Inter-Racial Progress, and the
Church Federation of Los Angeles formed a Council for Civic Unity. Governor
Earl Warren, then being mentioned as a possible Republican candidate against
Roosevelt should the President seek an unprecedented fourth term, moved quickly
to distance himself from the anti-Mexican sentiments of Los Angeles. Disturbed
that the image of being the governor of a race-baiting, xenophobic state would not
serve his national candidacy, Warren asked Attorney General Robert Kenny to
chair a Citizens Committee to investigate the zoot suit affair. As a gesture to the
race and religion of the Mexican-Americans, Warren asked Auxiliary Bishop Joseph McGucken of the Archdiocese of Los Angeles to sit on the committee, as
well as the Mexican-American film actor Leo Carillo. According to some commentators in the national Catholic press, the Zoot Suit Riots in Los Angeles had
revealed, once again, the prevalence of a white fundamentalist anti-Catholicism,
linked to anti-Mexicanism, in the City of Angels.

Or, as black shipyard worker Bob Jones puts it in Chester Himes's novel *If He
Hollers Let Him Go* (1945), "Los Angeles is the most overrated, lousiest, countriest,
phoniest city I've ever been in." An African-American writer of growing reputation,
Himes lived in Los Angeles from 1940 until 1944. During that time, he accumu-
lated background material for two powerful novels set in the wartime city, *If He
Hollers Let Him Go* and *Lonely Crusade* (1947). Before arriving in Los Angeles,
Himes believed that he had encountered the worst of white America. In the South,
where his father taught mechanical arts at various black schools, the Himes family
had experienced a heavy dose of racial discrimination. His father, among other
things, had been warned against driving too expensive an automobile. Moving
with his family to Cleveland, Himes had worked as a bus boy, fallen down an

elevator shaft and been seriously injured, and flunked out at Ohio State University because of poor health and bad grades. Drifting into crime, he found himself a convicted felon at age nineteen, facing a twenty- to twenty-five-year sentence in the Ohio State Penitentiary for armed robbery. In prison, where he spent seven and a half years, Himes survived a disastrous fire on Easter Monday 1930 in which 330 convicts were burned to death in their cells. Like Malcolm X, Himes taught himself to write in prison through laborious self-instruction. By 1936, the year of his parole, he was publishing short stories in *Esquire*. Four fitful years followed as Himes, married in 1937 to Jean Johnson, an educated black social worker, struggled as a laborer with the WPA before landing a position as a research assistant in the Cleveland Public Library, assigned to help research and write an official history of Cleveland for the Ohio Writers' Project. He also served briefly as the valet to writer Louis Bromfield, then living at Malabar Farm near Pleasant Valley in Ohio. Bromfield encouraged Himes's writing ambitions and suggested a second start in Southern California.

In 1940 Himes secured the restoration of his citizenship from the Ohio Parole Board, and he and Jean moved to Los Angeles, where Himes hoped to find work as a screenwriter and freelance journalist. A possible assignment to do a profile of Lena Horne for *Collier's* fell through when it was transferred to a white writer. For a while, Himes was being considered for a job as a reader at Warner Brothers, until Jack Warner said: "I don't want no niggers on this lot."[8] While his wife secured a prestigious job as co-director of women's activities for the USO in Los Angeles, Himes was forced to work at menial jobs in the defense industry. Despite the fact that he had learned such skills as reading blueprints, elementary carpentry, plumbing, electric wiring, bricklaying, and roofing from his father, together with the operation of a number of machine tools, and was a fairly skilled typist, he could find only menial work, with the exception of brief stints as an apprentice shipfitter in the Kaiser Shipyard in Richmond on San Francisco Bay and one as a shipwright's helper at the Los Angeles Shipyard in San Pedro Harbor, helping install a ventilation system in a floating drydock. In three years, Himes held twenty-three jobs, moving from job to job in search of better opportunities because federal law allowed a defense worker to leave his position if he was not employed at his highest level of skill.

Humiliated by his wife's success and envious of her close working relationship to the black establishment of Los Angeles, Himes grew progressively more embittered. "Los Angeles hurt me racially as much as any city I have ever known," he later remembered, "much more than any city I remember from the South. It was the lying hypocrisy that hurt me. Black people were treated much the same as they were in an industrial city of the South. They were Jim Crow-ed in housing, in employment, in public accommodations such as hotels and restaurants." Under "the mental corrosion of race prejudice in Los Angeles," Hines lamented, "I had become bitter and saturated with hate."[9]

During the Second World War, more than seven hundred thousand African-

Americans moved into industrial cities seeking employment in defense industries. Some 150,000 of them moved to the Pacific Coast, mainly to Los Angeles County and the San Francisco Bay Area. Shipbuilding proved a magnet to African-American workers, and by late 1944 nearly two hundred thousand black Americans were employed in the nation's shipyards, some two-thirds of them on the Pacific Coast. Such a massive relocation of black America into California and the shipping industry was obviously fraught with social problems. At the outbreak of the war, fully half of all defense jobs were either overtly or covertly closed to African-Americans. Two powerful unions, the International Association of Machinists and the Boilermakers Union, which together represented 20 percent of all shipyard workers, excluded blacks from union membership or admitted them only to segregated locals, with no right to vote in industry-wide negotiations. On 28 June 1941 Franklin Delano Roosevelt signed Executive Order 8802, mandating fair employment practices in all war industries, and the situation slowly improved. By 1944 black Americans held 7.5 percent of all jobs in the war industries.

Such enforced integration came at great personal cost to African-Americans and others, including women, who were facing discrimination in the shipyards. Early in the war, social worker and sociology researcher Katherine Archibald signed on as a welder at the Moore Dry Dock Company in Oakland, where she eventually rose to shop steward. Archibald also kept meticulous notes on patterns of racial, social, and gender prejudice she encountered in the industry. Her post-war monograph *Wartime Shipyard: a Study in Social Disunity*, published by the University of California Press in 1947, depicts a shipyard industry racked by prejudice and distrust: a chilling paradigm, in short, of America in the 1940s.

The power of *Wartime Shipyard* lies in its frank evocation of just how deeply divided were the American people now migrating to California in such great numbers. The industrial shipyards, as Archibald develops them, function as accelerated communities, reflecting both the strengths and the limitations of American society. Here was the capacity of ordinary Americans for hard work, their sinewy resilience under deadline and stress; but here also was the fundamental weakness of social disunity born of racial and gender prejudice and discrimination. Racial, social, class, and gender prejudice, Archibald believed, was tearing America apart; and the shipyards proved it. Every group, it seemed, distrusted and frequently hated everyone else, singly and collectively. The Portuguese, Archibald noted, were held in almost the same contempt as blacks by white workers, despite their European origins. Asians were dismissed as Mongolians. Only the few Native Americans who managed to find work in the shipyards seemed to escape prejudice; indeed, Native Americans held universally high status. Even the Okies near the bottom of the status ladder boasted of their Cherokee blood.

Like blacks, Dust Bowl migrants, derisively known as Okies, flooded into the shipbuilding industries, finding in these industrial jobs their California Dream come true. Despite their white skins, Archibald noted, Okies encountered pervasive contempt from their fellow workers. OKIE, THIS IS A DOOR, Archibald found crudely chalked over one bulkhead passageway. Over a urinal was inscribed OKIE DRINKING FOUNTAIN, with a tin cup placed nearby. Many Oklahomans confessed to Archibald that they were hurt by their treatment in California. "Why, back in my hometown," one Okie told her, "we treat stray dogs better than they treat men out here."[10]

Universally, white workers, Okies and non-Okies alike, talked against Jews, although they admired what they believed to be Jewish intelligence and cunning. From the perspective of the shipyard worker, Jews belonged in the world of the front office. They were the merchants and the money boys, the administrators, at once admired and despised. Archibald was shocked not only by this pervasive anti-Semitism but by a disconcerting element of class envy she encountered in her fellow workers. Shop foremen, she noted, became almost noticeably servile when front-office men in shirts and ties were about, men whom they gave the title Mister; but as soon as the front-office people went back to the front-office, they were excoriated behind their backs as lazy blood-suckers. Front-office people of Jewish identity were especially lambasted. This distrust of the front office extended to union officials as well. A form of continuing warfare existed between the union rank and file and salaried officials, whom the workers generally despised as conniving crooks. Most shipyard unions affiliated with the American Federation of Labor were reactionary in their policies, Archibald believed. Elite shipyard unions such as the Steamfitters would not allow women or blacks to join the union, nor would they allow Okies to rise to elective office.

Women, Archibald observed, could get jobs in the shipyards and could function competently (women she claimed, had special skills as electricians); but they could not escape discrimination based on gender, which constantly took the form of an imputation of sexuality. Men might be excessively courteous or excessively hostile to their fellow shipyard workers who were female, Archibald noted; but both the courtesy and the discourtesy represented a male response to the element of sexuality male workers believed women brought to the workplace. Shop foremen, for example, rigidly insisted that no female hair ever emerge from a bandanna and that no nail polish, lipstick, or make-up be worn to work. Sweaters could not be worn unless covered by a shirt or bulky outer jacket. In the front office, where women worked in more traditional roles as bookkeepers and secretaries, they were allowed to wear sweaters and knee-high skirts and use make-up to their hearts' content; but when they came into competition with men as welders or electricians, they were forced to suppress all signs of femininity. A pervasive piece of folklore in the wartime shipbuilding industry, Archibald noted, was the widespread notion that female shipyard workers entertained lovers in the lower holds of Liberty ships under construction or moonlighted as prostitutes. Given human nature, Archibald agreed, incidents such as this did occur—but not to the epidemic extent of folkloric report. Such stories, Archibald believed, were just one way men coped with their anxiety about working next to women as equals. Stories of sexual activity, in other words, symbolically reduced a competitive female worker to a sexual object.

The good news was that this same attitude of resistent standoffishness, whether expressed as exaggerated courtesy or open hostility, tended to minimize actual sexual assaults against women, or what a later generation would call sexual harassment.

At the bottom of the shipyard pecking order were African-Americans. Disconcerted by the prejudice she encountered against other groups, Archibald was appalled, even depressed, by the racism directed against blacks, whom so many of the other workers treated as an almost sub-human species. Excluded from union membership, relegated to unskilled labor, African-American workers fought a daily battle for their rights and dignity. Despite the deep prejudice held against them, however, Archibald was surprised to note, at least some African-Americans made it into steamfitting and pipefitting—and many others worked closely and successfully alongside whites who were being forced for the first time in their lives, by wartime necessity, to work alongside blacks as equals.

Chester Himes's fictional protagonist Bob Jones, a black shipyard worker with two years of college education, finds himself enmeshed in just such a miasmic, paranoid atmosphere of racism.

If He Hollers Let Him Go is set in 1944, a particularly difficult year for blacks in California. If 1942 represented the high point of Japanese-American bashing, and 1943 constituted the high-water mark of Mexican-American bashing, 1944 proved an especially difficult year for African-American migrants to California, now that their numbers were growing, and competition for housing had reached crisis proportions, and it was beginning to dawn upon white California that black America, hitherto a demographically restricted sector of the state's population, was rapidly emerging as a new social presence. As the Detroit riots of June 1943 proved, black-white conflict was not the exclusive prerogative of California. Yet because California was not officially a Jim Crow state, its discrimination against blacks, as Himes noted of Los Angeles, was at once more subtle, more virulent, and more unexpected, hence more damaging.

Published two years apart, *If He Hollers Let Him Go* and Himes's next novel, *Lonely Crusade*, share similar protagonists, college-educated black men working in the defense industry; the same *mise-en-scène*, wartime Los Angeles; and the same theme, racism Los Angeles style. Robert Jones, the protagonist of *If He Hollers Let Him Go*, has come to Los Angeles from Ohio, like Chester Himes himself, to work at the Atlas Shipyard in San Pedro. Lee Gordon, the central character in *Lonely Crusade*, a Pasadena-born UCLA graduate, has worked his way up to serve as a CIO organizer at the Comstock Aircraft Corporation in Burbank. Jones and Lee are fast-paced, frenetic, even fugitive men, running not so much from the law, although the law would soon prove a problem for each of them, as from the pervasive racism of Los Angeles, which embitters and corrupts their lives.

Each man has risen from the ranks. By the spring of 1943, Jones has become a leaderman, or sub-foreman, and Gordon has become the first black union organizer in the aircraft industry. Bob Jones's challenge is to install shipboard ventilation systems with his all-black crew despite white foremen who call him "boy," clerks who refuse to issue him the proper blueprints, white workers who refuse to work with their black counterparts, and, worst of all, white women: one especially, Madge, a thirty-something peroxide blonde cracker showing plenty of mileage yet still sexy in a late-night honky-tonk sort of way. Madge plays Fay Wray's terrified virgin to Jones's King Kong every time Jones is forced to squeeze past her between decks. Lee Gordon, for his part, walks an equally delicate tightrope as the first black unionizer in an anti-union Jim Crow town.

Jones and Gordon are especially sensitive to racial affronts, which seem to be constant, because each of them, like Chester Himes himself, is a middle-class college man feeling most intensely and bitterly the disjunction between what America promised and what it delivered. While Jones's background in Ohio is left unsketched, Lee Gordon's origins provide a paradigm of the black experience in pre-war Southern California. Born to domestic servants on a Pasadena estate, Gordon is raised in his parents' cottage on the property. Because he is a resident of the city, the Pasadena public schools must take him in, and to a certain extent Southern California presents itself to young Gordon as an equal opportunity state. As a boy, Gordon feels himself equal to his white schoolmates in terms of physical abilities and intelligence. What is this thing called race, he asks himself? Why is it made so much of by everyone, including his parents? Gordon soon finds out when he is expelled from school for spying on the girls' locker room, and his family is forced to leave Pasadena in disgrace.

Scarred by racism, Jones and Gordon share similar responses to a Los Angeles mishmash of cars, cops, color, Communism, and sex. Chester Himes's father had always insisted on keeping a big new car, even in the South, where such an automobile was considered uppity. In Los Angeles, Himes discovered, the automobile and competitive driving was an even more frenetic (and frequently dangerous) symbol of racial equality. Each novel begins with a mad dash across Los Angeles from home to work: Jones in the 1942 Buick Roadmaster that serves as his zoot suit equivalent, a defiant symbol of identity; Gordon in an equally jazzy, equally speeding coupe. For Bob Jones, hot-footing his Buick down Central Avenue to Slauson, then east to Alameda, then south to the harbor, each moment on the streets of Los Angeles, jockeying for advantage, giving and receiving hostile stares at stoplights, is a form of racial competition. "Time and again," Jones says, "I cut in front of some fast-moving car, making rubber burn and brakes scream and drivers curse, hoping a paddy would bump my fender so I'd have an excuse to get out and clip him with my tire iron."[11]

Enter the cops. In both novels, the LAPD and the deputy sheriffs of Los Angeles just love to pull blacks off to the side of the road for speeding, which happens to both Jones and Gordon. Jones is merely insulted with racial epithets; Gordon is severely beaten, a Rodney King before his time (and their name was legion), only with no hidden video camera on hand to record the incident. (Ironically, it was just such a traffic incident ten years later, in 1953 in New York City, a gratuitous arrest on charges of reckless driving, followed by a booking in the county jail, that motivated Himes to expatriate to Europe.) Mistaking Lee Gordon's father, a night-time janitor, for a burglar as he leaves the department store where he worked, a Los Angeles cop shoots him dead.

Bob Jones fears that now that the Japanese-Americans have been interned, black Americans will be next. White America, after all, has clearly shown its ability to mass-incarcerate entire sectors of its citizenry. As far as color is concerned, how-ever, Jones and Gordon share a secret sympathy for the Japanese, who are, after all, a people of color confronting whites on their own terms and causing the white folk a lot of grief. During the false air raid on Los Angeles in February 1942, Lee Gordon stands with his wife Ruth in their backyard and watches the furious bar-rage overhead. "They're here!" he cries exultantly. "They're here! God-dammit, they're coming! Come on, you little bad bastards! Come on and take this city!"[12]

While Jones and Gordon share a concealed admiration for the Japanese, each is contemptuous of the Communist critique they encounter from certain fellow workers or union organizers or whites sympathetic to the black cause, almost all of them Jewish. In each novel, Chester Himes hovers on the outer edge of, or crosses into, an equation of Communism with Jewishness and vice versa, with its strong overtones of anti-Semitism, that has caused so much anguish, then and thereafter, between blacks and Jews on the left. Jones dismisses pro-Communists at the shipyard as just another species of white liars. Getting more involved, Gor-don attends Communist-sponsored fundraisers in Westside Los Angeles, where Marxism blends with a boozy, promiscuous bohemia. Himes later claimed that a pro-Communist element among booksellers and literary reviewers buried *Lonely Crusade*, which Alfred A. Knopf had reluctantly published, because of its contro-versial themes, only at the insistence of Blanche Knopf, the wife of the publisher. In any event, each of Himes's protagonists, while believing that white capitalist America stinks, holds equal contempt for a Communist alternative.

Cars, cops, color, Communism—and sex! Chester Himes can often seem the most sexually obsessed American writer of note prior to John Updike. No novelist in America, white or black, has ever presented the nexus of race, sex, and power in America with more telling frankness, which is perhaps the main reason, along with Himes's anti-Communism and aura of anti-Semitism, that reviewers balked at reviewing his books and booksellers balked at selling them. In Los Angeles, Himes had grown estranged from his college-educated wife Jean Johnson Himes, whose success as a USO official contrasted with his own menial employment. Like Himes, Bob Jones and Lee Gordon are estranged from the black women in their lives. Jones's girlfriend Alice Harrison is light-skinned and upper-middle-class and has close friends who are white. Jones almost says "I told you so" when two cops stop them on Santa Monica Boulevard and treat them with contempt, despite Alice's protestations that her father is a prominent, well-connected citizen of the city. Lee Gordon is likewise estranged from his wife Ruth, whom he simultane-

ously reveres and mistreats. Subconsciously obsessed by white women (at one point
he notes that at the time of his graduation from high school he had never said
more than a dozen words to any white girl), Gordon drifts into a liaison with a
white Communist activist, who is Jewish. Bob Jones, by contrast, gets sucker-
punched by Madge (entrapment, followed by a charge of attempted rape) in a
manner expressive of the tensions faced by black workers in the defense industry,
many of them functioning for the first time in an integrated environment.

Madge, after all, is in her own twisted cracker way attracted to Jones. In *Wartime
Shipyard* Katherine Archibald noted that so much of the prejudice against African-
American men in the shipyards consisted of anxieties on the part of white men
that black men would play up to white women or vice versa. On one ship on
which Archibald was working, two young white girls found themselves stringing
cable next to a group of black machinists. The girls chose to be friendly, exchang-
ing a joke or two; and indignation spread throughout the white men in the immediate vicinity. The girls were not flirting or acting in an untoward manner,
Archibald noted. They were merely treating the black men in the same way that
they would treat white men alongside whom they might be working. Yet the
tension resulting from their few innocent sallies was electric.

Bob Jones encounters the same tension in his dealings with Madge. Initially,
Madge goes through her Fay Wray routine every time Bob passes. She refuses to
take orders from him. Yet even in her defiance and racial contempt, there is a
magnetism on her part for him and on his part for her. The magnetism is corrupt,
however, as Jones finds out one evening in Madge's hotel when she invites him
to rape her. Not wishing to be Los Angeles' first wartime lynching candidate, Jones
flees; but Madge later gets her revenge, faking a rape incident on the ship when
Jones once again rebuffs her overtures. Jones is arrested, then sent to the Army
when Madge, faking patriotism, refuses to press charges lest the incident pit white
workers against black workers at the Atlas Shipyard.

In 1943, the real-life counterparts to Bob Jones were entering a segregated Army.
Not until 1947 would the armed forces of the United States be desegregated.
During the war, African-Americans, while segregated, found their best opportu-
nities in the Army Air Force and in certain Army ground units. The Navy and
Marine Corps, by contrast, were reluctant to allow blacks to serve in combat units.
The Navy assigned blacks almost exclusively to steward duties or to stevedore work
in labor divisions, despite the fact that Navy Steward Dorie Miller had won the
Navy Cross at Pearl Harbor for seizing the controls of an anti-aircraft gun aboard
the USS *Arizona* after its crew had been killed and downing six Japanese Zeros.

By 1943 African-American Navy stevedores were serving at Port Chicago, an
ammunition depot on the south shore of Suisun Bay north of San Francisco.
Loading Liberty ships with ammunition for the Pacific constituted a dangerous,
back-breaking, unglamorous job, akin to forced labor; and the Navy confined such
assignments almost exclusively to black enlisted men, who worked under the su-

pervision of white lieutenants and black petty officers. As the war in the Pacific stepped up its scope and pace, the African-American stevedore crews at Port Chicago found themselves working three shifts around the clock, seven days a week. Typically, a division of men, numbering between 100 and 125, would load ships for seven hours a day for three consecutive days, followed by a half day of barracks duty and an afternoon of athletics, followed by three more days of ammunition loading, followed by one day of liberty, during which they might leave the base on pass. It was grinding, unrelenting, and perilous work. Many of these African-American stevedores had enlisted in the Navy in the hopes of becoming gunners, mechanics, radiomen, or similar positions calling for skill and responsibility in the fleet; but here they were instead, doing a job so grim, so grueling, that the Navy assigned it only to African-American enlisted men.

As the tempo of shipments of ammunition from Port Chicago to the Pacific increased, so did the risks. On the night of Monday, 17 July 1944, shortly after ten o'clock, a horrendous explosion racked Port Chicago as two Liberty ships, a fire barge, and a loading pier disappeared in a blast that was equivalent to five kilotons of TNT, which is to say, an explosion comparable to that of the atomic bomb dropped on Hiroshima thirteen months later. An Army Air Force crew flying overhead at the time reported a fireball that covered approximately three miles and sent metal fragments nine thousand feet into the air. Three hundred and twenty men — 202 of them black enlisted stevedores — lost their lives in an instant. Only fifty-one bodies were recovered sufficiently intact to be identified. Another 390 military and civilian personnel, including 233 black enlisted men, suffered injuries, many of them serious. It was the most significant home-front catastrophe of the war.

Needless to say, the surviving black stevedores were in a state of shock, and the Navy began to consider the possibility of assigning white enlisted men to Port Chicago. Before that could occur, however, more than two hundred black enlisted men balked at returning to work until the disaster could be investigated, a report made, and corrective steps taken. Such a refusal in wartime on the part of so many men sent a current of amazement and dread through the entire Naval establishment.

The contrast between the refusal of the Port Chicago sailors to return to work and the rioting of the white servicemen in Los Angeles the previous year is revealing. The white servicemen, edging dangerously into the borderlands of mutiny for the trivial purposes of rioting and pantsing zoot suiters, were ordered back into their barracks with no punishment. The African-American sailors, traumatized by the instant annihilation of hundreds of their colleagues, found themselves facing court-martials. Was their refusal an expression of collective anxiety, akin to the crowd behavior of the zoot suit rioters, only more serious? Or were the individual black sailors truly capable of mutinous action? President Roosevelt personally reviewed the matter and decided that the majority of the 208 men who balked at returning to work should be given only summary punishment because they were understandably the victims of mass fear. He left it up to the Navy, however, without recommendation, as to what should be done to the fifty other sailors identified as ringleaders.

On 14 September 1944 fifty black sailors went on trial at the naval installation on Treasure Island on charges of mutiny. Each of them faced a possible sentence of death or a long prison term, if convicted. The NAACP sent its top attorney, Thurgood Marshall, to monitor the Navy defense team. Marshall quickly strategized a defense. No sailor had ever refused a direct order, he argued. "The men actually don't know what happened," Marshall told the press on 10 October. "Had they been given a direct and specific order to load ammunition and they had refused to obey that order, then the charge would be legitimate. But they say no direct order to load was issued them. They were asked whether they would load and they replied that they were afraid. They have told me they were willing to go to jail to get a change of duty because of their terrific fear of explosives, but they had no idea that verbal expression of their fear constituted mutiny." A week later, Marshall became even more aggressive. "This is not fifty men on trial for mutiny," he told the press, emerging from a meeting with local NAACP officials. "This is the Navy on trial for its whole vicious policy towards Negroes. Negroes are not afraid of anything anymore than anyone else. Negroes in the Navy don't mind loading ammunition. They just want to know why they are the only ones doing the loading!"[13]

On Tuesday, 24 October 1944, after only eighty minutes of deliberation, with time out for lunch, the trial board of naval officers found all fifty defendants guilty of mutiny. Each of the men was to be sentenced to fifteen years in prison, followed by a dishonorable discharge. In a separate proceeding, the other 208 black sailors who had balked at returning to work were given bad conduct discharges through summary court-martial proceedings. By November 1944 208 young black men had had their records permanently damaged by a dishonorable discharge, and another fifty were beginning their sentences at the Terminal Island Disciplinary Barracks in San Pedro.

The fictional Bob Jones, and certainly Chester Himes himself when he was working in the San Pedro shipyards, might very well have looked across the water to Terminal Island and seen the Disciplinary Barracks where fifty black Americans were serving hard time for nothing more than being afraid to do work—horrendously dangerous work—that only black sailors were being asked to do. Thurgood Marshall, meanwhile, was taking their case to Secretary of the Navy James Forrestal and other defense officials. Why were only blacks assigned to Port Chicago, Marshall asked Forrestal? Why were they not given proper training in the handling of ammunition? Why were their white officers encouraged to compete with each other in the amount of ammunition loaded so as to win promotion or even monetary bets? Why were the black sailors in the stevedore battalions given virtually no promotions? Why were they not allowed to rotate out of their dangerous, backbreaking assignment after a stated period?

Marshall also prepared a brilliant appeal brief, which he presented to the judge advocate general of the Navy at the Pentagon on 3 April 1945. Although the judge advocate did not reverse the convictions, he did admit procedural errors, specifically the admission of hearsay evidence during the trial, and directed that the 12th Naval District reconvene its court and reconsider whether hearsay evidence had tainted the proceedings. In June 1945 the 12th Naval District upheld its verdict and penalties, although the admiral in command, Carleton Wright, did reduce some sentences. Already, Eleanor Roosevelt had expressed her sympathy for the convicted sailors in a personal letter to Secretary Forrestal, and the NAACP continued its campaign to have the men released. Not until after the war, however, in January 1946, were forty-seven of the Port Chicago sailors released from prison. (Two others were in the hospital, and a third had acquired a bad conduct record while in confinement.) Ironically, a number of the men were given ship assignments, which is what so many of them had wanted in the first place.

Mexican-American soldiers, by contrast, were not segregated. The assignment of Mexican-American soldiers, sailors, Marines, and airmen as individuals into white units, in fact, constituted a swift form of desegregation that would forever transform the Mexican-American experience in the United States. Nearly half a million Mexican-American young men served in the armed forces during World War II, despite the fact that Mexican-Americans constituted less than 3 percent of the nation's population. Special schools were established to teach English to Mexican-Americans whose only language was Spanish. The acquisition of the English language enabled many of these young men to compete with increased self-esteem in the larger society in the post-war period. This self-esteem came, in part, from the distinguished record of Mexican-Americans in the armed forces.

In the service, in fact, hundreds of thousands of Mexican-American young men experienced for the first time the acceptance — indeed, the admiration and respect — of Anglo society. Mexican-Americans constituted the most highly decorated ethnic group in the Second World War. Thirty-nine Mexican-Americans won Congressional Medals of Honor, most of them posthumously. Of the nine thousand men who fell at Bataan, a quarter were Mexican-Americans belonging to the New Mexico National Guard: artillery units, called up before the war and sent to the Philippines in part because of the men's skills in Spanish. Because young Mexican-American men tended to gravitate toward elite combat units, Spanish surnames figured prominently on casualty lists. Surveying Los Angeles newspapers during the war, Beatrice Griffith estimated that approximately one-fifth of the casualties from the City of Los Angeles were Mexican-Americans, despite the fact that this group constituted only one-tenth the population of the City of the Angels. Mexican-American young men were especially fond of the paratroops. In a number of airborne classes at Fort Benning, Georgia, one-third of the men earning their paratrooper wings were Mexican-Americans. Interestingly enough, the Mexican-American body type — small, sinewy, strong — was ideally suited to paratroop duty.

And besides: Mexican-Americans liked the special uniform worn by airborne troops. It reminded them of a zoot suit. By 1944 the hated zoot suit and *pachuca* styles of 1943 had made their way into mainstream feminine fashion. Heavily padded shoulders, sharp lapels, single-button jackets, knee-length pleated skirts, high pompadours, a blotch of lipstick above the upper lip: by 1944 the Andrews Sisters and millions of other young women had adapted a stylized version of the attire. On 13 June 1943 the Los Angeles City Council had passed an ordinance prohibiting the wearing of zoot suits within the city limits, classifying it as a misdemeanor. There is no record of the City Council or the LAPD having served a warrant of any kind on the Andrews Sisters.

5

1944 ✶ Swing Shift

TOWARD four in the afternoon in early 1944, the bells and sirens at the Douglas plant in Santa Monica shrieked loudly enough to be heard over the din of aircraft construction. The day shift streamed off the assembly line, and the swing shift took its place. All over Los Angeles County at approximately the same time — at Douglas, Lockheed, Vega, Northrop, North American, Convair — the day shift was going off, and the swing shift was coming into position. After Pearl Harbor, all six Los Angeles County aviation plants had accelerated into a three-shift, around-the-clock schedule that yielded an immediate 30 percent increase in productivity. By early 1944, the height of wartime production, most aviation plants were supporting three eight-hour, or the equivalent, shifts.

The swing shift came on in the late afternoon and worked until eleven or midnight, depending upon starting time. Toward dusk, great floodlights illumined the vast plants till dawn and the arrival of the day shift. By 1944 more than 230,000 men and women were at work in aviation in Los Angeles County, up 50 percent from 1943, which was up 100 percent from 1942. Photographs in *Life* depict the departure of the day shift and the arrival of the swing shift as great rivers of humanity, the men strangely formal in their fedora hats, the women more industrial-appearing in their bandannas. Few workers were carrying lunch pails, as in the case of the shipyards, for most aviation plants provided a low-cost, highly subsidized cafeteria service.

At the end of the swing shift, not everyone went home. The hours after midnight, after all, constituted time off for the swing shift. Newspapers published swing shift editions. Motion picture theaters scheduled films in the early morning hours. Bowling alleys stayed open until dawn. On weekends, plants sponsored post–swing shift dances in their recreation halls or at nearby clubs. Changing into white blouses, putting gardenias into their hair, women transformed their daytime uniform of dark slacks and denim shirts into festive nighttime attire and headed to dances beginning after midnight and lasting until dawn. Even with the war—especially with the war!—this was their time, 1944, to be young and have fun. For the day shift, dances and entertainments were held over the lunch hour. A photograph from *Life* depicts workers dancing to the Douglas Welfare Band. Hollywood stars and other celebrities made frequent appearances at these noontime rallies. At Douglas and Northrop, the workers themselves organized and produced a minstrel show. Aviation companies also sponsored Saturday or Sunday picnics, softball games, and beach parties.

Were these wartime factories, one might legitimately ask, seeing the men and women dancing in the pages of *Life*, half-hearing the big band music from sixty years ago; or were these scenes from an industrial utopia, a social democratic experiment more suitable to Scandinavia than to the *laissez-faire* United States? The question might be even further justified in view of the full range of social benefits afforded aviation workers.

Aviation plants maintained an extensive program of industrial medicine, with an integrated system of emergency clinics and preventive health programs, including short-term psychological counseling for those experiencing difficulties in the workplace or, more tragically, those who had suddenly lost a loved one to the war. Each worker received a health code number, which indicated handicaps, deficiencies, and job descriptions. Thousands of the handicapped, moreover, had found work. The hearing-impaired were assigned to the noisiest tasks and departments. The sightless proved especially skilled at hand-assembly, and seeing-eye dogs became a common presence in aircraft factories. Management also facilitated the countless tasks of day-to-day life—banking, postal services, car registration, optometry and dental care, payment of telephone and utility bills—by setting up kiosks and other service centers adjacent to assembly lines.

Rather than have workers bring their lunches, always a difficulty in a rationed economy, or leave the premises to eat, which wasted time and money, aircraft companies maintained a highly subsidized program of on-site food service. In February 1944 the Lockheed plant in Burbank unveiled its new cafeteria, the largest in the world, capable of serving sixty thousand meals a day, six days a week. Designed by the distinguished Los Angeles firm of John and Donald Parkinson (Bullock's Wilshire, City Hall, the Union Station), the Lockheed cafeteria covered an entire city block. Within, it was a dramatically attractive space, set off by re-inforced concrete columns, its lower walls lined in terra-cotta tile. Up to seventeen hundred workers could be seated at a time, channeled in six lines past gleaming steam tables. Another thirty-six thousand hot meals were rushed each day to twenty-two canteen locations in outlying Lockheed factories. At North American, fifty cents dropped into a turnstile entitled a worker to eat all he or she wanted from an ample menu. The Douglas plant in Santa Monica provided free Eskimo Pie ice creams, twelve thousand of them daily, at break time. Not only were such food service programs a boost to morale and efficiency, they also ensured that workers enjoyed a standard of nutrition essential to their health in the rationed wartime economy. One cannot help but think, sixty years later, of the slave labor, starved and abused, that was becoming increasingly characteristic of Axis production.

When it came to getting to work, the aviation plants of greater Los Angeles proved equally accommodating. With Southern California so vastly decentralized, and housing near plants at a premium, commuting had become a fact of life. In 1944 more than a hundred thousand Los Angeles County defense workers were commuting more than fifty miles each day. The average daily commute through the entire industrial population was twenty-two miles round-trip. Despite gasoline rationing, travel to and from work by private automobile remained high. As of April 1942, for example, an estimated 85 percent of aviation workers were still commuting by private car. Management laid out extensive parking lots and staggered shift times so as not to gridlock the heavily burdened roads. Douglas, Lockheed, and North American each established its own bus system. With a total of 117 buses in service by 1944, making 480 round-trips for an average of 12,000 miles per day, carrying 69,238 Lockheed workers to and from work each month, Lockheed found itself running one of the largest bus-commute systems in the country. For workers fortunate enough to find housing in neighborhoods adjacent to plants, Lockheed provided six thousand bicycles at cost. Today, in retrospect, the spectacle of thousands of employees commuting to and from work by bicycle reinforces the Scandinavian social democratic comparison.

So do the extensive day-care programs also in operation. Working with state and local government and private nursery schools, the Aircraft War Production Council by 1944 had established 126 nursery centers, accommodating more than 4,000 children, and another 118 day-care centers where an average of 3,300 children were being cared for. Many of these nurseries and day-care centers opened as early as five in the morning. A photograph in *Life* depicts women workers from Vega Aircraft picking up their children at the end of the day shift, one tow-headed boy seeming especially immaculate in his sailor suit.

The presence of so many women in the aircraft industry was in and of itself the most telling evidence that, if only for the duration of the war, American industry as represented in the aircraft plants of Los Angeles County had evolved overnight into a new stage of industrial culture. Never before in the history of an American industry had women workers played such an extensive and crucial role. This introduction of women into the work force, however, came not as a matter of conscience or social equity but as one of necessity.

The Tuesday following Pearl Harbor, 2,533 men enlisted in Los Angeles County alone, foreshadowing the personnel shortages that would soon afflict the aviation industry. Between 1942 and 1945 more than a hundred thousand men holding aircraft industry jobs were drafted. The aircraft industry energetically sought draft deferments for its professional engineers and its skilled production workers, but these were the very men whom the armed forces also desperately needed. And besides: draft boards were reluctant to grant draft deferments to any one industry on a blanket basis, lest that industry be stigmatized as a haven for draft dodgers. Aviation companies could secure individual deferments for workers on a six-months by six-months basis, but eventually just about every eligible male worker, with the exception of a small sector of specialized engineers, received his draft notice. At Lockheed and Vega, for example, more than twenty-four thousand men left their jobs for military service. A total of 394 of them lost their lives. Consolidated-Vultee of San Diego experienced an 88.7 percent turnover in 1944 alone.

To counter such losses to the draft, aircraft companies launched a nationwide recruitment of draft-exempt or draft-deferred family men, relocating entire families to Los Angeles. Locally employed professionals and other draft-exempt men were encouraged to work part-time shifts in aviation as a patriotic contribution. Policemen, firemen, and servicemen stationed in the vicinity were also integrated into the industry at the rate of a shift or two per week. Age barriers were dropped, especially for veterans; and thousands of World War I, even Spanish-American War, veterans worked full- or part-time on the assembly line. Working with local boards of education, aircraft companies devised programs that would allow high school students over the age of sixteen to work a half-day shift, making up class time on Saturdays. In many cases, such programs were coordinated with technical instruction in the high schools to create a comprehensive apprenticeship program. More than four thousand young men of high school age, including nearly the entire football team from Burbank High School, were at work at Lockheed by the summer of 1943. All in all, some seventy-seven Southern California high schools participated in such work-study programs, which were in and of themselves notable achievements in industrial culture.

Yet all this was not enough. Even before Pearl Harbor, Vega and Vultee were hiring women for the assembly line. Immediately after Pearl Harbor, Lockheed and Vega hired sixty women who had lost their husbands in the attack. Smaller in height and body size, women proved adept at welding in tight spaces. (Short men were in demand for the same reason; so were midgets and dwarfs.) Vega had eight hundred women on its staff by January 1942, the same month that personnel officials at Douglas, having studied the matter, announced that women would eventually constitute one-third of the total Douglas work force. That figure was reached within months. The shortage of male workers in the aircraft industry reached crisis proportions in the summer of 1943 and precipitated a wholesale shift to women workers. By July 1943 some 113,028 women were on the job: 42.4 percent of the total work force in Southern California aviation. This ratio was nearly identical to the figure for the female work force in the United Kingdom, which stood at 45 percent, and surpassed by more than 10 percentage points the percentage of women employed in defense industries throughout the United States.

For a brief few years, it seemed as if a major social revolution were occurring in American industry: the introduction into the work force of women on an in-creasingly equal basis. Never before in the history of American industry had so many women worked side by side with so many men at comparable levels of wages, working conditions, and skills. By definition, a new relationship between men and women in the workplace and hence in private life was being forged: one suggested brilliantly in director Jonathan Demme's *Swing Shift* (1984), starring Goldie Hawn as a young aircraft worker who rises to leadership status in an aircraft factory while her husband is serving in the Navy in the Pacific. In *Swing Shift* Hawn's character and her fellow workers begin their employment amidst catcalls and sexual harass-ment. By the end of the film (and the war it depicted), there is at the minimum a begrudging respect and at the maximum a flourishing work relationship between the women defense workers and their male counterparts.

Like the young woman played by Goldie Hawn, an Iowa girl who had married her high school sweetheart before moving to Southern California, thousands of women experienced new levels of income, job satisfaction, responsibility, and self-esteem working in defense industries. One woman, cited in a Department of Labor study just after the war, had been a general helper in a cafeteria before Pearl Harbor. In May 1942 she became a welder in the aircraft industry. By September 1943 she had been promoted to senior welder. By May 1944 she had become an inspector. Married women throughout greater Los Angeles found their lives equally in transition as thousands of housewives reported for work, many of them for the first time since their marriage. The aircraft industry favored such married women, because they already had their housing organized, and offered women with heavy family responsibilities shorter shifts, another example of the evolving industrial culture. The minimum wage for women in California during the war was forty cents per hour. Aviation factories began women at sixty cents. Married women working in aviation found themselves making, even at a minimum wage, up to $40 per week, a substantial subsidy for any household budget.

With some adjustments by the women to the technology (and some adjustments of the technology to the women), females made excellent assembly line workers. Lockheed retained the services of a female physician, Dr. Marion Dakin, to work at various tasks in the line into which women were being introduced. Dakin analyzed these tasks, then made specific recommendations regarding adjustments and retooling based upon average female heights, weights, and body strengths. Women workers at Vultee developed a "lazy arm" to move heavy tools, which soon became standard throughout the industry. A true revolution was at work, anthropologist Margaret Mead believed, with young women coming into Los An-geles on their own, getting jobs in the defense industry on their own, experiencing anonymity and mobility on their own, in contrast to the restrictions of their pre-vious environments. That revolution extended to the male-female relationship as well. Surveyed at Lockheed at the beginning of the war, the majority of women described their male supervisors as impressive, even brilliant, technical wizards. Fifteen months later, a similar survey at the same plant revealed a high level of disenchantment on the part of the same women with their male bosses. Only the promotion of women to supervisory roles could alleviate the impasse.

Anxieties over sexuality in the workplace surfaced most intensely in 1942 as more and more women joined the line. Douglas Aircraft, for example, ran a major article on gonorrhea and syphilis in the company newspaper at the same time that women began to come into its plants in significant numbers. Only one such story ran. Personnel managers at Vultee were so disturbed by the problem of sexuality in the workplace that personnel officers were instructed not to hire overly attractive young women. When word got out that Vultee and other companies had such a policy, young women presented themselves for interviews with no make-up and unruly hair so as to look as unattractive as possible. The joke went around personnel circles that you would hire a plain jane in the afternoon and the next morning a starlet would show up for work. Personnel officers were also wary of hiring high-strung, blue-blooded Katharine Hepburn types or arty bohemians.

By and large, women in both the aircraft and shipbuilding industries were women of the blue-collar and middle classes: high school graduates, not college co-eds; the wives, sweethearts, and sisters of enlisted men, for whom war work represented, as it does for the blue-collar heroine of *Swing Shift*, a step up in the world. There were, of course, exceptions, such as the upper-middle-class Mrs. Hilton wife and mother played by Claudette Colbert in *Since You Went Away* (1944), who takes to welding out of patriotic motives, and in real life the very Junior Leaguish Mrs. Prisalla Maury, whose father and husband, respectively a colonel and a major in the Regular Army, were missing on Bataan. While her mother-in-law stayed home with her four children, Mrs. Maury went to work in the aircraft industry. A photograph of her in *Life* for 12 October 1942 catches her blue-blooded good looks, emanating caste despite her bandanna and denim. More typical is another and equally attractive defense worker, twenty-two-year-old Mabel Aldahl of North Dakota, most recently a waitress. More Miss Aldahls than Mrs. Maurys showed up for work in the aircraft industry: young women from ordinary backgrounds, migrating out to the Coast from Oklahoma, Missouri, Texas, and the Midwest to accompany husbands and boyfriends in the service, powerful and compelling in the direct and placid presence, the physical vigor of their mid-America femininity.

The year 1942 witnessed the tight-sweater controversy. One aircraft factory in the East sent fifty-three women home in one day for wearing sweaters to work. Even the chauvinistic 1940s could not surface with the real cause for such a violent resistance to sweaters: the revelation of the female form in such a manner as to distract male workers. Instead, it was argued that sweaters were unsafe around heavy equipment and were liable to catch fire from welding sparks. Very soon, sweaters, dangling bracelets or earrings, long hair, and heavy make-up were banned entirely from the assembly line. After hundreds of women caught their Veronica Lake–like tresses in machinery, aviation officials prevailed upon the Hollywood star to adopt an upswept hairdo for the duration of the war. Patriotically, Miss

Lake complied, although her change in hairstyle can be said to have endangered her career.

In compensation for these restrictions, the aircraft industry in Southern California did its best to develop attractive working attire for its female employees. Following up on uniform designs for WACS, WAVES, WRENS, and Women Marines, Lockheed employed a Hollywood designer to create a serviceable but smart slack-suit for its female employees. North American prescribed blue slacks. These blue slacks caught on with other young women workers, for they were dressy as well as serviceable and required only a change of blouse for after-work socializing. Photographs from the period depict women aviation workers rather well dressed in slacks, denim shirts, and bandannas, in contrast to the overalls and heavy denim jackets of women employed in the shipyards. Aviation, in other words, had a glamour that included its spiffy uniform.

Initially fearful of sexuality in the workplace, the aviation industry was beginning to see it as an asset by 1943. Companies sponsored swing bands and dances as morale boosters. North American initiated a date-counseling bureau, which matched women newly arriving in Los Angeles with suitable gentlemen already at work in the aircraft industry: a species of industrial matchmaking that raised to new heights the social outreach programs of Los Angeles aviation. There was no comparable need for assisting unmarried men. By 1944 the entire population of unmarried men between the ages of twenty and thirty-four working in the defense industry dropped to 1.7 million. At the same time, there were more than 4.1 million single females in the same age range and employment category.

While reports of sexual activity in the holds of ships under construction were grossly exaggerated as part of shipyard folklore, on-the-job sexual activity in the aviation industry seems more extensive and better documented. Civil defense shelters seemed especially convenient. Lockheed had a constant problem with amorous couples using its bomb shelters for lovemaking on the lunch break; management requested that employees refrain from leaving garments and discarded condoms on the floor. Despite state and federal requirements that air raid shelters had to be kept accessible, management at the Douglas plant in Santa Monica closed off its civil defense shelters with heavy tar paper because too many couples were repairing there for lunchtime trysts. On the home front, the Second World War was, in general, a sexually intense, venturesome, and unstable time: a situation made even more compelling in the aircraft factories of Southern California by the increasing presence of young and attractive women and the decreasing presence of available men.

Many attractive young women flocked to the aircraft industry in Los Angeles County from around the nation with the hope of eventually getting into the movies: so many, in fact, that a new type emerged combining the attributes of a defense worker and a starlet. Naturally, Hollywood capitalized on the situation. The Hollywood Guild, which ran the Hollywood Canteen, recruited young women from Lockheed to act as dance hostesses at the Canteen after the swing shift. Formally designated the Blue Stars, the young women would work an eight-hour shift, get off at around midnight, then dance with servicemen at the Hollywood Canteen until three in the morning. At North American, some five hundred young women volunteered as dance hostesses for nearby Army Air Forces training detachments.

Norma Jean Baker Dougherty, whose husband had shipped out to Australia in the merchant marine, took a job in 1944 as an assembly line worker at the Radio Plane Company in Van Nuys, where she helped make parachutes for target aircraft before she was promoted to painter in the dope room, where she sprayed a liquid plastic called "dope" over the fuselage cloth that would be used as the outer skin of the target plane. A beautiful young Southern Californian, raised in Hawthorne, a blue-collar community near Mines Field, later the Los Angeles International Airport, Norma Jean had no trouble complying with the no-sweater prohibitions of aircraft work. Ever since adolescence, she had been self-conscious and shy regarding her development. With her husband away, Norma Jean drifted into an affair with an Army photographer named David Conover, who was serving under First Lieutenant Ronald Reagan as part of the 1st Motion Picture Unit based in the Hal Roach Studio in Culver City, more commonly known as Fort Roach. Conover discovered Norma Jean in the dope room at Radio Plane, where she had already won a certificate for excellence as a production worker. He asked if he could photograph her. She agreed.

Even as Conover was photographing her in various work-related poses, Norma Jean, just another female defense worker in Los Angeles, glimpsed the possibilities of what haunted so many young women in the defense industries there: the chance to make the transition to starlet. With Conover's encouragement, Norma Jean took sick leave from Radio Plane and enrolled at the Blue Book Modeling Studio and Agency headquartered in the Ambassador Hotel on Wilshire. The agency got Norma Jean a job as a hostess for the Holga Steel Company at an industrial show then being held at the Pan-Pacific Auditorium. A few weeks later, Blue Book sent Norma Jean out to Douglas, where she earned the extraordinary salary of $25 a day modeling as a defense worker for publicity stills. The aircraft industry that had sought to suppress sexuality in its female workers was now hiring a young woman explosive with sexuality to model as an aviation employee. The industry that had once demanded that young women cover themselves in baggy denim shirts was now sponsoring the introduction to Hollywood of Marilyn Monroe.

The emergence of the starlet–defense worker comes as no surprise. Hollywood and aviation had developed side by side in Southern California as parallel industries, each of them expressing and reinforcing the distinctiveness of the region. By 1908 Los Angeles already supported an Aero Club of California, which had two hundred members by 1909. In January 1910 the Chamber of Commerce sponsored a pioneering international air meet on Dominguez Hill, a table-like plateau halfway between Los Angeles and the ocean. Glenn Curtiss established a new speed record of sixty miles an hour, and the French aviator Louis Paulhan (earlier that week, Paulhan and his beautiful wife had led the Grand March opening the annual Charity Ball at the Hotel Maryland in Pasadena) established a new altitude record of 4,165 feet. The Dominguez Hill event had been promoted to dramatize the appropriateness of the Southern California climate to aviation, offering as it did 350 flying (and filming) days a year. Almost simultaneously, the film industry was discovering that same climate. Quite soon, aviation and the film industry, now known as Hollywood, came into synergy. Each industry was dependent upon good weather, open spaces, an abundant supply of electricity, and an intelligent work force. Each industry blended technology and dreams.

On 20 February 1911 Charles Walsh of San Diego, the first licensed pilot in California, took his wife and two children up for a spin—the first recorded passenger flight in American history. Given the distances of Southern California, the remoteness of its cities, and the flourishing of aviation culture, it is not surprising that a new idea, commercial passenger service, should first surface in the Southland—and under the auspices of the film industry. In May 1919 Cecil B. DeMille and a number of Hollywood investors established the Mercury Aviation Company, headquartered at DeMille Field No. 2. Mercury Aviation offered the first regularly scheduled commercial airline passenger service in the United States, with connecting flights from Los Angeles to Venice Beach, Long Beach, Pasadena, Bakersfield, and Fresno. A flight to Pasadena cost $12; a round-trip to Catalina Island (Glenn Martin had made the first successful flight across the channel to Catalina on 10 May 1912) cost $40.

Within the next decade, Los Angeles became the air travel capital of the United States. In early 1927 Maddux Air Lines, in which Cecil B. DeMille held controlling interest, inaugurated twelve-passenger Ford Tri-Motor service to San Diego, Baja California, and Phoenix. By the end of 1928, five Los Angeles–based passenger companies—Western Air Express, Maddux, Standard Air Lines of California, Pickwick Airways, and Transcontinental Air Transport—were connecting Los Angeles with San Diego, Phoenix, and Tucson to the south and Bakersfield, Fresno, and San Francisco to the north, with connecting flights via West Coast Air Transport to Portland and Seattle. On 25 October 1930 Transcontinental Air Transport inaugurated service between Los Angeles and New York, with part of the journey by railway. Los Angeles was now within forty-eight hours of New York, and New York had an equally convenient connection to the Coast. By that time, 1929, the combined aviation industry in Southern California—manufacturing, freight, mail, and passenger flight—approached a billion dollars in cumulative value. Los Angeles County alone had fifty-five airports and landing fields, together with twenty-seven accredited aviation schools with more than 1,500 students of aviation and aviation mechanics. Southern California handled 30 percent of all airmail traffic in the United States and had three thousand of the four thousand licensed pilots in the country.

There were twelve major airplane factories, and one of them, the Ryan Aeronautical Company in San Diego, founded by T. Claude Ryan in 1922, had already manufactured, in February and March of 1927, the most famous sub-orbital aircraft of the century, the *Spirit of St. Louis*. While Californians had missed beating the Wright brothers to the sky in heavier-than-air flight, the design and construction of the *Spirit of St. Louis*, the first aircraft to cross the Atlantic non-stop, implied a measure of catch-up on the part of Southern California aviation. On display today in the National Air and Space Museum of the Smithsonian Institution in Washington, D.C., the *Spirit of St. Louis* remains a primary icon not just of flight itself, and the heroism and romance of flight in the 1920s, but of American technology in general. Life and society, war and peace, were changed inalterably the morning of 20 May 1927 when Charles Lindbergh, the twenty-five-year-old Lone Eagle, taxied the *Spirit of St. Louis* onto the runway at Roosevelt Air Field on Long Island and then at six minutes before eight lifted off for a thirty-three-and-a-half-hour non-stop flight to Paris.

But first the airplane had to be built. For two months, February and March 1927, Franklin Mahoney, president of Ryan Aircraft, and Donald Hall, chief engineer and designer, worked personally with Lindbergh, a sometime Southern California mail pilot, to design and construct the airplane in which Lindbergh hoped to cross the Atlantic and win the $25,000 prize offered by hotelman Raymond Orteig for the first non-stop flight between Paris and New York. On 26 April 1927 the *Spirit of St. Louis* was rolled out of its construction hangar at Ryan Aircraft—almost! It was too big to get through. During construction, ten feet had been added to the wingspan, and the plane now had to be tipped in a complicated maneuver involving derricks and pulleys to fit it through the hangar door. Two days later, 28 April 1927, on Dutch Flats below San Diego, Lindbergh revved his air-cooled J-5 Whirlwind engine and headed skyward. It took only seven and a half seconds and 165 feet of runway for the oversize wings to lift the *Spirit of St. Louis* into the air. After a fortnight of test flights, during which Lindbergh mastered the art of periscope navigation and learned to control the wobbling of his aircraft, the young pilot took off from San Diego at five minutes to four on the afternoon of 10 May 1927 en route to St. Louis on the first leg of his historic journey.

The distance and the load capacity of the *Spirit of St. Louis* had more than peacetime implications. Throughout the 1920s General Giulio Douhet of Italy and Brigadier General William (Billy) Mitchell of the United States were advocating the high-level precision bombing of long-range military targets. As early as the Dominguez Hill air meet of January 1910, German representatives had been on hand to see aviator Roy Knabenshue demonstrate, for the first time in aviation history, the practicality of dropping explosives from a lighter-than-air ship. Four years later, on the verge of the outbreak of the war in Europe, at an air meet held in April 1914 at the Los Angeles County Fair Grounds, Glenn Martin dropped mock explosives on ground positions held by the California National Guard in a pioneering demonstration of the use of airplanes against troops. At the same event, Martin took his aircraft to an altitude of 14,200 feet—1,625 feet higher than the previous record—and a Miss Tiny Broadwick made a pioneering parachute drop from 1,500 feet. It was as if the entire panoply of the combat aviation soon to come were being given a dress rehearsal in Los Angeles. That July, less than a month before the war broke out in Europe, Congress authorized the first Aviation Section within the Army Signal Corps, to be headquartered on North Island, San Diego. In contrast to the doctrine later expounded by Billy Mitchell, Congress did not establish an independent air corps but allowed the Army, the Navy, and the Marines each to develop aviation units. In all three cases, however, Southern California maintained, or at the minimum shared, preeminence as military aviation developed during and after the war. San Diego divided naval and Marine aviation with Pensacola, Florida; and Army aviation was equally divided between California and Texas. Southern California, however, showed a stronger hand in showcasing military aviation, especially the possibilities of long-range bombing as advocated by Douhet and Mitchell.

From 8 to 16 December 1928, Los Angeles County sponsored the National Air Races at Mines Field. It was the largest air show held thus far in the United States. Some $2 million in equipment was displayed, and a paid attendance of more than two hundred thousand spectators crowded Mines Field to see more than five thousand take-offs and landings and innumerable demonstrations by Army, Navy, and Marine Corps pilots, including Charles Lindbergh, now a colonel in the Army Reserve. Intended as a booster event for Los Angeles–based aviation, the National Air Races constituted an early gesture in the direction of the war everyone suspected was coming. The final day of the meet featured a mass formation of 160 military aircraft, including the Martin MB, an American bomber developed in the 1920s, flying in coordination over Mines Field as if to prophesy the waves of fighters and bombers that would, very soon, be flying over Abyssinia and Spain, Poland and Czechoslovakia, Russia and England. In 1935 another suggestion of things to come occurred when the Boeing Company of Seattle began development of a prototype for a long-range bomber called the Flying Fortress. Boeing had an experimental prototype in the air by 1937. The Army Air Corps ordered thirteen.

Although Boeing of Seattle took the lead in developing the Flying Fortress, the companies of Southern California possessed the mass and the depth necessary for large-scale production. By 1937 Southern California had surpassed New York, meaning Long Island, as the leading center of aircraft manufacture, and the California Institute of Technology in Pasadena had become the leading center of aeronautical research and teaching in the nation. In early 1938 General H. H. (Hap) Arnold, chief of staff of the Army Air Corps, met with Southern California companies and discussed the probability of a major gearing-up of the industry. Already, a number of companies were expanding to fill British orders. On 23 June 1938, for example, the British Purchasing Commission headed by Arthur Purvis placed a $25 million order for two hundred planes from Lockheed. Within the next three years, the British had a total of $34 million in orders with Northrop alone. By the summer of 1940, Douglas Aircraft had so much business, a backlog of nearly $140 million in orders, it was forced to inaugurate a three-shift, around-the-clock schedule. With six thousand employees working on a backlog of $85 million, North American went on two shifts. To fill its $169 million in back orders, Lockheed, at 9,600 employees, added an extra half shift. When even more British orders poured in, Lockheed expanded its work force to ten thousand and, running out of plant space, established outdoor assembly lines. All in all, the aircraft industry in Southern California doubled its floor space in 1940 to nine million square feet, then doubled that again in 1941.

By this time, the orders were not only French and British but American as well, coming from the Army Air Corps and the Navy Bureau of Aeronautics, which also purchased for the Marine Corps. In May 1940 President Roosevelt called for the aircraft industry to gear up to produce fifty thousand planes a year. No one knows exactly where Roosevelt got this figure. It meant, however, that the President was asking the aircraft industry to turn out in one year as many planes as had been manufactured in the United States since the invention of flight. By Pearl Harbor 113,000 men and women were at work in the aircraft industry in Los Angeles County, up from 13,000 in January 1939. Taken together, the six Los Angeles County–based aviation companies were soon to surpass citrus and motion pictures as the leading industry of the region. In his State of the Union message of 7 January 1942, a month after Pearl Harbor, Roosevelt upped the ante even further, calling for the construction of 60,000 planes in 1942 and 125,000 in 1943. The industry would never reach these goals, although it did produce 100,000 aircraft in the peak year of 1944.

National press coverage of the burgeoning Southern California aviation industry, incidentally, again and again made reference to the Hollywood connection. In March 1941 *Fortune* described the industry as "an arsenal next door to Hollywood, in a Southern California atmosphere of orange groves, neon signs, movie stars, race tracks, chiropractors, leg art, radio studios, and pension movements." Said *Fortune*: "They are making dive bombers in the Land of Oz."[1] By 1942 a dramatic shift had occurred. Aviation had by now replaced the film industry as the important action in the Southland. Douglas Aircraft, said *Life* on 12 October 1942, employed more people than all the Hollywood studios put together. On the other hand, *Life* noted, the aircraft industry showed the same eclectic mix of people as the Hollywood studios (the pretty girls hoping to be starlets, the merely star-struck, the Folks from the Midwest, the anonymous people who had left behind other lives; one aircraft company reported that there were enough trained musicians in its employ to form two orchestras) and conducted its employee relations with "a fine air of Hollywood razzle-dazzle." There were free bands at noon, entertainment specials at least once a week. Lockheed mounted fashion shows, using models from local department stores.

If aircraft had replaced film in local chic, then the heads of the aviation companies became the new producers, and the aviation factory replaced the film studio as the preeminent industrial structure. Concentrating itself in Los Angeles County, Lockheed eventually encompassed some 250 buildings, for a total of 7.6 million square feet of floor space. Aerial photographs show the North American plant at Inglewood doubling, then tripling, then quadrupling its size as the war progressed. In the spring of 1943, North American took over the Hollywood Park Race Track for its administrative headquarters. Photographs in *Life* show aircraft factories rising up alongside agricultural fields, with field crews harvesting crops in full sight of aviation workers flowing in and out of the facility. (So too did photographs of the 1920s and 1930s show film studios likewise arising amidst lima bean fields on the west side of Los Angeles County.) Gigantic plants such as the Douglas plant in Santa Monica and the Convair plant in San Diego were cities unto themselves, incorporating the full spectrum of urban functions—fire, police (with 162 officers, Douglas had the sixth largest police department in California), transportation, branch city halls, lending libraries, voting booths. While the major film studios had achieved impressive levels of social organization by the late 1930s, the size and social intricacy of the aircraft plants represented a quantum leap in comparison.

Like the Hollywood studios, moreover, aviation plants, while industrial, did not seem so. There were no smokestacks belching pollutants into the air from the aviation factories, no open furnaces spraying sparks and molten metal, no grime on the walls. Like the studios, the aircraft plants exuded an atmosphere of skilled production and technology. Extremely well lit, as were the studios, plant interiors were obviously industrial spaces, but they also bespoke an advanced technology and a level of workmanship that were post-industrial in implication. Like film, aviation was not a heavy industry. Although the word did not exist at the time, aviation was high-tech, hence futurist in its a esthetic appeal. Like a film studio, an aviation plant—its ultra-modern product, the airplane, showcased in orderly production lines and under klieg lights as in a film set—suggested something powerfully creative, something touched by dream and myth, hence glamorous in a Hollywood sort of way. As if to intensify the comparison even further, aviation plants employed Hollywood set designers to camouflage their facilities from possible air attack. Set artists devised cunning color patterns to integrate plants in agricultural areas into the surrounding landscape. In the case of the Douglas plant in Santa Monica, a replica of an entire Santa Monica neighborhood, complete with mock houses and cars, was spread across the roof. Los Angeles might have gone industrial, *Fortune* noted, but it certainly did not look that way.

A photograph in *Life* for 12 October 1942 showed the all-male members of the Aircraft War Production Council in session. Growing out of informal pre-war talks hosted twice a month by Donald Douglas at his Santa Monica plant, the council coordinated the aircraft industry in the Southern California region. Briefly, in January 1942, Washington had been contemplating the appointment of an aircraft czar to coordinate the entire industry; but West Coast aviation leaders had balked, pointing out that they already were accustomed to cooperating and sharing ideas. Obviously, such an emergency wartime council suspended just about all anti-trust provisions of American law and created what was in effect a coordinated industrial policy operating through a temporary instance of capitalist-syndicalism parallel to those of Germany and Japan. Under the guidance of the Aircraft War Production Council, Southern California aviation incorporated liberal and conservative elements in its structure and operations. On the one hand, it was an industrial cartel, but then again: it was government-sponsored. In terms of its employee relations and benefits, it was a planned social democratic utopia.

No studio producer faced the camera with more polished assurance than these new *magnificos* of aircraft manufacture. Not yet fifty, Donald Wills Douglas was the *paterfamilias*, the Louis B. Mayer (or the Henry Ford) of the industry. The first person to take a degree in aeronautical engineering from MIT, graduating in 1914, Douglas had journeyed to the Coast to build planes in Los Angeles for Glenn Martin. In 1920 he had established his own Douglas-Davis Company, appropriately located in an abandoned movie studio at the corner of Wilshire Boulevard and Chelsea Avenue at the eastern border of Santa Monica. His partner David Davis was a sports writer from the Los Angeles *Times* who put up most of the money. Jack Northrop and Gerard Vultee joined Douglas as engineers.

The Douglas company specialized in larger aircraft. Its first plane, the Cloudster, was the first aircraft capable of lifting a load equal to its own weight. In 1928 Douglas moved his operation to Clover Field in Santa Monica and built a new plant. There he pursued the implications of the Cloudster for passenger flight, evolving a series of transports designated the DC-1, the DC-2 (in 1934 the World War I ace Captain Eddie Rickenbacker co-piloted a DC-2 from Los Angeles to Newark, New Jersey, in thirteen hours, four minutes), and finally the DC-3, arguably the most serviceable aircraft in the history of aviation. Announcing the DC-3 in 1935, Douglas sold 803 of these aircraft in the next two years. By 1937 DC-3s were carrying 95 percent of the civilian traffic in the United States. Through the DC-3 Donald Douglas made airplane passenger traffic, if still a luxury, then at least a luxury within the reach of more than just the super-affluent few. During World War II more than ten thousand DC-3s — redesignated the C-47 Skytrain or the C-54 by the Americans, the Dakota by the British — ferried hundreds of thousands of troops and an uncountable amount of freight. Some thirteen thousand DC-3s were in the air by 1945, and almost a half century later stubby, sturdy surviving DC-3s are still taxiing to and from terminals in remote regions of the planet.

As befitted a founder of the industry, Douglas sustained a quasi-Hollywood lifestyle. He lunched daily in a private dining room at the Santa Monica plant and sailed on weekends in his seventy-five-foot yacht *Endymion*. Expanding his parent plant in Santa Monica before and after Pearl Harbor until it became a city unto itself, and expanding a second plant in El Segundo as well, Douglas built in 1942–43 his third and largest plant (it covered 142 acres) adjacent to the municipal airport in Long Beach.

Sitting with Douglas in the *Life* photograph of the Aircraft War Production Council was another founder of the industry, T. Claude Ryan of Ryan Aircraft in

San Diego. If Douglas was the Louis B. Mayer of the aviation industry, the head of the largest and most lavish of the studios, Ryan was the David O. Selznick, the sturdy independent. Ryan's equivalent of Selznick's *Gone with the Wind* had been his airplane *Spirit of St. Louis*, the one masterpiece that justified an entire career.

Donald Milar, president of Vultee, also in the *Life* photograph, was in and of himself a Hollywood-aviation hybrid. In 1938 Milar had come to Vultee from Universal Pictures, making the transition from one primary Southern California industry to another. Located in Downey in southeastern Los Angeles County, adjacent to dairy and chicken farms, Vultee Aviation had been founded as a military manufacturer in 1936 by the dashing, charismatic twenty-seven-year-old Gerard Vultee, who was killed in a plane crash two years later. To the Vultee Company must be given credit for an important innovation, first employed in 1939: an electronically powered assembly line that carried fuselage frames on an overhead track through twenty-five different assembly stations. Borrowed from the automobile industry, Vultee's moving assembly line represented an important departure from the crafts-oriented construction techniques employed in aviation manufacture since the beginning. Photographs of airplane plants from the 1920s and even the 1930s depict groups of craftsmen assembled around a stable airframe, each of them performing his task. Photographs from 1940 onward depict airframes, wings, partially completed fuselages, cockpits, and other components being moved down an assembly line electrically, with each worker performing one task on each component as it passed. Only when these components were completed were they then brought together as a single airplane. Reorganized in 1939 and again in August 1942, Vultee operated as Consolidated-Vultee until 1943, when it was fully merged with Consolidated Aircraft of San Diego to form Convair, which was the Twentieth Century–Fox, the conglomerate giant, of the industry.

Located on a thirty-acre site near the Hawthorne Airport in south-central Los Angeles County, Northrop Aircraft—Jack Northrop, president—was another company that, like Douglas, Ryan, and Vultee, powerfully represented the corporate extension of one charismatic figure. Like Donald Douglas, Jack Northrop was a founder still very much on the scene. Beginning his career with the Loughead Aircraft Company of Santa Barbara in 1916, Northrop, a skilled aeronautical engineer and designer, joined in the early 1920s with the Loughead brothers, Allan and Malcolm, to co-found the Lockheed Aircraft Company of Burbank. Northrop then went on to work for Douglas before forming the Northrop Corporation as a Douglas subsidiary in 1931. In 1939 Jack Northrop, restless, inventive, visionary, left his company, then wholly owned by Douglas, to open a new and independent Northrop plant in Hawthorne. Like T. Claude Ryan and Donald Douglas himself—like D. W. Griffith or Thomas Ince or David O. Selznick, one is tempted to say—Northrop worked best as an independent, which is what he remained throughout the war.

In contrast to these founders, J. H. (Dutch) Kindelberger and his company, North American, located in Inglewood, were imports, North American Aviation having moved to Los Angeles County from Cleveland in November 1935. Like a small independent studio—Republic, say, or Monogram—North American remained conservative, even secretive, in its style. It initially resisted, for example, the hiring of women but by 1944 had accommodated itself to the prevailing mores.

From the start, the Vega Aircraft Corporation, represented by Cortlandt Gross in the *Life* photograph of the Aircraft War Production Council, operated in close symbiosis with Lockheed, which absorbed it in the final days of 1941. Lockheed designated the former Vega plant as Plant A and the original Lockheed plant as Plant B. Vega remained, however, if only as a name, like the Metro in Metro-Goldwyn-Mayer, the vestige of an earlier corporate identity.

Represented in the *Life* photograph by its president Robert Gross, Lockheed was the most dynamic, the most creative, and the most progressive of the aircraft companies: the United Artists of aviation, if you will. Like United Artists, Lockheed had a multi-phased founding, beginning with the Loughead Company of Santa Barbara founded by the Loughead brothers in 1918, which manufactured the Navy seaplane HS2L designed by Glenn Curtiss. The Lockheed company was organized and reorganized in the 1920s, its name simplified from its original Scottish spelling. The last incorporation occurred in 1932 when Lockheed was brought out of receivership. From the start, Lockheed was a design-oriented company. In 1927 it produced the Vega, the first aircraft to depart from the boxy kite-like configuration of conventional aircraft. Although constructed of wood, the Vega employed single cantilevered wings, internally braced, and a shaped monocoque fuselage. Throughout the 1930s Lockheed-Vega continued to design and produce innovative prototypes that distanced the airplane further and further from its origins in the kite and the bicycle. In May 1932 Amelia Earhart soloed across the Atlantic, the first woman to do so, in a Lockheed-Vega. In 1934 Lockheed test-flew the Electra, a pioneering ten-passenger transport. By 1940, thanks to the efforts of such internationally known aviators as Charles Lindbergh, Amelia Earhart, Wiley Post, Sir Charles Kingsford-Smith, Major James Doolittle, and Howard Hughes, Lockheed enjoyed a worldwide reputation as the designer and builder of cutting-edge aircraft. By Pearl Harbor, Lockheed had fifty-four thousand employees, which grew to ninety thousand by 1944, making it the single largest employer in Los Angeles County.

Lockheed was also the most progressive of the aviation companies. Many of the employee policies and services that made Southern California aviation seem an industrial utopia—transportation, food service, counseling, day care, medical, banking, and public utility services, on-site optometry and dental care—first appeared at Lockheed. As a boost to employee morale, Lockheed went so far as to persuade the city of Burbank to rescind an ordinance prohibiting dancing on Sunday. Lockheed welcomed women into its work force and rather early in the war hired 150 sight-impaired workers and five hundred other physically challenged employees.

Southern California aviation was initially a white person's game. As of June 1941 there were only four—four!—African-American production workers on the assembly lines in all of Southern California aviation. In its March 1941 article, *Fortune* noted the overwhelming whiteness—indeed, the Anglo-Saxon blondness—of Los Angeles aircraft workers, so many of them from the Old English stock of Appalachia via the Dust Bowl. Seeking the prototypical aviation worker, *Fortune* selected Cole Weston, a riveter at Lockheed, age twenty-two, "fair, straight-nosed and ingenious, a typical young Anglo-Saxon American worker." *Fortune* also suggested that anti-Semitism was rampant in the industry, especially among management, who perceived Jews as having radical, which is to say, unionizing, tendencies. Shortly after Pearl Harbor, Gerard Tuttle of Vultee openly confessed in a letter to the National Negro Congress that his company hired only workers of the Caucasian race. In June 1941 President Roosevelt had issued Executive Order 8802 establishing a Committee on Fair Employment Practices in an effort to protect the rights of black Americans seeking work in the defense industry. Eighteen months later, Northrop was still hiring no African-Americans.

Lockheed and Douglas pursued a different policy. By the end of 1942, Douglas was employing 1,800 black workers. By the end of the war, African-Americans filled 4.5 percent of all jobs at Douglas. Lockheed ran special bus lines into black neighborhoods to bring workers to its Burbank plant. When the one hundredth black worker was hired at Lockheed, the company brought in heavyweight champion Joe Louis, then a sergeant in the Army, to welcome him onto the line. Lockheed also got a local defense housing project, where many black workers lived, named in honor of Louis. Lockheed public relations made much of the fact that relatives of such black celebrities as Jackie Robinson and Jesse Owens were with the company. Lockheed also supported the construction of an African-American-oriented YMCA in Burbank. In the summer of 1942, Lockheed placed the first black female on the production line. By 1943 Lockheed was employing some three thousand African-American workers. Even such progressive companies as Lockheed and Douglas, however, initially maintained all-black sports teams, canteens, choral groups, and dances, although segregation tended to break down as the war progressed.

In further testimony to its social democratic progressivism, Lockheed maintained excellent relations with its unions both before and during the war. Remarkably, the United States did not require a labor draft during World War II. All labor needs, rather, were met on a voluntary basis. On the other hand, the question of union representation and such union sanctions as the strike became especially controversial in wartime. Nowhere was this more true than in Southern California, the most unorganized region outside the South for a variety of reasons: the mobility of a population comprised of strangers from elsewhere, hence lacking group identity; the fluidity of social and economic conditions, in which few Southern Californians saw themselves as permanently fixed in any one or another class or occupation; the lack of heavy industry, in which union organization was the norm; and, perhaps most important, the effective organization against unions by the oligarchy, led by the fiercely anti-union Los Angeles *Times* and the Los Angeles County Chamber of Commerce, which repeatedly outmaneuvered whatever union sentiment managed to coalesce.

The war changed this, bringing the union movement to a previously impregnable fortress of the open shop. By late 1944 *Fortune* was reporting that Los Angeles could no longer be considered a predominantly open-shop city. The Teamsters, for one thing, had forty thousand members in Los Angeles County alone. The CIO had organized the waterfront and gained a foothold in oil and the garment industry. The major breakthroughs in the anti-union battle lines through which the Teamsters, the AFL, and the CIO raced, like Patton breaking through the German lines with his tanks, were centered in the aircraft industry. Organizing this newly expanded sector, the unions went on to further and further gains, adding a significant Southern Californian component to the 4,250,000 new union members enrolled throughout the United States between Pearl Harbor and V-J Day.

Two unions vied for power in the aircraft industry: the International Association of Machinists (an AFL union) and the United Auto Workers (of the CIO). Of these two unions, the IAM was the more skills- and craft-oriented, hence the more conservative. The UAW, by contrast, pursued a more comprehensive CIO agenda of industry-wide organization, regardless of craft or skills specialties. The CIO union also possessed a more encompassing attitude toward women and minorities, while the IAM remained, at least implicitly, resistant of females and persistently Jim Crow. The UAW also pursued a more aggressive program of confrontation. While the IAM rather easily struck collective bargaining agreements with Consolidated Aircraft of San Diego and Lockheed-Vega in Burbank, the UAW confronted the union-resistant North American Aviation in Inglewood and played hardball. On 5 June 1941 Local 683 of the UAW walked off the line at North American in a wildcat strike. Sixteen hundred pickets barricaded the entrance to the plant. The national leadership of the UAW was appalled by this radical action and claimed that Communist troublemakers were fomenting the strike.

For such a militant CIO union as the United Auto Workers, itself constantly Red-baited by others, to cite a Communist presence in its Southern Californian local represents a most unusual moment in American unionism and leads one to suspect that the national leadership might very well have known what it was talking about. On the verge of entering the war, the United States was being confronted with the spectacle of a vital defense industry being shut down by militant unionists controlled by a local leadership that, if it were not Communist, was at least out of the control of its national.

On 9 June 1941 President Roosevelt stated that he would seize the North American plant if the strike was not called off. That very morning, pickets clashed with police, and Roosevelt ordered in the Army. Soldiers with fixed bayonets established a no-picketing zone around the plant. Over the next two days, the leadership of Local 683 came to recognize that it did not have the support of its parent union and, even more compelling, that a wartime attitude now prevailed in the aviation

industry, which made strikes counter-productive or, worse, unpatriotic, even trea-
sonous. By the 11th everyone had returned to the assembly line, although Army
troops stood guard at North American until July. North American recognized the
UAW in March 1942. Consolidated and Lockheed-Vega had already signed with
the IAM. Eventually, with the exception of Northrop, every aviation company in
Southern California recognized either the IAM or the UAW as a collective bargaining agent. With the exception of a few localized disputes, there were no further
strikes or walkouts in Southern California aviation during the course of the war.

This is not to say that conflict was lacking, especially at Douglas, where Donald
Douglas fiercely resented and resisted unionization. As far back as February 1937,
Douglas had fired all CIO organizers in his Santa Monica plant. A sit-down strike
followed. Some strikers poured flammable solvent on the floor and threatened to
torch the place. Douglas went to court and secured indictments against 345 workers for forcible entry and occupancy. It took 350 police and sheriff's deputies to
clear the plant. If Donald Douglas hated unions before this event, he certainly
hated them after; and Local 683 returned the sentiment, excoriating Douglas as
Donald Duck, the quacking union-basher. Throughout 1942, Douglas warded off
the organization of his plants by matching union gains in other companies. By
the end of 1943, however, his El Segundo plant had gone over to the other side,
and in February 1944 Local 683 of the UAW won collective bargaining elections
at Long Beach, leaving only the Douglas plant at Santa Monica unorganized. And
finally, in October 1944, a majority of workers in the Santa Monica plant elected
the IAM as their collective bargaining agent. Only Northrop now remained unorganized, pointing proudly to the 1943 findings of the Truman Committee investigating wartime procurement and production that absenteeism was heaviest in
union-controlled aircraft plants, especially those with CIO contracts, and lowest
at Northrop.

Not too much credence should be given to this little bit of pique from the Truman
Committee. The productivity statistics of aviation in Southern California remain
today an impressive chapter in the history of American industry: inspiring to Americans of a later era, yet tormenting as well with the possibility that the best days
of the United States as a manufacturer are long past. First of all, there is the
impressive example of the tooling up of an entire industry from 1939 onward and
the training, almost overnight, of a vast skilled and semi-skilled work force. In
industrial terms, aviation workers were by definition an elite. Up to 90 percent of
all jobs connected with airplane manufacturing were at least at the semi-skilled
level. A good percentage of the tasks involved skilled or highly skilled labor. Yet
no one had ever done such work before, the mass manufacture of aircraft, at least
on such a scale. Aviation had a way of attracting not the unemployed but the
skilled and semi-skilled worker already employed elsewhere. Aviation skimmed the
cream from other industries. One cannot overestimate the industrial accomplishment of bringing together so many intelligent, skilled, highly motivated men and

women and transforming them into the single most accomplished corps of industrial workers outside the specialized crafts.

In 1940 West Coast aviation companies strained to produce 3,050 airplanes. In 1944 these same companies were producing 43,312 aircraft. Production tripled between 1940 and 1941 then more than doubled itself in 1942. By 1944 productivity had almost doubled itself again. So too did the productivity of the individual worker. In January 1941 an average worker could produce twenty-three pounds of airframe in a stated period. By November 1943 this same worker was producing seventy pounds of airframe in the same time. In mid-1944 productivity reached ninety-six pounds, where it remained for the duration. All this had its desired effect on price. A Flying Fortress that cost Lockheed $268,373 to produce early in the war cost $136,473 by late 1943. Boeing of Seattle, which built even more planes, could produce a Flying Fortress for as low as $105,560.

There were few, if any, precedents for this productivity and cost-effectiveness, other than those techniques borrowed from the automobile industry. Everything, each tool, each technique, had to be invented on the assembly line. Thousands of workable suggestions came from the rank and file. In 1942 alone, more than thirteen thousand proposals came from the assembly line to management. A third of them were acted on. As the war progressed, more and more suggestions for design changes or modifications came from combat crews and mechanics overseas. Aviation companies established numerous overseas installations, in Northern Ireland and North Africa especially, to handle modifications in the field. Much of what was being built in the aviation plants, together with the techniques employed in manufacturing, was secret, even top secret. Workers could not discuss what they were doing, even with their families; thus security breaches were rare, and aviation plants remained free of sabotage.

Because it was a new industry, and because workers were involved and management was listening, the aircraft industry pioneered ergonomics, the science and art of fitting tools and machinery to human capacities and limits. Workers were constantly making suggestions as to how tools and production techniques could be made more efficient and less fatiguing. As women became more central to the work force, a number of ergonomic adjustments were made on their behalf, such as the lazy arm for moving machinery, which increased productivity throughout the entire work force.

By its very nature, aircraft manufacture necessitated a near-heroic level of synchronized cooperation. Each airplane involved a minimum of 587,000 bits and pieces. From diverse points of origin, these 587,000 parts had to be made, transported, assembled, then further assembled into the component parts of an individual aircraft. Thirty-eight percent of the work was subcontracted. Hundreds of feeder plants prepared airplane parts and systems for assembly at the major sites. Sometimes these feeder plants were subcontractors; sometimes they were owned by the company. Douglas, for example, had sub-assembly sites in Anaheim, El Monte, Fullerton, Elsinore, Santa Ana, and Long Beach, each of these places now transformed into an industrial suburb. All this intricacy of manufacture—thousands of parts flowing together into a river of aluminum and other metals that came to rest, at last, in one plant, then one airplane—had to be tracked and monitored without benefit of computers, through the simple technique of establishing index cards for each bit and part, then each component, then each aircraft. Each shipment generated its own cards, to be shuffled and reshuffled with other index cards so as to track and control the flow of aluminum parts into, eventually, a single aircraft.

Not only did each airplane involve thousands of parts, hence thousands of index cards, planes were manufactured in a consortium. Four companies in addition to Boeing, for example, built Flying Fortresses. By 1944 500 B-17 Flying Fortresses were being produced by the major companies each month: more bombers per month, that is, than all the bombers operative in Germany and Japan. Like component parts themselves, thousands of engineers were combined and recombined in shifting design teams, according to need. At Lockheed, Douglas, Convair, and the other plants, row upon row of engineers at drafting boards extended almost as far as the eye could see beneath equally extensive rows of fluorescent lights. Hundreds of men, and some women, bent silently over their desks designing new aircraft, producing solutions for planes that were of their own design or completing designs for planes sent to them, like the Flying Fortress, from another company. Freed from restrictions of anti-trust, functioning across company lines as a vertically and horizontally integrated cooperative, the aircraft industry was functioning, paradoxically, in an industrial structure similar in some ways to that of Germany and Japan.

At the culmination of the assembly line emerged for shipment to the military the integration of the 587,000 parts: the individual aircraft. Each plane embodied a design solution that met a specific combat requirement and at the same time advanced the state of aviation art. Impressive in size and capacity, the lead element in the manufacturing effort, were the great bombers: the Flying Fortress, first of all, the B-17, first developed by Boeing in 1935 as a weapon for hemispheric defense, capable of carrying ten tons of bombs over a tactical radius of 750 miles, a plane now described by General Hap Arnold, chief of staff of the Army Air Forces, as "the guts and backbone of our worldwide aerial offensive"; the North American Mitchell (B-25), also a pre-war product, which Lieutenant Colonel James Doolittle and his men had taken in low over Tokyo on 18 April 1942 from the deck of the aircraft carrier *Hornèt*; the Convair-Vultee Liberator (B-24), which came in at low altitudes over the oil fields of Ploesti in the spring and summer of 1944; and finally, toward the end of the war, the Boeing Superfortress (B-29), Moderne in its sleek lines and futurist fenestration, capable of speeds over 350 miles per hour and of great altitudes with its pressurized cabin for the crew: an aircraft that embodied the impending possibility of large passenger planes flying great distances at great heights in a world in which oceans and continents could be reduced to mere hours of travel time. It would be this final great bomber, this Superfortress, a

B-29 named *Enola Gay*, that would drop the first of two terrible bombs on the Japanese people, ending the war but also culminating six years of mass destruction from the air. All these bombers were fierce war machines, and they looked so even as they rolled off the line and were taxied by their crews to assembly points for deployment overseas. Lined side by side in long rows on the runways of Southern California, great flying creatures at rest, emanative at once of life and destruction, the bomber aircraft en route to war both exhilarated and terrified those who walked beneath their silent wings.

So too did the fighter aircraft, ranging from the workhorse Mustang (P-51) from North American, designed and produced in a hundred days with the lessons of the Battle of Britain kept in mind: a versatile plane, capable of low-level strafing as well as functioning as a medium-altitude fighter-bomber. Then, later on in the war, came the Northrop Black Widow (P-61), the Stealth Bomber of its era, designed and manufactured under the strictest secrecy: black, sleek, ominous, crouching on the runway before shipment like a panther preparing to strike. The superstar of the fighter class was the Lockheed Lightning (P-38), a twin-fuselage fury, perhaps the most versatile fighting plane in the war: a fighter capable of functioning either as a light bomber, an attack craft, a photo-reconnaissance plane, or, with a compartment pod slung to its underside, a small but effective troop transport. In its fighter mode, the P-38 could soar to an altitude of twenty thousand feet in six minutes at speeds of up to 360 miles per hour. It could dive with even more speed and ferocity. The Germans called it *der gabelschwanz Teufel*, "the fork-tailed devil." Referring to its twin booms, the Japanese designated the P-38 with an ideograph meaning "two airplanes, one pilot." With the P-38 so successful in combat, orders poured in to Lockheed, where the P-38 production line extended out of the plant itself and down an adjacent runway.

Perhaps the most elegant of all the aircraft being produced in Southern California — suggesting civilian value as well as perfection of design — were the great Flying Boats: the Boeing Clipper (C-98), the Consolidated-Vultee Catalina (PBY) and Coronado (PB2Y): great seaplanes, part aircraft, part ship, with their enduring suggestions of trans-Atlantic and trans-Pacific passenger travel before the war. Igor Sikorsky had designed the first twin-engine S-38 Flying Boat for Juan Trippe of Pan American Airways in 1928. In 1931 Sikorsky expanded his design to four engines, then augmented it further into the Sikorsky Clipper S-42: a hotel in the air featuring a cocktail bar where passengers might sip iced martinis before sitting down to an elegant meal served with silver and porcelain china on white linen and then, later, after brandy and conversation, retiring for the night into private sleeping compartments. The S-42 had a range of 2,500 miles at cruising speeds of 150 miles per hour, perfect for transoceanic travel. Next was developed the Martin Flying Clipper (M-35) of 1935: four engines, twenty-one tons, capable of carrying forty-eight passengers for even longer distances and with even greater amenities. Boeing entered the Clipper market with its B-314, the last of the pre-war Flying Boats, designed to carry seventy-four passengers across the Atlantic. Twelve were built between 1939 and 1941. With the outbreak of the war, Martin introduced the Mars, the last in its great Flying Boat series. The Mars weighed seventy tons, had a wingspan of 200 feet, and was powered by four two-thousand-horsepower engines. Six were built during the war, and four remained in naval service until 1956. A Mars Flying Boat had a cargo capacity of thirty-five thousand pounds and could be configured to carry either 133 troops or eighty-four litters with twenty-five seats.

This dream of lifting great numbers of men over the ocean by Flying Boat brought together two of the most intriguing industrialists of the Second World War, each of them California-based: Henry Kaiser and Howard Hughes. No more eccentric collaboration can be imagined than this between the tall, lanky, forty-two-year-old Texan Howard Hughes, heir to the Hughes Tool Company, a dashing test pilot, a movie producer and collector of beautiful women, whom he hoarded like art in a museum, yet for all his flamboyance a man growing progressively more secretive; and the rotund, extroverted, self-made Henry Kaiser, age sixty, faithful to his one and only Bess. At the point of their brief collaboration, in the spring and summer of 1942, Kaiser was already, whether or not his colleagues acknowledged it, one of the most important industrialists—in terms of industrial and social practice—in the entire war effort. Although they differed in so many respects, Howard Hughes and Henry Kaiser had in common a streak of eccentric greatness turned to industrial creativity.

Henry J. Kaiser, as he always called himself, was largely a product of self-invention. Born and raised in upstate New York, he turned to photography as a teenager, then moved west to the state of Washington, where he got into the road-paving business, there and in Cuba. Not that Kaiser initially knew anything about paving roads, or about photography for that matter; he merely threw himself into a pursuit and learned it through practice. Road-paving on a large scale in Cuba in the 1920s trained Kaiser in the management of men and equipment. From there he went into the construction business, making a stunning debut as the president of the consortium of Six Companies that built Boulder/Hoover Dam in the early 1930s. From this experience evolved a structure of organization and procedure which Kaiser maintained for the rest of his professional career.

Stout, manic, citified, Kaiser was anything but a field man. His genius consisted, rather, in determining great projects, assembling teams, then handling the politics and finance. During the construction of Boulder/Hoover Dam, for example, Kaiser spent most of his time in Washington, D.C., working on finance and governmental regulations. During his next big project, constructing the dams and aqueducts of the Metropolitan Water District of Southern California and the Grand Coulee Dam in western Washington for the Bureau of Reclamation, Kaiser remained headquartered in his corporate office in Oakland, a city that eventually became for all practical purposes a Kaiser company town.

Kaiser had a knack for spotting talent, young men usually, far younger than normal for the responsibilities he assigned them, beginning with his son Edgar, a

talented field manager, Clay Bedford, Edgar's fraternity brother, and Eugene Tre-
fethen, another young Cal Berkeley graduate. These young men, well before they
were thirty, played major roles in the construction of Parker Dam, Imperial Dam,
and Grand Coulee Dam by the Kaiser Companies. Kaiser, meanwhile, was doing
what he did best: wrangle, wheedle, finagle, prod, finesse—most of this in the
course of *blitzkrieg* calls on government officials or telephone conferences with
his men in the field. Kaiser loved the telephone. He played it like a Stradivarius
violin. Subordinates could expect calls any time of the day or night, seven days a
week.

Living for work, the Wizard of Oz behind the green curtain of countless construction projects, Kaiser relaxed with the same heedless prodigality with which
he worked. Loving fine food, good scotch, and even better cigars, he grew to
gargantuan proportions, which he enveloped in great double-breasted suits whose
lapels flapped in the wind like the sails of a schooner. In middle age, he grew
bald and cherubic behind his rimless glasses, smiling through a pronounced overbite. He was an indoor man by inclination, despite the outdoor nature of construction; his favorite sport consisted in terrifying Lake Tahoe with his speedboat, an
activity that did not, alas, burn many calories.

His Tahoe speedboat, in fact, was the closest Kaiser had come to matters maritime by 1940. Within five years, however, Kaiser had built 1,490 ships, for a total
budget of $4 billion, in his California, Oregon, and Washington shipyards: 821
Liberty ships—small, fast, ten-thousand-ton freighters; 219 Victory ships, a larger
version of the Liberty; fifty small escort aircraft carriers; and an assorted number
of tankers, tenders, and other craft. All in all, the Kaiser shipyards built 30 percent
of American wartime shipping. Napa vineyards did a solid business during the war
preparing bottles of champagne with red, white, and blue streamers for the launching of ships built by Henry J. Kaiser.

Kaiser's shipbuilding career was based on the same formula as his construction
career: a big project, a bold approach, and lots of government money. In late 1940
a British commission came to the United States with contracts for sixty cargo ships.
Representing the Six Companies, Kaiser traveled with his young staff to New York
to bid on the contracts. He had no previous shipbuilding experience. One of his
staffers later claimed that he was sent to the New York Public Library to secure
books on shipbuilding design and terminology for Kaiser and his staff to study
before making a successful presentation to the British commission. Wisely, the Six
Companies joined with the experienced Todd Shipyards to secure the British
contracts. Thirty ships were to be constructed on each coast. Two companies were
organized: Todd–Bath Iron Shipbuilding in the East and Todd-California in the
West. Kaiser put his financial interest into Todd-California. As soon as he had
secured the British contracts, Kaiser phoned Clay Bedford, then constructing a
naval air station in Corpus Christi, Texas. Kaiser informed Bedford that they were
going to get into the shipbuilding business in Richmond, a small bayside town
north of Oakland. Within six months, Clay Bedford had the Richmond shipyards

ready for work, and on 14 April 1941 the keel was laid for the *Ocean Vanguard*, the first of the 747 ships that would be built at Richmond over the next five years.

All this sounds like a fable, even a fantasy, of American know-how; but it happened. Under Clay Bedford's supervision, Kaiser's construction teams scooped bay-side drydocks from the earth, as if the land itself were being prepared to germinate ships, and assembled with equal haste the cranes and derricks that would soon be used to swing into place entire sections of ships that had been pre-assembled in adjacent sites. For a half century and more, naval vessels had been built on the Pacific Coast, most noticeably on Mare Island in San Francisco Bay and at the Union Iron Works in South San Francisco, but never before on such a scale. In traditional shipbuilding techniques, a keel was laid and a ship was constructed, section by section, in its totality, just as craftsmen once stood around an airframe and built airplanes one at a time. Like their counterparts in the aircraft industry, the Kaiser shipyards mastered the art of pre-assembling entire sections of ships, then fitting these sections together in fast-track construction.

To show the country that a new player was on the shipbuilding scene, but also to boost morale among workers, Clay Bedford produced a Liberty ship at Richmond in November 1942 in record time. The keel for the SS *Robert E. Peary* was laid on Sunday morning, 6 November. Four days, fifteen hours, and twenty-six minutes later, the ship was launched. Fourteen days from the laying of the keel, the *Peary* was sailing out of the Golden Gate, fully loaded with war supplies from the Pacific. Some traditional shipbuilders scoffed, calling this a stunt. They pointed to the fact that large portions of the SS *Robert E. Peary* had already been pre-assembled before the keel was laid. That, Henry J. Kaiser replied, was precisely the point.

And besides: Henry J. Kaiser was always being criticized. In testimony before the Truman Committee in the summer of 1942, Kaiser was prodded to admit that he had never even seen a ship launched. He came back before the Truman Committee on a number of subsequent occasions, becoming especially red-faced when one of his ships, the SS *Schenectady*, an oil tanker, broke apart shortly after being launched in Portland in January 1943. Kaiser was also forced to grit his overbite when critics called his escort carriers Kaiser Coffins. Kaiser had personally come up with the idea of small aircraft carriers to be used for pursuit and convoy protection and sold the idea to President Roosevelt, who personally approved the program. Despite the alliterative sobriquet, resembling the Dugout Doug charge leveled against General Douglas MacArthur, Kaiser's pocket carriers played a crucial role in extending air power on convoys and throughout the fleet.

As in the case of his pre-war dam-building, Kaiser tended to leave his son Edgar and Clay Bedford in charge of field operations while he took care of the government. He encouraged the two men—Edgar in charge of the Portland/Vancouver shipyards, Clay Bedford in charge of Richmond—to compete against each other. The two young men finished the war in a virtual dead heat, 747 ships for Bedford, 743 for Edgar Kaiser. Roosevelt saw Henry Kaiser as the essence of the New Deal industrialist, a man capable of working with government on the largest possible scale. Kaiser's critics used this against him, claiming that Kaiser had never been successful unless he was publicly employed. Kaiser, they claimed, was a socialist industrialist, not a capitalist entrepreneur.

Kaiser's critics were partly correct. Of all major industrialists of the period, Kaiser had the broadest, most encompassing social philosophy. He maintained close relations with his unions, much to the disgust of many industrialists, who accused him of fostering featherbedding and other non-productive practices. Kaiser also insisted that African-American workers get an even break in his shipyards, although he was forced, finally, to go along with many of the Jim Crow restrictions favored by the shipbuilding unions. Despite this, thousands of black workers migrated to Richmond to work for Kaiser, attracted in part by his reputation for fair play. During the war, Kaiser gave a number of speeches regarding the necessity of pensions and pre-paid comprehensive medical coverage in the post-war era. Astonishingly, he provided such coverage for a significant percentage of the two hundred thousand men and women working in his shipyards and associated companies. Obsessed with medicine (he would later keep available a doctor's black leather bag for his own medications, which he sometimes dispensed to others when emergencies arose), Kaiser went so far as to claim that his mother had died in his arms because of inadequate medical attention. Although this was not true, the story was not so much a lie as it was a magician's fable, a fictional parable intended to illustrate a point. Henry J. Kaiser, after all, was constantly creating his own reality, and much of what he created came true.

In the mid-1930s, Kaiser began to offer workers on his construction projects in the deserts of Southern California a program of pre-paid comprehensive medical coverage. The idea was simple: everyone contributed a small amount per month, whether sick or healthy. These pre-payments created a fund sufficient to support a program of comprehensive medical care for all Kaiser employees. To run this system, Kaiser recruited a young surgeon from the USC–Los Angeles County Hospital surgery program, Sidney Garfield, a freckle-faced, sandy-haired physician of Russian Jewish background whose entrepreneurship in matters medical equaled that of Kaiser. From Desert Center, Garfield took the program up to the Grand Coulee project in Washington; and when Kaiser got into the shipbuilding business in 1941–42, he secured Garfield's release from the Army Medical Corps to run the health care program at Richmond and Portland/Vancouver. The 4-Fs of America, meanwhile—the sick, the lame, the halt—were pouring into the Kaiser shipyards to build Liberty ships. One physician in attendance described the working population at Richmond as an ambulatory museum of American diseases.

Under Garfield's supervision, physicians established a Permanente Field Hospital in Richmond, named in honor of a permanently running creek near Kaiser's Permanente Cement Plant in Cupertino south of San Francisco. Kaiser liked the word *Permanente*, with its suggestion of healing waters and permanence. Organized as a health plan foundation, the Kaiser-Permanente program continued autonomously after the war until it was providing, by the 1980s, prepaid comprehensive medical care to more than five million Americans. In the case of his health care program, in which he played an equal role as founder along with Garfield and his physicians, Kaiser bridged the public philosophy of the New Deal and private capitalism. Criticized in the 1940s and 1950s as socialized medicine, the Kaiser Health Plan and its affiliated Permanente Medical Groups in reality had the very opposite effect. They proved that private social medicine could remain free of government while meeting mass health care needs. By the 1960s nearly a third of the entire population of the San Francisco Bay Area was enrolled in the Kaiser Health Plan. Toward the end of his life, surveying all that he had created, Kaiser stated in a rare moment of self-reflection that the health program that he co-founded and that bore his name, Kaiser-Permanente, represented his most lasting contribution to society.

By late 1944 *Fortune* was describing Henry J. Kaiser as in and of himself one of the major industrial resources of the West. The one wartime industry Kaiser was failing to enter successfully, however, was aviation. In May 1942, as German submarines devastated Allied shipping in the Atlantic, Kaiser had yet another idea: the construction of great Flying Boats, Liberty ships of the air, which could ferry cargo and troops above the submarine-infested Atlantic. Kaiser proposed that such giant Flying Boats weigh as much as five hundred tons—half the weight of a Liberty ship! Such aircraft, inspired as much by Jules Verne and H. G. Wells as by any real-life aviation precedent (Kaiser's Flying Boat was fifteen times the weight of any existing Flying Clipper), could ferry hundreds of fully equipped troops and tons of supplies directly from the continental United States to theaters of operation. Kaiser was fully confident that he could bring such Flying Boats into operation by late 1944, just in time for the invasion of Europe. After all, he had not known port from starboard two years earlier and was now producing Liberty ships galore.

In the weeks that followed, Kaiser refined his proposal. Instead of the gigantic five-hundred-ton Flying Boat he first proposed, he now leveled his sights on something more plausible: the mass construction of five thousand seventy-ton Flying Boats, each of them capable of carrying one hundred fully equipped soldiers. A fleet of five thousand such craft, Kaiser argued, could rapidly land a half-million-man Army in Europe. While Kaiser's first proposal of a five-hundred-ton plane seemed fantastic, and hence threatened no one, his second proposal sent shocks of apprehension into the aircraft industry. After all, it was thoroughly plausible that Kaiser could pull together and implement the Flying Boat project in his shipyards. If Kaiser could learn to build Liberty ships, why not airplanes? Fearful of being upstaged, of being forced to have the entire aircraft industry on the West Coast share equal billing with Henry J. Kaiser, who would soon dominate resources and the spotlight, the aircraft companies went into high-gear opposition. Robert Gross, president of Lockheed, and Donald Douglas were especially effective lobbying in Washington against Kaiser's bid to build five thousand Flying

Boats. At the end of the wrangling, Kaiser had funds only to build one experimental prototype in partnership with Hughes Aircraft of Culver City.

The Flying Boat prototype soon dropped from the radar screen of Kaiser's attention. He had so much else to do. Howard Hughes, on the other hand, kept the project alive through the war at Hughes Aircraft, a small, experimental subsidiary of the Hughes Tool Company. In short order, the Flying Boat became one of Hughes's many obsessions, like test-piloting, producing movies, or putting actresses under contract. Hughes spent hundreds of hours through 1943 and 1944 with his engineers, designing and testing miniature prototypes. By October 1943, plans for a spectacular Flying Boat had emerged: a two-hundred-ton craft, powered by eight Pratt and Whitney engines, with a wingspan of 320 feet, the largest airplane ever built.

In nature and the arts, genres frequently reach a point of gigantism, of epic proportions, just before they go permanently into decline. Emergent in the 1930s, Flying Clippers would remain in use through the 1950s, especially in the Indian Ocean and the South Pacific; but their best moment had already passed, and Hughes's Flying Boat represented a culmination, a defiant gigantism, before obsolescence. In aesthetic terms, Hughes's Flying Boat was also a culminating masterpiece of Art Deco: the Rockefeller Center, if you will, of maritime aircraft. Because he and Kaiser had lost the political battle in Washington, Hughes was prohibited from using scarce metals and was forced to build his Flying Boat of plywood on a spruce frame. Hand-crafted, hand-sanded, the Spruce Goose, as it was called, represented a very expensive throwback to the laborious crafts-construction of aircraft in the 1920s and early 1930s. Hughes was forced to scour the forests of Minnesota for wood and the entire nation for available skilled cabinetmakers to work, secretly, in Culver City.

The Flying Boat was still under construction when Japan surrendered. Under pressure after the war from the Senate Committee to Investigate the National Defense Program to justify the cost of continuing to build the great craft, Hughes had it disassembled in the spring of 1946 and shipped in sections by truck convoy to an assembly site and dock on Terminal Island off Long Beach. By November the reassembled colossus was floating in the water, awaiting further testing. With Howard Hughes at the controls, the Flying Boat taxied from its dock on 2 November 1947, a Sunday morning, on what was supposed to be a taxi checkout. Hughes, however, lifted the behemoth into the air for a brief flight. He did this on impulse, but also because the ship, so beautifully designed, wanted to fly. What Henry J. Kaiser envisioned as great fleets crossing the Pacific came down to one gigantic aircraft lifting off at seventy knots for a brief flight that was in effect a hail and farewell to the golden age of Flying Boats.

In taking care of the health of his shipyard workers, Henry J. Kaiser assumed a formidable task. Shipbuilding—the swinging into place of unwieldy bulkheads, the ceaseless welding that pitted super-charged fire against resistant steel, the noise, the grime, the heat, the constant possibility of terrible accidents—attracted a much more rough-and-ready class of workers than aviation. World War II–era photographs depict aircraft workers streaming into and out of their plants in almost casual attire, so many of them smiling, as on a college campus. Shipyard workers walked to their work sites in bulky denim, lunch pails in hand, and emerged from work more noticeably fatigued, peering at the world through grime- and sweat-stained faces. Aviation workers were discernibly middle class. Many of the women in their midst were glamorous and photogenic. Shipyard workers, by contrast, so many of them migrants, had the gaunt, lined faces of the Dust Bowl or the ebony features of the African-American South. Their power was not that of glamour or prettiness but of industrial Labor with a capital L.

The aircraft industry housed its people in Los Angeles and its suburbs. Many of them, in fact, were middle-class residents of the region, already housed. Shipbuilding, by contrast, created entirely new towns such as Richmond, California, a Wild West frontier boomtown, World War II style. Before the war, Richmond was a sleepy bayside town of twenty-four thousand. Then came Kaiser and the construction over the next three years of 486 Liberty ships, one-fifth of the Liberty ships produced in World War II, each of them launched an average of 48.5 days from the laying of the keel. The population of Richmond quadrupled during the war as seventy-five thousand workers and their families poured in. The black population jumped from four hundred to fourteen thousand. In 1943 housing was so scarce in and around the Richmond shipyards, single men would deliberately work the night shift, sleep through the morning and early afternoon in public parks, clean up in gas stations, then spend the evening in restaurants and bars before going to work. In the first year or so of the war, arrests averaged four thousand a month. ("Drunks," noted a local police officer, "knifers, rapists, attackers, hop-heads, harlots, wife-beaters, murderers—anything you like.")[2] With schools operating in double shifts, truancy soared by 25 percent as boys cut classes to shine shoes outside shipyards or in taverns, run errands (cigarettes, liquor, numbers, prophylactics), or otherwise get into mischief. Police officers assigned to the juvenile division in Richmond in 1944 handled an impressive average of 240 cases a month. This represented a delinquency arrest rate of eighty-seven per one thousand juveniles as compared to the California average of twenty-five. Prostitution proved a perennial problem. To discourage soliciting, Richmond bars such as the Nut Club, the Denver Club, and the Red Robin—packed from early morning to the wee hours after midnight, jukeboxes blaring, crap games out back, hustling everywhere—posted signs saying UNESCORTED WOMEN MUST REMAIN WITHOUT ESCORTS, an ordinance more honored in the breach than in the observance.

The housing shortage at Richmond had been significantly corrected by 1944. Through the second half of 1942 and throughout 1943, the city of Richmond and the Kaiser shipyards joined the Maritime Commission, the Federal Public Housing Authority, the Farm Security Administration, and private developers to build some thirty thousand dwelling units, including dormitories for single men and women. With federal assistance, the city of Richmond shipped a Third Avenue Elevated Railway train from New York City and ran it between Oakland and Richmond via San Pablo Avenue, thereby enabling shipyard workers to commute from existing housing stock in Oakland and Alameda. The contrast between ship-yard housing and housing for aircraft workers followed true to form. The shipyard-related housing created at Richmond and Vallejo in the East Bay, Marin City in Marin County, and Potrero Hill, Hunters Point, and Candlestick Cove in San Francisco was overtly industrial in appearance. Everything bespoke hasty construc-tion, inexpensive materials, wartime necessity. Most of these structures, sitting on mud flats or hastily bulldozed hills, easily made the transition to low-income pub-lic housing projects after 1945.

In Los Angeles, by contrast, private developers, sensing the long-term middle-class ambitions and financial capabilities of many aircraft workers, developed whole neighborhoods of one-story, two-bedroom bungalows for sale to them. A photograph in *Life* for 12 October 1942 showed the families of the 1400 block of Oak Street in West Los Angeles standing in front of their newly purchased bun-galows, lawn after lawn filled with smiling aircraft workers and their families. The city of San Diego, which experienced a 75 percent growth between 1942 and 1945, thanks to Consolidated-Vultee/Convair, Ryan Aircraft, the Navy, and the Marine Corps, showed this same burgeoning of middle-class ambition. The Linda Vista Housing Project in San Diego, for example, built by the National Housing Agency for the workers at Consolidated-Vultee, was featured in design critic John En-tenza's *Arts & Architecture* magazine in November 1944 as a prime example of how wartime housing, properly designed, could anticipate the amenities of the post-war era. The 4,846 dwelling units of Linda Vista encircled a thirteen-acre Commercial Center, carefully designed by Whitney Smith and Earl Giberson, which featured the layout and conveniences of the post-war shopping center. Traf-fic, parking, pedestrian, freight, and shipping access and other retail conveniences were carefully planned. Linda Vista anticipated, almost on the level of utopian statement, what could be achieved in urban and suburban neighborhoods and shopping centers following the war.

Of the three major civilian-administered shipbuilding facilities in California—the California Shipbuilding Corporation shipyards on Terminal Island in Los An-geles Harbor, the Kaiser shipyards in Richmond, and Marinship in Marin County—only Marinship displayed a middle-class texture analogous to that of the aircraft factories. Part of this was due, no doubt, to the fact that Marinship was small (fifteen thousand workers by 1944) and located in the picturesque town of Sausalito in affluent Marin County. Small, selectively staffed, Marinship was al-most a boutique operation in comparison to its sprawling counterpart on the east-ern side of San Francisco Bay. Established in March 1942 by former members of the Six Companies who had built Boulder/Hoover Dam, Marinship was directed by a who's who of California corporate and industrial blue bloods, including Ken-neth and Stephen Bechtel, Felix Kahn, and John McCone, a Bechtel employee who would soon be serving as high commissioner in Germany and later founding director of the CIA. In the course of the war, Marinship built fifteen Liberty ships and thirty single-screw tankers of the Mission class. Standing as launch sponsors along with the usual celebrities, highly placed, and socially prominent were the wives of yard workers, machinists, electrical engineers, materials managers, hull inspectors, and paint superintendents. Such inclusiveness suggested the shared, and middle-class, social culture of Marinship during the war. Even the names chosen for the ships reflected it: the T-2 tankers were named in honor of California missions; the fleet oilers in honor of Native American peoples; and the EC-2 Liberty freighters in honor of prominent figures from California history, including Jack London and Sun Yat-sen, the sometime San Franciscan who served as first president of the Republic of China.

Like the aircraft factories of Southern California, Marinship anticipated the well-being that could characterize the post-war period, should the enlightened industrial policies of wartime continue. In doing this, moreover, Marinship, the Kaiser shipyards, the aviation companies, and the other enlightened California-based wartime industries stood as evidence that California, north and south, had become industrialized—and in many instances in a socially progressive manner. In Northern California, San Francisco Bay was ringed with shipbuilding, ship repair, and port facilities. In Southern California, aircraft manufacture had put the south coast at the center of a national industrial network. Los Angeles County stood second only to Detroit in total war production. By early 1945 the value of the aircraft industry in Southern California exceeded in dollar volume the entire industrial value of Detroit prior to the war. Los Angeles, in short, had become the Detroit of American aircraft.

Other industries rode the crest of this wave. By 1944 Los Angeles and Orange counties had more than four thousand separate defense plants involved in every aspect of manufacture. The garment industry alone had grown by 475 percent, transforming Los Angeles into the fourth largest center of garment manufacture in the United States. Southern California stood second only to Akron, Ohio, in the manufacture of tires. Manufacturing and industrial communities were scattered through the region: in Torrance, Wilmington, Long Beach, El Segundo, Santa Monica, Culver City, Burbank, Glendale, Pasadena, Alhambra, Azusa, and El Monte.

California even had its own steel mill, the Kaiser Steel plant at Fontana, fifty miles east of Los Angeles amidst the vineyards and orange groves of San Bernardino County. Ever the master of the bureaucratic end run, Kaiser was initially able to finagle sufficient steel for his shipyards. In the early fall of 1942, however, Kaiser ran afoul of the Office of Price Administration for buying steel on the black market. Requiring cement when he entered the construction business, Kaiser had built his own cement factory near Permanente Creek in Cupertino. He was now determined to build his own steel mill, financing it with more than $115 million in loans from the Reconstruction Finance Corporation. Initially, Kaiser wanted to build his steel plant near the seashore for shipping convenience, but federal officials made him locate it eighty miles inland in case of invasion or bomber attack. By 30 December 1942, Kaiser had the first blast furnace at his Fontana steel mill in operation, three months ahead of the equally new government-owned steel mill in Geneva, Utah, forty miles south of Salt Lake City. Built by the Defense Plant Corporation, the government-owned and-operated Geneva Steel Company was being run by U.S. Steel as a non-profit subsidiary. Beating Big Steel into production in the far West—this from an industrialist never before in the steel business— Henry J. Kaiser tweaked U.S. Steel in Geneva and the Big Steel men of Pittsburgh.

Even before the war was over, Kaiser was describing his Fontana steel mill as proof and symbol of the new industrial economy in Southern California. When the war was over, Kaiser wanted Fontana to produce tin plate, cold-rolled steel sheets, tubular steel for plumbing and natural gas, pipes for the oil industry, and whatever else it would take to back the post-war building boom that Kaiser was certain would happen. In July 1945 Kaiser had the *chutzpah* to bid against U.S. Steel for the right to purchase the Geneva mill after the war. U.S. Steel eventually purchased the Geneva facility for the bargain basement price of $47.5 million. In November 1950 Kaiser presented a check to the Reconstruction Finance Corporation for $91 million. He eventually paid off the entire RFC loan for Fontana, returning $1.23 for every dollar he had borrowed from the federal government.

By February 1945 *Fortune* was announcing that the Pacific Coast was no longer an economic colony of the East. Previously, the Coast had exported raw materials for manufacture elsewhere and was dependent upon outside financing. Now, as the war drew to a close, the Coast reveled in its newfound financial and industrial power. Henry J. Kaiser, as an example, had secured much of his financing from the San Francisco–headquartered Bank of America, whose founder and chairman A. P. Giannini shared much of Kaiser's social philosophy and saw his bank as the bedrock of California's financial independence. Southern California even had a new industrially related problem, smog, although the term had not yet entered the general vocabulary; and on 28 October 1943 the Board of Supervisors of Los Angeles County established a Smoke and Fume Commission to deal with it.

Even as *Fortune*, the New York *Times*, and others were announcing this obvious and stunning debut of California as an industrial and financial power, however, a counter-current of anxiety chilled the optimism. Could or would it last after the war? Had California experienced an enduring transformation or merely a wartime mobilization? As early as April 1942, economist Robert Pettengill of the University of Southern California was enumerating the problems that the defense industry in the Southland would face after the war. Eastern industries, Pettengill emphasized, existed before the war with specific tooling and established markets. Converted to wartime production, Eastern industry would revert to its normal functioning with the coming of peace. Southern California industry, by contrast, was almost purely war-related. Could these wartime industries, Pettengill asked, adapt themselves to post-war markets? In late 1944 and early 1945, this question became an articulated fear in corporate and governmental circles. In 1944 the state of California established a Reconstruction and Reemployment Commission, which began to address, among other things, the problem of continuing the present level of employment in peacetime. How could the state cope with the loss of an esti-mated eight hundred thousand jobs in shipbuilding and aircraft manufacture, not to mention the other defense industries, each with its attendant economies? The problem became further compounded with the estimate that as many as eight hundred thousand servicemen and -women would return to California, or relocate there, following their release from the armed forces. Cumulatively, then, more than 1.6 million jobs, possibly more, remained in uncertainty. Discussion of the problem of post-war readjustment reached such intensity by early 1945 that both the Reconstruction and Reemployment Commission and the defense industry, fearing a drop in morale and productivity, organized behind the slogan "Let's Finish the War First!"

There were many optimistic scenarios. Pointing to the steel mills at Geneva and Fontana, Henry J. Kaiser stated that California had passed a point of no return. It now possessed an industrial economy, which would create its own markets. Even though others forecast the demise of shipbuilding, Kaiser was proposing by late 1944 nothing less than the complete revamping of the American merchant fleet through the mass construction of container-cargo freighters keyed to automated dockside facilities. Even longshoreman leader Harry Bridges partially agreed, al-though he had serious reservations regarding the new technologies of loading and unloading ships. That same year, the Ports of Los Angeles, Long Beach, and San Diego launched multi-million-dollar programs of improvement. Buoyed by the fact that the various ports on San Francisco Bay—the Port of San Francisco, the Port of Oakland, the Port of Stockton, the various shipbuilding and military in-stallations at Sausalito, Mare Island, Alameda, and Redwood City—had made the San Francisco Bay Area, taken collectively, the largest port in the nation, the Port of San Francisco began drawing up plans in February 1945 for a $30 million World Trade Center on the Embarcadero.

State officials, meanwhile, were encouraged by the fact that California was fin-ishing the war with half a billion dollars in unemployment insurance reserves. Progressives, including Governor Earl Warren, began discussing a new era of pub-lic works, highway and water projects especially, as a way of creating post-war employment. Prior to the war, after all, highways and motor transportation had accounted for an estimated 430,000 jobs in the state. On the local level, the Bureau of Power and Light of the City of Los Angeles embarked upon a three-year plan to spend $35.5 million on new power production and distribution facilities and an eight-year plan to spend $23 million on the improvement of water distribution. In augmenting its electricity and water, the Los Angeles oligarchy was determined to keep both the city and the county as a competitive industrial center.

What would happen to the aircraft industry? The doomsday scenario spoke for itself. Aviation, it could be argued, would revert to near pre-war levels of production. More positively, aircraft economists pointed to the fact that the reduction of the three-shift schedule to one shift could keep the industry economically viable in peacetime. In late 1944 Convair signed a contract with Greyhound to develop a new lightweight bus. Other plans included the transfer of aircraft technology to the manufacture of lightweight automobiles, household appliances, and pre-fabricated homes. Other economists looked to aviation itself. After the war, they predicted, a market would emerge for private aircraft among the two million qualified pilots in the United States. Futurist illustrations from the period showed Californians commuting to and from work by gyro-copters capable of vertical and horizontal deployment.

By late 1944 Northrop, Convair, Douglas, and Lockheed already had post-war projects in development. Northrop was working on a passenger version of its still-secret Flying Wing. Convair had plans for a four-hundred-passenger liner. On the drawing boards at Douglas was the DC-7, intended to carry 108 passengers. Pan Am and other airlines, meanwhile, had orders in at Douglas for a total of 130 DC-4s, DC-6s, and the DC-7 under development. Even before the war, in 1939, engineers at Lockheed had begun work on the four-engine L-049 Constellation, which Lockheed had in the air by late 1944. Not fully ready until 1946, the hump-backed, triple-tailed Lockheed Constellation Transport, refitted as a passenger plane, would dominate transcontinental and transoceanic passenger service through the 1950s. Also in the air by early 1944: the P-59 and the P-80, jet-propelled aircraft capable of speeds of up to 550 miles per hour. Two years earlier, on 2 October 1942, the XP-59A, America's first jet aircraft—airframe by Bell Aircraft, engines by General Electric—was test-flown at Muroc Dry Lake, now Edwards Air Force Base, in south-central California. Designated the P-59, sixty-six of these aircraft were built and used as trainers. Lockheed and North American built a total of 243 Shooting Stars (P-80) before the war ended. Neither the P-59 nor the P-80 jet fighters were ever used in combat, but they did prefigure a whole new aviation economy.

This was little consolation to the three out of four aircraft workers in Southern California who had lost their jobs by 1946. These men and women had geared themselves up to unprecedented levels of skill and productivity. They had chosen to become Southern Californians. (As early as 1943, more than 75 percent of six thousand surveyed employees at North American stated that they wanted to remain in Southern California after the war.) Now, they worried, what would become of their skills, their jobs, their lives? This question, powerful enough for men, bore a special intensity for women. They, after all, had made the most significant gains, in Southern California and throughout the nation. In aviation they had become production workers, lead-women, sub-forewomen, in some cases the forewoman herself. Even in shipbuilding, a more restrictive industry, they had won a place for themselves as welders. At the California Shipbuilding Corporation, women had been trained in reading blueprints, which was a primal form of power in the industry. At Marinship, women had accounted for 40 percent of the work force. How could they now return to waitressing, file-clerking, the typing pool, when they had held such well-paid jobs in industry? How could millions of housewives, so many of them holding the first job of their careers, revert to an exclusively domestic life and a one-income family structure, provided their husbands were able to keep their jobs? And what about the benefits for women, especially in the aircraft industry: the tendency toward parity in wages, the nursery and day-care centers, the Social Security and unemployment insurance, the subsidized transportation and meals, the availability of postal, banking, and public utilities facilities, the medical, dental, and counseling services? Would the post-war employment picture contain such benefits for women workers? Or would industry revert to its pre-war habit of offering women workers lower wages and next to no benefits?

In the second half of 1945, more than 1.32 million American women were discharged from their jobs in defense industries. There was talk in some circles of a social revolution, which is to say, a refusal by women to relinquish their jobs; but as dramatic as the war had been, it had not totally eradicated the social anthropology of the American people. The defense industry mounted a sophisticated advertising and public relations campaign that suggested to female defense workers that, just as it had been their patriotic duty to replace men on the assembly line, it was now, equally, their duty to go back home and make room in the economy for returning servicemen. Just how voluntary was this relinquishment of position (for it did occur) remains a mystery. In early 1944, 62 percent of all women surveyed in Los Angeles County war plants said that they wanted to continue working after the war. On the other hand, 64 percent of the women who listed their occupation as housewife before the war stated that they were willing to return to the home. Two-thirds of the housewives, in other words, could be persuaded to return home. The other third were adamant about staying on the job. Single women, by contrast, were by and large not so willing to relinquish their positions. What would happen to these industrial women after the war? Where would they find work? For three glorious years, these women had experienced an unprecedented boost in their income and self-esteem. They were necessary. They were appreciated. They were well paid. Then suddenly, in late 1945, they were history. What happened to their anger? How did they deal with such dislocation? Public health reports from Southern California in 1945, 1946, and 1947 show a rise in the caseload of social and psychiatric services being extended to former female defense workers of both blue-collar and white-collar backgrounds.

The good news was that many women had made permanent improvements in their sense of personal capacity and self-esteem. Many of those who found jobs after the war can be seen to have improved their lot in life significantly. By late 1946 surveys were showing that a majority of female aircraft and shipyard workers, even though they were no longer in these industries, had gone on to jobs different and more demanding than their pre-war employment. A waitress before the war, for example, had become a riveter during the war. After the war, she had qualified as a beautician and had opened her own shop. An unemployed widow before the war, age forty-four, had become an aircraft assembler. By June 1946 she was working in a textile printing and dyeing establishment. It is difficult to measure inner life, especially a half century and more later, but one suspects that many, perhaps a majority, of married women who returned to homemaking nurtured within themselves in the years to come a fond memory of the time when, as the character played by Goldie Hawn in *Swing Shift* puts it, "We really showed them, didn't we?"

For a few brief years in shipbuilding and aviation, but perhaps aviation most dramatically, California as well had showed them—showed the nation, showed the world: showed forth the possibilities of an industrial culture keyed to worker creativity, productivity, and self-esteem. From 1939 until 1945 more than one million workers, men and women, had been recruited, trained, and employed in the aircraft industry in Southern California. Most of them remained Californians after the war. They brought to the post-war economy and to the social psychology of their adopted state a capacity for large-scale enterprises and a philosophy of skills development and work satisfaction. Equal to all this, war work had given rise to an intensified expectation of a better life at home and in the workplace. California would never be the same, now that its men and women had worked the swing shift.

6

1945 * Hollywood Canteen

IN both its films and its live entertainment programs—bond rallies, USO tours at home and abroad, the Hollywood Canteen in downtown Hollywood—the film industry sought to position itself, for reasons of patriotism and profit, as one hundred percent behind the war effort. More subtly, Hollywood sought to position itself as a key player in the mobilization, second only to the military and the defense industries, and certainly on a par with civilian government. Not only did Hollywood want to win the war, the film studios wanted to emerge from the war as something much more important than a mere industry. In the war, film moguls saw the opportunity—and Darryl F. Zanuck of Twentieth Century–Fox spoke openly of this wish—for the entertainment industry to become a fixed and proper part of the national establishment, something akin to Wall Street, the Ivy League, the State Department, the Senate, even the White House.

Zanuck had entered the Army as a lieutenant colonel in the Signal Corps. Dressed in a tailored uniform and armed, incongruously, with a tommy gun, he had toured the North African theater as a special advisor. In Zanuck's only combat experience, he fired his tommy gun at a passing German plane, hoping for a lucky hit. Back in Hollywood by October 1943, Zanuck, resplendent in his tailored uniform and promoted to full colonel, addressed a Writers Congress meeting on the UCLA campus under the auspices of the Hollywood Writers Mobilization. In his recent tour of the front, Zanuck reported, he had talked to thousands of average fighting men for whom the war was proving an intellectual awakening. "In some cases, dimly, and in others, sharply," Zanuck reported, "the fighting men are beginning to perceive that somehow their leaders failed them in a crisis in human history. They know now that some such a device as a League of Nations, some scheme of world cooperation, must come if we are to escape further agony and bloodshed. It is up to us to help focus and channelize these thoughts. It is up to us to help give them substance and reality. We can do so. We have the talent, the know-how, and the resources. We have an incomparable medium for education and enlightenment—the greatest the world has ever known."[1]

Zanuck was obviously gearing himself and his audience up for his forthcoming film *Wilson* (1944), directed by Henry King, then going into production: at $5 million (Technicolor, a huge cast, $500,000 in sets, including exact replicas of the House of Representatives and key rooms in the White House) the most expensive movie thus far made in Hollywood. Written by Lamar Trotti, with Alexander Knox in the title role, *Wilson* was intended, in Zanuck's phrase, "to show the mistakes of the past so they could be avoided in the future." He had originally proposed *Wilson* as a government documentary, but this idea had been rejected, and so Zanuck produced the film as the most lavish ever made by Hollywood and the prefigurement, in his belief, of the type of great big message movie that would characterize Hollywood in the post-war era when it had become a fixed and primary component of the American establishment.

Warning Americans not to squander the peace after World War II as they had after World War I by rejecting the League of Nations, *Wilson* was not only a message movie. The lavish biopic sought to speak for the nation at the highest possible level of establishment discourse. Six thousand people attended its premiere in New York on 1 August 1944, including Wendell Willkie, Wilson's widow, Wilson's daughter Mrs. William Gibbs McAdoo, and James Cox, the Democratic presidential nominee for 1920. Although moderately successful at the box office (ten million had seen it by February 1945), *Wilson*, an over-long, preachy, and very expensive film, would never earn back its cost. Hence, in Hollywood terms, which is to say, in terms of the bottom line, *Wilson* was a flop. Yet Zanuck's explicit effort to guide public policy through a motion picture purporting through reference to World War I to lay down conditions in the post–World War II social and political order tipped Hollywood's hand as to its deepest intentions: not just to make money but to edge itself alongside government as a channel and determinator of national policy.

In thrusting itself so boldly forward as a creator of national policy, Hollywood was acknowledging once again that the best defense is a good offense; for ever since the late 1930s, the federal government, specifically the Justice Department, had been at war with Hollywood over the matter of its monopolies. Like baseball, Hollywood considered itself beyond the reach of anti-trust legislation. Unlike baseball, however, which in 1919 the Supreme Court exempted from anti-trust restrictions, the major studios had been investigated by the Justice Department for five years, beginning in 1933, for their practice of integrating film production, distribution, and exhibition—and for fixing prices at every step of the process. Throughout the 1920s and the 1930s the film industry had increasingly functioned as a vertically and horizontally integrated syndicate, fully justifying the decision of Harry Cohn of Columbia to decorate his offices as an exact replica of Mussolini's office in the Palazzo Venezia. Each executive, after all, headed a syndicalist operation. And besides: Italy and Germany remained good markets for Hollywood films through 1940.

In 1938 the Justice Department had filed an anti-trust suit against Paramount, MGM, Twentieth Century–Fox, Warner Brothers, RKO, Universal, Columbia, and United Artists, charging these studios with a wide array of monopolistic, price-fixing practices. In November 1940 five of the major studios signed consent decrees, but the matter was not fully settled. The studios, for one thing, mounted an appeal to higher courts, and the Justice Department, on its part, opened further linkages and practices to investigation. In August 1944, the very month *Wilson* premiered, the Justice Department renewed its attack, in this case against Paramount, asking the Federal District Court to modify even further certain aspects of the 1940 consent decree. In 1946 the Justice Department would renew its attack on the industry, and the suit would drag on through the courts until 1949. The federal government, in other words, had Hollywood by the throat throughout the war and hence had no trouble in exacting from Hollywood its full cooperation in the war effort; and Hollywood for its own reasons—profits, most obviously, but also hopes of becoming a fixed part of the American establishment—was more than willing to cooperate.

And yet it must be admitted that Hollywood had remained attached to its European markets even after war broke out in September 1939. As late as December 1940, a group of studio heads might listen in silence—not outrage, but the silence of businessmen hearing a report from the field—as Joseph Kennedy, one of their own, a sometime Hollywood producer, recently returned from the Court of St. James, warned his colleagues to lay off the anti-Nazi movies lest anti-Semitism flare up in the United States. Kennedy was especially distressed by the film *Confessions of a Nazi Spy* (1939), in which Nazis link up with supporters among German-Americans in the United States, and by Charlie Chaplin's mockery of Hitler in *The Great Dictator* (1940). Was Kennedy merely giving a warning, or making a threat, or simply talking good business? In any event, only Warner Brothers was conspicuously guilty of what would soon be termed premature anti-fascism. Most of the other studios bided their time and kept servicing their European markets until the last possible moment.

The film *To Be or Not to Be* (1942), directed by Ernst Lubitsch, demonstrated this transitional confusion. First of all, it was a comedy, starring Jack Benny as the head of a Shakespearean troupe caught in the Nazi invasion of Poland. Charles Chaplin had already tried to make Hitler seem funny with mixed results, but could anyone, even Ernst Lubitsch, master extraordinaire of the light touch, make the Nazi invasion of Poland a background for humor? When a Gestapo colonel said of Jack Benny playing a hack actor, "What he did to Shakespeare, we're doing to Poland," American audiences gasped in shock or remained silent. Returning from selected sneak previews, friends and associates of Lubitsch begged him to clip the

comment from the film, but Lubitsch refused, and the controversy followed him
to his death in 1947. The callow joke, in fact, can be said to have ended Lubitsch's
career.

After Pearl Harbor, Hollywood got enthusiastically on the anti-Nazi, anti-
Japanese bandwagon. Sixty-odd years later, the racist portrayal of the Japanese,
foreign and domestic, in such films as *Little Tokyo, USA* (1942), *Wake Island*
(1942), *Air Force* (1943), *Gung Ho!* (1942), *Danger in the Pacific* (1942), and *Halfway
to Shanghai* (1942) can engender responses of shocked and embarrassed silence
akin to those that greeted Lubitsch's Gestapo colonel's remark. It took specific
directives from the Bureau of Motion Pictures of the Office of War Information
to tone down this initial racist and bloody-minded response. Recent research has
disclosed how liberal and internationalist-minded censors of the bureau, headed
by Lowell Mellett, a former Scripps-Howard editor, worked with the studios, script
by script, to coax Hollywood in the direction of a more high-minded view of the
conflict. George Cukor's *Keeper of the Flame* (1942), released at the low point of
the first wave of racist war pictures, represents the first appearance of a Hollywood
message film that sought to establish a commanding—and, more important, a
respectable—leadership position *vis-à-vis* the American people. Written by Donald
Ogden Stewart, a wealthy Harvard-educated screenwriter who had joined the
Communist Party in the 1930s, *Keeper of the Flame* put forward an ultra-liberal
anti-fascist message: namely, that fascism was a distinct possibility in the United
States. Sixty years later, *Keeper of the Flame*, so skillfully directed by Cukor and
acted by Katharine Hepburn and Spencer Tracy, remains astonishing in its bold
effort to shape American public opinion. It is a film that preaches a hard-line
Popular Front message, the possibilities of fascism within American culture, that
hovers just on the edge of insulting a population even then sending its boys to
fight the Axis.

The polarizations of 1942 as represented in the Japanese-bashing war films of that
year and, more subtly, in *Keeper of the Flame* underscore the sheer achievement
of *Casablanca*, written, filmed, and premiered in New York in 1942 and put into
general release in January 1943. Where most films of 1942, even the subtly crafted
Keeper of the Flame, sought to propagandize, *Casablanca* sought to show complexity and ambivalence. Written and filmed in a white heat, helmed by a director,
Michael Curtiz, who prided himself on always coming in on time and on budget,
Casablanca seemed almost to stumble into greatness, taking the prize that eluded
Wilson while at the same time fulfilling Darryl F. Zanuck's notion that American
audiences and the films that entertained them were capable of messages and meanings speaking directly to the best possibilities of American culture. Sixty years later,
Casablanca, an almost spontaneous work of art, continues to instruct successive
generations regarding the ambiguities and ambivalences of Americans at war or
otherwise involved in the international arena.

Internationalism, in fact — the sheer necessity, however inconvenient, of American involvement in world events — pervades and structures *Casablanca*, reflected in its setting, theme, cast, and director. While he has never attracted a cult following, Michael Curtiz must be considered in the top ranks of Hollywood directors in terms of the range, versatility, and overall excellence of his oeuvre, one hundred films in all, forty-six of them A-budget, including at least three masterpieces, *The Sea Wolf* (1941), *Casablanca* (1942), and *Mildred Pierce* (1945). Born in Hungary in 1888, Mihaly Kertesz got his start as a film actor in his native country before moving to Vienna in 1919, where he became active in the Austrian film industry. Kertesz's most important breakthrough occurred when he collaborated with his fellow Hungarian Alexander Korda in the costume drama *The Slave Queen* (1924), one of the most ambitious spectaculars of the European silent cinema and a film that had a great effect on Cecil B. DeMille. *The Slave Queen* brought Kertesz to the attention of the Warner brothers, Harry and Jack, who brought him to Hollywood to direct their own spectacular, *Noah's Ark* (1928), which the Warners hoped would out-DeMille DeMille. Anglicizing his name to Michael Curtiz, the émigré director slogged through a series of lesser-budget efforts, acquiring a reputation as a thorough professional, capable of turning to any type of film vehicle and getting the job done. Curtiz's American breakthrough came with *Captain Blood* (1935), in which he directed the second debut of Errol Flynn, who had previously played the non-speaking part of a corpse in Curtiz's *The Case of the Curious Bride* (1935). Despite Flynn's tendency to blow his lines or otherwise misbehave on the set, the Tasmanian ocker with English mannerisms and the partially Anglicized Hungarian director were made for each other; and through such vehicles as *Captain Blood, The Charge of the Light Brigade* (1936), *The Adventures of Robin Hood* (1938), and *The Sea Hawk* (1940) — productions that continue to define the costume adventure — Curtiz took Flynn to stardom.

Jack Warner prized Curtiz's versatility and timeliness. Curtiz could do action-adventure; or gangster films such as *Angels with Dirty Faces* (1938), in which James Cagney contrives a coward's death for himself in the electric chair so as to dissuade other young men from following in his footsteps (perhaps one of the most emotionally gripping sequences in film history); or westerns such as *Dodge City* (1939), an important milestone in the evolution of this genre in its combination of frontier action and psychological motivation; or musicals such as *Yankee Doodle Dandy* (1942), in which Cagney, playing George M. Cohan, turns in one of the greatest song-and-dance sequences of any Hollywood musical ever. Throughout his Hollywood career, which lasted through 1954 with two final efforts, *White Christmas* and *The Egyptian*, Michael Curtiz communicated in an idiosyncratic pidgin patois that blended Hungarian, German, and English. It was rumored that only one person, a British grip nicknamed Limey, truly understood Curtiz and that he moved from Curtiz film to Curtiz film as his translator. Many of the malapropisms attributed to Samuel Goldwyn, in fact, may have actually originated with Curtiz.

When questioned by Jack Warner regarding the accuracy of the background of *Casablanca*, for example, Curtiz was reputed to have replied: "Vell, Jock, the scenario isn't the exact truth, but vee haff the facts to prove it."[2]

Interpretations of *Casablanca*, and they are multiple, range from straight allegory, with Rick (Humphrey Bogart) as Roosevelt, Captain Louis Renault (Claude Raines) as Churchill, and Casablanca as exactly that, the White House. Rick and Renault, Roosevelt and Churchill, agree at Casablanca that, in Renault's phrase, theirs is going to be a beautiful friendship. Other interpretations see Rick as an early version of the existentialist hero soon to be developed by Jean-Paul Sartre and Albert Camus. Others detect a submerged homosexual attraction between Rick and Renault or at least a strong homoerotic bond, while others, more plausibly, see *Casablanca* as a paradigm of the new world order brought on by the Second World War with its mixing of cultures, nations, and languages. Each of these interpretations, together with others as well, has its plausibility, for every work of art encodes in itself multiple meanings. From the perspective of Hollywood's effort to take a leadership position in the war, however, *Casablanca* can be interpreted as a triumph of the studio system: an almost unconscious masterpiece, cranked out like hundreds of others, yet possessed from the start of a formal, thematic, and symbolic intensity that would make it, eventually, an icon of American identity.

In nothing except the final result was *Casablanca* anything more than a routine Hollywood production from a studio, Warner Brothers, known for its volume production. Purchasing the film rights to an unproduced play by Murray Burnett and Jean Alison entitled *Everybody Comes to Rick's*, Warner Brothers sent the vehicle to the Epstein brothers, Julius and Philip, who batted out the first draft of a script. When the Epsteins were called to Washington for war work, Howard Koch inherited the project. A tall, preppie New Yorker raised on the Upper East Side, Koch had initially thought of the Episcopal priesthood before attending Columbia Law School. Dissatisfied with the law, he joined the Mercury Theatre of the Air as a staff writer, producing the famous "Invasion from Mars" script based on H. G. Wells's *War of the Worlds* (1898), which caused such a panic when it was broadcast on 30 October 1938. In Hollywood Koch did the screenplay for Curtiz's *The Sea Hawk* and *The Letter* (1940), directed by William Wyler, based on a short story by Somerset Maugham, then went on to write *Sergeant York* (1941), which like *Wilson* used the First World War as an allegory for the Second.

Even as Koch was working on the Epstein script (Jack Warner delighted in playing his writers off against each other), Warner Brothers began casting and set a production deadline for late 1942. George Raft turned down the role of Rick, and Louis B. Mayer would not release Hedy Lamarr to play Ilsa Lund. There was talk of dropping the film into the B category, with Ronald Reagan and Ann Sheridan in the leads; but then Jack Warner secured Ingrid Bergman from David O. Selznick in exchange for two months of Warner contract player Olivia de Havilland's time and cast Warner regular Humphrey Bogart as Rick. Koch was still writing as director Michael Curtiz went into production. Although Koch did not know it at the time, the Epsteins, returned from Washington, were also back on the project. Their revisions of Koch's revisions were returned to Koch, who as yet did not know their source, and Koch's revisions of the Epsteins' revisions of Koch's revisions of the Epsteins' first draft also had the input of Humphrey Bogart, who began consulting with Koch as the film went into production and must thus be accorded some of the writing credit. Bogart and Curtiz, meanwhile, were constantly quarreling on the set, and Paul Henreid, playing the freedom fighter Victor Laszlo, was chafing at being in a subordinate role to Bogart. Music director Max Steiner, meanwhile, was trying to have the song "As Time Goes By," which he loathed, eliminated from the score.

No contemporary reviewer seems to have discerned the enduring greatness of *Casablanca*, which is no surprise. Many masterpieces go unrecognized or even fail at their debut. But to a later generation *Casablanca* embodies a subliminal message akin to that emanating from Marlene Dietrich on the front eighteen months later: war is a disaster; it demands sacrifice; its mixture of idealism and tragedy, justice and injustice, precludes fancy speeches; and when caught up in it, do your best to remember Paris. Rick's farewell speech to Ilse in the Casablanca airport regarding the countless people whose lives will be disrupted, even destroyed, by the war, against whom one's own sacrifices do not amount to a hill of beans, pulsates with as much high-mindedness as the American temperament can honestly tolerate. Rick is a liberal. We know this elliptically. He ran guns to the Ethiopians, fought with the Loyalists in Spain, but by the time we encounter him in his café he is a burnt-out case, suffering from that quintessential American malady (according to liberal interventionists, at least) cynical isolationism. Part of the power of *Casablanca* lies in its combination of pro-Allied propaganda and its subversive existentialism that knows, as Albert Camus was even then putting in his novel *L'Etranger* (1942), that most high-flown certainties are not worth the strand of a woman's hair. Like Marlene Dietrich on the front, *Casablanca* encouraged Americans to do the right thing while remaining convinced of war's absurdity and defiantly committed to private pursuits. Rick does the right thing, but at the end he and Renault are still committed to playing all the angles.

In Hollywood's terms, the angles tended to serve success at the box office. The Second World War proved a windfall to Hollywood. Despite wartime restrictions and the onerous task of producing training films, production dropped only slightly below the pre-war level. Approximately eighty-five million tickets were sold each week in the United States alone during the war years. Yet even as it improved its product—the crudities of 1942 giving way to the romantic existentialism of *Casablanca*; the multi-cultural, indeed multi-racial, tolerance of Alfred Hitchcock's *Lifeboat* (1944); the attempted honesty of William Wellman's *Story of G. I. Joe* (1945) and the post-war *A Walk in the Sun* (1946), directed by Lewis Milestone— Hollywood worried about its moral relationship to its audience. Doing the right thing, assisting the war effort, Hollywood was making big bucks. But what about the millions of little guys in uniform and the hundreds of thousands of them who were being killed and wounded? It would take thirty years for the existential subtleties of *Casablanca* to reveal themselves, and then it would be to a younger, college-educated audience shaped by the complexities of Vietnam. True, the mobilization of America for war sold tickets at the box office through 1942 and 1943, but by early 1944 it began to dawn on the industry that a straight diet of war films had its limits. Audiences were becoming restive with the crude propaganda vehicles in the style of 1942.

An America capable of pushing ahead of Hollywood in its tastes, of growing weary of propaganda with the end of the war not yet clearly in sight, was a dangerous audience to Hollywood's way of thinking. By 1944 Hollywood subconsciously understood that it stood in danger of having its profiteering, and perhaps even its facile messages, discovered by an American public growing increasingly sophisticated under the demands of mobilization. The war was taking ordinary Americans and transforming them into something beyond themselves. And this was true not only of the military. On the home front, nearly half the defense work force, the female half, was experiencing an enhanced range of new capacities. In such an environment—of country and city kids in uniform mastering the complexities of a vast war machine on land, sea, and air, of civilians servicing the equal if less dangerous complexities of national industrialism—Hollywood began to fear the loss of its grip on its mass audience. Once before, in the early 1920s, the American people had turned in judgment on Hollywood, and it could happen again, after the war especially, if there were scores to settle. Hence patriotism and the desire to sustain profits merged with a more haltingly understood motivation: the need to sustain its hold on an audience that was providing its sons for the battlefield and showing dangerous signs of rejecting propaganda as young men came under fire and mothers placed Gold Star flags in their windows. Searching about for counter-moves, Hollywood happened upon Marlene Dietrich, Bob Hope, and the Hollywood Canteen.

Knowledge of the need to connect directly, physically, in the flesh with its audience during wartime was nothing new to Hollywood. In most such efforts, however—the bond drives especially—Hollywood played its part under the direction of the government. Of significance to the effort of Hollywood to establish itself as more than a business, to become a fixed element of the American establishment, like baseball and Harvard, were the programs that Hollywood itself supported and controlled: programs that reevoked and reintensified the preeminent, almost magical, presence of Hollywood among ordinary Americans, even those coming under fire.

This effort to connect, culminating in the tours of Dietrich and Hope, began in early 1942 with the establishment of the Hollywood Canteen. Bette Davis, at thirty-four at the height of her powers as an actress, and John Garfield, feeling uneasy about being classified 4F, came up with the idea just after Pearl Harbor as they sat together over lunch in the Green Room (stars only) at the Warner Brothers commissary. Davis and Garfield discussed the thousands of servicemen who were already stationed in greater Los Angeles and the even larger number that could be expected to be coming through now that the United States had joined the war. The scene resembled one of those Andy Hardy films in which Judy Garland and Mickey Rooney decide to fix up the old barn and produce a show, only in this case Davis and Garfield decided to fix up a well-known but temporarily abandoned building at 1451 Cahuenga Boulevard just off Sunset Boulevard and open it as a USO center staffed by Hollywood celebrities. Built as a livery stable, the building had recently served as a little theater and a nightclub.

Devoting eighteen hours a day to the project, Bette Davis faced three obstacles: the Victory Committee chaired by James Cagney, the unions, and money. The Victory Committee, an organization of film stars, agents, and other members of the industry loath to squander their talent, even for patriotic purposes in wartime, claimed total jurisdiction over all appearances by Hollywood stars in war-related causes. The habit of monopoly ran deep in actors and actresses whose every move was controlled by the studios to which they were under contract. Initially, the Victory Committee did not like the Hollywood Canteen idea. As Davis and Garfield envisioned the Canteen, it would be open twenty-four hours a day, seven days a week. How in the world, asked the Victory Committee, James Cagney especially, could such an operation feature Hollywood celebrities without burning them out completely or, worse, over-exposing them to the servicemen: pressing too much flesh in person, that is, hence diminishing the value, the magical presence, of the Hollywood star? In later years, Bette Davis considered it one of the greatest achievements of her life that she succeeded in persuading the Victory Committee to allow such an open-ended staffing pattern, so contrary to the cautious exposure characteristic of tightly managed Hollywood careers. Davis also persuaded more than forty-two Hollywood guilds and crafts unions to bend their equally draconian rules and donate their services for the refurbishment of the Canteen, which she had leased for $100 for the duration of the war plus six months. For fundraising, Davis turned to Jules Stein, head of the Music Corporation of America, who advised her to establish a Hollywood Canteen Foundation as the non-profit vehicle to raise money and administer the program. Stein persuaded Harry Cohn of Columbia to do a premiere benefit for its new film *Talk of the Town* (1942), which netted $6,500, and raised additional funds throughout the film community by direct solicitation.

By October 1942 the Hollywood Canteen was ready for business. As if to showcase even further the Hollywood nature of the event, Jules Stein ran the opening as a premiere benefit, with bleachers built on either side of the entrance to the Canteen. Stars and celebrities bought tickets at $100 a seat, and, sitting in the bleachers, they watched three thousand servicemen enter the Canteen on opening night. The reversal of roles, the Hollywood stars watching the incoming servicemen, netted $10,000 for the Canteen and as a public relations gesture further reinforced the notion that Hollywood would be making every effort to extend itself to servicemen and servicewomen — on Hollywood's terms. As if to underscore this point, another premiere benefit was held, this time for *Thank Your Lucky Stars* (1943) from Warner Brothers. Not only were the proceeds of this film donated to the Canteen, Jack Warner paid its stars $50,000 each for their appearances in the film, whose plot was a self-congratulatory cavalcade of Hollywood talent, and the stars in turn agreed to donate their salaries to the Canteen. As always, there was the bottom line. Even as a non-profit venture, the Hollywood Canteen played well, finishing the war with half a million dollars in the till.

Hollywood thus found the means of servicing military men and women while congratulating itself and positioning itself to remain profitable during the conflict and, more important, to announce itself as a constituent part of the American establishment. Deep down, although this notion never surfaced until the controversy attached to the film *Hollywood Canteen* (1944) flared forth, the young men and women in uniform were expected to be grateful, to think something really important had happened in their ordinary lives, because they now had the chance, for a moment or two, to dance with Hedy Lamarr or have Rita Hayworth serve them a sandwich.

Remaining open until V-J Day, the Hollywood Canteen entertained an estimated three million servicemen and -women during the war. Hedy Lamarr poured coffee and danced with the young men. Marlene Dietrich and Rita Hayworth served coffee and sandwiches, prepared by such stars as Basil Rathbone, Fred MacMurray, and Roddy McDowall, under the direction of Mrs. John Ford, who spent the war, she later noted, making mountains of sandwiches and brewing a Niagara of coffee. Hayworth also danced and sang. Other performers included Harry James and Betty Grable, Eddie Cantor, Joe E. Brown, who had lost a son to the war, Bing Crosby, and Kay Kyser, whose orchestra performed just about every Saturday evening, even if Kyser had to fly his musicians back from another engagement. Classical musicians such as Yehudi Menuhin also performed, and Roy Rogers came by with Trigger. Servicemen crowding into the Canteen were asked to stay only an hour on the premises, so as to make room for others waiting outside. Significantly, the Hollywood Canteen was not segregated, although black and white servicemen tended to remain in their own groups and space. If any trouble broke out, the band played "The Star-Spangled Banner," which brought everyone to attention; Bette Davis later claimed that they had to play the national anthem only twice during the war. Hundreds of young women from the aircraft factories volunteered as dance hostesses. Altogether, some six thousand volunteer workers, only a few of them celebrities, worked at the Hollywood Canteen during the war, assisting a paid staff of nine.

A number of celebrity volunteers at the Hollywood Canteen — Fred MacMurray, for example, or Roddy McDowall, John Garfield, and Roy Rogers — were for one reason or another not in the service. Other celebrities who remained civilians included John Wayne, Frank Sinatra, Errol Flynn, Kirk Douglas, Humphrey Bogart, Bing Crosby, Cary Grant, Gary Cooper, Randolph Scott, Fred Astaire, and Bob Hope. The reasons why such stars did not serve are varied. John Garfield and Frank Sinatra were classified as 4F, Sinatra because of a punctured eardrum. Bogart, Crosby, Cooper, Scott, and Astaire were all beyond draft age and would have had to make a special effort to enlist. The reasons for John Wayne's failure to enlist remain mysterious; they had something to do with Wayne being miffed at not being able to secure a direct commission. Australian by birth, Errol Flynn avoided the military like the plague, preferring to see service, like Bogart, Wayne, and Garfield, in a series of war films, culminating in the notorious *Objective Burma* (1945), written by Alvah Bessie and directed by Raoul Walsh, in which Flynn led an American detachment in the Burma campaign, leaving the impression that only Americans were serving in this theater. (The British were outraged.) Garfield performed credibly in such war films as *Air Force* (1943) and *Destination Tokyo* (1944). Bogart played a crusty tank commander in *Sahara* (1943) and a merchant marine deck officer in *Action in the North Atlantic* (1943). Errol Flynn saw plenty of action as well, earning himself two charges of statutory rape, which he beat, thanks to the help of defense attorney Jerry Giesler. Ironically, one of the enduring phrases to emerge from the war, "in like Flynn," celebrated Flynn's home-front activities.

Earlier in the war, Flynn had slugged a Marine for asking him why he was not in uniform. The Marine was an ordinary soldier asking a commonsense question. Why should the many serve while the privileged but eligible remained civilians? Altogether, it must be noted, Hollywood made a reputable showing in wartime enlistments, with approximately 2,700 men and women, 12 percent of the film industry work force, in uniform by October 1942. (This impressive percentage, it must also be emphasized, was attained by the enlistments of low-ranking technicians and set workers who in the course of events would have been drafted anyway.) Hollywood made sure to send its product to the armed forces along with that 12 percent of its manpower. By 1943 an estimated 630,000 men and women in uniform, either in the continental United States or overseas, were each evening enjoying a Hollywood film in barracks or in the field.

Among the crowd might be the celebrity star himself. A number of Hollywood actors enlisted in the ranks. Cesar Romero, for example, rose to chief boatswain's mate in the Coast Guard. William Holden joined the Army as a private under his real name, William F. Beedle Jr., and Henry Fonda, despite his advanced age of thirty-seven, enlisted in the Navy after two tries, with the ambition of becoming a gunner's mate. (Darryl Zanuck blocked Fonda's first effort to enlist, telling Washington that Fonda was still needed at Twentieth Century–Fox.) Sabu the Elephant Boy joined the Army Air Forces and flew a full combat tour as a tail gunner. Two stars, Jimmy Stewart and Tyrone Power, enlisted as privates, then attained commissions as pilots. Stewart won the Distinguished Flying Cross as an

Army Air Forces bomber pilot over Germany and finished the war with the well-earned rank of colonel. Power won his aviator's wings in the Marine Corps and served as a combat transport pilot in the Pacific.

A number of stars—David Niven, Robert Montgomery, Douglas Fairbanks Jr., Ronald Reagan—already held commissions or were commissioned directly into the service. A graduate of Sandhurst and a former officer in the Highland Light Infantry, Niven returned to England in late 1939, rejoined the army, and finished the war as a lieutenant colonel in the famed Phantom Reconnaissance Regiment. Robert Montgomery rose to the command of a destroyer in the Atlantic. A notable war hero, Douglas Fairbanks Jr. also attained, like Montgomery, the three gold stripes of a naval commander in the course of serving in North Africa and Europe as the field commander of a super-secret commando team. Ronald Reagan, a second lieutenant in the cavalry reserve, was kept in Hollywood with the Army Motion Picture Unit stationed at Fort Roach. So many Hollywood people managed to secure direct commissions, in fact, or were commissioned after their enlistments, that Senator Harry Truman of Missouri, chairing a Special Committee Investigating the National Defense Program, made it a frequent point to ask the embarrassing question: why were so many Hollywood producers, directors, film stars, screenwriters, and publicity men commissioned officers? Didn't any of these boys wish to serve in the ranks?

The Army Signal Corps was especially quick to enlist producers and directors for its Pictorial Service, the agency responsible for the production of training films and documentaries. Darryl Zanuck, as has already been pointed out, entered the Signal Corps as a lieutenant colonel and was initially assigned to London, where he lived at Claridge's, then went on to North Africa to produce a documentary. Director Frank Capra joined the Signal Corps as a major and had risen to the rank of colonel by 1945. As commander of the 834th Photo Signal Detachment, Capra produced the *Why We Fight* series: seven documentaries that were shown to millions of servicemen and -women in basic training.

Of all the American military, the United States Army Air Forces, the newest of the services, was the most anxious to employ film and public relations to justify its new form of aerial warfare, long-range daylight bombing. Throughout the war, the USAAF maintained an extensive program of public relations and self-promotion, carried on, in many instances, by former Hollywood agents, public relations men, filmmakers, and stars. To his great credit, an over-age Clark Gable voluntarily enlisted in the USAAF, after his wife Carole Lombard died in January 1942 while on a war bond tour when her TWA DC-3 crashed in Nevada. But Lieutenant General Arnold, chief of staff of the Army Air Forces, had other plans for Gable, and within two months of his enlistment Gable was commissioned and assigned to produce training films. Again to his credit, Gable maintained a low profile in the service and eventually flew a number of combat missions over Europe as a photo-reconnaissance officer. General Arnold also brought Jack Warner into the Army Air Forces in 1942, making him yet another instant lieutenant colonel. After ordering a costume press of suitable uniforms from the studio, Warner proceeded to produce the recruitment and training film *Winning Your Wings*, which General Arnold claimed helped the USAAF recruit more than a hundred thousand airmen. Warner also produced another important USAAF training film, *Rear Gunner*.

While in uniform, three Hollywood directors—John Ford, John Huston, and William Wyler—created documentaries that attained the status of filmic art. Commissioned in the Navy despite his defective eyesight, Ford produced and directed *The Battle of Midway* (1942), dealing with that crucial Pacific battle of June 1942, and Huston, an Army captain in the Italian campaign, made *The Battle for San Pietro* (1945), concerned with a smaller-scale, lesser-known, but equally bloody clash. As might be expected from a director known for his epic westerns, Ford captured the scale and sweep of the Midway conflict, in which two great fleets, advancing into uncertain waters, each probed and sought the presence of the other before engaging in the largest naval air battle in history. Again, as might be expected for a director known for his gritty realism, Huston produced a film so graphic in its depictions of death and casualties among Americans at San Pietro that the War Department sequestered the film in its original format and released only a sanitized version.

While also capable of graphic realism, William Wyler's *Memphis Belle* (1944) avoided direct images of bloodshed and became the best known and most effective of these war documentaries. Having just finished the direction of *Mrs. Miniver* (1942), the pro-British film Franklin Roosevelt said had helped cement the Anglo-American alliance, Wyler was recruited directly into the USAAF as a major by Major General Carl Spaatz, commander of the newly formed (and still secret) 8th Air Force, scheduled to commence bombing operations over Europe from England. Wyler was introduced to Spaatz in Washington in early 1942 by Spaatz's aide USAAF Captain (later Major) Sy Bartlett, the Hollywood screenwriter who after the war would write the script for the film *Twelve O'Clock High* (1949). The very fact that Spaatz would have a screenwriter as one of his aides spoke for itself. Like most Air Force generals, Spaatz knew the value of good publicity. As far as he was concerned, Wyler had one mission: film the air war over Europe. Assigned to the 8th Bomber Command in England, commanded by Major General Ira Eaker, Wyler qualified as an aerial gunner as a prerequisite for flying with the *Memphis Belle* on combat missions. Vincent Evans, bombardier of the *Memphis Belle*, later remembered the sight of Wyler standing in the catwalk of an open bomb bay five miles above Germany, on oxygen and in full flight gear against the sub-zero temperatures, pointing his hand-held camera at flak bursts and Luftwaffe fighters attempting to break up the formation of B-17s. Aside from the danger of combat, Wyler stood in special jeopardy should the *Memphis Belle* be forced down in Europe. A Jew born in Alsace-Lorraine, Wyler had just directed one of the great propaganda films of the war, *Mrs. Miniver*, and, like Marlene Dietrich, might have encountered, if captured, special attention of an unwelcome sort.

The overseas tours of Bob Hope and Marlene Dietrich were under the auspices of the USO—the United Service Organization, which worked in conjunction with the Special Service Units of the various branches of the military. There were an estimated 122 major overseas tours by celebrities during the war, and the number of shows at military bases in the continental United States is impossible to document. Such entertainers as Bud Abbott and Lou Costello, Martha Raye, Kay Francis, Joe E. Brown, and Al Jolson were especially active on the USO circuit. Its champion performer, however, was Bob Hope, in whose tours the efforts of the film industry to position itself as, simultaneously, member of the establishment, tribune of the people, and royalty amidst loyal commoners reached unprecedented heights. Touring the combat zones with his well-crafted repertoire of gags, his featured singer Frances Langford, and his second banana Jerry Colonna, with sideman Tony Romano on guitar, Hope created the genre Dietrich would help perfect: the presence of Hollywood on the front as the palpable embodiment of home and civilian life, past and future, amidst the loneliness and dangers of the wartime present. This was the central message, and it was as sincere as anything can be sincere amidst the dishonesties of war; but the USO tours, the Bob Hope tours above all, also communicated a more subliminal message: the war was important because Hollywood was there, helping keep it a celebrity event in which non-celebrities were doing most of the dying.

In late 1943 Luftwaffe fighters still reigned supreme over Europe. In daylight bombing raids over Schweinfurt and Regensburg, nearly 20 percent of the B-17s went down: sixty bombers for an approximate loss of six hundred men, either killed, wounded and captured, or merely captured. In their nighttime bombing attacks, the British alone suffered fifty-five thousand dead. When bombardier Second Lieutenant James M. Brown (last encountered as an air cadet on leave in Big Bear, Southern California) reported to the 97th Bombardment Group in North Africa for bombing runs over Italy, the briefing officer told the men: forget home, forget your wives and sweethearts, forget worrying about your own survival, consider yourself already dead—get the job done. A significant percentage of the airmen who crowded Bob Hope's shows in England and North Africa, together with the ground forces in North Africa, poised for the invasion of Italy, were marked men, and somehow, in the deepest recesses of their being, they must have known it, however subliminally, as they cheered and whistled at Hope's gags or stilled themselves momentarily as Frances Langford sang that she would be seeing them in all the old familiar places.

Born in Eltham, England, in 1904, Leslie Townes Hope immigrated as a boy with his family to Cleveland, where he grew up as just another local kid, hanging around pool halls, taking a stab at soft-shoe routines and humorous pitter-patter, until he was twenty-one and Fatty Arbuckle, banished from Hollywood in the aftermath of starlet Virginia Rapp's death, hired him for the vaudeville act through which Arbuckle was supporting himself in exile. In vaudeville, Hope discovered that his future lay not in his dancing, which was marginal, nor in his looks which were idiosyncratic (a ski nose, an equally angular chin), but in his abilities as master of ceremonies and stand-up comic capable of a rapid-fire delivery in an off-handed style with a quick comeback when there were hecklers in the audience. From vaudeville Hope graduated to Broadway, with parts in such musical comedies as *Roberta*, *The Ziegfeld Follies*, and *Red, Hot, and Blue*, in which he starred alongside Ethel Merman and Jimmy Durante.

Radio made Bob Hope a star. He had a character, a voice, a personality that communicated well over the airways, projecting a brassy insouciance that came almost naturally to a young man without education or background, indeed without any single outstanding talent—with the exception of the talent of being himself, the average American guy, interested in girls, golf, the ponies, a good time. Signed on by Pepsodent toothpaste after a shaky start on the air under the sponsorship of Bromo-Seltzer and Lucky Strike, Hope found his persona and voice: brassy middle-brow, the cheekiness of a vaudeville comic and, most brilliantly, a self-deprecating humor that not only masked the necessary ego of the vaudevillian master of ceremonies but reinforced it by allowing Hope to win for losing in every comic routine. Buoyed aloft by a gaggle of gag men who wrote the jokes he consumed at a furious pace, Hope pioneered the persona, Mr. Average Guy with sizzle (*Time* described it as Hope's "strenuous averageness—which paradoxically managed to set him apart"), with droll overtones of a mild lechery and an obsession with golf, that would survive through the 1990s as a fixed genre in American humor. From radio, Hope went on to Hollywood, where he found his métier alongside Bing Crosby in a series of *Road* pictures and other comedies that made him one of the top-drawing stars by 1942; at that point Hope was making approximately $1 million a year from his broadcasts and pictures, the comedy *Caught in the Draft* being his most recent release. Very soon Hope would become, like his occasional co-star Crosby, one of the wealthiest men in Hollywood and, eventually, one of the wealthiest men in California.

The film industry, meanwhile, had organized the Hollywood Victory Caravan, a special train packed with entertainers scheduled to whistle-stop the country in May 1942, raising funds for Army and Navy Relief. The Victory Caravan tour symbolically inaugurated three continuous years of fundraising by Hollywood that would see millions of dollars raised in war bond drives and more than $2 million raised for Army and Navy Relief efforts. On board the Hollywood Victory Caravan was an array of film and radio stars whose presence testified to the eagerness of Hollywood to take a leadership position in the war effort. From the movies came James Cagney, Charles Boyer, Claudette Colbert, Joan Bennett, Joan Blondell, Olivia de Havilland, Cary Grant, Merle Oberon, Pat O'Brien, Spencer Tracy, and Eleanor Powell. Comics included Bert Lahr, Laurel and Hardy, and Groucho Marx. Bing Crosby headed a list of actor-performers that included Desi Arnaz and

Risë Stevens. Chosen to emcee this three-hour variety show on its national tour, Hope became by definition the leading spokesman of the entertainment industry in the war effort. His Pepsodent shows, meanwhile, were being broadcast each week from various military bases around the country. When the Victory Caravan finished its tour in Houston, Hope simultaneously emceed its final performance before a capacity crowd of twelve thousand in the Houston Coliseum while broadcasting the Pepsodent program in an adjacent theater packed with airmen from Ellington Field. At this point, Hope's career was at its peak. Paramount was set to release the *Road to Morocco*, the best of the series. Hope's autobiography *They Got Me Covered* (1941) had sold an astonishing three million copies, and Hope had positioned himself as the wartime voice of the entertainment industry. As if this were not enough, Hope followed the Victory Caravan with a tour of Alaska and the Aleutian Islands, accompanied by guitar man Tony Romano, comic Jerry Colonna, and singer Frances Langford, with whom Hope shared something approaching equal billing.

Married, with two adopted children, the thirty-nine-year-old Hope was safe from the draft, yet his civilian status bothered him, especially on evenings like the Academy Awards ceremonies at the Cocoanut Grove in the Ambassador Hotel in Los Angeles on 4 March 1943, with Hope serving as master of ceremonies, when Marine Private Tyrone Power and USAAF Private Alan Ladd displayed an oversized flag carrying the names of 27,677 men and women from the film industry who were in the service. "Some night I'll be out there telling my jokes," Hope told syndicated columnist Ed Sullivan, shortly after this event, "and some big guy will stand up in the front row and he'll give me a Bronx cheer and yelp, 'Why in hell aren't you in the service, Hope?' and that is the $64 question I won't be able to answer."[3] Sullivan shared Hope's concerns with his readers and a few weeks later reported that John Q. Public, as Sullivan put it, believed that Hope should be deferred.

After this brush with conscience, Hope resolved his dilemma by devoting a major portion of his energies in the war years to USO tours in Europe and the Pacific. Slightly after midnight on 25 June 1943, Hope left for his first USO tour of the European theater—England, North Africa, and Italy—via a Pan Am Clipper from the La Guardia Marine Terminal in New York. On board the flight to Ireland for transfer to a second plane to England were Langford, Romano, and second banana Jack Pepper, a chubby song-and-dance man who was officially an Army private. Hope and his troupe spent five weeks in England and Northern Ireland before flying from Prestwick, Scotland, to North Africa, followed by a tour with Patton's troops in Sicily. All in all, the Hope show covered twenty thousand miles and did more than 250 shows in eleven weeks. The crowds were enormous. At Prestwick, where he performed before enplaning for Morocco, Hope attracted an audience of ten thousand defense workers. At Ferryville, a base near Bizerte, Morocco, Hope played to a crowd of seventy-five hundred. At Palermo, in Sicily, an estimated sixteen thousand troops, many of them fresh from battle, jammed a natural amphitheater. Hope's tour received extensive coverage from the wire services and from such prestigious byline correspondents as Quentin Reynolds, Bob Considine, Ernie Pyle, and John Steinbeck. *Time* gave him a cover profile on 20 September 1943. Naturally, Hope's publisher, Simon and Schuster, was interested in a book, which Hope produced in ten weeks with the help of ghost writer Carroll Carroll and a rotating group of gag men. The resulting manuscript, *I Never Left Home* (1944), humorously illustrated by Carl Rose, sold 1.5 million copies.

I Never Left Home comes closest to probing the inner dynamics of Hope's role as avatar *par excellence* of Hollywood as tribune of the people, endowed with a touch of healing royalty: of an entertainment industry that saw itself as a central event of a global conflict that, from Hollywood and Hope's perspective, sometimes seemed to be being brokered by and on behalf of celebrity culture. Page by page, base by base, Hollywood and other celebrities, most of them in uniform, make cameo appearances. On the flight to England, Hope chats amiably with Lord Beaverbrook and Averell Harriman at the hotel at Botwood, Newfoundland. In London, where he stays at Claridge's and hangs out at the Embassy Club (the El Morocco or Stork Club of London, Hope tells us), Hope runs into Major Sy Bartlett, screenwriter turned General Spaatz's aide and arguably the single most influential Hollywoodite in the European theater. Hope also runs into Captain Burgess Meredith, also with the 8th Air Force, Captain Gene Raymond, and John Steinbeck, who held officer's rank as an accredited correspondent. Also in London, staying at Claridge's, are Captain John Mahin—one of Hollywood's top screenwriters, Hope tells us—USAAF Captain Mack Kriendler, owner of "21" in New York, and Lady Cavendish, the former Adele Astaire, Fred Astaire's sister. Returning to London from Belfast, Hope plays a big show at the Odeon with his troupe, alongside Adolphe Menjou, the Blossom Sisters, and a swing band under the direction of Warrant Officer Frank Rossotto. The King and Queen are in attendance. A few days later, five touring American senators invite Hope to a cocktail party at the Dorchester where Hope hobnobs with the senators and such notables as Averell Harriman (again), Anthony Drexel Biddle, Ambassador John Winant, and Ira Eaker, now the commanding general of the 8th Air Force. The senators also invite Hope to accompany them on a visit to the House of Commons. En route, they stop off at Number Ten Downing Street, where Ambassador Winant introduces the senators and Hope to Winston Churchill.

Playing a base near Bristol, Hope pals around with Major David Niven, through whom he gets word of Major Jimmy Stewart, Major Clark Gable, Commander Douglas Fairbanks Jr., Commander John Ford, Captain John Huston, and Major William Wyler. At another Flying Fortress base, Hope has Major Clark Gable himself in the audience, to whom he directs a number of personal jokes intended to let the rest of the airmen in on some in-group Hollywood banter. Gable, for example, had been banished from the B-17s, Hope claimed, because his ears destroyed the streamlining. (In later years, one wonders, did the boys who survived tell stories of how they were privileged to serve alongside Clark Gable and hear him bandy words with Bob Hope?) A raft of celebrity correspondents make an appearance—Bob Considine in Belfast, Ernie Pyle at the Hotel Excelsior in Palermo—together with certain other Hollywood fringers also on commissioned service: Lieutenant Jimmy Smith of the Airborne in North Africa, Hope's old friend from the Stork Club, and Lieutenant Bob Peoples at the naval base at Lake Bizerte, a well-known USC football player. One must search diligently for the names of enlisted men in *I Never Left Home*, and when these occur, if they occur at all, cameo appearances are granted only to the most highly decorated or those who are praising Hope's show, mainly in letters home. Senator Truman might fume, but, as Hope suggests, all Hollywood is wearing brass on its shoulders or gold stripes on its sleeves and doing more than its bit to win the war.

And as far as brass is concerned, Hope is greeted at each point of the tour by no officer below the rank of bird colonel. One after another, European theater greats—Brigadier General Frank Armstrong, the highly decorated bomber commander, Major General Jimmy Doolittle, Lieutenant General George S. Patton Jr., and General Dwight D. Eisenhower himself—play prominent roles in the narrative. Armstrong welcomes Hope to a bomber base in England. Doolittle hosts Hope and his troupe to dinner at the Hotel Trans Atlantique at Tunis, and after dinner he and Hope match witticisms. In Algiers Hope has a long visit with Eisenhower and pays him the compliment of noting that Ike spoke with the same intonations and tonal registers as Clark Gable. Pushing on to Palermo, Hope meets with Patton in the palace in which Patton had established his headquarters. Patton and Hope discuss mutual friends in Southern California. Patton has his own camera and takes Hope's picture. That night, after performing for Patton's troops, Hope and his troupe attend dinner with the general and his staff, with Patton showing them personally around the palace. After dinner Hope, Langford, Tony Romano, and Jack Pepper put on an impromptu performance for Patton and his staff. (In *I Never Left Home*, Hope defended Patton in the slapping incident that almost cost Patton his command. "As far as I'm concerned," Hope argued, "a general can have war fatigue, too.")[4] Hope, in short, is treated like royalty, down to the enumeration of the special meals—porterhouse steaks, bacon and eggs, other scarce items—that mess sergeants seem able to conjure up for him and his troupe from base to base. On the other hand, *Time* made much of the fact that Hope also stood in the chow line with the men, like royalty rubbing shoulders with commoners. In London Hope is presented to the King and Queen, and in Morocco he is presented to the son of the ruling pasha, yet he is himself a royal from Hollywood, granted this status by the culture of mass entertainment.

The subtleties of sustaining such a status amidst young men facing death are many and complex. Standing in line with the troops for chow is one of them. Hospital visits are another. In *I Never Left Home* Hope is careful to present in detail his visits to the wounded. He and Frances Langford move through the rows of beds of the wounded, some of them dying, many disfigured for life, in what seems, sixty years later, almost a carefully organized ritual: Hollywood healing the wounded, the royal touch, which in the medieval world was believed to have the ability to cure sickness. Now and then—in a discussion, for example, of how military psychiatrists treat battle fatigue—something of the horror of it all seeps through; but then the drums roll, and Hope and his ghost writers intone a paean to American courage. "No group of men is ever going to top in spirit and courage," Hope tells us, "the kids from the streets of American cities, from American farms and factories, Sunday school rooms, poolrooms, shipping rooms, and business offices. Their ability to take it really rocked German soldiers back on their heels."[5]

To deal with the incongruity of his position, a privileged civilian at the front, Hope adopted the defensive strategy of making his alleged cowardice part of his routine. He claimed that his classification was 7L, coward. At Bone in Tunisia, a point of embarkation for the invasion of Sicily, Hope was playing a mixed audience of American infantry and sailors, WACs, WRENS, and Red Cross personnel when from the back of the crowd was hollered the very question from a heckler that Hope had told Ed Sullivan he was most worried about. "Draft dodger!" the heckler cried. "Why aren't you in uniform?" There was a moment of stunned silence, then Hope, ever quick on the comeback, offered in riposte: "Don't you know there's a war on? A guy could get hurt!"[6] In *I Never Left Home*, however, Hope is careful to give in meticulous detail the three air raids he experienced, especially the third one: in Algiers, when he comforted a weeping Frances Langford.

Now and then, the troops could be restless. A frequent motif in Hope's routines and in his discussion of his tours in *I Never Left Home* is the fear of laying an egg. Hope notes constantly how men call out jokes from the audience, their one-liners meeting his one-liners in return. He is proud of his ability to hold his own; but is there not also in these encounters as well as in his fear a knowledge on Hope's part that he is playing a dangerous game, gagging for men in danger of their lives? Did Hope fear the boos as much as he relished the laughs and the cheers? From this perspective, Hope's performances involved an act of mastery over the men and over the situation, and when that mastery grew tenuous (and as a skilled comic Hope could always sense such a moment), he had Frances Langford, who as a woman embodied another principle of entertainment entirely.

Hope needed Langford, almost desperately, and personally begged her husband, actor Jon Hall, to give her permission to go on the tours. As an attractive American woman, resplendent in slacks, midriff blouse, and high pompadour, Langford got more than her share of the obvious kind of attention, including such corny remarks from Hope as "What an inspiration a pair of Hollywood legs were to those men! A few days later, Italy surrendered."[7] (Rimshot six from gag writer number three!) Hope is constantly making such harmless but patronizing remarks regarding Langford's appeal. After all, this was 1943. Yet for all the sexist humor, Langford emerges in *I Never Left Home* as fully Hope's equal—indeed, his respected superior—as far as the troops are concerned. In the hospital wards, Langford makes no jokes. She kisses the wounded, and her songs are capable of bringing tears to men's eyes.

More than Hope's jokes, she and the songs she sings embodied the sweetness of life as experienced by those in danger of dying or recently returned from the fray.

Hope returned to the United States and the canonization of a *Time* cover. "He was friendly," remarked *Time*, "ate with servicemen, drank with them, read their doggerel, listened to their songs. He was indefatigable, running himself ragged, with five, six, seven shows a day. He was figurative—the straight link with home, the radio voice that for years had filled the living room and that in foreign parts called up its image. Hence boys whom Hope might entertain for an hour awaited him for weeks, and when he came, anonymous guys who had had no other recognition felt personally remembered." Hollywood could expect no greater tribute. In Bob Hope, Hollywood had become the voice of the anonymous, the masses, while remaining in elite circumstances and operating at a profit. Hope had brought Hollywood to the soldiers and let some of it rub off. At the conclusion of *I Never Left Home*, Hope would append a long quote from a letter from a young lieutenant to his parents back in the States testifying to the thrill of seeing Bob Hope in person in a USO show in Sicily. "When the war ends," Hope told *Time*, "it'll be an awful let-down."[8]

In films such as *Stage Door Canteen* (1943), *Star-Spangled Rhythm* (1943), *Thank Your Lucky Stars* (1943), *This Is the Army* (1943), and *Follow the Boys* (1944), Hollywood continued to congratulate itself on its patriotism and to showcase the power of the film industry to advance the war effort. Then, in December 1944, previewed for release in 1945, came *Hollywood Canteen* from Warner Brothers. The studio constructed an exact replica of the Hollywood Canteen on one of its sound stages and gathered the talents of sixty-two stars to play themselves in a story loosely scripted by Delmer Daves, who also directed. The plot of *Hollywood Canteen* was virtually non-existent. The point of the film was to show the Canteen in operation and to showcase Warner Brothers celebrities exactly as they might be performing there on any given night. Bette Davis and John Garfield played themselves, making sandwiches, hosting servicemen and -women, organizing the entertainment. Davis even jitterbugged. Joan Crawford served soft drinks.

What was disquieting about all this, beyond the crass self-promotion, was the attitude shown toward servicemen in the picture. Los Angeles *Times* critic Edwin Schallert was especially disturbed by a scene in which the sophisticated actor Paul Henreid, whose heart was most recently on fire for humanity as Laszlo in *Casablanca*, baits a simple serviceman played by Dane Clark in what was supposed to be a comic routine. For a brief horrifying moment of honesty, the aristocrat-peasant relationship between star and ordinary American surfaced, whether the audiences of the time realized it or not. Even more offensive, although not mentioned by Schallert, was the scene in which a serviceman has to be convinced by Hedy Lamarr that she is the real Hedy Lamarr: the serviceman, a slow-talking country boy, finally cannot believe his luck. Not a single serviceman in *Hollywood Canteen* emerges with any discernible autonomy when fortunate enough to meet a real live Hollywood star from Warner Brothers. They melt, rather, in grateful awe before these representatives from the kingdom of enchantment. *Hollywood Canteen* was not a film, even a sappy film, about how brave these young men were as they headed into harm's way. *Hollywood Canteen* was, rather, a celebration of how good Hollywood was to be on hand personally to send them off. Many enlisted men, seeing the film, were outraged, and a group of them signed a joint letter to the press protesting this "slur on the intelligence and acumen of every member of the armed services."[9]

No servicemen protested the presence of Marlene Dietrich on the Italian, French, and German fronts. If Bob Hope represented Hollywood as comic routine and only incidentally allowed Frances Langford to speak for deeper things, Dietrich deepened and expanded the implications of Langford's femininity and singing. In a very profound way, despite her genuine loyalty to her new country, Dietrich came from both sides of the conflict. In her sexuality, Dietrich was as much Berlin as Hollywood; and in this sexuality, as a matter of body and soul, seethed a radical apprehension of the futility of war, for all its comradeship and bravery, that supplemented and reinforced Hope's more comic (albeit equally necessary) perspective.

Blonde, blue-eyed, Prussian to the core, Dietrich had been born in Berlin, the upper-middle-class daughter of a Prussian war hero who held the Iron Cross for gallantry under fire as a major in the elite Uhlan Cavalry Regiment in the Franco-Prussian War. In 1937 Adolf Hitler had sent Marlene Dietrich Christmas gifts, including a German-grown Christmas tree, and had suggested to her through intermediaries that if she chose to return to her native country and formed a connection with the Führer she might preside gloriously at his side as First Lady of the Third Reich. At this suggestion, Dietrich had thrown back her head and laughed, in much the same way that her character Lola-Lola had laughed to scorn Professor Unrat in *The Blue Angel* (1930), the film that had launched the Berlin actress and cabaret singer into international stardom. The Führer was not amused. Had Dietrich been captured by the Germans in either the tour of 1944 or the tour of 1945, she stood in danger of being executed as a traitor to Germany. Just a month earlier, in December 1944, during the Battle of the Bulge, such a capture and execution had become a distinct possibility when Dietrich found herself with a unit surrounded by Germans commanded, interestingly enough, by German General Sepp Dietrich. Fortunately, Dietrich had been rescued from the sky by paratroopers from the 82nd Airborne Division personally led by division commander Major General James Gavin. An eyewitness to the rescue claims that Gavin, one of the youngest and most dashing general officers in World War II, personally knelt at Dietrich's feet before sweeping her up and placing her in a jeep for the escape back to Paris.

Marlene Dietrich had a powerful capacity to communicate to men, whether they be major generals, non-coms, or PFCs, a distinctive amalgam of sexuality and comradeship. Here, after all, was the great and good friend, the pal, of Clark Gable, Gary Cooper, and a younger actor, John Wayne, with whom Dietrich had hunted and fished in the backcountry of Southern California and gone to USC football games in 1940 and 1941. Dietrich's capacity for comradeship—for at once attracting men sexually yet remaining their pal as well—was evident throughout her career. It was, in fact, an essential aspect of her identity as a Berliner: a daughter, that is, of a culture in which sexuality possessed a public, even defiant streak that was part of the strong anti-establishment strain that ran through the Berlin psyche.

Prior to her departure for Hollywood, Dietrich had been a fixed figure in the café life of Berlin in the late 1920s. Despite marriage and motherhood, and her own proper upbringing, Dietrich liked to hang out with a rat pack that included Billy Wilder, then a journalist in Berlin, the novelist Erich Maria Remarque, with whom she conducted a longtime affair, Ernest Udet, the German air ace, novelists Leonhard Frank and Heinrich Mann, cabaret singer Fritzi Massari, and the celebrated comedian Max Pallenberg. Dietrich could also be found at the various transvestite clubs of Berlin, to which she frequently wore male dress; the Ring Club favored by ex-convicts, the bar at the Hotel Eden; or such vibrant cafés as the Silhouette, the White Rose, the Always Faithful. Everywhere she went, Dietrich exuded a comradely demeanor toward one and all, gay or straight, high or low in the social hierarchy. "She was like a free and easy boy," film director Geza von Sziffra later remembered, "and with her buddy-like comradeship she stifled every possible emotion of her would-be dates."[10]

In Hollywood Dietrich resumed her café-crawling, as much as one could in a city devoid of Berlin's night life. She shifted the scene of her socializing to private parties and premieres in addition to hotel bars and restaurants. As in Berlin, she preferred to hang out with men as one of the boys. She electrified Hollywood in 1932, for example, when she appeared with Maurice Chevalier and Gary Cooper at the premiere of *The Sign of the Cross* wearing a man's fedora and tuxedo. Dietrich loved to cross-dress. She played one of her Berlin films, *The Ship of Lost Men* (1929), almost exclusively in male attire. In Hollywood, aside from her tuxedo, she pioneered the wearing of slacks and pants suits. The public relations team at Paramount, after some confusion, got the point. They issued publicity stills of Dietrich in slacks and other forms of male attire, which they packaged with the slogan "The woman even women can adore!"[11] In her first American film, *Morocco* (1930), Dietrich did the closest thing to a lesbian love scene that American censors would allow or American audiences tolerate.

Marlene Dietrich, in short, compellingly communicated *eros* in its many guises: an *eros* that was, most basically, a species of comradeship. Dietrich knew how to be the good comrade to men (and sometimes to women as well), and never more so than when young men were in danger. This ability to communicate comradeship with men, so crucial to the Dietrich mystique, extended to German soldiers as well, who even more than their American counterparts knew Dietrich as a living legend as actress and singer. In 1942 the Office of Strategic Services asked Dietrich to record a number of American standards—"Time on My Hands" and "Taking a Chance on Love" among them—in German for broadcast to German troops. These songs, sung in a husky soulful style bridging singing and the spoken word, a technique Dietrich had mastered in the cabarets of Berlin in the 1920s, made her a cult figure among German troops. When visiting American hospital wards on her combat zone tours, Dietrich would also call on wounded German POWs and speak to them in German, and these German boys, many of them still teenagers, would find, like their American peers, a moment's release in the compelling presence of an attractive older woman who was at once their temptress and their comrade.

Deep within the Dietrich aura, as fact as well as subliminal message, spoke a subversive text—war stinks, it kills young men on both sides—that might have disconcerted the USO officials and certainly General Patton, another Dietrich admirer, if it had ever explicitly surfaced. For a later generation Dietrich's recording of "Where Have All the Flowers Gone?" served as a rallying cry for the antiwar movement. In 1944 and 1945 Dietrich's presence among the troops—she wore their uniform, she stood with them in the chow line, she joined with them to right an overturned jeep, she finally found herself confined with them to an Army hospital, the victim of exhaustion and a viral infection—communicated to the men, without explicit statement, a message that their lives were imperiled but that they were acting bravely nevertheless in the midst of this terrible conflict. War stank, and Marlene Dietrich was on hand to keep company with the soliders, sailors, and airmen.

Dietrich left the United States for her first USO tour in February 1944 in the company of her master of ceremonies, the young Lebanese-American comedian Danny Thomas, singer Milton Frome, and pianist Jack Schneider, who also played the accordion. She traveled with fifty-five pounds of baggage, which included four wrinkle-resistent sequined evening dresses and her musical saw, which she had learned to play in Berlin. Traveling from base to base in North Africa, Dietrich usually opened her act with a rendition of "See What the Boys in the Back Room Will Have" (which she had sung in the 1939 film, *Destry Rides Again*), followed by a performance on the saw, held between her legs like a cello. The troops inevitably went bananas, filling the tent or the outdoor amphitheater with a whining, high-pitched noise.

This noise filled a theater one night in Italy, after Dietrich had followed the troops from Anzio up the peninsula. Playing a routine with singer-actor Milton Frome, Dietrich began to compare film and stage kissing techniques. She then turned to Danny Thomas and asked him: "Do you want to learn how to kiss?" Thomas stammered back: "N-n-no, n-no, th-thank you!" At this, the men in the audience began to shout their willingness to volunteer. "Suddenly," Danny Thomas later remembered, "I heard the most amazing thing I've ever heard in my life. As she walked towards me, pawing her thighs, thrusting up her breasts, there was a groan from the thousands of men. The sensuality of this incredible woman had gotten to them. She was the *female* incarnate! What I was hearing was the orgasmic cry of humans in heat. I knew what was going to happen, and I stopped the show cold: I called the MP's. They jumped on the stage with machine guns. It's a good thing they did, because the men had started to rush the stage."[12]

It was the cry of *eros* over *thanatos*, life over death, which Sigmund Freud had grappled with in *Civilization and Its Discontents* and finally believed to be the real issue behind the First World War and any coming conflict: whether the destructive forces of darkness and death would, in their ancient enmity, rise up once again and extinguish life. Hollywood had no greater theme; yet nothing comparable to *All Quiet on the Western Front* would emerge from its studios in the 1941–45 period: a film, that is, capable of honestly presenting the fundamental absurdity and ultimate horror of war, even when entered upon for righteous purposes. John Huston's *The Battle for San Pietro* achieved such depth; but this was combat reportage, not a studio effort. And besides: once Huston had told the truth, the authorities knew instantly that the film could never be released. It was too terrible, and too true.

And so Frances Langford and Marlene Dietrich sang from impromptu stages near distant battlefields, and young men were reminded of home and the wives, fiancées, girlfriends, sisters, aunts, and other women in the lives they had momentarily—or perhaps forever—left behind. Singing in an unequivocally American voice, Frances Langford was instantly recognizable to the young men as one of their own. In the German accent of Marlene Dietrich and the spirit of pre-Nazi Berlin that had formed and sustained her and remained with her still, the young men were asked to recognize, at least subliminally, something much more complex and demanding about the life they loved, the dangers they faced, the fear they felt, their hope that they would not be forgotten. Telling them that they were remembered, each of them, even as they were being asked to go into harm's way, the Hollywood Canteen as represented by Frances Langford, Marlene Dietrich, and sometime second banana Bob Hope made some amends for the rotten movie of 1945.

7

1946 ✶ *Homecoming*

Atotal of 26,019 Californians serving in the armed forces since the declaration of unlimited national emergency on 27 May 1941 had lost their lives to battle and non-battle causes by 1946. For them, there would be no homecoming, no excited return to familiar places, no embrace from family and loved ones, no visiting old haunts while still in uniform, no resumption of prior identities, no weddings, no jobs, no new homes in the suburbs, no children. Had they lived, they would have taken their places in all ranks of society and witnessed the transformation of California into a world commonwealth. Their lives, which might have been such a welcomed addition to the California story of the next half century and more, remained now memorialized only in the laconic records of the War Department, on tombstones in foreign or American cemeteries, on bronze plaques in public spaces listing the war dead, in commemorative entries in high school or college yearbooks, the fading memories of successive class reunions, but, most important, in the deep and grieving entombment in loving and forever broken hearts.

When Les Ewing's mother was notified that her son, an infantry enlisted man with the 34th Division in Italy, had been killed during fighting just below Bologna on 24 October 1944, she left Les's room in the family's Westwood home untouched and intact, just as Les had left it when he went off to Camp Roberts in September 1943. Here, then, in the terrible months that followed the notification by the Army, Les's family might still find evidence of Les's days at Beverly Hills High School, where he had served as captain of the baseball and basketball teams, and UCLA, where Les had played baseball as well while majoring in economics and enjoying good times at the Zeta Psi fraternity house.

Throughout 1946, *UCLA Magazine* was running pictures and profiles of all of Les's friends and classmates who had died in the war. William Thompson, for example, who had volunteered for Army service in June 1940, had been killed by artillery on Corregidor the night before that bastion fell. In the chaos, no casualty lists were available; and for another three years Bill Thompson's family sustained a desperate hope because Bill was still being carried on the missing list, as was another UCLA Bruin, Staff Sergeant Chester Wuertley, a radio operator and gunner on a B-24, missing in action since his bomber went down off the Philippines in late 1944. Not until 15 March 1946 did the War Department move Wuertley from the missing to the presumably dead category since, as the telegram put it, "no information had been received which would support a presumption of his continued survival." Don Brown, son of the film comedian Joe E. Brown and a pal of Les Ewing's at Beverly Hills High School and later at UCLA, also lost his life early in the war, in 1942, in a training accident while serving as a cadet in the Army Air Corps. Hitoshi (Moe) Yonemura, a respected UCLA cheerleader and ROTC cadet, had been interned at Heart Mountain, Wyoming, in 1942. Released when he enlisted in the Army, Moe Yonemura lost his life in fierce fighting in France as a member of the 442nd Regimental Combat Team.

As 1945 turned into 1946, Les Ewing's mother continued to keep his room just as he had left it. When, if ever, can a mother forget? Or a father, for that matter, as was the case of San Francisco industrialist Charles Kendrick, brooding since 1943 over the loss of his beloved son Charles, a Marine aviator lost in the jungles of Guadalcanal. Les Ewing's mother knew where her son was buried, in the American Military Cemetery at Bologna. The remains of Charles Kendrick Jr. had been hastily interred by advancing Marines on the jungle knoll where the young aviator had crashed. Unsettled, unwilling to let go, Charles Kendrick Sr. used his military connections to wrangle a flight to Guadalcanal and, with the help of a local Marist missionary priest, hacked through the impenetrable jungle, fighting heat and insects and his own fatigue, until he found the site where his son's Grauman F4F had gone down four and a half years earlier. Digging up the knoll with the help of local natives, Kendrick recovered the skeleton of the son of whom he was so proud, wrapped and buried in the plane's rubber emergency raft, which the Marines had used as a makeshift shroud. Kendrick wept to see what time and death had exacted, then brought his son's remains back to Henderson Field, where, the next day, the Marist missionary offered a requiem mass; and Charles Kendrick Sr.—Major Kendrick from World War I, holder of the Legion of Honor, assured industrialist and civic leader of San Francisco—wept once again as he thought of the short life of his heroic son and heard the angelic voices of children from the mission school, near naked and in bare feet, singing "Nearer, My God, to Thee." With Charles Kendrick Jr.'s remains safely ensconced in the family crypt south of San Francisco, the Kendrick family achieved a measure of closure and resignation to the loss of its beloved son and brother.

So too as 1946 progressed did Les Ewing's mother begin to feel a measure of healing for her bereavement. Les's younger brother Frank, who had flown for American Airlines during the war and was now in the insurance business in Tulsa,

Oklahoma, had named his fourteen-month-old son Leslie Newberry Ewing III in honor of his older brother. Mrs. Ewing, meanwhile, was hearing and reading of the housing shortage for returning veterans at UCLA. Contacting the university, she rented Les's room to a returning veteran and his wife, with full kitchen privileges and use of all common spaces. It was good to have young people in the house again.

Hundreds of thousands of California veterans and those who had chosen to become Californians were flooding back into the Golden State, anxious to restart, repossess, reinvigorate, or, if need be, reinvent their lives. James Milton Brown of San Francisco, among so many others, was back, resplendent in his first lieutenant's uniform and the medals he had won in fifty missions over Italy and the continent as a B-17 bombardier and nose gunner with the 341st Bomb Squadron of the 97th Bombardment Group, including a low-level raid on Ploesti for which surviving crew members were given double mission credit. Awarded the Air Medal for downing a German fighter and given partial credit for two others, Brown had trouble believing he was still alive (eight of his original crew would not survive the war) that morning of 27 April 1944 as he returned from his last mission. Writing his mother and sister the next day (he had been too nervous to write between his fortieth mission and his last), Brown inscribed an over-large "50" atop his letter, which he underlined three times, and described himself as belonging to a "select and, unfortunately, small group called 'Fifty Missioners.'" How he had sweated out those last ten missions, Brown exulted! Yet "yesterday as we were coming back I'd look out over the sky at all those hundreds of beautiful 'Fortresses' flying alongside of me and I got the biggest lump in my throat and I felt just as alive as can be."[1]

And now he was back! First there had been the emotional return to the family home on Cole Street in the Haight-Ashbury district fronting Golden Gate Park, followed by a series of reunion parties with his pals from St. Ignatius High School and the University of San Francisco (scores would not be returning), including the resumption of the touch football games his gang had enjoyed before the war in the great meadow near Kezar Stadium, followed by a few beers at the nearby Kezar or Lucky clubs. What an amazing thing for Brown to awake now each morning, late, not in the middle of the night as before a mission, with the duty orderly shining his flashlight in your face and suggesting you rise for chow, a briefing, and take-off; but to awaken on a more leisurely basis, with yet another day of your terminal leave awaiting you as well as plans for the evening that might include dinner at Omar Khayyam's, the Blue Fox, or the Fairmont, with one or another of the executives from the Leo J. Meyberg Company anxious to re-recruit Brown back into the sales force—which is what happened as soon as Brown's terminal leave ended and he was released from active duty: a better version of his old job, this time covering Marin County and the north coast as far as the Oregon border (and this, as soon as possible, in a sleek green Chrysler sedan, once such a car became available), representing the distributing company for which Brown's late father had worked. By 1946 the Meyberg Company held a near-monopoly on RCA and affiliated products—radios, phonographs, and 78 rpm vinyl records, refrigerators, kitchen ranges, and other appliances, washing machines—all, in short, that bespoke in the language of consumerism the good life that Jim Brown and America had regained, indeed fully earned, by winning the war.

How sweet it was, on V-E Day, 8 May 1945, for Robert Easton of Santa Barbara to be with his infantry battalion in Bielefeld, Germany, knowing that he, too, had survived some of the fiercest combat of the war. Easton's unit passed in review before the commanding general of the division and the regimental commander; then there was a memorial service for battalion dead. Back home in Santa Barbara, meanwhile, the bells of the old Franciscan mission joined those of the rest of the city in celebrating the victory. But even as they pealed, Jane Easton was worried about the reassignment of her husband's unit to the invasion of Japan. Then came the dropping of the atom bomb in August and the rerouting of Bob's unit, already heading to the Pacific theater. On 9 November 1945 Robert Easton was standing in the courtyard of the home in Santa Barbara he had never seen. "The months, the years," he would later remember, "have boiled down to this." Jane was waiting inside nervously, her two girls freshly dressed, Katherine, the younger, saying that she had to go pee-pee. Jane took Katherine upstairs; just as she was holding the child over the toilet, her older daughter, Joan, shouted from the top of the stairs: "It's Daddy!" Jane and the two girls swept downstairs into Robert's arms. "Then Jane and I cling to each other," Bob later remembered, "just the two of us, laughing and crying, while our little girls gaze up in wonder. It is all over—and it's all beginning."[2]

Equally fulfilling was the return of Irma Leyres Flannery to her teaching job at the Roosevelt Junior High School in Compton. Flannery had joined the Marine Corps in 1943, shortly after receiving her master's degree from USC, and while on active duty had married another Trojan on duty in the submarine service. Trojan alumna Oloanne Dykeman, meanwhile, a WAC command librarian responsible for tracking military documents, was being released in February 1946 after two and a half years of duty at various Army Air Forces bases around the country. After eighteen months in Italy and Africa with the Signal Corps, WAC T/5 Gertrude Elaine Beame, another Trojan, was back in Los Angeles in the same month, February 1946, considering her options, as was Red Cross field director Evelyn Johnson, also a USC alumna, who had moved with her unit, the 300th General Hospital, just behind the lines at Anzio, up the boot to Italy, then through France and Germany, only slightly behind the combat lines. Assigned to the 27th Evacuation Hospital of the 7th Army on the French Riviera, Johnson had arranged innumerable bridal teas for American soldiers taking French, English, and Polish young women for brides. Back in civilian clothes, Johnson was enjoying a loafing vacation at her Los Angeles home and thinking about returning to her former position as a teacher in the Mark Keppel High School in Alhambra.

Freshly released from the Navy, in which he had enlisted in 1944 at the age of seventeen, Cesar Chavez returned to Delano in north central Kern County after a tour of duty in the Mariana Islands and Guam as a deckhand and painter. In contrast to the more positive recollections of so many of his Anglo contemporaries, Chavez would later remember his two years in the Navy as the worst two years in his life, given the discrimination he had experienced in an organization in which Mexican-Americans were confined to the lowest possible jobs and ratings. Yet young Chavez had received medical attention for the first time from a qualified doctor while in the Navy. He had also discovered, to his amazement, that various white ethnic groups were warring with each other, not just with people of color, and this insight broadened Chavez's horizons as to the more complex causes and patterns of discrimination. While on leave just before shipping out for the South Pacific, Chavez, dressed in his civies, had—almost as a spur-of-the-moment de-cision—refused to sit in the colored section of the movie theater in Delano on the upper right side of the aisle reserved for Mexicans, Filipinos, and African-Americans. The theater manager had called the police, and Chavez had been taken briefly into custody. Cesar Chavez had joined the Navy in 1944 because he was tired of the back-breaking work of thinning sugar beets. Returning to Delano after the war, he married his sweetheart Helen, and, after a brief honeymoon, the two returned to a one-room shack in a labor camp, heated by a kerosene stove, and Chavez went to work picking grapes and cotton.

More privileged was the return of former UCLA quarterback Bob Waterfield, medically discharged from the Army in 1944. Joining the Cleveland Rams, Wa-terfield led his team to a National Football League championship and was named Most Valuable Player of the year. And now, in 1946, married to his Van Nuys high school sweetheart, film star Jane Russell, currently appearing in Howard Hughes's controversial film *The Outlaw*, Waterfield was returning to Los Angeles with the Rams, the first National Football League team to move west. Like every-thing else in the United States, the Second World War had been a war of privilege. Men with college degrees had an easier time getting into officer training programs; and men with connections and special skills, be they football or typing, had a way of being assigned to the safer sectors—even if they preferred otherwise. Alan Cran-ston of Los Altos, for example, a Stanford graduate with an impressive record as a foreign correspondent before the war, had voluntarily left a cushy assignment at the Office of War Information to volunteer for the Army in 1944 at the age of twenty-nine. Nearly everyone in his basic training unit was assigned to an infantry battalion and sent directly overseas; but Cranston, who had himself hoped for front-line service, was specifically reassigned to the Army Service Forces to perform basically the same task he had performed at the Office of War Information, only this time as a private first class earning $21 a month. While on active duty, Cran-ston managed to write a book on the League of Nations controversy, *The Killing of the Peace*, which the New York *Times* rated one of the ten best books of 1945 because of its telling use of the failure of the League of Nations as a reverse paradigm for what the newly formed United Nations must do following the end

of the war. By 1946 Cranston, a discharged sergeant, was back in Los Altos just
south of the Stanford campus with his wife Geneva, whom he had married while
in the service. Joining his father in the family real estate and house-building business, Cranston was looking forward to a career in politics.

Paul Smith, meanwhile, was settling back into his pre-war life as editor of the
San Francisco *Chronicle*. A *Wunderkind* up from nowhere, managing editor of
the *Chronicle* while still in his mid-twenties, Smith had turned down an offer of
a direct commission in the Navy and, despite the fact that he was in his thirties,
had enlisted in the Marine Corps as a private. After combat service in the Pacific
and an earned advancement into the commissioned ranks, Smith had been reassigned to the Navy as a high-level admiral's aide and public affairs officer. As such
Smith—a mere sixty hours out of his watery foxhole in Okinawa—had found
himself on the cocktail circuit in San Francisco, based out of a suite at the Mark
Hopkins Hotel during the founding of the United Nations, on special assignment
from Secretary of the Navy James Forrestal. His diplomatic and intelligence-
gathering tasks completed (off-the-record conversations with, among others, foreign
ministers Lord Halifax and Jan Masaryk), Smith spent a poolside and tennis-court
weekend with State Department officials Adlai Stevenson and Archibald MacLeish
at *Chronicle* publisher George Cameron's estate in Hillsborough, where the talk
was all of the coming post-war world order, followed by a weekend at Cave Man
Camp at the Bohemian Grove presided over by Herbert Hoover, who had given
Smith his start fifteen years earlier when Hoover had hired Smith as his private
secretary. Then back to Guam, with an assignment to handle all press coverage
for the Navy and Marine Corps in the invasion of Japan, which never happened.
After another half year of high-level duty with the fleet and in occupied Japan,
including fact-finding tours of atom bomb–leveled Hiroshima and Nagasaki, Paul
Smith was back at his desk at the *Chronicle*, age thirty-seven, "youthful and ready,
willing, and able to help put the world back together again."[3]

Almost immediately, Smith resumed his pre-war parties in his duplex apartment
atop Telegraph Hill, upon which bachelor Smith was by 1946 lavishing a significant percentage of his $40,000-a-year salary in restoration and furnishing while
maintaining a full-time chef and full-time bartender-houseman. A regular at
Smith's soirees was another returned young *Chronicle* staffer, Herb Caen, who had
served under Smith before the war and had now been released from a stint in the
Army Air Corps as a London-based press officer. When Caen, a Sacramento native
and self-described junior college dropout, was returned from Europe and released
from the service, Smith gave him back his gossip column, which resumed in the
Chronicle on 1 January 1946 under the heading "One Man's San Francisco."

In Herb Caen's first post-war column was distilled the controlling paradigm of
the thousands of daily columns to follow over the next half century. In item after
item—a sailor and a WAC kissing outside the Clift Hotel at 2:00 A.M., Pulitzer
Prize–winning photographer Joe Rosenthal (the Marine flag-raising at Iwo Jima)
quitting the Associated Press, café society socialite Dave Falks and his wife going

fini, but Joe and Dorothy DiMaggio floating rumors of a reconciliation for the umpteenth time, a beribboned GI identifying himself at the money order desk in the Mission Street Post Office by whipping out his false teeth and revealing his name inlaid in gold letters on the upper plate—Caen was once again amusing his readers and corroborating their deep desire to see San Francisco as a magical place. For fifty years, Caen would successfully ply this beat, columnist laureate of "Baghdad by the Bay," as he dubbed San Francisco, telling and retelling an implied meta-narrative of how the World War II generation, having fought the good fight, was now settling into a Bay Area version of the good life.

Former Navy Lieutenant JG Neil Morgan, meanwhile, who would soon be performing a similar function for San Diego for an even longer period, was getting his start as cub reporter for the San Diego *Daily Journal*, an afternoon Democratic paper seriously engaged in covering the strike at Convair. While an undergraduate at Wake Forest College near Raleigh, North Carolina, Morgan had worked as assistant state editor for the Raleigh *News and Observer*, responsible for coordinating some two hundred stringers. Just before his release from the Navy in April 1946, Morgan had returned to Raleigh and to the *News and Observer*, expecting to spend the rest of his life there. After two short evenings in Raleigh, however, Morgan realized that he was even recognizing the same trash cans from before the war at the *News and Observer* office. If things could be so stable in Raleigh, Morgan asked himself, that even trash cans survived the war intact, then what would his future life in Raleigh be like? San Diego, by contrast, where Morgan had spent eight months assigned to the Kearny Naval Auxiliary Air Station at Miramar, offered an uncertain but challenging future. Hitching a ride back to San Diego on a MATS DC-4, Morgan took his discharge in that city and, on the basis of his Wake Forest degree, Phi Beta Kappa key, and pre-war experience as assistant state editor for the *News and Observer*, landed a job covering the Convair strike.

Some, then, returned to old jobs. Others had new jobs thrust upon them. For some, like Paul Smith, it was sweet to begin once again at the top, as it was for Army Major William Knowland, age thirty-seven, scion of the powerful East Bay publishing and political family that had given Governor Earl Warren his start. Appointed by Warren to the United States Senate on 14 August 1945 to fill out the remaining term of the recently deceased Hiram Johnson, Knowland arrived in Washington in his Army uniform, trousers tucked into combat boots, and was honorably discharged from the service so he could be sworn into the Senate. A somewhat rumpled naval lieutenant, meanwhile, Richard Milhous Nixon, a graduate of Whittier College and Duke University Law School, after a tour of duty in the South Pacific, was working in Baltimore handling contract termination negotiations between the Navy and the Glenn L. Martin Company. In early October 1945 Nixon received a letter from Whittier Bank of America branch manager Herman Perry that made a rather startling proposal in three one-sentence paragraphs in something like fifty words: "Dear Dick: I am writing this short note to ask you if you would like to be a candidate for Congress on the Republican ticket in 1946. Jerry Voorhis expects to run—registration is about 50–50. The Republicans are gaining. Please airmail me your reply if you are interested."[4] Lieutenant Nixon was interested. Within the year, he was a congressman. Within four years, he was a United States senator. Within six years, the former reserve naval lieutenant was Vice President of the United States.

An attorney with degrees from Whittier and Duke, Richard Nixon was capable of launching himself into his new career without the need for further education. Hundreds of thousands of returning veterans, by contrast, considered themselves in need of further training, and thanks to Title 2 of the Servicemen's Readjustment Act of 1944, signed by Roosevelt on 22 June 1944, they would get it. Public Law 346, as it was officially designated (but more popularly known as the GI Bill of Rights, as the American Legion, its primary sponsor, named it), guaranteed returning veterans health care for the disabled or sick (Title 1), education or training in any accredited school (Title 2), 50 percent of a loan for the purchase of a home, farm stock or equipment, or a business property for private enterprise (Title 3), employment counseling (Title 4), and unemployment insurance (Title 5). Under Title 2 veterans were entitled to a maximum of forty-eight months of training and/ or education, depending upon their length of service. The Veterans Administration would pay up to $500 a year in tuition and fees, together with a $65-a-month living allowance for married veterans, $50 a month for singles. Across the next ten years, some 7.8 million veterans, more than half of the total of those who served in uniform in World War II, received education or training under the GI Bill, some 2.2 million of them at colleges and universities.

Millions received technical or vocational training. Philip Soto, for example, a returning Mexican-American from East Los Angeles, recently employed as a gunner on B-17s over Europe, used his benefits to study basic electronics at the National School in Los Angeles for a year, followed by a six-month course in advanced electronics. Qualifying for a second-class license from the Federal Communications Commission, Soto went into the television and radio transmission repair and service business, with a sideline in the repair of radios, phonographs, and tape recorders. Married shortly after his release from the service, Soto also used the GI Bill to buy a home in La Puente in eastern Los Angeles County. With even further assistance from the GI Bill, Soto was able to establish his own company, Bandini Television, in a onetime nursery facility in the city of Commerce. Thus the GI Bill assisted the former combat airman to receive training in electronics, to buy a home, to start a business, and, eventually, to enter politics and become a pioneering Mexican-American member of the California state assembly.

Another Mexican-American veteran, Daniel Luevano, released from the Navy, used his benefits to become a pioneering Latino undergraduate at UCLA, where, thanks to an offer from undergraduate Eugene Lee, later a noted political scientist at UC Berkeley, Luevano joined the Phi Kappa Psi fraternity, another pioneering venture for a Latino in that era. Completing undergraduate and law degrees, Luevano went on to a career in state administration culminating with his appointment in 1960 as chief deputy director of finance in the administration of Governor Edmund G. (Pat) Brown. Arthur Alarcon, meanwhile, yet another Mexican-American who had gone to UCLA on the GI Bill after military service (four battle stars as a combat infantryman in Europe), was serving as Pat Brown's clemency and, later, executive secretary prior to an appointment to the Los Angeles Superior Court and, later, the Court of Appeal.

By 1946 California campuses were brimming with young men and a lesser number of young women wearing mix-and-match amalgams of military, co-ed, and Joe College attire. By September 1947, for example, 43 percent of the entire UCLA student body was comprised of returned veterans on the GI Bill. Their elected student body president, Ken Kiefer, had spent four years as a Navy enlisted man. Kiefer was the first married person to be elected president of the Associated Students of UCLA. He and his wife Virginia lived in a trailer on Kiefer's GI Bill stipend and the extra $50 a month he earned as bookstore janitor. The *UCLA Magazine* for November 1946 featured a photo of Army Air Force veteran Gene Dunn carrying his wife Gwyne across the threshold of their apartment in the new UCLA veterans' housing project: a complex of more than three hundred three-room units (bedroom, bathroom, a combination living room–kitchen) in twenty-two two-story wooden housing units, renting for $29 a month unfurnished, $33 a month furnished. Built during the war to house Kaiser shipyard workers in Vanport, Oregon, the units were acquired by UCLA from the federal Public Housing Authority, dismantled, shipped to Los Angeles, then reassembled on Gayley Avenue. To accommodate wheelchair-bound veterans, UCLA installed ramps on all its campus buildings decades before such ramping became national law.

At USC veterans comprised more than half of the 12,249-student body by June 1946, many of them housed in Army barracks that had been purchased from the federal government and brought in from nearby training camps. Among the returning veterans were future Assembly Speaker Jesse Unruh, future Congressman Philip Burton, future columnist Art Buchwald, and future political scientist and Democratic Party guru Francis Carney. The youngest of five children born to illiterate Texas sharecroppers, Unruh had come to USC after spending the war as an aircraft mechanic in the Navy, assigned initially to the Aleutian Islands and later to aircraft carriers, where, he later claimed, he had read every book in the library. After the war, Unruh's wife Virginia Lemon, a USC graduate, insisted that her spottily educated but voraciously read husband enroll at USC. Phil Burton, by contrast, a doctor's son from San Francisco, had already been assigned to USC in 1944 as a seventeen-year-old seaman apprentice in the V-12 program combining officer training with a college degree. Discharged from the Navy, Burton continued his education in place and graduated from USC in June 1946. Art Buchwald had enrolled at USC after enlisted Marine service in the South Pacific. Already, as an undergraduate writer, Buchwald was showing signs of a political intelligence combined with a wry sense of humor that would make him a syndicated columnist of national reputation. Francis Carney, who had left Stanford in the spring of 1943 to join the Army Air Forces, was resuming his education at USC after twenty-eight missions over enemy territory as a radioman on a C-47 Dakota. Supporting himself on the GI Bill and from earnings as a part-time staffer at the Los Angeles *Times*, Carney finished USC in short order, then went north to Stanford, where his good friend Eugene Burdick was pursuing a Ph.D. In time, with advanced degrees from Stanford and UCLA, Carney, a member of the pioneering faculty at UC Riverside, would serve as political scientist in residence, along with Burdick and Eugene Lee of UC Berkeley, to a generation of Democratic Party activists who would transform the political landscape of California.

At the Claremont Colleges thirty-five miles east of Los Angeles, in fact, so many returning veterans were applying it became necessary to jump-start the founding of a third college, the Claremont College Undergraduate School for Men, which opened its doors—almost at the last minute—on 23 September 1946, with $1 million in the bank and an enrollment of 150 students. Enrollee Morris Slack had flown B-17s and B-24s in the South Pacific, then taken charge of air intelligence in Kunming, China, before being discharged with the rank of lieutenant colonel, the same grade held by school director George C. S. Benson, who had served in Africa, Italy, and Austria in civil affairs and military government. Robert Eachus, also registering the morning the Claremont College Undergraduate School for Men opened, had won a battlefield commission in a tank destroyer battalion. Donald Phillips had likewise won a spot promotion from the ranks to ensign. James Wilcox had served in the South Pacific as a sergeant in airborne infantry and artillery. William Cronin had spent part of the war in Brazil as an enlisted technician in the Army Airways Communications Service.

Up north, in the Bay Area, meanwhile, returning veterans were pushing enrollment at UC Berkeley past twenty thousand and sparking a campus construction boom. A few miles away, at Mills College, former Army musician and occasional infantryman (at the Battle of the Bulge) Dave Brubeck was using his GI Bill to study composition under the renowned composer Darius Milhaud. Post-war music, Brubeck believed, jazz especially, would become more cerebral and complex. The days of the sweet-songed reedy dance band playing from simple charts would soon be over. What was needed by an ambitious jazz pianist such as Brubeck, an East Bay native with a musical performance degree from the University of the Pacific, was a knowledge of Music with a capital M: a mastery of harmonics, of counterpoint, polyrhythms, polytonality, and all the other intricacies of musical theory that Milhaud had mastered as a composer and a theoretician and taught with such patient skill, even to such a challenging student as Brubeck, who showed up at Mills lacking the ability to read a complex score.

As a graduate student, Brubeck organized the Dave Brubeck Octet and worked gigs at the Geary Cellar in San Francisco alongside saxophonist Paul Desmond, a student at San Francisco State, in what would turn out to be one of the longest and most fruitful partnerships in jazz history.

The education boom was not confined to the California campus. By 1946, as tens of thousands of veterans were returning to college, a younger generation of grammar and high school students in California were attending half-day sessions in temporary buildings and overcrowded classrooms. Local cities and towns could not build schools fast enough, or employ teachers fast enough, to keep up with the population boom. The little country town of Pomona, for example, in west Los Angeles County was growing at the rate of approximately four hundred families per month. When California governor Earl Warren was a freshman at Berkeley in the early 1900s, he had attended a lecture by Lord James Bryce, author of *The American Commonwealth* (1895), second only to Alexis de Tocqueville's *Democracy in America* (1835) as a perceptive account by a non-American of American life. In the course of the lecture, the Viscount predicted that California would one day have a population of fifty million. Although Bryce's prediction might have to await the second or third decade of the twenty-first century to come true, the equation of California with growth, articulated by one of the most astute analysts ever to turn his or her attention to the Golden State, remained powerfully fixed in Warren's mind.

In his campaigns for governor in 1942 and 1946, Warren ran first and foremost as an advocate of planned growth. He did not have long to wait. Between 1940 and 1950, the population of California grew from 6.9 million to 10.6 million, a gain of 53 percent. Growth was especially dramatic between 1943 and 1947. The population of California increased by two million, or 30 percent, during the war. In December 1945 alone, a total of 29,793 cars carrying a total of 82,179 people entered California from Arizona through Blythe, practically all of them intending permanent residence. Between July 1945 and July 1947, more than one million people migrated to California. Swelled by migrants and California-born baby boomers, the population of the Golden State reached nine million by 1946, ten million by 1948.

Most new residents came to California on their own, new Californians such as Dr. Harry Falk, formerly of Minneapolis, who spent three years in California as an Army medical officer and was, as of June 1946, practicing in a lean-to in a Los Angeles County suburb under construction, awaiting a proper office; or John Linder, a onetime grocery clerk from Ramsey, New Jersey, who caught a glimpse of California when passing through as a sailor and returned after the war, GI loan in hand, and bought a milk truck. By the time *Life* profiled Linder on 10 June 1946, the ex-sailor had bought four more milk trucks and was making payroll. On a macro scale Linder's entrepreneurship was reflected in the six hundred new factories established in California between 1945 and 1948. In 1947 California passed Iowa as the biggest agricultural producer in the nation, with all that this implied for increased business in processing, shipping, and distribution. Boston retail drug

executive Justin Dart brought his entire headquarters staff and their families out
to Los Angeles in early 1946, flying them to the Coast free of charge in a converted
B-17. By June, Dart was announcing the construction of the headquarters of
United-Rexall, the largest drug store chain in the world, at the corner of Beverly
and La Cienega. Dart's wife, the former Jane Bryan, a onetime Warner Brothers
starlet, was thrilled to be back in the Southland.

How to employ, house, clothe, feed, transport, educate, inoculate, recreate, and,
if necessary, incarcerate such an overnight population became an overwhelming
challenge to the public and private sectors alike. Everything was in short supply.
Recently discharged Navy lieutenant Ed Fant, for example, opened a Buick agency
in Los Angeles in 1946 but could not get any Buicks, so he went into the Buick
repair business until Detroit began shipments. Living in a society in which too
much was happening too soon, Californians were forced to line up to rent an
apartment, to buy a home or an automobile, to register a child in school, to
purchase any number of durable goods in short supply, or to eat in a restaurant.
Nothing was easy, especially driving on the crowded pre-war road and highway
system. In 1946 traffic deaths in California — 3,800 of them — outstripped the combined total of New York and Pennsylvania, despite the fact that these two states
had three times the population. The following year, 2,150 Californians lost their
lives in highway accidents, giving California the highest automotive death rate in
the nation. "The stampede has visited us with unprecedented civic problems,"
Governor Earl Warren admitted in 1948, "partly because we did not expect to
digest so much population in so short a time, and partly because even if we had
been forewarned we could have done but little to prepare for the shock during
the stringent war years. So we have an appalling housing shortage, our schools are
packed to suffocation, and our highways are inadequate and dangerous. We are
short of water and short of power, and our sanitation and transportation systems
are overtaxed. Our hospitals and our corrective institutions are bursting at the
seams."[5]

The housing crisis led the list of Warren's headaches. By August 1948, when
Warren was running for Vice President, nine hundred thousand new homes were
still needed, yesterday, if Californians were to be properly housed. Warren cited
this statistic in an article he wrote for the *Saturday Evening Post*. Even in 1948
dollars Warren's itemization of expenses being allocated by state government to
meet the boom is impressive: $55 million in state aid to schools, ten times that
on the local level; comparable sums for public health, higher education, the expansion and upgrading of the state park and recreation system; and, most dramatically, $1 billion over a ten-year period for highways.

Approximately 850,000 veterans settled in California following the war, the majority of them from elsewhere. Having trained in California or passed through the
state en route to the Pacific, these veterans were determined to resume the best
years of their lives in California circumstances: men such as John Norman, the
twenty-five-year-old protagonist of Frank Fenton's tightly written, highly philo-

sophical second novel, *What Way My Journey Lies* (1946). With minimalist realism, Fenton presents Norman's readjustment to Los Angeles life after the horrors of combat in Italy. After much turmoil and indecision, Norman decides to do the obvious: marry the girl, Mary Carter, a schoolteacher from Glendale; buy the house in West Los Angeles, $500 down; take the job in the bookstore in Westwood near UCLA, recognizing that UCLA was a rising university, Westwood a rising district, and the book business a good business to be in. The novel begins with Norman a tormented veteran psychologically and philosophically at odds with ordinary life after being wounded at Salerno. It concludes with Mary fixing him a breakfast of bacon and eggs in their little stucco house in West Los Angeles. As Zorba the Greek puts it, Norman accepts it all—the house, the job, the wife, the kids, the whole catastrophe!

For many young men, the maimed, the wounded in body and mind, the whole catastrophe would have been paradise itself, as Army nurse Betty Basye knew all too well, working as she did at Hoff General Hospital in Santa Barbara, Dibble General Hospital in Menlo Park, and the Vista del Arroyo Hospital in Pasadena through 1945 and 1946. A lively young woman from Oroville, a small mining town eighty miles north of Sacramento, Basye had enlisted in the Army Nurse Corps after Pearl Harbor. The young woman had red hair and a full figure and a special walk, or so the men on the wards told her, the more recuperative of them calling her Red or Hayseed or Basie or even Countess instead of Ma'am or Lieutenant as required by Army protocol, whistling and hollering their approval when she came by in her white uniform, despite the fact that she was an officer and they were enlisted men. Lieutenant Basye did not mind. And besides: she did not believe that a nurse had to be an officer to be a nurse. Over time, she had become convinced that the Army made its young female nurses officers so as to keep them off-limits to enlisted men.

The hollering guys were the boys en route to recovery. Others were not so lucky. One patient, "the Nose" he was called, had lost his, together with his ears and much of his facial tissue. The first time she met the Nose, Basye went to the bathroom and threw up. The worst patients were kept secreted in private rooms. First Lieutenant Molly Birch, Basye's superintendent at Hoff General Hospital, took Basye into these rooms only gradually, one room a day, one day at a time, so she could get used to it. The Nose kept a photograph next to his bed of himself as a handsome pilot beside his P-38. "Hi, Red, look. This is me." The Nose—real name, Bill—told Basye he was not getting out of the bed until the doctors brought him back to what he looked like before the war. Red eventually persuaded Bill to take her for a drink at the Officers Club as a way of boosting his morale. The two sat opposite each other, the beautiful young nurse and the equally young man with one eye lost, together with his nose and half his face, pedicles of flesh hanging from his head like peeling paint. "He looked around and saw other cases there," Lieutenant Basye later remembered. "So he began to get used to it." Bill was later transferred to Pasadena, where Basye was also posted, and once again she took him out, this time for a walk downtown. Nicely dressed women stared at Bill as they walked along the street. Basye was tempted to cuss out one glaringly staring matron. ("It's like the war hadn't come to Pasadena until we came there.") The Pasadena newspapers ran letters to the editor complaining about the deformed veterans on the downtown sidewalks. It might scare the children.[6]

Bill's adjustment and efforts at recovery paralleled those of the handless war veteran Homer Parrish in the award-winning 1946 film *The Best Years of Our Lives*. Produced by Samuel Goldwyn, directed by William Wyler, with screenplay by Robert E. Sherwood from the novel *Glory for Me* (1945) by Mackinlay Kantor, this RKO Radio Pictures saga of three returning veterans earned more than $10 million after its initial release, making it the biggest commercial success of the decade. It also won eight Oscars, including Best Picture of 1946, together with the Irving Thalberg Award for producer Samuel Goldwyn; and for the next half century sustained its reputation as one of the best—and most relevant—films Hollywood has ever produced. Nineteen forty-six was a banner year for Hollywood, with three blockbusters—*The Jolson Story, Duel in the Sun,* and *The Best Years of Our Lives*—contributing to a record $1.7 billion gross, up from $1.45 billion in 1945. Even more impressive, net profits practically doubled from $66 million in 1945 to $120 million in 1946. For the time being at least, Americans were going to the movies in record numbers; and the film industry was doing its best to respond to the burgeoning market with an array of 1946 releases—westerns, biopics, classics, best-sellers, comedies, costume dramas, musicals, and film *noir*—thoroughly impressive in quality and variety. Virtually the only genre not represented in this banner year was the combat action drama. *They Were Expendable*, after all, had been released in December 1945, and the only combat film of 1946, Lewis Milestone's *A Walk in the Sun*, fared badly at the box office, despite the fact that film critics today consider it one of the finest and most truthful war movies ever made, worthy of comparison to *The Big Parade* (1925), *What Price Glory?* (1926), and *All Quiet on the Western Front* (1930).

Despite Milestone's brilliant directing and the first-rate acting of Dana Andrews, Richard Conte, John Ireland, and Lloyd Bridges playing a squad of Army infantrymen on patrol in Italy, viewers stayed away from *A Walk in the Sun*, a story of war almost documentary in its realism, and flocked to a spate of films—*The Razor's Edge, Adventure, Deadline at Dawn, From This Day Forward, Pride of the Marines, Till the End of Time, Somewhere in the Night,* and *The Best Years of Our Lives*—dealing with the problems of returning veterans who had survived combat. Even such a bellwether 1946 film as Frank Capra's *It's a Wonderful Life* was by indirection an offering to the veteran homecoming genre in that it is the return of his war-hero brother that prompts James Stewart, playing a man who had remained on the home front during the war, disparagingly to review his entire life until the angel played by Henry Travers sets him straight. Capra's 1934 screwball comedy *It Happened One Night* was reworked by Mervyn Leroy into the 1946 offering

Without Reservations, in which, once again, Claudette Colbert makes unorthodox bunking arrangements, this time with returning veterans played by John Wayne and Don DeFore as the three of them are assigned to an over-crowded Pullman car. The films of 1946, in fact, even the comedies, were replete with returning veterans in uniform.

Within this returning-veteran genre, then, *The Best Years of Our Lives* emerged as the most memorable film among many similar efforts, with second place awarded to *Till the End of Time*, produced by Dore Schary and directed by Edward Dmytryk, also for RKO, with Guy Madison, Robert Mitchum, and Bill Williams as three Marine veterans struggling to adjust to civilian life. One Marine, played by Williams, has lost his legs in a storyline echoing the plight of the ex-sailor played by Harold Russell in *The Best Years of Our Lives*. Guy Madison's romance with war widow Dorothy McGuire, moreover, is equal in emotional strength to any of the romantic subplots of the great William Wyler film. As good as *Till the End of Time* is, however, it cannot equal the epic sweep of *The Best Years of Our Lives*: an understated epic, to be sure, filled with the homey details of domestic life, powerfully photographed by Gregg Toland (director Wyler and Toland had each spent the war doing documentaries), but an epic nevertheless in its ability to suggest an entire generation returning to the home front: Fredric March as the ex–infantry sergeant returned to banking, Dana Andrews as the ex–Army Air Force bombardier returning to an uncertain future, and Harold Russell as the handless ex-sailor struggling to return to the self-confidence of his pre-war identity. Socially, March, Andrews, and Russell embody an inclusive class structure. Al Stephenson (Fredric March) is a high-ranking bank executive living in solid upper-middle-class circumstances who deliberately chose to remain a non-commissioned officer so that he could serve alongside ordinary Americans and not spend the war in privilege. Before the war, Fred Derry (Dana Andrews), now so dashing in his captain's uniform, was a soda jerk. Stripped of his airman's wings and his captain's bars, returned to a clerk's job at a local hardware store, he loses not only his wife, who had married him for his uniform, but his sense of self as well, as his soda-jerk past threatens to become his post-war future. Harold Russell, playing the handless sailor Homer Parrish, was in a way playing himself; for Russell, then a sergeant in a demolition squad, had lost his hands when a defective fuse exploded on a North Carolina training field. So taken was General Omar Bradley, head of the Veterans Administration, with *The Best Years of Our Lives*, he ordered it shown to all his top subordinates and wrote Samuel Goldwyn: "You are not only helping us to do our job, but you are helping the American people to build an even better democracy out of the tragic experiences of this war."[7]

As head of the Veterans Administration, Bradley was responsible for the physical and psychological recovery of hundreds of thousands of veterans maimed in mind and body. Just exactly what the mental state of returning veterans might be after the war had been a topic of frequent speculation before the war ended. Two important investigations of this topic—*The Veteran Comes Back* (1944) by Columbia University social scientist Willard Waller and *Back to Life: The Emotional Adjustment of Our Veterans* (1945) by Herbert Kupper, staff psychiatrist at the Marine Hospital on Ellis Island—despite all their optimistic discussions of education and rehabilitation programs, sustained a strong undercurrent of anxiety as to just exactly how an entire generation could throw off the long-term effects of militarization and the trauma of war and return to normal civilian life. Even worse: should a significant number of veterans not be able to readjust, society could become destabilized.

To back up his assertions regarding maladjustment, Waller cited Shays's Rebellion by Revolutionary War veterans, the founding of the Ku Klux Klan by Confederate veterans, and the advocacy of fascism by veterans of World War I. Face facts, Waller urged his readers: an entire generation of young Americans had been taken from society, taught to exalt courage above all virtues, taught to survive on the battlefield in moments of fierce combat, and now that very same veteran was expected, almost instantly, to resume life where he had left it. Taught to hate, the returning veteran was now expected to become a loving and trusted husband and father. Taught that he was saving the world, the returning veteran was now expected to compete for a job alongside everyone else. The returning veteran, Waller argued, was an immigrant in his native land; and—here Waller's concerns become almost paranoid—an irredentist core of maladjusted veterans could soon, given the proper encouragement from demagogues, become the storm trooper center, a *freikorps* of violent political action on either the left or the right.

Waller's fears might have seemed to have come true over the Fourth of July weekend 1947 when some four thousand members of a Los Angeles–based motorcycle club calling itself the Booze Fighters, the majority of them veterans, roared into the sleepy town of Hollister south of San Jose and for three days held the city in a virtual state of occupation as they roared up and down the streets, drank innumerable cases of beer, pulled a bar out of a tavern and set it up on Main Street, got drunker and drunker, relieved themselves indiscriminately in the streets, and ended their spree only when the Highway Patrol poured into town to quell the takeover. Two weeks later, *Life* magazine ran a picture (most likely staged, as it turned out) of an open-shirted Booze Fighter, a bottle of beer in each hand, staring drunkenly at the camera from atop his parked but dangerously tilting motorcycle.

Psychiatrist Kupper feared a condition of buried psychoneurosis in a large number of veterans, especially combat veterans, who might at first glance seem to be coping. "The aftereffects of this great mass endeavor will remain with us for many years," wrote Kupper of the just completed war. "And those effects cannot be measured merely in terms of the men who are grossly and obviously ill. A more accurate yardstick might be offered by our ability to measure the alteration of feelings which the war has produced in every man!"[8] Many psychiatrists believed that colleagues such as Herbert Kupper were exaggerating. "We can't generalize on the problem of the returning veteran," Dr. Karl Bowman, president of the

American Psychiatric Association and medical superintendent of the Langley Porter Clinic in San Francisco, was saying in late March 1945. "There is no such
person as GI Joe. Each veteran is an individual case. Many will come back physically and mentally better than when they left." If *The Best Years of Our Lives* and
Till the End of Time were the only measurements, then Hollywood could be said
to share Bowman's point of view: his belief that the average returning veteran was
essentially normal and that time, love, and work would do their healing best in
even the most trying of circumstances. "Don't force the veteran to talk of his
experiences if he doesn't want to," Bowman argued. "Don't attempt to ignore his
physical disabilities, accept them normally; commend his efforts and his successes
and allow time for him to get acquainted with his surroundings. If things don't
go well, don't be afraid to ask for professional advice."[9]

Still, there was film *noir* to consider, with its mistrust of society, its themes of
alienation and obsession, together with Hollywood's continuing interest throughout 1946 in themes of psychoneurosis, amnesia, and false identity in such films as
Crack-Up, *Somewhere in the Night* (John Hodiak as a veteran with amnesia, looking for his identity), and *The Stranger*, which brought the problem of de-
Nazification to the post-war United States. And in the case of Audie Murphy, the
most decorated soldier in American history (thirty-seven awards in all, eleven of
them for valor), there was unfolding a Hollywood story equal in paradigmatic
power to any script making it to the silver screen. After all, Murphy—a small and
wiry sharecropper from Hunt County, Texas, the seventh of twelve children, abandoned by his father when he was sixteen, losing his mother before he was seventeen—had become by his majority a Medal of Honor–winning second lieutenant
of infantry who had personally dispatched 240 German soldiers in Italy, France,
and Germany in some of the fiercest fighting of the war. In contrast to Sergeant
Alvin York, who had killed twenty-five Germans and captured 132 in one continuous action on the Western Front in October 1918, Murphy had fought in ferocious combat for two long years. *Life* featured the photogenic Murphy on its cover
for 16 July 1945, smiling for the camera with a boyish grin that at the least 240
German soldiers would have found misleading, had they been around to do so.
Now what to do? became the question for this fifth-grade dropout (Army press
releases had upgraded Murphy to the eighth grade) with an almost impenetrable
Texas twang and a farmer's way of walking, swinging from side to side as if following a mule and plow down a Texas furrow. He could stay in the Army, of
course, including the option of temporarily putting aside his commission and
entering West Point. Certainly, the most decorated soldier in World War II, once
a West Point graduate, would have every expectation of a distinguished military
career. Then there was the prospect of attending Texas A&M and becoming a
veterinarian, which Murphy was also considering. But both West Point and Texas
A&M demanded that Murphy play catch-up for the three years of grammar school
and four years of high school he had missed, and that was a daunting prospect,

made even more so when Murphy contemplated the academic demands of the academy or pre-medical and veterinary school.

Actor James Cagney, meanwhile, like millions of other Americans, had been impressed by Murphy's good looks on the *Life* cover. At the time, Cagney was organizing his own production company. Through a Texas friend, he contacted Murphy and invited the young lieutenant, now on terminal leave, to come out to Hollywood. Cagney himself met Murphy at the Los Angeles airport, shocked at how frail and nervous, even distraught, the young Texan seemed. Cagney moved Murphy into his own home on Coldwater Canyon in Beverly Hills and told him to rest for a few weeks before making any decisions regarding his future.

And so, throughout 1946, Audie Murphy struggled to shed his Texas drawl in elocution classes at the Actors Lab studio behind Schwab's drugstore on Sunset Boulevard and to lose his country hayshaker way of walking, in part with the help of Cagney's own dance teacher, Johnny Boyle, who had choreographed and trained Cagney for his amazing dance performances in *Yankee Doodle Dandy* (1942). Murphy even took fencing lessons at the Actors Lab in an effort to acquire physical grace: this from a man who had stayed alive, one of the few men in his infantry company to do so, in significant measure because of his agility and was still suffering from a hip wound. Murphy's stomach bothered him constantly, and his headaches lasted a week at a time. He found it difficult to fall asleep at night, and he would frequently awake screaming from nightmares of being back in combat and would vomit in the morning after a restless night. Eventually, Murphy took sleeping pills to keep the nightmares in check. Cagney's production company failed to get off the ground, and by August 1947 Audie Murphy was living with seven other veterans in a gymnasium health club on La Cienega Boulevard, which reminded Murphy of life in an Army barrack, sleeping on a cot, working out every day, pulling some light duty. Not until 1948 would Murphy get a part, the briefest of parts, in a forgettable film called *Beyond Glory*.

Murphy met starlet Jean Peters at the Actors Lab: a greenish-grey-eyed girl of twenty-one from Canton, Ohio, so Louella Parsons described her, "much like an average co-ed in appearance," and very intelligent.[10] Peters was, in fact, a college girl, Miss Ohio State for 1945, hence considerably up the social scale from Murphy, with whom she immediately clicked. Some of Murphy's pent-up reservoir of tension, sexual and otherwise, was evident in his almost satyr-maniacal response to Peters in the nights they spent together in the summer of 1946. But it was more than just sex. It was a dream of life itself: a better life for the sharecropper orphan turned war hero. Jean Peters, Miss Ohio State, was class, real class, the best thing that had ever happened to a onetime Texas plowboy who had become a national icon, then almost as quickly had found himself doing yard work and serving drinks at Jimmy Cagney's. Jean Peters was the kind of girl that Audie Murphy dreamed of when in combat, the kind about whom he would soon be writing (or remembering to his friend publicist David McClure, who would do the actual composition) in *To Hell and Back* (1949), one of the finest combat memoirs of World

War II. After it was all over, Murphy tells us, after two years of killing, he was capable of envisioning his return to normal life only in terms of a girl whom he had never met but could imagine. "I will go back," Murphy had ended *To Hell and Back.* "I will find the kind of girl of whom I once dreamed. I will learn to look at life through uncynical eyes, to have faith, to know love. I will learn to work in peace as in war. And finally—finally, like countless others, I will learn to live again."[11]

In Jean Peters, Audie Murphy believed he had found the girl he had dreamt of across two long years of combat—and hence his new life. Then Howard Hughes, another Texan like Murphy, a people-collector, invited Murphy and Peters to fly out with him to Catalina Island on his private plane for a party. Hughes set to work on Peters almost instantly: this multi-millionaire who collected starlets almost as a hobby, only this time he had met his match in the girl from Ohio, who soon decided that she very much wanted to become Mrs. Howard Hughes, which eventually happened. Initially, Peters proposed to Murphy that he accept a secret ménage à trois with Hughes, which Murphy refused; and when Peters left him finally, Murphy stormed out of the guest house on Jimmy Cagney's estate on a mission, so he later claimed, to kill Howard Hughes, and came within one bodyguard of the fat cat who had stolen his girl.

Murphy was feeling betrayed, cuckolded even, and certainly beaten down by big money, and he remained in this frame of mind until another starlet, Dixie Wanda Hendrix, came into his life. But until that happened, Murphy was experiencing a sense of aggrieved misogyny similar to that pervading the films being produced by the industry he hoped to enter. True, most of the women of *The Best Years of Our Lives*—Millie Stephenson (Myrna Loy), who deals patiently with her husband's restive readjustment; Peggy, their daughter (Teresa Wright), who helps former captain Fred Derry back to self-confidence; and Wilma Cameron (Cathy O'Donnell), who marries her pre-war fiancé Homer despite the loss of his hands—were noble figures, and as such more than enough to offset Fred's floozy first wife (Virginia Mayo). And yes, comedies such as *Easy to Wed* (1946) made it seem the most natural thing in the world for an entire generation of returning veterans to marry the girl of their dreams. But an even stronger undercurrent in the year's films depicted women as murderous, deceptive, adulterous, or just plain bitches.

In the late 1945 Twentieth Century–Fox release *Leave Her to Heaven*, Gene Tierney plays a young bride who out of obsessive jealousy murders her husband's crippled brother and kills herself, framing her husband (Cornel Wilde) and sister for the crime. In *The Strange Love of Martha Ivers* (1946), Barbara Stanwyck reprised the homicidal female role she had brought to such perfection in *Double Indemnity* (1944). Other women in the films of 1946—Bette Davis in *A Stolen Life*, Rita Hayworth in *Gilda*, Olivia de Havilland in *The Dark Mirror*, Linda Darnell in *Fallen Angel*, Ingrid Bergman in *Notorious*, Jennifer Jones in *Duel in the Sun*, Merle Oberon in *Temptation*, Joan Crawford in *Humoresque*, Lana Turner in *The Postman Always Rings Twice*, even Paulette Goddard in *The Diary*

of a Chambermaid—were by turns, or in various combinations, murderous, unfaithful, manipulative, deceptive, or tart-tongued. What is going on here, one
might legitimately ask, given the ability of Hollywood to express and gratify the
subliminal in American life through storylines and characterizations speaking directly to inner anxiety and need? Women's fashions might be taking on a softer
look in 1946, with lots of feminine drapery and embellishment; but the on-screen
female was hardly celebratory of the kind of girls GIs such as Audie Murphy had
dreamt of when overseas.

In his *Sex Problems of the Returned Veteran* (1946), psychiatrist Howard Kitching
discussed the fear that veterans could be expected to have that their wives or
girlfriends had been unfaithful to them when they were in the service, especially
if they themselves had been unfaithful. In *The Veteran Comes Back* (1944), Willard
Waller of Columbia had suggested that the story of Uriah the Hittite might serve
as an almost universally applicable gloss on the mindset of returning veterans:
King David seduced Bathsheba, the wife of Uriah, when the Hittite captain was
in the field campaigning for David. Having formed this sexual connection with
his wife, David gave orders that Uriah be sent to the thickest part of battle, where
he lost his life. "Uriah did not come home," Waller concluded ominously, "but
many millions of veterans have come home to confront those who have betrayed
them in matters great and small. Veterans have written many a bloody page of
history, and those pages have stood forever as a record of their days of anger. Many
times has their blind, understandable fury changed the course of human events."[12]

Which was very much on Audie Murphy's mind as he headed in the general
direction of Howard Hughes that vaguely remembered day in 1946. To add injury
to insult, as far as the combat-fatigued Murphy was concerned, Hughes had not
only used his money to steal Jean Peters but had been exempted from military
service in the war (bad hearing) despite his much-vaunted talents as an aviator
and had profited as an aircraft and munitions supplier, surrounded by gorgeous
young women, while Murphy and his friends were dying in Europe and the Pacific. Hughes, in fact, had seemed to corner the market on sex with his film *The
Outlaw*, finished in the spring of 1941 but not released until 1943, on a limited
basis in San Francisco, then withdrawn until 1946, when it was re-released before
being intermittently withdrawn yet once again in the course of a number of local
censorship and court challenges.

In retrospect, it remains easy to dismiss *The Outlaw* as trash, as most critics did
then and many still do. Audiences in San Francisco, in fact, during the brief
release of the film in 1943, laughed at all the wrong places. It is another thing,
however, to ask what this film might have meant in the context of the psychological drama of *eros* and *thanatos*, life versus death, unfolding during the war years.
The Outlaw, it must be remembered, was filmed before Pearl Harbor; hence
Hughes's obsession as director with Jane Russell, her frontal anatomy especially,
fits self-evidently into the context of *eros* ascendant so characteristic of those twenty-
six months of 1939, 1940, and 1941 when Europe and Asia were killing fields and

the United States was trying to remain focused on life perceived as pleasure and sexuality. Young Jane Russell, after all, was in and of herself a self-evident admonishment to young men everywhere to make love, not war. Yet under the contract system, she was also in a very evident way the property of Howard Hughes; and through the war years Hughes collected attractive women—Russell herself, Faith Domergue, Jane Greer, Ursula Thiess, Carol Gallagher—whom he placed under contract to RKO, providing them with a salary, an apartment, even a live-in older couple as houseparents and chaperones.

While most of these women were merely kept under contract and never cast in a picture, Hughes in 1940 chose Ernestine Jane Geraldine Russell—a tall, leggy, busty nineteen-year-old brunette from Van Nuys, then working for $10 a week as a doctor's receptionist—to star in a film tentatively entitled *Billy the Kid*, later changed to *The Outlaw* when Metro-Goldwyn-Mayer released a film by the same name. Russell made only that one film for Hughes during the entire time she was under contract and would not star in any other picture until he briefly released her from her contract in 1946. Yet she became one of the best-known actresses of the war years, and certainly one of the most popular pinups, because Hughes had her promoted ceaselessly, especially to servicemen once the war broke out. If all the pictures that were taken of her at one military base or another, Russell later joked, were added to all the pinups of her in barracks, they would circle the planet. They would also suggest a near-ritualized display of Russell's feminine charms to millions of servicemen who may or may not have known that she was under contract to the millionaire playboy producer Howard Hughes, who would not have to go to war but would profit immeasurably by the conflict. But Howard Hughes knew, and that was somehow part of the satisfaction of an obsessive relationship that saw him film and refilm Russell through hundreds of takes and retakes and be forever fiddling with the rushes.

From one perspective, *The Outlaw* had the makings of a reasonable film. Photographed by the legendary Gregg Toland, it starred the respected actors Thomas Mitchell as Pat Garrett and Walter Huston as Doc Holiday and the unknown but competent Jack Beutel as Billy the Kid. True, Hughes could be an exasperating director, and Mitchell once threw down his hat and went into a screaming and swearing fit when Hughes demanded a twenty-sixth retake; but what really destabilized the picture was Hughes's growing obsession with Jane Russell as Rio, specifically Russell's breasts, which in time dominated virtually every scene in the film. The eroticism of *The Outlaw*—a rape scene, controversial dialogue, a scene in which Rio warms a wounded Billy by crawling beneath the covers with him, the voyeuristic obsession with Jane Russell, especially in one scene in which she is tied between two posts—would keep it from being nationally released until 1950, and then only in a highly censored form after a number of lengthy court challenges. But it must also be remembered that *The Outlaw* was an assertion of power and ownership by a producer-director who used the contract system to collect women as near-private possessions. Hughes's obsession with Jane Russell (he designed a special bra for her, which she claimed she never wore), while it might have meant one thing in 1940–41 (hooray for life; make love, not war), meant something else entirely by 1943 (I own what you cannot possess, Jane Russell, and I am safe from the war and will profit from it) and would have yet another layer of meaning by 1946 (the war is over, and this is what we fought for: Jane Russell).

From this perspective, Hughes the aircraft and munitions manufacturer turned voyeur-director might very well embody what he certainly must have embodied to Audie Murphy when he stole Jean Peters from him in 1946: money, the home front, the established order of things, the big shots in the military-industrial complex who had played it safe during the war and had been on hand for the girls when other men were away. For Audie Murphy (and for all the others) to come back, after what he (and they) had been through, and to find that the Howard Hugheses of the world were still in charge, still enjoying their pick of women, retold the Uriah story: only this time the Hittite soldier was back from the battle-field and plenty angry—or at the least highly suspicious. Hollywood instinctively understood this; hence the spate of betraying females in the movies of 1946.

One of the most popular songs of the war, with words and music by Gordon Jenkins, was the 1944 hit tune "San Fernando Valley (I'm Packin' My Grip)." Sung by Bing Crosby, the song represented a wartime expression of hope for the good life in California following the war. That meant a home, preferably in the suburbs, in the San Fernando Valley or elsewhere, a new car, a good job, a community with decent schools, parks, and public services. By 1946 Detroit was doing its best in the car department, with the introduction of its newly stylized automobiles, swept-back in design, assertive in grilles, exuding an ambience of jaunty optimism. July 1946 saw the introduction of the 1947 Studebaker, which was even more innovative in its torpedo shape and repeated design for hood and trunk. While the automobiles of 1940 had taken one last lingering glance at a rapidly vanishing war-threatened elegance, the cars of 1946 seemed to say *Welcome home, here is the good life you have waited for.* So too would the homes of 1946 be saying *Welcome back,* or, more correctly, *Welcome to the suburbs!*

In the final year of the war, two Project Committees on Postwar Home Building were meeting in Northern and Southern California under the auspices of the State Reconstruction and Reemployment Commission to assess the housing needs of post-war California. Chaired by two formidable builders, each of them already experienced in the creation of mass housing—David Bohannon in Northern California, Fritz Burns in the Southland—the committees in July 1945 issued a report, *Postwar Housing in California,* calling for the creation of 625,000 new single-family housing units within the first five years following the war if California were to be able to cope with its projected growth. Northern California would require approximately 300,000 new houses; Southern California, 325,000. This housing, moreover, would have to be within the financial reach of ordinary wage earners in a post-war economy that as yet had not defined itself. What was doubly interesting in the *Postwar Housing in California* report was its conviction that already in California there existed a building tradition that between the two wars, even during the Depression, had shown itself capable of bringing on-line affordable single-family housing in attractive urban and suburban communities. The California ranch home, the report argued, offered a proven prototype of the best possibilities of California expressed through and nurtured by housing. "California houses," argued the report, "lived in by people who came west to enjoy a garden or to live more out of doors, began to break down the division between outdoors and indoors. The ranch house is only one manifestation of this desire. Authorities see many more opportunities for taking advantage of California sun, flowers, climate, and natural beauties in postwar housing."[13]

Architectural critic John Entenza and the other editors of the Los Angeles–based *Arts & Architecture* magazine, while respecting the prototype offered by the ranch house, believed that the design and development community of California, especially its architects, had to go even further in the development of prototypes for post-war housing. Marshaling the talents of many of the best architects of the state, Entenza and the editors of *Arts & Architecture* launched in late 1944 a Case Study program that over the next five years (the program actually lasted until the early 1960s) sponsored the design and construction of numerous Case Study houses, the majority of them in Southern California, intended to demonstrate the architectural styles and materials of post-war California and serve as paradigms for housing development. Case Study houses favored horizontal rhythms of glass, aluminum, wood, stone, and tile at once simple in design and industrial in materials, yet possessed as well of the poetry of place and an ambience of new beginnings after wartime. The editors of the Northern California–based *Sunset* magazine understood the power of such architecture immediately. This was no time to build a house, cautioned *Sunset* in March of 1946, due to the scarcity of materials; but if one must build, then clear-cut, simple, and efficient solutions employing plywood, aluminum, and other industrial materials were in order. The few homes that *Sunset* showcased throughout 1946, in fact, were very much in the Case Study style and foreshadowed some two decades of construction to come in the more prosperous suburbs of the Bay Area, including housing that Stanford University would develop for its faculty and senior staff.

In Los Angeles County, which had grown by seven hundred thousand new residents between 1940 and 1946, lucky veterans, including those enrolled at USC and UCLA, had the benefit of Quonset huts. Others were forced to live in converted streetcars, four two-room apartments to a car, renting for $25 to $32.50 per month. Others lived in converted airplane fuselages shorn of their wings and tail structures and moved onto a site like house trailers. There were reports of families living in automobiles and at least one documented instance of a family living on a sidewalk in Los Angeles, the household furniture arranged with care, as if the family were camping in the countryside. Calling the legislature into special session in January 1946 to deal with the many problems brought on by rapid growth, Earl Warren backed, among other programs, low-cost housing loans—$7,500 for a house, $13,500 for a farm—to be administered by the California Department of Veterans Affairs. Payable in thirty years at an interest rate of 3 percent, these Cal-Vet loans played a key role in financing the post-war creation of suburban California. In 1948 alone, precisely 5,492 homes selling for approximately $7,000, aimed at blue-collar workers and returning vets, were built on the slopes and plains of the Los Angeles suburb of Westchester near the municipal airport, an area previously devoted to the cultivation of lima beans.

Magazines and newspapers of the period are replete with stories describing and illustrating the construction boom. On 10 June 1946 *Life* ran a series of photographs depicting construction signs in empty fields in Los Angeles County, the San Fernando Valley especially, where announcements of developments burgeoned like a new crop. So scarce was housing, prospective buyers would line up in the early morning hours outside real estate offices. Lots that sold for $850 during the war jumped to $5,000 by 1946. Even buyers who had made their down payment frequently had to wait up to eight or nine months, even a year, as materials shortages, compounded by a shortage of carpenters, electricians, plumbers, and other building trades workers, brought development after development to a grinding halt.

For all the difficulties, then, growth was in the air. Even the city of San Diego, ever ambivalent to growth, was building an aqueduct connection to the water lines of the Metropolitan Water District, which it joined by popular vote on 5 November 1946. Inherited from the Navy, which had begun the project during the war, the pipeline was being financed by a $2 million bond issue passed by an electorate notoriously stingy when it came to financing public works. Placed in service in late November 1947, the seventy-one-mile San Diego Aqueduct at long last accessed for San Diego the waters of the mighty Colorado River and in doing so made possible the impending expansion of the city. A privileged and protected resort and naval enclave now stood on the verge of metropolitanization.

So did the San Fernando Valley, which had been annexed by the City of Los Angeles in 1915 but had remained for nearly thirty years a Chicago-sized region of ranches, farms, and market towns, with a total population of approximately 170,000 by late 1944. As late as 1946, the San Fernando Valley sustained 1,500 poultry ranches, eighteen large dairies with a total of 5,000 producing cows, 18,000 acres of citrus, 7,500 acres in deciduous fruits and nuts, 26,000 acres in field crops, 12,000 acres in vegetables, and a goats' milk industry valued at $1.35 million, as any member of the San Fernando Valley Goat Society, founded in 1940, would be happy to tell you. Aviation, of course, had begun to change the nature of the western San Fernando Valley before and during the war. The Burbank-based Lockheed-Vega aviation company was employing some ninety thousand people by late 1944. That meant housing and a kind of makeshift urbanization on the southeastern edge of the valley—temporary housing, of course, and even temporary urbanization, but housing and urbanization nevertheless, including the Lockheed Air Terminal: 374,474 passengers passing through it annually by 1943, making it one of the busiest air terminals in the world. Aviation, together with the presence of the Warner Brothers and Republic studios in Burbank, foreshadowed a growing industrial base for the post-war San Fernando Valley, where, as Crosby sang, so many returning veterans were planning to make their homes. Between V-J Day, 14 August 1945, and November 1946, the urbanized portions of the San Fernando Valley completed the subdivision of 10,514 housing lots. Nearly ten thousand new homes were completed in 1947, and a total of 24,858 building permits were issued.

Industrialist Henry J. Kaiser, meanwhile, was announcing—and building!—some two thousand new homes on the 411-acre Panorama Ranch between Van Nuys and San Fernando, fifteen miles from downtown Los Angeles. In this effort, Kaiser was joined by Fritz Burns, chair of the state-sponsored Southern California Project Committee on Postwar Home Building and one of the two or three most successful developers in California. As in the case of nearly everything Henry J. Kaiser did—the building of dams and Liberty ships, the creation of a large-scale pre-paid health plan, the bringing of a heavy steel mill to California, his advocacy of workers' pensions, vacations, and medical benefits—Kaiser Community Homes, developer of mass housing in the Westchester district of West Los Angeles and at Panorama City in the San Fernando Valley, was characterized by interactive notions of industrial production, mass marketing, and social progressivism. To the depth of his being, Henry J. Kaiser understood the hope expressed in *Postwar Housing in California* that the homes of post-war California—88 percent of them single-family dwellings in 1946 alone—would at once be affordable to a broad population ($4,000 to $5,000 a home, Kaiser was promising, $150 down, the rest in installments), well built, efficient, and possessed of a respectable level of amenities. Houses such as these, Kaiser believed, houses with garages, backyards, dishwashers, would promote in returning veterans a renewed sense of having a stake in society: of having fought for something and gained what they had fought for.

The writers of *Postwar Housing in California* correctly predicted a shortage of materials after the war and a consequent rise in housing prices. By December 1945, certainly by early 1946, President Harry Truman, worried about the same thing, was threatening to bring real estate under price controls. Kaiser, of course, had made a wartime specialty of getting scarce materials to where they were needed, even if it meant building the first heavy steel mill in the state. A master of industrial production, Kaiser was by late 1944 envisioning the homes of post-war California as being partially pre-fabricated in industrial plants, which would prepare standardized parts for assembly at the housing site. Early in 1946 he and Burns established such a production facility on a sixteen-and-a-half-acre site on west Manchester Boulevard in the Westchester district of Los Angeles. Here, in three separate zones, carpenters and other specialists pre-cut and partially pre-fabricated housing components and prepared such non-wooden utilities as metal kitchen cabinets, toilets, bathtubs, and dishwashers for on-site installation.

Whereas Kaiser himself claimed to be taking the technology and techniques of the automobile industry into the production of mass housing (Kaiser was at the time also getting involved in automotive production), USC architecture and planning historian Greg Hise argues that wartime aviation plants provide a better model for the way in which Kaiser and Burns were mass-producing houses from previously prepared components. True, the homes rising by 1948 in endless rows on the flatlands of Panorama Ranch, now renamed Panorama City, did not possess the studied elegance of the Case Study houses. Yet to Panorama City residents working at the nearby Fisher Body Division and Chevrolet Assembly Plant, completed in February 1948 at the cost of $12 million, or shopping in the Panorama City commercial district along Van Nuys Boulevard, or enjoying the new amenity of television over the pioneering stations KTLA, KWIK, or KGIL, or driving on Sunday in their General Motors or Kaiser Frazer sedan, life in the San Fernando Valley seemed fully worth the promise of the Gordon Jenkins song.

To the contrary, bohemian writer and all-round rebel Henry Miller might very well have snorted. Life in Panorama City was just another example of the Air-Conditioned Nightmare. Miller had first used the phrase "air-conditioned nightmare" as the title of a book he completed late in the war while living in Big Sur on the central coast. Based on a year-long auto tour of the United States from October 1940 to October 1941 and published by New Directions in late 1945, *The Air-Conditioned Nightmare* can be taken as a prophetic anti-statement to everything that Panorama City stood for: conformity, routine, philistinism, sexual repression; the long gray death, in short, to Henry Miller's way of thinking, of middle-class life in America.

Born in Brooklyn in 1891, Henry Valentine Miller—Val to his friends and intimates, who were legion—had spent only a few months in Southern California in 1910, doing odd jobs in Los Angeles and San Diego, before returning to New York. Like Walt Whitman, whom he resembled in so many respects, Henry Miller, both the man and the writer, was hard to classify. Was he the last representative of the 1920s generation, so infatuated with Paris, as Edmund Wilson claimed? Was he a social critic of prophetic importance, warning against the increasing conformity and mechanization of American life? Or was he a cad, a heel, a shameless sponger, whore-mongering pornographer, a poseur and blowhard, the perpetrator of some two million words of stream-of-consciousness prose that seemed to be saying everything, hence nothing, simultaneously?

The answer was yes to each query. In some vast and nearly impenetrable way, Henry Miller was managing by the mid-1930s, when his autobiography *Tropic of Cancer* (1934) was published in Paris and banned in the United States, to have contained within himself all the contradictions and paradoxes that two of Miller's favorite writers, Ralph Waldo Emerson and Walt Whitman, considered a salient characteristic of the free-thinking, free-spirited American man of letters as social and cultural critic. Whatever Henry Miller might have become by 1940, when he returned to the United States after a tour of Greece resulting in *The Colossus of Maroussi* (1941), which some believe his best book—hierophant or shameless lech, free spirit or sponging bum, ingrate or reformist visionary in the Americanist tradition—Henry Miller was well on the way, as man, writer, and legend, to becoming one of the most influential writers ever to be based in California; for what Miller wrote, together with what he acted out and stood for, would in time pervade the value system of an entire generation and shift the sensibility of the entire nation.

All this was a big order for a down-and-out writer nearing fifty in 1940, with only one important book available to the general public: a writer turned down by the Guggenheim Foundation when he applied for funds to tour the United States, just as he had recently toured Greece, and write a book about his travels and observations. Thanks to an advance from Doubleday Doran, Miller made the trip anyway, after learning to drive in five lessons from aspiring poet Kenneth Patchen and buying for $100 a 1932 Buick sedan, which terrified him as he headed it into the Holland Tunnel into New Jersey, then turned south toward New Hope, Pennsylvania, and from there into America itself.

In the course of this year-long journey of return and anti-homecoming, Miller drove, worked, crashed, and sponged his way across America: an over-age-in-grade Parisian expatriate returning to America along with a whole generation of émigrés, the vast majority of them more solvent and respectable than Miller, which was not a difficult accomplishment. A decade later, another rebel, Jack Kerouac, would make a similar journey in part under Miller's inspiration; for the important thing about Miller's journey was that it brought him, once again, to California, where he hung out with, among other like-minded people, John Steinbeck's friend Ed (Doc) Ricketts in Monterey and Lawrence Clark Powell, a literary critic and former French expatriate, then settling into a career as librarian and writer at UCLA.

Like so many expatriates, Henry Miller liked California—inasmuch as he could find anything to like about the United States—and decided to settle there. Thanks to the generosity of two friends, Margaret and Gilbert Neiman, he could now do exactly that: settle into the Neimans' home in the Beverly Glen district of Los Angeles as a more or less permanent non-paying guest. Two years later, in May 1944, Miller accepted a further offer of hospitality, moving in with artist Lynda Sargent (no monkey business, Miller assured a friend in one of his ceaseless stream of letters) in Sargent's Log House on the Big Sur coast, later famous as the site of the Nepenthe Restaurant. Miller had first seen the Big Sur in the course of his 1941 automotive journey and now, seven dollars in his pocket, he was glad to be back. This was Tibet, he claimed in another one of his letters, a place where nature itself—the coastline running abruptly into the sea at the height of a thousand feet, the canyons with their tangled thickets and secretive streams, the morning and evening fogs, the blazing noontime sun, the hawks, vultures, ospreys, and condors gliding overhead, borne aloft atop a continuous river of updrafts—seemed to bespeak, like Tibet, a place out of time, a retreat, a paradise, a Shangri-la. In

May 1944 yet another patron came to Miller's rescue, Keith Evans, the former mayor of Carmel, then in the service, who offered Miller the use of his cabin on Partington Ridge for the duration of the war: and a good thing, too, for Lynda Sargent had just sold Log House to Orson Welles.

Settled in on Partington Ridge, beyond civilization itself, hauling in his own food and water up a steep grade, lighting his own fires, cooking his own food, Henry Miller continued to work on *The Air-Conditioned Nightmare*, which he had begun before Pearl Harbor. From one perspective, *The Air-Conditioned Nightmare* can be seen as a bitter, dismissive, contempt-ridden indictment of American life as ordinary men and women lived it—or were being asked to die for it in wartime. The moment he stepped off the boat in Boston, Miller wrote, he encountered the great American ugliness, the great American chill. "I didn't like the look of the American house," he remembered; "there is something cold, austere, something barren and chill, about the architecture of the American home. It was *home*, with all the ugly, evil, sinister connotations which the word contains for a restless soul. There was a frigid, moral aspect to it which chilled me to the bone."

It got worse for Miller throughout the year-long journey. America, he opined, was a long nightmare, an air-conditioned nightmare: routinized, surreal, mechanical. "I had to travel about ten thousand miles," he claimed, "before receiving the inspiration to write a single line. Everything worth saying about the American way of life I could put in thirty pages. Topographically, the country is magnificent— and *terrifying*. Why terrifying? Because nowhere else in the world is the divorce between man and nature so complete. Nowhere have I encountered such a dull, monotonous fabric of life as here in America. Here boredom reaches its peak." Take that, Norman Rockwell! And take that, all you New Dealers and artistic fellow travelers, with your Thomas Hart Benton murals and Aaron Copland fanfares extolling a noble land and a free and virtuous people. "To call this a society of free peoples is blasphemous," Miller argued. "What have we to offer the world besides the superabundant loot which we recklessly plunder from the earth under the maniacal delusion that this insane activity represents progress and enlightenment?"[14]

Such was the searing indictment from the prophet of Big Sur, and much more was to follow in the years to come. Already, by 1946, Henry Miller had become something of a cult figure: in France, certainly, where his royalties continued to mount but could not be transferred to the United States because of currency laws (and would soon be dramatically devalued along with the franc), but in the United States as well, in Northern California especially, in the regions between Big Sur and Berkeley where a new bohemia was forming, with Henry Miller as its guru and pied piper. In his many writings, Miller had condemned war, and after the war a phalanx of conscientious objectors, released from their Western camps, made a pilgrimage to the Sage of Big Sur. In all his writings, as well, Miller had drenched himself in sex. That is what kept *The Tropic of Cancer* and *The Tropic of Capricorn* (1939) banned from the United States; but sex is also what made each of these books circulate underground and be read by GIs in Europe, and

When Vice President and Mrs. John Nance Garner invited President and Mrs. Franklin Delano Roosevelt to dinner in early February 1939, FDR's naval aide, Captain Daniel Callaghan, accompanied the President. Three years later, Rear Admiral Callaghan, a native of Oakland, led his ships into the last major direct-fire ship-of-the-line gun battle in naval history. INTERNATIONAL NEWS SERVICE, SAN FRANCISCO HISTORY CENTER, SAN FRANCISCO PUBLIC LIBRARY (SFHC/SFPL).

Fritz Wiedemann—German consul general in San Francisco, alleged spymaster, Hitler's commanding officer in World War I—returned to Germany in mid-July 1941. Like so many others in San Francisco, stewardess Bee Hensley found Captain Wiedemann to be a most charming fellow. ASSOCIATED PRESS, SFHC/SFPL.

Fearing an attack by Japanese airplanes, San Franciscans darkened their city on the night of 8 December 1941. It was an imperfect blackout. By the 12th, however, the blackout was near-perfect. CALL-BULLETIN, SFHC/SFPL.

For the next three years, Japanese-American internees would re-create, as best they could, the very same American life they had already been living before their imprisonment. ASSOCIATED PRESS, RHC/USC.

Because they were Japanese-Americans, this young couple found themselves in an assembly center in San Pedro, tagged and ready for shipment. LOS ANGELES EXAMINER, REGIONAL HISTORY COLLECTION, UNIVERSITY OF SOUTHERN CALIFORNIA (RHC/USC).

The War Relocation Authority would only release photographs showing internees as smiling Americans. There was, however, another side to the story. WAR RELOCATION AUTHORITY, RHC/USC.

Like all American boys, the internees loved baseball. ASSOCIATED PRESS, RHC/USC.

On the aircraft carrier *Hornet*, meanwhile, Lieutenant Colonel James Doolittle was attaching a Japanese medal to one of the 500-pound bombs his raiders would soon be dropping on Tokyo. WIDE WORLD, SFHC/SFPL.

Doolittle's raiders had trained in the Bay Area, and their B-25s had been manufactured in Southern California. Making such airplanes took men, thousands of them, such as this swing shift forming up to go on line at the Douglas Aircraft Company in Santa Monica. U.S. ARMY AIR FORCES, RHC/USC.

And when the men were drafted and came into short supply, women began to take their places on the production line. WIDE WORLD, RHC/USC.

Women acquired new skills. VIC STEIN, RHC/USC.

Overnight, an aviation technocracy emerged, engineers and technicians capable of fast-track design and monitoring hundreds of thousands of parts as they coalesced into the creation of a single aircraft. LOCKHEED AIR-CRAFT, RHC/USC.

Aviation was an industrial social democracy of sorts, with such extended services as transportation, housing, and daycare. WIDE WORLD, RHC/USC.

Industrial genius and social democrat Henry J. Kaiser fostered worker-oriented social programs. His employees, Kaiser insisted, should be housed, fed, rested, recreated, and given medical care. KAISER COMPANIES, RHC/USC.

That way, Kaiser reasoned, workers would build better ships more quickly and stay steadily on the job in greater numbers. KAISER COMPANIES, RHC/USC.

At its Richmond shipyards, the Kaiser Companies sponsored attached wartime housing notable for its efficiency and convenience. Fifty years later, such housing seemed a prophetic paradigm of the future. CALL-BULLETIN, SFHC/SFPL.

In both aviation and shipbuilding, women took to the nitty-gritty of welding and riveting, as did Mrs. Lois Butcher, apprenticed to Bill Harrison, a seventy-six-year-old retiree who had returned to work for the duration. ELEVENTH NAVAL DISTRICT, RHC/USC.

In working together, women achieved a solidarity that would eventually have long-term effects on the way that they, their daughters, and their granddaughters would regard their lives. CALL-BULLETIN, SFHC/SFPL.

Recuperating at the Letterman Hospital in the Presidio of San Francisco in June 1943, these wounded veterans of the Attu campaign, receiving awards and decorations, were happy that they had made it through the worst. Staying alive, making it through, was a gift beyond description. CALL-BULLETIN, SFHC/SFPL.

Before going into harm's way, there were the good times, whether in the honky-tonk International Settlement on the Barbary Coast of San Francisco . . .

or the more respectable USO Hospitality House at Civic Center. CALL-BULLETIN, SFHC/SFPL; GABRIEL MOULIN, SFHC/SFPL.

May 1944, an air base in Foggia, Italy. Bombardier James Milton Brown of 830 Cole Street, San Francisco, has just completed the fiftieth and final mission of his combat tour. U.S. ARMY AIR FORCES, SFHC/SFPL.

The trumped-up indictments in the Sleepy Lagoon case underscored the strength of anti–Mexican-American sentiment in Los Angeles. LOS ANGELES EXAMINER, RHC/USC.

On the other hand, there was evidence that the Zoot Suit riots a year later represented a little more than a rumble between teenagers in and out of uniform. ASSOCIATED PRESS, RHC/USC.

Hollywood went to war in various ways. Kept from overseas deployment by bad eyesight, Ronald Reagan helped produce training films for the Army Air Forces. LOS ANGELES EXAMINER, RHC/USC.

Robert Montgomery served in active sea-going command, winning the admiration of James Cagney. LOS ANGELES EXAMINER, RHC/USC.

From air bases in England, Jimmy Stewart flew bombers over Europe and rose to command pilot and operations officer. Joining the Army Air Corps as a private, Stewart finished the war a colonel. ASSOCIATED PRESS, RHC/USC.

Back on the home front, the Andrews Sisters prepared *hors d'oeuvres* for servicemen and servicewomen attending the Sisters' at-home USO entertainments. LOS ANGELES EXAMINER, RHC/USC.

In between trips to the front, Marlene Dietrich served sandwiches at the Hollywood Canteen. INTERNATIONAL NEWS, SFHC/SFPL.

Using the GI Bill, Navy veteran John Cooledge enrolled at UC-Berkeley. His wife Yvonne taught part-time. The couple lived in a trailer in El Cerrito. CALL BULLETIN, SFHC/SFPL.

In Los Angeles, Bob Hope and singer Frances Langford played cards with sailors wounded at the Battle of Leyte Gulf. LOS ANGELES EXAMINER, RHC/USC.

When Japan surrendered, there was time for celebration and the resumption of postponed dreams. CALL BULLETIN, SFHC/SFPL.

Other veterans on the GI Bill and their families found temporary housing in quonset huts. ASSOCIATED PRESS, RHC/USC.

The Earl Warren family, on the other hand, had been projecting wholesome family values since the 1930s. INTERNATIONAL NEWS, SFHC/SFPL.

Following the war, master developers Henry J. Kaiser and Fritz Burns joined in the creation of such instant suburbs as Panorama City. In one day alone, 21 February 1947, forty veterans and their families moved their furniture, unpacked their bags, and began their future. ASSOCIATED PRESS, RHC/USC.

For an entire generation, the governor's daughters—Nina (Honey Bear), left, and Dorothy (Dotty), right—embodied the sunshine promise of postwar California. LOS ANGELES EXAMINER, RHC/USC.

Agness Underwood, the first woman in the country to hold a city editorship on a major metropolitan daily, covered, assigned, and edited the big stories of front-page Los Angeles. CALL BULLETIN, SFHC/SFPL.

Elizabeth Short, the cruelly tortured and murdered Black Dahlia, had known better times. After her death, a photo of Short with the late Matt Gordon, whom Short claimed to be her husband, was found among her effects in a trunk in the Los Angeles Greyhound Bus Depot. INTERNATIONAL NEWS, SFHC/SFPL.

Celebrity Los Angeles gangster Michael (Mickey) Cohen had no idea whatsoever how his sometime colleague, the recently late Hooky Rothman, had succumbed to a shotgun blast outside Cohen's haberdashery store on Sunset Boulevard, or how another associate, Albert Snyder, had been left on the sidewalk critically wounded in the same encounter. He had stepped into the restroom at the time, Cohen told police officers, and could thus, regrettably, be of little help in the investigation. ASSOCIATED PRESS, RHC/USC.

When labor leader Harry Bridges toasted Soviet Foreign Commissar Vyacheslav Mikhailovich at a party in the Borgia Room at the St. Francis Hotel in San Francisco on 8 May 1945, it all seemed so innocent: except, of course, to those federal officials who would spend the next half decade and more trying to deport Bridges for being a member of the Communist Party, perhaps even an agent of the Soviet government. INTERNATIONAL NEWS, SFHC/SFPL.

Republican State Senator John Tenney, chairman of the California State Joint Fact-Finding Committee on Un-American Activities, claimed to have proof that California was in the grip of a vast Communist conspiracy. On 26 March 1947, visiting Washington, Tenney presented evidence to that effect to Representative J. Parnell Thomas (R-NJ), chair of the House Un-American Activities Committee, and another member of the Committee, first term Representative Richard M. Nixon (R-Calif.). ASSOCIATED PRESS, RHC/USC.

When Korea became a hot war, four young Mexican-Americans—Corporal J. V. Fernandez, on floor; Private J. M. Valenzuela, with duffle bag; Corporal J. V. Marin, hanging up his uniform; and Private George Jiminez, holding his rifle—found themselves back in uniform at Camp Cooke with the 40th Division of the California National Guard, heading for more training in Japan and front-line duty in Korea. LOS ANGELES EXAMINER, RHC/USC.

The Korean police action could not be won, at least the way it was being fought, believed Major General Daniel Hudelson (center), the oil executive commanding the 40th Division. In February 1952, Hudelson conferred at the front with theater commander General James A. Van Fleet (right) and Major General Willard G. Wyman (left), commanding the 9th Corps. In Southern California, many shared Hudelson's pessimistic prognosis. U.S. ARMY, RHC/USC.

smuggled back into the United States, to be passed in battered copies across the high school and college campuses of the nation: the dirty books of a generation, in one sense, but also a call, however muddled, to transcendence and liberation through eros. From this perspective, Henry Miller's brief book *The World of Sex*, published in 1940, was yet another cry of *eros* against the dark night of *thanatos* that was descending that year over the world.

Others, however, considered Miller's books purient—and, worse, radical—trash, speaking with an especially corrupting power to the young. Already, well before the war had ended—indeed, because of the war—America was finding itself uneasy about its youth: not so much the young men and women in uniform, but the half-generation just behind them, the *pachucos* and V-girls, the growing number of young offenders from the inner city. Writing in *Look* magazine in January 1946, FBI director J. Edgar Hoover predicted an outburst of juvenile delinquency in the post-war era. Already, Hoover pointed out, seventeen-year-olds had the highest arrest rate of any age group in the country. Then there was the recently released veteran, only a few years older, to be watched, the sort who had made up the bulk of the motorcycle gang that had taken over Hollister in July 1947: an event that would six years later be made the basis of a film, *The Wild One*, in which Marlon Brando as Johnny, the motorcycle gang leader, would establish a paradigm of rebellious youth that would encourage an entire generation—and not just James Dean, or even Montgomery Clift in a different sort of way—to seem to be so troubled, so oppressed, by the established order of things that only jeans and a T-shirt and a mumbled way of talking could manage to express a massive rebellion and thus in some obscure manner hold a troubled identity together.

Rebellion, then, was in the air and would grow steadily throughout the next decade, and Henry Miller, the man and his books, was in some palpable way emerging as the guru and avatar of an emerging alternative vision. Berkeley economist Mildred Edie Brady, a part-time Big Sur resident, had firsthand experience of this new movement early on, through 1946 and 1947, and described it for *Harper's* magazine as a new cult of sex and anarchy. The entire story of this radical bohemia, Brady argued, began with the arrival of Henry Miller in Big Sur in late 1943. By his very presence, his personal mystique, and through the influence of his writings, Miller had played a significant role in activating the Northern California axis between Berkeley and Big Sur as a new post-war bohemia and center of political dissent. From Miller, Brady claimed, a generation of alienated young people, especially pacifists but veterans as well, were imbibing "an engaging potpourri of mysticism, egoism, sexualism, surrealism, and anarchism."

Accentuated and enhanced by Miller's own eclectic and chaotic religiosity, which emphasized astrology and the occult, a certain free-wheeling mysticism dovetailed easily with the already flourishing tradition of religious cults in California and the persistent mysticism of Carmel and Big Sur as an American Tibet. "His appetite for the mysterious," noted Brady of Miller at Big Sur, "was soon widely known and a host of dealers in occult lore came to see him: astrologers, faith healers, sexologists, and spiritualists laid their experiences in the wonderful at his feet and marveled with him over the grandeurs of the Lost Continent of Mu." The egoism of this new bohemia, Brady continued, was fueled quite vividly by the near-cultic example of a writer-guru autobiographical to the core: a writer, in fact, who could rarely write about anything else but himself as being the most interesting subject and the measure of all things, a prophet unto himself and against the masses, as in *The Air-Conditioned Nightmare*.

Sexual rebellion had always been part of bohemia, Brady admitted, but now it had the reinforcement of not only Henry Miller's works but the writings of Wilhelm Reich, whose *Function of the Orgasm* (1942) was even more revered than Miller's writings as covenantal text. All evils, Reich had argued (or so Brady was interpreting him), all physical and spiritual ills from cancer to fascism, stemmed from what Reich called "orgastic impotence." Sexual repression had made modern civilization a sick place. Into this landscape, the new bohemians of Berkeley–Big Sur believed, was gathering a generation of sexual liberationists who would renew civilization itself: the men at least, for Mildred Brady found the women of this new bohemia strangely silent and compliant. "No budding Edna St. Vincent Millay or caustic Dorothy Parker appears at their parties," she noted. "If the girls want to get along they learn, pretty generally, to keep their mouths shut, to play the role of the quiet and yielding vessel through which man finds the cosmos."[15]

The surrealism, finally, of the movement came from the Big Sur coast itself—a place that was so detached from everyday life and landscape and, although Brady did not cite this influence, perhaps from the worldview of Miller himself, as revealed in his writings. In Miller, after all, in his pornography and grotesquerie, in the nightmarish sexual scenes of *Tropic of Cancer* and *Tropic of Capricorn*, there was a quality of surreality that was doubly reinforced in his social commentary by the idiosyncratic, indeed hyper-eccentric, view he often took of conventional social reality. There was in Miller's worldview a hallucinogenic quality transcending drug-induced visions, although lesser beings would need drugs to get there: a view of the world, that is, as nightmarish and deceptive—and only true and beautiful on the other side, however one got there.

The point was: as early as 1946, one observer at least was seeing in the gathering Berkeley-Big Sur bohemia the makings of an alternative view of American life that could in time become the makings of a mass movement. Over the next decade and a half, the attitudes described by Brady would emerge as the beat movement; and this sensibility, in turn, quickened by generational revolt and a hated war in Vietnam would become the hippie movement, the free speech movement, the anti-war movement, the anti-corporate movement, the anti-establishment movement, the anti-everything movement: that congeries of resentments and shifting values and attitudes, in short, that would coalesce in the 1960s as a whole new way of looking at American life. The judgments of Henry Miller in *The Air-Conditioned Nightmare* were harsh and presumptuous; yet, soon, many would find in them a compelling critique and alternative way of life.

8

1947 ✶ Black Dahlia

I T was a *Front Page* kind of city, the Los Angeles of 1947: a city of cops, crooks, and defense lawyers; a demimonde of rackets, screaming headlines, and pol-iticians on the take; a town of gamblers, guys and dolls, booze and sex; a place for schemers, also-rans, suckers and those who deceived them: the kind of city in which a private detective such as Philip Marlowe might make his way down mean streets in search of the ever-elusive truth and get sapped with a blackjack for his effort by parties unknown. Being all these things, it was also a golden time for newspapers, a *Front Page* time in a *Front Page* town. In 1947 the City of Los Angeles alone had five competing newspapers covering the action. Within the county, there were also important newspapers in Glendale, Pasadena, and Long Beach, together with dozens of smaller publications. Greater Los Angeles seemed greedy to devour stories about itself, to savor every gory detail of each spectacular crime, each Hollywood scandal, and there were plenty of these to go around. Then there was sports news; and coverage of the beach, bar, and restaurant scene; and real estate, so important to the burgeoning region.

Leading the pack was the stately Los Angeles *Times*, grand dowager of the newspaperworld, destined to outlast every one of its competitors. William Ran-dolph Hearst had entered the Los Angeles market with the *Examiner* in 1914 by popular request, a good part of the city resenting the dominance of the region by *Times* publisher Harrison Gray Otis, a fire-eating hierarch so conservative, so op-posed to organized labor, as to define in and of himself a new species of American ultramontane. For the *Examiner*, Hearst architect Julia Morgan, soon to be busy as well on San Simeon to the north, created a multi-colored Moorish castle on Olympic Boulevard. It was the most distinctive newspaper building in the United States. At ground level, one could stand on the sidewalk and look through large plate glass windows and see the giant presses rolling out the competition for the morning *Times*. Hearst also had an afternoon paper, the *Herald-Express*, devoted, as veteran reporter Jack Smith later remembered, to sex, crime, and wrong-doing. The *Herald-Express* was sharp, sassy, scandalous, and very Hearst. It was also superbly directed by managing editor John B. T. Campbell and city editor Agness Underwood, who had risen through the ranks as an ace stop-the-press reporter. There was also the *Daily News*, aimed mainly at commuter traffic on the streetcars, and the *Mirror*, a blue-collar-oriented tabloid, popular in East Los Angeles, in South Central, and around the betting parlors and the track.

Hundreds of men and women had their employment on these newspapers, and a number of them became living legends. Jim Murray flourished at the *Herald-Express* and the *Examiner* before going on to help found *Sports Illustrated* and win a Pulitzer Prize for sports reporting at the Los Angeles *Times*. Jack Smith made a similar hegira, winding up as the leading *Times* columnist. Medically discharged from the Coast Guard with a hole in his right lung, Gene Fowler, son of the famous New York newsman of the same name (Fowler's father had been managing editor of the New York *American* at age thirty-three), went to work at the *Examiner* in 1944, at the age of twenty-one, later transferring to the *Herald-Express*. Fowler was a great reporter (and he would be among the first to tell you that). Fowler was also an arm-wrestler of preternatural strength, which really impressed the cops and earned him respect in the demimonde; and in the midst of it all, he managed to bat out a number of very fine books. Richard O'Connor, the skilled chief rewrite man on the *Herald-Express*, managed to write more than fifty published books across his career, including well-received biographies of Jack London, Bret Harte, and Ambrose Bierce, together with a study of American involvement in the Far East. Eccentric even by Los Angeles standards, O'Connor neither owned a car nor had a driver's license, a form of eccentricity verging upon willful self-destruction in Southern California.

Newspaperwomen Adela Rogers St. Johns, Hedda Hopper, and Louella Parsons, together with their male colleagues Jimmy Starr and Harrison Carroll, brought Hollywood reporting into its greatest era. Matt Weinstock wrote a city-side column for the *Daily News* filled with Damon Runyonesque dialogue and incident. Bevo Means covered the sheriff's beat, which meant crime throughout Los Angeles County, which meant an enormous capacity for constant driving and swift movement on Means's part, which Means managed to do despite his more than five hundred pounds. News photographers had to be equally mobile to negotiate the great distances of metro Los Angeles. Now and then, some of them got lucky, as in the case of *Examiner* photographer Frank Powolney, who, in the course of photographing film star Betty Grable in a swimsuit, caught her, at Gene Fowler's request, from the other side, her right arm on her hip, despite the fact that the Hays Office explicitly banned *derrière* poses, especially in high heels and swimsuits. Powolney caught the moment, and Miss Grable's smile, and the resulting snapshot became the number one pinup of the Second World War.

Naturally, there were hacks aplenty, with so much writing to be done each day, each hour, each minute, to feed the rolling presses of five newspapers; yet in retrospect, it is amazing how much fine writing was accomplished by Murray, Fowler, O'Connor, St. Johns, and the others—provided, of course, that they had the booze under control, for life on the fast track of *Front Page* Los Angeles involved the ability to live constantly in the company of John Barleycorn. On his first day at the *Examiner*, Gene Fowler was taken to lunch by Jim Murray at Betty's Broadway Circle on Broadway—two bourbons before lunch and two bottles of ale to accompany the ham on rye, all this for sixty-five cents. Fowler returned to his desk feeling like a real newsman. Before the afternoon buzz wore off, there was always a chance to get across the street and visit the bar at the Carillo Hotel. For *Front Page*-ers, booze was an occupational hazard. Louella Parsons, a monumental toper, was known frequently to phone her column in when under the influence, which challenged the best of the rewrite staff at the *Examiner* to transcribe her gibberish. Liquor almost killed *Examiner* managing editor Jim Richardson, whose doctor had told him in the late 1930s, after Richardson had come to in the hospital after a monumental bender, that one more drink, literally one more drink, and Richardson's liver would collapse and he would be dead. After innumerable firings for drunkenness, Richardson went on the wagon and was given one final chance by managing editor Ray Van Ettischof. Newspapering became Richardson's life, his way of coping with his condition as a recovered alcoholic: a story told in fictional form by another Los Angeles newspaperman, Harlan Ware, whose novel *Come, Fill the Cup* (1952), based on Richardson's life, became a best-seller and a film starring Jimmy Cagney.

Jack Smith, who worked for Richardson, later described him as "sadistic . . . the worst kind of a drunk—a reformed one," by which Smith was suggesting Richardson's ferocious management of such reporters as himself, Gene Fowler, Richard O'Connor, and Jim Murray.[1] In one of his boldest coups, this as city editor of the *Examiner* in 1938, Richardson had authorized an undercover reporter, William Bradford Huie, to penetrate the household of gangster Bugsy Siegel. Employed as a houseboy, Huie reported to Richardson that Siegel's basement was filled with smuggled Chanel No. 5. Richardson tipped off the customs office; but by the time revenue agents pulled a raid, all the Chanel had been removed, and Siegel greeted the officers at the door with a smile on his face. Undaunted, Richardson ran a series of stories exposing Siegel's career as a gangster on the East Coast. The bad publicity cost Siegel his membership in the Hillcrest Country Club. Like so many literate Los Angeles reporters, Huie went on to achieve fame as a novelist and writer with such works as *The Execution of Private Slovik* (1954), *The Americanization of Emily* (1959), and *The Revolt of Mamie Stover* (1951), each of them the basis for a successful film.

Richardson's counterpart over at the *Herald-Express*, managing editor John B. T. Campbell, was equally tyrannical: a cigar-smoking managing editor from Central Casting, barking orders, chewing out reporters, tearing up the front page minutes before the final deadline. The son of a prominent San Francisco judge, Campbell had been raised in splendor in the Palace Hotel in that city and begun his career as a reporter on the San Francisco *Chronicle*. A conservative Republican, Campbell managed the impossible: to work for Hearst while remaining socially prominent. Campbell's city editor Agness Underwood shared San Francisco as a birthplace in common with Campbell, but little else, save for a mutual love of newspapering; for Underwood had come from the most narrow and difficult of circumstances. Orphaned as a child and shunted from relative to relative in the Midwest, Agness Underwood arrived in Los Angeles as a young woman of seventeen, supporting herself as a clerk in the Broadway Department Store on 4th Street in the Downtown. Within months, she was married, and then a mother, and shortly thereafter a mother of two, and only left her home to work as a temporary switchboard operator on the Los Angeles *Record*, a small Eastside working-class, community-oriented newspaper, when her husband could not afford to buy her a new pair of silk stockings. Lacking background or education, Underwood learned the newspaper business by paying attention to the messages that flowed back and forth through her switchboard. She later graduated to supervising community toy, food, and clothing drives at Christmas time, and then, being a superb typist, she was allowed to do backup work on rewrite, amazing one and all with her ability to transcribe on her Underwood Number 5 even the most rapid-fire dictation from reporters in the field. It took Underwood six years to work her way into a reporter's position on the *Record*, but her career did not go into high gear until she joined the *Herald-Express* in January 1935, age thirty-two, a married woman, raising her thirteen-year-old daughter and her nine-year-old son.

As a crime reporter, Aggie Underwood turned in scoop after scoop through the late 1930s and early 1940s, based initially out of her unpretentious, lower-middle-class home at 112th and Figueroa streets near Florence Avenue in South Central, where her husband managed an automobile agency. Named city editor in 1947, the first woman to hold this position in a major metropolitan newspaper in the United States, Underwood moved her family to the more upscale San Fernando Valley, although this meant that she had to rise slightly past four in the morning to be downtown by six in order to push the *Herald-Examiner* toward its noon deadline for copy and its 12:35 P.M. deadline for pictures. On hot days, once she became city editor, Aggie would order up a case or two of cold beer for the city room. Direct in manner, skilled in her calling, Underwood remained, simultaneously, a homemaker, famous for her impromptu spaghetti dinners for sixty or more of the press gang, and a dynamic city editor who, like so many other Los Angeles reporters, also wrote a very fine book, *Newspaperwoman* (1949), her autobiography and a lively social history of the city.

As reporter and city editor, Aggie Underwood covered the big and little stories of the Front Page era at a time when even the little stories were big on the day they happened. During the war, for example, there was the bizarre incident reported by Bill Zelinsky of the young woman, a devout Christian, married to an infantryman in the European theater of operations, who found herself pregnant despite the fact that she had been faithful to her husband and he had been gone for two years. The woman was distraught, on the verge of suicide. What happened? Then Zelinsky ran a background check on the woman's dentist and found that he had been previously charged with raping female patients under anesthesia, which is what happened to the young woman in question. Or the terrible scandal that broke out when the President's son, Colonel Elliott Roosevelt, USAAF, husband of screen actress Faye Emerson, was alleged to have secured a priority flight for his dog Blaze, bumping an enlisted man trying to get home. When General George S. Patton Jr. and Lieutenant General James H. Doolittle, both from the Los Angeles area, returned for receptions in June 1945, Mrs. Patton quarreled terribly with Mrs. Doolittle, believing that her husband and she were trying to upstage the Pattons, their seniors in rank. Aggie Underwood had to coax Mrs. Patton to pose with Mrs. Doolittle for photographers. Then there was the more serious catastrophe of Thursday morning, 20 February 1947, when a terrible explosion at the O'Connor Electro-Plating Building at 922 East Pico Boulevard killed thirty and injured three hundred.

Like every good crime reporter, Agness Underwood got to know the courts and, more important, the cops: Detective Lieutenant Harry Fremont, for example, allegedly the toughest and meanest cop on the LAPD. Fremont was known to have nearly beaten a prisoner to death at the 77th Street Substation, and Gene Fowler was convinced that the homicide detective had killed a number of criminals in back alleys. Fowler claimed to have been an eyewitness to the time when Fremont was interrogating a man who had just shot and killed Fremont's partner. The man was wounded and lying on a gurney at the receiving hospital on Georgia Street. Fremont told the man to get up off the gurney and run for it. Fowler caught the look in the arrested man's face as he started his run, knowing he was doomed. Coolly, Detective Fremont put six shots into the fleeing suspect. There was no investigation.

Some years earlier, criminologist and crime reporter Ernest Hopkins, writing in *Our Lawless Police* (1931), had claimed that the LAPD had an absolute disregard for the constitution, or for law of any sort, for that matter. Hopkins described how the LAPD as a matter of course used rubber hoses to beat suspects under interrogation, since a hose left no visible marks. Throughout the 1930s a reputation for lawlessness, for being a kingdom unto itself, clung to the LAPD and its allied departments. The areas policed were so vast (three thousand square miles under the jurisdiction of the sheriff's office alone), and the officers and deputies so scattered, and the alliances among law enforcement so tight, that it was not surprising that the LAPD and allied agencies achieved a high level of administrative and even political autonomy.

When C. B. Horrall retired as Los Angeles police chief in the late 1940s, Mayor Fletcher Bowron appointed William Worton, a retired major general in the Marine Corps, to come in from the outside and whip the department into shape. Worton, a tough combat veteran of thirty-plus years of Marine service, was soon complaining: "I can't trust a soul in the whole department."[2] On the other hand, the LAPD was responsible for 453.3 square miles, the largest municipal area in the world, and was forced to manage this with a staff of 4,333 in 1947, a thousand of whom were assigned to traffic. The LAPD had 150 radio cars that year and three hundred patrolmen walking beats. Homicide had to deal with an average of one murder every two or three days. When General Worton admitted defeat and departed in 1950, Deputy Chief William Parker took over and revolutionized the department. Thanks in great part to actor Jack Webb's portrayal of Sergeant Joe Friday in the *Dragnet* radio and television series, the LAPD was also able to soften its image of conspiracy and corruption, although suspicions and hostilities still ran high and would remain that way for most of the rest of the century.

But that would be a later time. For the 1940s the LAPD homicide detective, as Agness Underwood encountered him and as Raymond Chandler depicted him in confrontation with private detective Philip Marlowe, flourished as an almost folk-loric figure, a law unto himself: even something of a dandy in his double-breasted suit, snap-brim hat, loud tie, gold watchband, gold name-bracelet, gold ring, and gold mechanical pencil for taking notes. Such dandyism was part of the *esprit de corps* of homicide, whose detectives moved in their own world: an elite cast of characters—some corrupt, some not, some in between—in a detective story writing itself in the City of Angels. How, one might ask, could cops afford so much jewelry on the salary of a detective sergeant or, for a smaller number, detective lieutenant? Part of the answer was innocent. So acute was the housing shortage in these years, homicide detectives frequently made calls to real estate agents before the body was removed from the premises. There were cases in which a body was moved in the morning and the apartment was cleaned in mid-day and rented by late afternoon. Naturally, the rental agency expressed its gratitude to the detective in question. Agness Underwood noted that most LAPD homicide detectives retired in middle age, getting their twenty years in and getting out, and that many of them had ranches in Oregon or in rural California. Finally, she noted, most of the detectives at homicide were large and physically robust, capable of holding their own in a violent situation, capable of using their fists, as the fictional Philip Marlowe sometimes discovered to his distress.

On the morning of 15 January 1947, an alert crackled over the shortwave radios of Los Angeles Police Department patrol cars. "A 390 W, 415 down in an empty lot one block east of Crenshaw between 39th and Coliseum," droned the dispatcher. "Please investigate. Code Two." Translated into more complete English, the message suggested that a drunk female, indecently exposed, was lying in an empty lot in South Central. The nearest patrol car should proceed in all haste but without red lights or siren. Riding in his car with his photographer partner Felix Paegel, *Herald-Express* reporter Will Fowler heard the call over his shortwave monitor, and Paegel, who was driving, turned south on Crenshaw, heading toward 39th. Fowler and Paegel had every reason to believe that they were on the trail of yet another bizarre Los Angeles story, a drunken naked dame this time, passed out in an empty lot. Turning east on 39th, they were shocked to find that the young woman in question was not only naked, she was also dead and sawed in half.

A reporter for three years on the crime beat, Fowler had witnessed many an autopsy in the county morgue in the basement of the Hall of Justice in the Downtown, which each week yielded its harvest of corpses done in by various forms of mayhem, and had been further instructed by Ray Pinker, head of the LAPD crime lab, in the techniques of quickly analyzing a corpse. Fowler was thus able to note that the body, "lying there like a discarded marionette, separated from itself by about one foot," was clean of blood, indicating that it had been bisected, then scrubbed down at some other place, before being deposited in the lot. "The top of this young woman's right breast," Fowler also observed, "had been cutaneously excised along with its nipple. Her generously formed left breast had been horizontally incised (about twelve millimeters) to the left of and away from the nipple and exposed an outer sheet of muscle." Later, he would get access to the coroner's report to make more precise his initial impressions. The dark color of the blood and its coagulation on the forehead and slashed mouth of the corpse, together with the purple bruises around her neck, arms, and wrists, indicated that the woman had been tortured before her death, perhaps for days. Below her navel and directly above the *mons veneris* was a vertical incision cut to resemble a hysterectomy scar. There was also evidence that pubic hair had been pulled from the skin in the course of torture. The left leg had been deeply cut, and part of the femur bone was exposed. An equilateral triangle of skin was missing, which was later located in the rectum and found to be marked with a rose tattoo. The hair of the corpse, which was chestnut in color, as evidenced by the roots, had been dyed a deep black. Even in its mutilated state, the face, together with the proportions of the figure, indicated that the woman had been young and attractive.[3]

A few minutes after Fowler and Paegel arrived on the scene, LAPD Detective Sergeant Harry Hansen, wearing the fedora hat, loud tie, double-breasted suit, and expensive watchband that were *de rigueur* in homicide, arrived on the scene and commenced his investigation. Thirty-five years later, long after his retirement and almost until the time of his death, Sergeant Hansen was still investigating what had long since become the Black Dahlia murder case.

A fingerprint check soon revealed the identity of the deceased. She was Elizabeth Short, twenty-two. Born and raised in Medford, Massachusetts, Short had dropped out of high school at sixteen and headed west to Hollywood with the vague ambition of becoming a movie star. She had become, instead, one of thousands of juvenile V-girls who hung around military bases in hopes of romance and marriage. In Los Angeles terms, she was one of a horde of anonymous nobodies fleeing from elsewhere during the war years, bringing along the terrible obscurity of their lives, their desperate hopes for something better, their flawed and frequently disastrous dreams. Most recently, Short had worked at the PX at Camp Cooke 160 miles north of the city. Her last known address had been in

Santa Barbara. Before that, she had lived in Long Beach, where people who knew her had nicknamed her the Black Dahlia because of her dyed jet-black hair, which she wore in a bouffant pompadour, and her preference for black clothing; and this became how the Los Angeles press designated her, the Black Dahlia, then and for all time to come.

Elizabeth Short had spent the final month of her life in Pacific Beach, a lower-middle-class suburb of San Diego, as the guest of a certain Mrs. Elvira French. French's daughter Dorothy, a cashier at an all-night motion picture theater, had met Short late on the evening of 8 December 1946 when Short, broke, alone, homeless, was buying a ticket to sit up all night in the theater. Dorothy French took pity on the attractive young woman and took her home, and Mrs. French looked after her through the Christmas season. Around six o'clock in the early evening of 8 January 1947, Elizabeth Short took her leave of the Frenches in the company of a young man she called Red. Short told the Frenches that Red was driving her to Los Angeles. Red came by in a 1940 black Studebaker and piled Short's luggage into the car, and the two of them drove off into the early winter darkness.

Police soon found Red and brought him in for questioning. He was Robert (Red) Manley, twenty-five, of 8010 Mountain View Avenue, Huntington Park, married to Harriet Manley. The couple had a four-month-old infant. Manley admitted to the police that he had picked up Elizabeth Short on impulse on a street corner in San Diego, wanting to test whether he still loved his wife, and spent a sex-less night with her in a local motel before dropping her off in front of the Biltmore Hotel in Los Angeles at approximately six-thirty on the evening of 9 January 1947. Short told Manley that she had a date to meet someone there. A former Army Air Force musician who had been discharged from the service for homicidal tendencies, Red Manley came under immediate and total suspicion; but his alibi held—a married man at home with his family on the most likely date of the murder and dissection of Miss Short—and he was eventually released from custody.

Through the enterprise of *Examiner* and *Herald-Express* reporters, Elizabeth Short's luggage was recovered from the Greyhound station in downtown Los Angeles, and a trunk with her clothes, picture album, and correspondence with servicemen through the war years was located at the warehouse of the Railway Express. Short's correspondence testified to relationships, real or imagined, she had established in Southern California during and after the war with servicemen. In her handbag, recovered along with her luggage, was found a newspaper clipping concerning the marriage of Army Air Forces Major Matt Gordon. The name of the bride had been scratched out. Major Gordon had been killed in an air crash in India in 1943. Had Short corresponded with him? Had she perhaps fantasized that she had been married to the dashing young aviator, keeping this altered clipping as a form of pseudo-proof? Or had she used the clipping to pass herself off as a war widow?

Elizabeth Short had obviously formed a number of relationships with servicemen, and each of them had failed. The police knew why at the time, and so did the newspapers, but they did not let it be known that Short, so tragic in her brief life, also suffered a physical deformity: an infantile entrance to her vagina, which had no doubt caused the many breakups. Plastic surgery could have corrected the deformity and allowed Short to lead a normal life; but there was no one to guide her in this matter or to bring her to a doctor. There were only a number of young men to recoil from her in anger—and one, whether young or middle-aged, to torture her heinously in such a way as to mock her defective femininity, which was not her fault and deserved pity and surgery, not the horrible kind of cutting she endured in the ghastly last hours of her life.

The Los Angeles *Examiner*, the *Herald-Express*, and the other papers kept the Black Dahlia case on the front page for thirty-two days. Somewhere in the vast anonymity of the city, her killer followed the publicity and called Jim Richardson, city editor of the *Examiner*, and told him that he had the Black Dahlia's address book and birth certificate and a few other items from her handbag; two days later, postal inspectors intercepted a parcel with these items addressed to the *Examiner* by the murderer of Elizabeth Short, who had clipped his words from the newspaper to avoid detection. Among other items were the locker receipt stubs that led to the purse itself and the luggage.

Desperate, terrible, obscene in its cruelty, the Black Dahlia case mesmerized Los Angeles throughout January and February of 1947 not only because of its graphic horrors but because (whether this could be fully grasped at the time or not) the brief and unhappy life of Elizabeth Short said something about Los Angeles itself: something about the anonymity, the desperation, the cruelty and brutality life could have in the City of Angels. The war precipitated innumerable acts of violence in Los Angeles as servicemen did violence to servicemen, servicemen did violence to civilians, civilians did violence to servicemen, and civilians continued to do violence to each other. In June 1945, for example, Ernest Bougher, age thirty-eight, returning from the merchant marine, learned that his wife Audrey, also thirty-eight and the mother of their two children, had been unfaithful to him with defense worker Alex Haproff, twenty-five. Bougher invited Haproff out to his home in Lynwood, promising an afternoon of free liquor and free love. Instead, Bougher, assisted by his repentant wife and a friend, Donald Lawhead, thirty-seven, another merchant marine veteran, beat and shot Haproff to death.

By 1947, Gene Fowler noted, Los Angeles had so many murders that approximately fifty of them—which is to say, at least half—warranted little more than a minor paragraph in the back pages of the newspaper. Each day, the receiving hospital on Georgia Street welcomed the shot, the maimed, the stabbed, or the otherwise wounded, and the county morgue received its corpses. Murderers such as Louise Peete, the second woman executed in the history of the state (this at San Quentin on 11 April in the murderous year of 1947), did continue to receive front-page treatment; but then again, this was Mrs. Peete's second conviction for first degree murder for gain. All three of Mrs. Peete's husbands, moreover, defying actuarial tables, had committed suicide. Mrs. Peete was plump and wore matronly print dresses and epitomized in so many other ways the matriarchal virtues of the Folks despite the three mysteriously deceased husbands; despite the wealthy mining engineer, Jacob Denton, forty-nine, whom she had shot and buried in the cellar of her home on South Catalina Street in the 1920s, and the body of Mrs. Margaret Logan, sixty, whom Mrs. Peete had recently shot and buried under an avocado tree in the yard of the Logan home in Pacific Palisades. With the Black Dahlia case, the execution of Mrs. Peete, the Overell murders, and the assassination of the Los Angeles–based mobster Bugsy Siegel, 1947 proved a banner year.

Springing as it did, once again, from the Folks, and involving overtones of American Gothic as grand guignol, the Overell case — with its admixture of parenticide and tawdry romance — fascinated as well as baffled someone as generally detached from his environment as German émigré novelist Thomas Mann, who followed the case avidly, if somewhat shamefacedly, in the newspapers. On an otherwise warm and peaceful Saturday night in Newport Beach, 15 March 1947, the forty-seven-foot yacht *Mary E.*, belonging to Walter Overell, owner of one of Los Angeles's better-known furniture companies, exploded and sank. On board were Overell and his wife, Beulah. As the blast shook the harbor, the couple's daughter, Beulah Louise Overell, seventeen, and her boyfriend George Rector (Bud) Gollum, twenty-one, sat eating hamburgers at a lunch counter near the beach. When the bodies of Walter and Beulah Overell were recovered, it was alleged by the coroner that they had been beaten to death with a ballpeen hammer just before their yacht was blown sky high with dynamite. Two days later, the police arrested Beulah Louise and her boyfriend on charges of murder, and they remained in jail awaiting trial.

The case fascinated reporters because it showed the Folks as *haute bourgeoisie* afflicted with delinquent offspring: a foretaste, perhaps, of an even more familiar pattern in the 1950s. While in prison awaiting trial, Louise and Bud exchanged a series of letters in which each of them expressed undying love and admiration for the other. "I dream of your beautiful chest," Louise at one point wrote her tall, bespectacled boyfriend, a pre-pre-med student at the Los Angeles City College. "Darling, no one will ever have as beautiful chest as you. My wonderful, beautiful, gorgeous Pops. My intelligent, handsome Pops. Never leave me. You're an unlifted [*sic*] human being. You're the most intelligent person I ever heard of. Einstein was a moron compared to you." On his part, Bud was equally ardent. "I love you, I love you, I love you," he wrote in a series of letters secured by the Los Angeles *Examiner* and published. "I am yours my darling. I am going to have you as my wife. Because I love and adore and worship and cherish you with all my heart. If necessary, I'll kidnap and carry you off somewhere so that no one will ever be able to find us and I'll make passionate and violent love to you."[4]

For the time being, the Overell-Gollum letters bespoke the younger generation of the Folks as a demotic Heloise and Abelard en route to James Dean and Natalie

Wood in *Rebel Without a Cause* (1955). The children of the Folks had graduated—or so it was being alleged—to parricide. The Overell trial lasted nineteen
weeks. The prosecution called ninety witnesses; the defense, thirty. A million
words of testimony were transcribed, but not the one hundred jailhouse letters,
which Judge Kenneth Morrison refused to have read in court or entered into the
record. A Santa Ana jury acquitted Louise and Bud, describing them as victims
of circumstance. Walter Overell and his wife, the jury decided, had not been
beaten to death with a ballpeen hammer, nor had the *Mary E.* been dynamited
into oblivion. Walter Overell, the jury decided, had been in a depressed condition,
and the Overells had met death due to "the accident of suicidal tampering with
dynamite by Walter Overell" on the *Mary E.* Beulah Louise Overell and Bud
Gollum left the court in freedom. Thomas Mann was appalled, but the Folks
understood.[5]

A year later, the Folks were not so understanding with another one of their own.
Caryl Chessman, twenty-six and a two-time loser, was brought to trial in May 1948
on eighteen felony counts, including two kidnapping charges carrying the death
penalty. Chessman was accused of being the notorious "red light bandit" who had
terrorized Los Angeles County throughout 1947. Patrolling lovers' lanes and back
roads in Malibu, or the open spaces surrounding the Rose Bowl in Pasadena, or
the hilly areas along Mulholland Drive and the back roads of the Flintridge Hills
in a late-model Ford equipped with a red spotlight that made it seem a police car,
the red light bandit would approach couples, who initially thought he was a po-
liceman. Armed with a .45, he would rob his victims in most instances; at other
times, however, he would force his female victims to perform fellatio on him at
gunpoint.

Born in Michigan in 1921 of church-going white Protestant stock, Chessman
had been brought as a boy by his parents to Los Angeles and grew into a precocious
child. The Depression hit Chessman's parents hard. Twice, his dispirited father
attempted suicide. The boy himself suffered from asthma and was severely weakened by an attack of encephalitis, which he later claimed completely changed his
personality. Strongly religious in his upbringing, Chessman grew morbid, intro-
spective, convinced that he was worthless. He began to act out this conviction
through petty delinquencies, followed by more serious offenses that landed him
in reform school, followed by two felony convictions and terms in San Quentin
and Folsom.

Whatever else he was, Caryl Chessman remained a sort of genius, even in the
midst of his self-destructive life of crime. (As a boy, he was alleged to have been
able to recite "The Night Before Christmas" verbatim after hearing it only once.)
His two adult prison terms served as his Harvard and his Yale, giving him plenty
of time to read as well as further hardening his heart against society. Chessman
admired the life and poetry of François Villon, the fifteenth-century French poet
who combined a literary career with a life of crime. In any event, when his case
came to trial before Superior Court Judge Charles Fricke, Chessman chose to

defend himself against Deputy District Attorney J. Miller Leavy, confident that the descriptions of the red light bandit—a slender man, even slight, dark in appearance, most likely Italian, speaking with a slight accent—would in no way match Chessman's six feet, 190 pounds, and fair complexion. And besides: Chessman, a skilled (if twice convicted) burglar, hijacker, enforcer, and would-be racketeer, had contempt for the red light bandit as a bungling amateur and sex creep, or so he later alleged in his best-selling autobiography *Cell 2455 Death Row* (1954), one of the most powerful instances of prison literature to be written and published in the United States.

He who has himself for a lawyer, runs the proverb, has a fool for a client. Chessman insisted on representing himself, and he insisted on testifying in his own defense. The prosecution succeeded in getting much of Chessman's prior record before the jury and painted him as a criminal genius sociopath. More damagingly, the prosecutor succeeded in having admitted to evidence a previous confession, which Chessman claimed the police had extracted from him through physical and psychological torture. Sentenced to the gas chamber in San Quentin, Chessman carried on a twelve-year defense from death row, writing numerous briefs and motions and two best-selling books. By the late 1950s Caryl Chessman — a brilliant writer, a self-taught lawyer, an existentialist figure straight from the pages of Albert Camus's *The Stranger*—had become an icon of resistance to a growing protest movement. His execution in 1960 would have enormous consequences for both California and the nation. Indeed, it can be argued that the Chessman case played a major role in defining the 1960s, which in turn played a major role in defining the emergent culture of the United States in the last third of the twentieth century.

But that would happen later. For the time being, the 1930s and 1940s, the more intriguing dramas of crime in the Southland involved Hollywood, which stood in strong symbiosis to the Folks and experienced along with them an abundant measure of murder, suicide, and other modes of mayhem down through the 1940s. In his classic study *Hollywood Babylon* (1960), followed by *Hollywood Babylon II* (1984), Hollywood antiquarian Kenneth Anger (he grew up in Hollywood and in 1935 played the stolen boy in Max Reinhardt's *A Midsummer Night's Dream*) presented the macabre side of filmland with such outrageous detail that critic Susan Sontag, another Hollywood kid, later ranked *Hollywood Babylon*, part one, as a *sui generis* work of art, possessed of an intensity equal to the best screen production. Indeed, Anger does describe the dark star of Hollywood as it collapses into itself—in murder, suicide, brawls, drugs, alcoholism, and miscellaneous modes of wickedness—allowing no light to escape.

From Anger and from contemporary eyewitnesses, including Clinton Anderson, chief of police of Beverly Hills, one has no difficulty encountering case after case in which the vagaries of the Folks and Hollywood run in tandem. After the demise of director Desmond Taylor in February 1922, murder was not all that common in Hollywood, at least in the upper echelon. On the other hand, in April 1927 actor Paul Kelly did get into a serious fistfight with song-and-dance man Ray Raymond, the two of them blind drunk at the time, and Raymond died as a result. Kelly spent five years in San Quentin. Released in 1933, he defied the odds and made a complete comeback as a stage and screen character actor. On 15 August 1931 Florine Williams, widow of Earl Williams, a silent picture star, murdered her two children and her aged mother, and then committed suicide after a confidence man had bilked her of $500,000. At the end of the decade, on the night of 26 June 1939, Campbell MacDonald, twenty-six, beat his mother, film actress Margaret Campbell, fifty-six, to death with a claw hammer. Investigation yielded strong evidence of an incestuous relationship between mother and son, and MacDonald was committed to the Mendocino State Hospital for the criminally insane. Then there was the attempted murder in 1938 of pianist Myrl Aldermann, lover of singer Ruth Etting, by Miss Etting's divorced husband Moe (the Gimp) Snyder. The story of this domestic dispute was later filmed as *Love Me or Leave Me* (1955), starring Jimmy Cagney and Doris Day.

Hollywood suicides too numerous to mention in detail included the suspicious death on 5 September 1932 of studio executive Paul Bern, husband of film star Jean Harlow, who allegedly shot and killed himself in the bedroom of the couple's house in Benedict Canyon. Some suspected Harlow of being more than a horrified bystander. Nor was everyone satisfied that actress Thelma Todd had done herself in through carbon monoxide poisoning on 13 December 1935. Dressed in the mink coat and blue and silver sequined evening gown she had worn that Saturday night to a party on the Sunset Strip, Todd's body was found on the front seat of her brown Lincoln behind the closed doors of a garage at 17531 Posetano Drive in Malibu near a café she owned. It was rumored that the mob had disposed of Miss Todd when she refused to turn her restaurant into a drug emporium. Lupe Velez's suicide, by contrast, on 14 December 1944 was less ambiguous. Pregnant by her latest lover, Velez, the divorced wife of Tarzan actor Johnny Weissmuller, filled the bedroom of her Rodeo Drive home with flowers and gave a farewell dinner for her two closest girlfriends. Swallowing seventy-five Seconals, Miss Velez wished to be discovered gracefully in bed the next morning. Sadly, she died kneeling before the toilet, vomiting.

The war and post-war period produced more instances of assault with intent to commit murder, or mere felonious assaults, than murder itself. On the night of 5 August 1944, in the Sunset Strip apartment of bandleader Tommy Dorsey, actor Jon Hall got into a fight with Dorsey, Allen Smiley, a close associate of gangster Bugsy Siegel, and others at the party. Hall was beaten, and his face was disfigured to the point that he almost lost his nose. Actor Franchot Tone almost lost his nose as well — indeed, his entire face had to be reconstructed through surgery — after he was beaten by actor Tom Neal on the lawn of the home of actress Barbara Payton on the night of 14 September 1951. Four months later, on the afternoon of 13 December 1951, producer Walter Wanger, suspicious that his wife actress Joan

Bennett was having an affair with her agent Jennings Lang, waited in a parking lot across the street from the headquarters of the Beverly Hills police for the couple to return in Lang's blue Cadillac convertible from an afternoon assignation. Fifty-seven years old at the time, Wanger had produced such hits as *Algiers* (1938), *Stagecoach* (1939), and, most recently, *Joan of Arc* (1948), starring Ingrid Bergman. Spotting the Cadillac entering the lot, Wanger approached the car and shot Lang in the scrotum and lower body with a .38.

No wonder that Jerry Giesler, defense attorney to the stars, was being kept so busy! Acquiring his training in the offices of the legendary Earl Rogers, whom even Clarence Darrow had for a lawyer, Giesler had come into prominence in 1931 when he won a new trial and an acquittal in the rape conviction of theater magnate Alexander Pantages. Giesler spent the next two decades, or so it seemed, getting his clients, many of them celebrities, acquitted. The war years, 1944 especially, were banner years for Giesler's practice. He won two of his most celebrated cases but lost the third. When Dorsey and Smiley were indicted on felony charges of assault against Hall, Giesler defended Smiley and won a dismissal for both men. In one of the best-known cases of its type, Giesler successfully defended Errol Flynn against three felony charges of statutory rape. When the rising young actor Robert Mitchum was set up and busted for smoking marijuana at a party in Laurel Canyon on 31 August 1948 (a peroxide blonde had only just handed Mitchum the reefer when the cops burst in), Giesler defended Mitchum directly to the judge, no jury, on the basis of the grand jury transcript. Mitchum escaped with a misdemeanor conviction and a sixty-day sentence in the county jail, which he served as a model prisoner, emerging more popular than ever. Giesler employed a similar strategy of jury avoidance in April 1952 when defending Walter Wanger on charges of attempted murder against his wife's lover. Wanger was facing a felony conviction and some very hard time. Instead, Judge Harry Borde of the Superior Court in Santa Monica reduced the charges to simple assault and sentenced Wanger to four months. Wanger served his time at the Wayside Honor Farm in Castaic, north of the city, where he worked as camp librarian and ran the projector on movie nights.

The mysterious death of Thelma Todd, like the presence of gangster Allen Smiley at Tommy Dorsey's party, leads to an issue that remains an obscure, albeit fascinating, aspect of the Hollywood story: its relationship to the mob. Al Capone was alleged to have visited Los Angeles in 1927 with an eye to organizing the city. By the mid-1930s, Phil Capone, Al's brother, Bugs Moran, Bugsy Siegel, and others had established themselves in Los Angeles. Marino Bello, Jean Harlow's stepfather, had mob connections. In the late 1930s gangster Willie Bioff penetrated and took over the International Alliance of Theatrical and Stage Employees and shook producers down on a regular basis. The sheer dispersion of metropolitan Los Angeles — indeed, the decentralized nature of Southern California in general — precluded a full-blown Chicago-style organization of the region, although now and then gangsters did act true to Chicago form, as in April 1933 when the bodies of gangsters Earl Withrow and Victor Ayeres were found on the Downey Road in an unincorporated part of the county, victims of an internecine slaying.

The 1930s also witnessed a fusion of mob and Hollywood interests in the evolution of the gangster movie and the rise to stardom of an actor, George Raft, who bridged the cultures of Hollywood and the hoods. Although he pleaded guilty to one count of income tax evasion in later life, George Raft was not a gangster. He was, rather, a gangster *manqué* who as an actor traded on his early mob connections and whose successful on-screen depiction of bad guys helped determine the way gangsters behaved in real life. Raft brought to Hollywood a new persona, the movie star as gangster or, conversely, the gangster as movie star. For most of his career, the public believed that Raft had active gangland connections, a notion Raft reinforced by an occasional fistfight, which always made the front page, and his open friendship with Bugsy Siegel.

Hollywood fit George Raft superbly. Right from the start, after all, George Ranft, now Raft, had been a creature of his own invention, a Great Gatsby figure coming of age as a boxer, tango dancer, gigolo, friend of gangsters, and occasional rum-runner in New York and now living in the Great Gatsby of American cities, Los Angeles–Hollywood, where nearly everyone was playing a role. Aware of his lack of education, ashamed of his near-illiteracy, Raft kept his counsel. In public he remained reserved, not talking unless he had something definite to say; and this taciturnity, with its suggestion of a smoldering inner life kept tautly in control, became central to his appeal. Up from the streets, Raft spent a fortune on his tailoring: high-waisted suits, long pointed collars, luxuriant ties, a fedora tilted at just the right angle. Only Adolph Menjou and Cary Grant had comparable success as fashion plates, and they emphasized an Anglo-American Savile Row look, while Raft was strictly Broadway. Soon, gangsters across the country were dressing like George Raft, and some of them were even flipping coins the way Raft did in *Scarface* (1932) when he felt that his character, gangster Guido Rinaldo, was being upstaged.

The vehicle in which George Raft, gangster *manqué*, achieved fame, the gangster film and its sub-genre the prison film, continues to intrigue cultural historians. There were more than two hundred identifiable gangster or gangster-prison films released in the 1930s, a figure falling by more than half in the 1940s. George Raft, in fact, scored his greatest triumph as an actor in perhaps the best prison film of all time, *Each Dawn I Die* (1939), directed by William Keighley and co-starring James Cagney. The prison film was even more schematic than the gangster movie, for here there were no distracting themes of social class and urban sociology, as there so often were in gangster films. In the prison film, society was collapsed back into its basics, prisoners and guards, the powerless and the all-powerful, in a setting that awaited the analysis of French theorist Michel Foucault for its more complete construal: the prison, in short, as the perfect metaphor for the drama of power and control in modern society.

This drama of power and control, together with the subliminal appeal the gangster-prison films held for the American imagination as a displaced paradigm of the national culture, was dramatically corroborated and reinforced during the first four days of the May 1946 convict revolt at the maximum security federal prison on Alcatraz Island in San Francisco Bay. During the revolt and the military siege that followed, a theater in Oakland arranged for a hasty showing of the 1938 Paramount film *King of Alcatraz* depicting a similar, if more successful, attempt by convicts to take over the Rock. Thousands crowded Fisherman's Wharf, Coit Tower, the Marina Yacht Harbor, Aquatic Park, and other vantage points in San Francisco to watch the Marines and the correctional officers launch their final attack. It was just like a movie.

And so too, like the movie they eventually became, were the last days of George Raft's good friend Benjamin (Bugsy) Siegel, then busy with the construction of a gangland institution of another sort, the Flamingo Hotel in Las Vegas. (Raft had personally loaned Siegel $200,000 in cash for the venture.) At some point during the war, Siegel had taken up with a rather mysterious woman from Chicago named Virginia Hill. Born in Alabama in 1916, Hill had arrived in Chicago in 1933 at the age of seventeen, had been briefly married, then seems to have prospered as an associate of gamblers who admired her for her good looks and impressive head for business. Siegel and Hill guided their relationship by Mildred Cram's novel *Forever* (1938), which concerned a man and a woman who, denied a life together in this world, believe that they will be united as lovers in eternity. Although Virginia Hill was always true to Bugsy Siegel in her fashion, discreetly taking a lover or two on the q.t. when Bugsy was out of town, she nevertheless saw her relationship with the handsome gangster as the great big love of her life: something grand and sweeping and for eternity, as in *Forever*, something worthy of Hollywood. It took Hill time to detach Siegel from his wife Esta, the mother of his children, the wife of his youth who spoke so powerfully to his Jewish identity; but Siegel's open association with Hill eventually proved too much for Esta, and she sued for divorce in Reno in December 1945, and in the fall of 1946 Siegel and Hill were secretly married in Mexico.

By this time, Siegel had discovered the one great venture that would give him everything he wanted in life—glamour and power, legitimacy, respectability: a resort hotel in the Las Vegas desert, shimmering by day in the sunlight, resplendent at night in neon, its lobby teeming with affluent gamblers and Hollywood stars. Los Angeles had nurtured Hollywood, and now the Los Angeles–Hollywood dream, operating in and through a jumped-up Brooklyn mobster, was improbably giving birth or at least rebirth to a new American city. Every dream, however tawdry and meretricious, that had pulsated through the collective imagination of Los Angeles–Hollywood, Bugsy Siegel now brought to Las Vegas. Siegel had promised his associates—among them Meyer Lansky, an old friend, and Charles (Lucky) Luciano, an old but not so friendly colleague—that the Flamingo, which they bankrolled, would cost $1 million. Siegel hired Del Webb to build the hotel.

Through his good friend United States Senator Pat McCarran, Webb arranged priorities for construction materials still scare in the post-war period. Siegel interfered constantly with his architects and with Webb, ordering expensive adjustments, and the cost of the project pushed toward $6 million. Part of the money Siegel raised from loans and the sale of hotel stock (no one ever fully accounted for how many shares Siegel issued); much of it came from Siegel's colleagues on the East Coast.

On 26 December 1946 an unexpected storm kept a promised Hollywood crowd from flying in to Las Vegas to celebrate the grand opening of Siegel's hotel. Only such second-tier stars as Charles Coburn, Sonny Tufts, George Sanders, George Jessel, and Jimmy Durante were spotted in an embarrassingly empty lobby—and Jessel and Durante were on the payroll. In January 1947 Siegel was forced to close the Flamingo so as to finish construction and get it in operating order. He opened the Flamingo a second time on the first of March. A month earlier, Siegel had been summoned to Havana for a meeting with Luciano, Lansky, and others regarding the continuing losses the hotel was incurring. Siegel stalked out of the meeting, and a vote was most likely taken at that time to kill him for his defiance. The Flamingo continued to lose money, and the relationship between Siegel and Hill, now living openly as husband and wife in penthouse suite 401, rapidly deteriorated. Hill grew morose and jealous. Quarreling with Siegel, she struck him with the spike heel of one of her shoes, cutting a deep gash in his head. She fled Las Vegas until Siegel cooled down. Upon her return, she physically attacked a hatcheck girl whom she accused of making a play for Bugsy. After this incident, Hill took sleeping pills in a suicide attempt and had to be rushed to the hospital to have her stomach pumped.

Siegel's checks were bouncing; and besides, word was out that he was a marked man. The 20th of June 1947 was Siegel's last day on earth. At 12:53 that morning Siegel and an associate, Swifty Morgan, boarded Western Airlines flight 23 for Los Angeles. In Siegel's briefcase was $600,000 in cash. (Was Bugsy making a payment on his debt or skimming the profits?) Flight 23 landed at Mines Field in Los Angeles at 2:30 A.M. Siegel went directly to Virginia Hill's house on Linden Drive in Beverly Hills and went to bed. That morning and afternoon, Benjamin Siegel seemed to be taking farewell of life, as if he knew the end was near. He embarked upon a prototypical day that seemed almost choreographed in its evocation of Siegel's personal version of the good life, Los Angeles style. He spent the morning with his associate Mickey Cohen, a tough guy out of Chicago, and his longtime friend George Raft. In the afternoon, Siegel went to his favorite barbershop in Beverly Hills, where he ordered a shave, a haircut, a manicure, a neck and shoulder massage, and a shoeshine. In the early evening he phoned the Hollywood office of *Daily Variety* and thanked columnist Florabel Muir for her favorable review of the floor show at the Flamingo. Later that evening, he went with his associate Allen Smiley, Virginia's brother Chick, and Chick's girlfriend Jerri Mason out to Ocean Park for a seafood dinner at Jack's at the Beach.

As if he had not a care in the world, Siegel ate dinner with his back toward the door, as opposed to the usual gangster style of always eating back to the wall, facing the entrance of a restaurant. Leaving Jack's shortly after nine, Siegel picked up a complimentary copy of the next day's Los Angeles *Times*. GOOD NIGHT, the front page was stamped. SLEEP WELL WITH THE COMPLIMENTS OF JACK'S. On the way home he stopped off briefly at the Beverly-Wilshire drugstore for some Campho-phenique for a stuffy nose. Opening the door to Virginia's home, he switched on the hall light and said that he smelled flowers in the room, perhaps carnations. He asked Chick to see if there were any fresh flowers in the room or elsewhere in the house. Chick went searching from room to room, remembering what his mother had told him as a boy in Alabama: "When someone smells flowers and there aren't any in the house, it means they're going to die."[6] As Chick and Jerri went upstairs, Siegel sat on the chintz-covered divan in Virginia Hill's living room, talking to Allen Smiley.

Three men, meanwhile, driving an old Pontiac sedan—an unusual sight in Beverly Hills, where cars tended toward Cadillacs and Lincoln Continentals— pulled alongside Yellow Cab driver Arthur Day Jr., parked just outside the Beverly Hills Hotel. One of the men said to Day in a strong Brooklyn accent: "Hey, Mac, how do we get to North Linden Drive from here?" Day told them they were just about four blocks away: three blocks to Whittier Avenue, a left, then Linden. Shortly thereafter, one of the three men, using a .30–30 carbine, which he rested on a lattice frame outside the living room window, pumped nine bullets into Bugsy Siegel. Allen Smiley was untouched. The next day, a photograph of Siegel's body in the Los Angeles County Morgue—his bare feet protruding from beneath the sheet, an identification tag with his name misspelled tied to one big toe—went out on the wires. Just about the same time, Moe Sedway and Morris Rosen walked into the lobby of the Flamingo in Las Vegas and assumed control of the hotel in the name of its Eastern investors. A few days later, Jewish services were held at Groman Mortuary on West Washington Boulevard. Only five people showed up, Virginia Hill not among them. She and Siegel's other friends were very much frightened as to who might be next.

Reaching the end of the arc of one identity but not yet advancing into its next, Los Angeles and its hinterlands grew even more eccentric and colorful as the area approached its new status, reached in 1949, of being the third largest metropolitan region in the United States. Thirty-two percent of the population of greater Los Angeles had arrived since 1940. The largest number of inmigrants had come from either the west south-central census area (Arkansas, Louisiana, Oklahoma, Texas) or the west north-central census area (Minnesota, Iowa, Missouri, Nebraska, Kansas, the Dakotas). Los Angeles, in other words, remained the whitest big city in America. On the other hand, it had more Mexicans than any other city outside of Mexico itself and nearly fifty distinguishable tribes or nation-groups of Native Americans: all this augmented by the returning Japanese-Americans and a growing black population, forecasting the diversity in place by the 1970s. Aside from the City of the Angels proper—the fourth largest city in the United States since 1945, 1.9 million people spread over 451 square miles, divided by the City Planning Commission into fifty-nine distinct communities with a total of 932 recognizable neighborhoods—the greater Los Angeles region encompassed forty-five cities and nearly ninety unincorporated areas. One critic compared it to an aggregation of movie sets.

After the war, American observers began to respond to what English residents such as Aldous Huxley had long since noticed, the delightful singularity of the region. Los Angeles, opined one observer in the *Saturday Evening Post*, "is New York in purple shorts with its brains knocked out."[7] Los Angeles, noted *Daily News* columnist Matt Weinstock, was "the most insulted city in the world"—and frequently deserved it. "With some basis," Weinstock observed, "Los Angeles has been described as a glorious climate wasted on an undeserving, vulgar, boorish people."[8] Ten thousand people, in fact, were pouring into the City of Angels each month. "The town is hopelessly overcrowded," noted Sam Boal in the *New York Times Magazine*. "It is short of houses, short of restaurants, short of stores, even short of filling stations. Its traffic problem, because it lives on wheels, is complex almost beyond description."[9]

Despite the fact that the streetcars were still running, and would continue to run for nearly another decade, one could not efficiently function in Los Angeles unless one owned an automobile, as Man Ray discovered once he had secured a car, thereby changing his life, or as Thomas Mann discovered by insisting upon a daily walk. Frequently, Katia Mann tells us, a driver would stop his car and accost the Manns as they walked along the palisades above the seashore or headed toward a back canyon. "May we give you a ride?" the motorists frequently asked. "No thank you. I'd rather walk," Thomas Mann would reply. Just as frequently, any and all unleashed dogs in the neighborhood would walk along with the Manns, up to half a dozen of them, delighted to have human company.[10] "Here in Los Angeles, you cannot walk," novelist and screenwriter Vicki Baum, a German émigrée who otherwise liked the city, noted. "That's part of my feeling of being an exile. Try to take a walk and you are among three million cars that honk furiously for you to get out of the way."[11] Pre-freeway Los Angeles, moreover, was in the process of losing its battle with traffic. In 1948 there were 1,720,253 registered motor vehicles in Los Angeles County alone, nearly half the automobiles in the state. A six-hour check of traffic at Sunset and Figueroa counted more than thirty-four thousand cars. The demolition of older structures and the construction of parking lots was now a leading form of public works.

Every criticism of Los Angeles, however, every sarcasm, implied a compliment and a possibility for art. Sprawling, eccentric, traffic-choked, peopled by oddballs of every sort, Los Angeles was achieving a density, if only in its negatives, that could not help but nurture imaginative expression. The region possessed, among other things, the most colorful demimonde in the nation, which was one of the things that helped keep defense attorneys such as Jerry Giesler busy and well paid. First of all, there were the criminals, no new thing in the Big Orange. An article in the Los Angeles *Examiner* for 13 August 1931 estimated that there were approximately fifteen thousand swindlers, confidence men, and other illegal promoters at work in the region. The war only intensified this trend. "Los Angeles," noted lawyer Bernard Potter in the late 1940s, "has become the dumping ground for the riff-raff of the world. Racketeers of every type, bootleggers, bookmakers, black-market operators, thugs, murderers, petty thieves, procurers, rapists, fairies, perverts, reds, confidence men, real estate sharks, political carpetbaggers and opportunists. Ask for any violator of any law and we can promptly fill the order."[12]

With the sudden departure of Benjamin Siegel, wiseguy Michael (Mickey) Cohen assumed the mantle of number one mobster. A Chicagoan, Cohen had come to Los Angeles in 1939 and announced himself locally by holding up a bookie joint on Franklin Avenue. Interestingly enough, the bookie joint belonged to Siegel, who put the word out on the street that he wanted Cohen to call on him at the Hollywood YMCA. The two met. Cohen agreed to make restitution. Siegel admired Cohen's style, and, after one more meeting, asked him to join his organization. Soon Cohen was sharing honors with Benny (the Meatball) Gamson as Siegel's top deputy; and when the Meatball was gunned down in 1946 and Siegel was killed in 1947, it left Mickey Cohen in charge of organized crime in Los Angeles, specifically some ten thousand bookies spread throughout the region. Gambling was a staple of life in Hollywood, either legitimately at Hollywood Park, Santa Anita, or Del Mar in San Diego County (a chartered DC-3, equipped with piano bar, left Los Angeles daily for the racetracks of the San Francisco Bay Area) or through any one of thousands of full-time or part-time bookies working the bars, clubs, and cigar- and newsstands.

Like his mentor, Mickey Cohen was not afraid to kill people, although he insisted: "I never killed nobody that didn't deserve killing by my standards."[13] In 1945 Cohen killed Maxie Shaman over a disputed bet but won acquittal on the basis of self-defense. In 1948 one of Mickey's top aides, Hooky Rothman, died in a hail of gunfire while standing in Cohen's new haberdashery on Sunset near Beverly Hills. Mickey convinced the grand jury that he had just stepped into the washroom to pee when the unfortunate incident occurred. Small and ferocious-looking, a gangster from Central Casting (high-waisted pants, draped jackets, an oversized fedora, two-toned shoes), a pit bull to Siegel's well-brushed Afghan, Mickey Cohen was a well-known figure around town after 1947, gathering hundreds of headlines. People stopped him on the street for his autograph. With his bookmaking income, Cohen built a lavish home in Brentwood, where he lived with his wife La Vonne (whose maiden name he claimed he could never remember) and his bodyguard and ever-present pal Sam Farkas. In late 1949 Mickey posed for *Life* on his Brentwood lawn with his dogs and protested: "I take my oath on my mother and my dogs—and I'm very fond of my dogs—I ain't guilty of what they say about me."[14] The same article presented an Illustrated Crime Map of Los

Angeles with sixteen designated sites, including Sherry's Restaurant, where Mickey Cohen was fired on; Mickey's home in Brentwood; his haberdashery on Sunset; the site where he killed Maxie Shaman; and the headquarters of the Guarantee Finance Company, the alleged front for Mickey's bookmaking syndicate.

In great part because of the lure of Hollywood, Los Angeles in the mid- to late 1940s was noticeably peopled by attractive young women. It was also an important American divorce capital, granting twice as many divorces as Reno, three times as many as Miami, the two other contenders for divorce centers in the United States. The judges in wartime and post-war Los Angeles County were especially liberal and hasty in granting divorces, which began to approach the one-hundred-a-day mark in the post-war era. Sixty percent of the divorces in 1945 went uncontested and had an average hearing time of less than ten minutes. Divorce lawyer Sammy Hahn, for example, who had worked his way up the ranks from newsboy and, later, newspaper reporter before passing the bar, could handle a quickie divorce for fees ranging from $75 and up, depending. Photographers made a specialty of photographing newly minted divorcées crossing their legs and smiling for the evening newspapers in full celebration of their reavailability.

Not so usual, however, was the divorce of Ellsworth (Sonny) Wisecarver. At the age of fourteen, Sonny eloped to Yuma with divorcée (so she claimed, although the marriage license had been lost) Elaine Monfredi, age twenty-one, the mother of two, who soon found herself arrested on charges of child-stealing and sent back to Los Angeles for trial. In March 1945, confronted with overwhelming evidence that it was Sonny who had done the wooing, the judge dropped felony charges against Elaine and placed her on probation for three years. Eight months later, Sonny, now a ward of the juvenile court, ran off with Mrs. Eleanor Deveny, twenty-five, a married mother of two. "Sonny boy is the kind of guy every girl dreams about but very seldom finds," Mrs. Deveny told the press upon the occasion of her arrest for contributing to the delinquency of a minor. "He is more of a man at sixteen than a lot of men are at thirty-five. I love him more than I do my own husband." Committed to the California Youth Authority, Sonny escaped in July 1946 and eventually wound up in Las Vegas, where he met Betty Zoe Reber, a seventeen-year-old theater usherette, whom he married in a Mormon ceremony. The couple settled down in a house trailer in Las Vegas, and Sonny told the press: "My kid mistakes are behind me."[15]

Impressions from the post-war period suggest a city of waitresses and carhops wanting to be starlets, hustlers of various sorts in sport coats and large-collared gabardine polo shirts open at the neck, living in single rooms or cramped bungalow court apartments, everybody from elsewhere, nobody putting his or her cards fully on the table. Who would know, for example, that Helen Lee Worthing, who died in 1948 in her three-room apartment off an alley in Hollywood, her estate valued at $16.80 by the public administrator, had once starred in the *Ziegfeld Follies* in New York, or that Harrison Fisher, one of the premier illustrators of the period, had claimed that she had the most beautiful profile in the nation? Moving to Hollywood in the late twenties, Worthing had had a brief career in the silents, then spent twenty years in progressively alcoholic obscurity, the more-than-occasional guest of the Los Angeles County psycho ward.

Los Angeles so often seemed a city of people on the edge, people pushing it to the breaking point, either from an excess of resources and opportunities or from desperate scarcity. Nowhere was this more true than in the matter of booze or sex or some combination thereof. It was, after all, a hard-drinking place, Hollywood especially, whose master of alcoholic revels, W. C. Fields, had made his departure from this earth on Christmas Day 1946. Fields's gang of boozing pals, headquartered at the home of artist John Decker at 419 North Bundy Drive on the Westside, included John Barrymore, also recently deceased, courtesy of the grog, and Errol Flynn, who would keep alive the roistering tradition for another decade. Also in the group: actors Thomas Mitchell, Burgess Meredith, John Carradine, and Anthony Quinn and poet Sadakichi Hartmann, who because he was half German and half Japanese had decided to spend the war on a Native American reservation near Banning.

Post-war Los Angeles, one writer claimed, was one big cocktail lounge, with every stool occupied by a female available for pickup. An infinite array of restaurants, nightclubs, and watering holes, ranging up and down the social scale, from dives to such reservations-only establishments as Ciro's, Chasen's, the Brown Derby, Perino's, and Romanoff's, extended from the Chateau Gardens in San Fernando to Shanghai Red's at the San Pedro Harbor. Beacon Street in the Harbor district — a phantasmagoria of bars, bordellos, pawn shops, tattoo parlors, and bail bond offices — monopolized the low-end market. On weekends during the war, more than a hundred thousand shipyard workers, together with countless soldiers, sailors, and Marines in training or in transit, would pack the numerous joints on Beacon, and after the war the party continued at such hostelries as the Club Del Rio, where a young black singer named Nat King Cole had a breakthrough gig; the Bank Café, where loan sharking was common; the Silver Dollar, with its exotic Oriental murals; Goodfellows, where Scandinavian sailors danced with one another to accordion music; Johnny Reno's, the Chateau Gardens, the Gay Way; and Shanghai Red's at Fifth and Beacon, the roughest bar in the district, where Shanghai Red himself, the proprietor, a gentleman holding significant interests in two Harbor-area whorehouses, ran gambling in the back room and where order was maintained by two lesbian bouncers, Big and Little Stormy. Big Stormy was six feet tall and weighed two hundred pounds. Little Stormy was small and weighed a lot less. She wore a blonde wig and was equally as effective as her larger partner.

Other demimonde joints across the Los Angeles basin included the bar at the Town House Hotel in inner Wilshire, where rooms were rented by the hour, no questions asked; the Little New Yorker in Hollywood, where Mickey Cohen and other bad guys hung out; and the Back Room bar, favored by the newspaper crowd, along with Moran's, where the permanent cast of characters included, as of 1947,

resident bookie Lou (Cocky) Gregorius, who specialized in taking bets from reporters, and Taxi Bill, a cab driver who had arrived in Los Angeles during World
War II from Manhattan, having picked up two soldiers and a sailor at Grand
Central Station and driven them across the country in five days. Newspaper people
also took their nourishment at Betty's Broadway Circle in the Downtown, which
had a full-service liquor license, and the Pantry on Figueroa and 9th, which served
prodigious meals, seven days a week, twenty-four hours a day, to a mixed clientele
of newsmen, truckers, tourists, cops, bookies, nighttime workers, and, after two in
the morning, strays from the bars, which were closed until six. Higher on the
evolutionary scale were such hangouts as Charlie Foy's Supper Club in the San
Fernando Valley; the Tail o' the Cock on La Cienega and Musso & Frank on
Hollywood Boulevard, a favorite among screenwriters, along with Lucey's on Mel-
rose Avenue, just across the street from Paramount; Jack's at the Beach on Ocean
Park, where Bugsy Siegel enjoyed his last meal; the Pacific Dining Car in the
Downtown, favored by politicians and upper civil servants; and two other downtown places, the original Taix on East Commercial Street, where antiquarian bookseller Jacob Israel Zeitlin ran a literary round table, and the Good Fellows Grotto
on South Main, packed each lunchtime with the business crowd.

   Historians of American night life might justifiably pass over Los Angeles 1947
as a significant restaurant city, its major claim to fame in this regard having been
the invention of the cafeteria in 1905, an eating style perfected by the Boos brothers, John and Horace, and Clifford Clinton in the 1920s and 1930s. Yet, being a
singles city, Los Angeles was a place where people frequently ate out, and hundreds of establishments, great and small, rose up to meet this market. Lawry's on
La Cienega helped Los Angeles celebrate the post-war return of beef with heroic
servings of prime rib. Mama Weiss's served goulash and Central European specialties good enough to win the approval of the émigrés. Paul's Duck Press catered
to hunters, who brought in their own birds and venison, which Paul prepared in
the style of the Tour d'Argent. As one of the most expensive restaurants in the
city, Perino's on Wilshire catered to a mixed show biz and upper-crust WASP
clientele, being one of the few places in the city to show signs of such a joint
tenancy by the two elite communities of greater Los Angeles, which tended to co-
exist side by side but rarely mingle. The same sort of all-city inclusiveness, at least
among the affluent, could be had in the restaurants and lounges of the Biltmore
Hotel downtown on Pershing Square and in two nightclubs, the Cocoanut Grove
at the Ambassador and Earl Carroll's on Sunset, with its all-girl review. Slapsie
Maxie Rosenbloom's on Beverly likewise attracted a distinctive blend of show biz
and mainstream Los Angeles.

   It was a time of pre-television twilight splendor for the studios; and the restaurants and supper clubs favored by people in film—Ciro's, Chasen's, the Brown
Derbies (proprietor Bob Cobb was the first to install telephone hook-ups at every
table; he also created the Cobb salad, which remains a local favorite), the Mocambo, the Chi Chi, Billingsley's (an import from New York), and Romanoff's—

each enjoyed that special incandescence that emanated from Hollywood in its final years of studio feudalism. Located just off Wilshire in Beverly Hills, Romanoff's was the creation of the Brooklyn-born Harry Gerguson, otherwise known as Prince Michael Alexandrovitch Dmitry Obolensky Romanoff. No one seemed to mind Gerguson's assumption of Russian nobility. After all, a good part of his clientele were acting under different names or otherwise flying under false colors. A restaurant is only as good as its owner's personality, opined Gerguson.

In a town known for its flamboyance, the Prince held his own with the best of them. Visiting Hollywood in May 1947, publisher Bennett Cerf noted that Prince Mike and his minions seemed to have a monopoly not only on the restaurant business in Hollywood but on catering private dinner parties as well. When Walter Wanger was languishing in the Beverly Hills jail on charges of attempted homicide, Prince Mike showed up with his head waiter and personally supervised a dinner service for Wanger in his cell, using china and cutlery from the restaurant. Like all Hollywood restaurants and nightclubs (like Hollywood itself, in fact), Romanoff's thrived on snobbery and selection. Nobodies were asked to wait at the bar despite an array of empty tables being held on reserve in the main dining room, all evening if necessary, for Hollywood celebrities. Romanoff's eventually went broke because of this practice of allowing celebrities to keep a table empty and non-productive until they arrived. By 1950 annual profits had dropped to a mere $16,000. Even in Hollywood, Americans could grow tired of paying Prince Mike for a chance to be humiliated.

The English, including writer Raymond Chandler, continued to flourish in Los Angeles in the post-war era, although they were showing signs of Americanization. Like many other English-born actors and actresses—Cary Grant, Ray Milland, the child star Elizabeth Taylor, Ida Lupino, Deborah Kerr—and director Alfred Hitchcock, Charles Laughton perceptively Americanized his persona in the 1940s, beginning in the war years. Even Ronald Colman, crown prince of the Hollywood Raj in the 1930s, began to evolve in the 1940s into the more mid-Atlantic persona of an Ivy League college professor in the radio series *Halls of Ivy*. Errol Flynn, an Australian from Tasmania, had an Australian ability to seem either American or English, depending. In the late 1940s, Flynn gravitated toward a more American demeanor. Even David Niven seemed less old-boyish when he returned from the war. By 1947, in short, the Hollywood Raj was acquiring an American or at least a mid-Atlantic accent. As if to signal this transformation, the Raj's longtime leader, the character actor Sir C. Aubrey Smith, president of the Hollywood Cricket Club, died of double pneumonia at the age of eighty-five on 20 December 1948. It was the end of an era of unalloyed, unashamed Anglophilia, Anglo-dulia even, in Hollywood and its American audiences.

It was all more than a little fake or at least somewhat overwrought: a show put on for the locals, which is to say, Hollywood and its American audience, the acting out of an imagined England peopled by Public School men never at a loss for what to say or do. In February 1947 the visiting English novelist Evelyn Waugh, in town to negotiate a possible film contract for his novel *Brideshead Revisited* (1945), saw this immediately—the quasi-fakery of the Raj, the posturing of Sir Aubrey—and satirized it brilliantly in his novella *The Loved One* (1948), in which Sir Aubrey is depicted as Sir Francis Hinsley, president of the Hollywood Cricket Club, author of the Edwardian classic *A Free Man Greets the Dawn*. In the opening scene of the satire, Sir Francis and his friend Sir Ambrose Abercrombie are taking their gin and tonics on the porch at sundown, discussing the locals, as if Hollywood were an outpost in Kenya. Even Sir C. Aubrey Smith himself, however, knew he was dealing in an illusion. Just before the war, the then Mr. C. Aubrey Smith had returned to England only to find that the imagined Empire of his youth and young manhood was only a memory. He attended cricket matches but knew no one in the pavilion. He went to his club, but only the ancient wine steward remembered him. He and his wife drove out to a long remembered and favorite country house, a Tudor pile, but instead found a newly built block of cheap cottages. "I went back to London and booked my passage back to California," Sir Aubrey later admitted. "I wasn't sorry to leave."[16]

Novelist and screenwriter Raymond Chandler, by contrast—Chicago-born but raised in the London suburb of Upper Norwood in Anglo-Irish impoverished gentility, a Public School man (Dulwich) and a World War I veteran of trench warfare with the Gordon Highlanders of Canada—continued to believe that beyond Los Angeles there would ever be an England. Chandler drank gin with lime juice, the universal drink of the Raj, cultivated his Public School accent, affected English manners, read English books and magazines. In later life, he wore yellow gloves, like an Edwardian dandy, to conceal a skin complaint. In the 1940s he formed a friendship with Christopher Isherwood. He wanted Cary Grant to star as detective Philip Marlowe, despite the fact that Marlowe was a decidedly non-British Los Angeleno born in Santa Rosa, California, and educated at the University of Oregon. When England treated him as a serious writer, he was deeply gratified.

Raymond Chandler belonged to the Lost Generation, which went through life a drink in one hand, a cigarette in the other. Even by the standards of his era, however, Chandler set new records. In the 1920s drinking brought him at least once to the verge of suicide. Drinking helped end his business career. Drinking provided the leitmotif of his career in the 1940s as a Hollywood screenwriter. Billy Wilder, his officemate at Paramount, noted that Chandler kept a bottle in his desk drawer and started to pull at it around three or four in the afternoon. (Part of the problem was the fact that Wilder was conducting his active dating life loudly over the telephone; the sheer carnality of it all made Chandler—already driven to frenzy, Wilder later claimed, by the scores of beautiful young women on the lot— even more manic, hence liable to reach for the bottle: and this compounded by the fact that Wilder was a Jew with a winning way with *shiksas* and Chandler was a notorious anti-Semite.) In order to overcome a writer's block when he was writing *The Blue Dahlia* (1946), Chandler stayed drunk for two weeks, launching himself with three double martinis before lunch at Perino's, followed by three double stingers. A friendly doctor provided Chandler with vitamin and glucose injections during the marathon. Chandler would drink, write, pass out; wake, drink again, write some more, pass out. Meanwhile, the first portion of *The Blue Dahlia* was being filmed at the studio, with the local draft board breathing down Alan Ladd's neck. As soon as Chandler finished a page or so of script, it was rushed down to the studio for filming.

Perhaps only someone as bleak, as desperate, as displaced as Raymond Chandler—bleak in his career prospects, bleak in his emotional life and thwarted sexuality, bleak in his constant drinking—could capture the essential bleakness of life in what so often seemed the bleakest city in America. Only James M. Cain and Nathanael West equal Chandler in an ability to depict the minimalist grimness of life in the instant suburbs of the Southland. Raymond Chandler was essentially a 1940s writer. His *Black Mask* stories of the 1930s are significant, but many of them were recycled into the later novels. More important, Chandler's point of view, his style, his tone, his obsessions were 1940s: 1940s Los Angeles, more precisely, the city of Bugsy Siegel and George Raft; the city of Detective Lieutenant Harry Fremont, capable of shooting a suspect down in cold blood, and all the other LAPD cops not reluctant to administer to Philip Marlowe, or anyone else for that matter, a beating; the city of five daily newspapers and sixteen hours of headlines; the city of the Black Dahlia and the dives on Beacon Street and the furtive homosexual action in Pershing Square and the sex jungle on the palisades above Santa Monica Beach.

Philip Marlowe lives and works in this *mise-en-scène*, in part an idealized version of what Chandler might have wished for himself, in part an unconscious expression of some of Chandler's more submerged traits. Much has been made of Marlowe's repressed sexuality, for example. He couples but once, possibly twice, in the entire Chandler oeuvre and is driven to disgust and rage when he finds the nymphomaniacal Carmen Sternwood in his bed. He practically delivers himself up as a willing victim for beatings by dominant men, gangsters or cops, beatings he seems to relish in ways best left to the explanations of psychiatry. Pansies (Chandler's term) are everywhere in Marlowe's world, as metaphor and villain. Like Chandler, Marlowe frequently gets his courage from the bottle. More profoundly, he is an honorary Public School man, an urban knight-errant (the comparison is explicit in *The Big Sleep*): "an English gentleman transplanted to one of the bizarre colonies," Matthew Bruccoli describes him, "setting an example for the natives."[17] Philip Marlowe, in short, is, like Chandler, a sexually repressed boozer, living in isolation (no wife or girlfriend, no family, few if any friends, not even a cat for company), keeping to his chivalric code despite the venality of the natives, caught forever between the romance of sordidness and the unattainable blonde with cornflower blue eyes.

Chandler despised Los Angeles. He claimed that it had eaten up his life, kept him on the edge of nothing, as he put it. After 1946, when Chandler had moved to La Jolla, his criticism of the City of the Angels became more vehement. "Los Angeles," Chandler wrote in March 1951, "has become a grotesque and impossible place for a human being to live."[18] Yet without Los Angeles he would be less than nothing, less than zero; for the city had energized his imagination, and he in turn had brought the city further into being through his art. Without the cops, the crime, the gangsters, the shakedowns, the payoffs, the seedy hotels of greater Los Angeles, what would Raymond Chandler have to write about?

Not accidentally, Chandler's brief career as a writer coincided with Hollywood's film *noir* years, in which Chandler himself played an important part as screenwriter and story source. Six of Chandler's novels were made into movies in his lifetime, and Chandler himself was nominated for Academy Awards for his work on *Double Indemnity* and *The Blue Dahlia*. Inspired, in part, by German Expressionism, with a preference for bleak people in claustrophobic settings, film *noir* was suited perfectly to 1940s Los Angeles as Chandler, the cops, the crime reporters, and the gangsters themselves were encountering it: a restricted and restrictive city, angular, grim, asking no quarter and giving even less. Chandler bore major responsibility (the dialogue is unmistakably Chandlerian) for *Double Indemnity* (1944), considered by many the best film *noir* ever made and certainly the single most Los Angeles–oriented of the genre. Described by one critic as "a film without a single trace of pity or love," *Double Indemnity*, which Billy Wilder directed, can also be said to announce the debut of Los Angeles as *mise-en-scène*: not only for the film *noir*—down through *Mildred Pierce* (1945), *The Postman Always Rings Twice* (1946), *Sunset Boulevard* (1950), the last Los Angeles–set film *noir* in black and white, and *Chinatown* (1974), the first Los Angeles film *noir* in color—but for the use that James M. Cain, Nathanael West, and Raymond Chandler had already made of the city in fiction.[19]

Among other accomplishments—some of the most brilliant dialogue ever to appear in an American film, for example, and some of Hollywood's greatest acting—*Double Indemnity*, under Chandler and Wilder's guidance, is also an exploration of Los Angeles as place and psychological state: insurance salesman Walter Neff (Fred MacMurray), his paramour Phyllis Dietrichson (Barbara Stanwyck), and insurance executive Barton Keyes (Edward G. Robinson) play out their drama of lust, murder, and betrayal in the homes, streets, supermarkets, train stations, and downtown office buildings of Los Angeles at the peak of its pre- and post-war fulfillment as a built environment and a state of mind. True, *Double Indemnity* could have been set in Indianapolis, but it would not have had the same sense of evil beneath the sunny surface of palm-lined streets and such settings as the Spanish Revival home in the Los Feliz district where Neff first calls upon his fateful client, the Hollywood Bowl where Neff, now entangled in murder, tries to recover his innocence in a new romance, the supermarket where Neff and Dietrichson carry on their plots in a setting suggestive of consumer abundance, and the Art Deco Oviatt Building in the Downtown, headquarters of the insurance company that figures so strongly in the plot.

Chandler's *The Blue Dahlia* (1946) takes us further down the social scale of the City of Angels into a world of neighborhood bars and bungalow courts, the Los Angeles of the lower middle class, as opposed to the upper-middle-class imagery of *Double Indemnity*. Of all post-war films *noir*, *The Blue Dahlia* (one of Chandler's two original screenplays, adapted for Paramount from a novel-in-progress) offers the most explicit evocation of Los Angeles as post-war city of *noir*: a dark and shady labyrinth for which the sleazy Blue Dahlia nightclub on Sunset Boulevard and the equally *noir* Cavendish Court Hotel provide the perfect *mise-en-scène* and metaphor for a city willingly in love with the night. To this deceptive and violent city return three Navy veterans—Johnny Morrison (Alan Ladd), George Copeland (Hugh Beaumont), and Buzz Wanchek (William Bendix). On their arrival, George and Buzz set up a household that some critics have found crypto-homosexual (Chandler bitterly resented the imputation), and Johnny discovers that his wife Helen (Doris Dowling) had spent the war as the mistress of draft-dodging gangster Eddie Harwood (Howard Da Silva). Later that same night, Helen is murdered—and what better suspect than an aggrieved husband. Evading the cops, Johnny links up with Eddie Harwood's wife Joyce (Veronica Lake), and the two of them, each cheated by the other's spouse, set out to find Helen Morrison's killer: which gives Chandler and veteran director George Marshall the perfect opportunity to evoke Los Angeles as a city of gangsters, gamblers, grifters of every sort, shakedown artists, rogue cops, and shady ladies—the standard Raymond Chandler cast of characters that is in so many ways reflective of the post-war city.

Chandler originally wanted the returning veteran Buzz Wanchek, wounded in combat, with a metal plate in his head, to be responsible for Helen's death, killing her in a fit of rage when she bad-mouths Johnny, then blanking the entire incident from his memory; but censors from the Department of the Navy forbade such an ending because it would cast discredit on returning veterans and reinforce the fear in certain quarters that many of them were unstable. Stymied by the Navy censor, Chandler had to go on a monumental binge to finish the script, making an elderly house detective at the Cavendish Court Hotel the culprit. In terms of post-war Los Angeles, however, the details of the final plot are secondary to the prism of ominous ambiguity through which Chandler views the City of Angels.

Elizabeth Short, no doubt, saw *The Blue Dahlia* sometime in 1946, sitting in the darkened theater and seeing perhaps in Veronica Lake the image of all that she wanted to be, all that she had come to Los Angeles in search of. She was most likely pleased when those few people who knew of her shadowy existence nicknamed her "the Black Dahlia" in reference to the film. Any connection with the silver screen would be welcomed in a life heading nowhere. Unlike Veronica Lake, however, Elizabeth Short would find no Alan Ladd to stand alongside her on Sunset Boulevard as the neon lights of the Blue Dahlia were going dark, the two of them having found each other through a maze of miscues and deceptions. For Elizabeth Short the *noir* of Los Angeles would soon become all too real—so horribly real.

9

1948 ✶ Honey Bear

O N the afternoon of 25 June 1948 in Convention Hall, Philadelphia, Earl
Warren, fifty-eight, the thirtieth governor of California in its American
era, accepted the nomination of the Republican Party to the vice presidency of the United States. As he had in 1944, Warren had come to the convention
with the California delegation pledged to him as a favorite son. When Governor
Thomas Dewey of New York needed thirty-three more votes to win the nomination, Warren released his delegates. Four years earlier, Dewey had unsuccessfully
attempted to interest Warren in the vice presidency. This time, Dewey prevailed
with a promise that he would expand the responsibilities and assignments of the
position. Joining Warren on the platform that afternoon before the cheering delegates was the redoubtable Warren family: the governor's handsome wife Nina
Palmquist Warren; son James Lee Warren, twenty-four, and his wife Margaret
(Maggie) Jessee Warren, twenty-seven, a well-known California tennis star; Earl
Warren Jr. (Ju-Ju), seventeen; and his tow-headed younger brother Robert Warren
(Bobby), thirteen; and the three Warren daughters, smiling and waving to the
crowd like California itself, Virginia (Ia), twenty, Dorothy (Dotty), sixteen, and
fourteen-year-old Nina, whom the Warren family called Honey Bear. Photogenic,
blonde, tan, fit, the Warrens thrilled the convention with their presence on the
platform. Here was the very emblem and spirit of California. Here was a new kind
of American on the national political scene.

Throughout the campaign, the Warren family, especially the girls, charmed the
press. When the Warrens called on the Deweys at the Dewey farm near Pawling,
New York, after the convention, the Warren girls and the Deweys' two teenage
sons captivated the press with their obvious attraction to each other. Fifteen-year-
old Tom Dewey Jr. had trouble keeping his eyes off Dorothy when the two families
stood together for photographs. "Look at the camera, please, Tom," Governor

Dewey admonished.[1] After the photo session, the Dewey boys and the Warren girls ran off together down a grassy slope leading away from the main house. A young woman of twenty, Virginia Warren proved especially adept at campaigning alongside her father. Later that fall, Virginia joined her parents in the *Aleutian*, the Warrens' private car in the fifteen-car Warren Special campaign train whistle-stopping the West. The atmosphere aboard the *Aleutian*, *Newsweek* reported, was congenial, informal, relaxed, just what people expected of Californians.

Throughout the 1940s the father of this handsome family, Earl Warren, dominated the politics of California and served the aspirations of its burgeoning middle class. The rise of Earl Warren coincided with the rise of California, and the governor was shaped almost exclusively by the state's culture and institutions. Earl Warren was at once the last of the High Provincials, in Josiah Royce's phrase, with roots in the frontier, and among the youngest of the New Men, the Progressive generation led by Hiram Johnson and Herbert Hoover, the public men in the vanguard of California's rise to national prominence. A native Californian, Earl Warren was born in Los Angeles on 18 March 1891 when that city had slightly more than fifty thousand citizens. He was reared in Bakersfield in southern Kern County when that community was still a raw and sometimes violent frontier town. Only four previous governors—Romualdo Pacheco, George Pardee, Hiram Johnson, and James Rolph Jr.—had been native sons; and only one governor, Hiram Johnson, had ever been elected to a second term. Earl Warren was elected three times, in 1942, 1946, and 1950. He served as governor of California for ten years and eight months, the longest gubernatorial term in California history. He then assumed an office, Chief Justice of the United States of America, second only to the presidency in importance, and in that office earned a secure place in the history of his country.

From this perspective, Earl Warren seems to have lived a charmed life. He came into public office at a young age and remained in distinguished positions—district attorney, attorney general, governor, Chief Justice—for a half century and more. He married happily and had a large healthy family who prospered. Six feet tall, weighing an acceptable 215 pounds for most of his adult life, Warren radiated physical well-being. Although he was operated on for abdominal cancer in 1952, he survived for another twenty-two years in robust health. Many found Warren bland, intellectually limited, yet he pursued one of the most successful and influential public careers in twentieth-century America. As Chief Justice, he became a revered figure among the very intellectuals who had once dismissed him as a Babbitt from the Coast.

As governor of California, Earl Warren embodied the middle-class California Dream of the 1940s and early 1950s: the family, the home, the lawn, the dog, the middle-class success. In his family, as in no other mode (with the possible exception of his doomed quest for the presidency in 1952), Earl Warren allowed himself a measure of display and ego aggrandizement. Before the Kennedys, Warren understood the power of family and family values in political life. Californians, in turn, worshipped the Warren family, especially the girls, and followed their progress through life with unflagging interest. Through the prism of the Warren family—Mrs. Warren ironing her husband's shirts, even as First Lady of California, James Warren returning from the South Pacific, shiny lieutenant's bars on his Marine uniform, Honey Bear jumping her horse Flash and winning a blue ribbon, Ju-Ju and Bobby riding their bikes on the tree-lined streets of Sacramento or fishing with Dad on the American River or hunting ducks with him in the marshlands of the Delta—Californians glimpsed their own desires for an Ozzie-and-Harriet, Leave-It-to-Beaver life in the post-war era. Through the Warrens, Californians could glimpse the triumph of Midwestern, mid-American values, very white and tending toward the suburban, which motivated an entire era and propelled California into the forefront of national consciousness. The Warren family was proof positive that California was not dominated by the bizarre, the eccentric. California was a normal American place, only more so, and the Warrens proved it.

And a very white place as well, just as mainstream Californians wanted it to be. The Earl Warren family was white, very white, as only Scandinavians can be white. Warren's mother was born in Halsingland, Sweden, and brought to Illinois as an infant. Warren's father was born in Norway, where the family name was Varran. Warren's wife, Nina, was born in Sweden and brought to the United States as an infant and raised in a Swedish-speaking household. Earl Warren himself had fjord-blue eyes, and the Warren family was unmistakably blond, fair-skinned, blue-eyed.

Earl Warren was a Methodist who attended Baptist services in deference to his wife. He read the Bible to his children each evening. Shortly after World War I, Warren joined the Masons. In 1935 he was elected Grand Master for California, with responsibility for seven hundred lodges with a membership of 150,000. Like his fellow Mason Harry Truman and millions of other Masons throughout the nation, Earl Warren favored rimless glasses and double-breasted suits with lapels the size of schooner sails, which one is tempted to see as required Masonic uniform in the 1940s. Reticent regarding his religious beliefs, Warren derived great psychological strength from Masonry, which provided him with his theology, his ethical system, and his club.

Earl Warren lived in Oakland by deliberate choice. Even when he was attorney general of the state, Warren kept his family in their home at 88 Vernon Street in Oakland, doing his work in the California State Building in San Francisco's Civic Center, with occasional trips to Sacramento. He had first seen the San Francisco Bay Area in 1908 when he arrived there to enroll at the University of California in Berkeley. For the rest of his life, Warren remembered his first crossing of San Francisco Bay by ferry. "As I stood on the bow of the ferryboat," Warren later wrote in his memoirs, "surveying the beautiful bay and looking over to the Golden Gate, I filled my lungs with refreshing air and said to myself, 'I never want to live anywhere else the rest of my life.' And I have never really changed my mind." [2] Oakland was the whitest and most middle-class of California places, a Midwestern city plunked down on the eastern shore of San Francisco Bay, and Earl Warren was the quintessential Oaklander: a Republican, a Methodist, a Mason, a family man. He settled in Oakland in 1920 when he joined the district attorney's office as a young lawyer.

The following year, at a swimming party one Sunday at the Piedmont Baths, he met his wife-to-be Nina Elisabeth Palmquist Meyers, recently widowed when her husband Grover Meyers, a musician, succumbed to tuberculosis shortly after the birth of the couple's son James. The buxom young widow, the daughter of a Baptist minister, supported herself and her son managing a women's specialty shop. Earl and Nina Warren were married in October 1925. Earl Warren adopted his stepson James, and the couple proceeded to have five children of their own. The last was Nina, born in 1933, whom the other Warren children nicknamed Honey Bear the day she was brought home from the hospital. Nina and Earl Warren devoted themselves to their family. Putting aside her business career, Nina Warren cooked and kept house with all the skill and passion of her old-country upbringing. Earl Warren spent Sundays with his children, taking them on excursions to the park or to the San Francisco Zoo, finishing the day with dinner in Chinatown and a ride on the ferry back to Oakland.

The tendency of the Warrens to live privately, within the family, was intensified by Earl Warren's career as a crusading district attorney. Now and then, he received threats against the children. A private man, with a prosecutor's temperament and just the slightest touch of his father's isolation, Earl Warren had few, if any, close personal friends and no hobbies outside raising his children. By the late 1930s Warren had come to discover the political value of his tow-headed clan. When Warren ran for governor in 1942, he was photographed with his family in the backyard of their Oakland home, the entire family marching abreast, arm in arm, toward the camera: Warren in his dark double-breasted suit, Mrs. Warren in something sensible, Ju-Ju in his Boy Scout uniform, Dotty in her Girl Scout uniform, Bobby in the military uniform of his school, Honey Bear resembling a blonder Shirley Temple—the perfect picture of the perfect California family, vaguely mobilized in their various uniforms, as appropriate for wartime. It was one of the most effective campaign photographs of Earl Warren's career.

So reticent in every other aspect of his life, Warren was more than willing to bring his family on stage for photographers to convey the message that kept him in elective office for more than thirty years: California as a family-oriented society and the Warrens as the paragons of family values. In doing this, in stressing the triumphal presence of the white middle class in California, Earl Warren was reaffirming the dimension of his own background and identity in which Tom Sawyer had triumphed over Huckleberry Finn. Like Tom Sawyer, Earl Warren had ultimately chosen family, career, optimism, commitment. But like Huckleberry Finn, Tom Sawyer's good friend and alter ego, Earl Warren had also glimpsed the darker side of life in both his father and himself.

Warren celebrated the Tom Sawyer side of his identity at great length in the memoirs he was writing at the time of his death. The town of Sumner just outside Bakersfield, and eventually incorporated into it, was little more than a Southern Pacific railroad stop, a small village peopled by single men working for the SP and by French and Basque sheepherders in from the countryside. Two passenger trains came through each day, one heading north to San Francisco, the other heading south to Los Angeles. Warren's father worked as a railroad car repairer, supporting his family in a modicum of comfort in a little row house across the street from the SP repair yards. Warren's mother sent him to school in a Little Lord Fauntleroy suit, and a photograph survives of Warren in this outfit, with long ringlet curls, standing with his other classmates in front of the Baker Street School in East Bakersfield. (Actually, the entire class of children, Anglo and Mexican alike, looks beautifully scrubbed and groomed: the boys in suits of one sort or another, including at least three other Fauntleroys, the girls in freshly starched pinafores.) Warren carved his initials into his first grade desk, an assertive E W, and the desk is now in the archives of the Supreme Court. Another photograph, this from 1902, shows young Earl, age eleven, kneeling alongside his favorite hound dog in the backyard.

Young Warren loved to roam the Bakersfield countryside with this dog or ride his burro Jack bareback on hunting and fishing expeditions, guiding Jack with a slap on his neck or pressure on his flanks. Warren loved Jack, and the burro was strongly responsive to the boy. When Warren was forced to put Jack out to board, the burro brayed piteously at the separation. When Warren stopped by for a visit, Jack would chase him around the paddock, nibbling at the boy's pockets for the sugar he knew was there. Writing his memoirs in his chambers at the Supreme Court, the retired Chief Justice of the United States spent a surprisingly large amount of space on the story of his boyhood burro Jack. He wept, Warren remembered, when Jack had to be put down. Seventy years later, he confessed that he still felt sadness when he thought of Jack's death.

By the time he was eleven, Earl Warren had two paper routes, the Los Angeles *Herald* in the morning, the Bakersfield *Californian* in the afternoon. Later, he helped deliver bakery goods from a truck and ice from a wagon in the sweltering summers when the temperatures could reach 120 degrees Fahrenheit. When he was fifteen, Warren spent his summers as a call boy for the SP, earning twenty-two cents an hour for notifying crew members in their homes or in the saloons when their train was scheduled to depart or running other messages and errands in the repair yard. As a high school student, Warren played on the town baseball team. He also played clarinet in the Bakersfield town band. Warren studied the clarinet under George Kuhn, a local music teacher who, with the magic of Professor Harold Hill in *The Music Man*, organized the Bakersfield town band into a formidable group (albeit featuring fewer than seventy-six trombones), available for parades, political rallies, and Saturday night concerts in the park throughout the summer. Warren's best friend Albert Cuneo also played clarinet in the town band, and in 1907 the two of them took their first trip away from Bakersfield, heading over to the coast to see the Great White Fleet steam through the Santa Barbara channel.

To this Tom Sawyer idyll, on the other hand, must be added the stressful aspects of daily life in frontier California more than one hundred years ago, together with the chilling presence of Warren's father, who in his youth had suffered too much for later laughter. When Warren was still a boy, Bakersfield witnessed one of the last big shoot-outs in California history. Two deputy sheriffs lost their lives. Nor would Warren ever forget the horrible moans of the teenaged girl in the house next door, as she died slowly, agonizingly, from spinal meningitis, or the squeals of thousands of rabbits rounded up for an annual massacre, first driven by local residents into a fenced enclave, then clubbed to death with sticks. "I have never heard such sounds," Warren remembered. "The victimized rabbits remained in my mind as babies screaming, and I could not sleep well for weeks."[3]

From his father, Earl Warren absorbed a sense of just how grim life on the nineteenth-century frontier had been for many immigrants. Born in Haugesund, a small maritime city in southern Norway, Methias Warren had been brought to the Minnesota frontier as an infant and was raised in Minnesota and Iowa in the atmosphere of poverty and hard work, compounded by a Scandinavian tendency toward gloom, which Knut Hamsun and O. E. Rolvaag made the staples of Norwegian-American literature. There were twelve brothers and sisters in the family. Four died in infancy or youth, including one brother who died of tuberculosis on Christmas Eve in Methias's arms. Five of those who survived, Earl Warren's aunts and uncles, remained single throughout their lives, as if unable to establish lasting emotional contact with others or, even worse, as if they did not wish to bring others into the world. Although Methias spoke only obliquely of his childhood, Earl Warren sensed this legacy of youthful deprivation in his father, something silent and withdrawn. In high school, the Chief Justice later recalled, he came closest to the inner texture of his father's life when he read of the youthful hardships of Oliver Twist.

Methias Warren grew into a man who went his own way and kept his own counsel. He neither smoked nor drank. Throughout his life he scrupulously saved a portion of every paycheck. Mildly attracted to radicalism, Methias joined the American Railway Union led by socialist Eugene Debs. For this affiliation, the SP fired Methias Warren and blacklisted him from his job in Los Angeles. Methias was forced to move to San Bernardino and to find employment with the Santa Fe. Only later, when the SP lifted its ban, did he accept a position in the SP repair shops outside Bakersfield, where he rose to master car repairer. To his credit, Methias Warren did not belabor his children with stories of his deprived boyhood. The father's early suffering, rather, manifested itself in his lifelong frugality and abstemiousness, the absence of friends and social life, a tendency his son would inherit and check through his large family and his expansive domestic routines.

A loner father brought up a loner son who made being a loner his foremost political principle.

Forced to leave school after the seventh grade, Methias Warren read dutifully throughout his life in an effort to catch up. Earl Warren detected an enduring sadness in his father over the fact that Methias's lack of education, in mathematics and engineering especially, prevented him from advancing into railroad construction and design. Forced to remain repairing what others designed and built, Methias Warren was determined that the same thing would not happen to his son. He taught Earl to read when Earl was barely out of infancy and insisted that his son start school at the age of five in the second, not the first, grade and be rapidly skipped to the third. And so Earl Warren went through grammar school, high school, college, and law school as the youngest member of his class. Methias bought a copy of the *Century Encyclopedia* for Earl and his sister Virginia, the same encyclopedia Earl Warren later bought for his own children. He tutored Earl through his grammar school subjects. To Methias's embarrassment, he was forced to stop tutoring Earl when Earl went on to high school, for Methias was ignorant of algebra, geometry, and physics. Out of his own pocket, Methias paid for his son's high school, college, and law school education. There were no scholarships.

As the years went on, Methias Warren became even more bleak and isolated. His wife began to spend protracted periods of time in Oakland with her daughter. Earl Warren's mother was on one such lengthy visit to Oakland when, early on the evening of Saturday, 14 May 1938, an intruder broke into Methias Warren's home on Niles Street in east Bakersfield. Methias was asleep in his armchair. The intruder bashed the sleeping man's skull with a short piece of pipe and robbed the house.

Was it a transient, as Earl Warren himself believed (and took great pains all his life to justify), a random killing by a hobo who saw Methias Warren asleep in his chair through the window, killed and robbed him, then hopped a freight out of town? Or someone with a grudge against the frequently difficult Warren, by now a prosperous landlord? Called in to help investigate the case, Oscar Jahnsen, Warren's chief investigator in the Alameda County district attorney's office, remained convinced that Matt Warren knew who hit him. Jahnsen also believed that while robbery was a motive, it was not the exclusive motive. Someone, Jahnsen suggested, was settling a score. Notified of his father's murder as he was addressing a Masonic breakfast in the Claremont Hotel in Oakland, Earl Warren left immediately for Bakersfield. Entering his father's small home, where Methias's narrow, pinched life had come to such a violent end, the crusading district attorney of Alameda County, candidate for the office of attorney general of California, looked around, then wept.

Methias Warren left an estate valued at $177,653, an impressive sum in 1938 dollars. Did such later wealth assuage the pain of his early years? Certainly, his son's flourishing public career had proved a consolation. The ticket to this career had been the University of California in Berkeley, where Warren arrived as a sixteen-year-old freshman in 1908. In later life, Earl Warren epitomized the Old Blue, the boys and girls from public high schools throughout the state, urban and rural, for whom the University of California — Cal, as they called it — had proven a wondrous passport to upward mobility. Toward the end of the century, UC Berkeley would become an elite, internationally ranked university. In 1908 when Warren arrived, however, Cal was a struggling land grant institution committed to the education of as many qualified young Californians as possible, including those who earned a prevalance of C's in high school.

Supported in great part by his father, Earl Warren seems to have had a pleasant time at Cal. He passed his courses, even made an occasional honors grade, but was never a grind. He fulfilled his ROTC requirement by playing clarinet in the cadet band. The drum major was Robert Gordon Sproul, Class of 1913, later president of UC and a lifelong friend. Warren earned extra money playing in a dance band. An avid fraternity man, he took up residence in his freshman year at the La Junta Club, soon to be affiliated with Sigma Phi, and remained in fraternity digs throughout his six years in the combined bachelor of arts–doctor of jurisprudence program. Warren's fraternity brothers nicknamed him Pinky, the name by which a college nurse had summoned him in the infirmary when he was suffering a case of pinkeye. He also joined Skull and Keys, a secret society founded a decade and a half earlier by undergraduate Frank Norris, the future novelist. The members of Skull and Keys met in a replica of an Egyptian tomb for beer drinking, secret rituals, and other forms of good fun. Other favorite haunts of Warren's included Bill the Dog Man's hot dog stand, the Waldorf Bar, which served a free lunch, Gus Brause's restaurant, where there was always a group of students on hand to devour the beef and cheese sandwiches made by Mother Brause or sit over a game of cards and a stein of beer, and Pop Kessler's Rathskeller in downtown Oakland, where Warren went once a week for beer, dinner, and poetry readings.

An avid reader, Warren loved poetry and could recite many poems from memory. He also revered the writings of Jack London, a sometime Oaklander. Occasionally, Warren and his friends would go over to the First and Last Chance, a saloon on the Oakland-Alameda estuary where London used to hang out. There, California's future governor would sit and listen as London expounded his philosophies or told tall tales of the South Seas and the Far North. At the end of his junior year, Warren entered the law school; he took his bachelor's degree in 1912, after his first year of legal studies. As a boy, he had sat in the Bakersfield courthouse listening to the lawyers argue their cases, and these early impressions had led to his choice of a legal career. In 1914 Earl Warren was graduated as doctor of jurisprudence. His thesis: "The Personal Liability of Corporation Directors in the State of California." Shortly thereafter, he was called to the bar by the District Court of Appeal in San Francisco upon motion of a member of the law school faculty.

Like Masonry, the University of California quickened in Earl Warren affections and loyalties otherwise reserved for his family. For Warren and for many of his generation, the University of California was a continuing connection, a way of life, a loyalty akin to religion. The very model of the Old Blue, Warren faithfully attended the annual Big Game between Cal and Stanford. When the Big Game was played in Berkeley every other year, Warren would get together with his fraternity friends at Pop Kessler's Rathskeller for reminiscences and readings of such old favorites as Rudyard Kipling and Robert W. Service. He remained a close advisor of his ROTC bandmate Robert Gordon Sproul when Sproul became president of the university in 1930 and was active in the Cal Alumni Association, serving as vice president and president-elect, a post he resigned when elected governor in 1942 so as to avoid conflict of interest. At the annual summer encampments of the Bohemian Club of San Francisco at the club's redwood grove in Sonoma County, Warren belonged to the heavily UC-oriented Isle of Aves Camp founded by UC history professor Henry Morse Stephens in the early 1900s. At campfire songfests at the Grove, or in the communal singing before the theatrical performances called Low Jinks, no one rose more enthusiastically to sing "Hail California!" than Earl Warren.

At the 1948 Philadelphia convention, Warren asked Robert Gordon Sproul to nominate him to the presidency. Throughout his governorship, Warren watched zealously over the expansion and improvement of the University of California campuses, which eventually numbered nine. All six of his children attended UC: Jim and Virginia, UC Berkeley; Earl Jr. and Robert, UC Davis; Dorothy and Honey Bear, UCLA. In his memoirs Earl Warren gives six pages to his efforts on behalf of UC. He mentions the California State University system, the two-year community colleges, and the other state-supported special schools in a simple paragraph.

Graduated from his beloved UC, admitted to the bar, Earl Warren joined the law department of the Associated Oil Company (as governor he would take on the oil companies with a vengeance), followed by a position with the Oakland law firm of Robinson and Robinson. When the United States entered World War I, Warren enlisted in the Army as a private and rose rapidly to the position of first sergeant at Camp Lewis, Washington, before attending Officers Training Camp and receiving a commission as second lieutenant of infantry. Significantly, for one who would make his reputation as a crime-busting prosecutor, Earl Warren excelled in the thrust and parry, the brutal attack, of the bayonet. His expertise with the bayonet, together with his administrative skills, kept him from going overseas. Warren spent the war as a training officer at Camp Lee, Virginia, and a bayonet instructor at the Officers Training Camp at Camp McArthur in Waco, Texas. He was still wearing his Army uniform when he took up his duties as clerk of the Judiciary Committee of the California state assembly in Sacramento. Shortly thereafter, he joined the city attorney's office in Oakland. In the spring of 1920, Warren transferred to the office of the district attorney of Alameda County. With the exception of that brief period after graduation, Earl Warren was to spend his entire career in public service.

He made his political reputation as a hard-charging, showboating, crime-fighting prosecutor, giving no quarter, for whom the slamming shut of prison doors on convicted felons sounded better than the marching band at Cal. Earl Warren had a prosecutor's temperament, which is to say, he was at once repelled and fascinated by crime and criminals. When he was a boy in Bakersfield, the Warren family had defined itself against the drinking, gambling, and whoring of a wide-open railroad town. The single most important public event in Warren's boyhood had been the Bakersfield shoot-out of 19 April 1903. A bandit by the name of Jim McKinney was alleged to have shotgunned to death City Marshal Jeff Packard and his deputy Will Tibbet. McKinney was in turn slain by Burt Tibbet, Will's brother. Just before he died, however, Marshal Packard declared that McKinney was innocent. According to Packard, one of his own deputies, Al Hultse, had fatally shot Packard and Tibbet. Convicted of second degree murder, Hultse committed suicide in prison, slitting his throat from ear to ear with a razor blade. Obviously, this affair was of greater importance for another boy, Lawrence Tibbet, age six, the future (as Tibbett) opera star, whose father had been murdered; but it left a profound impression on Earl Warren as well. As retired Chief Justice, Warren gave the event extensive coverage in his memoirs. He lavished equal time on a number of the grand guignol murders he investigated and prosecuted in his years as district attorney.

Warren remembered his district attorney years because without them he would never have gone to Sacramento, much less Washington. Warren was elected district attorney at the age of thirty-three in 1925 on a narrow vote, three to two, by the Alameda County Board of Supervisors when his mentor and predecessor Ezra DeCoto resigned to take a seat on the Railroad Commission in Sacramento. By the end of the Roaring Twenties and the G-man Thirties, Warren was considered by many observers to be the best crime- and corruption-fighting DA in the nation. He began his career simply, by closing down Caddy Well's Parlor House, a well-known bordello a mere three blocks from the Alameda County Courthouse in Oakland. Guided by Franklin Hichborn's The System (1915), an incisive analysis of political corruption in San Francisco and the San Francisco graft trials of 1908–9, Warren chipped away at the network of prostitution, gambling, bootlegging, and political payoffs orchestrated by Alameda County sheriff Frank Barnett and centered in Emeryville, where juries were notoriously reluctant to convict in vice or gambling cases. Warren next rooted out and prosecuted a web of bribery associated with paving contracts.

In raw numbers, Alameda County had as many murders as London, many of them gruesome. Unlike many prosecutors, Warren was not content merely to present evidence in court. He took a personal interest in police investigations leading to arrest, especially when a violent crime was involved, and maintained a top-flight investigative unit in his department. As district attorney, Warren served as chairman of the State Board of Criminal Identification and Investigation, which he developed as a California version of the FBI. During these years, Warren became known by his staff as Chief, and Chief remained his favorite title throughout his entire career. It was, interestingly enough, totally appropriate to his last office.

Politically ambitious, Earl Warren never lost an opportunity to get favorable press. He once allowed two reporters from the San Francisco *Examiner* to accompany him on a stake-out and arrest. Photographers seemed ever on hand when Warren and his men charged in, wielding axes, to sunder whiskey barrels in a seized distillery. In 1938, when State Attorney General Ulysses Webb announced that he would not run for reelection, Warren filed and was elected. As his first act in office, he prosecuted Mark Megladdery, the nephew and secretary of the outgoing governor, Frank Merriam, for taking a bribe to secure a pardon for a convicted murderer. Megladdery had been scheduled to take a seat on the Superior Court in Alameda County. Thanks to Earl Warren, he found himself in a prison cell in San Quentin. Warren next went after a statewide bookmaking network, breaking it through indictments and convictions and by getting its telephone service disconnected through a court order. In the most flamboyant raid of his already flamboyant career, Warren went after the gambling ships *Rex*, *Texas*, *Tango*, and *Showboat* owned by bootlegger Tony Cornero, anchored off Santa Monica and Long Beach.

For Attorney General Earl Warren and Governor Culbert Olson, each of them taking office in 1938, it was loathing at first sight. There could be no greater contrast than that between Olsen, the committed New Dealer—insecure, neurotic, a jumped-up member of the Folks, an immigrant to the state—and the assured, non-partisan native son. Fifteen years older than Warren, Olson had known a hardscrabble life on the Utah frontier. Coming under the influence of William Jennings Bryan, Culbert Olson had remained throughout his life a fierce partisan Democrat of the populist persuasion. Warren, by contrast, now approaching fifty, exuded the self-confidence of the Grand Master Mason and the successful Old Blue. Warren later claimed that Olson spoke to him only once in the four years they served together, on the first day of the job, when Warren informed Olson that he would be investigating the selling of pardons by the executive secretary to Olson's predecessor. Even after Pearl Harbor, when Warren's role as chairman of the Civilian Defense Council assumed great importance, Olson refused to speak to Warren directly.

According to Warren, he had already become fed up with Olson in the months just before Pearl Harbor and had tried to persuade Robert Gordon Sproul, president of UC, to run for governor. Sproul demurred, saying that politics and academic presidencies did not mix. Over dinner at the Bohemian Club in San Francisco in early 1942, Warren urged Los Angeles mayor Fletcher Bowron to run. Bowron, in turn, urged Warren to enter the race. (Were Warren's urgings sincere or merely a way of flushing out Bowron's intentions and possibly getting his support?) Declaring his candidacy in April 1942, Warren persuaded Bowron to become his campaign chairman with the suggestion that Warren, as governor, would back Bowron for the United States Senate in 1944 when Sheridan Downey came up for reelection.

Warren ran under the rubric "Leadership, Not Politics." In his speeches he stressed his father's boyhood in Iowa and his mother's childhood in Minnesota, making himself seem less the native son and Old Blue and more one of the Folks, just another Midwesterner come to the Golden State. Under California's system of cross-filing, Warren, himself a Republican, entered the Democratic as well as the Republican primary. Knowing that he would do miserably in the Republican primary, Olson refused to cross-file. Warren swept the Republican primary and polled 404,778 votes to Olson's 514,144 in the Democratic, virtually assuring himself a victory in the runoff. In the course of the campaign, Earl Warren made the mistake—only once—of debating Olson face to face, over a statewide radio broadcast from studios in San Francisco. Feisty, aggressive, an enraged terrier, Olson savaged the bland and generalizing Warren, who avoided any such debates throughout the remainder of his career.

In the general election, Warren carried every county in California with the exception of Butte, which he lost by sixty votes. (As attorney general, Warren had enforced an unpopular opinion in a local school board controversy in Butte, and the voters of that rural county had not forgotten.) Moving into the governor's office in January 1943, Warren discovered that Olson had wired his office and the offices of his staff for eavesdropping. The final days of the Olson administration had been that paranoid! Warren dispatched his chief investigator Oscar Jahnsen to detect the bugs and sweep them clean. For years, a closet in Warren's office suite stored the tangled wires and recording equipment Olson had installed.

Due to wartime restrictions and protocols, Earl Warren was inaugurated as the thirtieth governor of California on 4 January 1943 with no ceremonies or celebrations. Virtually three quarters of his first administration occurred during the war. Already, however, Earl Warren was looking forward to the post-war era. Among his most notable wartime achievements was his establishment in 1944 of the Reconstruction and Reemployment Commission under the direction of Colonel Alexander Heron, formerly director of finance for the state, who was released from active duty with the Army in Europe to take up this crucial position. Warren, Heron, the members of the commission, everyone was asking: what would happen to California after the war? Would California return to its pre-war situation: an agricultural state that for all the glittering urbanism of Los Angeles and San Francisco remained under-populated and under-developed, geographically and psychologically remote from the centers of political and financial power in the East? Or was something else in store: a peopling of California without precedent since the Gold Rush and the creation of a new society? Some Californians were predicting a boom. (They were right. The boom would last for nearly a half century.) Others were predicting diminished expectations, even a bust.

In the interim, Earl Warren, wartime governor, brought his family forward as the image of a once and future California. During the war, the Warren family, so representative, so photogenic, came increasingly into the spotlight. They were

California's paradigmatic family on the home front: a long-running daytime radio serial in which the Warren children went to public school, ventured on their first dates, played football, won horse-riding competitions, served with the Marines in the Pacific, as Mom and Dad stood proudly by. It was good politics, all this family life and tow-headed kids and the oldest brother in the Marines; but it was also a way of projecting the post-war future, the family future, amidst uncertainties.

James Warren, first of all, did his part by getting drafted into the Army. A high school football injury kept him from Officers Candidate School. He was so ashamed of this fact—of the solitary PFC stripe on his sleeve and his clerk's job in the Presidio in San Francisco—that he refused to attend his father's inauguration. He later managed a transfer to the Marines and won admittance to OCS. Once James Warren had won his lieutenant's bars, he returned proudly to Sacramento to pose in uniform with his parents, brothers, and sisters on the steps of the governor's mansion. He served with distinction with the 3rd Marine Division in the Pacific, and when he married an attractive tennis champion named Margaret Jessee, and the couple had a son, and James survived the war and returned home, it was *The Best Years of Our Lives* in living color.

Mrs. Warren, meanwhile, was running the governor's mansion, raising her family, cooking meals, ironing the governor's shirts. Nina Warren personally refurbished the Victorian wedding cake of a governor's mansion, a ramshackle structure at the corner of 16th and H streets built in 1878. Never before had the mansion housed a growing family. The entire third floor was boarded off, its empty rooms a haven for bats. When Mrs. Warren first saw the structure, she wept. She remained with the children in Oakland, commuting to Sacramento as necessary, while the house was being cleaned and renovated. It took until April 1943 to unboard, clean, and refurbish the mansion and to furnish it from the W. & J. Sloane department store in San Francisco. The governor, meanwhile, lived in bachelor's quarters at the Sutter Club across from the capitol.

When the family moved in, the governor had himself listed in the Sacramento phone book: WARREN, EARL R 1526 H STREET GI-2-3636. A California Highway Patrolman answered the phone and routed the calls. At lunchtime during the week, Warren strolled alone in the park surrounding the capitol or sat on a bench with his face held to the sun in a characteristically Scandinavian fashion. On Saturdays, the governor performed family errands around town, walking to the shoe repair shop on H Street near the mansion, where shoe repairman Randall Butler took care of the many pairs of shoes necessary to keep the Warren family well shod. Household help virtually disappeared during the war, including from the governor's mansion. In the autumn of 1943, the governor, convalescing after an illness, received permission from his physician to get out of bed ahead of schedule and help his wife with the dishes.

Throughout the war and after, 1526 H Street bustled with the life of the Warren clan. Nina Warren did the cooking, even for state dinners. The press praised her preserves, pastries, chocolate cake, Swedish pancakes, her ration-stretching meat loaf, and her lamb stew, the governor's favorite dish. The children loved their mother's penuche, a type of Scandinavian fudge. The halls of the mansion teemed with tennis rackets, baseball bats and mitts, roller skates and ice skates, fishing rods, scooters, bicycles, Bobby's secondhand cornet. (Following in his father's footsteps, Bobby Warren played cornet in a Sacramento marching band.) Luxuriously for the era, each child had his or her own room. True to Scandinavian tradition, each of the children's rooms had its own small tree during the Christmas season. The darling of the family, Honey Bear, was awarded the ornate Governor's Bed Chamber on the first floor because it had a shower, which she loved, and a large, old-fashioned, free-standing claw-footed bathtub. Dotty was an active Girl Scout, and there were frequent Girl Scout parties, supervised by Mrs. Warren. Each evening, unless he was traveling or officially engaged, the governor came home for dinner. Enjoying a bourbon and soda (he later switched to scotch), Warren repaired to the dining alcove off the kitchen (the formal dining room was reserved for state occasions) and ate dinner with Nina and the children, discussing their schoolwork and events of the day. At night he read to them from the Bible, the smaller children snuggling in their pajamas on the governor's bed. When the boys got older, the governor, an inveterate outdoorsman, would take them duck hunting in the Delta or fishing in the north or south to the Gulf of California. Part of every summer was spent at Uplifters Ranch in Rustic Canyon in the Santa Monica Mountains below Malibu.

In the yard of 1526 H Street there was a large tree that Ju-Ju, Bobby, and Honey Bear, who was a bit of a tomboy, loved to climb and swing from the branches. Virginia, then fourteen, entered McClatchy High School. The younger children attended Crocker Grammar School or California Junior High before going on to McClatchy. California Highway Patrolman Edgar (Pat) Patterson drove Honey Bear and Bobby to school every morning and picked them up in the afternoon. When Pat Patterson wore civilian clothes and drove the family Chevrolet, Bobby and Honey Bear would allow him to take them right up to the school. When Pat was in his CHP uniform, however, or was driving the governor's shiny black Cadillac limousine, the children had him drop them off a block away so as not to attract the attention of their classmates. After school, Patterson would sit with the children in the kitchen, all of them enjoying an afternoon snack of Mrs. Warren's devil's food cake and a tall cool glass of milk. Initially, there was a Dalmatian named Jerry at 1526 H Street, but Jerry once tore the pants of a young man taking Virginia to a dance. Mrs. Warren repaired the boy's trousers with her own needle and thread, and Jerry was turned over to the Army K-9 Corps for wartime duty and replaced by three more malleable springer spaniels.

As the youngest of the Warren children, Honey Bear soon became the Caroline Kennedy of California: the adorable little girl in whom so much is invested and expressed. Already, in 1939 when she was six, Honey Bear had stolen the show at groundbreaking ceremonies for the Golden Gate International Exposition on Treasure Island, wielding a shovel with childish charm. In Sacramento, Honey Bear proved equally photogenic. A happy, smiling child, loved and loving, she had an open, willing disposition and took spontaneous joy in the world around her. When Nina Warren did housework, Honey Bear helped. Taking a big broom into the guards' quarters, she swept it clean.

Honey Bear had a special affinity for a succession of Warren household dogs — Bow, Spade, Rocky, Chris, and Sheriff — and was delighted with the arrival of a pinto horse named Peanuts, whom she and Bobby shared. Honey Bear graduated from Peanuts to competitive riding and jumping on her horse Billy Sunday, kept in Sacramento, or Flash, kept at the Barbara Worth Stables in Santa Barbara. Mrs. Warren decorated Honey Bear's room with the ribbons she won at horse shows.

Earl Warren let the photographers from *Life* into the mansion and kept the press fed with details of Warren family life because he was proud of his family and it was good politics. Californians, in turn, adored the Warrens, seeing in them the wholesome verve they wished for themselves. The Warren family — Governor and Mrs. Warren, Jim and Maggie, Virginia, Dotty, Ju-Ju, Bobby, and Honey Bear — embodied the dreams and aspirations of the home-coming, suburbanizing 1940s, on the verge of a nationally significant quest for family, homes, and happiness in the Golden State.

Yet who was this Earl Warren? Was he the crusading prosecutor or the bland Dad in a Sacramento version of *Father Knows Best*? Was he what he presented himself to be, friendly and smiling in his rimless glasses and double-breasted suit, or was he, behind the image, someone else? How could such a seemingly benign figure have been so successful as a prosecutor, which was all that Earl Warren had ever been before assuming the office of governor? Was there a darker dimension to his character, and how did this dark side, if it existed, this possible Warren *noir*, affect his philosophy and style of political leadership?

Carey McWilliams, for one, ever believed that Warren's deepest instincts were darkly on the right. Practically the first thing Warren did upon becoming governor was to fire McWilliams, as he had promised to do in the campaign, from his job as commissioner of immigration and housing. McWilliams counter-attacked in the *New Republic* and the *Nation*, which he edited after 1950, charging that William Randolph Hearst was behind Warren and wanted to see him in the White House as soon as possible. McWilliams cited a combination of Hearst newspapers, the Los Angeles *Times*, the Oakland *Tribune*, the Associated Farmers of California, and other big business and agribusiness interests as being behind the Earl Warren for President boomlet, which surfaced as early as 1944. While never fully saying so, McWilliams suggested that Earl Warren, family man, played one role for the cameras while remaining in his basic nature a grim, hard-boiled prosecutor with reactionary tendencies, given to leaking secret grand jury testimony to the press if it suited his purposes, constantly opposing any effort to grant pardons or even parole to Tom Mooney and Warren K. Billings, framed for the 1916 Preparedness Day bombings in San Francisco. As proof of these statements, McWilliams pointed to the *Point Lobos* case of 1936, the Max Radin case of 1940, the evacuation of Japanese-Americans from California in 1942, and Warren's appointment of William F. Knowland to the United States Senate in 1945.

The *Point Lobos* case would continue to cause trouble for Warren among liberals throughout his career. On the night of 22 March 1936, George Alberts, chief engineer of the steamer *Point Lobos*, then docked in the Oakland estuary, was beaten to death aboard his ship. Alberts was known to have been in active opposition against Communist influences in the Oilers, Wipers, and Tenders Union. The two men most likely responsible for Alberts's death fled the state and remained at large. Investigating the case, Warren learned the names of the four union activists who were part of the six-man delegation that had called on George Alberts that fateful night. Warren secured indictments and convictions of the four for second degree murder, getting them sentenced to San Quentin for terms of five years to life. These convictions enraged unionists and liberal Democrats, including Culbert Olson, who considered them flawed in procedure and motivated by Warren's Red-baiting anti-unionism. As governor, Olson paroled three of the men whom Warren had convicted.

It was now Warren's turn. In mid-summer 1940 Olson nominated Boalt Hall law professor Max Radin to the Supreme Court of California. Learned, impassioned, ultra-liberal, Radin was a champion on the far left. Among other things, Radin had criticized Earl Warren's handling of the *Point Lobos* case. Radin had also supported eighteen employees of the State Relief Administration when they had refused to yield a list of their colleagues belonging to the CIO to an assembly committee chaired by Assemblyman Samuel Yorty of Los Angeles that was investigating subversive activity. Yorty had the state workers arrested and jailed on charges of contempt. Radin wrote two spirited letters to the court asking for leniency. In order to take his seat on the Supreme Court of California, Radin had to be approved by the California Commission on Judicial Qualifications, a three-person panel consisting of Chief Justice Phil Gibson, John Nourse, presiding justice of the District Court of Appeal, and Attorney General Earl Warren. In a stormy two-hour session, Warren persuaded Nourse to vote against Radin's appointment on the basis that Radin's support of the CIO activists indicated a lack of judicial temperament. Rebuffed in his appointment, Governor Olson turned to another Boalt Hall professor, Roger Traynor, a tax specialist, who was confirmed. From Carey McWilliams's point of view, Warren's hardball attack on Radin—a brilliant, charismatic, liberal Jewish intellectual—showed the limits of Warren's much-vaunted liberalism. Warren might be a Progressive, McWilliams argued, but in Warren Progressivism veered sharply to the right.

Carey McWilliams had outspokenly opposed the removal of the Japanese from the Pacific Coast. Earl Warren, by contrast, had played a decisive role in the evacuation through his testimony before the Tolan Committee and through his chairmanship of the Civilian Defense Council. In later years, Warren found himself in an unusual conversation regarding the evacuation, which he never liked to discuss. Recalling the confusion and pain of Japanese-American children as they were taken under the escort of soldiers from their homes and schools, their playgrounds and familiar surroundings, and shipped with their parents to distant locations, Earl Warren, Chief Justice of the United States of America, broke into tears.

In August 1945 United States Senator Hiram Johnson died, and Warren appointed the thirty-seven-year-old former assemblyman William F. Knowland, scion of the powerful and conservative Oakland family, to the Senate. In so doing, Warren was repaying a longtime political debt to Knowland's father, Joseph Knowland, the arch-conservative publisher of the Oakland *Tribune*, who had supported Warren throughout his career as district attorney, attorney general, and governor. In 1946 Knowland defeated Congressman Will Rogers Jr. for a full six-year term in the Senate. In 1952 Senator Knowland nominated Warren to the presidency in Chicago in Warren's second attempt at that office. Carey McWilliams saw in the appointment of the ultra-conservative William Knowland proof positive that Earl Warren was a reactionary in his deepest convictions.

Beyond the restricted regions of the left-liberal intelligentsia, however, McWilliams's attacks against Warren never stuck. What McWilliams failed to grasp — and McWilliams was California's most astute political observer, despite his in-your-face commitment to liberalism — was that Earl Warren had succeeded in becoming a Knight of Non-Partisanship, as one observer called him, the leader of a pan-California movement that transcended party identification, a Party of One. Earl Warren led the Party of One, and he made it the Party of California. He was its sole spokesman and elected member, and between 1942 and 1952 the voters of California continually reendorsed this distinctive political program and persona.

Warren could do this, first of all, because of cross-filing, a direct legacy of the Progressive era that had formed him as a young man and with which he maintained his deepest political identification. The Progressive years 1911 to 1923 witnessed the enactment of a series of political reforms in California that warred against the traditional political organizations of most Eastern states. In an effort to establish direct democracy, Progressive legislators in California approved the direct primary, cross-filing, the referendum, the initiative, and the recall. The referendum allowed the voters to bypass the legislature and make law directly. With a mere 250,000 signatures, an initiative could qualify for the ballot and be voted into law in a general election. Robinson and Company of San Francisco specialized in gathering initiative signatures for a fee.

In 1909, during the first administration of Progressive governor Hiram Johnson, California enacted the direct primary system. Political candidates could now go directly to the people without the approval of their party. In 1913 California established cross-filing. Now, not only could a candidate go directly to the people, he (and later she) could enter both primaries, Republican and Democrat, without the necessity of stating party affiliation. Not until 1954 did a political candidate in

California have to declare his or her party affiliation to the voters. Cross-filing lasted until 1959, when Democrats, swept in by the landslide of 1958, abolished it.

Not only did the Progressive era promote bipartisanship on the state level, it outlawed partisan politics in local elections. Candidates for city and county offices were forbidden to run as Republicans or Democrats. Indeed, quite frequently, voters in local elections were not even aware of the party affiliation of a candidate. California thus disestablished the traditional party politics of the older states. Empowered as a sovereign Party of One, the California voter cast his or her ballot for the candidate of his or her choice, ignoring party affiliation at will. Naturally, the California voter grew increasingly independent of party loyalty in this system. At the same time, political identifications, frequently crossing party lines, grew strong on the local level. At the county, the regional, even the statewide level, California voters tended to organize as pressure groups behind one or another cause, again bypassing party structures. Freed from party control, but also party discipline, California became susceptible to cause-driven movements, many of them extreme, such as the Ham and Eggs pension crusade of the late 1930s.

Democrats waned under this system, and Republicans flourished, which was paradoxical in that California was only recently becoming a Democratic-dominated state. From the 1880s to the 1930s, California had been predominantly Republican. Even the Progressives in power from 1910 to the early 1920s maintained a tenuous relationship with the Republican Party. During the 1930s, however, Democrats pulled ahead of Republicans in registration figures as Democrats flocked into California from the Dust Bowl. Led by banker A. P. Giannini, California Democrats played a key role in engineering the election of Roosevelt in 1933. Roosevelt continued to carry California through 1944. Harry Truman carried California in 1948.

Yet behind the drama of national politics, a paradox was at work. In California, liberal Democrats had the most old-fashioned party, and conservative Republicans had the most innovative. In open-shop Southern California, the Democrats, cut off from their traditional link to big labor, remained exclusively in the hands of a left-liberal intelligentsia. Figures such as Upton Sinclair, Carey McWilliams, Culbert Olson, Jerry Voorhis, and Helen Gahagan Douglas come immediately to mind. While some liberal intellectuals could attain office (Voorhis and Douglas went to Congress), they were forced to go directly to the voters, so many of them suburbanized Republicans, without the benefit of a strong Democratic Party apparatus. In Northern California, by contrast, the Democratic Party, centered in San Francisco, stood in a classic alliance to labor and controlled the local pork barrel, insofar as pork was possible in California after the Progressives had reformed the civil service and public works system. As Earl Warren completed his first term as governor, San Francisco was under the political control of William Malone, state chairman of the Democratic Party. A close friend of Harry Truman's, Malone — himself a Trumanesque figure in his rise from the ranks, his love of reading, his diminutive stature and feisty integrity — ran the only classic big-city political machine in the state, and one of the few such machines on the entire Pacific Coast. The politicians coming out of San Francisco in this era—State Senator John F. Shelley, Assemblyman Edward O'Day, Board of Equalization member George Reilly, even Republican Assemblyman Thomas Maloney—were Irish politicians right from the pages of Edwin O'Connor's *The Last Hurrah* (1958), only, as Jimmy Breslin would later say of Oregon, the ocean was on the wrong side.

The Democrats had the numbers, but only in Northern California, with its strong ethnic and union identifications, could the Democrats even begin to guarantee the vote. In the shifting sands of suburban Southern California, traditionalist Democratic structures did not work. In the 1950 census, for example, nearly a quarter of the people responding had not lived at their present address one year earlier. No grass-roots political system, such as that controlled by William Malone in San Francisco, could survive amidst such fluidity.

Wealthier, better organized, more focused in their political allegiance, more in tune with the Californian sensibility, which outside San Francisco was suburban and individualistic, Republicans were better able to take advantage of the cross-filing system. Only once, in 1918, did Republicans run afoul of cross-filing. An amendment passed in 1917 said that no candidate could run on the ticket of another party if that candidate had not received the nomination of his or her own party as well. In 1918 San Francisco mayor James Rolph Jr., a Republican, won the Democratic nomination for governor but lost the Republican primary. Rolph was barred from the general election despite the fact that his cumulative showing in the Republican and Democratic primaries taken together indicated a victory. The 1917 amendment could also result in the absurdity of there being no candidates whatsoever in the general election if and when a Democrat won the Republican nomination but lost in the Democratic primary and a Republican won the Democratic nomination but lost in his own primary. Each candidate would then cancel the other out—which was exactly what occurred in 1948 in the Thirty-sixth Assembly District.

Republicans proved especially adept at winning Democratic votes. In general Republicans fielded good candidates and better campaign organizations. Republicans were also willing to cater to Democratic needs. Running for reelection to Congress in 1948, Richard Nixon ran as an incumbent on both tickets and did not endorse other Republican candidates. Nixon won the Democratic nomination. Three of the most strategically placed newspapers in the state—the Los Angeles *Times*, the San Francisco *Chronicle*, and the Oakland *Tribune*—were skilled at persuading Democrats to vote for Republican candidates.

Not only did the Republicans use the cross-filing system more skillfully, they seemed—at least until 1958—to have sociology on their side. Dust Bowl migrants had swollen the ranks of the Democratic Party in the 1930s, but in the post-war era the underlying suburban individualism of California, with its orientation toward personal freedom and the enjoyment of wealth and private life, began to reassert itself. Democratic strength was associated with big cities, ethnicity, unions, and academic intelligentsia: but in California this traditionally Democratic sector was being swamped in the 1940s by the arrival of millions of suburbanizing middle-class migrants untouched by such affiliations. There, in the Phantom Cities of California, as one team of political scientists described the maze of overlapping districts that governed the suburbs, traditional politics, so favorable to the Democrats, did not reassert itself because the fundamental basis of such politics—the neighborhood, the ward, the district, the union, the ethnic or religious organization, indeed the city itself—did not exist. An increasing number of post-war Californians lived in suburbs, which were governed by service-providing districts (fire, police, school, water) that did not inspire traditional political loyalties or associations. Increasingly, the new California suburban resident took his or her identity from home and family, job and workmates, church or synagogue, but from little else in the way of public identities. Whatever politics there was in the special districts was concerned primarily with the delivery of a service and not with governance in the broadest sense of that term. Even the most astute ward-heeler from Chicago would have trouble organizing a suburb in Southern California. Where would he start? What would be his leverage? Whom should he contact? Who on earth would care?

Skillfully, Republicans, Earl Warren most conspicuously, targeted the individual California voter through mass media campaigns. As district attorney, Earl Warren mastered the art of provoking favorable publicity through the press. In his first campaign for governor, he retained the services of the San Francisco–based public relations firm of Campaigns, Inc., better known as Whitaker and Baxter. In the early 1930s, Clem Whitaker and his partner (later his wife) Leone Baxter virtually invented the systematic mass-media-oriented political campaign in its modern form. As a reporter and editor in Sacramento in the 1920s, Clem Whitaker had organized a press service, which he sold to United Press International in 1929, designed to feed state capital coverage—articles, cartoons, political commentary—into newspapers too small to maintain their own capital bureau. Leone Baxter, meanwhile, was learning promotional techniques as manager of the Chamber of Commerce of Redding in Shasta County. The couple met in 1933 and formed a press agency and campaign service. In their first big election, they defeated the efforts of Pacific Gas & Electric to sink the Central Valley Water Project. (Shortly thereafter, PG&E put them on retainer for life.) The next year, the pair was retained by a temporary alliance of Republicans and conservative Democrats to defeat the candidacy of Socialist-turned-Democrat Upton Sinclair for governor. Whitaker and Baxter destroyed Sinclair in a mass media blitz that remains a textbook study.

Whitaker and Baxter grasped a simple but essential truth—true initially for California, true later for the nation at large. Californians, later Americans in general, could be reached individually—by the millions!—through the mass media: which in the 1930s meant pamphlets, leaflets, newspaper and magazine advertising, planted stories, commentary and cartoons, billboards, spot announcements on radio, slides and trailers in motion picture theaters, and direct mail. To this program of managed media, Whitaker and Baxter added the values of contest, image, and timing. Americans, they realized, could relate best to political questions if there was a clear-cut argument. Such an argument was best advanced through precise, tightly controlled imagery. It also had to be released most intensely in the final weeks of a campaign. Do not lay out to the voters a too complex program, Whitaker and Baxter advised their clients. Pick one dominant issue and run with it. Characterize the opposition in a single negative slogan and your own position in a single positive image. Unleash the full force of your campaign just weeks before election day, when voters tend to make up their minds. Today, seventy years later, the Whitaker and Baxter revolution seems commonplace, so prevalent has it become in our national political life. In the 1930s and 1940s, however, Whitaker and Baxter evolved their system, a forecast of things to come, in the special context of California politics.

By and large, Whitaker and Baxter handled only Republican candidates. (One of their few Democratic clients, George Reilly, lost his campaign for mayor of San Francisco in 1946.) Republicans had more money, for one thing, and could afford the expense of a mass media campaign. Outnumbered in registration, Republicans had to reach the broadest possible audience. More important, Republicans realized that the California voter stood alone in the universe and could be reached through mass media and hence could be persuaded.

Earl Warren mastered the distinctive political culture of California. In 1938, in his first and only run for attorney general, Warren won the Republican, Democratic, and Progressive primaries and was saved the time and expense of running in the general election. The same thing happened when he ran for a second term as governor in 1946. Warren became a Republican, he tells us, "simply because California was then an overwhelmingly Republican state."[4] As a young man, Earl Warren came to intellectual maturity during the golden age of Republican Progressivism. As he began his career, Republicans controlled Oakland, seat of Alameda County, dominated by arch-Republican publisher Joseph Knowland of the Oakland *Tribune*, and so Earl Warren continued in his Republican mode, going along to get along. And besides: he could always enter Democratic primaries.

As a candidate thriving in the cross-filing system, Earl Warren downplayed his Republicanism in favor of a bipartisan image. Only gingerly did he involve himself in Republican Party politics on the national level. In 1928 he went to Kansas City as an alternate delegate and returned to California to campaign for Herbert Hoover. He attended the 1932 convention in Chicago as a voting delegate. Between 1932 and 1936, Warren was thrust increasingly into statewide leadership in Republican Party circles as Senator Hiram Johnson, the highest-ranking Republican in the state, grew detached from party affairs. Warren went to the 1936 Republican Party convention in Cleveland as the chairman of the Republican State Central Committee, a Republican national committeeman, and a favorite-son candidate for President. Not only did Warren win the governorship in 1942, he led a Republican sweep of the assembly, which resulted in the election of a Republican, Charles Lyon, as speaker. Only rarely in any state did a Republican governor have a Republican speaker to back his programs.

The Republican sweep of 1942, coming as it did so closely upon the lean years of the Depression, brought Earl Warren to the attention of the national media and the national Republican Party leadership. At the 1944 convention in Chicago, which he again attended as a favorite-son candidate, Warren was invited to give the keynote address after retired Chief Justice Charles Evans Hughes declined the honor. Presidential nominee Tom Dewey begged Warren to accept the vice presidential slot. Only two years into his first term as governor, Warren was reluctant to show signs of interest in another office. Yet after receiving so much flattering attention at Chicago in 1944, Earl Warren became a little more willing to sound an occasional partisan Republican note in his generally bipartisan repertoire.

In Sacramento, Earl Warren kept only one photograph in his office, that of former governor and United States senator Hiram Johnson. In 1910, an insurgent special prosecutor from San Francisco, Johnson had won the governorship in his first try for political office. As an undergraduate and law student at Berkeley, Warren had lived through the heady years of Progressive reform. Singlehandedly, Hiram Johnson kept the Progressive Party alive in California as a sub-group of Republicanism until his death in August 1945. Johnson knew that at any time the right wing of the Republican Party could engineer a coup against him in the primary. By keeping the Progressive Party active as a third party, Johnson ensured his ability to be on the statewide ballot for the Senate should such a coup ever succeed. More than four hundred thousand registered voters in California continued to register as Progressive through the lifetime of their chief. While Warren was not one of them, he frequently described himself as a Progressive, spelled with a capital *P*: an independent suspicious of party machines; a middle-class reformer beholden neither to big business nor to big labor; an elected official committed to non-partisanship on the state and local levels, and to the efficient conduct of government by trained professionals appointed through civil service.

Despite his Republicanism, Earl Warren remained sympathetic to his Democratic supporters. After all, Democrats had given him the nomination of their party in 1938 and 1946. Darkly, Carey McWilliams suggested that Warren was merely seeking to mask his conservativism through imitating FDR as much as he could within the limits of his Republican affiliations and instincts. Columnist Marquis Childs, however, described Warren as "a New Deal wolf in Republican sheep's clothing." More flatteringly, Harry Truman said to a train-side audience during a whistle-stop in Sacramento on 12 June 1948: "He's a Democrat and doesn't know it."[5] Was Carey McWilliams or Harry Truman correct? Was Warren masking his conservatism behind a hypocritical show of non-partisanship? Or did he possess a genuine liberal streak? There is much in Warren's career to suggest sincere albeit submerged liberal instincts running alongside the hard-boiled stance of the prosecutor.

Within the limits of the Old California myth, for example, Warren had excellent relations with Mexican-Californians. As a boy in Los Angeles, he had attended Mexican festivities in the Plaza and been enchanted by the dancing and singing, the gaily colored horses, of these gatherings. Like so many Protestant Californians, Warren revered the myth of Old California as a Spanish Arcadia of white-walled, red-tiled haciendas and a colorful, pastoral way of life. Whenever possible, he attended the annual Old Spanish Days Fiesta in Santa Barbara. When Warren ran for governor in 1942, the actor Leo Carrillo, a sixth-generation Californian and a registered Democrat, campaigned for his *compadre* among Mexican-American voters. Carrillo, in fact, became the closest thing to a pal Earl Warren seems to have had in public life: Pancho to Warren's Cisco Kid, a combination factotum, court jester, master of ceremonies, and sometime hatchet man of the sort most politicians, even Earl Warren, seem to find necessary.

As far as the African-American community was concerned, Earl Warren was the first statewide politician in California to seek out black support and to identify with the advancement of African-Americans. As a boy in Bakersfield, he had gone to school with black children. As district attorney, he had taken on the Ku Klux Klan. As attorney general, he had ended the practice of banning black boxers from the Hollywood Legion Stadium. As governor, he integrated the National Guard and brought blacks into the civil service. Warren also made possible one of the first conspicuous public careers of an African-American in California, that of Walter Arthur Gordon. Like Warren, Gordon had attended UC Berkeley, where he achieved All-American honors in football and graduated from Boalt Hall, the law school, before going into practice in Oakland. While a law student, Gordon had worked as a police officer in Berkeley under Chief August Vollmer, a pioneering professional in police administration. In 1945 Warren appointed Gordon to the Adult Authority, which elected him chairman. Warren also brought Gordon to the attention of the Eisenhower administration, and in 1955 Eisenhower appointed Gordon governor of the Virgin Islands. In 1958 Gordon became one of the first African-Americans to sit on the federal bench.

Warren also had strong and continuing support from the Jewish community of San Francisco, many of them Republicans, led by the distinguished lawyer and philanthropist Jesse Steinhart. Nor was he without union support. Throughout his life, Warren maintained an active membership in Local 263 of the Musicians Union. Despite the *Point Lobos* affair, Warren sailed through his entire political career with strong backing from unions. CIO chief John L. Lewis once told Warren not to mind the official endorsements of his opponents by the CIO or to pay much attention to any CIO criticism. It was part of the game unions had to play with Democrats, Lewis told Warren. On election day, he would get the CIO votes. In March 1946 the American Federation of Labor endorsed Warren for governor and Democrat John Shelley for lieutenant governor, a split ticket. As a sign of his close connection to labor, Warren appointed Cornelius Haggerty, the San Francisco–based secretary of the State Federation of Labor, to a sixteen-year term on the Board of Regents of the University of California, the California equivalent of a life peerage. Throughout his years as governor, Warren nominated an almost equal number of Democrats and Republicans to statewide office. When Harry Truman visited Sacramento, Warren greeted him warmly in public, despite the warning of many die-hard Republicans that such a greeting could return to haunt Warren in the general election. When Democratic candidate Adlai Stevenson passed through Sacramento four years later, Warren extended him an equally friendly public greeting, despite the fact that Warren's future, if he had any, was in the hands of Dwight David Eisenhower.

Masons and Roman Catholics were oil and water in these years, yet Earl Warren, Grand Master Mason, sustained deep and warm personal and intellectual connections with members of the Roman Catholic community, especially with those of the Irish persuasion. In 1925 Warren had been given his start in public life by Alameda County supervisor Johnny Mullins, the swing vote in Warren's three-two appointment to district attorney. Throughout Mullins's life, Warren stayed close to the former supervisor and his wife, who lived simply in a modest Oakland apartment. In 1948 Warren invited the Mullinses to travel with the Warrens in the private car of the Warren Special. Later, when the Mullinses were unable to attend the wedding of one of the Warren daughters, Warren and his wife rang the doorbell of the Mullins apartment in Oakland, with Earl Warren, governor of California, carrying in hand the top tier of the wedding cake.

Warren was intrigued by Roman Catholic intellectuals, especially the social democratic aspects of their political philosophy. The single most influential person in the Warren administration was William Sweigert, a brilliant Irish Catholic attorney from San Francisco, a Democrat, strongly influenced by the liberal social teachings of the papal encyclicals. Accompanying Warren to Sacramento as chief of staff, Sweigert became Warren's liberal alter ego. Sweigert guided Warren into liberal programs of workers' compensation, health care, equal opportunity in employment, and other social supports. Or was it more subtle than a question of guidance? Did Warren choose Sweigert as his alter ego, the two of them forming a Masonic-Catholic odd couple, because Warren wanted precisely the same things that Sweigert wanted and chose to operate through his liberal Democratic deputy? Did Sweigert dare speak and propose Warren's suppressed liberal dreams and thus, with Warren's approval, allow the Chief to retain his mantle of non-partisanship?

Warren was equally friendly to another liberal intellectual Irish Catholic Democrat strongly influenced by the social teachings of the papal encyclicals, Attorney General Robert Kenny. To the manor born (an old Southern California family, long active in banking), Kenny grew up in Los Angeles, graduated from Stanford and Stanford Law, and had worked as a foreign correspondent in London and Paris before returning to Los Angeles to pursue a career as a lawyer and a judge. In 1938 Kenny won election to the state senate, where he replaced Culbert Olson when Olson became governor. As state senator, Kenny was one of the few important state officials—perhaps the only one—to speak out against the internment of the Japanese. Oddly enough, this did not prevent him from being elected attorney general in 1942, replacing Earl Warren.

Warren and Kenny rode up together to Sacramento to be inaugurated. Like everyone else, Earl Warren enjoyed Robert Kenny's conversation. The Daniel Patrick Moynihan of his time and place, Robert Kenny blended the good-humored demeanor of a wit, a raconteur, a snowman-shaped *bon vivant*, with that of a heads-up reporter with the memory of an elephant, a razor-sharp legal mind, and a powerful commitment, religiously reinforced, to social justice. When reporter John Gunther, visiting California to research the first edition of *Inside USA* (1947), first met the attorney general, Kenny was in a San Francisco watering hole enjoying a drink with labor leader Harry Bridges, Father Andrew Boss, a Jesuit specialist in industrial relations at the University of San Francisco, and an unnamed chorus girl. Gunther was enchanted by Kenny, whose wit and affable worldliness stood in such contrast to the Masonic blandness of Earl Warren, and saw in the attorney general the coming Democrat of California, even national, politics.

In 1946 the Democrats practically begged Kenny to run for governor against Earl Warren. Kenny agreed, as a duty. At the same time, he accepted the offer of his friend Supreme Court associate justice Robert Jackson, the American prosecutor at Nuremberg, to attend the trials as an observer. To the despair of Democratic Party officials, Kenny agreed to go, despite the fact that he would be out of the country for the first month of the campaign. "Most campaign mistakes are made during the first month," Kenny told the press drolly. "I figured that if I wasn't around, I wouldn't make those mistakes."[6] To no one's surprise, Earl Warren won the Republican, Democratic, and Progressive primaries, thus saving Kenny the drudgery of running in the general election.

In 1946 Artie Samish, a powerful Sacramento lobbyist representing liquor and racetrack interests, was in search of an easy-going candidate to replace Kenny as attorney general, since Kenny had reluctantly entered the governor's race. Samish backed Frederick Napoleon Howser, the lackadaisical district attorney of Los Angeles County. A strong recommendation for Howser, Samish cynically pointed out to his confrères, was that Howser's name closely resembled that of the popular incumbent lieutenant governor, Fred Houser, and Samish correctly guessed that most voters would vote for Howser thinking they were voting for Houser. To oppose Howser, the Democrats nominated Edmund G. (Pat) Brown, district attorney of San Francisco. A Republican turned Democrat, Brown paralleled Warren in his successful career as a prosecutor and in the attractiveness of his wife and four children—Barbara, Cynthia, Jerry, and Kathleen. Although Warren loathed Howser as the tool of Samish, he could not bring himself to endorse Brown openly. Howser, a Republican, was elected, and Samish got his wish; not only was Howser willing to look the other way as far as Samish's clients were concerned, the attorney general's own coordinator for law enforcement was secretly running a string of slot machines in Mendocino County.

Infuriated, Warren created a statewide Commission on Organized Crime under the chairmanship of retired admiral William Standley, formerly chief of naval operations and ambassador to the USSR. To administer the Commission, Warren appointed his longtime associate Warren Olney III. Attorney General Howser initially refused to authorize Olney's salary, correctly determining that Governor Earl Warren had established a second investigative and prosecutorial office at the state level. By 1950 Warren had completely undermined Howser, who failed to win the Republican nomination for reelection. In the general election of 1950, the Republican candidate Edward Shattuck was defeated by Pat Brown, with the *sub rosa* approval—but not the open endorsement—of Earl Warren. Warren got along famously with his Democratic attorney general. The bond between the two men, in fact, constitutes the central political continuity of California between 1950 and 1966, when Pat Brown was defeated for governor by Ronald Reagan. Earl Warren, Republican, recruited Pat Brown, Democrat, into the Party of California, committed to an essentially bipartisan, growth-oriented, neo-Progressive program strongly based in public works. Between the Protestant Mason Republican, friendly yet reserved, never losing the demeanor of the prosecutor, and the Irish Catholic San Francisco Democrat, amiable, chatty, never forgetting a name or a face, there grew up a cordial association based on a shared vision of the California moment, of which they were the leading stewards and political spokesmen.

Warren's refusal to endorse candidates can be attributed to his non-partisanship. It can also be seen as a cloak for the essential isolation of Methias Warren's son. One thing about being a Party of One: it precluded the contacts, trade-offs, loyalties, and antagonisms of ordinary political life. The more one pushes into the Warren mystique, the more one is tempted (at least tempted!) to detect behind the non-partisanship, behind the lifelong refusal to endorse other candidates, an egotism so great as to be heroic, for all its unpretentiousness.

The good news was that Earl Warren was unbeholden to the corporate sector that exercised such a continuing influence in Republican circles. As a prominent Republican elected official, Earl Warren was taken into the Bohemian Club of San Francisco and the Sutter Club of Sacramento, but he was never fully impressed by the corporate types around him; indeed, his dignified reserve in these places suggested that the clubs were lucky to have him as a member and not vice versa. In 1942 San Francisco investment banker Charles Blyth, a fellow Bohemian, raised enormous amounts of money for Warren in his first campaign for governor. Blyth wanted veto rights on all appointments to the Railroad, later Public Utilities, Commission so as to ensure that his investment firm, Blyth-Witter, would continue to handle all of the commission's bond business. Warren refused to give Blyth veto rights, and Blyth-Witter lost the bond business to a more competitive bid. Charles Blyth spent the next ten years, or so Earl Warren believed, trying to engineer the competing candidacy for governor of Lieutenant Governor Goodwin Knight. When it came to Big Oil, for whom Earl Warren had briefly worked as a young attorney, the governor was even less intimidated; indeed, he sometimes seemed eager to settle an old score. In 1947 Warren called for a tax of three cents per gallon on gas to pay for a billion dollars of highway construction over a ten-year period. With the assistance of Whitaker and Baxter, Big Oil resisted, but Warren prevailed. William Keck, president of Superior Oil, spent over $1 million backing the anti-Warren candidacy of Bakersfield congressman Thomas Werdel, to no avail.

Like California itself, whose aspirations it so vividly expressed, the Warren family continued to flourish in the boom years of Warren's second and third terms. Over time, the Warren daughters were progressing from cute little girls to handsome teenagers to sorority co-eds at Cal, and the Warren boys were making comparable progress, all of this expressing a life cycle of family fulfillment that in one way or another most Californians wanted for themselves. At twenty-two in 1950, Virginia, a Berkeley graduate, was showing signs of the sophistication and elegance that would eventually win her wide social acceptance in New York and Washington. Dotty was enrolled at UCLA, thus strengthening her father's connection to the southern part of the state. Honey Bear was attending McClatchy High School in Sacramento, where she was a cheerleader. She was also studying the cello and improving her skills on the ski slopes.

Californians were shocked in November 1950 when Honey Bear contracted poliomyelitis on the very day her father was elected to a third term. She had felt poorly the previous day but had insisted that her parents drive down to Oakland to vote in their old precinct as was their custom. Later that day, the Warrens were notified that Honey Bear had been rushed by ambulance to Sutter Hospital in Sacramento, paralyzed from the waist down and in great pain. The Warrens sped north to Sacramento. Honey Bear was conscious when her parents entered her room. She told her father not to worry. "It's not so bad," she said. She then said to Nina Warren: "Mother, take him home and make him rest." Earl and Nina Warren left Honey Bear's hospital room. Standing by himself in the hospital corridor, Earl Warren, elected that day to his third term as governor, wept publicly for the second time in his life.[7]

Two weeks later, Dorothy Warren was being driven home from a fraternity dance at UC Davis. There was an automobile accident. Dotty suffered five broken ribs and was in shock when the California Highway Patrol reached the scene. At the hospital, X-rays revealed a punctured lung. Honey Bear's polio and Dorothy's automobile accident represented every parent's worst nightmare come true. Empathy, moreover, was now compounded by a new medium, television. A year earlier, three-year-old Kathy Fiscus of South Pasadena wandered away from home and fell into a dry well, where she languished for fifty hours as rescuers struggled to reach her. The entire ordeal was carried live on pioneer television station KTLA, which set up uninterrupted, commercial-free coverage of the rescue attempt. Some time into her ordeal little Kathy Fiscus died, and when her body was recovered on live television, a wave of grief swept over greater Los Angeles, unified for the first time by the power of the new broadcast medium.

The ordeal of the Warren girls, Honey Bear especially, provoked a similar intensity of mass identification. What would happen to this teenaged California icon now that she had been struck by the polio scourge, which was terrorizing an entire generation? When the news was released that Honey Bear would not suffer permanent paralysis and would recover, Californians, united by radio and television, breathed a collective sigh of relief. Honey Bear seemed to be fighting polio on behalf of the entire state. Thousands of letters, cards, and telegrams poured into Sutter Hospital. On the day before Christmas Eve 1950, a recuperating Honey Bear was interviewed by the press, propped up in her bed in the master suite of the governor's mansion, a selection of cards, letters, and telegrams plastering her walls. On Christmas Eve itself, Honey Bear was allowed to leave her bed for the first time since her hospitalization to open presents. The next day, Christmas, she was allowed to sit with her family at dinner.

The following November, an official of the Young Republicans took an oblique strike at Honey Bear in a speech. "I took a strong dislike to a dog named Fala," said the Young Republican in reference to FDR's White House pet, "and I'm afraid I might take a strong dislike to Teddy Bears or Honey Bears or what have you."[8] The Young Republican was using Honey Bear to say that he did not want the Earl Warren family in the White House. As political comments go, it was innocuous. Yet Honey Bear was still recovering from poliomyelitis, and the reference shocked Californians as a tasteless attack on a likable teenager who had been stricken by a disease everyone dreaded. The Young Republican decided upon a career in private life. A recovered Honey Bear graduated from McClatchy High School in 1951 and entered UCLA, where she lived in the Kappa Alpha Theta house, majored in psychology, and added surfing and tennis to her repertoire of sports.

The disgraced Young Republican made his offensive remarks in the course of discussing Earl Warren's fifth and very heartfelt campaign for the presidency. In 1936, 1940, 1944, and 1948, Warren had gone to the Republican convention as a favorite son, the head of the California delegation, expected to release his delegates to a more serious contender. This time, in 1952, Warren wanted to attend the Republican convention as a serious candidate. He was especially convinced that he could do a better job campaigning than two-time loser Thomas Dewey. On election day in November 1948, Earl Warren had gone to bed in his suite on the eleventh floor in the St. Francis Hotel in San Francisco believing that he would wake up Vice President of the United States. The next morning, Warren drove up to Sacramento to resume his duties as governor. Despite Truman's upset victory, Warren seemed almost relieved that the campaign was over. He and Dewey had a polite but distant relationship. They had spoken to each other only twice during the campaign. Warren felt that Dewey lacked the common touch. He later wrote that one of the pivotal events in the campaign happened when an engineer tested the air brakes of the campaign train while Dewey was giving a speech from the rear platform. The train gave a sudden jerk. Dewey told the crowd that they "should take that engineer out and shoot him at sunrise." Dewey thought that he was making a joke, but the remark, Warren believed, so chilling in its suggestion of patrician hauteur, compounded by Dewey's background as a prosecutor, helped him lose the 1948 election.[9]

What did Earl Warren bring to his pursuit of the presidency? He was the governor of a dynamic state, most obviously, second only to New York in population, and he enjoyed a solid record of administration and reform, in the prison system especially. As attorney general, Warren had inherited a correctional culture so lackadaisical that two well-heeled convicts from Folsom used to bribe their way to weekend furloughs in San Francisco, where they ensconced themselves in one or another of the better hotels with liquor and women. Having sent so many people to the slammer, Warren took a personal interest as attorney general and governor in the administrative reform and physical rehabilitation of the prison system. When an earthquake leveled the Women's Prison at Tehachapi fifty miles south of Bakersfield, Warren flew to the sight in his gubernatorial C-47 and personally supervised the housing of the women in hastily erected tents. As a goodwill gesture for their cooperation during the crisis, Warren shortened every inmate's sentence by thirty days.

Although the term had not yet been invented, Earl Warren was an avid environmentalist in the style of outdoorsmen who love to hike, camp, hunt, and fish. Warren knew by heart the environment and natural resources of California, river by river, mountain range by mountain range, forest by forest. As governor, Warren loved to fly across California in his converted C-47, named the *Grizzly Bear*. All in all, he racked up 250,000 air miles criss-crossing the state. To revitalize the Division of Forestry, Warren turned to Professor Emanuel Fritz of the Department of Forestry at UC Berkeley, a leading expert. As chairman of the state commission, Fritz oversaw the expansion and improvement of the Forestry Division and established a program of timber replenishment. To improve the conservation and management of wildlife resources in California, Warren turned to General of the Army Henry H. (Hap) Arnold, the retired chief of staff of the Army Air Forces, then living in Sonoma. As chairman of the Fish and Wildlife Commission, General Arnold put California in the forefront of the wildlife conservation movement, while at the same time maintaining a responsible fishing and hunting program under strict licensing.

To supervise the reform of California's overburdened and lethal road and highway system, Warren turned to Charles Purcell, the person most responsible for the successful construction of the San Francisco–Oakland Bay Bridge. Serving as state engineer at the time of his appointment, Purcell represented the essence of the Progressive public servant connected to that most beloved of all Progressive activities, public works. Summoned to Warren's office at the beginning of Warren's first term in 1943, Purcell brought along his maps and charts, believing that he was to be replaced as state engineer. To the contrary, Warren promoted him, putting him in charge of an ambitious new highway program. During the war,

Purcell devoted his best energies to keeping the road and highway system of California functional for defense shipments and troop movements. After the war, Purcell drew up plans for an entirely new system that was long overdue. Despite the prevalence of automobiles in California—one car for every 2.5 persons—more than one third of the fourteen thousand miles of highways in the state were two-lane roads no more than twenty feet in width. Purcell replaced this system with a billion-dollar master plan of freeways, highways, and county roads scheduled to take a decade to complete. Warren, meanwhile, fought to get through the legislature a tax of 1.5 cents per gallon on gas and 2.5 cents per gallon on diesel to finance this ambitious program. It took until 1953 for him to overcome the opposition of Big Oil and for the money to start rolling in.

As governor, Warren promoted an aggressive program of publicly sponsored health care. He reorganized and improved the state's Department of Public Health, paying especially close personal attention to programs in polio prevention, remembering initially the dying girl next door in Bakersfield, then the ordeal of Honey Bear. Going further, Warren established a Department of Mental Hygiene, which pioneered the employment of preventive and treatment-oriented mental health programs as part of the public health outreach of the state. In the liberal side of his complex cluster of liberal and conservative values, Warren was outspokenly in favor of a statewide program of state-sponsored health insurance. As early as 1944, discussion of a pre-paid comprehensive health insurance plan for California first surfaced as a recommendation of the Reconstruction and Reemployment Commission. Warren came closest to getting such a compulsory health insurance program through the legislature in 1947, but it was defeated in the legislative sessions of 1945, 1947, 1949, and 1950. Ironically, it was the campaign firm of Whitaker and Baxter, working for its client the California Medical Association, that did the most to sink Warren's proposal, with the suggestion that such a program would take California into socialized medicine. Indeed, this suggestion of socialism in Warren's early version of Medicare provoked great hostility in the ultra-conservative California Medical Association and the growing number of ultra-conservatives in Southern California, where it first began to be whispered about that Earl Warren was secretly a Communist, or at least a Communist sympathizer.

The long resistance of Big Oil to the highway tax and the ability of the California Medical Association, assisted by Whitaker and Baxter, to sink Warren's health insurance program underscored the difficulty of governing California. The same political system that had created Earl Warren—the absence, that is, of parties and party discipline, hence the multiplicity of private agendas among legislators; and the isolation of the individual voter, hence the susceptibility of the electorate to manipulation by mass media—also made it difficult to govern in a traditional manner. No one knew this better than Earl Warren's Falstaffian nemesis Arthur H. (Artie) Samish, the three hundred-plus-pound political boss of the state. If any one figure stood between Earl Warren and a clear-cut path to greatness as governor and beyond that to the presidency, it was this larger-than-life lobbyist, heroic in his consumption of food and drink, garish in a straw boater and glen plaid suit, holding forth in a haze of cigar smoke, bourbon in hand, in his suite in the Hotel Senator across the street from the state capitol.

Like Earl Warren, Artie Samish had gotten his start as a clerk in the legislature. Only Artie, a grade school dropout with a mother to support, did not have the same opportunities as Earl Warren, bachelor of arts and doctor of jurisprudence. Warren was a lawyer, an Old Blue, an Army lieutenant in a Sam Browne belt when he took a position in the legislature. Samish was a nobody from nowhere, just another fat guy from working-class San Francisco. And so while Earl Warren left the legislature to become a crusading DA, Artie Samish left it to become a lobbyist. Earl Warren sensed that in party-weak California, one could go directly to the voter as a non-partisan. Analyzing the same circumstances, Artie Samish realized that one could go directly to each legislator on behalf of a well-organized—and well-paying!—special interest or, if necessary, take the case of the special interest directly to the voter in a heavily financed campaign or, if further necessary, pay others to use the referendum and initiative process to get favorable legislation directly enacted by popular vote.

If Earl Warren was the Party of One, the Party of California, Artie Samish was his shadowy counterpart, his *Doppelgänger*, a Party of Special Interests, a parodic anti-type of Warren as man of virtue beholden to nobody. Samish was beholden to everybody, and everybody—or so it often seemed—was beholden to him. Earl Warren got by on his modest governor's salary. Artie Samish was making hundreds of thousands of dollars a year. At the height of his influence in the late 1940s, Samish's combined salaries, retainers, and expense accounts—his and those of his lieutenants—equaled the compensation of both houses of the legislature. While Earl Warren was speaking in high terms regarding his programs and the destiny of California, Samish was running money, votes, liquor, and women on behalf of his clients. While Warren dined quietly with his family in the governor's mansion or read the Bible to his children at bedtime, Samish was giving legendary parties that lasted for days in his suite at the Hotel Senator.

History will remember Samish as a pioneer of the special-interest oriented politics that would come increasingly to dominate California—and the nation. He was the Whitaker and Baxter of juice. Because parties were weak in California, special interest groups tended to organize themselves as direct-action organizations, bypassing political parties. Instead of going to party officials with their problems and needs, the special interests hired lobbyists and took their case directly to individual legislators in Sacramento. By the 1940s the pool of lobbyists in Sacramento had become a *de facto* third house of the state legislature. Shamelessly, Samish would work the floor, legislator by legislator, when the assembly or the senate was in session as if he were himself an elected official. Artie Samish became the political boss of California by orchestrating the flow of campaign contributions to candidates favoring his clients or, conversely, by financing opponents of candidates who were showing signs of being unwilling to take guidance from Artie. Like Warren, Samish was a consummate bipartisan politician. He would work to elect or defeat Democrats and Republicans alike, depending on their attitude toward his clients. Earl Warren openly admitted that in matters that pertained to his clients' interests, Artie Samish had more power than the governor.

Was Artie Samish corrupt? To ask this question is to ask the question: was California corrupt? For Artie Samish was merely exploiting the system as Progressives had established it. Samish did not bribe legislators. He contributed to their campaigns. Investigated in the late 1930s by H. R. Philbrick, a private detective in the employ of the grand jury, Samish was shown in the Philbrick Report of 1938 to be at the center of a network of special interest lobbying with tentacles reaching throughout the state. The grand jury discovered, among other things, that Samish had helped get the law firm of the speaker of the assembly on the payroll of the Santa Anita race track. The speaker, William Moseley Jones, had in turn appointed assemblymen to the Committee on Motor Vehicles and the Committee on Public Morals who made sure things came out all right for Santa Anita. Samish put the Republican floor leader Charles Lyon on retainer ($3,000 per year) to Samish's firm, in addition to getting him another $5,000 a year in legal fees from Samish clients in the horse racing, pinball, slot machine, commercial fishing, and liquor businesses. There were no indictments forthcoming, however, for there was no conclusive evidence that either Samish or the legislators had violated the law as it was then written. There is no evidence that Earl Warren, as either attorney general or governor, ever took on Artie Samish; nor is Samish discussed at any length in Warren's memoirs. Warren was capable of sending three hundred men out against the offshore gambling ships of Tony Cornero, but as an experienced prosecutor, he knew that Artie Samish was most likely operating within the limits of the system — or at least within the parameters of reasonable doubt.

In 1949 Artie Samish self-destructed because, like Rodney Dangerfield, he was tired of getting no respect. Samish had power in California but no respectability. Poignantly, Samish, the grade school dropout, helped his clients acquire power and riches; but they — the brewery executives, the insurance men, the oil executives, the liquor magnates, the transportation owners — never invited Artie to the party. Even the legislators whom he created were reluctant to be seen in public with Artie, although they would, under proper circumstances, partake of his hospitality in the Hotel Senator. Toward the end of his career, Samish would set up operations in the very lobby of the hotel — like A. P. Giannini managing the Bank of America from an open desk on the floor, in full view of the public — just to get people to acknowledge him openly. When Lester Velie, an associate editor of Collier's, interviewed Samish in his suite at the Senator in the late spring and early summer of 1949, Samish began to boast with the outspoken bravado of a man who most likely had more than a little booze under his size fifty-plus belt but who was also tired to the point of gross indiscretion of being the bag man, of doing the dirty work, for the entire state. Talking and talking to Velie, Samish told all: how the deals were done, how he made or unmade candidates, how he took care of his clients' interests. At one point in the interview, Artie rummaged in his closet and came up with a ventriloquist's dummy. He sat the dummy on his lap. "How are you today, Mr. Legislature?" Samish asked. A photographer from *Collier's* was in the room and caught the moment on film. Published in two parts on 13 and 20 August 1949, Velie's article, "The Secret Boss of California," consisted primarily of Samish's rambling monologue, garnished by photographs of Samish in a straw hat, white shirt, and suspenders, or talking on the telephone in a dressing gown that must have once belonged to Sidney Greenstreet, or — most shocking — talking to the dummy Mr. Legislature, perched on his knee.

Telling it all, letting the world know California's nasty secret — that the reforms of the Progressive era had been subverted, that California had become controlled by corporate and other interests and not the We-the-People so frequently invoked by the Progressives — Artie Samish pulled the plug on himself, as he perhaps subconsciously intended to do. The dummy Mr. Legislature proved especially galling to the solons Artie had to keep happy to stay in business. Ever seeking to come out from under Warren's shadow, Lieutenant Governor Goodwin Knight, a Republican from Southern California, and leaders from both parties demanded an open investigation into Artie Samish and all his works. Warren was goaded into calling for a special session in December 1949 to investigate and reform the lobbying system.

Even then, Artie Samish did not go gently into the good night. He lost influence, but there were no indictments, state or federal, connected with his lobbying activities. When they finally got Artie, it was the usual rap — income tax evasion, government's conviction of last resort — that brought him down. In the spring of 1953, Artie Samish was convicted in federal court of avoiding $71,878 in income taxes. Samish paid this sum, a $40,000 fine, and a rumored settlement of $750,000 for back taxes. He also served twenty-six months of a three-year sentence at McNeil Island Penitentiary in Washington State, where he lost weight. Emerging from confinement on 16 March 1958, Artie told the press that he never looked or felt better. Returning to San Francisco, Artie was soon a familiar figure, albeit reduced in girth, at the lunch table at Jack's or Bardelli's, where, as in the old days at the Hotel Senator, you could still hear the laughter from the bar and the banging of dice cups.

Warren's reluctance to confront the lobbyists' culture of California, or at least his reluctance to take on Artie Samish *mano a mano*, bothered *Inside USA* reporter John Gunther as he surveyed the state for the 1951 edition. Appearing before the Senate Crime Investigating Committee chaired by Senator Estes Kefauver, holding hearings in San Francisco, Samish was in remarkably good form. "Relax," he said to Kefauver at one point, easing into a yarn, as if the two of them, Artie and Estes, were sitting over bourbon in the lobby of the Hotel Senator. "This is a good story."[10]

It did not look too good for Warren, presidential candidate, to have the political system of California under review by the Kefauver Committee in 1951. Here was a California governor, after all, who had been on the cover of *Time* as early as 1944 and won an unprecedented third term in 1950 against the Democratic candidate, the eldest son of FDR, James Roosevelt, a forty-two-year-old Los Angeles insurance broker in the vanguard of a new genre, the celebrity candidate, which would one day put Ronald Reagan in Sacramento. (Other celebrity candidates in California included Will Rogers Jr., who ran for the Senate in 1947, and actor-director Orson Welles, who was seriously being discussed as another Senate possibility in 1946. Actress Helen Gahagan Douglas, wife of screen star Melvyn Douglas, was already representing Westside Los Angeles in the House of Representatives.) Entering the Democratic primary as well as the Republican, Warren won a million votes in the Democratic primary alone, coming within a mere hundred thousand votes of winning the Democratic nomination, a near-repeat of the five-card trump of 1946. As it was, Warren beat Roosevelt by more than a million votes in the general election. When Eleanor Roosevelt came to California to campaign on behalf of her son, telling reporters that she thought Jimmy would make a good governor, Warren responded: "I don't like to argue with a mother about her boy."[11]

It was the closest Earl Warren had ever come to wit. Since the mid-1940s the national media had found Earl Warren . . . well, a little dull, not that bright, as *Time* subtly suggested in 1944. As in the case of his liberal/conservative bifurcation, Earl Warren showed two sides to his nature when it came to brain power. He was, in one side of his identity, the first graduate of the Baker Street School in Bakersfield to go on to high school, much less college. In high school, however, he was teased by his classmates for his ability to get by with as little work as possible. There and at Berkeley, he had trouble with math. He had to cram to pass his trigonometry requirement. In law school Warren was almost mulish in his refusal to recite in class. The law school dean, William Carey Jones, warned him that he could be flunked out of law school for not reciting, but still Warren balked. He did not see the point of recitation. Ultimately Dean Jones backed off and allowed Warren to graduate on the basis of written work alone. In later life, Earl Warren, the rah-rah Old Blue, refused to name any professor at Berkeley who had had a special influence on his development. That would be a form of endorsement.

Earl Warren kept very few papers, wrote even fewer letters. If it were not for his posthumously published *Memoirs* (1977), which Warren worked on from early 1970 until his death on 9 July 1974, he would have left next to no statements regarding the texture and significance of his early life. There exists hardly any documentation of conversations, exchanges of opinion, or shared moments in which Earl Warren analyzed his motivations, expressed doubts, or reflected upon himself in any way. He was said to read the Bible on a regular basis and was a nominal Methodist who attended Baptist services in deference to his wife; yet nothing about him was touched by evangelical Protestant piety or sentiment, nothing that got to the surface at least. He was alleged to read serious books on American history in his private time, but one detects no evidence of it: no references to figures in American history in any diary or public utterance, no citations of any philosopher or social scientist or even an influential journalist in Warren's conversation or papers. A reading of the collected speeches of Earl Warren, gathered into one slim volume, remains a fail-safe cure for insomnia. San Francisco newspaper reporter Pierre Salinger observed of him: "He can pronounce publicly a platitude with a reassuring tone of discovering as if here, with the help of God, he has stumbled upon a hitherto unsuspected but eternal verity."[12]

Reporter John Gunther was forced to acknowledge Warren's achievements as governor. Despite the flourishing condition of California, however, Gunther could only bring himself to write: "Earl Warren is honest, likable, and clean; he will never set the world on fire or even make it smoke; he has the limitations of most Americans of his type; he is a man who has probably never bothered with an abstract thought twice in his life; a kindly man, with the best of social instincts, stable, and well-balanced; a man devoted to his handsome wife and six splendid children; not greedy, not a politician of the raucous, grasping kind that has despoiled so much in the United States; a 'typical' American in his bluffness, heartiness, healthy apple-pie atmosphere and love for joining things; a man glad to carry a bundle for his missus in the neighborhood supermarket and have an evening out with the boys once in a while; a man with nothing of a 'grand line' and little inner force, to throw out centrifugal or illuminating sparks; a friendly, pleasant, average Californian; no more a statesman in the European sense than Typhoid Mary is Einstein; and a man who, quite possibly and with luck, could make a quite tolerable president of the United States."[13]

Thus assessed (and with him, California assessed as well) Earl Warren pushed toward the 1952 Republican convention in Chicago with a mixed reputation in the minds of the Republican establishment. Warren was small-town in background, public-school, and an Old Blue. The East Coast Republican establishment was prep-school and Ivy League, with strong connections to West Point and Annapolis. Warren was regional and untouched by foreign affairs. The Eastern Republican establishment was mid-Atlantic and internationalist. Warren read the Sacramento *Bee*. Eastern Republicans read the New York *Times*. The Eastern Republican establishment was very rich. Earl Warren lived on his modest income. There were no royalties, no honorariums, no sweet deals sent his way by loyal supporters, no connections to Wall Street. For all his prominence as governor of the most vividly ascendant state in the nation, there were for Earl Warren no prestigious speaking engagements, no invitations to exclusive forums, no honorary doctorates from Harvard or Yale. It took until 1950 for East Coast Republicans to invite Warren out for a speech, a Lincoln Day address to the Middlesex Club of Boston, the oldest Republican Club in the nation.

Yet Warren pushed on toward his goal, wanting the presidency, really wanting it, for the first time in his life. He was sixty-two. This was his last shot at a national career. Thirty-five years earlier, the two-term governor Hiram Johnson had shaken the dust of Sacramento from his feet and headed to Washington as United States senator with an almost audible sigh of relief. Johnson's wife Minerva (Minnie) hated the hot, dry, dusty country town where she had grown up and where California did its statewide business. As of 1952 the Warrens would have been in Sacramento for a decade. Time to push on, lest one be forced to contemplate an unprecedented fourth term as governor, or go on the bench, or return to private life, in which Warren had little interest and next to no experience.

As barriers between Warren and his goal stood two men, General of the Army Dwight David Eisenhower, on leave from his post as president of Columbia University to serve as Supreme Commander of NATO, and Senator Robert Alonzo Taft of Ohio, the eldest son of a former president. Taft was beatable, Warren believed, because he was devoid of liberal credentials, was in fact the co-author of the Taft-Hartley Act of 1947, which drove Warren's union friends to a condition of choler approaching apoplexy. Eisenhower was another matter.

Was Warren deluded in his aspirations? Doomed perhaps — but not deluded. In seven short years, he had become a respected national figure, despite his lack of links to the Eastern Republican establishment. A Gallup poll taken in late 1951 showed that Earl Warren could beat Harry Truman if Truman ran for a second full term and if Earl Warren was the Republican nominee. Beyond a mere victory, the poll predicted a landslide. A poll of union leaders throughout the country determined that Earl Warren would run better than any other Republican candidate among rank-and-file working people.

In the fall of 1951, Earl Warren suffered a major setback, a diagnosis of abdominal cancer, and was operated on. Former President Herbert Hoover, among others, spread the rumor that the doctors had opened Warren, taken a look, and sewn him up as a hopeless case. The rumor was false. Warren recovered rapidly and seemed in full strength when he announced his intention to run for President at a press conference in his office in the capitol on 4 November 1951, but continuing rumors regarding his health weakened his campaign. Warren entered the Wisconsin primary in the spring of 1952 and placed a very respectable fifty thousand votes behind Taft. To no one's surprise, Warren swept the California primary. Eisenhower, who was still in uniform in Europe, entered neither race. Warren recognized the attraction of the charismatic general, who had only recently declared himself a Republican, biding his time in high command, but the Californian still saw himself as a plausible alternative should Taft and Eisenhower cancel each other out at the convention. Still, Warren bristled when reporters suggested he was a mere stalking horse for Ike. Again and again, Warren insisted that he was a viable candidate.

Enter the junior senator from California, Richard Milhous Nixon. The day after Warren had declared his intention to run, Nixon was asked to comment. "I would say Senator Taft and General Ike are the front runners," Nixon said, "with Governor Warren the strongest dark horse."[14] The fact that Nixon was correct in his assessment was almost beside the point. The junior senator was not planning to play an observer's role.

In June 1945 Nixon, an obscure Navy lieutenant attached to a legal unit in New York City, had watched from his twentieth-floor office window on Church Street as Eisenhower passed in a ticker-tape parade. The gap between the rumpled reserve lieutenant and the triumphant five-star general twenty floors below could not have been greater. In 1949 Congressman Nixon first met Eisenhower, then president of Columbia University, when Eisenhower had requested a briefing on the internal security threat posed by Communists in the United States. As a member of the House Un-American Activities Committee, Nixon provided Eisenhower with the briefing. The young congressman was ecstatic at having been ushered into the presence of the great man himself. At the Bohemian Grove encampment of July 1950, Nixon, now running for the United States Senate, once again met Eisenhower, this time at Cave Man Camp, where former President Herbert Hoover gave a luncheon in Eisenhower's honor. Sitting, as he remembered it, "about two places from the bottom" of the long table, Nixon listened as Eisenhower spoke extemporaneously, without polish, applauded only when he endorsed the loyalty oath at Berkeley. From the perspective of the Southern California–dominated Hoover wing of the Republican Party in California—with Hoover himself presiding in rustic splendor at his camp—the barely articulate Eisenhower stood in no danger of replacing the charismatic and articulate Taft.

A year later at the Bohemian Grove, conversations at Cave Man took another turn entirely as liquor industry executive Ellis Slater, a close personal friend of Eisenhower's, made an impassioned plea on Eisenhower's behalf to the Chief, as Hoover was called in the Grove, and the other corporate bigwigs gathered at another Cave Man luncheon. Taft was a fine Republican, Slater remarked, but he could not win Democratic votes, and only a Republican with a strong constituency among Democrats, such as Eisenhower, could become President. A week later, at the Bohemian Club clubhouse in San Francisco, Slater gave another stirring talk on Eisenhower's behalf—and for the first time mentioned the newly elected United States senator Richard Milhous Nixon as a possible running mate. Five days later, Slater was at NATO headquarters in Paris, lunching and golfing with Eisenhower and informing him that Richard Nixon had strong support in the conservative wing of the Republican Party.

The rise of Richard Nixon in five years from naval reserve lieutenant to senator and a leading vice presidential possibility, working energetically, if discreetly, on Eisenhower's behalf, must have nettled Earl Warren, although he never said so, at least in public. Posed alongside each other in the presidential campaign of 1952, the sixty-one-year-old governor and the thirty-eight-year-old senator, as men, as types, embodied to perfection a contrast of generations, regions, values, and styles that juxtaposed one California against another. Genial and open in demeanor; calm, self-assured; fair, blond, bland, Warren stood in dramatic contrast to the neurotic and insecure Nixon, self-conscious, unfavored in features, plagued by an

ominous five-o'clock shadow and a tendency to break out in nervous sweats. Warren stood calmly and smiled to the crowd. Nixon had a tendency to hunch, clasp
his hands, and shift his eyes nervously above a feral smile. Each man had come
from simple circumstances in the southern tier of the state, but Earl Warren had
seemed to move serenely through life, from success to success, convinced that
everyone was on his side. Nixon never felt such approval (and rarely received it)
and was forced to calculate each move. Earl Warren wooed his wife effortlessly.
From the time they first met, it was just a case of when they could afford to get
married. Nixon was forced to lay siege to Pat Ryan in the face of her ceaseless
rejections. Merely to remain in contact with her, he drove her to dates with other
men. Warren established a powerful family identity in the mind of the public.
Although he was married to an equally beautiful woman and had two equally
beautiful daughters, Richard Nixon seemed oddly detached from his family as far
as public appearances were concerned. People seemed surprised that Nixon should
have such an attractive, kindly wife and such gracious and accomplished children.
Sharing their husbands' fates, Nina Warren went on from triumph to triumph;
Pat Nixon was forced to play out on behalf of her husband a role of Shakespearean
proportions.

   In geographical terms, Nixon represented Southern California, with its deep
connections to the rising plutocratic conservativism of the prosperous Sun Belt.
Warren, by contrast, was a Northern Californian by choice and a Progressive by
temperament, playing to the non-partisan center while Nixon played to the center-
right. Nixon cut his political teeth on the Alger Hiss–Whittaker Chambers case as
a junior member of the House Un-American Activities Committee. In his race for
the Senate in 1950, he savaged his opponent, Congresswoman Helen Gahagan
Douglas, for allegedly voting the Communist Party line. Warren shared Nixon's
anti-Communist fervor, but after the *Point Lobos* case and the scuttling of Max
Radin for the state supreme court he tended to float above discussions of Communist conspiracy. Warren also kept his distance from the corporate, legal, and
financial bigwigs who dominated Republican Party fundraising. Nixon welcomed
their help. Because of his federal career, Nixon developed a first-rate knowledge
of foreign affairs. Warren remained focused on California. Earl Warren represented the self-assured serenity of the Bay Area, where he had lived since his late
teens. Nixon epitomized the more fluid and insecure social structures of Southern
California, a region where men who had arrived did not feel it, and those who
had failed felt it too much. Northern Californians tended to pursue more stable
careers, and by and large they seemed more content to remain within more modest
limits. Southern Californians over-reached, connived, schemed, failed frequently,
reinvented themselves and began anew. Like Bostonians in New York, Northern
Californians such as Warren felt faintly aghast at the vivid spectacle of the Southland. Even the most successful of them confessed a lack of ease when moving
through its aggressively plutocratic savannahs.

   "We are not unfriendly," Richard Nixon said of Earl Warren. "We are two individuals going our own way."[15] Who was Nixon kidding? The two men distrusted each other from the beginning. Nixon resented Warren's refusal to endorse him or otherwise to help him in his campaigns of 1946, 1948, and 1950. As a delegate to the Republican National Convention in Chicago in July 1952, Richard Nixon was pledged to California's favorite son. Under California rules, Nixon was obligated to vote for Earl Warren on the first ballot and was expected not to campaign on behalf of any other candidate until released from his pledge by the governor. The other United States senator, William Knowland, favored Taft — was, in fact, Taft's most likely choice for the vice presidency, should Taft win the nomination — but Knowland kept his pledge to Warren; indeed, Knowland headed the California delegation that boarded the eighteen-car Warren Special heading for Chicago from the Bay Area in July 1952 and was scheduled to nominate Warren at the convention. The Warren family joined the governor in his private car. Once again, the Warren girls, blonde and tan, worked their magic. In the club car, one delegate sat down at the piano, and the Warren girls danced with others.

Richard Nixon flew out to Denver from Chicago, where he had already been busy on Eisenhower's behalf, and at nine-thirty on the evening of 4 July 1952 boarded the Warren Special. Warren supporters later described the ensuing day and a half as the Great Train Robbery. Once aboard, Nixon was ushered into Earl Warren's private car. Again, it was a scene of Shakespearean proportions: the fatally wounded Earl Warren, the older man ostensibly being soothed by the young senator, ski-nosed, his face dark with five o'clock shadow, thick in the middle of a barely concealed plot to hijack Warren's delegation and deliver it to Ike. The exact nature of Nixon's activities on the Warren Special remains a matter of controversy. There was strong evidence that Nixon moved from car to car, delegate to delegate, suggesting to each and all that Earl Warren could not win, that the California delegation should swing to Ike. As evidence, Nixon had in hand a private poll he had sent to twenty-three thousand contributors in his former congressional district asking them who they thought would be the strongest Republican nominee. As might be expected, Eisenhower won the popularity contest. (Warren supporters were furious that Nixon used his franking privileges to conduct such partisan activity.) Then there was the *Time* magazine article claiming that fully fifty-six out of seventy votes in the California delegation would go to Eisenhower if Warren would release them.

When the Warren Special pulled into the Chicago terminal, the California delegation posed *en masse* for photographers. Richard Nixon was nowhere to be seen. He had left the train at a suburb outside the city. After the photo session, the Warren delegation piled onto buses arranged for it by Nixon's aide Murray Chotiner. Plastered across the side of each bus were IKE FOR PRESIDENT banners. Warren flushed with anger at this Dirty Trick. He demanded that the banners be pulled from the buses before the delegation was driven to its hotel.

Two contenders, Warren and Taft, equally doomed, now confronted the conquering general who had never run for office. On the first ballot, Earl Warren received eighty-one votes. Eisenhower was only nine votes short of nomination. Only when Harold Stassen and the Minnesota delegation voted to make Eisenhower's nomination unanimous did Warren release his delegates. Although he had kept the California delegation pledged to his doomed hopes, he had earlier helped a pro-Eisenhower delegation be seated in a pre-convention dispute regarding credentials. Generously, when a deadlock between Taft and Ike might have represented his only chance for nomination, Warren favored the seating of two contested Eisenhower delegations. "If anyone ever clinched the nomination for me," Eisenhower later said, "it was Earl Warren."[16]

Warren played no role in the selection of Nixon as vice presidential candidate; indeed, he was excluded from all inner-circle meetings throughout the convention and the campaign. Once Nixon was the nominee, Warren behaved impeccably. At a reception in Whittier, Mrs. Warren held one of the Nixon girls on her lap. Eisenhower took California by more than seven hundred thousand votes.

Earl Warren never went so far as to accuse Richard Nixon of violating his oath as a delegate and working secretly for Eisenhower aboard the Warren Special, but he never dispelled the suggestion either. Already, at the convention, some California delegates, angry at Nixon's treatment of Warren, were muttering that Richard Nixon was the kept man of conservative Southern California interests. A few weeks later, it was perhaps a disgruntled Warren supporter who leaked to the press the allegation that Nixon was benefiting from a secret slush fund set up by Southern California Republicans to supplement the senator's income. The disclosure nearly cost Nixon his place on the ticket, until he recovered himself in late September by means of his nationally televised Checkers speech. During the height of the slush fund controversy, there was talk of replacing Nixon on the Republican ticket with Earl Warren.

At the Eisenhower inaugural in January 1953, the Warren girls, as usual, stole the show. In the spring, President Eisenhower asked Earl Warren to join the United States delegation to the coronation of Queen Elizabeth II at Westminster Abbey on 2 June 1953. It was a heady time for the Earl Warrens of Oakland and Sacramento, as they socialized at state occasions with the young Queen, the Queen Mother, and the Duke of Edinburgh. Once again Governor and Mrs. Warren brought their daughters along, and once again the Warren girls charmed everyone as they were presented to the highest circles of British society: these golden California girls, middle-class royalty from a middle-class state. At a dance in London during the coronation festivities, Michael Davie, an undergraduate at Merton College, Oxford, found himself dancing with Honey Bear Warren from UCLA. As Davie circled the floor with Honey Bear—blonde hair, tan skin, white teeth, picture-perfect features—he felt as if he were dancing with California herself. Years later, Davie confessed: "I still see California through a faint golden haze engendered among the pale London faces by the peach-fed Honey-bear from Sacramento."[17]

10

1949 ✻ Mexicali Rose

IN January 1949 James Corley, comptroller of the University of California, alerted UC president Robert Gordon Sproul as to the situation in Sacramento. Once again, Corley told Sproul, State Senator John Tenney, chairman of the Joint Fact-Finding Committee on Un-American Activities in California, was on the warpath against the university. The Los Angeles County state senator was planning to introduce a bill calling for a constitutional amendment removing the governance of UC from its autonomous Board of Regents and placing the university directly under the control of the legislature. The measure would demand a loyalty oath of every faculty member and employee. Tenney was also introducing bills outlawing the teaching of Communism in schools, requiring loyalty oaths of all candidates for public office, discharging subversives in the defense industry, and empowering unions to expel Communists from their ranks. On the one hand, Corley and Sproul had every confidence that Governor Warren, Old Blue extraordinary and *ex officio* chair of the regents, would head off Tenney's blatant maneuver, with its threat to make UC directly accountable to the people, which is to say, to such elected representatives of the people as State Senator Jack Tenney, a onetime dance hall pianist, composer of the song "Mexicali Rose." On the other hand, Tenney's threatened bill was worrisome. Tenney might very well have the votes. The rotund state senator, after all, chaired a committee responsible for ferreting out what was on everyone's mind in 1949: Communism with a capital C, the Soviet-directed conspiracy that had recently gobbled up Eastern Europe and was even now threatening, so Tenney was quick to point out, the existence of the Republic itself. The budget of the university was set by the legislature, and for nearly a decade Senator Tenney had been hounding UC with charges of Communist infiltration. Neither Corley nor Sproul, each of whom had come up through the financial and budgetary division of the university, underestimated

Tenney's ability to make mischief, if not with the governance of the university, then at least with its budget.

Comptroller Corley had an idea: why not have the Board of Regents pass a measure requiring a loyalty oath from the faculty and staff of the university as a way of outmaneuvering Tenney and his Red-baiting pals? After all, ever since 1940 UC faculty had been required to take an oath of allegiance as a precondition for appointment. Why not add to this oath an explicit rejection of membership in the Communist Party and adherence of any sort to Communist doctrine? Sproul agreed to take Corley's proposal to the regents.

On 25 March 1949 the regents met on the Santa Barbara campus of UC. High on their agenda for discussion was the ongoing investigation of alleged Communist infiltration at UCLA by the Tenney Committee. Being in Tenney's district and having the reputation of being a shade pinker than the other Cal campuses, UCLA was Tenney's favorite target in the UC system. The regents were clearly worried about UCLA, and Regent Edward Dickson, who had virtually founded the UCLA campus in the late 1920s, asked for a closed, off-the-record discussion to follow the afternoon meeting open to the public. In the course of this executive session, President Sproul proposed an expanded version of the loyalty oath. By resolution adopted by the regents in June 1942, Sproul pointed out, every appointee to the university was required to swear to support the Constitution of the United States and the Constitution of the State of California. Since the university was being hammered on all sides for, at minimum, its alleged vulnerability to Communist influence, Sproul continued, why not recast the oath to read: "I do solemnly swear (or affirm) that I do not believe in, and I am not a member of, nor do I support any party or organization that believes in, advocates, or teaches the overthrow of the United States Government, by force or by any illegal or unconstitutional methods; that I will support the Constitution of the United Sates and the Constitution of the State of California, and that I will faithfully discharge the duties of my office according to the best of my ability"? That, Sproul hoped, should take care of the Communist question.[1]

After some discussion and some further massaging of language, the regents voted the resolution into effect. Sproul and the regents (as president Sproul sat *ex officio* on the board) left the meeting fully convinced that they had outmaneuvered the troublesome composer of "Mexicali Rose." Such an oath (and Sproul had no doubt that he could persuade the faculty to take it) should disprove once and for all Senator Tenney's contention that the blue and gold of UC ran strong with streaks of subversive Red.

A few weeks later, in early May, Representative Richard Nixon and his friend and political supporter Frank Jorgensen, an insurance man living in San Marino, were sitting up late in their compartment in the Lark, the overnight Southern Pacific train connecting Los Angeles and San Francisco. That afternoon over lunch at the Pacific Union Club atop Nob Hill, Jorgensen had introduced Nixon to a group of prominent Northern California Republicans as "the next senator from the state of California." The group, gathered at the invitation of Albert Mattei, president of the Honolulu Oil Company, found Jorgensen's introduction of the young congressman perfectly plausible, and, in the discussion that followed, the Bay Area oligarchs began to list possible financial backers for a Nixon campaign for the United States Senate. While the *Lark* sped southward to Los Angeles that night, Nixon and Jorgensen, sitting in their shorts against the heat of a muggy evening, discussed the favorable reception they had met with that day. As the evening drew to a close, Nixon fell into long and quiet thought. Just before Jorgensen climbed into the upper bunk, Nixon said: "We're going to go." Before they slept, Nixon and Jorgensen agreed that Murray Chotiner, the Beverly Hills lawyer and political lobbyist who had run Nixon's 1946 campaign for the House, would be retained to run the Senate effort. "You make your deal with him," Nixon told Jorgensen, just before he turned out the lights.[2]

In 1946 Richard Nixon got his political start—very dramatically, going to the House of Representatives in his first try at elective office—in a campaign against the Democratic incumbent Jerry Voorhis that had one, and only one, issue: whether Voorhis had been soft on Communism. There could be no greater evocation of two Southern Californias, one in decline, the other rising, than the contrast between Voorhis, the paradigm of the Fabian patricians who had helped create Southern California earlier in the century, and the pragmatic conservative Richard Nixon, the essence of the New Man.

Like so many prominent Southern Californians of his generation, Jeremiah Voorhis had grown up rich, Episcopalian, and Republican in the Midwest. After Hotchkiss, Voorhis had gone on to Yale, graduating Phi Beta Kappa in 1923. Identifying with "the gospel of Christian involvement" as preached by J. Stitt Wilson, an evangelist and Socialist mayor of Berkeley, whom Voorhis had first heard preach at Yale, the idealistic young graduate turned his back on a life of country club prosperity in favor of factory work, a tour of German slums, a stint in an Episcopal orphanage in Wyoming, and, ultimately, the use of his family fortune to found the Voorhis School for Boys, a haven for homeless young men near San Dimas in the Pomona Valley, not far from Whittier. Initially a Socialist, Voorhis changed to a New Deal Democrat during the Depression. He helped local farmers organize cooperatives and walked on picket lines, ever in search of the Kingdom of God on earth. In 1934 Voorhis ran for the state assembly as a supporter of Upton Sinclair's EPIC (End Poverty in California) and was defeated. In 1936 he won election to the House of Representatives for the Twelfth District in eastern Los Angeles County, where for the next decade—rumpled, tweedy, pipe-smoking, more professor than politician—Jerry Voorhis earned a reputation as a liberal's liberal.

As long as the Twelfth District was a quiet enclave of ranches and small towns, and as long as Los Angeles County remained predominantly Democratic under Olson or bipartisan under Earl Warren, Jerry Voorhis fit his district. Men and women such as he, after all, educated Easterners with a touch of millenarianism, had played a major role in the creation of the Southland. But as the war came, and Southern California grew, and the post-war era set in, with its great stakes, its promise of financial windfalls as millions of new Californians poured in and the big boom began, Jerry Voorhis, despite the fact that he was only in his early forties, began to take on a dated mien. He belonged to a Southern California passing from the scene, a world of plain living and high thinking amongst the orange groves.

And besides: Jerry Voorhis had antagonized the big boys. He had opposed Standard Oil for its exploitation of federal oil reserves at Elk Hills, blasted the insurance companies for their exemption from anti-trust regulations, advocated public power, cited the necessity of public housing as well as private suburbs, supported strikers in Hollywood, and denounced the expansion of the Bank of America at the expense of small banks. Voorhis went so far as to refuse to prefix his name with "The Honorable," citing it as elitist and a waste of paper. Jerry Voorhis had definitely thrown down the gauntlet to the corporate interests in control of the great Southern California boom.

Backed by Southern California banking and insurance interests, by developers and oil men, Richard Nixon, assistant city attorney of Whittier, given to wearing his Navy uniform at public events, the two and a half gold stripes of a lieutenant commander on his sleeves, was more than eager to take up the challenge thrown down by Voorhis as to just exactly who would run post-war Southern California. Born to obscurity, repeatedly humiliated in his rise in life, Nixon had been nurtured in an atmosphere of lower-middle-class conservatism, with all its suspicions and resentments, and was in the process of moving even further to the right. Jerry Voorhis had had it all and had given it away. Richard Nixon had worn an apron in his father's store and sold fruit and produce, even after finishing law school, had been rebuffed by Wall Street, and had been sent home to a minor job in Whittier, even after his commissioned service in the Pacific. In the anachronistic and vulnerable Voorhis, so redolent of EPIC and the crackpot idealism of the Depression, Richard Nixon saw a one-way ticket out of Whittier. A year after his defeat, Voorhis was still in a state of shock at the *Blitzkrieg* with which Nixon had ended his political career. "The bitterest campaign I have ever experienced," he called it, a typical Voorhis understatement for a bruising assault, masterminded by Beverly Hills lawyer and lobbyist Murray Chotiner.[3]

First of all, Nixon had all the money he needed and then some. In October 1945, Voorhis claimed, a representative of a prominent New York financial house made calls on a number of influential people in Southern California and upbraided them for allowing Voorhis to represent their region in the House. Big Eastern money had joined Southern Californian money, Voorhis claimed, to back Nixon and blast the pipe-smoking former Socialist out of the Congress. Again and again during the campaign, Nixon hammered Voorhis with the charge that Voorhis had been endorsed by the Political Action Committee of the CIO, a Communist front. Nixon's charge that the CIO PAC was a Communist front could plausibly be argued, yet Voorhis had not been endorsed by this organization. He had been considered for endorsement, on the other hand, but rejected by the National Citizens Political Action Committee (Ronald Reagan was a member), a left-liberal organization that worked in concert with the CIO PAC.

Voorhis fought back with newspaper advertisements stating he was proud to have been endorsed by the AFL and the Railroad Brotherhoods, but he was also proud that the top leadership of the California CIO had refused to endorse him. Stumbling in his denial, Voorhis admitted in his ad that "there is at least grave question whether the Communist Party does not exercise inordinate if not decisive influence" in the state and county CIO leadership.[4] Thus, in the course of denying Nixon's charges, Voorhis poured fuel on the flames. Even he, a liberal's liberal, was admitting that the statewide and Los Angeles County CIO leadership was Communist-controlled. Voorhis found himself savaged in Twelfth District newspapers for voting the CIO PAC line in Congress forty-six times. Voorhis retorted that the votes in question were for such things as a school lunch program and a bill to allow soldiers in uniform to vote. Yet one of the votes at issue was a vote against allowing the House committee investigating un-American activities to continue, and Nixon made the most of it.

In a debate, the first of five, held in the auditorium of the South Pasadena–San Marino Junior High School on Friday, 13 September 1946, Nixon savaged Voorhis, not with the CIO PAC charge, which even Nixon had abandoned after Voorhis's newspaper rebuttal, but with a claim that Voorhis had been supported by the National Citizens PAC, an organization dominated by the Communist Party. As a point of fact, neither the CIO PAC nor the National Citizens PAC had endorsed Voorhis, but the point became moot as a packed auditorium, masterfully programmed by Chotiner, cheered Nixon and booed the hapless incumbent into history.

Nixon's anti-Communist crusade was only in part about Communism. In Southern California at least, the very heart of Nixon country, anti-Communism also framed the debate regarding development. For all its boom mentality, pre–World War II Southern California had paradoxically sustained within itself a quirky tendency to the left, even among developers. H. Gaylord Wilshire and John Randolph Haynes, for example, two of the most successful developers of the pre- and post– First World War era, were committed Socialists. Pasadena sustained a flourishing Fabian socialist circle among its millionaires. The post–Second World War boom, by contrast, was controlled by shadowy corporations and banks and equally shadowy developers who pushed the anti-Communism issue and supported anti-Communist politicians such as Richard Nixon. By so doing, the pro-development forces sought to create by implication and psychological association a strong counter-argument and counter-force in favor of laissez-faire growth. The anti-Communist crusade, in short, helped soften up innumerable city councils, planning commissions, and zoning boards, threatening them with the implied argument: regulation of growth replicates the planned economies and political controls of Communism.

In his best-selling novel *The Ninth Wave* (1956), UC Berkeley political scientist Eugene Burdick depicted this strategy in great detail. Burdick's protagonist Hank Moore is a Southern Californian up from nowhere, just like Nixon, who becomes, simultaneously, a Southern California developer and a behind-the-scenes political operative who hopes to use the anti-Communist issue to destabilize, then control, government in California, state and local, so as to create a government-weak environment in which developers might have the advantage. Among his contemporaries, only Eugene Burdick seems to have grasped the confluence of anti-Communism and runaway development that helped put Richard Nixon in the House and Senate.

As a freshman congressman, Nixon won a coveted seat on the House Committee on Un-American Activities, more commonly known as the House Un-American Activities Committee, an ironic reversal of words suggesting that the committee was designated to carry on un-American activities, an idea with which many might agree. The HUAC was chaired by Republican congressman J. Parnell Thomas of New Jersey—a burly man like State Senator Jack Tenney of Los Angeles, flush-faced like Tenney, and also given to pinstriped double-breasted suits, and like Tenney a politician up from nowhere: a man who had changed his name from John Parnell Feeney Jr. and his religion from Catholic to Mason-Episcopalian to evade his less than fashionable origins.

In October and November 1947, in hearings held in the Caucus Room of the Old House Office Building in Washington, Thomas and his committee returned to some unfinished business, Communism in Hollywood. In 1940–41, the committee, then chaired by Representative Martin Dies of Texas, had engaged in a preliminary skirmish against the Hollywood Reds but backed off when the Soviet Union and the United States became wartime allies. The Dies Committee had been curious about what it called "premature anti-fascism" in Hollywood, which is to say, anti-fascist activity the committee suspected was Communist-inspired, such as the formation of the Hollywood Anti-Nazi League in 1936, which sponsored the visit of French novelist turned Loyalist aviator André Malraux. Arriving in Los Angeles on behalf of the Spanish Republic in 1937, Malraux was lionized (fifteen movie stars contributed $15,000 each) and ended his visit with a mass rally in the Shrine Auditorium in the course of which hundreds of supporters, many of them in formal evening wear, returned Malraux's clenched-fisted salute. Dies was also interested in such prematurely anti-fascist films as *Confessions of a Nazi Spy* (1939) from Warner Brothers and Charlie Chaplin's *The Great Dictator* (1940) and was on the trail of suspected British agent Alexander Korda's efforts to involve the United States in the war on behalf of Great Britain; but Pearl Harbor ended that line of inquiry as well.

After the war, it was "no more Mr. Nice Guy" for Dies's successor, J. Parnell

Thomas. Internally and externally, Hollywood was in trouble on the Communist issue and on other matters. Among other things, there was television. By late 1947 sets were selling at the rate of two hundred thousand per month. The number of television stations had jumped to forty-one in less than three years. During World War II, movie tickets were selling at the rate of eighty-five million per week, peaking at ninety million a week in 1946. With the advent of television, ticket purchases dropped precipitously. By 1956 they averaged forty-seven million a week, slightly more than half the 1946 market. Studio employment fell by a quarter in 1948. As of February 1949 only twenty-two features were in production, half the output of the war and immediately post-war years. In 1948 the Justice Department successfully concluded its long-standing case against Paramount, Warner Brothers, RKO, Twentieth Century–Fox, and Loew's-MGM, forcing these vertically inte-grated giants to separate their production companies from their distribution agen-cies and theater chains.

What turned out to be a decade of woe for Hollywood opened in 1945 with two years of ferocious strikes in which Communist and anti-Communist elements in the various unions struggled for power. The 1945 strike lasted 238 days. On 5 October 1945 there was a tear-gas and fire-hose confrontation outside Warner Brothers. In late September 1946 picket lines went up once again outside Warner Brothers, MGM, RKO, and other studios. This time, the mood was even more angry, with striking workers belonging to the Conference of Studio Unions pre-venting other employees from entering or exiting the studios. There were frequent confrontations, mass arrests, and the trials of dozens of strikers on various charges. Hollywood became an industrial nightmare. (On the other hand, non-striking em-ployees frequently made the best of it. At RKO, for example, non-striking em-ployees trapped in the studio by pickets dined free in the commissary; poorly paid secretaries wolfed down meals more suited to burly stagehands and grips. Return-ing to his office at the conclusion of the strike, an RKO executive found it littered with empty liquor bottles and used condoms: evidence of the unexpected satur-nalia the strike had brought to at least one group of besieged employees.)

The strikes of 1945 and 1946 represented a three-way struggle among the studios, the International Alliance of Theatrical and Stage Employees, and the Conference of Studio Unions. Led by Roy Brewer, a crusading anti-Communist, IATSE was a main-line AFL union with a troubled past. In the late 1930s two of its leaders, George E. Browne and Willie Bioff, had shaken down studio officials, including Louis B. Mayer. Indicted, tried, and convicted, Browne and Bioff went to prison in 1941. Organized that same year, the CSU was in part a reform organization, a protest against the Browne and Bioff era at IATSE. Dominated by Herbert Sorrell, a former prizefighter, the CSU enlisted such critical organizations as the Screen Cartoonists, the Screen Office Employees Guild, the Film Technicians, the Ma-chinists Union, and the Motion Picture Painters. The Technicians (Local 683), Machinists (Local 1185), and Painters (Local 644) had previously belonged to IATSE, which found their defection to the CSU especially embittering.

It is uncertain whether Herbert Sorrell, leader of the CSU, was a Party member. It was apparent from the start, however, that the CSU had a strong Communist presence in its leadership structure. Whether or not he carried a card, Herbert Sorrell made every effort to align the CSU with Party doctrine. For two years Hollywood played out—sometimes violently on the streets—a scenario of industrial strife with radicals and Communists on one side, the anti-Communist IATSE on the other, and arch-conservative studio moguls playing both ends against the middle.

Executive Hollywood was on the defensive, then, when the House Committee on Un-American Activities sent out its subpoenas in the fall of 1947. First of all, there were the strikes themselves, which had brought the studios dangerously close to being dominated by the Communist-controlled Conference of Studio Unions, which did not look good to Washington. Then there was the embarrassing matter of the pro-Soviet films produced during the war. The war, in fact, offered pro-Soviet screenwriters the opportunity of a lifetime. Prior to the war, Hollywood demanded a distanced, at best satiric, approach to Soviet society as in the case of *Ninotchka* (1939), starring Greta Garbo as a Soviet commissar who falls in love with the Western way of life. By 1943 John Howard Lawson, the archdeacon of Hollywood Communists, could put a scene in the film *Action in the North Atlantic*, starring Humphrey Bogart, in which a Soviet plane is openly described by American merchant mariners under torpedo attack from Nazis as "one of ours." *Mission to Moscow* (1943), directed by Michael Curtiz from a script by Howard Koch, based on the book of the same name by Joseph Davies, former United States ambassador to the USSR, represented an uninterrupted paean to Soviet society in general and Josef Stalin in particular, including a whitewashing of Stalin for the purges of 1937. Although on the left, Koch was not a Party member, and there is some evidence that Roosevelt himself requested Jack Warner to do the film; but by 1947 this most openly pro-Stalinist film made during the war was proving an embarrassment: as were *North Star* (1943), directed by Party member Lewis Milestone from a script by Party sympathizer Lillian Hellman, two of Hollywood's most ardent Stalinophiles, and *Song of Russia* (1944), directed by the Russian-born Gregory Ratoff, in which Robert Taylor played an American conductor touring the Soviet Union as the Germans invade.

By 1947 Hollywood moguls such as Jack Warner had grown fearful at what they had done. They had celebrated Stalin as a great world statesman, musing over maps and spinning globes with Davies and Churchill. They had recognized Soviet aircraft as our own and depicted a utopian Russia—nightclubs, dancing peasants, Tchaikovsky music everywhere—more idealized than any Soviet propaganda would dare attempt. The mood of the nation had shifted abruptly to the right in 1946. A scene in *The Best Years of Our Lives* in which a home-town banker refuses a loan to a returning GI without sufficient collateral came under violent criticism for being anti-American.

The fact is: Hollywood did support a flourishing Communist community from

1936 onward. In her posthumously published *The Hollywood Writers' Wars* (1982), Nancy Lynn Schwartz chronicled the rich range and extent of Communist Party culture in Hollywood during these years. Schwartz's depiction is valuable because she herself was sympathetic to the Left, the Communist Party included; hence her account is free of both the witch-hunting from the Right and the denial from the Left that cloud most accounts of Communist Party activity in Hollywood during this period. For screenwriters especially, Schwartz suggests, so many of them from privileged backgrounds, the Party functioned as a means of redemptive release for the guilt many of them felt over the obscene salaries they were making as the rest of America suffered through the Depression. Hollywood writers knew that in literary terms, under the studio system, they were hacks, or at least quasi-industrial workers, yet they were making thousands of dollars every month. Since the Communist Party pursued an informal style of tithing—screenwriters were expected to pledge a certain percentage of their earnings to various causes as well as to the Party itself—it offered a form of redemption from guilt. And besides: the Party presented itself as something mainstream, genuinely American, thoroughly assimilated. "Once we were told that we could be Communist and still support the New Deal and Roosevelt," Budd Schulberg later remembered, "and that the Communist Party was simply a more advanced group going on in the same general direction, it was pretty heady and convincing stuff to us."[5]

In a milieu obsessed with status, Communist Party members considered themselves a moral and social elite. (Screenwriter Paul Jarrico attended his first Communist Party meeting at the Hillcrest Country Club.) The national Communist Party extended kid-glove treatment to its Hollywood organization, which was controlled directly by the national Party office in New York, bypassing state and regional headquarters. The Party was also fun. It was secret, for one thing, like a Masonic Circle in late eighteenth-century Vienna. No cards were issued, although members were known to each other and were expected to help one another professionally. In high-living Hollywood, the Communist Party was bohemian in style and tone. There were plenty of fundraising parties where one could enjoy oneself on behalf of Spain, striking cannery workers, or a workers' education center. Ring Lardner Jr. once proposed the slogan, tongue in cheek, "The Most Beautiful Girls in Hollywood Belong to the Communist Party" for Party recruitment but got nowhere. For the less bohemian, membership in the Communist Party, like membership in a church or synagogue, offered a conventional social life—picnics, potluck suppers, Sunday barbecues—for married couples who might otherwise be alone in the fragmented social scene of Southern California. Flourishing amidst the star system, the Hollywood Communist Party had its hard-driving studio boss, screenwriter John Howard Lawson, and its leading lady—its star, its poster girl—Virginia (Jigee) Ray, later Jigee Schulberg, later Jigee Viertel. A Los Angeles resident, educated at Fairfax High School in Hollywood, Jigee Ray had become a Goldwyn Girl with a difference: a chorus girl who read Marx and held Communist ideas. Angular, attractive, Jigee Ray was a *shiksa* from Central Casting. "All the Jewish Communists were attracted to her," remembered her brother-in-law Melvin Frank, a writer turned producer and director, "because she was this gorgeous gentile princess who was accessible because she was a Communist."[6]

On New Year's Eve 1936, Jigee Ray married Budd Schulberg, whom she had met in a Marxist study group meeting in Schulberg's home in Benedict Canyon. She had joined the Party sometime that year. For the next half dozen years, Budd and Jigee Schulberg flourished as the social center of the younger set among Hollywood Communists. Nearly fifty years later, when interviewed by Nancy Lynn Schwartz, seventeen male survivors from the circle confessed to having been, in various degrees, once in love with Jigee. Irwin Shaw portrayed her in *Two Weeks in Another Town* (1960). Ring Lardner Jr. made her the heroine of *The Ecstasy of Owen Muir* (1954), which he wrote in prison in 1950. Arthur Laurents put her into the film *The Way We Were* (1973). In 1944 Jigee divorced Schulberg and married Peter Viertel, Salka's son, a UCLA graduate and an accomplished novelist since writing the Southern California classic *The Canyon* (1940), an account of his Santa Monica boyhood, at the age of nineteen. Jigee then became the equally attractive center of her mother-in-law Salka Viertel's Sunday soirees. Peter, however, then on active duty with the Marines, was rabidly anti-Communist, and Jigee left the Party in 1945.

Already, her former husband Budd Schulberg later noted, the Communist Party in Hollywood was losing much of its glamour and certainly its amateur status. During the Hitler-Stalin Pact of 1939–41, signs of a tightening control surfaced when word came from national headquarters in New York to throw into reverse the anti-Nazi crusade launched with the formation of the Hollywood Anti-Nazi League in June 1936. During the pact years, Schulberg observed an increased presence of Party functionaries on the Hollywood scene as Communist Party or fellow-traveling screenwriters were suddenly being asked to reverse direction. Anti-Nazism now became the implied pacifism of Party member Dalton Trumbo's novel *Johnny Got His Gun* (1939), which vividly depicted the horrors of war as filtered through the consciousness of a severely maimed American veteran who was little more than a quasi-sentient corpse. When Hitler invaded the Soviet Union in June 1941, however, it became time once again to crank up the anti-fascist, pro-Soviet propaganda machine. Donald Ogden Stewart's screenplay for *Keeper of the Flame* (1942), directed by George Cukor, in which Spencer Tracy and Katharine Hepburn encounter home-grown fascism, represents an early and brilliant effort on the renewed anti-fascist front, followed in 1943 and 1944 by a spate of pro-Soviet films.

The first major sign that Hollywood was in trouble, deep trouble, with the American public on the Communist issue was the overnight reversal of the popularity of Charles Chaplin. Arriving in the United States on the SS *Cairnrona* in September 1910 (another English comedian, Stan Laurel, was also on the ship and tells the following anecdote), Chaplin stood at the rail of the vessel as it steamed toward New York. Flinging out his arms, he announced, like Balzac's Rastignac looking over Paris: "America, I am going to conquer you. Every man, woman, and child shall have my name on their lips—the name Charles Spencer Chaplin!"[7]

By 1917 Chaplin was making a million dollars a year under contract to First National and had achieved his wish. Yet for all his popularity, the Little Tramp missed something essential—whatever that was—in his connection to the American people. Americans flocked to his films and laughed, but they withheld a certain assent. For all his popularity, Chaplin remained an outsider. As early as March 1921, at the height of his popularity, Chaplin was humiliated when immigration officials refused to admit his mentally ill mother to the United States and confined her at Ellis Island, pending deportation. Chaplin was forced to plead publicly and demeaningly for his mother's release. He claimed that her mental illness came from shell shock from zeppelin air raids on London. When immigration officials relented and released Chaplin's mother to his custody, they required him to post a huge bond against her becoming a public charge. Something in Chaplin's smirk, while it amused the American public, also irritated it, especially after Chaplin showed no signs of taking out American citizenship, despite his fame and prosperity in the United States.

Chaplin's sex life, especially his penchant for young women of a tender age, also infuriated large portions of the American public. In 1939 the rumor surfaced that Chaplin and Paulette Goddard were not legally married, despite the fact that they lived together as man and wife. The couple claimed that they had been married by the captain of a ship at sea, but when Goddard could not produce a marriage certificate, she lost a starring role in *Gone with the Wind*. In 1942 a young woman by the name of Joan Barry launched the first of two paternity suits against Chaplin. In 1944 Chaplin was indicted on felony charges under the Mann Act for allegedly transporting Miss Barry to New York for immoral purposes. Never in his life, remembered defense attorney Jerry Giesler, had he experienced such hatred as he did when he escorted Chaplin down the corridor of the Federal Building in Los Angeles for arrest, booking, and fingerprinting following the indictment. Secretaries and other women came out into the corridor and literally hissed as Chaplin passed, like maenads in an ancient Greek tragedy preparing to tear apart their hapless victim. Giesler successfully defended Chaplin on the Mann Act charges, but the following year, in yet another paternity suit by Miss Barry, Chaplin was ordered to pay child support after a second trial, despite the fact that blood tests, to which he voluntarily submitted, cleared him of paternity. Los Angeles juries did not like Charles Chaplin. To make matters worse, Chaplin concluded the year 1946 by marrying Oona O'Neill, the eighteen-year-old daughter of playwright Eugene O'Neill, who repudiated his daughter for her decision to marry a man old enough to be her grandfather.

Émigré novelist Lion Feuchtwanger, a friend of Chaplin's, was among the first to determine that, while this unpopularity was linked to his non-citizenship, his sexual life, and his maddening air of intellectual superiority, Chaplin's ability to antagonize the American people had now become political in focus. Throughout 1942 Chaplin had argued publicly and constantly for a Second Front to assist the Soviet Union. After the war, the entire Second Front movement was considered so much Soviet propaganda. "You are the one artist of the theater," Feuchtwanger told Chaplin in 1946, "who will go down in American history as having aroused the political antagonism of the whole nation."[8] At this point, Chaplin began to become an active member of Salka Viertel's émigré circle, as if to reconfirm to himself that, for all the length of his American residence, he remained an outsider, holding on tenuously in a hostile country.

It took one last element, the hostility of Roman Catholics, to coalesce in final terms what soon amounted to a national hatred of the comedian. In 1947 Chaplin directed and starred in *Monsieur Verdoux*, a contemporary retelling of the Blue Beard story, based upon a real-life Frenchman who had disposed of a succession of wives and showed no remorse when mounting the guillotine. Chaplin caught the icy hauteur of Verdoux brilliantly, his smug superiority before God and man, and played a final scene, in which Verdoux out-debates a priest on the eve of his execution, with chilly contempt or, worse, with an attitude of amusement at the naive beliefs of the solicitous cleric. American Catholics, already incensed by Chaplin's unconventional love life, were outraged by his depiction of the amoral Verdoux besting a Catholic priest in theological debate. Clare Booth Luce and the Legion of Decency launched a vociferous anti-Chaplin campaign, and Catholic groups went so far as to disrupt a press conference by Chaplin in New York.

By 1947 Charles Chaplin had become not the beloved Little Tramp but the hated Dirty Old Man—worse, a Communist dirty old man, contemptuous of morality and religion. On 18 September 1952 Charles and Oona Chaplin sailed for London on the *Queen Elizabeth*. While en route, he received a telegram from Immigration informing him that he would be barred from reentry to the United States. Should he try to return, the telegram stated, he would be taken into custody and brought before a Department of Immigration board of inquiry to answer questions relating to his political affiliations and possible moral turpitude.

"Hollywood," W. C. Fields told Gene Fowler one night in the Mocambo, "is the gold cap on a tooth that should have been pulled years ago."[9] The American people, Fields might have gone on to say, would periodically try to pull the tooth. As Hortense Powdermaker suggests in *Hollywood, the Dream Factory: An Anthropologist Looks at the Movie-Makers* (1950), Americans assumed an almost slavish relationship to Hollywood. Yet the American public, in exchange for this devotion, was also forbidding Hollywood any full measure of creativity. As its part of the exchange, Hollywood had constantly to keep in mind just exactly what the public wanted. This straitjacket applied to off-screen life as well. Stars required the public's tacit approval of their personal and political behavior, whatever that might be. Hollywood, for its part, regarded its audience, the American people, who subtly controlled it, as "suckers whose emotional needs and anxieties can be exploited for profit."[10]

Taken as a symbolic drama, then, the ostracism of Charles Chaplin constituted a ritual act in which the slave-master relationship between Hollywood and its audience reversed itself on the grounds that, first of all, Chaplin had exceeded even the elastic boundaries of Hollywood sexuality without the permission of the American people and, second, his contempt for the public—which was the contempt of Chaplin's employers in Hollywood as well—had become too overt and, worse, had linked itself, as it had in the case of so many screenwriters, to the far left. During the Second World War, in short, Hollywood had overplayed its hand in telling the American people that Hollywood was winning the war, almost singlehandedly. While others fought and died, Hollywood had increased its status as a privileged enclave. In October 1947 American nobodies, most of them film fans, including freshman congressman Richard Nixon, took cyclical revenge on their Hollywood royalty on behalf of all those nobodies who together constituted the American people. From one perspective, the HUAC hearings repeated the Red Scare that followed the First World War. Yet they were also a replay of the mid-1920s when the American people had clamped down on Hollywood in the aftermath of the Desmond Taylor murder and the Fatty Arbuckle sexual scandal. Every so often in a monarchy, the peasants can grab their pitchforks and storm the gates.

The first group to testify before the committee, the anti-Communists associated with the Motion Picture Alliance for the Preservation of American Ideals, already understood that a populist reaction was brewing and that its justification, this time around, was Communism. The MPAPA itself had been forged in an early and prophetic confrontation, a National Labor Relations Board election in 1940 in which the older and very left-wing Screenwriters Guild prevailed over a conservative breakaway organization, the Screen Playwrights; in 1944 dissidents from the Playwrights founded the MPAPA. Out of self-interest or commitment, or a combination thereof, such Hollywood personalities as actor Adolphe Menjou, screenwriters Ayn Rand and Rupert Hughes, Mrs. Lela Rogers (Ginger's mother), actors Robert Taylor, Robert Montgomery, George Murphy, Ronald Reagan, and Gary Cooper, director Leo McCarey, and producers Walt Disney and Louis B. Mayer made their obeisance or otherwise established their peace with the committee on the basis that, as Gary Cooper put it, Communism was not on the level. Jack Warner, head of the most liberal of the studios before the war, met in secret with HUAC staffers a few months before the open hearings and named people in Hollywood he thought were Communists, a list that was read back to him in open session in October. Few of these people would ever work in the industry over the next fifteen years. At the conclusion of Warner's testimony—the most shameless, self-seeking, sycophantic, and evasive testimony in the history of the committee— Chairman J. Parnell Thomas warmly shook Warner's hand. Warner had gotten himself off the hook for *Confessions of a Nazi Spy, Action in the North Atlantic, Mission to Moscow,* and other wartime indiscretions.

Not so the Hollywood Ten, originally the Unfriendly Nineteen but soon reduced to Ten as many of the subpoenaed—including Bertolt Brecht, who testified on 30 October 1947—made their peace with the committee in one way or another, some naming names or, as in the case of Brecht, fleeing the country. The first thing to say about the Hollywood Ten is that it is ninety-nine percent certain that each of them was at some time a member of the Communist Party. All discussions of the Hollywood Ten are marred by the refusal of commentators—justifiably outraged by HUAC's abuses of constitutional rights and due process—to come to terms with the fact that the Hollywood Ten were Communists. Looking around the living room of director Lewis Milestone as attorney Robert Kenny, the former attorney general of California, outlined their defense strategy before the HUAC, screenwriter Lester Cole, one of the Ten, recognized sixteen of the Unfriendly Nineteen as members of the Party at one time or another.

Certainly John Howard Lawson was a Communist: the arch-Communist of Hollywood, in fact, between 1937 and 1950: the first president of the Screenwriters Guild in 1933, a primary organizer of the Hollywood Anti-Nazi League in 1936, "the great, exacting father figure" of Hollywood Communism, as Nancy Lynn Schwartz describes him—and, like so many exacting father figures, a frequent burden to others as he went through life exhorting, judging, meddling, and organizing radical activities throughout the Hollywood community. Arrogant, outspoken, John Howard Lawson was a witch-hunter's dream: a Jewish radical masquerading behind a WASP name, a brash doctrinaire activist incapable of discretion. Screenwriter Dalton Trumbo, another one of the Ten, claimed that he joined the Communist Party in 1943; but there is strong evidence—the testimony of Paul Jarrico, for example—that Trumbo joined the Party at the beginning of the Hitler-Stalin Pact. Certainly Trumbo's novel *Johnny Got His Gun*, published on 3 September 1939 and serialized in the *Daily Worker*, offered the most powerful statement possible, the depiction of the American veteran as a living corpse, for keeping the United States out of war or, for that matter, for dissuading Hitler from invading Russia.

Writing in the *Saturday Review of Literature* for 16 July 1949, historian Arthur Schlesinger Jr. attacked the Hollywood Ten as overpaid hacks who had gone Communist out of a mixture of guilt and arrogance and in the process had given mainstream liberalism a bad name. Schlesinger's assessment, as far as talent is concerned, is justified in the case of many, if not most, of the Ten. Alvah Bessie, for example, while personally courageous in terms of his beliefs (Bessie fought with the Abraham Lincoln Brigade in Spain) had only the slenderest of screenplays to his credit, including the grossly inaccurate Errol Flynn epic *Objective Burma* (1944), which depicts Americans as the only force fighting in the Burma theater. No one would confuse Ring Lardner Jr. with his father, and the rest of the Ten remain equally obscure, save for their contempt of Congress citations, with the exception of Edward Dymtryk, a director of some talent—*Tender Comrade* (1943), *Murder, My Sweet* (1944), *Back to Bataan* (1945), *Crossfire* (1947)—who later recanted.

Dalton Trumbo, by contrast, had real talent. Even within the hack conditions of Hollywood, Trumbo's abilities shone through, most dramatically in his pacifist novel, which—whatever its political sponsorship or intent—remains a quasi-underground American classic. Like the rest of the Ten, however, Trumbo was addicted to Hollywood for the money, the money, the money. He needed lots of it, and nothing else in the United States—with the exception of robbing banks—yielded cash like scriptwriting. Trumbo had other addictions as well, the inevitable by-products of the fast-paced, on-the-edge life he led. His personal physician Robert Riemer kept Trumbo liberally supplied—by April 1950 at least, when Trumbo was crash-completing three projects before going to jail—with Seconal, Benzedrine, and Dexedrine, which Trumbo used to go to bed or wake up on schedule and to fuel his over-burdened creativity.

What Trumbo, Bessie, Cole, Lardner, and Lawson (especially Lawson!) had in common was a cocky arrogance that came, perhaps inevitably, from fighting one's way to the top of the brutal Hollywood heap, however slender one's talent might be. This arrogance, appropriate to Hollywood, would prove their downfall (or their glory, depending upon one's perspective) when they faced the committee.

The Ten had a problem. They were Communists, or they had once been Communists; and the hunt—the Time of the Toad, as Trumbo called it, Scoundrel Time in Lillian Hellman's terms, in Alvah Bessie's phrase the Inquisition in Eden—the hunt was on. How one interprets such membership in the Party from a contemporary perspective is one thing. As Budd Schulberg pointed out, many perceived membership in the Party as but an avant-garde version of the New Deal. From the perspective of October and November 1947, however, membership in the Communist Party had grave consequences under the Alien Registration Act (the Smith Act) of 1940, the first anti-sedition act to be passed in peacetime since the Alien and Sedition Acts of 1798. Under the terms of the Smith Act, it was a felony to advocate the violent overthrow of the government. At the core of Communist Party doctrine was the notion of violent revolution. Hence the Hollywood Ten and others of their ilk, who considered membership in the Communist Party as a constitutional mode of political activity, now stood in danger—if they admitted their Party membership—of being indicted for advocating the violent overthrow of the government. On the other hand, if they lied under oath to the committee, they would commit perjury, also a felony, carrying with it five years of hard time. The Ten might consider the HUAC hearings a circus, but it was they who were in danger of falling from the trapeze.

Robert Kenny and his colleague Bartley Crum, joined by Charles Katz and Ben Margolis, the most powerful defense team possible in California at the time—a former attorney general (Kenny), a prominent Republican (Crum), the partners of Leo Gallagher (Katz and Margolis), who had helped win an acquittal for Georgi Dimitrov in Berlin in 1934 in the Reichstag fire trial—decided upon the strategy of having the Ten avoid all questions on First Amendment grounds, which is to say, freedom of speech and the right of free association, but not directly to refuse to answer the questions, merely to finesse them with prepared statements. Kenny, Crum, and their colleagues advised the Ten not to refuse to testify on the basis of the Fifth Amendment—that their answers, that is, might tend to incriminate them—which later became the strategy of unfriendly witnesses subpoenaed by the HUAC. The Ten lawyers believed that they could win their case on the more high-minded level of the First Amendment, which made no reference whatsoever to possible self-incrimination, hence did not even suggest that a crime might have been committed. Such a defense, furthermore, was intended to put the committee itself on the defensive as to whether it was proceeding in a constitutional manner. A quarter of a century later, Kenny, then a Superior Court judge in Los Angeles, was still defending the strategy, although it had exploded in his face.

Why had it exploded? The cunning of J. Parnell Thomas, for one thing, and the arrogance of the Ten, for another. Initially, all of liberal Hollywood had rallied to the First Amendment strategy. Directors John Huston and William Wyler and screenwriter Philip Dunne organized a glittering array of Hollywood Democrats into a Committee for the First Amendment. Taken in its entirety, the CFA represented many of the best-known names in Hollywood. A number of them released statements to the press. Flying at cut-rate prices on a chartered TWA Constellation, thanks to Howard Hughes (then still a liberal), a CFA delegation—it included Humphrey Bogart and Lauren Bacall, Danny Kaye, Gene Kelly, Sterling Hayden, Richard Conte, and Jane Wyatt—ensconced itself in the Statler Hotel, held press conferences on behalf of the Ten, and sought an interview with President Truman. The night before the delegation left Hollywood, it met at Chasen's restaurant, where William Wyler cautioned the group, as Lauren Bacall later recalled, not to look like slobs: skirts, not slacks, for the women, coats and ties for the men. Bacall's account of the trip, indeed, reads like an outing of student government, with its concern for a proper dress code and its excited belief that big things were happening. "The airport crowds," remembered Bacall, "were large and vociferous— cheers went up—God, it was exciting. I couldn't wait to get to Washington. Wouldn't it be incredible if we really could effect a change—if we could make that Committee stop?" Bacall went so far as to write a front page editorial for the Washington *Daily News*. "When they start telling you what pictures you can make," she opined, "what your subjects can be, then it's time to rear up and fight!"[11]

At the hearing, J. Parnell Thomas welcomed the delegation from the Committee on the First Amendment and had it seated in reserved seating. He then called upon John Howard Lawson as the first witness. Thomas was gambling that Lawson would disgrace himself. Taking the initiative after being sworn in, Lawson demanded the right to read a statement. Thomas examined the statement, then refused permission. He began his interrogation of Lawson. Lawson began to protest in a loud, braying voice. The hearing soon became a cacophony of Thomas asking questions and banging his gavel and Lawson making recriminatory retorts. "I am not on trial here, Mr. Chairman," Lawson managed to say at one point. "This committee is on trial here before the American people. Let us get that straight." When Lawson continued his disruptive behavior, Thomas ordered him escorted from the stand by a squad of Capitol police. The House committee then proceeded to read into the record a long list of Lawson's political activities, including his articles in the *Daily Worker*. The next day, Dalton Trumbo was equally disruptive. "This is the beginning," he shouted to Thomas as Thomas gaveled him out of the room, "of the American concentration camp!" Only Ring Lardner Jr. managed a bit of dignified wit on the stand, telling Thomas that he could name names to the committee but would hate himself in the morning.

The delegation from the Committee on the First Amendment fled Washington in horror. Far from conducting themselves in a dignified manner, the Hollywood Ten had postured and brayed and refused to answer questions as if they had something terrible to hide. Humphrey Bogart was especially furious. He told Lillian Ross of the *New Yorker* that the entire trip was a mistake. Privately, he was more emphatic. "You fuckers sold me out," he shouted at Danny Kaye before fleeing the capital. Shortly thereafter, he wrote an article in *Photoplay* entitled "I'm No Communist."[12]

The Hollywood studios, meanwhile, in the form of the Motion Picture Association of America, the Association of Motion Picture Producers, and the Society of Independent Motion Picture Producers, went into a posture of damage control. Convening on 24 November 1947 in the Waldorf-Astoria Hotel in New York, the group deliberated for two days, then issued the so-called Waldorf Statement condemning the actions of the Hollywood Ten before the House Committee on Un-American Activities. Congress voted a contempt citation, and the Ten went to trial and were convicted and each sentenced to a year in federal prison.

Hollywood Ten member Alvah Bessie later claimed that the HUAC had destroyed not only its victims' employment, family life, social standing, and ability to remain in the United States, it had also hounded to death a number of them, including actor John Garfield, who succumbed to a heart attack, and Frances Young, the actress wife of a blacklisted writer, and Madelyn Dmytryk, the former wife of the blacklisted Hollywood Ten director, each of whom committed suicide. (Bessie failed to mention another suicide from the period, under highly ambiguous circumstances, that of Louis Adamic, the historian of radicalism and good friend of Carey McWilliams.) Hollywood liberals fought back with *High Noon* (1952), directed by Austrian émigré Fred Zinnemann and starring Gary Cooper as a sheriff deserted by the entire community when a paroled gunslinger and three of his sidekicks come gunning for him: an obvious allegory for the solitary witness abandoned by the community as he or she is dragged before the HUAC or the Tenney Committee.

The cases of the Hollywood Ten were still on appeal in June 1949, when the Joint Fact-Finding Committee on Un-American Activities in California, more commonly known as the Tenney Committee, issued its *Fifth Report*. Seven hundred

and nine closely printed pages, the report exploded like a supernova before collapse. Written in great part by Edward Gibbons, editor of the Southern California
anti-Communist magazine *Alert*, the *Fifth Report* saw nothing less than a worldwide Communist conspiracy coming to fruition in California. The first 266 pages
presented an encyclopedic review of Communist doctrine, history, recent gains in
Europe, and ambitions to subvert the United States. As bad as Communism was,
the Tenney Report continued, it had become hideously compounded in its evil
by its link with Stalinism: Russian aggression, that is, compounded by the Stalinist
dictatorship, which used Communist doctrine as its program for, and justification
of, world conquest. "The conflict between Americanism and Stalinism," the report
argued, "is irreconcilable and cannot be compromised."[13] Hardly the language of
a bureaucratic report—but then again, the Tenney Committee was no ordinary
committee. It had as its goal nothing less than the routing out of Stalinist Communism from the very fabric of California. To judge from the report, moreover,
the battle for California hung precariously in the balance; for the report listed
more than seven hundred individuals and scores of organizations in California
who, according to the Tenney Committee, revolved within the various Stalinist
orbits.

    The Tenney Report, an official publication of the State of California, consti-
tuted a virtual Who's Who of California in its list of alleged Stalinist-Communist
agents and/or dupes. Indeed, in its lengthy list of allegedly compromised individuals, the *Fifth Report* suggested that all California—its academic, literary,
entertainment, and journalistic establishment—was one inter-connected Communist front. The argument could be made, in fact, that you were nobody in
California unless you had made the Tenney list. From the world of architecture
there was Gregory Ain of the University of Southern California; from science,
future Nobel laureate Linus Pauling of Cal Tech and even the name of occasional
Californian Albert Einstein. Literary Californians making the list included detective novelist Dashiell Hammett, novelist and social critic Louis Adamic, poet William Rose Benét, historical novelist Lion Feuchtwanger, writer Irwin Shaw,
bookseller-poet Jake Zeitlin, and Thomas Mann. Professor Max Radin of Boalt
Hall represented the academy, along with F. O. Matthiessen of Harvard, who had
been born and raised in Pasadena and thus deserved mention. From the world of
music came émigré studio composer Hanns Eisler and that avid *agent provocateur*
Artie Shaw. Representing bench and bar, former attorney general Robert Kenny
made the list as well as defense attorneys Bartley Crum (a Republican) and Leo
Gallagher and federal judge Leon Yankwich of Los Angeles, who had made the
mistake of being born in Rumania. Show business Stalinists, according to the
Tenney Committee, included José Ferrer, Gregory Peck, Edward G. Robinson,
John Huston, and Orson Welles. Los Angeles lawyer-journalist Carey McWilliams,
whom Senator Tenney considered "one of California's outstanding Communists,"
made multiple appearances in a variety of categories. No wonder Artie Samish
said: "Meet Tenney on the street and say 'hello' to him, he calls you a Red."[14]

Screenwriter Emmett Lavery, among others, would have no trouble acknowledging the truth of what Artie Samish had just said. A prominent Roman Catholic (as was Samish in his own way), Lavery had also been Red-baited by the irascible senator. President of the Screenwriters Guild in the mid- to late 1940s, Lavery came from a left-liberal Roman Catholic tradition, with its social democratic orientation rooted in the teachings of Pope Leo XIII, represented in the United States by such figures as Peter Marin and Dorothy Day and the magazine *Commonweal*. Conservative screenwriter Rupert Hughes, in fact, had once called Lavery "a Communist masquerading as a Catholic" — which is exactly the point that John Tenney tried to establish in his heated interrogation of Lavery on 7 October 1946.[15] In the course of this grilling, Tenney drew numerous parallels between Lavery's positions and those of the Communist Party. Refusing to budge an inch under Tenney's cross-examination, Lavery deftly traced his beliefs to the encyclical *Rerum Novarum* (1891) of Leo XIII and the political philosophy of the French Catholic philosopher Jacques Maritain, at the time the French ambassador to the Holy See. Interestingly enough, a Communist Party pamphlet entitled *Catholicism in San Francisco*, mimeographed and distributed around 1947, urged Party members to drop their arrogance vis-à-vis the Roman Catholic working classes of San Francisco and to seek points of agreement between Communism and Catholic social doctrine with Italian workers in North Beach and Irish workers in the Mission district. On the other hand, Hollywood screenwriter and producer Roy Huggins left the Party after a brief membership, saying: "Lapsed Catholics make bad Communists — it's too much like the Church."[16]

While Emmett Lavery's liberal Catholicism represented an authentic expression of the mind of the Church as far as social teachings were concerned, this was more true in Europe, with its long-standing social democratic traditions, than it was in the laissez-faire environment of the United States. The bishops of the United States tended to come from Irish or German blue-collar or lower-middle-class families, and as religious leaders they were inclined to share a generally conservative, AFL-oriented point of view, as opposed to the CIO-oriented *Commonweal* Catholics in the intellectual elite. A polished and assured member of the hierarchy, Monsignor (later Bishop) Fulton J. Sheen, a doctor in philosophy (with the very highest distinction) from the University of Louvain, forcefully advanced the anti-Communist line. Privately, many in the Roman Catholic hierarchy hoped that the polish of Bishop Sheen would in some way compensate for the crudities of Senator Joseph McCarthy, the most notorious anti-Communist of Irish Catholic descent.

In Hollywood, another Irish Catholic, director Leo McCarey, also contributed to the cause by his outspoken anti-Communism. During the war, McCarey had directed *Going My Way* (1944) and *The Bells of St. Mary's* (1945), two films that, along with *Knute Rockne: All-American* (1940) and *The Fighting 69th* (1940), heralded the acceptability of ethnic Catholics as *bona fide* Americans. (Although Rockne himself was a Protestant Norwegian, his strong identification with a Catholic team made him an honorary member of the club.) *Going My Way* and *The Bells of St. Mary's* were two favorite films of Pius XII, the Pope of anti-Communism. Pius believed that the priest as played by Bing Crosby represented the best possibilities of Roman Catholic clerical culture in the United States. In 1952 McCarey made *My Son John,* in which Helen Hayes plays a Roman Catholic mother who turns her Communist son over to the authorities. Even among the regents of UC, the Roman Catholic issue asserted itself, with John Francis Neylan and the other Catholic regents leading the pro-oath forces. In discussing the oath controversy, The *Christian Century* described Neylan pointedly as "a product of Catholic schools," as if this fact alone explained Neylan's ultra-conservativism.[17]

The majority of Roman Catholics in the United States were pro-union. Paradoxically, in becoming a strong component of the anti-Communist crusade, Catholics found themselves aligned with a movement that brought with it strong anti-union currents. A favorite target of John Tenney's, for example, was the California Labor School located in the Broadway Arcade Building in Los Angeles. The fact is: many labor unions in California—AFL as well as CIO, the International Longshoremen's and Warehousemen's Union, the Sailors' Union of the Pacific, the constituent unions of the Conference of Studio Unions in Hollywood—sustained a significant Communist presence or influence among union officials and, in the case of certain unions, among the rank-and-file. In San Francisco, rank and file members of the otherwise conservative Building Trades AFL locals formed the McNamara Club, which was openly affiliated with Communist Party headquarters at 942 Market Street. San Francisco also had a Communist-oriented California Labor School paralleling that of Los Angeles. Within the San Francisco–based Sailors' Union of the Pacific, a fierce battle was raging between anti-Communist labor leader Harry Lundeberg and radical elements. As an outspoken anti-Communist, Lundeberg aligned himself explicitly against ILWU president Harry Bridges, who had emerged in the 1934 coastwide maritime strike as the most powerful and charismatic labor leader on the Coast.

During the war, Harry Bridges had fulfilled his promise that the ILWU would not strike. In 1948, however, Bridges supported Henry Wallace and began openly to oppose the Marshall Plan and the European Recovery Program, which earned him expulsion from the CIO by a national leadership trying to realign the CIO to a respectable position on the center-left. In December 1948 the House Un-American Activities Committee specifically named Bridges as a Communist, a charge the Australian-born labor leader had repeatedly denied under oath. In May 1949 a federal grand jury indicted Bridges for perjury and fraud in conjunction with his denial that he had ever been a member of the Communist Party. Bridges was convicted in April 1950 and sentenced to five years in prison. Released while his case was under appeal, Bridges continued as president of the ILWU. When the Korean War broke out in June, he spoke bitterly against American involvement and was briefly jailed as a security risk. That same year, RKO released the film *I Married a Communist,* which specifically depicted a Bridges-like figure, played by

Thomas Gomez, as a murderous Communist agent. As late as December 1992, historians Harvey Klehr and John Haynes, in the course of preparing a three-volume collection of documents from Soviet archives for Yale University Press, claimed to have found evidence in Soviet files that Bridges was known to the Central Committee of the Communist Party as a secret member, identified by the pseudonym Rossi. If true, this meant that Bridges had repeatedly perjured himself—so Klehr and Haynes claimed—when he denied under oath in 1938, 1941, 1945, and 1949 that he had ever joined the Party.[18]

If one were to send to Central Casting for someone to embody the Folks of Southern California in all their hope, glory, and occasional grotesquerie, then John B. Tenney might very well turn up on the set. But then again: Tenney himself—hard-drinking, paranoid, dyspeptic—could have been played by W. C. Fields in one of that actor's grouchier moods. Born in St. Louis, Tenney arrived in Los Angeles as a boy of ten in 1908 with his parents as they joined the great migration of Folks to the Southland. During the war, he fought with the American Expeditionary Force in France. Upon his return, Tenney, a pianist, formed the Majestic Orchestra and spent the first half of the 1920s driving from dance hall to dance hall throughout the southern tier of the state. When bookings in the better dance halls or hotels were lacking, the Majestic played places like the Owl in Mexicali. Situated across the border from Calexico, Mexicali functioned as a funnel for Mexican farm workers passing to and from the Imperial Valley. In January 1923 Tenney and the Majestic Orchestra were playing the Imperial Dance Hall in Mexicali. For some weeks previously, Tenney had been fiddling with a tune in his mind, a modified waltz. A regular at the Imperial was a woman named Rose, who ran a boardinghouse for railroad men in Brawley, which is to put the best possible interpretation upon the establishment. Rose would come into the Imperial after midnight, already a bit drunk, and was wont to break into tears, especially when Tenney and the Majestic played the waltz tune Tenney had composed. Seeing Rose in tears one night, Tenney was inspired to attach lyrics to his melody. He later described "Mexicali Rose" as a tribute to all beautiful, black-eyed señoritas. Like the Ramona myth, "Mexicali Rose" took on a life of its own. Two movies were made, and the sheet music sold steadily throughout Tenney's lifetime. "Mexicali Rose" became one of the most recorded songs in the history of Tin Pan Alley. Banal, sentimental, touched with spurious Hispanic romance, the song embodied the hopes and dreams of the Folks as they settled into their new identity as Southern Californians.

Cole Porter Tenney was not. The third-tier orchestra leader knew he had to find a better way to make a living lest he spend the rest of his life motoring between dance halls throughout the Southwest. Graduating from night law school and passing the bar, Tenney entered local politics, and in 1936 he won election to the assembly from Los Angeles County as a populist Folks-oriented Democrat, more than a little to the left. Tenney entered elective politics via the usual route in

California: political boss Artie Samish. According to Samish, Tenney called on him in Sacramento and told the rotund boss of his interest in getting elected. "What's your background, what have you done?" asked Artie. Replied Tenney: ' I've written the song 'Mexicali Rose.' " To which Samish responded: "That's good enough for me," and John Tenney, erstwhile pianist and bandleader with the Majestic Orchestra, went to the assembly along with his pal Samuel Yorty, another son of the Folks, Nebraska-born, and like Tenney a night law school graduate.[19]

The Los Angeles County Tenney and Yorty represented had strongly supported Upton Sinclair in his campaign for governor in 1934. The Folks were mostly Democrats and mad as hell against the prevailing plutocracy of Southern California. Successively, the Yorty-Tenney constituency supported such radical measures as Upton Sinclair's End Poverty in California (EPIC) campaign of 1934, the pension plan advocated by Dr. Francis E. Townsend of Long Beach under the rubric Old Age Revolving Pensions, Ltd., the Ham and Eggs pension plan that went before the voters in 1938, the crypto-millenarian United States Senate campaign of Sheridan Downey that same year, which was successful, and the equally successful gubernatorial campaign of Culbert Olson, which at long last brought the New Deal to California. The Folks of Los Angeles County, in short, were decidedly to the left. The House Un-American Activities Committee chaired by Martin Dies, in fact, had affidavits in its possession to the effect that John Tenney and Samuel Yorty had been members of the Communist Party between 1936 and 1937. (A few years later, in January 1946, George Campbell, who had worked with Tenney in the Musicians Union, boldly challenged Tenney in an open hearing: "I've heard it said, Mr. Tenney, that you joined the Communist Party under an assumed name, and tried to get a friend to join, also under a fictitious name.")[20] Tenney was also listed with the Dies Committee as a supporter of a large number of left-wing causes, including the Friends of the Abraham Lincoln Brigade. No sooner had they reached the assembly than Tenney and Yorty joined together to sponsor a bill to repeal the Criminal Syndicalism Act of 1919, which had been used with such telling effect against left-wing agricultural unions throughout the 1930s.

In December 1932 Tenney was elected to the lucrative post of president of Local 47 of the American Federation of Musicians. No one was expected to live on an assemblyman's salary. And besides: Tenney loved the job. It put him at the center of the Hollywood studios, the hotel and nightclub scene, even the serious music world, where Tenney rubbed elbows with important people who treated him deferentially for being what he was, one of the most powerful union officials in the single most glamorous industry, entertainment, in Los Angeles County. Throughout his tenure as president, 1938–39, Jack Tenney remained a well-supported and prominent left-wing politician. We find him in August 1938, for example, speaking to a rally of the Anti-Nazi League of Hollywood, which he would later investigate as a Communist front. Then, in August 1939, Tenney lost the union presidency— his job, his income, his prestige, his identity—in a closely contested election. Tenney blamed the Communists for organizing his ouster. He returned to Sacramento a bitter man: he, Jack Tenney, the composer of "Mexicali Rose," bounced from Local 47!

Already, Tenney's friend and colleague Sam Yorty was turning right. In December 1939 Yorty had become chairman of the Assembly Relief Investigating Committee, which in 1940 turned into a witch-hunt for Communist social workers in the State Relief Administration. By the fall of 1940, Jack Tenney had followed Yorty to the right. In September Tenney led a drive in the legislature to ban the Communist Party from the ballot. The bill passed and was signed by Governor Olson, but the California Supreme Court declared it unconstitutional in 1942, the year that Tenney, now a Republican, won election to the state senate. As state senator, Tenney achieved the chairmanship of the Joint Fact-Finding Committee on Un-American Activities in California, formed in 1941. The rotund boozy piano player, just another good old boy, now emerged as the Grand Inquisitor of the Great State of California: an ominous figure in a pinstriped double-breasted suit, peering inquisitorially from the dais of the hearing room through rimless glasses at an endless parade of witnesses subpoenaed before the committee to explain their alleged Communist or Communist-front activities. Senator Tenny had become the worst nightmare of the liberal intelligentsia come true: an avenging inquisitor from the Folks, smart enough to be dangerous, publicly placed to do mischief, and out to avenge the loss of the Musicians Union presidency.

Initially, during the war years, Jack B. Tenney dipped his toe into the waters of anti-Communism only gingerly, very gingerly. The United States, after all, was an ally of the Soviet Union, and domestically the Communist Party had put itself solidly behind a United Front. In December 1941 and again in October 1944, the Tenney Committee questioned William Schneiderman, secretary of the Communist Party for California, almost deferentially. After the war, by contrast, in hearings held between late 1945 and 1948, the Tenney Committee aggressively concerned itself with allegations of Communism in unions, at the University of California, in local elections in San Francisco and Marin counties, in high school curricula, and among teachers, including the sex education program in Chico. Tenney and his chief counsel R. E. Combs, who asked most of the questions, increasingly badgered witnesses. Tenney, in turn, was frequently baited during hearings by audiences packed with supporters of the subpoenaed, who would laugh when he was out-debated, which was frequently, or said stupid things, an equally frequent occurrence. His face flushed, Tenney would pound his gavel and threaten to order the bailiffs to clear the room. On a number of occasions, Tenney was not above jumping up from his chair and arguing with attorneys; in at least one instance, he came close to fisticuffs. His remarks to defense counsels were frequently intemperate.

The night-school lawyer enjoyed his power over the sleek, well-paid graduates of accredited institutions. On 19 February 1948 Tenney had the pleasure of cross-examining federal judge Leon Yankwich, a distinguished legal scholar, who frankly admitted that he had lectured at the People's Educational Center in Los Angeles, a favorite target of investigation by Tenney. Born in Rumania and naturalized as a boy, Yankwich exuded an almost rabbinical ambience of legal scholarship. In his line of questioning, Tenney did his best to make a learned judge seem, at best, a communist Party dupe. Without any evidence whatsoever, Tenney later listed Yankwich in a Committee report as a Communist Party fellow traveler. The more socially advantaged the witness, the more educated, the more prominent, the more Tenney and counsel Combs enjoyed the cross-examination, with its humiliating spectacle of a subpoenaed witness—Mrs. Fredric March, for example (stage name: Florence Eldridge), UCLA provost Clarence Dykstra, Judge Yankwich—people who might otherwise have never given Jack Tenney the time of day, now forced to sit before microphones under the lights and be cross-examined under oath by a committee before which they had already been tried and convicted.

The transcripts of the interrogation of Mrs. Fredric March on 18 February 1948 seethe with barely suppressed rituals of social revenge, as Tenney and Combs grill the elegant Broadway actress mercilessly regarding her participation as an American delegate to the Congress of Women convened in Paris in November 1945 to deal with post-war problems of broken families and homeless children. Tactfully, Mrs. March informed Tenney that Eleanor Roosevelt herself had asked her to attend the Paris conference. To which Tenney replied: "Mrs. Roosevelt [has] admitted many times that the Communists had fooled her."[21] No doubt Tenney and Combs had a file on Eleanor Roosevelt herself. The central investigative resource of the Tenney Committee was an elaborate system of index cards compiled by Combs, who subscribed to hundreds of journals and newspapers, including Communist Party publications. Painstakingly, Combs would enter onto cards the names of each organization and each individual listed as a supporter. By 1943 he had nearly fourteen thousand filed, indexed, and cross-indexed cards.

In many cases, Combs did not have to search very exhaustively for his data. The Communist Party of California, after all, was more or less an open affair. In 1938 the Party had launched its first openly Communist newspaper, the *People's Daily World*, edited and published in San Francisco. Party functionaries such as Dorothy Healy, secretary of the Communist Party in Los Angeles County, were in the late 1930s and into the war years increasingly operating in the open and aligning themselves with scores of other organizations; indeed, Healy—a genuinely committed individual, living ascetically for naught save radical politics—resisted the cult of secrecy that characterized Communist Party activities in Hollywood, believing as she did that more was lost than gained through undercover activity. A 1939 pamphlet, *The Communist Party: Whom and How to Recruit in California*, set forth an ambitious program to make the Party become perceived as a mainstream political organization by working people up and down the state. "Nine of the ten people you know are good prospects for the party," the pamphlet noted, urging Party members to avoid dogmatism and arrogance in the effort to recruit new members. On the evening of Saturday, 25 October 1942, the Los Angeles County Communist Party joined representatives from Governor Culbert Olson's and Lieutenant Governor Ellis Patterson's offices, together with Assemblyman Augustus Hawkins and a representative of State Senator John Tenney's campaign for attorney general, for a Victory Election Symposium held in the Embassy Auditorium on South Grand Avenue in the Downtown. With Anita Whitney on the stage as Communist Party candidate for state controller, the evening was intended as a united front among liberal and Communist candidates.

To review Communist Party literature produced in California in the war years and through 1948 is to encounter a tone of optimism and confidence, especially after the Party had beaten back in the California Supreme Court an attempt to bar it from the state. Attorneys for the Party had argued successfully that it was "a duly organized and existing political party of the United States and the state of California" and that its officials — Anita Whitney, chairman of the California State Central Committee, and William Schneiderman, secretary — were citizens of the United States and duly elected to their Party positions. By 1947 Communist candidates such as Oleta Yates, running for the Board of Supervisors in San Francisco, were making every effort to run as candidates acceptable to a broad spectrum of the population. That year as well, the Communist Party of California launched a drive to build its membership to ten thousand by September. Pamphlets and instructional manuals supporting this drive stressed a pro-labor, pro-union, pro-third-party, and pro-Negro front.

In this last emphasis, the securing of civil rights and economic opportunity for African-Americans, Communist Party literature from the period anticipated the civil rights drive of the 1960s. As early as 1941 the Communist Party had joined with other individuals and organizations to sponsor a California Action Conference for Civil Rights, held in San Francisco on 27 and 28 September. This two-day conference obsessed State Senator John Tenney, as did the Hollywood Writers Conference at UCLA held in October 1943. Tenney had wanted the entire Civil Rights Action Conference investigated as a Communist front, but Pearl Harbor put his plans on hold. "A firm and unbending alliance with the Negro people," stated the 1947 pamphlet *The Negro Question*, "is required by the present struggle against reaction. This demands, in the first place, a constant fight against the doctrines and practices of white chauvinism, and their eradication in whatever form they may be present from the labor and progressive movement." As part of its organizational structure, the Communist Party of California supported a state-wide Negro Commission to pursue its civil rights agenda on behalf of African-American rights. "Raise the Negro question throughout," urged a manual for new members of the Party issued in 1947.

Tenney was especially angry with lawyer-activist-historian Carey McWilliams, who had played a major role in civil rights agitation, including an important role in the 1941 civil rights conference in San Francisco. Cross-examining McWilliams in 1947, Tenney coaxed from him a refusal to condemn interracial marriage. The 1947 report of the Tenney Committee castigated McWilliams for advocating the marriage of blacks and whites, "part of the Communist philosophy," the report claimed, "of breaking down the races."[22] This playing of an anti-inter-racial mar-riage race card represented the most ugly line of attack ever taken by the intem-perate inquisitor from Los Angeles County.

The 1948 third-party Progressive movement led by former Vice President Henry Wallace offered a renewal of the United Front of World War II for the Left in California as well as the rest of the nation. Communist Party pamphlets from 1947 are uniformly favorable to the third-party movement. William Schneiderman, for example, chairman of the Communist Party of California, argued in the *Daily People's World* for 18 and 19 June 1947 (articles shortly thereafter published as a pamphlet entitled *Political Perspectives and the 1948 Elections*) that Wallace's third-party movement offered Communists an opportunity to align themselves openly with other organizations on the left and thereby renew their mainstream identity. Nothing could be more respectable, in fact—glamorous, even—than the star-studded rally held on behalf of Wallace on 19 May 1947 at Gilmore Stadium in Hollywood, organized by a left-liberal coalition calling itself the Progressive Citi-zens of America. The group had initially tried to secure the Hollywood Bowl but had been turned down by the board of directors on political grounds. Twenty-eight thousand people filled the stadium that evening to hear Katharine Hepburn, dressed in bright scarlet, denounce the HUAC and the Tenney Committee in a rousing speech that might have afforded Hepburn a political career in her own right, had she been so inclined.

The celebrity status of Hepburn suggested the dynamics of State Senator Ten-ney's demise. In an article published in the *Nation* on 23 July 1949, following the release of the *Fifth Report*, Carey McWilliams suggested that the Tenney Com-mittee in general and its chairman in particular were riding a tiger. As long as Tenney stayed focused on true Communists, McWilliams argued, he could main-tain his popularity. After all, the opposition would come mainly from the Com-munist Party. But Tenney was dangerously casting a wider and wider net. The witnesses subpoenaed before his committee were becoming more and more estab-lishment. Too many prominent Californians had been raked over the coals for Tenney to maintain his position. "Once witnesses of this kind are brought before the Inquisition," McWilliams noted, "two concurrent developments are usually noted: the opposition is strengthened, and the position of the Committee is un-dermined, for it begins to look ridiculous even in the eyes of the less progressive elements of the community."[23]

Without saying it openly—for that would represent a species of snobbery un-acceptable to the Left—McWilliams was suggesting that Chairman Tenney had over-reached himself socially in such events as the grueling cross-examination he gave Mrs. Fredric March and his presumptuous encounter with Judge Yankwich, not to mention making a fool of himself in his ridiculous inquiries into the sex education program in the public schools of Chico, a quiet and proper state-college town in Butte County. Among others, McWilliams noted, Chairman Tenney had smeared such respected Californians as Mrs. Edward H. Heller of San Francisco, a Democratic National Committeewoman, a regent of the University of California, the wife of an important shipping executive; Oliver Carter, the state chairman of the Democratic Party; Congresswoman Helen Gahagan Douglas; San Francisco district attorney Edmund G. (Pat) Brown; Marine Colonel James Roosevelt, son of the late President and a decorated combat veteran; Judge Isaac Pacht, president of the Los Angeles Jewish Community Council; and—most dangerously of all— the San Francisco *Chronicle*, the San Francisco *News*, and the Los Angeles *Daily News*. In attacking the press, McWilliams continued, Tenney was most noticeably setting in motion his own demise. McWilliams was prophetically on target. Shortly after the appearance of the *Fifth Report*, Tenney's fellow state senators, fearing the establishment, the newspapers especially, more than they feared a Tenney smear, voted him out as chairman of the Joint Fact-Finding Committee on Un-American Activities.

Not one person named in the five reports of the Tenney Committee, and there were hundreds, was ever indicted for, much less convicted of, subversive behavior, although a number of known Communists, including some of the Hollywood Ten, made the various Tenney lists. But the Hollywood Ten, it must be remembered, went to jail not for subversion but for contempt of Congress, a misdemeanor. In its hearings, the Tenney Committee egregiously violated due process, and in its listings of so-called subversive organizations, it smeared hundreds of groups as Communist Party fronts merely because of the presence of one or another name on a letterhead. Hectoring witnesses, calling everyone (as Artie Samish had noticed) a Red, John Tenney became a parodic paragon of the very un-Americanism he claimed to be exposing. In 1949 Tenney placed a poor fifth in the race for mayor of Los Angeles. He subsequently failed in two attempts to reach the House of Representatives. In 1952 he ran for Vice President of the United States on the Christian National Party ticket alongside General of the Army Douglas MacArthur. By 1959 Jack Tenney was back where he began, in the desert, practicing law in Banning, a Mexicali Rose sort of town.

11

1950 ☆ Police Action

*I*DEOLOGICAL battles rarely have but one meaning. In California, the anti-Communist crusade, as led by State Senator Jack Tenney and, soon, the UC regents, was obviously energized by the rapidly developing Cold War, which became a hot war, albeit limited, when North Korean forces invaded South Korea on 25 June 1950 and, five days later, President Harry Truman authorized American military intervention on behalf of the south. A week later, another fifteen members of the United Nations joined the American effort, and General Douglas Mac-Arthur was appointed supreme commander. Initially, the Korean War—which was not a war at all in legal terms but a police action by the United Nations—seemed to many to be but the prologue to the World War III that must inevitably follow. Although the shooting war was contained to the Korean peninsula over the next three years, the prospect of a wider conflict, so apocalyptically palpable in June 1950, anchored the anti-Communist crusade even more solidly on a foundation of realities that included the loss of Eastern Europe and the Balkans, the near-loss of Greece, the vitality of Communist parties in Western Europe, the steady rise of the Soviet Union as an aggressive military power with atomic capabilities, the Communist victory in China, and the growing strength of the Communist-inspired insurgencies in Southeast Asia. Across the globe, then, locally, nationally, geopolitically, titanic forces were vying for dominance in conflicts ranging from peasants' revolts to the threat of nuclear retaliation. The anti-communism of 1950, therefore, cannot be dismissed in retrospect as a hallucinatory response—however reckless or unconstitutional the behavior of some of its key protagonists might have been.

For the citizen-soldiers of the 40th Infantry Division, California National Guard, the global conflict with Communism suddenly became highly personalized when, on 1 September 1950, the division was called to active duty and nationalized. A

Southern California–based unit, with a distinguished record of combat in the Pacific during World War II, the 40th was commanded by Major General Daniel Hudelson, a forty-eight-year-old executive with the General Petroleum Corporation in Los Angeles. Outspoken and flamboyant, Hudelson had won a Silver Star, a Bronze Star, and the French Croix de Guerre as a regimental commander with General George Patton in fierce fighting in Europe and was wont to claim, only half facetiously, that it was General Patton who was imitating Colonel Hudelson's mannerisms and not vice versa. In any event, Hudelson ended the war as a federally recognized brigadier general in the California National Guard, assigned to the command of the 40th Division. By September 1950, when it was called to active duty and federalized, it stood at ten thousand strength, eight thousand men short of its authorized cadre; but Hudelson had managed to instill in the 40th the very proficiency and *esprit de corps* that had made it a prime candidate for activation.

And so, in the autumn of 1950, some ten thousand Southern Californians converged on the Exposition Park Armory in Los Angeles for shipment to Camp Cooke in rural Santa Barbara County, where they were scheduled for twenty-eight weeks of training before deployment overseas. Hudelson was convinced that the 40th would be heading for Europe, where it would be engaging Soviet troops in World War III, and he trained his men accordingly, with specific reference to their forthcoming battle with the Russians: something that his former commanding officer Patton had always wanted to do. At the re-activated Camp Cooke, meanwhile, it was déjà vu all over again as citizen-soldiers, many of them veterans of the Second World War, commanded by senior officers who had earned their rank in the Second World War, were issued World War II–era supplies by the Quartermaster Corps and, as they had done a few short years earlier, began their training according to Second World War drills and exercises. Once again, Hollywood celebrities arrived at Camp Cooke to entertain the troops. There were new names, of course — Debbie Reynolds and Vic Damone, for example — but also a number of stars such as Dorothy Lamour and Harpo Marx, who were veterans of the World War II USO circuit.

On 18 December 1950 Supreme Commander Douglas MacArthur requested of the Joint Chiefs of Staff that four National Guard divisions be sent as soon as possible to Japan so that Japan-based American Army units could be sent to Korea. And so the 40th received its orders for Japan, not Europe. To Major General Hudelson's credit, the 40th — now augmented by replacements from the Regular Army, including a cadre of seasoned non-coms — required only a month to get ready for deployment to Japan, a third of the time usually allowed. And so it was déjà vu all over again as well when in late March and April 1951 the men of the 40th Division, wearing their World War II uniforms and carrying their World War II weapons, entrained for Fort Mason, San Francisco, where they boarded World War II–era troop transports and, for the second time in the case of many, sailed beneath the Golden Gate toward combat in the Pacific.

The 40th spent a year in Japan before deployment to the front line in Korea. Governor Earl Warren, a first lieutenant in the First World War, visited the 40th in Japan in late August 1951, standing in the chow line with the men in a poncho on a drizzling day, mess kit in hand, meeting with non-coms and soldiers after chow in the field, the brass pointedly asked to wait off in the distance. The soldiers and non-coms gave Warren an earful regarding their shabby and out-of-date equipment, as did Hudelson. The general also encouraged Warren to resist the intention of the Regular Army to cannibalize National Guard divisions as sources of replacement for units already on the front lines rather than deploy National Guard units at division strength. Thanks in part to Warren and the California congressional delegation, a flow of better equipment to the 40th soon ensued, and the division remained intact until its deployment to Korea in early 1952. In its half year on the line as a National Guard division before rotating its citizen-soldiers back to California and reorganizing itself as a Regular Army unit, the 40th Division experienced something resembling the trench warfare of World War I, with stable and well-dug-in units facing each other across a no-man's-land where combat patrols fought by night and there was a constant danger from snipers, mortars, and artillery.

Eighty-two soldiers lost their lives during the time the 40th was a National Guard division, 298 were wounded, and five were missing in action: relatively low casualties, attributable at once to the stable nature of the lines at the time and the high level of training Hudelson had instilled in his men. Still, it had been a steep price to pay for veterans who had already fought in World War II and an unexpected price to pay for young men who had enlisted in the National Guard as a way of avoiding the draft and staying home in California. Because the 40th Division was predominantly Southern California National Guard, moreover, each aspect of its deployment, training, and combat service was reported extensively in Southern California newspapers. Each Southern Californian who died in training or combat tended to be well known in his community or the son of a well-known and respected family. In such cities as Alhambra, Whittier, San Gabriel, Pasadena, San Bernardino, Santa Ana, Ontario, Santa Monica, Santa Barbara, and Cucamonga, where the officers and men of the 40th had come from, the National Guard was a community service organization and a social club as well as a military unit.

The young men of the 40th were the local high school athletes, the kids with promise whom everyone knew and hoped the best for. The NCOs of the 40th were the foremen in the local shops, the bosses in the local garages and repair shops, the refrigerator and television repairmen, the Scout leaders and coaches of local teams. The more senior officers (and some of these died as well) were the bankers and insurance executives, the principal of the local high school, the regional director of a state agency. The loss of such citizen-soldiers, then, in a far-off place to a Communist foe in a limited police action caused a special kind of

stress in local Southern California communities and underscored the real consequences of the Cold War against Communism when it became hot.

Had it been worth it, after all? What had been accomplished at the cost of such
loss of life? Just as Patton had done in 1945, Major General Daniel Hudelson did
in June of 1952: shoot his mouth off, that is, describing the Korean War as a no-
win situation as it was being presently fought. Called on the carpet by Secretary
of the Army Frank Pace Jr. and, later, by the commanding general of the 6th
Army, Hudelson claimed that he thought he had reverted to civilian status when
he spoke to the press. He left active duty on 16 June 1952 with a written admonishment in his permanent service record, which many in Southern California
considered an unfair muzzling of a combat-tested general by politicians in Washington, which was a long way from either Korea or Southern California.

This issue of outsiders calling the shots in California was not without relevance
to the multiple levels of meaning for the whole question of Communism and anti-
Communism. In domestic terms, whether on the national level or within California itself, the anti-Communist crusade had goals and levels of meaning that
were not related exclusively to questions of the Cold War, or even the Korean
Conflict. As in the case of State Senator Jack Tenney in California, for example,
the anti-Communist activities of Senator Joseph McCarthy on the national scene
were being multiply motivated by factors of religion, social class, regional rivalries,
and personal demons. In California, moreover, the anti-Communist crusade had
among its levels of meaning the question of just exactly who would run the post-
war Golden State. A conviction was taking hold of many established oligarchs in
California, great and small, that the state—in growing so rapidly during and after
the war, in being colonized increasingly by non-Californian talent—was falling
through the fingers of the establishment that had been running things since the
Progressive Era. Once again, this older establishment was not hallucinating. Ever
since 1942 California had been in the process of being rapidly recolonized by
Americans from elsewhere and by European émigrés whose talent, energy, credentials, and other resources were propelling them rapidly into leadership and/or
positions of control in every phase of California life. At the same time, previously
suppressed groups within California, transformed by their experiences during the
war years, were proving increasingly restive with their second-class status.

Such a bifurcated sensibility can be seen, with only the slightest risk of pushing
the envelope of interpretation (science fiction, after all, is frequently allegorical),
in the short stories that Los Angeles–based science fiction writer Ray Bradbury
began to publish between 1946 and 1950, gathered as *The Martian Chronicles*
(1950), revolving around the interactions between the original Martians and American colonizers. As in the case of Southern California's long-standing conception
of itself, the original Martians enjoyed a world in which nature and technology
were in creative synergy. While they knew and used technology, their primary

impulse was toward nature and the nurturing of their aesthetic, emotional, imaginative, and intuitive selves. Then came the invasion of the people who colonized Mars and bent it to their more technologically dependent and environmentally exploitative way of life. Mars became a bustling American place. The old Martians had one Mars, the Earth colonizers another. The old Martians lived a life of plentitude and gracious leisure. The new Martians were busy, overworked, and obsessed with promotional schemes. They were haunted by the old Martians as well: by the great canals they built, by their belief that the old Martians still survived in remote regions and could be seen sweeping by night across the plains on their great landships or reconvening by ancient pools for festivity and song. The old Martians, for their part, were disdainful of the newcomers and capable of counter-measures against them, some of them emotionally and mentally cruel to an extreme degree.

If one were to use *The Martian Chronicles* as a gloss, the regents of the University of California were old Martians/old Californians, indeed. They were the establishment such as it existed in mid-twentieth-century California, with many of them empowered by nineteenth-century lineages and fortunes. As regents, appointed for sixteen-year terms, they presided over an institution one of its alumnae, Joan Didion, would at the end of the decade describe as California's best idea of itself. Yet by 1950 the regents knew as well that the high provincial state in which they enjoyed their hegemony was filling, rapidly, with new Californians; and this awareness, this anxiety, was to become somehow entangled with the anti-Communist crusade.

On 2 May 1949 Robert Underhill, secretary to the Board of Regents, published a notice in the *Faculty Bulletin* stating that the new oath adopted by the regents in their March meeting at Santa Barbara must be signed by all faculty and staff of the university for their employment to continue into the next fiscal year, which extended into the first half of 1950. Through the summer, President Robert Gordon Sproul had every confidence that he could bring the faculty along regarding the new requirement. After all, there was still looming on the horizon Tenney's Senate Constitutional Amendment 13, which would enable the legislature to bypass the regents altogether and impose a loyalty oath on the UC faculty and staff on its own authority. In Washington that June, another ominous cloud surfaced: the investigation by the House Un-American Activities Committee into alleged subversion at the UC Radiation Laboratory in Berkeley during the war.

President Sproul approached these things in a practical spirit. He was, after all, not a faculty man. He had done no graduate work. He was a no-nonsense administrator. Taking his bachelor's degree from UC Berkeley in 1913, Sproul had gone directly to work in the controller's office and worked his way up the ladder to secretary of the Board of Regents, comptroller, vice president for finance, and then, in 1930, president. It was Sproul who had brought the idea of the expanded loyalty oath to the Board of Regents in the first place: a practical solution from a seasoned administrator.

But Sproul had already failed to understand the obsessive hold academic issues have for a university faculty. The loyalty oath the regents were now demanding clashed head-on with two entwined academic notions, academic freedom and tenure, for which American professors had fought long and hard. These conjoined rights — the freedom to teach and write without outside interference and the right to hold one's job for life after an agreed-upon period and process of probation — constituted the fundamental privileges of the American academy. Other professions might receive more remuneration or prestige, but the American professorate was free and unsackable, save for proven instances of moral turpitude. In the American university, high-mindedness and self-interest fused in the alembic of these twinned prerogatives. And now the regents — businessmen, politicians, union leaders, not an academic among them, including the president himself — were threatening to reduce a privileged profession to the status of mere employment.

How did the matter look, on the other hand, to the majority of the regents? Eight of the twenty-four — the governor, the lieutenant governor, the assembly speaker, the president of the state board of agriculture, the president of the Mechanics Institute of San Francisco, the state superintendent of public instruction, the president of the university, and the president of the alumni association — came in one degree or another from the political sector. Such people were used to deals and compromises as part of daily life. The remaining sixteen regents, however, were, as they had been since 1920, lawyers, businessmen, and bankers, with a union official or clergyman thrown in now and then for good measure. In the case of the Ivy League and other distinguished private universities — Chicago, Stanford, Duke, Vanderbilt, Northwestern — capitalism had directly and privately created institutions of higher learning; but even in the case of land grant institutions such as the University of California, the corporate and financial sector had soon exercised hegemony, and these public institutions edged toward a system of *de facto* private control. Appointed by the governor to sixteen-year terms, governing their institution autonomously once their budget was secured from the legislature, respected as one would respect a federal judge (Alexis de Tocqueville's definition of an American peer of the realm), the Board of Regents constituted the House of Lords of California, with the regents serving as enpaneled barons.

Like the House of Lords, or the United States Senate before the direct election of senators, the Board of Regents was a conservative body. During the New Deal, the regents were reluctant to accept much PWA or WPA money from Washington with the result that University of California campuses did not enter the 1940s with the array of federally assisted structures one might expect, given the pervasiveness of PWA and WPA assistance to community colleges and high schools throughout the state. Dominating the board were such congenital conservatives as citrus rancher and onetime Republican congressman Charles Teague, a founder of the Associated Farmers of California, Mario Giannini, president of the Bank of America, and such former Progressives turned conservative as Edward Dickson of Los Angeles, father of the UCLA campus, and John Francis Neylan, chief counsel to

William Randolph Hearst and arch-priest of conservatism in the state. Throughout the controversy to come, Dickson, Giannini, and Neylan led the pro-oath forces on the board. Son of A. P. Giannini, founder of the Bank of America, L. Mario Giannini openly stated in the course of the controversy: "I want to organize twentieth-century vigilantes, who will unearth Communists and Communism in all their sordid aspects, and I will, if necessary." A vote to rescind the oath, Giannini opined, would result in the flying of flags from the Kremlin.[1]

Less inflammatory in his rhetoric, John Francis Neylan was more effective in his advocacy. A brilliant Irish Catholic lawyer trained at Seton Hall in South Orange, New Jersey, Neylan had come to California as a young attorney and had gone to work as a reporter for the Hearst newspapers in San Francisco. Newly elected governor Hiram Johnson took Neylan to Sacramento in 1910 and made him the first director of state finance. Returning to the private sector, Neylan grew rich as an investor, a real estate developer, and the attorney for all Hearst interests on the Pacific Coast. (Throughout the loyalty oath controversy, the Hearst-controlled newspapers in California—the San Francisco *Examiner*, the San Francisco *Call-Bulletin*, the Los Angeles *Herald-Express*, and the Los Angeles *Herald-Examiner*—pounded away at the resistent faculty.) Neylan had seen the endless American graves in France after World War I, and his politics had taken a radical turn to the right, as had those of his mentor Hiram Johnson, as well as those of Herbert Hoover and Edward Dickson and most of the once-young men of the Progressive generation. Authoritative, assured, opinionated, and well read (he owned a vast private library), John Francis Neylan embodied the very essence of a generation of New Men who had risen to wealth, prominence, and power within the framework of pre–World War II California.

Neylan frequently hosted dinner meetings of the Board of Regents in the Pacific Union Club atop Nob Hill in San Francisco, where the regents met on 13 January 1950 at the height of the controversy. Here, in the onetime Flood mansion converted and expanded by architect Willis Polk, the regents were on Neylan's turf in more ways than one, although the very idea of having a public body meet for business in an exclusive private men's club barred to minorities and women boggles contemporary laws and sensibilities. Neylan also used the device of clubby lunches at the Pacific Union Club with key faculty as a way of bringing them around, impressing the academics, self-made men on limited salaries, with the power and prestige, the assurance and polish, of at least one regent, John Francis Neylan, whom the faculty, it was suggested, should think twice about crossing.

In the research- and information-oriented decades to come, the University of California and its spin-off affiliates in agriculture, medicine, engineering, aerospace, weapons research, high technology, and, eventually, biotech would constitute the essential engine of the California economy. Already, with eight university campuses and affiliated institutions and its distinguished faculty of 3,200 academics, Cal had become the largest university in the nation and was on the verge, in its Berkeley campus, of becoming the most distinguished public university of its kind. The University of California had become, in short, California as utopia, as future: the best possibilities of the state distilled and institutionally expressed, given support and privilege beyond measure. Here was the intellectual blast furnace for a high-tech post-industrial economy destined to become the sixth largest economy in the world by the 1990s, then in its take-off phases. What a prize! And who was to control it?

The loyalty oath controversy represents a watershed between one California— regional, locally governed, as was the University of California, by resident oligarchs and politicians—and a post-war behemoth in the making, global in sweep and importance. Struggling blindly with each other on the issue of the oath, valid in its own terms as an intellectual and moral debate, the regents and the faculty were having it out, for the first time, as to who exactly would be running the post-war California show. From the perspective, perhaps subconscious, of the regents, the loyalty oath controversy was about Communism, true, but only secondarily. The regents had no hard evidence of Communist Party membership on the part of a single UC faculty member, although there were some who had been Communist in the 1930s; nor did the regents seem to be taking any pains to uncover such evidence. The Red Scare, rather, offered the regents an opportunity to regain control, if only symbolically, of an institution that was no longer local and hence moving beyond their grasp.

Who were these faculty members anyway, the regents were at least subconsciously asking themselves, recruited as they were from national and international institutions? What were their loyalties to the California that was now welcoming them to its university? Prior to World War II, the regents could assuredly dominate UC. Distinguished professors had then too been recruited on a national and international basis; but such academic stars as Henry Morse Stephens, recruited from Cambridge University, or Herbert Bolton, recruited from the University of Texas via Stanford, had soon become part of the local establishment. Stephens, for example, the first tenured professor of history at the university, soon became a beloved and pivotal figure at the Bohemian Club in San Francisco. This was even more true of university presidents Benjamin Ide Wheeler, David Prescott Barrows (also a major general in the California National Guard), and Robert Gordon Sproul, the classmate and close friend of Governor Earl Warren. The president and faculty of Stanford University enjoyed similar status. The presiding *numen* of Stanford, Herbert Hoover, Class of 1895, longtime trustee, ran Stanford University as a near-personal fief and established there a great research library that bore his name. Only once had the UC faculty truly flexed its muscles on a matter beyond the departmental; that had been in the late 1920s, to force from office President Barrows, a non-published political scientist more interested in the National Guard than the university. In the main, the UC faculty had tended, even through the radicalized late 1930s, to enjoy its status and the good life that came with it and to mind its own business.

Nor can one fully discount an element of anti-Semitism, however masked, in the confrontation. The regents most vociferous in their advocacy of the oath— Teague, who died in the midst of the affair and was replaced by L. Mario Giannini, Dickson, Neylan—invite such speculations, given who they were in their time, leaders of a plutocratic gentile Right; and it must also be pointed out that the most consistent defenders of the faculty, attorneys Walter Heller and Sidney Ehrman, came from the German-Jewish San Francisco elite. Anti-anti-Semitism, for sure, had gotten Hollywood into trouble with the HUAC in 1947, the same year that President Truman recognized the newly formed State of Israel. Two films had proven especially galling: *Crossfire* (1947), directed by Edward Dmytryk, and *Gentleman's Agreement* (1947), directed by Elia Kazan, which starred Gregory Peck as a gentile reporter who passes as a Jew in order to research an article on anti-Semitism (thereby prompting Ring Lardner Jr. to say that the moral of the movie was that you never should be mean to a Jew because he might turn out to be a gentile). Kazan also directed *Pinky* (1949), starring Jeanne Crain as an African-American passing for white who returns to the South and encounters the realities of racism. The Right considered such films Communist propaganda; and Congressman John Rankin, in the course of welcoming the star-studded Committee for the First Amendment to the HUAC hearings in Washington, had delighted in baiting the Hollywood delegation by giving the original names of such committee members as June Havoc (Hovick), Danny Kaye (David Daniel Kaminsky), Eddie Cantor (Edward Israel Iskowitz), Edward G. Robinson (Emmanuel Goldenberg, mistakenly given by Rankin as Goldberg), and Melvyn Douglas (Melvyn Hesselberg), as if such name changes were *de facto* proof of Communist sympathies.

The University of California faculty as of the late 1940s was not predominantly Jewish; nor was resistance to the oath among the faculty predominantly Jewish. The leadership of the resistance in its first phases—philosophy professor Edward Strong, English professor George Stewart, chemistry professor Joel Hildebrand, history professor John Caughey, economics professor Emily Huntington, psychologist Warner Brown—came from the Protestant ascendancy that had dominated UC since the nineteenth century. As of the late 1940s, however, the growing UC faculty represented men and women from an American and European background, many of them refugees from Hitler, who had distinguished themselves in the most exacting sectors of their profession. They had been recruited to California rather than promoted from within. Hence, they embodied the impending internationalism of the university, of the state itself, with its more diverse and subtle network of loyalties and identities. Many of them were Jewish, either American-born or naturalized émigrés. A number of regents, men who had come up through the ranks of high provincial California in the Progressive Era, sensed the changing nature of the faculty and had problems with it. The loyalty oath offered them a means of counter-attack through symbolic discipline and control.

Nor did the investigations of the House Un-American Activities Committee in June 1949 into the Soviet penetration of the Manhattan Project at Los Alamos help either the cause of oath resistance or anti-anti-Semitism in the minds of the regents. Klaus Fuchs, David Greenglass, Harry Gold, Julius and Ethel Rosenberg—the names associated with the penetration of Los Alamos and the conveying of atomic secrets to the Soviet Union—represented an anti-Semite's daydream come true. At the center of the controversy was the most charismatic faculty member in the history of the university: J. Robert Oppenheimer, whose younger brother Frank, also a Los Alamos scientist, admitted to the HUAC on 14 June 1949 that he and his wife Jackie had been members of the Communist Party, an admission resulting in his instant dismissal from the University of Minnesota and provoking headlines across the nation.

In the first half of the 1930s, J. Robert Oppenheimer, holding a joint appointment in physics at Cal Berkeley and Cal Tech, had stayed away from politics. He had neither a telephone nor a radio in his apartment in Berkeley or his room in Pasadena, and he read no magazines or newspapers. In 1936, however, Oppenheimer became involved with Jean Tatlock, the daughter of a conservative professor of medieval literature at Berkeley. Then in her mid-twenties, Tatlock was working on a doctorate in psychology while herself undergoing psychoanalysis. Jean Tatlock was also a card-carrying member of the Communist Party. In a reversal of the stereotype that it was Jewish Communists who were corrupting the goyim, this WASP princess—tall, leggy, well-bred, a vanilla milkshake straight from the Junior League—brought the reclusive Oppenheimer out of his shell and into a variety of associations on the left. In the course of their affair, which lasted three years before she ended it in 1939, Tatlock introduced the brilliant physicist to a number of prominent West Coast Communists and encouraged Oppenheimer's involvement in a growing number of left-wing causes, most notably the effort to form a teachers' union on the Berkeley campus. By the late 1930s, Oppenheimer was donating $1,000 a year to various Communist Party–affiliated causes. He was also attending many meetings that were, whether he knew it or not, Communist-dominated. There is strong evidence that he helped write a series of pamphlets entitled *Reports to our Colleagues* issued by the College Faculties Committee of the Communist Party of California.

Oppenheimer later claimed that Frank and Jackie—both of whom had joined the Party in 1936—brought him to the only recognizable Communist Party meeting he had ever attended, a gathering held in Frank's home in Pasadena to protest racial segregation at a local swimming pool. In sworn testimony before the Tenney Committee in May 1950, however, Sylvia Crouch stated that in 1941 she and her husband Paul attended a top secret gathering of Communist Party members hosted by Robert Oppenheimer at his home at 10 Kenilworth Court in Berkeley. Crouch was eventually to become a paid consultant of the Justice Department, so her testimony before the highly compromised Tenney Committee can be discounted. But in a letter to Oppenheimer dated 23 July 1964, Haakon Chevalier, a member of the Berkeley French department in the late 1930s, referred to "your and my membership in the same unit of the CP from 1938 to 1942," a clue which even

Oppenheimer's sympathetic biographer finds credible, although Oppenheimer denied throughout his life that he had ever joined the Party.[2]

He did, however, marry the widow of a Communist hero. Her name was Kathryn (Kitty) Puening, and her second husband had been Joe Dallet, the Dartmouth-educated son of a wealthy investment banker who had joined the Communist Party and been killed in the Spanish Civil War. Oppenheimer met Kitty Puening at a garden party in Pasadena in August 1939, and once again he found himself involved with yet another privileged radical. Born in Germany in 1910, Kitty Puening had been brought to the United States at the age of two and raised in a wealthy suburb of Pittsburgh, where her father was prospering as an engineer in the steel industry. Kitty attended the University of Pittsburgh before going on to the Sorbonne and the University of Grenoble. While hanging out in Paris, she married a jazz musician but had the marriage annulled after a few months when she discovered he was a drug addict. In 1933 Kitty returned to the United States and enrolled at the University of Wisconsin at Madison, where she met and married Joe Dallet, the All-American upper-class boy turned Party activist, a sort of Robert Redford of the American Communist Party. Joe and Kitty separated briefly before he went to Spain to fight for the Loyalists, but they had a brief reunion in Paris in June of 1937 just before Joe's death. After Joe Dallet was killed, Kitty was extremely close to Steve Nelson, later the official organizer of the Communist Party in Alameda County. Nelson was responsible for recruitment to the Party on the Berkeley campus.

A heavy smoker and drinker, hard-edged and neurotic, Kitty Puening married her third husband, Richard Harrison, a British doctor studying for his boards, after meeting him at the University of Pennsylvania, where she was taking courses in biology. She was living with Harrison at the time she met Oppenheimer in Pasadena, and the two of them began a clandestine affair almost immediately. The affair lasted a year; then Kitty, pregnant with Oppenheimer's child, went to Reno for a quickie divorce, which was granted on 1 November 1940. She married Oppenheimer, her fourth husband, the same day. Kitty and Opje, as he was known to friends and familiars, set up housekeeping at Number One Eagle Hill in Berkeley, a rambling Spanish Revival bungalow, which they purchased in August 1941 and which soon became the center of a boozy bohemian left-wing circle. In May of that year, Kitty introduced her husband to her good friend (and perhaps former lover) Steve Nelson: an indiscreet gesture, to say the least, in that Oppenheimer was already involved in the biggest secret of the war.

Although other American universities contributed to the Manhattan Project, UC Berkeley provided the key contribution of technology, expertise, and—in the figure of J. Robert Oppenheimer—leadership in the drive to unleash the power of the atom. Oppenheimer's colleague Ernest Orlando Lawrence, another Berkeley *Wunderkind*, had constructed the first cyclotron—a magnetic resonance accelerator for the production of high-energy particles—at Berkeley in 1930 when he was only twenty-eight. Establishing the Radiation Laboratory, Lawrence built increasingly larger cyclotrons over the decade. The eleven-inch cyclotron chamber of 1930 grew to the 148-inch chamber of the Calutron of 1943, named in honor of UC. By 1943 Lawrence was four years into his Nobel laureate, having won that coveted prize in 1939 at the age of thirty-seven for laying down the experimental foundation of high-energy physics. Oppenheimer and Lawrence were Castor and Pollux, twin polarities: the theoretical and the experimental; the charismatic Disraeli-esque Semite and the freckle-faced, sandy-haired, apple-cheeked All-American boy. They became, if not close personal friends, then at least friendly colleagues. A photo exists of Oppenheimer and Lawrence in the snow at Oppenheimer's ranch in New Mexico in the early 1930s: two of the most gifted physicists in the world, so amazingly young, from whose twinned efforts would come so much of the atomic age.

In 1943 Kitty and Opje gave a festive farewell dinner for themselves and some friends — among them, Professor and Mrs. Max Radin (whom Earl Warren had kept off the California Supreme Court) and Professor and Mrs. Haakon Chevalier — in an upper room at Jack's restaurant in San Francisco, with Opje securing an exquisite roast beef, despite wartime rationing, and an array of the best wines from Jack's formidable cellar. The Oppenheimers were off to Los Alamos. Discussions and meetings leading to the atomic bomb project had been underway for more than a year in Le Conte Hall on the Berkeley campus, where Oppenheimer had his office. The gathering of scientists from around the country at Los Alamos was under the overall command of Major General Leslie Groves, with Oppenheimer directing the scientific research.

As early as 10 October 1942, FBI agents, using bugging devices, had monitored a discussion at Alameda County Communist Party headquarters in Oakland in which organizer Steve Nelson had made reference to a secret weapons project at Berkeley and a Communist Party sympathizer very high in the project with whom he had spoken. The sympathizer, Nelson noted, had been a member of the Teachers Committee. Almost routinely, the FBI report drew the inference that Nelson was referring to J. Robert Oppenheimer. Both the FBI and Army Counter-Intelligence were aware of Kitty Oppenheimer's Party-oriented past, her marriage to Party hero Joe Dallet, her friendship with Steve Nelson. They also had the transcription of Nelson's remarks. The most top secret project of the war was by sheer necessity being staffed by many scientists from California, including the director himself, who were suspected of possessing one form or another of Communist Party affiliation or sympathies. Throughout the war, an incredible cat-and-mouse game swirled around the Los Alamos Project, whose scientific coordinator, J. Robert Oppenheimer, was under constant surveillance by the FBI, by agents of Colonel Boris Pash, chief of Counter-Intelligence for the 9th Army Corps on the West Coast, by Colonel John Lansdale, security aide to General Groves, and by Captain (later Major) Peer de Silva, chief of security at Los Alamos.

On 12 June 1943 Oppenheimer committed what was at best a glaring indiscretion, staying overnight at the Berkeley home of his former girlfriend Jean Tatlock,

still a member of the Communist Party. Tatlock's house was under FBI surveillance, and there is a strong possibility that it was electronically bugged, which
meant that the FBI and Army Counter-Intelligence had a transcription of conversations relating to Oppenheimer's probable adultery and who knows what references to Los Alamos or other privileged matters. Seven months later, Jean Tatlock
committed suicide in her Telegraph Hill apartment in San Francisco.

The scene now shifts to Haakon Chevalier, formerly president of the Teachers
Union at Berkeley, a half-French, half-Norwegian literary scholar and novelist, not
up to Oppenheimer intellectually perhaps (who was?) but compensating for that
inequity with a devotion that soon won Oppenheimer's friendship, especially after
his marriage to Kitty. In late 1942 or early 1943, as Haakon Chevalier would later
tell his side of the story, Chevalier had a conversation with George Eltenton, a
chemical engineer with Shell Oil who had lived for several years in Leningrad,
where he had worked with a British firm and where one of his two children had
been born. Fashionably British (Dolly Eltenton was a first cousin of Sir Hartley
Shawcross, chief prosecutor for the United Kingdom at the Nuremberg Trials),
left-leaning, and active in the proper causes, the Eltentons had fit quite comfort-
ably into the academic-professional social scene in Berkeley. In this alleged conversation at Eltenton's house one afternoon when his wife was out with the
children, the Shell Oil engineer, as Chevalier tells it, after some general remarks
on "the uncertainty, the odds against which the Allies were fighting, and the fact
that the Soviet Union and the United States were brothers-at-arms and were bearing the brunt of the responsibility for winning the war," got down to cases, specifically "the importance of the work being done by American and Soviet scientists." What was needed, Eltenton told Chevalier (according to Chevalier's later
testimony) was the sharing of strategic information between American and Soviet
scientists so as to facilitate the war effort. Would Chevalier's good friend Oppenheimer, so sympathetic to the right causes, perhaps be willing to facilitate such a
scientific exchange in conjunction with certain parties Eltenton only vaguely suggested he was representing?

Chevalier later claimed that it dawned on him then and there that the unidentified people behind Eltenton, who seemed so embarrassed, so roundabout in his
phrases, "were really interested in the secret project Oppenheimer was working
on." "I told Eltenton," Chevalier said, "something to the effect that whoever had
thought this up had got his signals mixed; that I was not one to involve myself in
such a thing, and that I was sure Oppenheimer would be horrified at any suggestion of this kind." Eltenton seemed eager, according to Chevalier, to let the matter
drop, as if he really did not want to be involved in it himself, as if a great weight
had been taken from his shoulders when the conversation was over.

A short time later, the Oppenheimers invited Chevalier and his wife for dinner
on Eagle Hill. As Oppenheimer mixed martinis in the kitchen, Chevalier told
him of his conversation with Eltenton. "Neither Opje nor I have the slightest
recollection," Chevalier later asserted of the incident. "I remember only the sub-

stance: that I reported the conversation I had had with Eltenton because I thought he should know of it, and that he [Oppenheimer] agreed I was right in telling him. He [Oppenheimer] was visibly disturbed. We exchanged a remark or two. And that was all. We went back into the living room with the cocktail shaker, the gin and the vermouth, and joined our wives. I dismissed the whole thing from my mind."[3]

Six months later, in August 1943, Oppenheimer voluntarily went to a low-ranking Army officer, a lieutenant serving as chief of military security at UC Berkeley, and informed him that a local individual was putting out the word that he, Oppenheimer, was willing to pass on classified information to the Soviet Union via the consulate in San Francisco. Oppenheimer neither mentioned Haakon Chevalier's name nor related his kitchen conversation. Lieutenant Johnson contacted Colonel Pash, and the next day, 26 August 1943, Pash interviewed Oppenheimer in Durant Hall, recording the conversation on a hidden wire recorder. Oppenheimer told Pash that it would be all right by him if President Roosevelt informed the Russians regarding the project: "At least I can see there might be some arguments for doing that, but I do not feel friendly to the idea of having it moved out the back door." Under Pash's almost deferential questioning—Oppenheimer was, after all, director of Los Alamos—Oppenheimer named George Eltenton as the man in question. Skillfully, Colonel Pash pressed his case and eventually gleaned from Oppenheimer the fact that someone else, not Eltenton, had contacted two of Oppenheimer's close associates at Los Alamos. And there had been references as well, Oppenhenheimer continued, to someone from the Soviet consulate who had a lot of experience in microfilming—"a lot of experience in microfilm work, or whatever the hell" was how Oppenheimer put it. Colonel Pash finally elicited the admission that the contact person was a member of the faculty at Berkeley, but Oppenheimer said he did not wish to reveal his name because he felt that the Professor X in question (so the name was listed in Pash's report) was acting in good faith. Surprisingly, Oppenheimer also told Pash that Professor X had approached a total of three people—two at Los Alamos, one at Berkeley—within a week. Oppenheimer did not name himself as one of these people contacted.

Like the assassination of President Kennedy, the Oppenheimer-Chevalier incident could provoke a library shelf of research, and almost has. Was Oppenheimer nervous over the fact that one of his staff scientists from Berkeley, Giovanni Rossi Lomanitz, had been drafted into the Army in order to remove him from Los Alamos for security reasons, thus making Oppenheimer anxious to dissociate himself in the minds of FBI and Army Counter-Intelligence from Lomanitz and his ilk? Had the Haakon Chevalier conversation over the martini pitcher been something other than Chevalier later claimed? Had it been an actual invitation to espionage; and was Oppenheimer, again, trying to dissociate himself?

Astonishingly, nine years later, in April 1952, under cross-examination by Roger Robb, counsel to the Personnel Security Board of the Atomic Energy Commission,

Oppenheimer testified that he had invented the other two Los Alamos figures who had allegedly been approached by Professor X, now revealed as Haakon Chevalier: which meant that he had lied to Lieutenant Johnson and to Colonel Pash. "Why did you do that, Doctor?" Robb asked. Oppenheimer, the god-like Shatterer of Worlds in the Sanskrit phrase he had used in the New Mexican desert when the Trinity fireball first mushroomed into the sky at five-thirty on the morning of 16 July 1945 ("I have become death, the Shatterer of Worlds"), slumped in his seat, visibly shaken, then answered: "Because I was an idiot."

Did Oppenheimer lie to Pash in an effort to establish his loyalty by dissociating himself from the contacts? Or did such contacts truly occur, and did Oppenheimer only say in 1952 that they were fabricated so as to avoid perjury charges based on earlier testimony to the HUAC? In any event, Oppenheimer gave Haakon Chevalier's name to General Groves within a year of his interview with Colonel Pash. Yet even here circles move within circles, for Chevalier was sent as a translator to the Nuremberg Trials with the rank of colonel. But then again: the FBI and Army Counter-Intelligence and the soon-to-be-formed Central Intelligence Agency were perfectly capable of allowing Haakon Chevalier to function in a responsible position as an unwitting mole — if, that is, Chevalier were, even indirectly, a Soviet agent.

The entire affair is a labyrinth. As late as New Year's Day 1946, Oppenheimer was entertaining Communist Party members David Adelson and Paul Pinsky at his Berkeley home, and the FBI was aware of it: aware that Adelson and Pinsky had hopes of getting Oppenheimer to speak to the forthcoming Communist Party convention in Sacramento. Oppenheimer did not speak, but an FBI report filed shortly thereafter stated: "On January 3rd, Barney Young told David Adelson that he and Paul Pinsky had had a talk with J. Robert Oppenheimer and that Oppenheimer had gone over some material that Paul Pinsky was to take up to the legislature in Sacramento, and that Oppenheimer had boiled it down for him." The director of the Los Alamos Project, the man as responsible as anyone for the creation of the atomic bomb — a secret now safely in the hands of the Soviets — boiling down material for a Communist Party convention in Sacramento: the entire affair being monitored by the FBI! Was J. Robert Oppenheimer so self-destructive — or so arrogant — or was there some other scenario at work, worthy of a novel by John le Carré in its ambiguity and complexity?[4]

It has never been satisfactorily explained, for example, why Oppenheimer was treated so gingerly, so deferentially even, in his appearance before the House Un-American Activities Committee in 1949. By this time, after all, Oppenheimer must have had an FBI dossier five inches thick. And yet chairman John Wood virtually thanked Oppenheimer — whose brother Frank, also a Los Alamos scientist, was now admitting to membership in the Communist Party — for taking time out of his busy schedule and appearing before the committee. Individuals with far less probable cause for suspicion — low-ranking technicians, functionaries in the State Department, assorted Hollywood hacks — were meanwhile being raked over the coals for far less than even one of the many compromising items the FBI must have had gathered in Oppenheimer's file. Had Oppenheimer, confronted with what he knew to be damaging evidence, named names? Or was he innocent of any misbehavior beyond being overly friendly to individuals under surveillance? The very fact that the Berkeley Radiation Laboratory was being investigated as a possible nest of Soviet spies, however, upset the regents and made them fear the worst scenario of all: a full-scale HUAC investigation of UC. The Washington hearings, moreover, threatened to reinforce in the mind of the public what State Senator John Tenney and his committee had been saying all along: that the University of California was Red, very Red.

As early as 1940, Tenney had sought special permission to investigate Communism at UC. The 1942 committee report stated that at UC "a considerable number of instructors and faculty members" were either Communists or fellow travelers. In September 1946 the Tenney Committee investigated allegations that Communists had taken control of the Berkeley branch of the YMCA. Triumphantly, Tenney established the fact that Aubrey Grossman, educational director for the Communist Party in San Francisco, was known to Harry Kingman, director of the Berkeley YMCA. From the perspective of the Tenney Committee, Kingman's admission under oath that he had known Grossman when Grossman was an undergraduate Party activist at Berkeley constituted proof positive that the UC Berkeley YMCA was a Communist front. In the post-war period, Tenney became obsessed with the University of California, which he equated in his mind with the left-leaning, Communist-front academic-intellectual establishment of California. "The University of California is not a sacred cow," opined the 1947 Tenney Committee report in language more than a little suggestive of populist-right resentment of what it considered the privileged liberal academic establishment.

Situated in his home territory, UCLA provided Tenney with a continuing target of opportunity. Indeed, stress from testifying before the Tenney Committee throughout the post-war period may very well have helped bring on UCLA provost Clarence Dykstra's early death from a heart attack in the spring of 1950. From 1 to 3 October 1943, UCLA and an organization calling itself the Hollywood Writers Mobilization held a two-day Hollywood Writers Conference at the UCLA campus, which drew more than 1,500 writers and others, at five dollars per person, to hear speeches by the likes of Darryl F. Zanuck, Thomas Mann, James Hilton, Edward Dmytryk, and others on various aspects of the writer's role and responsibility in film, radio, and print media during the wartime mobilization. The conference sponsored workshops and panels on such touchy topics as the role of minorities in wartime, the relationship between propaganda and individual conscience, and other sensitive issues. A year later, the University of California Press published the proceedings of the conference as a book, which was widely reviewed as an almost revolutionary assertion of the primacy of the writer in the entertainment industry. Livid that Hollywood writer and suspected Communist John Howard Lawson had

spearheaded the founding of the Hollywood Writers Mobilization and the organization of the UCLA conference, Tenney had unsuccessfully tried to have the
conference canceled before it was given. For the remainder of the war, Tenney
brooded and lay in wait.

After the war, Tenney began to pound away at the UCLA campus and its
provost, Clarence Dykstra. Had not UCLA sponsored the Hollywood Writers Conference in October 1943, an obvious Communist Party front? Had not UCLA
students demonstrated on behalf of Communist-infiltrated unions during the violent strike at Warner Brothers in October 1945? Had not UCLA cooperated with
John Howard Lawson and other members of the Writers Mobilization to found
the *Hollywood Quarterly*, a highly suspect periodical? Had not Dean McHenry,
an assistant professor of political science at UCLA, become a member of the
provisional committee for the People's Educational Center in Los Angeles, aligning himself with, again, John Howard Lawson, with Dorothy Healy, secretary of
the Communist Party of Los Angeles County, and that well-known Communist
activist Carey McWilliams? Had not the UCLA Institute of Industrial Relations
invited Harold Laski of the London School of Economics, a prominent socialist,
to lecture on campus? Again and again, Provost Dykstra was bombarded with a
barrage of cross-examination, innuendo, outright accusation, all of it depicting
UCLA in various shades of red and pink.

However beleaguered, Dykstra was not one to run from conflict, or at least he
feared his faculty and public opinion among the liberal intelligentsia of Westside
Los Angeles more than he feared Chairman Tenney. In February 1949 Dykstra
authorized a lecture at UCLA by a University of Washington faculty member who
had been dismissed for membership in the Communist Party. The regents were
enraged. Taking the matter up in executive session on 25 February 1949, the board
criticized Dykstra for allowing a known Communist to appear on campus. As if
to fire yet another warning shot across the UC bow, the California legislature
voted on 17 March 1949 to commend the regents of the University of Washington
for firing Communists on their faculty.

The reputation of UCLA suffered yet another blow on 21 October 1950 when
the *Saturday Evening Post* ran an article by William Worden profiling Communist
infiltration on the UCLA campus. "The record of Communism at UCLA," Worden wrote, "is worth studying as a case history of what has been done at many
schools, and can be done anywhere, by Communists or any other cohesive group
which invades a school with a definite and continuing purpose."[5]

Worden began his article with an evocation of the seventeen-thousand-student
UCLA campus as an institution as new and ungainly (a streetcar university, a
poor-boy's college, he describes it) as Los Angeles itself. By 1950 UCLA was barely
twenty years into its existence at Westwood in the Westside of Los Angeles, and
it had only received its full autonomy from Berkeley after the war. Such a university, Worden argued—growing, urban, a commuter student body, recruiting
faculty at a rapid rate—offered ample opportunity for Communist infiltration.

What Worden did not explicitly say, although he came close to it, was that UCLA was also the favored school of students from the Fairfax district of Los Angeles, something like a City College of New York with palm trees, liberal, Jewish, racially mixed. In 1950 an African-American, Sherrill Luke, was elected student body president of UCLA, the same year an African-American alumnus, Ralph Bunche, won the Nobel Peace Prize. Another African-American alumnus, Tom Bradley, was working his way up the ranks of the LAPD and going to night law school. Worden pointed to the presence of professed Communist Helen Edelman as a political writer on the *Daily Bruin*, the campus newspaper edited by allegedly left-wing students James Garst and Clancy Sigal.

Warden also chronicled a number of anti-discrimination agitations on campus: the picketing of a Westwood barbershop, for example, by a Students for Wallace group for its refusal to cut the hair of African-Americans; and a broadly based campaign carried on by the Committee for Campus Equality (the coalition included representatives of the Labor Youth League, the Mike Quin Communist Club, the Young Progressives, the Westwood Socialist Club, and the Marxist Student Forum) to force Alcu Thige, a private for-profit dormitory for women, to accept African-American applicants. There were probably no more than fifty Communist Party members on the UCLA campus, Worden admitted, "but this small group—call it branch or cell or faction—has been able to give the entire University a damaging reputation. . . . UCLA is not a Communist school by a majority of some 400 to 1. But it has been affected and hurt by Communists. Should you be a Party member and need a model for operations on a university campus, here it is."[6]

Unable to ignore the *Saturday Evening Post* article, the regents grew even more distressed. The loyalty oath controversy had erupted into a bleeding ulcer. Reacting to the unexpected faculty resistance to the oath, President Sproul had secured the release of September 1949 checks for non-signers. Sproul had also secured an agreement from the regents to approve contracts for the academic year 1949–50, which would give him time, he argued, to bring around the non-signers and resolve the dispute. Throughout the academic year 1949–50, the Year of the Oath, as Berkeley English professor George Stewart described it, the controversy raged as Sproul sought to win over a stiffening resistance centered in the faculty senate at Berkeley.

On 27 June 1949 faculty resisting the oath had held their first meeting at the Faculty Club on the Berkeley campus. This group was large and broadly based. Impressively, its sympathizers included Monroe Deutsch, provost emeritus of Berkeley, the academic administrator most responsible for the rise of Berkeley to distinction in the 1930s. Deutsch's opposition must have proved embarrassing to Sproul, who was, after all, not an academic but a jumped-up alumnus, however talented as a financial manager and however devoted to his alma mater. Professor Max Radin of the Boalt Hall law faculty joined the fray, another disquieting moment for Sproul: for Radin had just been appointed to the Institute for Advanced Study at Princeton (where J. Robert Oppenheimer was serving as director) and had helped spearhead Berkeley's growing preeminence in law. In the summer of 1950, Radin wrote an elegantly reasoned account of the controversy for the *American Scholar*, journal of Phi Beta Kappa, in which he turned the tables on the regents by suggesting that they were the ones who were darkening UC with the "shadow of a Kommissar."

Medieval historian Ernst Kantorowicz, a refugee from Nazi Germany, went even further. At a meeting of the academic senate on 14 June 1949, Kantorowicz, in a stirring oration, compared the oath being demanded by the regents to that demanded by Mussolini in 1931 and by Hitler in 1933. The first oath, Kantorowicz remarked, was innocuous enough, a pledge of faith to *Volk und Vaterland*. Shortly thereafter, there came a second oath demanding allegiance to Adolf Hitler as *Führer*. Those who refused this second oath were sent letters of inquiry regarding their actual or alleged Jewish ancestry. Given the luridness of such comparisons, plausible to so many because of the recent events in Europe (Kantorowicz, after all, had fled for his life from the Nazis), it is not surprising that paranoia gripped many members of the faculty, especially the émigrés. Many faculty believed that their telephones were tapped and refused to call each other on university lines. Even worse, some faculty grew suspicious that certain students were spying on them on behalf of the administration.

On 24 February 1950 the regents voted twelve to six that those faculty not signing the loyalty oath by 30 April would automatically be severed from the university as of 30 June. Regents voting against the majority included Governor Warren, President Sproul, Sidney Ehrman, Edward Heller (Ehrman was the son-in-law of I. W. Hellman, a regent from 1881 to 1918, and Heller was Hellman's grandson), Jesse Steinhart, and Admiral of the Fleet Chester Nimitz. The fact that a five-star admiral had sided with the faculty boded well for a softening of the regents' position, which did occur over the next few months. On 31 March 1950, meeting at Santa Barbara, the regents voted ten to ten on a motion to withdraw the ultimatum. The tie, however, enabled the ultimatum to stand. As the August deadline for signing approached, more and more leaders of the resistance — Professors Jacobus tenBroek of economics, George Stewart of English, Clark Kerr of economics, Edward Strong of philosophy, Joel Hildebrand of chemistry, Walter Horn of the art department — signed the oath. Horn had just been recalled to active duty as a captain in Army intelligence. He thus faced a double jeopardy, the loss of his job and the probable loss of his commission, if he remained recalcitrant.

It must be noted, however, that the vast majority of the UC faculty took the oath as a matter of course. The more California-connected the UC campus — which is to say, the more localized and rooted — the less the controversy. At the agricultural stations at Davis and Riverside, for example, with their deep roots and loyalties in California agriculture, compliance was nearly perfect. The core of resistance resided at Berkeley and Los Angeles, the two campuses with the most

nationally and internationally oriented faculties: the campuses with the most colonizers. Even those who signed the oath after much agonizing found the occasion
anti-climactic. The San Francisco *Chronicle* reported on 1 March 1950 how a
professor, after much soul-searching, went into the Administration Building on the
Berkeley campus to sign the oath and was surprised to find the dreaded process
being administered by a secretary who was also a notary public, who cursorily
swore him in, then tossed his signed oath onto a stack of others, saying she would
stamp it later when she got around to it.

This is not to minimize the threat of dismissal faced by those thirty-one hard-
core non-signers who organized themselves as the Group for Academic Freedom
on 6 July 1950, electing Charles Muscatine, an assistant professor of English at
Berkeley, as their secretary-treasurer. By this time, the regents had already fired
physics teaching assistant Irving David Fox for declining to testify before the
HUAC in its hearings on alleged security breaches at the Radiation Laboratory.
On 16 December 1949 Fox had been hauled before the regents. The hapless TA
admitted that he had belonged to a few Communist-front organizations in the
1930s and attended a few Communist Party meetings in 1942 but said he had never
signed up as a member of the Party. The regents fired Fox on the spot, paying
his salary through June. Since Fox had no tenure, it was an easy thing to do. Fox
was exactly that: a fox run to ground by the regent huntsmen, not even an important fox at that, just a little fox — but with some connection to the faculty, hence
giving some credibility to the need for a loyalty oath.

The next firing, that of Miriam Brooks Sherman, a pianist in the department
of physical education for women at UCLA, occurred in April and was tragi-comic
in its humorous poignancy. Sherman's assignment was to provide piano music for
calisthenics: UCLA co-eds would file into the gym in exercise clothes, a coach
would call various exercises, and Sherman would play the appropriate music. State
Senator Jack Tenney had long been on the trail of Miriam Brooks Sherman as an
alleged Communist; and the regents, in yet another effort to appease the portly
inquisitor, ordered Mrs. Sherman pulled from her piano in the gym at 11:45 on
the morning of 20 April 1950 during an exercise session and fired on the spot,
leaving the young women signed up for the Rhythms Class standing bewildered
in their rehearsal shorts as their pianist was escorted from the room.

On 25 August 1950, the regents, with a two-vote majority, followed teaching
assistant Fox and gym pianist Sherman with more significant prey, voting to fire
the thirty-one faculty members who refused to sign the oath. (One dismissed
younger scholar, David Saxon of UCLA, a physicist, would in 1975 become president of the university.) Many of the younger scholars — Charles Muscatine of
Berkeley, for example — had distinguished wartime records. As a lieutenant in the
Navy, Muscatine had participated in the landings in North Africa and Salerno
and had won a commendation ribbon from the commander of the Atlantic fleet
for rescue work on the D-Day landings in Normandy. Emily Huntington, one of
the few tenured women scholars at UC, had written three monographs and twenty-

plus articles on social economics and had served on the National War Labor Board. A former faculty member at Oxford, where he had served as visiting professor of history, Ernst Kantorowicz had written four major books and more than twenty articles on patristic and medieval history; at the time of his dismissal, he was a visiting professor at Harvard. A fellow of the American Physical Society and a leading nuclear physicist, Gian Carlo Wick had come to Berkeley from Notre Dame and consultantships with the Office of Naval Research and the Atomic Energy Radiation Laboratory in Berkeley. John Caughey, professor of history at UCLA, was ironically a pioneer in the field of California studies and a ceaseless promoter of the California heritage.

On 2 October 1950 *Life* magazine profiled the last days of dismissed professor of psychology Edward Tolman as he cleaned out his desk and enjoyed a final lunch with colleagues in the Faculty Club. Even the usually hard-boiled Luce publication grew uneasy at the prospect of such obvious non-Communists as Tolman, a thirty-two-year veteran of Cal teaching, forced from his job at the age of sixty-four, a year short of retirement. "At the University of California last week," *Life* stated, "a very sad fact was being proved. The fact was that in opposing Communism, Americans sometimes create another evil."[7] *Life* also featured a close-up photograph of a grim-faced Neylan, looking very much the thin-lipped Torquemada, sitting near one of his supporters, regent Ed Pauley, an oil man whom the Senate had rejected in 1946, *Life* tellingly pointed out, when Truman nominated him to be Undersecretary of the Navy.

Academics live and breathe status and prestige. It is their meat and drink, their oxygen. And now the University of California stood tarnished, even in the eyes of such a popular, hence dismissable, magazine as *Life*. There was talk of an embargo on Cal credits by other institutions. The faculty senate of the University of Chicago voted to create a fund to assist the dismissed UC professors. Expressions of support flowed in from Harvard, Columbia, Cornell, Princeton, Yale, Michigan, Wisconsin, and other major universities: heartening, no doubt, but also humiliating in that UC wished to associate with these universities as *primus inter pares*, the first among equals, and not as a lost leader, a runner who had stumbled. Already, on 7 March 1950, a group of Cal alumni—it included construction mogul Stephen Bechtel, mining magnate Donald McLaughlin, investment banker Paul Davies, Walter Haas and Daniel Koshland of the Levi Strauss Company, and Monsignor Charles Ramm, Vicar General of the Archdiocese of San Francisco, a member of the Class of 1884, each of them embarrassed by the turmoil and loss of reputation of their alma mater in non-Cal circles—had formed a committee in an attempt to mediate the situation.

It would take two years for the California Supreme Court to find that the regents had abused their authority and to order the non-signers reinstated. By that time, however, thanks to the Levering Act passed by the legislature in 1950 in the immediate aftermath of the controversy, all state employees in all branches of government were now required to sign a similar loyalty oath against belonging to any group advocating the overthrow through violence of either the state or the federal government. With the passing of the Levering Act, the regents withdrew the UC oath, having gained little and lost much in the course of the controversy.

Richard Nixon, by contrast, a non-UC man, found the entire affair beneficial to his campaign for the United States Senate. Four years after his victory over Jerry Voorhis, Nixon was back on the campaign trail with the same technique—a charge of fellow-traveling, hammered home repeatedly—in a race against Helen Gahagan Douglas. If Jerry Voorhis represented the Left as Pasadena socialist, Helen Gahagan Douglas embodied the Left as Seven Sisters in league with Beverly Hills. A beautiful stage and screen actress and occasional opera star, Douglas emanated a Helen Hayes–like authority: a combination of stage presence, assimilated preppiness, and that species of assumed moral superiority that can so frequently characterize Hollywood liberals and tends to drive their more folksy opponents on the right to apoplexy. Gahagan was married to the equally assimilated Melvyn Douglas, an American Jew who, like Douglas Fairbanks, had taken a new name and mastered a British demeanor, a British accent, and British tailoring. The Douglases were ardent liberals involved in a score of causes, and when Helen Gahagan Douglas went to Congress in 1945 to represent the liberal silk-stocking Westside Los Angeles Fourteenth District, she outspokenly aligned herself with the Left, including the effort to disestablish the House Committee on Un-American Activities. On 19 June 1949, moreover, Douglas had blasted the *Fifth Report* of the Tenney Committee in the pages of the *Congressional Record*.

Helen Gahagan Douglas entered the race against Nixon weakened from a brutal primary. Outgoing senator Sheridan Downey, for one thing, had vilified Douglas for refusing to support the Truman Doctrine and its programs in Turkey and Greece. Deciding against a third term, Downey threw his support to Los Angeles *Daily News* publisher (and La Cañada orchid and camellia grower) Manchester Boddy, another highly Anglophilic Southern Californian, whose newspaper was being secretly subsidized by William Randolph Hearst. During the Democratic primary, Boddy savaged Douglas in the *Daily News* for voting the Party line, and the Hearst papers echoed the chorus. To make matters worse, Nixon cross-filed in the Democratic primary and placed a strong second after Douglas, forcing the embattled liberal to face an opponent in the general election who had won the Republican nomination and was the second choice of her own party. In the general election, conservative Democrats led by San Francisco labor leader Emmet Haggerty and George Creel, a candidate for governor in 1934, formed an influential Democrats-for-Nixon group organized exclusively around the soft-on-Communism issue.

As in his 1946 race against Voorhis, Nixon hammered away at one cleverly packaged issue. As a congresswoman, Nixon claimed, Helen Gahagan Douglas had voted 354 times (354 times! count them! 354 times!) alongside that notorious Communist Party–liner Congressman Vito Marcantonio of New York. Nixon's campaign manager Murray Chotiner flooded the state with a flier printed on pink paper comparing the records of Marcantonio and Douglas on such crucial votes as a requirement for loyalty checks for federal employees, votes of contempt for persons and organizations that had refused to disclose to Congress whether they were Communist, the allocation of funds for the Un-American Activities Committee, the passage of the Subversive Activities Control Act of 1948, the Greek-Turkish aid bill, and other items. "After studying the voting comparison between Mrs. Douglas and Marcantonio," the infamous Pink Sheet asked, "is it any wonder that the Communist line newspaper, the *Daily People's World*, in its lead editorial on January 31, 1950, labeled Congressman Nixon as 'the man to beat' in this Senate race and that the Communist newspaper, the *Daily Worker*, in the issue of July 28, 1947, selected Mrs. Douglas along with Marcantonio as 'One of the Heros of the 80th Congress'?"[8]

The Pink Sheet unnerved Douglas, as did the disruption of one of her rallies on the University of Southern California campus in front of the Doheny Library. As Douglas addressed a crowd of students and faculty, a horse-drawn hay wagon appeared, filled with male USC undergraduates, all members of a secret society called Skull and Dagger. The young men were dressed in top hats, cutaway coats, and underpants. As they approached the crowd listening to Douglas, the Skull and Dagger men began squirting it with seltzer water. People scattered in every direction, and the Douglas rally collapsed in shambles. USC president Rufus B. von KleinSmid sent a letter of apology. A number of USC undergraduates involved in this incident later went on to specialize in Dirty Tricks in subsequent Nixon campaigns.

As the campaign pushed toward conclusion, Nixon received important assistance from the Roman Catholic Archbishop of Los Angeles, James Francis McIntyre. In September 1950 McIntrye sent a letter to every parish priest in the archdiocese directing them to preach against Communism on all four successive Sundays in October, just prior to the November election. Astonishingly, McIntyre further directed that his priests specifically take up the issue of Communist infiltration of high places in American government. (Helen Gahagan Douglas later claimed that some priests preached specifically against "the woman" who was seeking office.) Throughout October, Nixon campaign workers distributed copies of the Pink Sheet to prospective voters as they left mass on Sunday morning, their pastor's anti-Communist sermon still ringing in their ears. Rallying to Douglas's cause, liberal Catholics formed a Catholics for Douglas Committee, which issued a pamphlet entitled *A Message to Catholics from Catholics* defending the voting record of Douglas in light of the social teachings of the Church. "California is not France," objected one Douglas supporter, lawyer Richard Rogan, "and Archbishop McIntyre is not Richelieu."[9]

The Pink Sheet, together with the disruption of her USC rally and the open opposition of the Archdiocese of Los Angeles, unnerved and distracted Douglas, and she made the mistake of endorsing Jimmy Roosevelt against Earl Warren in the concurrent governor's race, which brought Earl Warren down from Mount Rushmore. Though he disliked Nixon, Warren was provoked to say that he invited Mrs. Douglas to guess how he would mark his ballot for senator, an oblique remark Nixon blew into a full-scale endorsement. On election day, Nixon defeated Douglas by seven hundred thousand votes. Even Nixon, who never gave quarter or expected any, expressed a small measure of remorse in later years regarding his savaging of Douglas in the 1950 race.

The Hollywood Ten, meanwhile, were observing the 1950 election from the various federal correctional institutions to which they had reported on the first of the year to begin serving their one-year sentences for contempt of Congress. Two of the Ten, Dymtryk and Biberman, received sentences of six months from a more lenient judge. Sent to the Federal Correctional Institution at Danbury, Connecticut, Lester Cole and Ring Lardner Jr. had the satisfaction of sharing their quarters with former HUAC chairman J. Parnell Thomas, who had pleaded guilty to payroll padding and kickbacks and had been sentenced to three years. The warden at Danbury was initially fearful that Cole and Lardner would try to harm Thomas, but the convicted screenwriters were merely content to see their onetime accuser, his formerly portly frame shrunken beneath his flapping prison denim, assigned to gather eggs each morning and clear away the droppings from the chicken coop. When he first spotted the former congressman in his new role, Lester Cole was cutting hay near the poultry yard with a scythe. "Hey Bolshi," cried the disgraced congressman, now a convicted felon, "I see you still got your sickle. Where's your hammer?" To which Lester Cole replied, almost inevitably: "And I see just like in Congress, you are still picking up chickenshit."[10]

"Before the Ten actually went off to the pokey," Robert Kenny later stated, "nobody believed anybody was going to jail. Even the judges who handed out the sentences thought this was nothing more than a test case."[11] If Kenny was correct in this assessment, then the test case of the Ten had revealed the obvious: the United States had moved very much to the right. For some time, the Hollywood émigrés had been noting this shift with increasing alarm. In 1946 Aldous and Maria Huxley had been stunned when their applications for citizenship were denied on the basis of their pacifism. Aldous Huxley was especially devastated and saw his rejection as a personal affront and a political sign of things to come. Then Elfriede Eisler, the sister of Gerhart Eisler and Hanns Eisler, the Hollywood composer, began writing accusatory articles under the name Ruth Fischer, which were later gathered into a book published by Harvard University Press. Fischer described her brother Gerhart as a key Soviet agent in the United States, a murderer and a terrorist, and her brother Hanns as, at the least, a philosophical Communist. Fischer also claimed that German émigré writers Bertolt Brecht, Lion Feuchtwanger, and Heinrich Mann each had strong links to German Communism. Within the year, Brecht and the Eisler brothers had fled the country.

Brecht appeared before the House Committee on Un-American Activities on

30 October 1947. His cunning behavior before the committee has since been hailed by sympathetic critics as a triumph of European ingenuity over the stupidity of the American Right. Unlike the Hollywood Ten, Brecht did not choose to defy the committee. He was, after all, an alien, hence not under the illusion of legal entitlements; and besides: he had already made up his mind to leave the USA, having secured an Austrian passport and a visa to Switzerland. Wearing his one good suit and smoking a succession of cheap cigars, Brecht spoke in heavily accented English (deliberately more accented so as to confuse his interrogators) and insisted on the presence of an interpreter for the more lengthy questions, which gave him time to frame his answers. Throughout October, investigators from the committee had pored over all the Brecht plays they could lay their hands on. It was a most unusual and amusing instance of literary study, calling perhaps, when dramatized, for treatment by *Saturday Night Live*. The decision of the committee to examine Brecht on the specific content of his work allowed the crafty Berliner to make total fools of the bewildered congressmen and their counsels. Throughout one line of questioning, Brecht answered as if the committee were talking about another play entirely, and the committee never caught on. There was also a curious exchange about the parallels between Brecht's drama and the No plays of medieval Japan, which brought the committee into unaccustomed waters.

Finally, in exasperation, HUAC counsel Robert Stripling asked Brecht pointblank: "Have you ever made application to join the Communist Party?" Brecht replied: "No, no, no, no, no, never."[12] In her book, Ruth Fischer had claimed that Brecht had joined the Communist Party in 1930. Brecht's close friend Hanns Eisler stated unequivocally that Brecht joined the Communist Party that year. If true—and there is much to indicate that Fischer and Eisler were speaking the truth—that would make Bertolt Brecht guilty of a six-fold perjury, five *no*'s and one *never*. Such an act of perjury could have resulted in his indictment, trial, conviction, and imprisonment. Shortly after Brecht's appearance, the committee came to the realization that it had been made a fool of, and a detention order was issued forbidding him to leave the country. By that time, however, Brecht was safely in Switzerland.

Gerhart Eisler, meanwhile, had skipped bail and fled to Europe, and his brother Hanns had been allowed to leave the country on the promise that he would never return to either the United States, Cuba, or Mexico. The Bavarian-born historical novelist Lion Feuchtwanger of Pacific Palisades, Los Angeles, was also coming under increasing suspicion. Feuchtwanger claimed that he had never joined the Party, but he was an obvious sympathizer. In 1937 he had interviewed Stalin in Moscow at the height of the treason trials. His report of this visit, published under the title *Moscow—1937* (1937) was extremely pro-Stalinist and earned Feuchtwanger some snide remarks in *Time* when the émigré author arrived in the United States. When Feuchtwanger moved to Los Angeles, his pro-Soviet reputation came with him and was featured strongly in the Los Angeles *Times* article covering his arrival. Feuchtwanger gave credence to his pro-Soviet connections later that year when he wrote a letter to Stalin regarding the whereabouts of Russian actor Alexander Granach, said to be in trouble with Soviet authorities. Suddenly, in 1942, Granach appeared in Los Angeles, seemingly out of nowhere, having been freed and cleared for emigration to the United States by no less a person than Stalin himself. Historical novelist Irving Stone claims that Feuchtwanger spoke openly to him in an afternoon conversation in Los Angeles in the late 1940s of his admiration for Stalin and the Soviet Union and his dismissal of the United States as a troubled society.

Lion Feuchtwanger made his first application for citizenship in 1941, and it was not granted. Throughout the 1940s and 1950s, in fact, Feuchtwanger was under FBI and Immigration Service investigation. Agents asked Feuchtwanger's friends many embarrassing questions, including questions about his chronic womanizing. Was he not, the agents suggested, a moral bankrupt, a dirty old man, a pro-Soviet Stalinist unworthy of American citizenship? In 1945, in an effort to clear his name and secure citizenship, Feuchtwanger wrote the pro-American novel *Proud Destiny*, based on the efforts of Benjamin Franklin to finance the revolution in Paris. A few years later, Feuchtwanger produced *The Devil in Boston* (1948), a play regarding the New England divine Cotton Mather, perpetrator of the witchcraft trials and executions, which Feuchtwanger used as a prototype of the anti-Communist crusade of the late 1940s. Since he could not secure citizenship for either himself or his wife, Feuchtwanger could not return to Europe, even for a visit, lest, like Charles Chaplin, he be refused reentry. Having already lost two villas and two libraries, Feuchtwanger was in no mood to lose his Villa Aurora in Pacific Palisades. There, elegantly imprisoned amidst his books, his legal status that of a resident alien under surveillance, Lion Feuchtwanger remained until his death from a stomach hemorrhage in December 1958. Since Germany had deprived him of citizenship in 1933, Feuchtwanger died stateless, a man without a country.

Heinrich Mann, perhaps the leading socialist among all the émigrés, died on 11 March 1950 as he was preparing to return to East Germany, where he had been offered the directorship of the National Academy, with the strong possibility that he would soon be promoted to the ceremonial position of President of the German Democratic Republic. An outspoken socialist, Heinrich Mann had never liked the United States. In Los Angeles, he had lived and died a recluse. His brother Thomas, by contrast, had become one of the most celebrated American citizens of the pre-war and wartime era. Even as he found refuge, however, "under the serene Egyptian-like sky of California," Thomas Mann nurtured numerous doubts. Initially, in the United States of Franklin Delano Roosevelt, Mann's good friend and the sub-textual protagonist of *Joseph the Provider*, Mann's difficulties with the United States in general and Southern California in particular were mainly cultural, certainly not political. He lived among the German-speaking émigrés, Mann wrote Bruno Walter on 6 May 1943, "and if occasionally an American countenance appears, it is as a rule so strangely blank and amiably stereotyped that one has had enough for quite some time to come."[13] In comparison to a later émigré, Vladimir Nabokov, who became an exquisite cultural anthropologist of American life, Thomas Mann only minimally connected with his surroundings. His letters and diaries, even the autobiographical *Story of a Novel* (1961), Mann's account of his composition of *Doctor Faustus* (1947), are characterized by a vast and shadowy distance between a generalizing Teutonic perception and the specifics of American experience.

After the war, Mann's disaffection began to assume a political dimension. He could never really recover from the death of his patron FDR, for one thing. (References to Harry Truman are next to non-existent in Mann's letters and diaries.) As early as November 1945, Mann was writing to Albert Einstein that he is growing frightened of the increasing xenophobia and anti-Semitism of the United States, its *Verdunklung*, or darkening, a term used by both Mann and Feuchtwanger. In a letter to his friend and patroness Agnes Meyer dated 1 December 1946, Mann speculated that the war had done major psychological and moral damage to the United States and that as a result the country could very well go to the right. "But if fascism comes," Mann noted mordantly, "I can point out that I was once Senator Taft's dinner guest. That perhaps may save me from the concentration camp."[14]

Throughout 1945 and 1946, Mann remained openly affiliated with such left-liberal organizations as the Independent Citizens Committee, which he joined along with Helen Gahagan Douglas and retired Marine brigadier general Evans Fordyce Carlson, himself an intriguing blend of Marine combat leader (the commanding officer of Carlson's Raiders, one of the crack commando units in the Pacific during the war) and a left-liberal spokesman showing every sign of running for the United States Senate before his premature death in 1947. Mann also formed a friendship with Charles Chaplin just as Chaplin was becoming progressively more alienated from the United States and hence a more active member of Salka Viertel's Sunday émigré circle. Although Mann's son Michael, father of grandsons Tonio and Frido, whom Mann adored, was flourishing as a violinist with the San Francisco Symphony and would later earn a Ph.D. in German literature at Harvard and rise to full professor at Berkeley, Mann's oldest son Klaus was, like his father, becoming increasingly anti-American in the years before his suicide in 1949, despite Klaus's distinguished service as a senior Army NCO in a psychological warfare unit on the front lines in Italy.

In January 1947, in a letter to the dean of the philosophy faculty of the university of Bonn thanking the University for the restoration of his honorary doctorate, Mann first surfaced with the idea that he was in the process of recovering his German identity in the course of writing *Doctor Faustus*. Ten months later, in another letter, written on the eve of the Hollywood hearings in Washington — a letter so bitter, and perhaps so dangerous, that it remained unsigned and unsent — Mann was even more gloomy regarding the United States. "We can already see the first signs of terrorism, talebearing, political inquisition, and suspension of law," he noted, "all of which are excused by an alleged state of *emergency*. As a German I can only say: That is the way it began among us, too."[15]

When the Hollywood Ten were indicted, Mann rushed to print with a statement in which he chastised "the ignorant and superstitious persecution of the believers in a political and economic doctrine which is, after all, the creation of great minds and great thinkers."[16] Mann was deeply disturbed when his friend Hanns Eisler was deported. "But I have a wife and children," Mann wrote Agnes Meyer on 10 October 1947, "and am not inquiring further into the matter."[17] Both Mann and his wife took great satisfaction in Bertolt Brecht's sly appearance before the HUAC, which they listened to on the radio.

In 1948 Mann supported Henry Wallace and the Progressive ticket. In 1949 he was listed as being a Communist sympathizer in the Tenney Report. The Beverly Wilshire Hotel refused to rent space to a group to whom he was scheduled to speak. The Library of Congress canceled a lecture. Congressman Donald Jackson criticized Mann from the floor of the House for sending birthday greetings to the poet Johannes Becher, then living in East Germany. On 26 March 1951 the *Free Man*, a right-wing magazine, published an article by Eugene Tillinger claiming that Thomas Mann was active in a number of Communist-front activities. The United Press syndicated the story to hundreds of American newspapers. Mann denounced the article in an open letter to *Aufbau*, the German-language newspaper in New York. He was not a Communist, Mann wrote, and had never been one. "At this opportunity, however," Mann continued, "it should be stated that the hysterical, irrational, and blind hate of Communism presents a danger for this country, whose citizenship was an honor and a joy for me. This danger is far more terrible than Communism itself; indeed, this insanity and persecution mania into which America has fallen and to which the people seem to be giving themselves over tooth and nail—all this can lead not only to nothing good but even to the most evil consequences unless the people come to their senses very soon."[18]

At this point, in mid-1951, Mann seriously began to think of returning to Europe. He could certainly afford to do so, thanks to publisher Alfred A. Knopf. During the war, the sale of Mann's works in German declined precipitously, and he became dependent upon royalties from the English translations of his work being published by Knopf. Both Knopf and Mann's English translator, Helen T. Lowe-Porter of Princeton, made the author a prosperous man. *Doctor Faustus* was a Book-of-the-Month Club selection, as was Mann's last novel to be written in the United States, *The Holy Sinner* (1951), which the club printed in an edition of a hundred thousand copies. At the same time, Mann was deeply disturbed by criticisms leveled against *Doctor Faustus* by American reviewers, who tended to find it too long, too discursive, too philosophical: too German, in other words, and perhaps too sympathetic to Germany. Such criticisms hurt Mann and dovetailed in his mind with his distress at the rise of the Right. *Doctor Faustus* was by Mann's own report his deepest, most personal book. While Europe praised it, the United

States accepted it only with reservation, and Mann brooded over this in his heart. It might even be said that the writing of *Doctor Faustus* through 1946, the very act of composing it in Pacific Palisades, had kept Thomas Mann rooted in the United States, despite his difficulties with American culture. Once *Doctor Faustus* was completed in January 1947, one notices a fall-off in Mann's attachment to his new country. The rejection of *Doctor Faustus* by American critics accelerated the process. From this perspective, not only the rise of the Right but also, more subtly, the European acceptance of *Doctor Faustus* prepared the way for Thomas Mann's triumphal return to Europe.

Had the country been in a mood to listen, Mann's repudiation of the United States in the summer of 1952 might have come as a great shock, but few were listening, and Thomas Mann — the Kaiser, the Magician, the friend of FDR, the consultant to the Library of Congress, the conscience of liberal German civilization in the darkest moments of the Nazi era, escorted on his visit to UC Berkeley by motorcycle police as if he were the President-in-Exile of a Free Germany — crept almost stealthily toward Zurich from New York on 29 June 1952 with only his briefcase and hand luggage. "I have no desire," Mann remarked bitterly, "to rest my bones in this soulless soil, which I owe nothing, and which knows nothing of me."[19]

What a loss to both Thomas Mann and to the United States that he should have become so bitter! And yet how justified, in most respects, was Mann's disillusionment — at least temporarily: for the United States would not, as Mann feared, degenerate into roundups and concentration camps. The nation would correct and restabilize itself. Ironically, Earl Warren, governor of the great state of California, the public figure who would most dramatically embody the corrective tendencies of American political and legal life in the decade to come, was also, like Mann, crossing the Atlantic that summer of 1952, only in the opposite direction, returning from the coronation of Queen Elizabeth II and a homecoming tour of Scandinavia.

Warren was in a troubled state of mind. Having reached the apex of his career, and then having failed to attain the presidency, the California governor was in the process of thinking seriously about leaving public life. Yet Warren had a problem — money. After thirty-five years of public service, he would be eligible, at the most, for a $900-a-month pension. With four of his children still in college, Warren realized the limitations of that sum, even in 1952. Despite the fact that he was one of the most prominent Republican officials in the country and a proven executive, Warren had been offered no seat in President Dwight Eisenhower's cabinet. What to do? En route to England, Warren had stopped off in Washington and discussed his plans with the new Attorney General, Herbert Brownell, who suggested that Warren would make an excellent Solicitor General of the United States. The governor left for England thinking that this might be his future, but Brownell's suggestion went nowhere.

The fact is: the relationship between Warren and Eisenhower had always been touchy. Perhaps they were too much alike: these two upwardly mobile men, so similar in their unpretentious origins, their hard-won middle-class dignity and middle-brow tastes, their essential friendlessness masked by their public popularity and leadership skills. They had crossed paths in the Bohemian Grove in the late 1940s but had not warmed to each other; indeed, it was generally believed that the two of them never met until the 1952 Republican convention, so standoffish was their relationship. Since Eisenhower already had the votes, Warren's help had been essentially symbolic at the convention. Seeing that a pro-Ike California delegation was seated had been a nice gesture, but Eisenhower did not need California's votes for the nomination. During the campaign, Warren had stood in danger of losing Eisenhower's regard altogether when he brought the general to address a sparsely attended rally of the Veterans of Foreign Wars in the Los Angeles Coliseum. A mere eight to ten thousand showed up in a stadium seating more than a hundred thousand. Worse: the podium had been so placed that Eisenhower found himself addressing ninety thousand empty seats.

Still, there had been some talk, even before the election, of a possible Supreme Court appointment for Warren in an Eisenhower administration. Or was Ike merely being kind, knowing, as everyone did, that the general had put a quick and humiliating end to Warren's presidential hopes? In Eisenhower, moreover, Warren had encountered a man more accustomed to being a Party of One than Warren himself. Behind his bland and smiling exterior, Eisenhower could be thin-skinned, resentful, suspicious. Warren, for his part, was always standoffish with Ike, especially after the humiliation of the Coliseum rally. Wont to please no man and giving no endorsements, Warren seemed slightly intimidated by Eisenhower, even eager to please. (Five stars and the presidency had a way of capturing the attention of even so self-regarding a man as Earl Warren.) Invited to attend the inauguration, Warren overruled his wife Nina, who wanted him to wear a top hat, and chose instead to wear a homburg because Ike was wearing a homburg. Who knows? Given the sensitivities on either side, that homburg might very well have helped Earl Warren save his career.

After Chief Justice of the United States Frederick Vinson had died in his sleep on 8 September 1953, Eisenhower did not turn immediately to Earl Warren. Far from it: Attorney General Herbert Brownell, in charge of the search effort, first approached Secretary of State John Foster Dulles, who refused, followed by two-time presidential candidate Thomas Dewey, who also demurred. Had either Dulles or Dewey accepted, Earl Warren would have continued on his inevitable course to oblivion as far as a national career was concerned. Given Ike's earlier overtures, Warren felt betrayed but remained stoic. He would later have his say in his memoirs.

On Friday, 25 September 1953, Earl Warren and his two sons, Earl Junior and Bobby, were hunting deer and wild pig on Santa Rosa Island forty miles offshore in the Santa Barbara Channel. Via the Coast Guard, Warren received a ship-to-shore message asking him to call Attorney General Brownell in Washington. Warren took a small plane to the mainland and called Brownell, who asked the governor to meet him at McClellan Air Force Base near Sacramento. At McClellan, Brownell informed Warren that Eisenhower wished to appoint him to be an associate justice on the Supreme Court, with a sitting justice being elevated to the chief justiceship. Warren went silent and momentarily considered the offer. He would be Chief Justice of the United States, Warren informed Brownell, or nothing. It was a vivid moment. Denied the presidency by Eisenhower, Warren was demanding of Eisenhower the only other public office in the nation comparable to the presidency itself. In common parlance, Earl Warren was going eyeball to eyeball with the Eastern Republican establishment that had denied him his lifetime dream. The establishment blinked, although it took four days for that to happen: four days during which Earl Warren might once again have sunk into oblivion. On 30 September 1953, however, the White House announced that President Eisenhower would nominate Earl Warren, governor of California, to the United States Senate for ratification as Chief Justice of the United States. On Sunday, 4 October 1953, Earl Warren, sixty-two, boarded a United Airlines flight to Washington to begin the final phase of his long public career. Sworn in as Chief Justice on the 5th, he lived in a hotel while Nina packed up the family's household effects in the governor's mansion in Sacramento for shipment to Washington.

The ensuing decade would witness Earl Warren emerge as one of the most influential—and liberal—Chief Justices in American history. Calm, majestic, Warren seemed destined for the marble corridors of the Supreme Court. Now, as Chief Justice, the other side of Warren's nature—the liberal side of the California duality—was free to emerge. Historians who would later describe Warren as reversing his philosophies and values after being appointed to the Court and turning liberal, even going soft, did not know the full complexity of Warren's California Progressive sensibility with its admixture of conservative and liberal values. The attorney general of California who had played as important a role as anyone in incarcerating Japanese-Americans in 1942 strictly on the basis of their race would very soon be presiding over the unanimous 1954 *Brown v. Board of Education of Topeka, Kansas*, decision that would end the legality of public schools segregated by race. The crusading prosecutor would in 1966 preside over the *Miranda v. Arizona* decision ruling that a criminal suspect must be apprised of his or her legal rights, including the right to remain silent, before being interrogated. The outspoken anti-Communist while district attorney, attorney general, and governor would soon find himself labeled on the floor of the Senate by Senator Joseph McCarthy as the best friend of Communism in the United States. Carey McWilliams had once denounced Warren as a reactionary. Now the John Birch Society would soon be mounting an Impeach Earl Warren campaign. The President who had appointed Warren would later describe the appointment as "the biggest damn fool thing I ever did." Flying to London on Air Force One for the funeral of Sir

Winston Churchill in St. Paul's Cathedral on 30 January 1965, Eisenhower would tell Warren that he was personally disappointed that Warren and his court did not take a more draconian attitude toward Communist subversion. "What would you do with Communists in America?" the Chief Justice asked the former President. "I would kill the SOBs," Ike replied.[20]

Harsh words, true—and sounding even more harsh, perhaps, since they were coming from a revered former president and current General of the Army. But the Cold War and the anti-Communist crusade that was taking hold of American life in the late 1940s represented an equally harsh confrontation and would remain so for more than forty years. As of 1950, however, this confrontation, while important, was not the entire American story and certainly not the entire story of California. Even as hostilities dragged on in Korea, California was entering the era, 1950 to 1964, that would witness the fulfillment of so much of what had been hoped for and dreamed of during the 1940s. By 1962 California would become the most populous state in the nation. More, it would become in significant measure the fulfillment of its best wartime and post-war hopes for itself. Already, by the late 1940s, despite the dissensions and neuroses of the Cold War, that fulfillment was more than manifest in a gratifying pageant of moving vans pulling up to newly built homes in cities, towns, and suburbs and newly educated and employed veterans and their families entering upon their futures.

Tensions and ambiguities would remain, of course. Just as the tensions and ambiguities of the late 1930s were suppressed on behalf of the war effort, only to reemerge in the late 1940s, so too would the 1950s witness the gradual gathering of future storms of social and political protest, only temporarily suppressed. In this regard, the 1940s—with its chiaroscuro of life and death, foreign wars and homecomings, *noir* and suburbia—was perhaps the most ambiguous yet transformative decade in the history of the state. Pervading the lifestyle and imagery of the late 1940s and the ensuing decade—the swimming pools and backyard barbecues, the school yards teeming with healthy children, the suburban tracts and freeways, the whole Ozzie and Harriet splendor of it all—was an awareness continuing from the first half of the 1940s that it was all so precious because it could be lost. No matter: whatever the dangers, the dream was there, energizing California with the conviction that a just war had been fought and won and that life, love, family, home, work, beauty, sunshine, even happiness, remained galvanizing possibilities.

Notes

Chapter 1
1940 * A Matter of Life and Death

1. Ernest Jones, *The Life and Work of Sigmund Freud*, vol. 3, *The Last Phase, 1919–1939* (1957), 274–75.
2. Sigmund Freud, *Civilization and Its Discontents* (1930), newly translated from the German and edited by James Strachey (1961), 92.
3. "United Air Lines Stewardesses Celebrate," San Francisco *Chronicle* (16 May 1940).
4. "Soprano—Bewitching—To Which We'll Be Switching," San Francisco *Chronicle* (9 October 1940).

Chapter 2
1941 * Shelling Santa Barbara

1. "Enemy Planes Sighted over California Coast," Los Angeles *Times* (9 December 1941).
2. Jacobus tenBroek, Edward Barnhart, and Floyd Matson, *Prejudice, War, and the Constitution* (1970), 35; Carey McWilliams, *Prejudice. Japanese-Americans: Symbol of Racial Intolerance* (1944), 16–17, quoting the San Francisco *Call* for 8 May 1900.
3. Edward K. Strong Jr., *The Second-Generation Japanese Problem* (1934), 137, quoting the San Francisco *Chronicle* for 23 February 1905.
4. Edward Conn, "Japan and America: [An] Interview with Viscount Kaneko," *Outlook*, 128 (8 June 1921), 252.
5. Baron Shimpei Goto, "The Anti-Japanese Question in California," *Annals of the American Academy of Political and Social Science* 93 (January 1921), 198. [Hereafter cited as *Annals*.]
6. Japan's Agitation over California," *Current History*, 13 (November 1920), 285–86; McWilliams, *Prejudice*, 59–60.
7. Clare Booth Luce, "Ever Hear of Homer Lea?" *Saturday Evening Post*, 214 (7 March 1942), 12–13, continued 14 March 1942, 27 ff.

8. Charles Downing, *The Reckoning* (1927), 218.

9. McWilliams, *Prejudice*, 39.

10. "The Japanese Bogey Reappears," *Current Opinion*, 69 (November 1920), 588.

11. *Annals*, 99.

12. Scherer, *The Japanese Crisis*, 68; Richard Austin Thompson, *The Yellow Peril, 1890–1924* (1978), 80, quoting the San Francisco *Chronicle* for 25 February 1905.

13. McWilliams, *Prejudice*, 58–59.

14. "Immediate Evacuation of Japanese Demanded," Los Angeles *Times* (27 February 1942).

15. "Stimson Says Fifteen Planes over City," Los Angeles *Times* (27 February 1942).

Chapter 3
1942 * Garrison State

1. Martin Blumenson, *The Patton Papers, 1940–1945* (1974), 68.

2. Samuel Eliot Morison, *The Struggle for Guadalcanal, August 1942–February 1943* (1949), 244, 258.

3. Frederic Wakeman, *Shore Leave* (1944), 12, 124.

4. Allan Berube, *Coming Out Under Fire* (1990), 114.

5. Leon Uris, *Battle Cry* (1953), 77.

6. Robert Easton and Jane Easton, *Love and War: Pearl Harbor Through V-J Day* (1991), 233.

7. Ibid., 292.

8. Studs Terkel, *The Good War* (1984), 243–44.

9. "Japanese Consul 'Quite Sorry,' " Los Angeles *Times* (8 December 1941).

10. Audrie Girdner and Anne Loftis, *The Great Betrayal: The Evacuation of the Japanese-Americans During World War II* (1969), 102.

11. Carey McWilliams, *Prejudice. Japanese-Americans: Symbol of Racial Intolerance* (1944), 116, quoting DeWitt's testimony before the House Naval Affairs Subcommittee, 13 April 1943.

12. Jeanne Wakatsuki and James Houston, *Farewell to Manzanar* (1973), 60.

Chapter 4
1943 * Zoot Suit

1. Beatrice Griffith, *American Me* (1948), 159.

2. Ibid., 47.

3. Carey McWilliams, *North from Mexico: The Spanish-Speaking People of the United States* (1948), 224.

4. Chester Himes, *Black on Black* (1973), 24.

5. McWilliams, *North from Mexico*, 223.

6. Mauricio Mazón, *The Zoot Suit Riots: The Psychology of Symbolic Annihilation* (1985), 85.

7. Ibid., 73–74.

8. Gilbert Muller, *Chester Himes* (1989), 21.

9. Chester Himes, *The Quality of Hurt* (1972), 73–76.

10. Katherine Archibald, *Wartime Shipyard: A Study in Social Disunity* (1947), 47, 54.

11. Chester Himes, *If He Hollers Let Him Go* (Signet edition, 1971), 17.

12. Chester Himes, *Lonely Crusade* (Chatham Bookseller edition, 1973), 46.

13. Robert Allen, *The Port Chicago Mutiny* (1989), 118–19.

Chapter 5
1944 * Swing Shift

1. "City of the Angels," *Fortune*, 23 (March 1941), 90, 174.
2. "Richmond Took a Beating," *Fortune*, 31 (February 1945), 267.

Chapter 6
1945 * Hollywood Canteen

1. Colonel Darryl F. Zanuck, "Do Writers Know Hollywood?" *Saturday Review*, 26 (30 October 1943), 12.
2. Bob Thomas, *Clown Prince of Hollywood: The Antic Life and Times of Jack L. Warner* (1990), 127–28.
3. William Robert Faith, *Bob Hope: A Life in Comedy* (1982), 170.
4. Bob Hope, *I Never Left Home* (1944), 153.
5. Ibid., 140.
6. Faith, *Bob Hope*, 178.
7. Hope, *I Never Left Home*, 165.
8. "Hope for Humanity," *Time*, 42 (20 September 1943), 46.
9. Charles Higham, *Bette: The Life of Bette Davis* (1981), 128.
10. Charles Higham, *Marlene: The Life of Marlene Dietrich* (1978), 70.
11. Ibid., 101.
12. Ibid., 212.

Chapter 7
1946 * Homecoming

1. Lieutenant James M. Brown to Mrs. M. E. Brown, 28 April 1944, World War II Letters collection, Special Collections, California State Library.
2. Robert Easton and Jane Easton, *Love and War: Pearl Harbor Through V-J Day* (1991), 370.
3. Paul Smith, *Personal File* (1964), 414.
4. Irwin Gellman, *The Contender: Richard Nixon, The Congress Years, 1946–1952* (1999), providing photostat of Herman Perry's letter of 29 September 1945.
5. Earl Warren, "California's Biggest Headache," *Saturday Evening Post*, 221 (7 August 1948), 20.
6. Studs Terkel, *The Good War* (1984), 128–32.
7. "Gen. Bradley Lauds Film," New York *Times* (11 December 1946).
8. Herbert Kupper, *Back to Life: The Emotional Adjustment of Our Veterans* (1945), 29–30.
9. "Danger Is Exaggerated, Psychiatrist Says," San Francisco *Chronicle* (22 March 1945).
10. Don Graham, *No Name on the Bullet: A Biography of Audie Murphy* (1989), 139.
11. Audie Murphy, *To Hell and Back* (1949, reprinted 1977), 273–74.
12. Willard Waller, *The Veteran Comes Back* (1944), 5.
13. State Reconstruction and Reemployment Commission, *Postwar Housing in California* (1945), 33.
14. Henry Miller, *The Air-Conditioned Nightmare* (1945), 11, 20.
15. Mildred Edie Brady, "The New Cult of Sex and Anarchy," *Harper's*, 194 (April 1947), 319–21.

Chapter 8
1947 * Black Dahlia

1. Jack Smith, "Extra! Extra!" Los Angeles *Times* (3 December 1991).
2. "Trouble in Los Angeles," *Life*, 28 (16 January 1950), 78.
3. Will Fowler, *Reporters: Memoirs of a Young Newspaperman* (1991), 73–74.
4. James Richardson, *For the Life of Me: Memoirs of a City Editor* (1954), 289–90.
5. Fowler, *Reporters*, 131.
6. Dean Jennings, *We Only Kill Each Other: The Life and Bad Times of Bugsy Siegel* (1967), 195–204.
7. G. S. Perry, "Los Angeles," *Saturday Evening Post*, 218 (15 December 1945), 14.
8. Matt Weinstock, *My L.A.* (1947), 1–2.
9. Sam Boal, "L.A. Has It, but What Is It?" *New York Times Magazine* (4 September 1949), 37.
10. Katia Mann, *Unwritten Memories* (1975), 120.
11. Jarrell Jackman, "Exiles in Paradise: German Emigrés in Southern California, 1933–1950," *Southern California Quarterly*, 61 (Summer 1979), 195.
12. Bernard Potter, *Los Angeles—Yesterday and Today* (1950), 28.
13. Jennings, *We Only Kill Each Other*, 208.
14. "Trouble in Los Angeles," *Life*, 80.
15. Weinstock, *My L.A.*, 164.
16. Sheridan Morley, *Tales from the Hollywood Raj: The British Film Colony on Screen and Off* (1983), 141–42.
17. Matthew Bruccoli, *Raymond Chandler: A Descriptive Bibliography* (1979), 131.
18. Raymond Chandler, *Selected Letters*, edited by Frank MacShane (1981), 268.
19. Charles Higham and Joel Greenberg, *Hollywood in the Forties* (1968), 28.

Chapter 9
1948 * Honey Bear

1. John D. Weaver, *Warren: The Man, the Court, the Era* (1967), 154.
2. *The Memoirs of Earl Warren* (1977), 34.
3. Ibid., 24.
4. Ibid., 122.
5. Leo Katcher, *Earl Warren: A Political Biography* (1967), 272; Weaver, *Warren*, 55.
6. Katcher, *Warren*, 206.
7. Weaver, *Warren*, 162.
8. Ibid., 174.
9. Warren *Memoirs*, 248.
10. John Gunther, *Inside USA* (revised edition, 1951), 29.
11. Weaver, *Warren*, 161.
12. Ibid., 102.
13. Gunther, *Inside USA*, 39–40.
14. Weaver, *Warren*, 178.
15. Ibid., 184.
16. Gladwin Hill, *Dancing Bear: An Inside Look at California Politics* (1968), 105.
17. Michael Davie, *California: The Vanishing Dream* (1972), vii.

Chapter 10
1949 * Mexicali Rose

1. David Gardner, *The California Oath Controversy* (1967), 25.
2. Roger Morris, *Richard Milhous Nixon: The Rise of an American Politician* (1990), 527–28.
3. Jerry Voorhis, *Confessions of a Congressman* (1947), 333.
4. Ibid., 336.
5. Nancy Lynn Schwartz, *The Hollywood Writers' Wars* (1982), 92.
6. Ibid., 92, 94.
7. John Baxter, *The Hollywood Exiles* (1976), 84.
8. Charles Chaplin, *My Autobiography* (1964), 429.
9. Will Fowler, *Reporters: Memoirs of a Young Newspaperman* (1991), 95.
10. Hortense Powdermaker, *Hollywood, the Dream Factory: An Anthropologist Looks at the Movie-Makers* (1950), 329.
11. Lauren Bacall, *By Myself* (1979), 159–62.
12. Otto Friedrich, *City of Nets: A Portrait of Hollywood in the 1940s* (1986), 324–27.
13. Edward L. Barrett Jr., *The Tenney Committee* (1951), 57.
14. Ibid., 169, 332.
15. Bruce Cook, *Dalton Trumbo* (1977), 182.
16. Schwartz, *The Hollywood Writers' Wars*, 116.
17. "The California Debacle," *Christian Century*, 67 (4 October 1950), 1158.
18. Harvey Klehr and John Haynes, "The Comintern's Open Secrets," *American Spectator*, 25 (December 1992), 34–43, esp. 34–35.
19. Barrett, *Tenney*, 332–33.
20. Ibid., 136.
21. Ibid., 227.
22. Ibid., 170.
23. Carey McWilliams, "Mr. Tenney's Horrible Awakening," *Nation*, 169 (23 July 1949), 80.

Chapter 11
1950 * Police Action

1. George R. Stewart, *The Year of the Oath* (1950), 94, quoting the San Francisco *Chronicle* for 22 April 1950.
2. Peter Goodchild, *J. Robert Oppenheimer, Shatterer of Worlds* (1981), 206.
3. Haakon Chevalier, *Oppenheimer: The Story of a Friendship* (1965), 54–55.
4. Goodchild, *Oppenheimer*, passim, esp. 91–93, 179–80, 182–83, 239–40.
5. William L. Worden, "UCLA's Red Cell: Case History of College Communism," *Saturday Evening Post*, 223 (21 October 1950), 42.
6. Ibid., 169.
7. "The Regents vs. the Professors," *Life*, 29 (2 October 1950), 431.
8. Pink Sheet, reproduced in Morris, *Nixon*, 583.
9. Helen Gahagan Douglas, *A Full Life* (1982), 322–23; Morris, *Nixon*, 603–4.
10. Lester Cole, *Hollywood Red* (1981), 320.
11. Bruce Cook, *Dalton Trumbo* (1977), 187.
12. Otto Friedrich, *City of Nets: A Portrait of Hollywood in the 1940s* (1986): 331; Martin Esslin, *Brecht: The Man and His Work* (1960), 157.
13. Thomas Mann to Bruno Walter, 6 May 1943, *Letters of Thomas Mann, 1885–1955*, selected and translated by Richard and Clara Winston (1971), 418.

14. Thomas Mann to Agnes E. Meyer, 1 December 1946, *Letters*, 513.

15. Draft letter to a Mr. Gray, 12 October 1947, unsigned and unsent, *Letters*, 536.

16. Thomas Mann, "Foreword," Gordon Kahn, *Hollywood on Trial* (1948), v.

17. Thomas Mann to Agnes E. Meyer, 10 October 1947, *Letters*, 534.

18. Hans Bergin and Hans-Otto Mayer, *Thomas Mann: A Chronicle of His Life*, translated by Eugene Dobson (1969), 236.

19. Friedrich, *City of Nets*, 413.

20. *The Memoirs of Earl Warren* (1977), 5–6.

Bibliographical Essay

Chapter 1
1940 * A Matter of Life or Death

Sigmund Freud's *Civilization and Its Discontents* was newly translated from the German by James Strachey in 1961. Ernest Jones, M.D., wrote *The Life and Work of Sigmund Freud* in three volumes: *The Formative Years and the Great Discoveries, 1856–1900* (1953), *Years of Maturity, 1901–1919* (1955), *The Last Phase, 1919–1939* (1957). Regarding the 1940s in general, see Cabell Phillips, *The 1940s: Decade of Triumph and Trouble* (1975). Regarding the lingering Depression in 1940, see Walter J. Stein, *California and the Dust Bowl Migration* (1973), especially chapter 7, "The Migrant Problem and the Federal Government, Phase Two." See also *Interstate Migration: Report of the Select Committee [of the House of Representatives] to Investigate the Interstate Migration of Destitute Citizens* (1941). Of interest as well is "Transient Workers Ride the Rails on Springtime Trek to California Farms," *Life* (18 March 1940). Regarding the population of California as a whole that year, see Doris Wright, "The Making of Cosmopolitan California," *California Historical Society Quarterly*, 19 (1940), 323–43; 20 (1941), 65–79.

The chronology of the war in 1939 and 1940 is taken from Marcel Baudot and others, editors, *The Historical Encyclopedia of World War II*, translated from the French by Jesse Dilson (1989). Popular attitudes toward the war in Europe and Asia in 1940 are readily available in a number of mass-circulation magazines. Of relevance to this chapter are the following 1940 articles in *Look*: General Hugh Johnson, "The High Cost of Killing" (16 January) and "The United States Has the Best Guns in the World—On Paper" (13 February); Dorothy Thompson, "What It Means to be Neutral" (27 February); General Johnson Hagood, "America Needs a Maginot Line" (26 March); Colonel William Donovan, "Draft the Old Men First" (30 July); Captain Eddie Rickenbacker, "We Need 250,000 Planes and 500,000 Pilots to Protect the United States from an Invasion by Air" (27 August); Paul Schubert, "How Good Is the U.S. Navy?" (22 October); Major Leonard Nason, "Why Our Maneuvers Are Useless" (22 October) and "How the United States Can Be Invaded" (19 November); and Eric Sevareid, "What Hitler's Bombs Are Doing to England" (31 December). Of interest as well are the *Look* photo layouts "The Chief of Staff of the U.S. Army" (24 September), "Your First Day in the Army" (3 December), and "Here's How to Tell a

Soldier's Rank" (3 December). Colonel Henry Sanborn wrote "Our Defense Problem in the Pacific" in the October 1940 issue of *Coast* magazine. In "War Posters," an advertisement in the May 1940 issue of *Sunset*, official French posters from the mobilization earlier that year were being offered for sale as decorative art.

Regarding the America First movement, see Justus Doenecke, editor, *In Danger Undaunted: The Anti-Interventionist Movement of 1940–1941 as Revealed in the Papers of the America First Committee* (1990); and Michele Flynn Stenehjem, *An American First: John T. Flynn and the America First Committee* (1976). Regarding Charles A. Lindbergh and the America First Committee, see A. Scott Berg, *Lindbergh* (1998); and Wayne Cole, *Charles A. Lindbergh and the Battle Against American Intervention in World War II* (1974). See also Walter Ross, *The Last Hero: Charles A. Lindbergh* (1964); and Leonard Mosley, *Lindbergh: A Biography* (1976). Lindbergh's appearances in California on behalf of America First in June and July 1941, including partial texts of speeches, were covered by the Los Angeles *Herald Examiner* on 21 June 1941 and the San Francisco *Chronicle* on 23 June and 2 July 1941. Novelist Kathleen Norris defended Lindbergh against attacks by columnist Dorothy Thompson in the San Francisco *Chronicle* on 27 April 1941. Regarding Norris's overall point of view, see Deanna Paoli Gumina, "Kathleen Norris: The Philosophy of a Woman," *Pacific Historian*, 18 (Winter 1974), 69–73. For the effort to connect Lindbergh to the far Right, see Samuel Grafton, "Why Congress Should Investigate Lindbergh," *Look* (12 August 1941). See also Drew Pearson and Robert Allen, "The Dies Committee: Is It American?" *Look* (2 January 1940); and "Coughlin and the Christian Front," *Look* (26 March 1940). See also Stanley High, "Alien Poison," *Saturday Evening Post* (31 August 1940).

Regarding the radio shows of 1940, see John Dunning, *On the Air: The Encyclopedia of Old-Time Radio* (1998). Regarding the Academy Award winners of 1940, see Robert Osborne, *Academy Awards Illustrated: A Complete History of Hollywood's Academy Awards in Words and Pictures*, foreword by Bette Davis (1966). See also Christopher Finch, with a special essay by Peter Blake, *The Art of Walt Disney* (1973); and, John Culhane, *Walt Disney's Fantasia* (1983). Of relevance to the hard-edged style coming into favor in Hollywood, see "Lupe Velez Gives a Party and Does a Barefoot Dance," *Look* (2 January 1940); and "*Look* Calls on Ann Sheridan," *Look* (13 February 1940). See also "Stars Test Show for Soldiers," *Look* (12 August 1941). For the best-sellers of 1940, see Alice Payne Hackett and James Henry Burke, *80 Years of Best Sellers, 1895–1975* (1977). Regarding William Saroyan's attitude toward the developing war, see Lawrence Lee and Barry Gifford, *Saroyan: A Biography* (1984). See also Jeffrey Hellman, "The Great Saroyan," *Life* (18 November 1940).

Sunset magazine for 1940 featured almost monthly advertisements for cruises to Japan. See also Gerald Nye, "We're Already in the War," *Look* (9 April 1940), regarding American scrap iron being shipped to Japan from Long Beach. The comings and goings of the charming Captain Fritz Wiedemann were covered by Herb Caen and others in the San Francisco *Chronicle* for 9, 10, and 14 July, 11 August, 22 and 23 November, and 13 and 27 December 1940. See also "Nazi Propaganda in America," *Look* (31 December 1940), for a description of Wiedemann as Hitler's spymaster in North and South America and "probably the most dangerous Nazi in the country."

For highlights of the marriage mania in 1940, see the following 1940 articles in *Look*: "They Couldn't Afford to Get Married, but They Did" (18 June); "The Home Life of Lana Turner and Artie Shaw" (18 June); and "There's a Population of Two in Love" (27 August). Regarding love and marriage in the military, see the two *Look* 1940 articles "102 Flying Cadets on a Blind Date" (14 January) and "Women of the Navy" (22 October). For Jane Russell as ambassador of *eros* to the military, see the two *Look* 1941 photo layouts "Jane Russell Visits Camp Roberts" (1 July) and "Jane Russell Calls on the Navy" (21 October). For the erotic implications of the new nylons, see "30 Facts About Nylon," *Look* (26 March 1940). See also "Tennis-Mad Los Angeles Inspires New Active Sports Dresses," *Life* (25

March 1940). The beach culture of 1940 can be seen in the following *Life* 1940 photo layouts: "This is How Venice (Calif.) Sells Self" (22 January), "Early Spring in California Takes UCLA Boys and Girls to Beach" (1 April), and "*Life* Goes to a Lifeguards' Party" (18 November). See also "Beach Latitude," *Sunset* (May 1940); "6,000 Boys Meet 6,000 Girls: California Students Take Over Balboa Beach for a Seven-Day Party," *Look* (4 June 1940); and "A Church Goes to the People," *Look* (24 September 1940).

Regarding the high school mania of 1940, see "The Students of Hollywood High School are a Cross Section of Young America," *Look* (14 January 1941). Regarding the jitterbug mania, see "Tommy Dorsey: Jitterbugs May Be Noisy, but I Love 'em," *Look* (27 February 1940) and "High School Kids Cut Loose!" *Look* (29 July 1941). For the private prep school scene, see, for the Webb School, "School for Spartans," *Coast* (February 1940); for the Cate School, Curtis Wolsey Cate, *School Days in California: The Story of a Santa Barbara School, 1919–1950* (1961); and for the Thacher School, *The Thacher School's Semicentennial Addresses* (1940), and LeRoy McKim Makepeace, *Sherman Thacher and His School* (1941). Regarding Mickey Rooney as teen idol, see "America's Favorite Movie Actor Steals the Show at President's Ball," *Life* (12 February 1940); and "You Are Cordially Invited to Meet the Gang at Our Party," *Look* (24 September 1940). For the upcoming college generation, see "One of America's 165,000 Graduates Gets Her Degree Cum Laude at USC," *Life* (18 July 1940). Regarding collegians opposed to the war, see "Youth Congress in Washington Hears President Roosevelt Tell Them They're All Wet," *Life* (26 February 1940). For collegians preparing for war, see "From College Boys to Warbirds," *Look* (4 June 1940). The 1940 *Blue and Gold* yearbook of the Associated Students of the University of California at Berkeley and the *Stanford Quad* yearbook of the Associated Students of Stanford University for the same year offer vivid impressions of student life at Cal and Stanford. See also "Bertram Russell Rides Out Collegiate Cyclone," *Life* (1 April 1940). For the football season that year, see the extensive coverage in *Coast*. See also Richard Neuberger, "Purity League," *Collier's* (9 November 1940); Hendrik Van Leuven, *Touchdown UCLA: The Complete Account of Bruin Football* (1982); and Ken Rappoport, *The Trojans: A Story of Southern California Football* (1974).

Impressions of the household appliances and automobiles of 1940 have been gleaned from numerous advertisements in *Life, Look,* and *Sunset. Sunset* for 1940 is an especially rich source of information regarding domestic architecture. In this regard, see "Kitchen Comfort" and "Fireplaces" (February); "What's New in Western Living" and "This is Sunset House" (May); "Building Materials" and "*Sunset's* Kitchen Cabinet" (July); "Eating Out-of-Doors" (August); and "Have You Solved These Problems?" (October). The spring 1940 list for Sunset Books included fifteen separate garden books covering every aspect of garden design. See also Charles Gibbs Adams, "Gardens for the Stars," *Saturday Evening Post* (2 March 1940). Impressions regarding the increasing coziness of domestic architecture in 1940 have been gleaned from numerous articles and photo layouts in *Architect & Engineer* for that year and "A Story in Design," *Sunset* (November 1940).

For impressions of the cuisine of 1940, see the *Sunset* articles "Backgrounds for Food" (April) and "Chefs of the West" (May). For a more popular cuisine, see the recipes offered by the members of the Areme Club, Social Order of Raisina Chapter No. 89 Eastern Star of Fresno, in *Areme Club Cook Book*, issued in June 1940. For the growing popularity of wine that year, see Albion Ross, "Grapes of Cheer: This Is the Wine Center of the Western World," San Francisco *Chronicle* (28 January 1940). See also Robert Lawrence Balzer, *This Uncommon Heritage: The Paul Masson Story* (1970); and Leon Adams, *The Wines of America* (second edition, revised, 1978).

In *Treasure Island: San Francisco's Exposition Years* (1973), Richard Reinhardt has caught the importance of that event to the sensibility of pre-war California. Regarding the elegant trains of the era, see "Design for Travel," *Look* (9 November 1940). For impressions of air travel in that year, see "United Air Lines Stewardesses Celebrate," San Francisco *Chronicle* (16 May 1940). That most Californians preferred baseball to politics is evident from even the most cursory of considerations of the administration of Culbert Olson. See, for example, H. Brett Melendy and Bejamin Gilbert, *The Governors of California* (1965), 395–407. Regarding the Pacific Coast League, see John Spalding, *Pacific Coast League Stars: One Hundred of the Best, 1903 to 1957* (1994); and Dennis Snelling, *The Pacific Coast League: A Statistical History, 1903–1957* (1995). See also John Spalding, *Sacramento Senators and Solons: Baseball in California's Capital, 1886 to 1976* (1995). The San Francisco *Chronicle* covered Joe DiMaggio's signing difficulties that year on 25 and 26 February, 2, 6, and 7 March, 29 May, and 24 and 30 September 1940. See also Tom Laird, "The DiMaggios of San Francisco," *Look* (18 June 1940); and Richard Ben Cramer, *Joe DiMaggio: The Hero's Life* (2000).

Information regarding the resorts, sporting events, fairs, festivals, excursions, plays, musical performances, art exhibitions, restaurants, and night life available to Californians in 1940 was gleaned from *Coast, Westways, Sunset,* and *Pasadena Playhouse News.* See also Joe Hendrickson and Maxwell Stiles, *The Tournament of Roses* (1971). Regarding Tahoe Tavern, see Edward Scott, *The Saga of Lake Tahoe* (1957); David Stollery Jr., *Tales of Tahoe* (1969); and "Tahoe Tavern Resort to Open June 20," San Francisco *Chronicle* (16 May 1940). Regarding the ice-skating craze, see "A Knight Puts God's Country on Ice," *Coast* (February 1940). Regarding the equestrian culture of California, see Harry Hoytt, "California-Bred," *Coast* (March 1940); and "Ranch Party," *Look* (31 December 1940). Regarding the 1940 San Francisco Opera season, see the San Francisco *Chronicle* for 6 February and 9 and 14 October 1940. See also Alexander Case, compiler and editor, *The Annals of the Bohemian Club for the Years 1907–1972* (1972).

Chapter 2
1941 * Shelling Santa Barbara

Prejudice. Japanese-Americans: Symbol of Racial Intolerance (1944), by Carey McWilliams, is basic to this chapter, as is Jacobus tenBroek, Edward Barnhart, and Floyd Matson, *Prejudice, War, and the Constitution* (1970). For the Japanese-American perspective on the events of 1941–42, see Bill Hosokawa, *Nisei: The Quiet Americans* (1969); and Eileen Sunada Sarasohn, editor, *The Issei: Portrait of a Pioneer, an Oral History* (1983). For the background and history of the Japanese in the United States, see Masako Herman, compiler and editor, *The Japanese in America, 1843–1973: A Chronology and Fact Book* (1974); Harry Kitano, *Japanese-Americans: The Evolution of a Subculture* (1969); Noel Leathers, *The Japanese in America* (1969); and George Goldberg, *East Meets West: The Story of the Chinese and Japanese in California* (1970). Regarding the Japanese community of San Francisco, see Christie Kiefer, *Changing Cultures, Changing Lives* (1974). See also Fumiko Fukuoka, "Mutual Life and Aid Among the Japanese in Southern California with Special Reference to Los Angeles" (M.A. thesis, University of Southern California, 1937); and Donald Fellows, "The Imprint of Japanese Buddhism on the Cultural Landscape of the Sawtelle Area of West Los Angeles" (M.A. thesis, San Fernando Valley State College, 1968). Regarding Japan and the United States, see William L. Newman, *America Encounters Japan: From Perry to MacArthur* (1963). See also Naoichi Masaoka, *Japan's Message to America* (1914); David Starr Jordan, *The Days of a Man* (two volumes, 1922); and Charles Lanman, *Leaders of The Meiji Restoration in America* (1931). See also *A Brief History of the Japan Society of Northern California, 1905–1995* (1995). For a history of travel between Japan and California, see John Haskell Kemble, *A Hundred Years of the Pacific Mail* (1950) and *San Francisco Bay: A Pictorial Maritime History* (1957).

The Complete Journal of Townsend Harris, First American Consul General and Minister to Japan, introduction and notes by Mario Emilio Cosenza, appeared in 1930. Early interest in a strong American presence in the Pacific can be gleaned from Alfred Mahan, *Interest of America in Sea Power* (1897); and Brooks Adams, *The Law of Civilization and Decay* (1896), *America's Economic Supremacy* (1900), and *The New Empire* (1902).

In the novel *Last Days of the Republic*, published in San Francisco in 1880, Pierton Dooner postulated the mass migration of Chinese to California as the first stage of military conquest. Two years later, in 1882, Robert Wolter returned to the same theme in his novel *Short and True History of the Taking of California and Oregon by the Chinese in the Year AD 1899*. In March 1905 the San Francisco *Chronicle* ran a series of articles on the "Yellow Peril" in which the Japanese takeover of California was depicted as already underway. The Yellow Peril position was most notably expressed in such statements as Madison Grant, *The Passing of the Great Race; or the Racial Basis of European History* (1916); Monteville Flowers, *The Japanese Conquest of American Opinion* (1917); and T. Lothrop Stoddard, *Rising Tide of Color Against White World Supremacy* (1920) and *Re-forging America: The Story of Our Nationhood* (1927). See also Richard Austin Thompson, *The Yellow Peril, 1890–1924* (1978). James Francis Abbott, *Japanese Expansion and American Policies* (1916), represents an effort to harmonize relations between Japan and the United States. See also Thomas Bailey, *Theodore Roosevelt and the Japanese-American Crisis* (1914). Other early efforts to confront the question of the Japanese in the United States include Sidney Gulick, *The American Japanese Problem* (1914); James Scherer, *The Japanese Crisis* (1916); Jesse Frederick Steiner, *The Japanese Invasion: A Study in the Psychology of Inter-Racial Conflicts* (1917); and Edward Strong Jr., *The Second-Generation Japanese Problem* (1934). See also Lincoln Steffens, "California and the Japanese," *Collier's* (25 March 1916).

Hostile attitudes toward the so-called Japanese picture brides are evident in "Japanese Picture Brides Become Frights in California," *Literary Digest* (9 August 1919); and "Jap Picture Brides Come No More, but California Fears New Importation Trick," *Literary Digest* (9 October 1920). The increasing ugliness of white attitudes toward the Japanese in California in 1920 and 1921 is evident in a spate of magazine articles, many of them hostile, appearing in these years. See in this regard the *Literary Digest* for 31 July, 2 and 9 October, and 20 November 1920 and 13 August 1921. See also Roger Lewis, "The Voice of California," *Collier's* (9 July 1921). Senator James Duvall Phelan led the anti-Japanese campaign in such articles as "Japanese Evil in California," *North American Review* (September 1919), and "Ethics of the Japanese Problem," *Overland Monthly*, new series (November 1920). In January 1921 The *Annals of the American Academy of Political and Social Science* devoted its entire issue to the question of Japanese immigration to California. Amidst the generally scholarly articles, Senator Phelan weighed in with "Why California Objects to the Japanese Invasion." Even *Sunset* got into the fray with G. G. Bordwell, "Who Says White Folks Won't Work? Substituting American Families for Asiatics in California Orchards" (December 1920). Especially hostile was the editor of the Sacramento *Bee*, V. S. McClatchy, in "California's Threatened Hegira of Japanese," *Overland Monthly*, new series (March 1924). More balanced reports came from the *Current History* magazine of the New York *Times* for October and November of 1920 and January and March of 1921. See also "Dilemma of White California," *Century* (December 1920) and "California and the Japanese," *Outlook* (8 June 1921). See also P. J. Treat, "California and the Japanese," *Atlantic Monthly* (April 1921). Defenses of the Japanese include Chester Rowell, "California and the Japanese Problem," *New Republic* (15 September 1920); and Bruce Bliven, "The Japanese Problem," and K. K. Kawakami, "California and the Japanese," *Nation* (2 February 1921).

The growing perception of Japan as a military threat can be traced through Homer Lea, *The Valor of Ignorance* (1909); James Francis Abbott, *Japanese Expansion and American Policies* (1916); and Hector Bywater, *The Great Pacific War* (1925). See also William Honan, *Visions of Infamy: The Untold Story of How Journalist Hector Bywater Devised the Plans*

That Led to Pearl Harbor (1991). The novel *The Reckoning* (1927), by Charles Downing, describes an air attack on California by an Asiatic power. In "Can Bombs Wreck L.A.?" *Saturday Night* (21 October 1937), Frederic Coonradt speculated on the possible effects of an air attack on Los Angeles. Regarding real attacks, see Burt Webber, *Silent Siege: Japanese Attacks Against North America in World War II* (1984). Regarding the shelling of Santa Barbara, see "Japanese Carry War to California Coast," *Life* (9 March 1942); and Clark Reynolds, "Submarine Attack on the Pacific Coast, 1942," *Pacific Historical Review* (May 1964). In "The Great Los Angeles Air Raid," published in *Los Angeles: Biography of a City* (1976), edited by John and La Rue Caughey, longtime Los Angeles columnist Jack Smith recalled the imagined air raid on Los Angeles. See also "Army Guns Open Up at Unknown Foe," *Life* (9 March 1942).

The rising tide of sentiment for the removal of Japanese-Americans from Southern California can be traced through the following February 1942 stories in the Los Angeles *Times*: "Summary Removal of Japs Demanded" and "Riverside Farmers Threaten Vigilante Ouster of Japanese" (the 25th), "Storm Grows over Alien Ouster Delay" (the 26th), and "Japs Ouster Demand Rises" (the 27th). See also the poignant "Japanese-Americans Pledge Loyalty to U.S." (8 December 1941). Regarding the evacuation of the Japanese, see *The Final Report, Japanese Evacuation from the West Coast, 1942* (1943), issued by the U.S. Army and the War Relocation Authority. See also Leonard Bloom, *Removal and Return* (1949); Allen Bosworth, *America's Concentration Camps* (1967); Audrie Girdner and Anne Loftis, *The Great Betrayal: The Evacuation of the Japanese-Americans During World War II* (1969); and Maisie and Richard Conrat, *Executive Order 9066: The Internment of 110,000 Japanese Americans* (1972). *Farewell to Manzanar* (1973), by Jeanne Wakatsuki and James Houston, is a classic account of life in the camps. See also John Tateishi, *And Justice for All: An Oral History of the Japanese-American Detention Camps* (1984); Mamoru Inouye, with an essay by Grace Schaub, *The Heart Mountain Story: Photographs by Hansel Mieth and Otto Hagel of the World War II Internment of Japanese Americans* (1997); and the magisterial anthology *Only What We Could Carry: The Japanese American Internment Experience*, edited with an introduction by Lawson Fusao Inada (2000). See also Violet Matsuda de Cristoforo (formerly Kazue Matsuda), *Poetic Reflections of the Tule Lake Internment Camp, 1944* (1987). Regarding those interned from the Class of 1942 at UC Berkeley, see Carolyn Jones, "From Manzanar to Zellerbach," *California Monthly* (December 1992). For later developments, see Roger Daniels, Sandra Taylor, and Harry Kitano, editors, *Japanese Americans: From Relocation to Redress* (1986).

Chapter 3
1942 * Garrison State

General considerations of the home front of importance to this chapter include Richard Pollenberg, editor, *America at War: The Home Front, 1941–1945* (1968); Richard Lingeman, *Don't You Know There's a War On? The American Home Front, 1941–1945* (1970); Donald Rogers, *Since You Went Away: From Rosie the Riveter to Bond Drives, World War II at Home* (1973); John Morton Blum, *V Was for Victory: Politics and American Culture During World War II* (1976); Roy Hoopes, *America Remembers the Home Front: An Oral Narrative* (1977); and Studs Terkel, *The Good War: An Oral History of World War II* (1984). Also of importance to this chapter are Gerald Nash, *The American West Transformed: The Impact of the Second World War* (1985); Roger Lotchin, *Fortress California, 1910–1961, From Warfare to Welfare* (1992); and David Kennedy, *Freedom from Fear: The American People in Depression and War, 1929–1945* (1999). Of special importance is the anthology of essays edited by Roger Lotchin as *The Way We Really Were: The Golden State in the Second Great War* (2000), especially the essays "Daily Life in Wartime California," by Arthur Verge;

"The Way We Thought We Were: Images in World War II Films" by Linda Mehr; "Music Goes to War: California, 1940–45" by Ronald Cohen; "California in the Second World War: An Analysis of Defense Spending," by Paul Rhode; "New Deal and Wartime Origins of San Francisco's Postwar Political Culture," by William Issel; "Ethnics at War: Italian Americans in California During World War II," by Gary Mormino and George Pozzetta; "War Comes to Chinatown: Social Transformation and the Chinese of California," by K. Scott Wong; and "Brothers Under the Skin? African Americans, Mexican Americans, and World War II in California," by Kevin Leonard.

Personal narratives of California on the morning of 7 December 1941 can be found in Terkel's *Good War*. See also the novel *A Time to Live* (1943), by Michael Blankfort. Regarding George S. Patton Jr. at the Desert Training Center, see Martin Blumenson, *The Patton Papers, 1940–1945* (1974) and *Patton: The Man Behind the Legend 1885–1945* (1985). See also George S. Patton Jr., *War as I Knew It*, annotated by Colonel Paul Harkins (1947). Regarding the Desert Training Center itself, see the following articles in *Desert* magazine: Elizabeth Ward, "Desert Memorial for Patton's Army" (March 1957); Weldon Heald, "With Patton on Desert Maneuvers" (July 1966); and Bill Jennings, "Patton Country" (September 1977). See also R. W. Koch, "The General Patton Memorial Museum," *California Highway Patrolman* (April 1993).

Regarding the career of Rear Admiral Dan Callaghan and the USS *San Francisco*, see Samuel Eliot Morison, *The Struggle for Guadalcanal, August 1942–February 1943* (1949), volume 5 of the *History of United States Naval Operations in World War II*. See also *Battle Report Pacific War: Middle Phase*, prepared from official sources by Captain Walter Karig, USNR, and Commander Eric Purdon, USNR (1947). Regarding Callaghan himself, see Francis X. Murphy, *Fighting Admiral: The Story of Dan Callaghan* (1952); and Herbert Holbrook, *The History of the USS* San Francisco *in World War II* (1978). See also *America's Medal of Honor Recipients, Complete Official Citations* (1981). The San Francisco *Chronicle* covered the return of the USS *San Francisco* to San Francisco on 17 November 1942, 12, 17, and 24 December 1942, and 18 January 1943. For the dedication of the USS *San Francisco* monument at Land's End, see the San Francisco *Chronicle* for 11 and 13 November 1959. Albin Krebs reviewed the career of James Doolittle in an obituary for the New York *Times* (29 September 1993).

The California State Library maintains a collection of ninety-seven yearbooks and other forms of annuals from military training schools and other installations in California during the war years. Of particular relevance to this chapter are the Victorville Army Air Field, *Bombs Away* (1943), issued by the Bombardier Class 43–12, attended by Air Cadet James Milton Brown; and *The History of U.S. Navy Pre-Flight School, St. Mary's* (1946). See also James Schneider, *The Navy V-12 Program: Leadership for a Lifetime* (1987). Alexander Cody, S. J., professor of English literature at the University of San Francisco, wrote memorials to two of Brown's classmates lost in training accidents, *A/C Jerry Kelly, A.A.F.* (August 1944) and *Lt. Albert J. Hogan, A.A.F.* (April 1945). An overall history and inventory of military installations in California during these years is given in Paolo Coletta and K. Jack Bauer, editors, *United States Navy and Marine Corps Bases, Domestic* (1985); and William Evinger, editor, *Directory of Miltary Bases in the U.S.* (1991). See also Robert Witty with Neil Morgan, *Marines of the Margarita: The Story of Camp Pendleton* (1970).

Impressions of San Francisco during the war were gathered from an array of clippings in the San Francisco Scrap Books in the San Francisco History Room of the San Francisco Public Library and the following articles: Lucius Beebe, "San Francisco: Boom Town de Luxe," *American Mercury* (January 1943); L. Bradley, "San Francisco: Gibraltar of the West Coast," *National Geographic* (March 1943); "War Stirs Golden Gate City," *Life* (12 July 1943); John Dos Passos, "San Francisco Looks West: City in Wartime," *Harper's* (March 1944); "*Life* Visits the Top of the Mark Famous for its Scenic Views of San Francisco,"

Life (31 July 1944); "Beautiful City of the Golden Gate," *Life* (30 April 1945); and R. L. Duffus, "Port of Men Going to War," *New York Times Magazine* (24 June 1945). See also Captain James W. Hamilton and First Lieutenant William J. Bolce Jr., *Gateway to Victory: The Wartime Story of the San Francisco Army Port of Embarkation*, foreword by General Douglas MacArthur (1946); and Earl Stewart, *Presidio History* (1959). Regarding the efforts to accommodate military on leave, see two 1944 *Business Week* articles: "Worried Hosts: Hotelmen Fear Crippling of City if the Army Takes Over Hotels" (12 August) and "Barracks in Hotels" (23 December). Frederic Wakeman's *Shore Leave* (1944) is a notable novel of San Francisco as a leave town. See also Herman Wouk, *The Caine Mutiny: A Novel of World War II* (1951). Regarding the USO Hospitality House at Civic Center, see Steven Chin, "GI Dance Hall Razed for Library," San Francisco *Examiner* (12 April 1992). See also *The Lady of the House: The Autobiography of Sally Stanford* (1966); and Allan Berube, *Coming Out Under Fire* (1990).

Regarding Los Angeles during the Second World War, see Arthur Verge, *Paradise Transformed: Los Angeles During the Second World War* (1993); and the following articles: "West at War: Southern California Does a Great Job," *Life* (12 October 1942); Roger Butterfield, "Los Angeles Is the Damndest Place," *Life* (22 November 1943); and "How a Playground Goes to War," *Travel* (December 1943). For the scene at Long Beach, see Hugh Young, *Furlough Den* (1949). The 1993 Winter-Spring issue of *Journal of San Diego History* was devoted to San Diego during the Second World War. See also Leon Uris's best-selling novel *Battle Cry* (1953) and John Sanford's novel *The Land That Touches Mine* (1953). The wartime letters of Robert and Jane Easton were published by the University of Oklahoma Press in 1991 as *Love and War: Pearl Harbor Through V-J Day*. The wartime letters of James M. Brown are on deposit in the World War II Letters collection of the California State Library in Sacramento.

Chapter 4
1943 * Zoot Suit

Charles Wollenberg edited *Ethnic Conflict in California History* (1970). In 1971 George Frakes and Curtis Solberg edited *Minorities in California History* as a special issue of the *California Historical Quarterly*. It was reprinted that year as well, as *Neither Separate nor Equal*. Two post-war classics in the field include Dorothy Baruch, *Glass House of Prejudice* (1946); and Katherine Archibald, *Wartime Shipyard: A Study in Social Disunity* (1947).

Carey McWilliams's *North from Mexico: The Spanish-Speaking People of the United States* (1948) was reissued in 1975 with additional material by Matt Meier. See also Ruth Tuck, *Not with the Fist: Mexican-Americans in a Southwest City* (1946); Beatrice Griffith, *American Me* (1948); Manuel Servin, *An Awakened Minority: The Mexican-Americans* (second edition, 1974); and Albert Camarillo, *Chicanos in California: A History of Mexican Americans in California* (1984). See also Ernesto Galarza, *Barrio Boy* (1971). For a defense of the Sleepy Lagoon defendants, see Guy Endore, *The Sleepy Lagoon Mystery* (1944). Regarding the relations of Mexico and Southern California during the war, see Michael Mathes, "The Two Californias During the War," *California Historical Society Quarterly*, 44 (1965), 323–32.

Mauricio Mazón, *The Zoot Suit Riots: The Psychology of Symbolic Annihilation* (1985) commands the subject. See also Marilyn Domer, "The Zoot Suit Riot: A Culmination of Social Tensions in Los Angeles" (M.A. thesis, Claremont Graduate School, 1955); Ismael Dieppa, "The Zoot Riots Revisited: The Role of Private Philanthropy in Youth Problems of Mexican-Americans" (D.S.W. dissertation, University of Southern California, 1973); and Patricia Rae Adler, "The 1943 Zoot-Suit Riot: Brief Episode in a Long Conflict," in Servin, *An Awakened Minority*. For contemporary coverage of the Zoot Suit riots, see "Zoot-Suit

Riots: 125 Hurt in Los Angeles Fights," *Life* (21 June 1943); "Portent of Storm," *Christian Century* (23 June 1943); Thomas McCarthy, "Report from Los Angeles," *Commonweal* (25 June 1943); and Ruth Tuck, "Behind the Zoot Suit Riots," *Survey Graphic* (August 1943), and "Pachuco Troubles," *Inter-American* (August 1943). See also Carey McWilliams's two reports in the *New Republic*: "Los Angeles' Pachuco Gangs" (18 January 1943) and "Zoot-Suit Riots" (21 June 1943). See also Arturo Madrid-Barela, "In Search of the Authentic Pachuco: An Interpretive Essay," *Aztlan, Chicano Journal of the Social Sciences and the Arts* (Spring 1973). Also of interest is the novel by Thomas Sanchez *Zoot-Suit Murders* (1978).

Chester Himes wrote his autobiography in two volumes, *The Quality of Hurt* (1972) and *My Life of Absurdity* (1976). See also Himes's *Black on Black* (1973). For critical appraisals, see James Lundquist, *Chester Himes* (1976); and Gilbert Muller, *Chester Himes* (1989). Robert Allen published *The Port Chicago Mutiny* in 1989. See also "Negro Problem Worries Coast," *Business Week* (23 December 1944); and the novel by Alexander Saxton *Bright Web in the Darkness* (1959).

Chapter 5
1944 * Swing Shift

Frank Taylor and Lawton Wright, *Democracy's Air Arsenal* (1947) and John Rae, *Climb to Greatness: The American Aircraft Industry, 1920–1960* (1968) remain the best comprehensive histories for this period. Regarding the rise of aviation and aircraft manufacturing in Southern California, see Kenneth Johnson, *Aerial California: An Account of Early Flight in Northern and Southern California, 1849 to World War I*; Arthur Dunning Spearman, *John Joseph Montgomery, 1858–1911, Father of Basic Flying* (1967); William Powell, *Black Wings* (1934); Art Ronnie, *Locklear: The Man Who Walked on Wings* (1973); Frank Cunningham, *Sky Master: The Story of Donald Douglas* (1944); and Carroll Glines, *Grand Old Lady: The Story of the DC-3* (1959). See also Andrew Hamilton, "Douglas: The Lengthened Shadow," *Westways* (February 1964); Raymond Holt, "Wings for War," *Westways* (May 1956); Arlene Elliott, "The Rise of Aeronautics in California, 1849–1940" *Southern California Quarterly* (March 1970). Regarding the Dominguez Field Air Meet of January 1910, see Mary Jo Clements, "The First United States Air Meet," *Westways* (June 1955); and J. Wesley Neal, "America's First International Air Meet," *Southern California Quarterly* (December 1961). Regarding the promotion of Southern California, Los Angeles County especially, as an aviation center in the 1920s, see two Los Angeles Chamber of Commerce pamphlets: Edwin Jones Clapp, *Los Angeles Should Be the Home of Aircraft Industries* (1926); and *Los Angeles County Spreads Her Wings* (1929). See also two articles in *Southern California Business*: A. W. Poole, "Where the Aviation Industry Centers" (May 1929); and James Collins, "Outpost — National Air Defense: Douglas Staff and Plant Second to None in Military Aircraft — And May We Keep It So!" (December 1931). Regarding the rise of San Diego as an aviation center, see Eugene Lyle and Charles Diffin, *The City of Wings* (1938). Regarding Long Beach, see the bound brochure *McDonnell Douglas' 50th Anniversary in Long Beach, 1940–1990* (1990).

Fortune devoted its entire March 1941 issue to military aviation. Of special importance to this chapter are the articles "Air Power as World Power," "Air Power and the Machine," and "Research and the Air." See also "The Air as a Trade Route" and "Captain Rickenbacker Looks Ahead." In February 1945 *Fortune* devoted an entire issue to the Pacific Coast. Of special importance to this chapter are the articles "Steel in the West," "After the Battle," "Detour Through Purgatory," and "Richmond Took a Beating."

William Glenn Cunningham, *The Aircraft Industry: A Study in Industrial Location* (1951) is crucial to this chapter. See also James Richard Wilburn, "Social and Economic Aspects of the Aircraft Industry in Metropolitan Los Angeles During World War II" (Ph.D. dissertation, University of California, Los Angeles, 1971). See also Arthur Gardiner Coons, "Defense Industry and Southern California's Economy," *Pacific Southwest Academy of Political and Social Science*, publication no. 20 (1941); and Leonard Levenson, "Wartime Development of the Aircraft Industry," *Monthly Labor Review* (November 1944). Regarding labor relations in the aircraft factories, the following proved of use: Army-Navy Conference of Industry, Labor, and Other Leaders, *War Report* (1944); U.S. Department of Labor, Bureau of Labor Statistics, *Southern California Aircraft Workers in War Time*, Work and Wage Experience Studies Report no. 6 (September 1946); and Gene Tipton, "The Labor Movement in Los Angeles During the Nineteen-Forties" (Ph.D. dissertation, University of California, Los Angeles, 1953). Regarding the Lockheed cafeteria, see "Lockheed Builds Nation's Largest Cafeteria," *Architect & Engineer* (February 1944). Regarding the Spruce Goose, see Charles Barton, *Howard Hughes and His Flying Boat* (1982). Regarding defense worker Norma Jean Baker, see Fred Lawrence Guiles, *Legend: The Life and Death of Marilyn Monroe* (1984).

Post-war considerations surfaced early in the aircraft industry. As early as 1940, in fact, the gigantic B-19 superbomber, then under development, was being presented in terms of its future use as a passenger aircraft. See "B-19, Army's Newest Super Bomber, Will Dwarf Any Plane Now in Air," *Life* (8 April 1940); and "Inside the World's Largest Bomber," *Look* (4 November 1941). As early as 1942, the Pacific Southwest Academy of the American Academy of Political and Social Science sponsored a one-day symposium at UCLA on the post-war future of the defense industries, most notably aircraft. See "Planning for Postwar Reconstruction in Southern California," *Pacific Southwest Academy* (11 April 1942). See also "Winning Both the War and the Peace," *Annals of the American Academy of Political and Social Science* (July 1942).

The pamphlet *Marinship* was issued in 1944 by the Marinship Corporation. Charles Wollenberg has chronicled this important shipyard in *Marinship at War: Shipbuilding and Social Change in Wartime Sausalito* (1990). Regarding the shipbuilding division of the Bethlehem Steel Company in San Francisco, see *A Century of Progress, 1849–1949, San Francisco Yard* (1949). See also Clifford Hollander, "Bethlehem's San Francisco Yard," *Shipmate, United States Naval Academy Alumni Association* (July-August 1978). Regarding the Kaiser Shipyards in Richmond, see Marilynn Johnson, *The Second Gold Rush: Oakland and the East Bay in World War II* (1993). See also "Richmond Took a Beating," *Fortune* (February 1945). Regarding Henry J. Kaiser, see Mark Foster, *Henry J. Kaiser: Builder in the Modern American West* (1989); and Albert Heiner, *Henry J. Kaiser, American Empire Builder: An Insider's View* (1989).

Chapter 6
1945 * Hollywood Canteen

For general background, see Hortense Powdermaker, *Hollywood: The Dream Factory* (1950); and Robert Stanley, *The Celluloid Empire: A History of the American Movie Industry* (1978). Regarding Hollywood in the 1940s, see Charles Higham and Joel Greenberg, *Hollywood in the Forties* (1968); Otto Friedrich, *City of Nets: A Portrait of Hollywood in the 1940s* (1986); and Thomas Schatz, *Boom and Bust: The American Cinema in the 1940s* (1997). Regarding Hollywood and the war effort, see Colin Shindler, *Hollywood Goes to War: Films and American Society, 1939–1952* (1979); and Clayton Koppes and Gregory Black, *Hollywood Goes to War: How Politics, Profits, and Propaganda Shaped World War II Movies* (1987). *Fortune* published "Hollywood in Uniform" in April 1942. In February 1945 *Fortune* returned to Hollywood with the in-depth coverage of "Hollywood's Magic Mountain: Movies for the Masses, the West Coast's Biggest Peacetime Industrial Export, Are Made on the

Highest Eminence of Earned Income in History." Regarding Hollywood in uniform, see also James Wise and Paul Wilderson, *Stars in Blue* (1997), *Stars in the Corps* (1999), and *Stars in Khaki* (2000).

Darrell Zanuck issued his wartime manifesto in "Do Writers Know Hollywood? The Message Cannot Overwhelm the Technique," which was published in the *Saturday Review* (30 October 1943). Also of importance to this chapter are the *Proceedings of the Writers' Congress, Los Angeles 1943* (1944). Regarding the filming of *Casablanca*, see Howard Koch and others, *Casablanca: Script and Legend* (1973); and Koch's *As Time Goes By: Memoirs of a Writer* (1979). Regarding Hollywood's anti-trust problems, see Michael Conant, *Antitrust in the Motion Picture Industry: Economic and Legal Analysis* (1960).

Bob Hope was profiled on the cover of *Time* on 20 September 1943. See also Bob Hope, *I Never Left Home* (1944), *Have Tux, Will Travel: Bob Hope's Own Story*, as told to Pete Martin (1954), and *The Road to Hollywood: My 40-Year Love Affair with the Movies*, with Bob Thomas (1977). See also William Robert Faith, *Bob Hope: A Life in Comedy* (1982). Regarding the founding of the Hollywood Canteen, see Charles Higham, *Bette: The Life of Bette Davis* (1981); and Bette Davis, *This 'n That*, with Michael Herskowitz (1987). Biographies of importance to this chapter include Charles Higham, *Marlene: The Life of Marlene Dietrich* (1978); Hector Arce, *The Secret Life of Tyrone Power* (1980); and Bob Thomas, *Clown Prince of Hollywood: The Antic Life and Times of Jack L. Warner* (1990).

Chapter 7
1946 * Homecoming

The *UCLA Magazine* and the *Southern California Alumni Review* for 1946 provide numerous vivid portraits of those who returned and those who did not. See also War Department, *World War II Honor List of Dead and Missing, State of California* (June 1946). Of importance to this chapter as well are the *Memoirs of Charles Kendrick*, edited and annotated with an introduction by David Warren Ryder (1972). For the return of certain veterans who were later prominent, see Paul Smith, *Personal File* (1964); Jacques Levy, *Cesar Chavez: Autobiography of La Causa* (1975), together with Susan Ferriss and Ricardo Sandoval, *The Fight in the Fields: Cesar Chavez and the Farmworkers Movement* (1997); Eleanor Fowle, *Cranston: The Senator from California* (1980); Gayle Montgomery and James Johnson, in collaboration with Paul Manolis, *One Step from the White House: The Rise and Fall of Senator William F. Knowland* (1998); and Irwin Gellman, *The Contender: Richard Nixon, The Congress Years, 1946–1952* (1999). Neil Morgan and Francis Michael Carney were interviewed by the author in October 2000. Herb Caen's "One Man's San Francisco" column returned to the San Francisco *Chronicle* on 1 January 1946.

Milton Greenberg, *The GI Bill: The Law That Changed America* (1997) is crucial to this chapter. Also consulted was a collection of related pamphlets at the California State Library. Of special importance were the brochures *California World War II Veterans*, issued in October 1945 by the California Department of Employment; *What Are My Rights to Readjustment Allowances Under GI Bill?* by the same agency; and *State Bonuses for World War II and Korean Veterans*, issued by the Tax Foundation, Inc. In "After the War: The Victories at Home," published in *Newsweek* for 11 January 1993, James Michener argued the premier historic importance of the GI Bill. In *Going to War and Going to College: Did World War II and the GI Bill Increase Educational Attainment for Returning Veterans?*, Working Paper 7452 of the National Bureau of Economic Research (December 1999), John Bound and Sarah Turner qualified some of the sweeping claims made for this program. Individual stories of returning veterans on the GI Bill were drawn from Carlos Vasquez, on behalf of the California State Archives State Government Oral History Program, "Oral History Interview with Philip L. Soto," "Oral History Interview with Daniel M. Luevano," and "Oral History Interview with Arthur L. Alacorn," all issued in 1988. See also John Jacobs, *A Rage for Justice: The Passion and Politics of Phillip Burton* (1995); and Doug Ramsey and Juul Anthonissen, *Dave Brubeck, Time Signatures: A Career Perspective* (publication included in a boxed CD, 1992). Details regarding the impact of returning veterans on selected California campuses were taken from, among other sources, Andrew Hamilton and John Jackson, *UCLA on the Move During Fifty Golden Years, 1919–1969* (1969); Verne Stadtman, *The University of California, 1868–1968* (1970); and Manuel Servin and Iris Wilson, *Southern California and Its University* (1969).

For the look, feel, and texture of California in 1946, see Joyce Muench, *West Coast Portrait* (1946); and Evelyn Neuenburg, *California Lure: The Golden State in Pictures*, prologue and epilogue by Oscar Lewis (1946). Regarding the post-war economic boom, see K. Monroe, "Our New Western Empire," *Nation's Business* (July 1946); and "California Boom: New Industries Follow Westward Wave of New Population," *Life* (10 June 1946). See also Robert Sellmer, "Super Druggist Dart," *Life* (5 August 1946). Carey McWilliams commented on the post-war boom in *Nation*: "California Looks to 1946" (1 September 1945) and "Lesson of California" (22 June 1946). See also McWilliams's later "Look What Happened to California," *Harper's* (October 1949) and his masterly evocation of the boom, *California: the Great Exception* (1949).

Regarding the adjustment of veterans, see Willard Waller, *The Veteran Comes Back* (1944); Herbert Kupper, M.D., *Back to Life: The Emotional Adjustment of Our Veterans* (1945); and Howard Kitching, M.D., *Sex Problems of the Returned Veteran* (1946). The question of sexual difficulties was also explored by Stuart Engstrand in the novel *The Sling and the Arrow* (1947). Regarding Dr. Karl Bowman's defense of returning veterans, see "The Public's Fear of Neurotic Veterans, Danger Is Exaggerated, Psychiatrist Says," San Francisco *Chronicle* (22 March 1945). *Life* covered the raid of the Booze Fighters on Hollister on 21 July 1947. Hollister still remembers and commemorates the event. Regarding the film *The Best Years of Our Lives*, see Axel Madsen, *William Wyler: The Authorized Biography* (1973); and Thomas Schatz, *Boom and Bust: The American Cinema in the 1940s* (1997). Regarding General Omar Bradley's praise of the film, see the New York *Times* for 11 December 1946. See also Foster Hirsch, *The Dark Side of the Screen: Film Noir* (1983). Novels centered on the adjustment of veterans returning to California include Frank Fenton, *What Way My Journey Lies* (1946); and Peter Packer, *The Inward Voyage* (1948).

Don Graham told the story of Audie Murphy in *No Name on the Bullet* (1989). See also Audie Murphy's *To Hell and Back*, as told to David McClure (1949, reprinted 1977). Jane Russell told her story in *My Path and My Detours* (1985). See the San Francisco *Chronicle* (27 April 1943) for coverage of Russell's marriage to quarterback Bob Waterfield. Regarding Howard Hughes, see John Keats, *Howard Hughes* (1966); Albert Gerber, *Bashful Billionaire: The Story of Howard Hughes* (1967); and Donald Barlett and James Steele, *Empire: The Life, Legend, and Madness of Howard Hughes* (1979). Regarding Jean Peters, see the obituary in the Los Angeles *Times* for 21 October 2000.

Planning for the post-war future can be traced through the pamphlets issued, beginning in 1944, by the California State Commission on Reconstruction and Re-Employment and its monthly digest *Postwar California*, edited by Dorothy Tompkins. Of central importance to this chapter is the commission's *Postwar Housing in California* (June 1945). See also National Committee on Housing, Inc., *Proceedings of the National Conference on Postwar Housing* (Chicago, 8, 9, 10 March 1944); and Dean McHenry, "California Looks Ahead: Papers Presented Before the Pacific Southwest Academy, 15 June 1946," *Annals of the American Academy of Political and Social Science* (November 1946). Also of relevance are C. H. Grattan, "California's Prospects," *Harper's* (March 1945); and R. L. Duffus, "California Ponders Her Great Destiny," *New York Times Magazine* (3 June 1945).

Greg Hise, *Magnetic Los Angeles: Planning the Twentieth-Century Metropolis* (1997) is of pervasive relevance to any question of growth in this era. Regarding growth in San Diego in this era, see volumes 6 and 7 of Richard Pourade's multi-volume history of San Diego, *Rising Tide* (1967) and *City of the Dream* (1977). For the San Fernando Valley, see Jackson Mayers, *The San Fernando Valley* (1976).

Regarding the acute housing shortage of 1946 and after, see J. Marshall, "Chaos on the Coast," *Collier's* (21 September 1946); and H. Lavine, "Crowded California: Land of Come-One, Come-All," *Newsweek* (11 October 1948). *Blueprints for Modern Living: History and Legacy of the Case Study Houses* (1989), edited by Elizabeth A. T. Smith, includes definitive essays on this topic by Esther McCoy, Thomas S. Hines, Helen Searing, Elizabeth A. T. Smith, Thomas Hine, Reyner Banham, Dolores Hayden, and Kevin Starr. Regarding the enduring popularity of architect Pierre Koenig's Case Study House no. 22, as photographed by Julius Shulman, see Bob Pool, "Thoroughly Beguiled by Modernist House," Los Angeles *Times* (5 November, 2000). *Sunset* took a brief and guarded look at the post-war house in "This Is No Time to Build a House, But . . ." (March 1946) and "Glass and Simple Construction" (June 1946).

New Directions published Henry Miller's *The Air-Conditioned Nightmare* in late 1945 and *Big Sur and the Oranges of Hieronymus Bosch* in 1957. Mildred Edie Brady attacked "The New Cult of Sex and Anarchy" in *Harper's* for April 1947. Of the writing of books by and/or about Henry Miller, there has been no end. Of relevance to this chapter have been Alfred Perles, *My Friend Henry Miller* (1955); Kingsley Widmer, *Henry Miller* (1963); Willam Gordon, *The Mind and Art of Henry Miller* (1967); and Jay Martin, *Always Merry and Bright: The Life of Henry Miller, an Unauthorized Biography* (1978). See also Burr Snider, "The Man Who Loved Women," San Francisco *Examiner* (20 August 1989). Regarding the specter of juvenile delinquency in this period, see Albert Binder, Gilbert Geis, and Dickson Bruce, *Juvenile Delinquency: Historical, Cultural, Legal Perspectives* (1988). See also J. Edgar Hoover, "I Predict—A New Gangster Era," *Look* (8 January 1946); and the novel *Incorrigibles* (1947), by Karl Brown. Frank Rooney published "Cyclists' Raid," a short story based upon the 1947 motorcycle raid in Hollister, in *Harper's* for January 1951. For the film *The Wild One* (1953), based on Rooney's story, see Ron Offen, *Brando* (1973); and Charles Higham, *Brando: The Unauthorized Biography* (1987).

<h2 style="text-align:center">Chapter 8
1947 * Black Dahlia</h2>

General studies of Los Angeles in and around 1947 include Max Miller, *It Must Be the Climate* (1941); Matt Weinstock, *My L.A.*, foreword by Fred Beck (1947), and *Muscatel at Noon* (1951); Lee Shippey, *The Los Angeles Book*, with photographs by Max Yavno (1950); Bernard Potter, *Los Angeles—Yesterday and Today* (1950); Robert d'Auria Houston, *This Is Los Angeles: A Complete Guidebook* (1950); and John and Laree Caughey, *Los Angeles, Biography of a City* (1976). Articles on Los Angeles from this same period include "Los Angeles at 160," *Newsweek* (15 September 1941); H. Smith, "Magnificent Paradox," *Saturday Review of Literature* (30 October 1943); George Session Perry, "The Cities of America—Los Angeles," *Saturday Evening Post* (15 December 1945); Bennett Cerf, "Trade Winds," *Saturday Review of Literature* (3 May 1947); Earl Wilson, "No Inhibitions," *Saturday Review of Literature* (4 October 1947); H. Sutton, "It's Not the Heat, It's the Instability," *Saturday Review of Literature* (19 February 1949); "California: The Pink Oasis," *Time* (4 July 1949); and Sam Boal, "Los Angeles Has It, but What Is It?" *New York Times Magazine* (4 September 1949).

Studies of metropolitan Los Angeles as an urban environment include George Bemis and Nancy Basche, *Los Angeles County as an Agency of Municipal Government* (1946) and *From Rural to Urban: The Municipalized County of Los Angeles* (1947); Eshref Shevky and

Marilyn Williams, *The Social Areas of Los Angeles: Analysis and Typology* (1949) and *Your Neighborhood: A Social Profile of Los Angeles*, with photographs by Max Yavno (1949); and Mellier Goodin Scott, *Cities Are for People: The Los Angeles Region Plans for Living* (1942) and *Metropolitan Los Angeles: One Community* (1949). For politics in the City of Angels, see Guy Finney, *Angel City in Turmoil: A Story of the Minute Men of Los Angeles in Their War on Civic Corruption, Graft, and Privilege* (1945); and Aldrich Blake, *You Were the Big Shoe: An Inquiry into the Politics and Government of the American City, with a Case Study of the Los Angeles Metropolitan Area* (1945). See also "Bowron's Boom Town," *Time* (11 October 1948).

The underworld and demimonde of Los Angeles in this period is evident in the photographic essay "Trouble in Los Angeles," *Life* (16 January 1950), and in Howard Whitman, "Don't Go Out Alone at Night in L.A.," *Collier's* (28 October 1950). Regarding the Alcatraz Rebellion, see *Alcatraz '46: The Anatomy of a Classic Prison Tragedy*, as told to Don DeNevi by Philip Bergen and Clarence Carnes (1974). For a historic perspective on crime in Los Angeles, see Veronica King, *Problems of Modern American Crime* (1924). See also J. Francis McComas, *The Graveside Companion: An Anthology of California Murders* (1962). Caryl Chessman made his statement in *Cell 2455 Death Row* (1954) and *Trial by Ordeal* (1955). For one point of view, see Dean Jennings, *We Only Kill Each Other: The Life and Bad Times of Bugsy Siegel* (1967); and Lewis Yablonsky's biography of Siegel's pal *George Raft* (1947). See also Clinton Anderson, *Beverly Hills Is My Beat* (1960). For the look of it all, see the photographs compiled by Jim Heimann in *Sins of the City: The Real Los Angeles Noir* (1999).

George Raft suggests the interactions in this period among Hollywood, the demimonde, and the sexual underground. From this perspective, Kenneth Anger's *Hollywood Babylon* (1975) and *Hollywood Babylon II* (1984) are in a class by themselves. See also Jonathan Fryer, *Isherwood: A Biography* (1978); Brian Finney, *Christopher Isherwood: A Critical Biography* (1979); Charles Higham, *Charles Laughton: An Intimate Biography* (1976); and Hector Arce, *The Secret Life of Tyrone Power* (1980). See also the *Memoirs* of Tennessee Williams (1975). For Los Angeles as a divorcees' paradise, see "Divorce Mill: Los Angeles Frees Many More Mismated Couples than Reno," *Life* (23 July 1945). For night life, see "Mike's Place: Romanoff's Restaurant," *Time* (6 November 1950).

Newspaper memoirs from the period include Agness Underwood, *Newspaperwoman* (1949); James Richardson, *For the Life of Me: Memoirs of a City Editor* (1954); Charlotta Bass, *Forty Years: Memoirs from the Pages of a Newspaper* (1960); Adela Rogers St. Johns, *Final Verdict* (1962); and Will Fowler, *Reporters: Memoirs of a Young Newspaperman* (1991). Regarding Underwood at retirement in 1968, see Walt Anderson, "The Holy Terror of the 'Her-Ex' Calls It 30," *Los Angeles* magazine (February 1968).

Evelyn Waugh's *The Loved One* (1948) and Aldous Huxley's *Ape and Essence* (1948) are the high points for the Los Angeles novel in this period. For background, see Sam Bluefarb, *Set in L.A.: Scenes of the City in Fiction* (1986). Waugh returned to England. Huxley, by contrast, became a representative, indeed prophetic, Southern Californian. In this regard, see Huxley's *Time Must Have a Stop* (1944), *Science, Liberty, and Peace* (1946), and *The Perennial Philosophy* (1957). See also Sybille Bedford, *Aldous Huxley: A Biography* (1974). Regarding Raymond Chandler and film *noir*, see Raymond Chandler, *The Blue Dahlia: A Screenplay*, with a memoir by John Houseman, edited with an afterword by Matthew Bruccoli (1976); and Bruccoli's *Raymond Chandler: A Descriptive Bibliography* (1979). See also Gene D. Phillips, *Creatures of Darkness: Raymond Chandler, Detective Fiction, and Film Noir* (2000); Al Clark, *Raymond Chandler in Hollywood* (1982); and William Luhr, *Raymond Chandler in Film* (1982). Also of relevance to this chapter are Frank MacShane, *The Life of Raymond Chandler* (1978); and Dorothy Gardiner and Katherine Sorley Walker, editors, *Raymond Chandler Speaking* (1962). For a wider perspective, see George Bluestone, *Novels into Film* (1957); and John Tuska, *The Detective in Hollywood* (1978). See also Charles Higham and Joel Greenberg, *Hollywood in the Forties* (1968).

Chapter 9
1948 * Honey Bear

The Earl Warren Oral History Collection in the Regional Oral History Office of the Bancroft Library at UC Berkeley includes a number of valuable reminiscences. Of special use to this chapter were the recollections of James Warren, Nina Warren Brien, William T. Sweigert, Merrell F. Small, and Irving Stone. In 1970–71 and 1976–78, Amelia Fry and Miriam Stein of the Regional Oral History Office tape-recorded extensive interviews with the children of Earl and Nina Warren. A bound 267-page photocopy of the typed transcript of these interviews is on deposit at the Bancroft as *Earl Warren: The Governor's Family* (1980). Two important magazine articles demonstrating the political effect of the Warren family can be found in Robert Coughlan, "California's Warren and Family," *Life* (24 April 1944); and Sidney Shalett, "The Warrens: What a Family!" *Saturday Evening Post* (3 February 1951). Michael Davie remembered dancing with Honey Bear in London in 1952 in the preface to *California: The Vanishing Dream*, photographs by Camilla Smith (1972).

Warren discussed the challenges facing him as post-war governor of California in "California's Biggest Headache," *Saturday Evening Post* (14 August 1948). *The Public Papers of Chief Justice Earl Warren*, edited by Henry Christman, was published in 1959. The *Memoirs of Earl Warren* appeared in 1977. In 1971–72, Amelia Fry and other members of the Regional Oral History Office tape-recorded a series of lengthy interviews with the recently retired chief justice. A bound 339-page typed transcript of these interviews is on deposit at the Bancroft Library as *Conversations with Earl Warren on California Government*, with an introduction by Ira Michael Heyman (1982).

Warren's good friend and fellow Old Blue novelist Irving Stone wrote the campaign biography *Earl Warren: A Great American Story* (1948). Biographies crucial to this chapter include John Weaver, *Warren: The Man, the Court, the Era* (1967); Leo Katcher, *Earl Warren: A Political Biography* (1967); and G. Edward White, *Earl Warren: A Public Life* (1982). Of special importance to an understanding of Warren as jurist is Ed Cray's *Chief Justice: A Biography of Earl Warren* (1997). For a brief but telling portrait of Warren as he made his debut on the national scene, see John Gunther's *Inside USA* (revised edition, 1951). For a less than complimentary view, see two articles by Carey McWilliams, "Warren of California," *New Republic* (18 October 1943) and the more sympathetic "The Education of Earl Warren," *Nation* (12 October 1974). Despite his removal to New York as editor of the *Nation*, McWilliams remains a perceptive analyst of California politics. See, for example, McWilliams's articles for the *Nation* "Machines, Political and Slot" (28 May 1949), "And Now, Jimmy Roosevelt" (4 June 1949), and "Population and Politics" (8 July 1950).

An investigation into the tangled and distinctive history and functioning of politics and government in California in the first half of the twentieth century begins with *California Politics and Problems, 1900–1963: A Selective Bibliography*, by David Leuthold with the assistance of William Reid and William Macauley (1965). Reviewed as background for this chapter were (chronologically by date of publication) John Bollens and Stanley Scott, *Local Government in California* (1951); David Farrelly and Ivan Hinderaker, *The Politics of California* (1951); Winston Crouch, John Bollens, Stanley Scott, and Dean McHenry, *California Government and Politics* (1956); Bernard Hyink, Seyom Brown, and Ernest Thacker, *Politics and Government in California* (1959); Philip Schlessinger and Richard Wright, *Elements of Government in California* (1962); Leroy Hardy, *California Government* (1964); Henry Turner and John Vieg, *The Government and Politics of California* (1964); Joseph Harris, *California Politics* (1965); John Owens, Edmond Costantini, and Louis Weschler,

California Politics and Parties (1970). In this maze of commentary, the work of UC Berkeley political scientist Eugene C. Lee is in a class by itself; see his *California Votes* (1963) and *The Challenge of California*, with Larry Berg (1970). Also in a class by themselves and of special relevance to this chapter are Gladwin Hill, *Dancing Bear: An Inside Look at California Politics* (1968); Michael Rogin and John Shover, *Political Change in California: Critical Elections and Social Movements, 1890–1966* (1970); and Royce Delmatier, Clarence McIntosh, and Earl Waters, *The Rumble of California Politics, 1848–1970* (1970). The annually issued *California Blue Book* remains an essential source of reference for state government.

Regarding the non-partisan philosophy of Warren, see Richard Harvey, "Governor Earl Warren of California: A Study in Non-Partisan Politics," *California Historical Society Quarterly* (Winter 1967); and Raymond Moley, "Knight of Nonpartisanship: Earl Warren," in *27 Masters of Politics* (1949). As background to the distinctive environment in which Warren practiced his non-partisan brand of politics, see (in chronological order of publication) Dean Cresap, *Party Politics in the Golden State* (1954); Leonard Rowe, *Pre-Primary Endorsements in California Politics* (1962); Raymond Wolfinger and Fred Greenstein, *The Political Cultures of California* (1966); Herbert Phillips, *California: The Dynamic State* (1966); Ruth Ross and Barbara Stone, *California's Political Process* (1972); and William Buchanan, *Legislative Partisanship: The Deviant Case of California* (1978). Also of relevance is Dean McHenry, "Cross-Filing of Political Candidates in California," *Annals of the American Academy of Political and Social Science* (November 1946). For historical background, see H. Brett Melendy, "California's Cross-Filing Nightmare: The 1918 Gubernatorial Election," *Pacific Historical Review* (August 1964).

For the Republican side of things, see Markell Baer, *Story of the California Republican Assembly* (1955). For the Democratic point of view, see Francis Carney, *The Rise of the Democratic Clubs in California* (1958). For later developments, see James Q. Wilson, *The Amateur Democrat: Club Politics in Three Cities* (1966); and R. Hall Williams, *Democratic Party and California Politics* (1973). Regarding the role of public relations and professional campaign management in California campaign politics, see: Stanley Kelley Jr., *Professional Public Relations and Political Power* (1956); Irwin Ross, "The Supersalesmen of California Politics: Whitaker and Baxter," *Harper's* (July 1959); and Robert Pitchell, "The Influence of Professional Campaign Management Firms in Partisan Elections in California," *Western Political Quarterly* (June 1958). Regarding the lobbying culture of California politics, see Edgar Lane, *Lobbying and the Law* (1964). Regarding Artie Samish, the master lobbyist of them all, see Lester Velie's explosive interview "The Secret Boss of California" in *Collier's* for 13 and 20 August 1949. See also Herbert Solow, "So They Did Business with Samish," *Fortune* (April 1954); and Artie Samish's colorful memoirs, with Bob Thomas, *The Secret Boss of California* (1971).

Richard Nixon's *Six Crises* appeared in 1962. Amelia Fry did a series of tape-recorded interviews regarding the role of Nixon in the 1952 Republican convention. A bound transcript of these interviews is on deposit in the Bancroft Library as *Richard M. Nixon in the Warren Era* (1980). See also Earl Mazo, *Richard Nixon: A Political and Personal Portrait* (1959); William Costello, *The Facts About Nixon: An Unauthorized Biography* (1960); Roger Morris, *Richard Milhous Nixon: The Rise of an American Politician* (1990); and Irwin Gellman, *The Contender: Richard Nixon, the Congress Years, 1946–1952* (1999). See also Donald Jackson, "The Young Richard Nixon," *Life* (6 November 1970). Of special relevance to this chapter are the autobiographies by Jerry Voorhis, *Confessions of a Congressman* (1947), and Helen Gahagan Douglas, *A Full Life* (1982).

Chapter 10
1949 * Mexicali Rose

Central to this chapter is Edward L. Barrett Jr., *The Tenney Committee: Legislative Investigation of Subversive Activities in California* (1951). In 1949 the California legislature issued the *Fifth Report of the Senate Fact-Finding Committee on Un-American Activities* in 709 closely printed pages. In the late 1960s former senator Jack B. Tenney was interviewed by staffers of the Oral History Program at UCLA. The four-volume bound typescript of these interviews is on deposit at UCLA as *Jack B. Tenney, California Legislator* (1969). See also these important articles: Carey McWilliams, "Mister Tenney's Horrible Awakening," *Nation* (23 July 1949); and Robert Pritchard, "California's Un-American Activities Investigations: Subversion on the Right?" *California Historical Society Quarterly* (Fall 1970). Regarding Tenney's cross-examination of Helen Gahagan Douglas, see "Helen Gahagan Douglas," *New Republic* (20 September 1948); and "Helen Gahagan Douglas: Reply with Rejoinder," *New Republic* (18 October 1948).

Regarding the history of Communism in California, see two articles by Ralph Shaffer: "Formation of the California Communist Labor Party," *Pacific Historical Review* (February 1967) and "Communism in California, 1919–1924," *Science and Society* (Winter 1970). See also Dorothy Healey and Maurice Isserman, *Dorothy Healey Remembers: A Life in the American Communist Party* (1990). The Oleta O'Connor Yates Collection of the Communist Party of California at the Bancroft Library includes many Party-sponsored pamphlets. Of relevance to this chapter are the 1947 pamphlets "Catholicism in San Francisco" and "The Negro Question." See also the pamphlet by William Schneiderman, chairman of the Communist Party of California, *California Political Perspectives and the 1948 Elections*, reprinted from the *Daily People's World* (18, 19, and 20 June 1947). For a hard-line anti-Communist point of view regarding the Wallace campaign, see the pamphlet on deposit at the Bancroft Library: Pasadena Anti-Communist League, "Know Your Neighbors? Independent Progressive Party Known as the Third Party" (1949). See also the pamphlet by L. Fry, "California Betrayed! The Factual Story About Communist Spies" (1951). Regarding the question of Communism on the San Francisco waterfront, see Stephen Schwartz, *Brotherhood of the Sea: A History of the Sailors' Union of the Pacific, 1885–1985* (1986). For the allegation that Harry Bridges was a Communist agent, see Harvey Klehr and John Haynes, "The Comintern's Open Secrets: The Archives of the Late Communist Party of the Soviet Union Reveal a Clear Picture of Subversion in the United States," *American Spectator* (December 1992).

Regarding the investigations in Washington, Walter Goodman, *The Committee: The Extraordinary Career of the House Committee on Un-American Activities*, foreword by Richard Rovere (1968), is central to this chapter. See also Abraham Polonsky, *A Season of Fear* (1956); Stefan Kanfer, *A Journal of the Plague Years* (1973); and David Caute, *The Great Fear: The Anti-Communist Purge Under Truman and Eisenhower* (1978). Regarding the alleged infiltration of Hollywood, the House Committee on Un-American Activities published its transcripts and conclusions in the 1947 government publication *Hearings Regarding the Communist Infiltration of the Motion Picture Industry Before the Committee on Un-American Activities, House of Representatives, 80th Congress*.

For the other side of the story, see Gordon Kahn, *Hollywood on Trial: The Story of the 10 Who Were Indicted*, foreword by Thomas Mann (1948); Alvah Bessie, *Inquisition in Eden* (1965); and Larry Ceplair and Steven Englund, *The Inquisition in Hollywood: Politics in the Film Community, 1930–1960* (1980). See also Eric Bentley, *Are You Now or Have You Ever Been: The Investigation of Show Business by the Un-American Activities Committee, 1947–1958* (1972); and the anthology edited by Bentley, *Thirty Years of Treason: Excerpts from Hearings Before the House Committee on Un-American Activities, 1938–1968* (1971).

Regarding the blacklist, see John Cogley, *Report on Blacklisting* (two volumes, 1956). See also Nora Sayre, *Running Time: Films of the Cold War* (1982); and John Stanley, "Reviving the Ghosts of 'High Noon,'" San Francisco *Chronicle* (24 November 1992). Nancy Lynn Schwartz, *The Hollywood Writers' Wars*, completed by Sheila Schwartz (1982), is crucial to this chapter, as is Walter Wanger, "The Hollywood Writers' Congress," *Saturday Review* (30 October 1943).

Personal perspectives are available in Lauren Bacall, *By Myself* (1979); Victor Navasky, *Naming Names* (1980); and Lester Cole, *Hollywood Red* (1981). See also Joe Hyams, *Bogie: The Biography of Humphrey Bogart* (1966); and Nathaniel Benchley, *Humphrey Bogart* (1975). Regarding the all-important presence of Dalton Trumbo, see Trumbo's *The Time of the Toad: A Study of Inquisition in America and Two Related Pamphlets* (1949) and *Additional Dialogue: Letters of Dalton Trumbo, 1942–1962*, edited by Helen Manfull (1970). See also Bruce Cook, *Dalton Trumbo* (1977). Trumbo's shocking novel of 1939 *Johnny Got His Gun* was reissued in 1967. In the early 1960s Hollywood writer Emmet Lavery was interviewed by staff members of the Oral History Project at UCLA. The bound 196-page typescript of these interviews is on deposit at the Bancroft Library as *Notes and Footnotes, Casual Recollections of Things Past—Things Remembered—Things Not Yet Finished* (1962).

Chapter 11
1950 * Police Action

Regarding the call-up of the Fortieth Infantry Division, see Kerry Diminyatz, "The 40th Infantry Division in the Korean Conflict: The Employment of the California National Guard in an Undeclared War" (M.A. thesis, history, Sonoma State University, 1990). Regarding the escalating crisis at the University of California that year, David Gardner's *The California Oath Controversy* (1967) commands the subject. See also these contemporary studies: Carey McWilliams, *Witch Hunt* (1950); Ernst Kantorowicz, *The Fundamental Issue: Documents and Marginal Notes of the University of California Loyalty Oath* (1950); and George Stewart and others, *The Year of the Oath: The Fight for Academic Freedom at the University of California* (1950). Newspaper and magazine coverage of the loyalty oath controversy was extensive. In this regard, see relevant articles in the *New Republic* for 27 March, 24 April, 7 August, 18 September, and 9 October 1950; and the *Nation* for 29 April, 10 June, 9 September, 30 September, and 4 November 1950. Coverage in *School and Society* included important articles on 29 April and 15 July 1950. See also Max Radin, "Loyalty Oath at the University of California," *American Scholar* (July 1950); H. W. Flannery, "Red Smear in California," *Commonweal* (8 December 1950); Dixon Wecter, "Commisars of Loyalty," *Saturday Review of Literature* (13 May 1950); and John Caughey, "A University in Jeopardy," *Harper's* (November 1950). *Life* chronicled the controversy in "Regents vs. the Professors: University of California Drops Forty Courses as Battle over Non-Communist Oath Is Carried into Court" (2 October 1950). Columnist Raymond Moley supported the regents in *Newsweek* on 14 August and 4 September 1950. *Time* covered the controversy on 10 April 1950.

Allegations of Communist influence at UCLA were put forward by William Worden in "UCLA's Red Cell: Case History of College Communism," *Saturday Evening Post* (21 October 1950). The ambiguous career of J. Robert Oppenheimer was chronicled by Peter Goodchild in *J. Robert Oppenheimer: Shatterer of Worlds* (1981). Haakon Chevalier had his say in *Oppenheimer: The Story of a Friendship* (1965). Ruth Fisher made her accusations in *Stalin and German Communism: A Study in the Origins of the State Party*, with a preface by Sidney Fay (1948).

For the reaction of Charles Chaplin to the anti-Communist crusade, see Chaplin's *My Autobiography* (1964); John McCabe, *Charlie Chaplin* (1978); and the authoritative *Charlie*

Chaplin and His Times, by Kenneth S. Lynn (1997). For the reaction of Lion Feuchtwanger, see Lothar Kahn, *Insight and Action: The Life and Work of Lion Feuchtwanger*
(1975); and the anthology of Feuchtwanger's writing edited by John Spalek under the title
Lion Feuchtwanger: The Man, His Ideas, His Work (1972). The sly and ambiguous comings
and goings of Bertolt Brecht and his sudden departure to Europe can be traced through
Martin Esslin, *Brecht: The Man and His Work* (1960); Frederic Ewen, *Bertolt Brecht: His
Life, His Art, and His Times* (1969); James Lyon, *Bertolt Brecht in America* (1980); Bruce
Cook, *Brecht in Exile* (1982); and Ronald Hayman, *Brecht: A Biography* (1983). The growing
alienation of Thomas Mann can be traced through Hans Burgin and Hans-Otto Mayer,
Thomas Mann: A Chronicle of His Life, translated by Eugene Dobson (1969); and *The
Letters of Thomas Mann, 1889–1955,* edited and translated by Richard and Clara Winston
(two volumes, 1970). See also Mann's *Essays of Three Decades,* translated by H. T. Lowe-
Porter (1947) and *The Story of a Novel: The Genesis of "Dr. Faustus,"* translated by Richard
and Clara Winston (1961). See also Katia Mann, *Unwritten Memories* (1975); and Nigel
Hamilton, *The Brothers Mann* (1979).

Acknowledgments

This book was researched at the Doheny Library of the University of Southern California, the University Research Library of the University of California at Los Angeles, the Doe and Bancroft libraries of the University of California at Berkeley, the San Francisco Public Library, the Gleeson Library of the University of San Francisco, and the California State Library in Sacramento, where my executive assistant Mattie Taormina is to be especially commended for her organizational skills. I remain grateful as well to the staff of Special Collections at the California State Library, so ably directed by scholar-librarian Gary Kurutz. In this regard I am most indebted to senior librarian John Gonzales for his assistance in multiple inquiries and the inter-library loan process. I am thankful to Dace Taube of the Regional History Center at the University of Southern California and to Pat Akre and Susan Goldstein of the San Francisco History Center of the San Francisco Public Library for assistance in selecting photographs. For encouragement and corrective guidance, I remain grateful to Peter O'Malley Pierson, University Professor of History at Santa Clara University. Wade and Jane Hughan and Monsignor Steven Otellini have generously helped with proofreading; and Sarah Ereira has prepared an excellent index. I continue to remain represented by the finest literary agent on the Coast, Sandra Dijkstra, and to be edited by a master, Sheldon Meyer of Oxford University Press, who has long since become my friend. I can imagine no finer copy editor than India Cooper or no finer production editor than Joellyn Ausanka of Oxford, and I remain grateful to Peter Ginna, executive editor at Oxford, for his continuing commitment to the Americans and the California Dream series.

This book was researched and written across a busy decade, sans grants, fellowships, or leaves of absence. It was also interrupted by a bout of cardiovascular disease necessitating quadruple bypass surgery. Without the constant assistance of my wife, Sheila Starr—as researcher, editor, critic, and friend—the Americans and the California Dream series would have come to a halt. In thinking of Sheila Starr, I have only to make reference to what Hilaire Belloc once said of his wife Elodie: namely, that Sheila Starr is the wife of my youth, and she abides with me still, and I with her. As the dedication of *Embattled Dreams* indicates, I remain grateful to the physicians, nurses, and medical and administrative staffs of Kaiser Permanente, San Francisco, for a second chance at life, and I remain grateful to Sheila Starr, my daughters, Marian and Jessica, my sons-in-law, and my six grand-children for making that regained life so worth living.

Los Angeles, San Francisco, Sacramento   K.S.
March 2001

Index